The Flaming Soul
Van Gogh's
Drawings and Paintings
燃燒的靈魂 梵谷

國立歷史博物館
National Museum of History

目次
Contents

序

　　梵谷是最受世人喜愛的畫家之一，國立歷史博物館非常榮幸地能舉辦他在台灣的第一次大規模個展，而時值他逝世即將屆滿120週年之際，更讓此展別具紀念意義。梵谷用色大膽的畫作印象，深深地烙印在每個欣賞他藝術表現的人心上，這次展覽作品中，除了有大家熟悉的梵谷風格油畫作品外，更難得的是庫勒穆勒美術館借展大量的素描和水彩作品，每幅作品呈現的是畫家追求不同題材完美表現的歷程，以及運用各種媒材嘗試創作出他所經驗感受的社會人生。炭筆、墨水筆、粉筆、水彩等各式媒材的交互運用，讓梵谷的素描呈現出新穎豐富的層次，未臻成熟的人物比例拿捏，更讓觀眾有機會一起想像窺探畫家成長的過程，配合梵谷勤寫書信的好習慣，有如他親自帶領大家領略他的藝術內涵與創作理念，真切地了解他對繪畫的執著與熱情。

　　儘管生前並不得志，又深為疾病所苦，梵谷對藝術的熱情與堅持，透過他的作品感動了海倫·庫勒穆勒夫人，促使她有計畫地收藏梵谷畫作，讓庫勒穆勒美術館成為全世界典藏梵谷作品的重量級美術館，並繼續秉持她「為大眾之益，為大眾之樂」的精神，願意與台灣觀眾分享梵谷97幅的重要作品，我謹在此表達最誠摯的感謝。同時也感謝聯合報系對藝文展覽的支持與投入，在去年成功的米勒展後，一起再度共創梵谷的美麗新巔峰。梵谷視米勒為典範，而國立歷史博物館能在米勒展後，以梵谷展延續大師級的藝術饗宴，實在再完美不過了！

　　本次展覽承蒙國內外眾多公私立機構的參與與支持，尤其是教育部大力支持本館在設備水準上的提升，特別藉此機會表達至高的謝意。其次日本POLA美術館以及願意為台灣藝文教育活動共盡心力的企業與基金會的共襄盛舉，終能成就此一展覽盛事。相信我們對藝術的熱情並不亞於梵谷對藝術的熱愛，或許就是這份相同的心意，才能有今天這美好的交流與呈現！

國立歷史博物館 館長

 謹識

Preface

Vincent van Gogh is one of the world's most popular artists, and the National Museum of History is very honored to commemorate this great artist by holding this first solo exhibition of his work in Taiwan as the 120th anniversary of his death approaches. Van Gogh is famous for his strong and bright colors, which had a deep impression on the minds of those who enjoyed his work. In addition to showing paintings in his more well-known style, we are also exhibiting much more rarely displayed drawings and watercolors from the collection of the Kröller-Müller Museum in Otterlo, the Netherlands, which reflect the processes by which Van Gogh pursued the best interpretations of various subjects, and his attempts to use different media to create what he had experienced in life. The use together of such media as charcoal, pen, chalk and watercolor lend Van Gogh's drawings layers of richness and depth. The not quite mature depictions of figures' proportions allow us a glimpse at his approach to becoming a great artist. Van Gogh was a diligent writer of letters, and the letters he bequeathed to posterity enable us, with him as our guide, to explore his ideas of art and comprehend his devotion and enthusiasm for artistic creativity.

Although he had a tough life as he struggled with mental illness, Van Gogh's love and insistence for art moved Mrs. Helene Kröller-Müller, who built up a collection of his work, and established the importance and renown of the Kröller-Müller Museum. To carry on the ideal "for the benefit and pleasure of the community" of Mrs. Kröller-Müller, the Kröller-Müller Museum has generously shared 97 treasured artworks of Van Gogh with us, and I would like to express my sincerest gratitude for their generosity. I would also like to acknowledge the United Daily News Group for their support, and their devotion to the arts, which have made this beautiful exhibition possible, and I believe this will be another great success to follow that of the Millet exhibition last year. Van Gogh admired Millet, and produced several drawings imitating his work. This exhibition will also be a wonderful opportunity to show the connection between these two masters.

This exhibition has been made possible with support from many quarters. I am very grateful to the Ministry of Education for assisting us with upgrading our facilities, and to the POLA Museum of Art for its participation, as well as to all enterprises and foundations which are willing to promote art education in Taiwan. I truly believe that our enthusiasm for art is no less than that of Van Gogh, and may be it is this same passion which brings us together for this wonderful exhibition!

Director
National Museum of History

序

　　梵谷的人生與創作吸引全世界的想像。他的創作是喜悅、安慰與靈感的來源，他對人生不屈不撓的毅力令人欽佩，也讓我們對必然的人生歷程有所領悟。他為生活的奮鬥，以及為其信仰而奮戰的渴望讓他成為典範。他的書信能夠回溯其令人印象深刻的自我意識之發展，卻也看到其中人性的脆弱之處。

　　上世紀初，荷蘭的庫勒穆勒夫婦認知到梵谷在藝術與對人類社會深遠的重要性，歷經二十餘年的歲月，他們持續地收藏大量且多樣的油畫與素描。這批藏品形成庫勒穆勒美術館的核心，1938年於荷蘭的厚荷扶鹿國家公園對外開放。

　　我非常榮幸與高興台灣首次有機會舉辦梵谷的展覽。本展專注於梵谷創作練習的基礎，尤其是畫素描的發展。在他能夠創作現今如此為人所熟知的作品前，他首先必需熟練素描的技法與技巧。如梵谷所言：「素描是一切的根基。」此外，本展亦展出他的精選油畫作品，其中有的直接源自素描，有的展現他藝術天份發展的過程。只有在精通素描的真髓後，才能進一步解放對色彩的運用。

　　我非常感謝聯合報系促成此展，同時也非常感謝國立歷史博物館的熱情以及對本展投入的心血。我希望梵谷展現藝術天才的作品，能為台灣觀眾帶來莫大的愉悅與啟發。

庫勒穆勒美術館 館長

埃弗特・范・斯達登

Preface

The life and work of Vincent van Gogh appeals to the imagination of people all over the world. His work is a source of joy, solace and inspiration, his life gives rise to admiration for his perseverance, and to the comprehension of the inevitable fate of human beings. His struggle for life and his desire to stand for something in the world have made him into an example. In his letters, it is possible to trace his impressive development towards self-awareness, but the bounds of human frailty can also be perceived.

At the start of the previous century, the Dutch married couple Helene and Anton Kröller-Müller recognized the enormous significance that Van Gogh would have for art and humanity. In the course of two decades, they succeeded in building up a large and varied collection of paintings and drawings. This collection forms the heart of the Kröller-Müller Museum, which opened its doors in 1938 in the centre of the Netherlands, in the De Hoge Veluwe National Park.

I am very honoured and delighted that, for the first time in the history of Taiwan, it is possible to realize an exhibition of work by Van Gogh. The exhibition focuses on the foundations of Van Gogh's artistic practice, namely following his development as a draughtsman. Before he was able to make the work for which he is now so famous, he first had to master the craft and technique of drawing. As Van Gogh said: "the root of everything is drawing". In addition to the drawings, the exhibition also includes an outstanding selection of his paintings, some of which stem directly from the drawings, while others show the development of his autonomous genius. The colour could only be liberated after having mastered the tracing of the line.

I am extremely thankful to the United Daily News Group for making this exhibition possible. I am also tremendously grateful to the National Museum of History in Taipei for their hospitality and the care with which they surround the exhibition. I hope that these works by this gifted artist prove to be a source of great pleasure and inspiration to the visitors in Taiwan.

Evert van Straaten

Director
Kröller-Müller Museum

序

　　「燃燒的靈魂‧梵谷」特展，是華人地區首見的大型梵谷畫展，也是台灣有史以來最重量級的國際大展，聯合報系金傳媒集團深感榮幸，能促成這項展覽，寫下歷史的新頁。過去二十年來，聯合報系致力於引介重要優質展覽，為社會大眾打造更能親近藝術的文化均富環境，並且藉以不斷挑戰極限，為台灣帶入的展覽越來越好。

　　去年「驚艷米勒—田園之美畫展」，已經交出令人驚艷的成績單，我們有信心，「燃燒的靈魂‧梵谷」特展一定能帶來更加打動人心的藝術饗宴。

　　米勒是梵谷的精神導師，啟迪他畫出人類的靈魂；梵谷卻青出於藍勝於藍，成為比米勒更影響深遠的偉大畫家。台灣第一次的梵谷大展，我們想讓大家看見真正的梵谷—大多數人只知道梵谷後期在法國南方的大膽色彩表現；這項展覽卻從梵谷27歲決心當畫家的起步開始，讓大家看見梵谷一步一腳印烙下的深刻足跡，進而瞭解梵谷之所以成為梵谷的關鍵密碼。

　　梵谷未必瘋狂，也不見得是天才，卻絕對是勤奮務實，將藝術創作當成生命戰場的人。從1880年至1890年的10年間，梵谷的創作能量驚人，他的刻苦、執著、忠於自我，才是成就梵谷留名青史的要件。如此重量級的國際大展，能夠來到台灣讓社會大眾親炙大師之作，得力於中國信託等眾多重視藝術文化核心價值的企業共襄盛舉。

　　最要感謝，是國立歷史博物館以史前無例的超大手筆，閉館兩個月進行硬體更新工程，讓展覽空間達於國際標準，台灣社會大眾也更加有福氣，能享受史無前例的優質展覽。梵谷真誠的創作態度，感動無數的人，相信我們以真誠打造出來的梵谷特展，也能感動台灣的廣大觀眾。

聯合報系金傳媒集團　執行長

楊仁烽

Preface

Van Gogh: The Flaming Soul is the first large-scale Van Gogh exhibition of the Chinese-speaking world, and is also the most heavyweight international exhibition in Taiwan's history. United Daily News affiliated Gold Media Group is honored to be able to present this event and write a new page in the annals of Taiwan's history. In the past twenty years, the United Daily News has strived to bring important, high-quality exhibitions to Taiwan, creating an environment of cultural equality, where everyone can experience art. We continually test the limits of how great an exhibition we can present.

Last year's *Millet and His Time: Masterpieces from the Musee d'Orsay* exhibition was a stunning show of what we can achieve; we are confident that *Van Gogh: The Flaming Soul* will furnish an even more inspirational feast for the artistic appetite.

Millet was a spiritual guide for Van Gogh, enlightening him on painting the human soul; Van Gogh eventually came to surpass his teacher and became an even more influential grandmaster painter. In this Van Gogh exhibition, Taiwan's first, we want to show you the real Van Gogh - most people only recognize him from his late-period daring use of color in the south of France; therefore, this exhibition starts from a twenty-seven-year-old Van Gogh, the age when he became determined to be an artist. We showcase each step Van Gogh took on his path to greatness, giving you an understanding of just what it is that makes Van Gogh Van Gogh.

He may not be mad; he may not be a genius; but Van Gogh is a hardworking realist who saw creative work as life's battlefield. His prolificacy in the decade from 1880 to 1890 is breathtaking: assiduous, persistent, self-loyalty - these are the traits that let Van Gogh leave his mark on history. Holding such an important international event in Taiwan could not have been possible without the help and support of Chinatrust and other corporations that value the importance of culture and the arts.

Most of all, we would like to thank the National Museum of History for taking on the costly task of a two-month renovation so that the exhibit area lives up to international standards, making the people of Taiwan lucky indeed to be able to enjoy an unparalleled high-quality exhibit. Van Gogh's sincere creative attitude has moved countless people; we believe that our sincerity in presenting this special Van Gogh exhibition will touch you as well.

CEO, Gold Media Group,
United Daily News Group

序

寄語「燃燒的靈魂・梵谷」特展

　　POLA美術館收藏之《薊花》（1890）能在台灣初次大規模之梵谷展展出，對我而言是極大的喜悅。

　　財團法人POLA美術振興財團，自1996年設立以來，進行對年輕藝術家之出國研修、美術館員之調查研究以及有關美術之國際交流之各範疇之促進事業，而為了擴展美術範疇使更多的人能夠親近美術，於2002年9月，於日本神奈川縣箱根仙石原設立了POLA美術館。總數達約9500件之POLA美術館之收藏品，是POLA集團之前總裁鈴木常司（1930-2000）經過40多年收集之美術作品，收藏品之核心為19世紀法國印象派或巴黎派畫家等之西洋繪畫400件，其他亦收藏日本之西洋畫、日本畫、東洋陶瓷、日本近現代陶瓷、玻璃工藝、化妝道具等為數不少，是範圍很大之收藏。

　　《薊花》為本館之西洋繪畫收藏品之代表作品。此作品為自1890年5月至7月間，梵谷在其一生最後的約兩個月，於巴黎近郊的美麗鄉村Auvers-sur-Oise的精神科醫師Gachet的家裏所描繪的數件野花靜物畫之一件。在此作品完成後約一個月，梵谷即在麥田中以手槍自殺，兩天後宣告死亡。承受精神病的痛苦而繼續進行繪畫製作的梵谷，以極生動的筆觸描繪了插在樸素的花瓶中的薊花與野花。希望梵谷親眼看到的樸素野花之可愛之美，與堅強的生命力能使大家感動而銘記於心。

財團法人POLA美術振興財團 理事長

鈴木鄉史

2009年12月

Preface

It brings me tremendous pleasure to have *Flower Vase with Thistles* (1890) from the POLA Museum of Art, participate in the first great Van Gogh exhibition in Taiwan.

POLA Art Foundation was established in 1996, and its mission is to encourage young artists to study abroad and support them in doing so, curatorial research and investigations, and international art exchange activities. The POLA Museum of Art was built in September, 2002, in Hakone, Kanagawa, Japan, to extend opportunities for people to experience art. The collection in POLA comprises about 9,500 artworks that were acquired by the late CEO of POLA Group Tsuneshi Suzuki (1930-2000) throughout a period of over 40 years. The collection focuses on 400 artworks of French Impressionists in the 19th century and artists of the Paris school. There is also a wide-ranging collection of Western painting by Japanese artists, traditional Japanese paintings, porcelain and ceramics, modern porcelain, glass art, and cosmetics tools.

Flower Vase with Thistles is one of the masterpieces in the POLA painting collection. This painting is dated in the period May to July of the year 1890, the last two months of Van Gogh's life. It is one of several still life paintings of wild flowers which were finished at the home of the psychiatrist, Gachet, in the beautiful countryside in Auvers-sur-Oise, near Paris. About one month after finishing this artwork, Van Gogh shot himself with a handgun in a wheat field, and passed away two days later. Suffering from mental illness but painting persistently, Van Gogh depicted thistles and wildflowers in a simple vase with very vivid brushstrokes. Hope, as represented by the lovely, vital wildflowers of Van Gogh's art will touch everyone's mind.

Suzuki Satoshi
Chairman of Board Directors
POLA Art Foundation

專文
Essays

梵谷的素描：初期（1880-1883）

泰歐‧梅登多普
歐克耶‧斐黑斯特

　　庫勒穆勒美術館（The Kröller-Müller Museum）擁有梵谷的179件畫作、2件石版畫及1件蝕刻版畫，素描當中有一部分為雙面作畫，因此紙本總數為164件。最主要的館藏是庫勒先生於1928年向收藏家Hidde Nijland取得的112件畫作。當時庫勒穆勒夫婦已擁有47張作品，剩下的5件則是在1941年之後，海倫‧庫勒穆勒及她的丈夫過世後才入藏的。這些收藏中，大部分的素描為梵谷在荷蘭時期（1880-1885）所作，只有少數是他在法國時期的作品。

　　這些收藏使得庫勒夫婦成為荷蘭最早的梵谷收藏家之一。這是目前世界上收藏梵谷畫作第二多的博物館：加總所有的畫作，庫勒穆勒美術館擁有超過250件這位因戲劇性筆觸及強烈的色彩而聞名的藝術家的作品。梵谷的素描作品數量比油畫多，如同大部分的畫家，在他的繪畫生涯初期是以素描作為練習。以下的文章將概略地敘述梵谷發展各個時期的素描：早期（The early years 1880-1883），在這個時期他先後居住在波林納吉、布魯塞爾、埃頓、海牙及德倫特；努南時期（Nuenen 1883-1885）；及最後的聖雷米時期（Saint-Rémy 1889-1890）。[1]

早期 1880年－1883年

> 我要做的事是學習如何畫素描，以成為一個大師，不論是用我的鉛筆，用我的炭筆，還是用我的筆刷。我沒辦法告訴你（雖然新的挑戰每天都會出現，未來也會繼續出現）我有多開心我又開始畫素描了。
>
> 　　　　　　　　梵谷給西奧的信，1880年9月24日，Cuesmes（波林納吉）（157/136）

　　1880年，梵谷決定要成為一個藝術家。當時他27歲，曾經做過國際知名的古比藝術貿易公司（Goupil & Cie）的銷售員、老師以及書店店員。當時他要研究神學的進取心受挫，在比利時礦區波林納吉作為福音傳播者的任期也沒能被續聘，他的弟弟西奧是第一個建議他當一名藝術家的人。

　　梵谷立刻就以一種相當計畫性的方式開始他的畫家生涯。1880年8月20日，在一封被認為是他決定成為畫家後寫給西奧的第一封信中，他說道：「如果我沒記錯的話，你應該還擁有米勒的《田間勞動》（Les traveaux des champs）。你能夠好心地把它寄給我，並借給我一段時間嗎？你應該知道我正在臨摹一幅米勒的素描……我在正在素描的時候寫給你，希望可以趕快回去繼續作畫。」[2] 他試圖自習素描的技巧，或多或少也效法了美術學院的正規課程的方法：模仿版畫及特殊範例。他臨摹了米勒作品的照片及版畫；作為一個法國農村生活畫家，米勒成為梵谷一輩子的

---

1. 在這些文章中，頻繁且感激地使用了許多出色的相關出版品，特別是梵谷美術館的圖錄《素描一、二、三和四》（*Drawings I, II, III and IV*）（Sjraar van Heugten[I-III]，Maeije Vellekoop [III-IV] 和Roeloe Zwikker [IV] 著，阿姆斯特丹，1996-2007）；*Van Gogh Draughtsman. The Masterworks*（Sjraar van Heugten著，阿姆斯特丹，2005）和庫勒穆勒美術館最新、對梵谷素描有詳盡說明的圖錄*Drawings and Prints of Vincent van Gogh in the Collection of the Kröller-Müller Museum*（Teio Meedendorp著，奧特羅，2007）。文中所摘錄的信件內容及信件編號是來自於*De brieven van Vincent van Gogh*（Han van Crimpen和Monique Berends-Albert編，海牙，1990）。
2. 梵谷給西奧的信 （155/134）

典範。《掘地者》（*Les Bêcheurs*，頁63 [KM 119.703]）和《晚禱》（*L'Angelus du Soir*，頁61 [KM 115.117]）描繪出辛勤工作的農人，梵谷臨摹向畫商借來米勒素描作品照片，完成了這兩幅畫作。

　　梵谷也從書本中獲取繪畫的技巧資訊，特別是Armand Cassagne的出版品，在梵谷作畫的第一年裡給了他很大的幫助。Cassagne討論了許多藝術方面的問題，像是透視法、深度效果、比例及結構學。他之後寫信給西奧：「解決了我疑問的是Cassagne的一本讓人能夠理解的透視法《素描入門》（*Guide de l'ABC du dessin*），八天後我畫了一幅小廚房的室內畫，當中的爐子、桌子、椅子和窗戶都以它們的腳站在適當的位置，之前要在素描中有深度和正確的透視法，對我來說是某種巫術，或是巧合。」[3] 這本書正確的名稱是*Cassagne, Guide de l'Alphabet du dessin*，當中包含了素描基本原則的簡易解釋。巴爾格（Charles Bargue）的散裝出版品《素描課程》（*Cours de dessin*）也是很重要的輔助。在最初的這幾個月裡，他幾乎都在摹仿出版品裡頭的畫作如《雅各‧梅爾之女》（*The Daughter of Jacob Meyer*，頁69 [KM 128.492]）。除了這些臨摹之外，他也創作了一些自己的作品像是《雪地裡的礦工》（*Miner in the snow*，頁59 [KM 111.966]），這幅素描的紙嚴重褪色及損傷，從人物輪廓線的許多修改痕跡，可以看出梵谷還不確定的筆跡。1880年10月，為了尋找更具藝術氣息的環境及希望能欣賞到更多畫作，梵谷搬到了布魯塞爾。他在皇家藝術學院（Académie Royal des Beaux-Arts）註冊，但並不能確定他是否有在那裡上過課。在布魯塞爾他向傳統海牙畫派的大師勒洛夫斯（Willem Roelofs）請益，同時也與年輕的藝術家接觸。在那裡他結識了凡‧拉帕德（Anthon van Rappard），一個已經作畫四年並且願意讓梵谷偶爾在他的工作室作畫的畫家。儘管最早的這個時期梵谷留下來的作品很少，布魯塞爾對他來說還是相當重要，因為他在這裡畫了詳細的人體結構習作和一些他自己的構圖。[4] 梵谷的生活費來自他的家庭，原本是他的父母在支付，但到了1881年2月，西奧擔負起這個責任，直到梵谷戲劇性地辭世。

埃頓時期

　　1881年4月，梵谷搬去和他的父母同住在北布拉邦（North Brabant）的埃頓村。在那裡他除了摹仿之外，也致力於描寫週遭的主題，而當地居民也提供了他充足的題材。凡‧拉帕德在那年夏初去拜訪了梵谷，他們一起尋找適合的風景主題。他的自信在此時增長了不少：「現在我終究是感受到了：『我有一雙畫素描的手』，我非常高興身上有這樣的工具，雖然它還是相當地笨拙。」[5]

　　在那個夏天完成的《庭園一隅》（*Corner of a garden*，頁67 [KM 115.487]）中，梵谷非常精確地描繪出一幅浪漫的景色：花園中一座涼亭靠著一面植物蔓生的牆。花園中空盪的家具突顯出人物的缺席。某些細節被非常精確地，同時也是「笨拙地」表現出來（地上的格子布和家具）：桌面沒有位在桌腳的中間，左邊的椅子看起來像在跳舞。庫勒穆勒夫人非常喜愛這件作品，證據就在她寫給密友山姆‧范‧德凡特（Sam van Deventer）的信中：「Salomon，現在你可對梵谷的畫有更深的了解？就是那幅有凳子、茶几、還有非常靜謐的小庭院的畫。你難道不能想像兩個人坐在那裡，剛剛才起身離開，他們沒有經驗到什麼，卻又經驗了這麼多，也發覺了這個庭院簡單卻偉大的美？在他們身後，房子成了庭院顯現的背景。再看一次這幅畫，它對我如此珍貴，也和梵

3. 梵谷給西奧的信（213/184）
4. 梵谷給西奧的信（163/142）
5. 梵谷給西奧的信（179/155）

谷其他畫作裡雄厚的情感形成如此的對比。」[6]

1881年的8月底，梵谷拜訪了他在海牙的表姊夫，海牙畫派的大師安東·莫弗（Anton Mauve），之後他開始體驗新的素材與技巧。在那之前，他主要是以鉛筆和沾水筆作畫，但莫弗建議他：「你應該要改變一下，嘗試使用炭筆、蠟筆、筆刷和用剩的筆頭。」[7]那個夏天他也收到了Cassagne送給他的《論水彩畫》（Traité d'Aquarelle）。起初他只結合水彩與其他的技巧作畫，例如他在8、9月間創作的《多德勒克的風車磨坊》（Windmills at Dordrecht，頁72 [KM 126. 249]）就表現出了許多的技巧：鉛筆、蠟筆、沾水筆、筆刷和不透明水彩。從海牙回來之後，他寫了一封充滿熱情的信，顯示出經常獨自摸索的梵谷一旦有其他的藝術家同儕的交流就會茁然成長：他充滿熱情地討論他在海牙看到的第六次Hollandsche Teekenmaatschappij展覽的作品，他希望這次觀展能夠成為「更深入瞭解莫弗和其他藝術家的第一步。」[8]

1881年秋天，他創作了許多以真實人物寫生的素描，他偏好取材自正在篩種、掘地、播種、削馬鈴薯或裁縫的農人及他們的妻子。庫勒穆勒美術館擁有從這個時期開始的許多素描，這些素描作品常常表現出些許的不自然：這些人物並不是真的在工作，而經常只是在擺姿勢。梵谷為了練習畫出正確的比例，偶爾會讓他的人物表現出複雜的姿勢。例如《持鐮鋤草的男孩》（Boy with a Sickle，頁87 [KM 111. 847]），他從側面畫一位一腳跪在地上另一腳蹲著的人物。這個模特兒是替梵谷牧師照料花園的17歲的考夫曼（Piet Kauffman），擔任模特兒讓他得到了一些報酬。《爐邊閱讀的人》（Man reading at the fireside，頁92 [KM 128.322]）和《爐邊的老人》（Old man at the fireside，頁95 [KM 120.849]）這兩幅室內習作的靈感則是來自於梵谷景仰的藝術家Jozef Israëls的類似作品「對於窮困人家」的寫實描述。透過鉛筆、畫筆、蠟筆和少量局部的色彩，梵谷能夠把貧苦農人家中的氣氛表現在畫作中。11月底他第二次前往海牙時，他把這些人物素描拿給莫弗看，莫弗注意到梵谷距離他的模特兒太近，以至於失去了視覺上的比例。然而在農人居住的狹窄小屋裡，並不是很容易能夠保持著距離作畫。

海牙時期

在莫弗的鼓勵之下，加上與父母的不和，梵谷決定在1881年搬到海牙定居，他從1869年開始就在那裡的古比藝術貿易公司工作了四年，因此海牙對他而言是個相當熟悉的城市。12月他在莫弗的畫室上了約三週的課程之後，全神貫注在人物寫生及街景的素描上，而那三週的課程也激勵他完成了他的第一幅油畫。同時他也向其他藝術家學習，像是與他一起在街上尋找適合主題的巴雷納（George Breitner）和委辛本（Hendrik Weissenbruch），但大多數時間梵谷還是獨自創作。

到了海牙之後，梵谷一開始住在Schenkweg（後改名為Schenkstraat）街旁、Rijnspoor車站（今為海牙中央車站）正後方的一間有凹室的房間，他也在這裡設立了他的畫室，在當時這裡是城市的邊

《爐邊的女人》，1881年10至11月，素描，
庫勒穆勒美術館，奧特羅 [KM 116. 182]

6. 庫勒穆勒夫人給S. van Deventer的信，1912年3月28日。當時這幅素描還不是庫勒穆勒夫人的收藏，但她對於Vincent van Gogh-100 Teekeningen uit de Verzameling Hiddle Nijland in hett Museum te Dordrecht （阿姆斯特丹，1905）當中的複製品十分熟悉。
7. 梵谷給西奧的信（170/149）
8. 同上。

緣地帶。在那裡他努力地以模特兒作畫，他初期的人物素描例如《爐邊的女人》（*Woman at the fireside*, [KM 116.182]），很清楚地表現出他還是在比例當中掙扎，像是女人過長的大腿，還有火盆與椅子間過遠的距離。然而照著莫弗的建議，梵谷已經和他的模特兒之間保持了較遠的距離。在這幅作品中，他用黑色蠟筆和尺描繪出了地板。1882年7月，他搬到了同在Schenkstraat街上鄰近的一棟房子裡，有了一間稍大的畫室及一間閣樓。

在平面上表現空間和比例關係的估算困擾了梵谷一輩子，為了在這方面變得更熟練，他在1882年開始使用一個方便的工具─透視框（Perspective Frame）。這個木製的框架可以與一到兩根桿子組合，拉緊的細線可以創造出特定的格局。例如一條水平和一條垂直的線，與兩條對角線相互交集在框架中心；或是一個垂直與水平線組成的方格。這些線條以相同比例被轉移到畫紙或畫布上，畫家透過透視框來觀察主題之後，便能夠快速而正確地完成合理的畫面構成。在海牙，梵谷很頻繁地使用透視框，在很多素描中還可以看到他沒有擦掉的格線痕跡。舉例來說，在《Schenkweg沿路的水溝》（*Ditch along Schenkweg*, [KM 113.904]）這幅素描中的天空部分，可以

《Schenkweg沿路的水溝》，1882年3月，素描，庫勒穆勒美術館，奧特羅 [KM 113. 904]

很清楚地看到格線。他在8月寫了一封信給西奧：「這個冬天我花在顏料的費用減少了，但為了學習透視及比例，我花了更多的錢在一件杜勒（Albert Dürer）的作品中有提到，也被傳統荷蘭大師所使用的工具上。它能夠用來比較近物和遠處的比例，以免畫家不能依照透視規則完成構圖。除非是受過訓練或經驗豐富，否則單靠雙眼要得到正確的透視比例，是很容易失誤的。」[9] 梵谷在他的作畫生涯中都使用這個工具，只有在最後的幾年較少使用。

在海牙的這段時間，梵谷實驗了各種不同的素描技巧。在西奧的堅持之下，梵谷開始畫水彩畫，在當時的藝術市場，水彩畫比黑白的素描更容易賣出。但梵谷在使用層層透明水彩來描繪構成時，遭遇了相當大的困難。他傾向於使用稀釋過的不透明水彩或樹膠水彩，在鉛筆或炭筆的草稿上作畫。他最喜愛的作畫工具是一種在橢圓木筆桿中有長條石墨，叫做木匠鉛筆的筆，這種筆能夠畫出粗細不同的線條。他偏好用這種筆在粗糙耐用的紙上作畫，並用稀釋的牛奶來固定他的素描。這個動作消去了石墨的光澤而使作品變得自然，梵谷認為：「比起一般的鉛筆素描要生動許多。」[10] 版畫蠟筆是另一樣他在粗糙水彩紙上作畫的主要工具。這種含油極多深黑色的蠟筆被用在石版作畫上，除了刮刀之外很難能夠消除筆跡，當然在紙上就更難消去。梵谷主要使用這種蠟筆來修飾鉛筆素描，使得畫作有更強烈的黑白對比。因此他不必在素描作品中「潤飾」太多，而且也「不需要檢查和拭去太多」。[11] 此外，在1883年初，他對於有著深咖啡色彩的天然粉筆相當著迷，在西奧寄給他之後，他甚至想要訂購50公升的這種粉筆。他也使用炭筆作畫，儘管他覺得這是一種很容易在作畫過程中被擦拭掉，不太容易使用的工具。然而使梵谷能達到他最吸引人的效果的工具，則是筆和墨水。

在那段時期，梵谷從雜誌像是《倫敦新聞畫報》（*The Illustrated London News*）和《畫報》（*The Graphic*）中剪輯，積極地收集木刻版畫。從他到倫敦替古比藝術貿易公司工作時，他就對這些雜誌相當地熟悉，同時他也很欣賞幾位在這些雜誌投稿的藝術家，包括了Hubert von

9. 梵谷給西奧的信（235/205）
10. 梵谷給西奧的信（216/187）
11. 梵谷給西奧的信（298/256）

Herkmoer。梵谷本身也很嚮往替雜誌工作。他的木刻畫收藏所包含的社會寫實主題，激勵他在1882年秋天和1883年夏末創作了石版畫，替自己成為一位插畫家鋪路。

　　梵谷在海牙街道上的速寫，為他帶來了第一件真正的委託。他的叔叔柯爾（Cor），阿姆斯特丹的藝術商Cornelis Marinus van Gogh，在參觀過梵谷的畫室之後對於「一幅小素描」非常有興趣。根據梵谷的說法，「我在一次與巴雷納於午夜十二點散步在Paddemoes（靠近Nieuwe Kerk的猶太區）時，速寫了從Turfmarket看到的景色。」柯爾立刻就向他訂購了一系列12幅小型的都市景色，梵谷自己開價每幅2.5法郎。如果這個系列讓人滿意，柯爾就會訂購另一系列較大幅、較高價的阿姆斯特丹街景，他的叔叔柯爾說：「這樣你就可以賺到一些錢了」。[12]《海牙一景》（View of The Hague ['Paddemoes']，頁105 [KM 118.997]）就是讓那位畫商如此著迷的素描，而Ditch along Schenkweg（[KM 113.904]）則是梵谷在兩週內完成

《木匠的工場和晾衣場》，1882年5月底，素描，庫勒穆勒美術館，奧特羅 [KM 116.039]

的第一個小幅街景系列之一。梵谷得到了第二次的委託，但是主題從阿姆斯特丹改為海牙，而件數也減至6幅而非12幅。為了第一個系列，梵谷概略地參訪了海牙的各個角落，以第一個系列為基礎，他的叔叔極力主張他應該要畫出更明確細緻的街景。梵谷在5月底創作的這幅動人的《木匠的工場和晾衣場》（Carpenter's Yard and Laundry, [KM 116.039]），就是第二次委託的一部份，最後這系列是由7張素描所組成。藝術家本人一直形容這些素描是透視法的習作。這幅充滿力量的素描，詳盡地呈現出梵谷畫室窗外的景色，在右邊有洗好正在晾乾的衣服，而在其後則有辛勤木匠勞動的木匠工場。《席凡寧根的晒鰈魚乾場》（Dab-drying Barn in Scheveningen，頁114 [KM 122.835]）也屬於第二次委託的這個系列。透過他的藝術商叔叔柯爾的仲介，這兩幅作品在1895年之前，就已經為收藏家Hidde Nijland所擁有，而在1928年，庫勒先生則直接向這位收藏家購買了他所有的梵谷收藏。

　　梵谷在海牙結識了席恩（Sien Hoornik）並與她同居。雖然遭到了家人的強烈反對，其他朋友也不看好他與這個懷孕的（前）妓女同時也是未婚媽媽的關係，梵谷還是很開心能夠組成這樣一個家庭。而席恩在7月初生下了一個男孩威廉（Willem）。此外，梵谷無法支付模特兒費用的問題也立刻得到了解決辦法：席恩與她的妹妹還有她們的母親，經常會來擔任他的模特兒。許多大幅或較小幅的坐姿、裁縫婦女和母子畫像習作，都是在海牙的這個時期完成，《母與子》（Mother with child，頁123 [KM 112.180]）這幅敏銳的素描，是其中一幅有上色的作品。

　　1882年9月，梵谷接觸了荷蘭改革宗老人之家（Nederlands Hervormde Oude-mannen-en-vrouwen-huis）的居民，並把這些人加入他的作畫模特兒清單之中。在這段時間裡，他也增加了二手勞工服飾的收藏，他大多要求這些人穿著這些服飾擺出姿勢：「工作服、合身夾克、舊大衣、圍巾、帽子，別忘了還有傳統的雨帽（sou'wester）。」在1883年1月，他設法留住最後這一件雨帽，使得一系列漁夫的習作得以完成。梵谷稱這些人為「孤兒」（orphan men），根據一張描繪其中一個人的速寫，這位模特兒的身分可以被辨識出來。換言之，梵谷在這張速寫的下方寫上了「199號」，這個號碼也被繡在夾克的袖子上；所有這裡的居民都被要求佩上一個註冊號碼，而這個擔任梵谷模特兒最頻繁的人是Adrianus Jacobus Zuyderland。梵谷寫信給西奧說道：「他有一顆友善

---

12. 梵谷給西奧的信（210/181）

《悲傷的老人》，1882年11-12月，素描，庫勒穆勒美術館，奧特羅 [KM 124.396]

的禿頭、（聾的）大耳朵和白色的鬢鬚。」[13] 戴著帽子或制服帽和經常穿著黑色長大衣的Zuyderland，在很多習作中都可以被認出來（頁128 [KM 118.619] 及頁127 [KM 113.952]）。Zuyderland也替《悲傷的老人》（Sorrowing Old Man, [photo KM 124.396]）這件與梵谷稍早的At Eternity's Gate相對映的作品擔任模特兒。文生寫道：「穿著他縫釘的衣服，還有他的禿頭，一位老勞工是如此地帥氣。」[14]

在將近兩年定居海牙的時間裡，梵谷花了大部分的時間在素描上。他的油畫創作只限於夏天的月份，他覺得他必須要先大量地素描，來使他的油畫能得到好的結果。

德倫特時期

在1883年大約8月的時候，梵谷第一次告訴他的弟弟，他想要搬到德倫特，荷蘭最北邊人口最稀少的一個省份。席恩跟她母親日益嚴重的爭執—她母親希望她「重操舊業」，海牙昂貴的物價，加上梵谷本身希望回歸自然，促成了他做出這個決定。此外，凡・拉帕德也使梵谷對於德倫特廣闊的荒原和風景如畫的村莊感到著迷。同時梵谷也想要把重心擺在比素描昂貴許多的油畫練習上，而他也希望能藉由住在物價便宜許多的德倫特來省下一大筆開銷。但事實上，所有事情都令人失望。他在那裡待了三個月（從9月初到12月初），但當地居民拒絕擔任他的模特兒，他在那裡沒有自己的畫室，實際上在那裡要取得作畫或素描的工具，是極度困難的。他一開始就發現那裡的景色像是沙漠一般，令人不快的無趣且使人厭煩，同時也是不適合居留和不友善的。[15] 只有在暮色低垂，景色有了變化時才能吸引他。在一封寫給西奧的信中他告訴他的弟弟：「我完成了幾張荒原景色的習作，等它們乾了我再把它們寄給你，同時我也開始使用水彩作畫。還有，我又開始畫墨水筆素描了，畫的其實和我剛剛提到的那些油畫是同樣的景色，因為素描能夠表現出油畫做不到的細節，而且我認為就同樣景色畫出兩種習作是個不錯的主意：一幅素描出畫面中的每一個細節，另一幅則是畫出色彩。」[16]

梵谷直接用筆在（書寫的）紙上畫了一幅婦女頭像，可能是在霍赫芬（Hoogeveen）到新阿姆斯特丹村的接駁船上，他就坐在婦女旁邊，因此沒有辦法保持足夠的距離，只能從很近的位置素描（頁155 [KM 128.378]）。她憂鬱的神情被梵谷完整地捕捉下來：從她深色有面紗的帽子來判斷，她可能正在服喪。梵谷也著迷於當地充滿特色的房屋和泥草屋：在泥沼中苦幹的勞工們所居住的貧瘠泥炭小屋（頁153 [KM 121.207]）。三個月之後，梵谷來到努南（Nuenen），再一次與他的父母及最年幼的妹妹同住。1882年，梵谷的父親被指派為努南的改革教會牧師，他的家人離開了埃頓，搬到了位於布拉邦的另一個城市—努南。

---

13. 梵谷給西奧的信（271/235）
14. 梵谷給西奧的信（288/247）
15. 梵谷給西奧的信（390/325）
16. 梵谷給西奧的信（391/326）

Van Gogh as Draughtsman: early years, 1880-1883

Aukje Vergeest

Teio Meedendorp

The Kröller-Müller Museum possesses 179 drawings, 2 lithos and 1 etching by Vincent van Gogh on a total of 164 sheets of paper: some have drawings on both sides. The majority of this collection was acquired by Mr Kröller from the collector Hidde Nijland in 1928: 112 drawings in total. At that time, the couple Kröller-Müller already owned 47 sheets, and the remaining 5 were added to the collection after 1941, after the death of Helene Kröller-Müller and her husband. In this collection, the drawings from Van Gogh's Dutch period (1880-85) are the most abundantly represented; only a few examples from his French drawing oeuvre are included.

This makes the Kröllers one of the earliest Dutch collectors of Van Gogh. Currently this is the second largest collection of work by Van Gogh anywhere in the world: together with the paintings, the Kröller-Müller Museum possesses over 250 works by this artist, who gained particular notoriety for his dynamic brushstrokes and intense colour palette. And yet, he made more drawings than paintings and, like most artists, at the start of his career Van Gogh first practiced by drawing. Below are a number of essays that sketch Van Gogh's development as a draughtsman in the periods: The early years 1880-83, when he lived consecutively in the Borinage, Brussels, Etten, The Hague and Drenthe; Nuenen, 1883-85; and finally Saint-Rémy 1889-90. [1]

The early years 1880-1883

> *The thing for me to do is to learn how to draw well, to become a master, whether of my pencil, whether of my charcoal, whether of my paintbrush. I cannot tell you (although new difficulties arise every day and will continue arising) how delighted I am that I have taken to drawing again.*
>
> Vincent to Theo, 24 September 1880, Cuesmes (Borinage) (157/136)

In 1880, Vincent van Gogh decided to become an artist. He was 27 at the time and already had careers behind him as a sales clerk at the internationally renowned art-dealers Goupil & Cie, as a teacher and a bookseller. When an initiative to study theology was unsuccessful and his temporary appointment as evangelist in the Belgian mining district the Borinage was not extended, it was his younger brother Theo who first suggested becoming an artist.

Van Gogh immediately began working in a systematic fashion. On August 20th 1880, in the first letter we are aware of since his decision, he wrote to Theo: 'If I'm not mistaken, you should still have *Les traveaux des champs* by Millet. Would you be so kind as to loan it to me for a while and send it by post. You should know that I am working on large sketches after Millet [...] I write to you while I am drawing and want to get back to work soon.' [2] He tried to master the drawing techniques independently, more or less following the methods of a regular course at an art academy: copying from prints and special examples. Thus he copied prints as well as photographs after the work of Jean-François Millet, the painter of the French peasant life,

---

1. For these essays, frequent and grateful use has been made of the excellent already existing publications on Van Gogh as a draughtsman, in particular the file catalogues of the Van Gogh Museum *Drawings I, II, III and IV*, by Sjraar van Heugten (I-III), Marije Vellekoop (III-IV) and Roelie Zwikker (IV) (Amsterdam 1996-2007), *Van Gogh Draughtsman. The Masterworks*, by Sjraar van Heugten (Amsterdam 2005), and the most recent file catalogue of the Kröller-Müller Museum, with detailed descriptions of the drawings from their own collection, *Drawings and prints of Vincent van Gogh in the collection of the Kröller-Müller Museum*, by Teio Meedendorp (Otterlo 2007). The fragments of letters quoted in the text are accompanied by a reference to the letter numbering used in the edition *De brieven van Vincent van Gogh*, edited by Han van Crimpen and Monique Berends-Albert, The Hague 1990.
2. Letter to Theo (155/134).

who would remain a lifelong example for him. *Les bêcheurs* (p. 63, [KM 119.703]) and *L'angélus du soir* (p. 61 [KM 115.117]) are drawings of hard-working farmers, which Van Gogh made from photographs of drawings by Millet that he had borrowed from an art-dealer.

Van Gogh also gathered technical knowledge from books. The publications of Armand Cassagne in particular, were an important aid in the first years. Cassagne dealt with various artistic problems such as perspective, depth effect, proportions and anatomy. 'The thing that has cured my doubting', he later wrote to Theo, 'is that I read a comprehensible book on perspective, Cassagne, *Guide de l'ABC du dessin*, and 8 days later, drew an interior of a small kitchen with a stove, table and chair & window in their proper places and standing on their legs, whereas previously it seemed to me some sort of witchcraft or coincidence that one had depth & correct perspective in a drawing.' This book, officially titled *Guide de l'Alphabet du dessin*, contains a simple explanation of the basic principles of drawing. The three part loose-leaf publication *Cours de dessin (Drawing course)* by Charles Bargue was also an indispensible aid. In these first months, he mostly made copies from this publication, such as the portrait of *The Daughter of Jacob Meyer* (p.69 [KM 128.492]). Apart from the copies, he also made a few drawings of his own, including *Miners in the snow* (p. 59 [KM 111.966]). In this drawing, the paper of which is heavily discoloured and damaged, Van Gogh's still uncertain hand can be seen in the many corrections to the contours of the figures.[3] Van Gogh moved to Brussels in October 1880, in search of a more artistic environment and wanting to see works of art. He enrolled at the Académie Royal des Beaux-Arts, but it is unclear whether he actually took classes there. In Brussels, he asked the older Hague School master Willem Roelofs for advice and sought contact with younger artists. There, he became acquainted with Anthon van Rappard, who had already been practicing art for 4 years and in whose studio he was occasionally permitted to work. Although very little work from this earliest period remains, Brussels was important for Van Gogh because there he made strict anatomical studies - and few compositions of his own.[4] For his living expenses he was dependent on his family, originally his parents, but as of February 1881, Theo increasing bore the responsibility, until the artist's eventual death.

Etten

In April 1881, Van Gogh went to live with his parents in the village of Etten in North Brabant. There, in addition to making copies he applied himself particularly to rendering motifs from the surrounding area, while the local population also provided him with ample subject matter. Anthon van Rappard visited him at the start of the summer and together they searched for suitable landscape motifs. His self-confidence grew: 'at present I feel that after all: "I have a draughtsman's fist", and I am so happy to have such an instrument on my body, although it is still rather awkward'. [5]

In the drawing *Corner of a garden* (p. 67 [KM 115.487]) from that summer, Van Gogh very precisely depicted a romantic scene: an arbour against an overgrown wall in a garden. The empty garden furniture emphasizes the absence of people. Some details are very accurately rendered (the chequered cloth on the ground, the furniture) but are at the same time 'awkward': the tabletop is not centred on its leg, the chair on the left seems to be dancing. Mrs Kröller-Müller loved this work, as is evident in a letter to her confidant Sam van Deventer: 'Salomon, you shall now better understand that picture of Van Gogh: the seat, the table and that oh so quiet garden. Could you not imagine that two people had been sitting there & had just left, who had experienced nothing & yet so much, who also saw that garden in such a simple and magnificent splendour? [...] Take another look at that picture, which I was always so fond of, & which contrasts so greatly with the intensity of feeling in the other works by Van Gogh'. [6]

At the end of August 1881, Van Gogh visited his cousin by marriage in The Hague, the established

3. Letter to Theo (213/184).
4. Letter to Theo (163/142).
5. Letter to Theo (179/155).
6. from H. Kröller-Müller to S. van Deventer, 28 March 1912. At that time the drawing was not yet in her possession, but she was familiar with the reproduction from the publication Vincent van Gogh - 100 Teekeningen uit de Verzameling Hidde Nijland in hett Museum te Dordrecht, Amsterdam 1905.

master of the Hague School Anton Mauve, after which he began experimenting with new materials and techniques. Until then, he had drawn mainly in pencil and pen and ink, but Mauve had advised him: 'you ought to try it with charcoal & crayon & brush & stump for a change'. [7] That summer he also received *Traité d'Aquarelle* as a gift from Cassagne. Originally he only used watercolour in combination with other techniques. *Windmills at Dordrecht (Weeskinderendijk)* (p. 72 [KM 126.249]) from August-September shows, for example, a multitude of techniques: pencil, crayon, pen, brush and opaque watercolour. From the enthusiastic letters he wrote after his return from The Hague, it is possible to deduce that Van Gogh, who was constantly slogging away on his own, thrived in the vicinity of art and other artists: thus, he enthusiastically discussed the works he had seen in The Hague at the sixth exhibition of the Hollandsche Teekenmaatschappij and hoped that his visit might be 'a first step towards getting to know Mauve & others more seriously'. [8]

In the autumn of 1881, he made dozens of drawings after live models, preferably working farmers and their wives: sifting, digging, sowing seeds, peeling potatoes or sewing. From this period, the Kröller-Müller Museum has various drawings in its possession, which often appear somewhat stiff: the figures are not truly at work, it often remains a pose. Van Gogh occasionally had his figures assume a more complicated posture, in order to practice drawing in the correct proportions. For example, he drew the figure in *Boy with a sickle* (p. 87 [KM 111.847]) from the side, while the figure is kneeling on the ground with one leg and squatting with the other. We know that this model was the 17-year-old Piet Kauffman, who tended the garden of the minister Van Gogh. He received a few pennies for sitting. *The Man reading at the fireside* and *Old man at the fireside*, two interior studies (p. 92 [KM 128.322] and p.95 [KM 120.849]), are inspired by similar realistic depictions of the 'impoverished people' by Jozef Israels, an artist admired by Van Gogh. Using pencil, pen, crayon and small accents of colour, Van Gogh is able suggest the atmosphere of a poor farmers hut. When Van Gogh made a second trip to The Hague in late November, he showed figure drawings such as these to Mauve, who remarked that he sat too close to his models, causing him to lost sight of the proportions. In the cramped huts where the farmers lived, however, it was not always easy to work at a distance.

The Hague

Encouraged by Mauve - and due to disagreements with his parents - in 1881, Van Gogh decided to move permanently to The Hague, a city he already knew well as he had worked there at the art-dealers for four years from 1869. He concentrated on drawing after live models and cityscapes, after initially taking classes at Mauve's studio for around three weeks in December, which spurred him on to make his first oil painting. He also learned from other artists such as George Breitner (with whom he searched for suitable motifs in the streets) and Hendrik Weissenbruch, but Van Gogh still did most things alone.

In The Hague, Van Gogh first lived in a room with an alcove on a side street of the Schenkweg (later named the Schenkstraat), just behind the Rijnspoor railway station (now The Hague Central Station), where he had also set up his studio. At that time, this was on the edge of the city. There he worked from models, and his first figure drawings, such as *Woman at the fireside* ([KM 116.182]), clearly show his continuing struggle with proportions, for instance, in the long upper legs of the woman, and the large distance between her chair and the brazier. Nevertheless, Van Gogh already maintained a greater distance to his model, as Mauve had suggested. He depicted the

Woman at the fireside, 1881 Oct.-Nov., drawing, Kröller-Müller Museum, Otterlo [KM 116. 182]

7. Letter to Theo (170/149).

8. Idem.

Ditch along Schenkweg, 1882 Mar., drawing, Kröller-Müller Museum, Otterlo [KM 113. 904]

floorboards by using a ruler to trace lines in black crayon. In July 1882, he moved into an adjoining building on the Schenkstraat, where he was able to set up a slightly larger studio and also had an attic.

The rendering of space onto a flat surface and assessing the mutual proportions remained problematic for Van Gogh throughout his entire life. In order to become more proficient in this, in 1882 he started using a convenient tool, the perspective frame. In this wooden frame, which could be attached to one or two poles, threads were stretched to create a certain pattern: for example, a horizontal and vertical line that, together with two diagonal lines, intersect each other in the centre, or a square grid of horizontal and vertical threads. These lines were transferred the paper or canvas in the same proportions, after which the artist viewed the motif through the perspective frame and was thus able to make a first layout of the composition reasonably fast and correctly. In The Hague, Van Gogh frequently used the perspective frame, which is often apparent from the traces of the grid that he did not take the trouble of erasing and which can still be seen in many of the drawings. In *Ditch along Schenkweg* ([KM 113.904]), for example, the remains of a grid are clearly visible in the sky section. 'While my expenses for paint have been lower this winter than others', he wrote to Theo in August, 'I have made higher expenses with regard to the study of perspective & proportion, for an instrument the description of which appears in a work by Albert Dürer and which was also used by the old Dutch masters. That which makes it possible to compare the proportions of nearby objects with those of a far distant plane, in cases where the construction cannot be made according to the rules of perspective. That which - unless highly experienced & trained - is constantly wide of the mark when one attempts it *with the eye*'.[9] Van Gogh used this aid throughout his entire career, though less frequently in the final years.

During his period in The Hague, Van Gogh experimented with various drawing techniques. At the insistence of Theo, he began making watercolours, which according to the prevailing rules of the art trade at the time were more saleable than black-and-white drawings. Van Gogh, however, had great difficulty with pure watercolour painting, the construction of a depiction in watery transparent layers of paint. He preferred to work with (thinned) opaque watercolour or gouache on top of an initial layout in pencil or charcoal. His favourite drawing material was the so-called carpenter's pencil, a broad rectangular stick of graphite in an oval wooden pencil shaft, with which both thin and broad lines can be made. He drew with this preferably on coarse and durable paper and used diluted milk to fix his drawings. This removed the silvery gloss of the graphite and made it nicely matt, according to Van Gogh, 'much livelier than one usually sees in a pencil drawing'.[10] Another material he used predominantly on coarse watercolour paper was lithographic crayon. The extremely oily, deep black crayon was used in lithography to draw onto the stone and could not be removed other than with a scraper, which is of course rather difficult with paper. Therefore, Van Gogh used it primarily to touch up pencil drawings and give them a more intense black and white contrast. Thus, he did not need to 'polish' too much in a drawing and could work 'without having to seek or erase much'.[11] Moreover, in early 1883 he was so enthusiastic about the natural chalk, that had a dark brown tint, which Theo had once sent him, that he wanted to order a 'half mud' (i.e. 50 litres). He did also work with charcoal, although he found it a difficult material that easily rubbed off during the drawing. The materials with which he was able to achieve perhaps the most appealing results - also later on - were pen and ink.

During that period, Van Gogh was an active collector of woodcuts, which he clipped out of periodicals

9. Letter to Theo (235/205).
10. Letter to Theo (216/187).
11. Letter to Theo (298/256).

such as *The Illustrated London News* and *The Graphic*. He was familiar with these magazines from the time he spent in London working for the art-dealers Goupil and Cie and admired various artists who contributed to them, including Hubert von Herkomer. Van Gogh also aspired to a job on a magazine. His collection of woodcuts, which often had social-realistic subjects, inspired him, for example, in the autumn of 1882 and later in the summer of 1883, to make lithos that were intended to pave the way to a position as illustrator.

The sketches that Van Gogh made in the streets of The Hague gave rise to his first real commission. His uncle Cor, the Amsterdam art-dealer Cornelis Marinus van Gogh, was very enthusiastic after visiting his nephews studio, about 'one small drawing', which according to Vincent, 'I had once sketched while parading around with Breitner at 12 midnight - viz the Paddemoes (that Jewish quarter near the Nieuwe Kerk), seen from the Turfmarkt.' Uncle Cor promptly ordered a series of 12 small cityscapes, which Vincent himself priced at f 2.50 each. If the series was satisfactory, C.M. van Gogh would order another series of Amsterdam cityscapes, in a larger format and at a higher price: 'then you'll earn some money', according to uncle Cor.[12] *View of The Hague ('Paddemoes')* (p. 105 [KM.118.997]) is the drawing that the art-dealer was so enthusiastic about, and *Ditch along Schenkweg* ([KM 113.904]) is also a small cityscape from the first series, which Van Gogh completed within two weeks. The second commission was also awarded, although for larger cityscapes of The Hague instead of Amsterdam, and six instead twelve. On the basis of the first series - for which Van Gogh had generally visited the edges of the city - his uncle had urged him to make more specific and elaborate cityscapes. The magnificent *Carpenter's yard and laundry* ([KM 116.039]) from the end of May was part of this second commission, which would eventually comprise seven drawings. The artist himself always described them as studies in perspective. The powerful drawing shows the view from his studio window and is rich in detail,

Carpenter's Yard and Laundry, 1882 late May, drawing, Kröller-Müller Museum, Otterlo [KM 116. 039]

with washing hung out to dry on the right and the carpenter's workshop further back, where hard labour is being performed. *Dab-drying barn in Scheveningen* (p. 114 [KM 122.835]) also belongs to this second series; before 1895, both works were already - via the art dealership of uncle Cor, C.M. van Gogh - in the possession of the collector Hidde Nijland, from whom Mr Kröller bought virtually his entire collection of Van Gogh drawings in 1928.

In The Hague, Van Gogh became acquainted with Sien Hoornik, with whom he would also live together. Despite the strong disapproval of his family and others concerning his relationship with this pregnant (ex) prostitute and unmarried mother, Van Gogh was happy to form a kind of family. Sien bore a son in early July, Willem. Moreover, Van Gogh's lack of expensive models was solved immediately: Sien and her younger sister, and their mother, regularly sat for him. Various large and smaller studies of sitting, sewing women, and scenes of a mother with child stem from this period in The Hague, one of which was also in colour, the sensitive drawing *Mother with child* (p. 123 [KM 112.180]).

In September 1882, Van Gogh came into contact with the residents of the Nederlands Hervormde Oude-mannen-en-vrouwen-huis (Dutch Reformed Old People's Home), who he added to his list of painter's models. In the meantime, he had also built up a fair collection of used (labourer's) costumes, in which he asked principally the men to pose: 'various smocks, tight jackets, old coats, scarves, hats, not forgetting the sou'wester'. He had managed to get hold of this last item in January 1883 and it led to a series of studies depicting fishermen. Van Gogh called the men 'orphan men'. Based on a sketch of one of these men, it was possible to ascertain the identity of the model. That is to say, Van Gogh had written 'No 199' under the sketch, the number that was also sewn into the long sleeve of the jacket; all the residents of the home were required to wear a registration number. This man, who would pose most frequently for Van Gogh,

12. Letter to Theo (210/181).

Sorrowing Old Man, 1882 Nov.-
Dec., drawing, Kröller-Müller
Museum, Otterlo [KM 124. 396]

was Adrianus Jacobus Zuyderland. 'He has a friendly, bald head, big ears (deaf) and white sideburns', he wrote to Theo. [13] Zuyderland can be recognized in many of the studies, with a hat or cap and often wearing a long black coat (p. 128 [KM 118.619] and p. 127 [KM 113.952]). Zuyderland also posed for the *Sorrowing old man*, a mirrored version of the print *At eternity's gate*, that he made a little earlier. Vincent wrote: 'How handsome such an old labourer is, in his patched bombazine suit and with his bald head'. [14]

Most of the nearly two years that Van Gogh stayed in The Hague was spent drawing. His painting with oils was restricted primarily to the summer months and he felt he had to draw a great deal first, in order to arrive at attractive results in his painting as well.

Drenthe

Around August 1883, Van Gogh informed his brother for the first time of his intention to go and live in Drenthe, one of the most northerly and sparsely populated provinces of the Netherlands. The escalating arguments with Sien and her mother - who wanted her to go 'back on the game' - the expensive city, but also the longing to be back amongst nature, led him to this decision. Furthermore, Van Rappard had made him enthusiastic about the countryside in Drenthe, with its wide heath lands and picturesque villages. Van Gogh also wanted to focus on the far more expensive practice of painting and thought he could save a lot of money by going to live in the much cheaper Drenthe. But in reality everything was disappointing. He stayed there for three months (from early September to early December), but the local inhabitants refused to pose for him, he had no studio there, it was virtually impossible to obtain painting or drawing materials and initially he found the landscape 'agaçant dull and tiresome as the desert, equally inhospitable and hostile, as it were'. [15] Only when the evening twilight fell, did the landscape undergo a metamorphosis that was to seduce him. In a letter to Theo he informed him: 'I have a few studies of the heath land, which I will send you when they are properly dry, and have also started making watercolours. And, I have started making pen drawings again, actually with a view to the painting, because it is possible to go into details with a pen that cannot be done in a painted study, and it is a good idea to make two studies: one entirely drawn to get everything in its place and one painted for the colour.' [16]

Van Gogh drew the head of a woman in pen directly onto (writing) paper - probably on the tow barge from Hoogeveen to the village of Nieuw-Amsterdam - from very nearby, as if he was sitting next to her and was almost unable to gain enough distance (p. 155 [KM 128.378]). Her melancholic expression is captured well; she is probably in mourning, judging by her dark, crêpe-veiled bonnet. He was also enchanted by the characteristic houses and huts in the region: the poor sod huts or peat sheds, where labourers who toiled in the peat bog would live (p. 153 [KM 121.207]). After three months, Van Gogh left Drenthe to once again live with his parents (and youngest sister) in Nuenen. In 1882, the Van Gogh family had moved from Etten to another town in Brabant, Nuenen, where his father was appointed as minister of the Reformed congregation.

13. Letter to Theo (271/235).
14. Letter to Theo (288/247).
15. Letter to Theo (390/325).
16. Letter to Theo (391/326).

梵谷的素描：努南時期（1883－1885）

泰歐‧梅登多普
歐克耶‧斐黑斯特

> 在這幅新的素描裡，我從軀幹的部份開始描繪人物，在我看來這樣做使他們變得更圓潤飽滿。如果50幅不夠，我就素描100幅，如果還是不夠我就素描更多，直到我確實地達成我想要的目標—所有東西都是豐滿的。這樣的形式沒有所謂的開始或結束的點，但它構成了一個和諧鮮活的整體。
>
> 梵谷給西奧的信，約1885年6月2日（509/410）

經過了兩年在海牙和德倫特的日子後，隨著梵谷在1883年12月4日回到家中，他與父母的衝突似乎和緩了一些。但很快地，他們的關係很明顯地變得相當糟糕，而且一直沒有好轉。梵谷和他父親兩個人的個性可以說是水火不容，梵谷回家約一週後，他寫信給西奧說道：

> 讓我留在家裡對他們來說，就像是讓一隻無賴的大狗待在家裡一樣地不情願。他帶著濕腳掌進入房間，如此地難以駕馭，**還有他大聲刺耳的吠叫。**簡單來說，就是一頭骯髒的野獸。……那條狗只後悔他沒有遠離這裡，儘管有他們的幫忙，住在這房子裡，比在荒原還寂寞。[1]

透過書信，西奧扮演起梵谷與父親的調解者，儘管關係這麼糟糕，梵谷還是得到了父母的支持。他的父母讓他使用洗衣的軋乾房作為畫室和儲藏室，在一封給西奧的信中，他很諷刺地描述了他的工作室，位在炭棚跟糞坑中間，前後被污水管包圍著。跟他在海牙的畫室相比，這房間只能算是勉強堪用。然而在1884年5月，他透過Schafrat夫婦找到了一間有兩個房間的套房，藉此除了食宿之外，他不需要再麻煩他的父母。一年之後，在梵谷的父親過世後，他也搬到那間套房住，而Schafrat是天主教的教堂司事這個身分，也使得梵谷新教牧師的家庭氣氛不再和諧。

在努南的這段時間，梵谷對他的工作及作品的市場價值終於有了更多的自信。從此開始，他希望能把一直以來西奧給他的生活費，當作是把作品寄給弟弟所得到的報酬。此外，梵谷希望，在古比藝術貿易公司的巴黎蒙馬特大道經營自己部門的西奧，能夠積極地試賣他的作品。這讓西奧相當為難，即便是他想這麼做，也很難在主管的注意之下公開讓大眾注意到哥哥的作品。[2]因為在1876年，梵谷就是被巴黎的主管給解雇的。雖然偶爾西奧會把某些作品給他的畫商朋友看，但他或許並未更進一步地安置梵谷的素描和畫作，這也導致了這對兄弟之間較為不愉快的書信。

梵谷的妹妹Willemien曾經向他描述過努南這個在布拉邦的美麗村莊景色，在他一抵達那個村莊後，便開始描繪當地的景色及居民。他高度的期望沒有落空：「文明」發展還沒有滲入到這個地方，這對梵谷來說是很重要的一點。他喜歡身處農夫和織布工之間，他認為他們是誠實而單純的，並且「與我們有教養的階層過著完全不同的生活。」[3]在十九世紀末工業化遽增的威脅下，梵谷變得更依戀鄉村的純樸。追隨著巴比松畫派，梵谷希望可以用他對鄉村生活的描寫，給鄉

---

1. 梵谷給西奧的信，約1883年12月15日（415/346）。
2. 在1884年Goupil家族退出之後，這間藝術貿易公司就改名為Boussod, Valadon & Cie, successerus de Goupil & Cie。
3. 梵谷給西奧的信，約1885年4月30日（501/404）。

村畫帶來新的動力。在海牙他讀了宋思爾（Sensier）所著的米勒傳記，米勒是他在這方面最好的榜樣。漸漸地他對人物素描發展出一種特殊的看法，只要畫中人物是「活的」，表現出絕佳的表情和個性，結構上的完美就不再是最重要的。梵谷也知道這需要非常多的學習才能實現。然而，素描習作再一次，甚至更勝以往地，成爲他繪畫的工具。他想成爲雜誌插畫家的企圖漸漸地消散了，取而代之的是想成爲全盤的藝術家。在努南他最常用來創作的工具是沾水筆和墨水（主要用於風景畫）、鉛筆（用於精細的素描）、黑色蠟筆（用來表現更生動的表情和更強烈的明暗對比）和他在海牙嘗試過的不透明水彩（稀釋過並常與其他素材結合）。

當時北布拉邦的紡織工業十分興盛，儘管在日益工業化的時代，在努南及周邊地區約有400名在家工作的紡織工人。[4]梵谷曾在波林納吉認識了一些紡織工人，他在當時對他們十分著迷。「如果有一天我被允許畫下他們，而這些從未，或者說幾乎沒有被出版過的畫作類型能夠問世，我會認爲自己相當幸運。」當時他這樣告訴西奧。[5]紡織工的確很少被當作畫題，在努南的前三個月裡，針對這個主題梵谷畫了大概10幅的油畫和大約16幅的素描。「這些人非常難畫，在他們狹窄的房舍裡很難有足夠的距離可以站著畫紡織機，我相信這是爲什麼畫他們常常注定失敗的原因。但我已經找到一個可以容納兩台紡織機，並讓我完成畫作的地方了。」[6]梵谷跟著他造訪努南約10天的朋友凡・拉帕德開始思考如何捕捉「織布工和戶外各種美好的景象。」[7]《在房間前的織

《在房間前的織工》，1884年5至6月，素描，庫勒穆勒美術館，奧特羅 [KM 121.558]

工》（Weaver in front of his room, [KM 121.558]）是一幅根據油畫《紡織機與織工》（Loom with Weaver，頁175 [KM 105.976]）的素描，現爲庫勒穆勒美術館收藏。[8]這幅素描非常強調加強亮度的部分，這使人聯想到蝕刻版畫或雕版畫。梵谷認爲這幅素描已臻完善，可能也具有市場價值，很明顯的證據就是他在作品右下角清楚的簽名。順道一提，原本在作品左下角有一個更大的簽名，但可能梵谷認爲它會使得構圖不均衡而抹去了它，那道痕跡還能夠模糊地被看見。

在1884年的3月到4月間，梵谷專注於風景畫的創作，於是完成了一個系列約7幅可算是他荷蘭時期傑作的大尺寸素描。這個系列很明顯地，如同在海牙替他的叔叔柯爾委託的系列所用的方法一樣，他回復以筆和墨水來素描，用這些工具他更常能達到令人印象深刻的結果。有一次他對畫家Jan Hendrik Weissenbruch承認，他觀看四周景色猶如用筆來素描它們一樣，Weissenbruch回應他：「那麼你就必須用筆來素描。」[9]舉例來說，名爲《翠鳥》（Kingfisher）的素描（梵谷美術館藏），有著有力的構圖並且是以許多不同的筆觸所完成。在這幅有著蕭條灌樹叢和許多樹群的冬天景色中，在池面上露臉的那隻鳥就佔了較少的重要性。不論是透過西奧或是他的朋友兼同儕

4. C. van der Heijden:「Een zeer armzalig volkje. Leef-en werkomstandigheden van de Nuenense wevers in de tweede helft van de negentiende eeuw」，摘錄於Van den Brink & Frijhof 1990，23-35頁。
5. 梵谷給西奧的信，1880年12月4日（157/136）。
6. 梵谷給西奧的信，約1884年1月2日（422/351）。
7. 梵谷給西奧的信，1884年5月底（450/369）。
8. 分別是《紡織機》（Weaver, 32/JH480）和《紡織機與織工》（Loom with Weaver, F35/JH478）。
9. 梵谷給西奧的信，1882年5月1日（221/195）。

凡‧拉帕德，梵谷都沒有能夠賣掉這些充滿企圖心的素描。這段不如意過後的一陣子，梵谷幾乎全神貫注在他還未純熟的油畫創作上。被色彩理論所吸引，他希望能藉由盡可能地多畫習作，來掌握許多油畫技巧上的問題。

1884年底，梵谷又完成了一些素描習作，這些素描常被拿來當作油畫的草圖。這個時期，以人物為模特兒的油畫佔據了梵谷的心思。很幸運地（特別是在多季，當地沒有太多事情可以做），他找到許多村民願意為了「一個下午或上午幾分錢」的費用擔任他的模特兒。[10]

《食薯者》，1885年4月，石版畫，庫勒穆勒美術館，奧特羅 [KM 126.762]

在他的畫室裡，梵谷有一批用來替他的模特兒著裝的服飾收藏。更有傳言說他有一個「櫥櫃，裡頭裝了至少三十個鳥巢、各類從荒原收集來的苔蘚和植物、一些鳥的標本、梭子、紡車、便盆、所有的鄉村用品、舊帽子、骯髒的婦女帽、木屐等等。」[11] 利用這些道具，梵谷能夠在室內呈現出各種不同的場景，雖然他也在戶外畫了一些速寫來練習某些姿勢。1884年冬天，梵谷完成了約40幅頭部、手部、半身或全身的素描習作。在一張素描（頁165 [KM 114.886]）的紙上畫了一些習作：婦女的頭部，在她左邊可能是同一個人物較粗略、明亮的版本，在那之上則是一個小小的頭。在左下角梵谷以農田為背景，畫了一個肩扛木頭右手持斧頭，走在小徑上的男性。

在梵谷美術館的收藏中可以找到更多頭部細節的習作，包括了大幅的《婦女頭像》（Head of a Woman，梵谷美術館藏），以黑色蠟筆完成的一位農夫妻子的人物側寫。畫中最醒目的就是她的醜陋，和充滿皺紋、疲憊的臉，或是像布瑞默（H.P. Bremmer）—海倫‧庫勒穆勒的藝術「導師」，同時也是顧問所說的，一個「怪物般的人」，有著「被野蠻地重筆描繪」的下頷。[12] 梵谷重視生理學，或者更確切地說是人相學的觀念。這種在18世紀末出現，19世紀末興盛的偽科學觀察方式，認為一個人的個性可以從他的外貌特徵來決定；而且常被拿來和動物做類比。

根據他的朋友所言，梵谷通常會選擇非常與眾不同的，最醜的人作為模特兒。他們的農人面容和與動物的相似之處，讓梵谷確信這些人十分接近自然。在他的信中，他提到這些習作是「人物頭像」（koppen uit het volk），這是他直接參考了《畫報》雜誌中一個描繪勞工特徵的畫像系列《人物頭像》（Heads of the people）。因此在他的頭像習作中，梵谷的用意並非要創作一幅精心的肖像，或是非常寫實的描繪。西奧偶爾會試著說服他的哥哥創作一些比較「怡人」的作品，但梵谷仍然堅守他原本選擇的道路。

回顧起來，梵谷從1885最初的幾個月開始創作的許多素描和油畫習作，可以被視作是他為了一幅大的人物作品所做的準備，這個理想終於在《食薯者》（The potato eaters）這幅畫上實現。他最大的希望就是成為一名人物畫家，以傳統來說，這是一位藝術家最被推崇的畫作類型。那年

10. 梵谷給西奧的信，約1882年10月10日 （279/238）。
11. A. Kerssemakers, Herinneringen aan Vincent van Gogh I De Amsterdammer, 1912年4月, nr. 1816.
12. H.P. Bremmer，Moderne Kunstwerken. Schilderijen, teekeningen en beeldhouwwerken，8（1910） instalment 11，nr. 82。

多天他總共完成了約100幅油畫及素描的人物頭像。此外，爲了對在小泥草屋中的光線狀況有更多的掌握（不論是從窗戶透射進來的自然光線，或是人工的油燈或火爐）他也完成了婦女縫紉或削馬鈴薯皮的室內習作。（頁170 [KM 113.109]）

《食薯者》，1885年4月，油畫，73.9×95.2公分，庫勒穆勒美術館，奧特羅 [KM 109.982]

《食薯者》，梵谷的第一幅同時也是最後一幅大型人物畫，在1885年4月完成。他在春天寫信給西奧，「整個冬天我把織布的線拿在手上，思索著明確的樣式。」時機一到，早期大量的作品使他能夠相當容易地完成構圖：在完成最後的傑作之前，他先畫了一張油畫習作和一件石版畫（[KM 126.762]）。然而，梵谷接著承受的批評卻是相當嚴苛的。西奧覺得這些人物相當單調，而凡‧拉帕德更是在收到這幅版畫之後，在給梵谷的信中非常嚴苛：

> 你一定也同意這件作品無法被認真看待，感謝老天，你可以做的比這個更好。那爲什麼每件事物都以同樣膚淺的態度觀察和處理呢？現在他們在擺姿勢了，後面那個女人賣弄風情的小手，多麼地不寫實！而咖啡壺、桌子和那隻在壺把上的手之間又是什麼關係？……爲什麼右邊那個男人必須沒有膝蓋沒有肚子也沒有肺？還是那些都被藏在他身後了？……爲什麼左邊那個女人的鼻子是一枝尾端有著骰子的煙斗柄？這樣的作畫水準，你怎麼敢提起米勒和布荷東的名字？拜託！藝術對我來說太值得尊敬，以致於不能被如此冷漠對待。

被激怒的梵谷退回了那封信作爲回應，並且寫下這些字句：「收到了你的信—我很驚訝。在此我把信還給你。　梵谷。」[13] 他在6月回覆了這封充滿批評的信，並試著解釋他是怎樣看待畫家的專業：「我的論點很簡單：畫出結構正確的人物，以及均整地思慮過的筆觸，與我目前的需求—那急迫的繪畫的需求，可說是幾乎沒有，或比一般以爲的，具有更少的關係。」[14] 梵谷與凡‧拉帕德的友情最終破裂了。

儘管經歷了這些事，梵谷還是很重視這些批評，他自己也清楚《食薯者》中的缺點，特別是在人物的描寫上。於是他繼續不屈不撓地畫人物習作，這幾乎佔去了他從5月到8月的所有時間：這段時間他的作品共有12件油畫和超過90件的素描。他讀過尚‧吉古（Jean Gigoux）的《論時代畫家》（*Causeries sur les artistes de mon temps*），這本內容描述知名法國畫家尤金‧德拉克洛瓦（Eugène Delacroix）作畫方法的書之後，試著以體積而非輪廓線作爲素描的基礎。西奧寄了這本書給他，梵谷在那個夏天很頻繁地引用這本書的內容，特別是當中有一段提到一個畫家帶著一座銅質雕塑拜訪德拉克洛瓦，並詢問他是否爲眞跡，根據德拉克洛瓦的說法：「這不是上古時期，

13. 凡‧拉帕德給梵谷的信，1885年5月24日（507/R51a）和梵谷的回信，d.d. 1885年5月25日（508/R51）。因爲信件被退還，這是唯一一封被保留下來凡‧拉帕德寫給梵谷的信。梵谷本身並不是個會妥善保管信件的人。

14. 凡‧拉帕德給梵谷的信，1885年6月的第二部份（513/R52）。

而是文藝復興時期的東西」，因為「它非常美麗，但它是由捕捉線條成形，而上古的藝術家捕捉的是體積（量塊與核心）。」然後他又說：「看這裡」，並在一張紙上畫了許多橢圓，他用幾乎看不見的線把這些橢圓給連接起來，創作出一匹騰躍的馬，充滿活力和律動。他說，「傑利科（Géricault）和格羅（Gros），從希臘人學習到那一點，首先描繪出體積（幾乎總是橢圓），並從這些橢圓的位置和比例來推斷出輪廓和動作。……我問你，這不是很偉大的事實嗎！然而……這有在學院的素描課程中教授給素描石膏像的人嗎？我想沒有。如果是這樣教的話，我會很開心地推崇這間學院，但我很清楚知道事情並不是這樣的。」[15]

庫勒穆勒美術館擁有梵谷在1885年5月到6月間，主要用黑色蠟筆完成的一組22件小幅素描，這些素描呈現出體格粗壯的人物、披著喪服頭紗的婦女、手中拿著桶子、鏟子或掃帚、在田裡工作的農夫，或是他們把手負在背後行走。在某些素描中可以清楚地看出梵谷企圖照著德拉克洛瓦所建議的，在畫中使用了大量的橢圓來建構「量塊」（頁193 [KM 114.398 recto]），梵谷共有40幅這類的作品傳世。

同一時期，一件不尋常的事引起了梵谷的注意：努南的舊塔要拆除了。這座塔位於這個地區中心，同時旁邊的墓園也是不久前梵谷父親下葬的地方，梵谷希望能夠記錄拆除的不同階段及過程。為了替一幅水彩素描（頁172 [KM 118.569 verso]）作準備，他在拍賣現場畫了許多速寫，村民們在那裡拍賣競標木材、石板和舊鐵器。在其中一件作品中，他速寫了村莊警察Johannes Biemans（穿戴著帽子和制服）的頭像，這幅水彩作品描繪出他正在監看著群眾的畫面。

在這小尺寸的人物畫系列之後，梵谷也開始以較大的尺寸作畫，大約有50幅這樣的作品流傳下來。當中的19幅被收藏在庫勒穆勒美術館，主題多為收穫和其他的農地活動。這些作品幾乎都是用黑色蠟筆完成的，同時梵谷也使用了他在海牙畫鉛筆素描用過的方式─用稀釋過的牛奶來定著蠟筆畫。通常他只針對人物部分使用這種方法而不及於整張畫紙，因此在人物的輪廓線上常能看到紙質的變色。從某些作品上的水滴狀痕跡，可以推測出梵谷有時候是用力地把這些液體甩到素描上。（頁186 [KM 122.483 verso]）他偶爾會用筆刷上定著劑，或在素描上用水來獲得細微的灰色調，或是他會用擦子或麵包屑來擦拭人物的部份，以得到更強烈的明暗對比，比方說，衣服皺褶的強調。

西奧曾經把他哥哥的作品拿給一些在巴黎的熟人看，像是畫商阿爾馮斯·波提爾（Alphonse Portier）和畫家兼石版畫家查爾斯·西瑞特（Charles Serret）─他們的評價並非是全然負面的。因此在一封長信中，梵谷再次試著解釋，他追求的是情感的表達，而不是為了技術上的完美：

告訴西瑞特，如果我的人物是好的，我會感到絕望，告訴他我並不想要他們在結構上是很正確的，告訴他我指的是，如果有人照相拍了一個掘地者，那麼那個人物就一定不會是在掘地。告訴他我覺得米開朗基羅的人物非常動人，儘管他們的腿太長，臀部太寬。

告訴他在我看來─米勒和雷赫密特（Lhermitte）才是真正的畫家，因為他們不照著事物的模樣畫，不依循枯燥的分析，而是照著他們─米勒、雷赫密特和米開朗基羅，對於這些對象的感覺來作畫。告訴他我最大的願望就是顯示這樣的不精確、這樣真實的偏差、修正和更改，這些可能都是─怎麼說呢，謊言，但卻比拘泥字義的事實還要真實。[16]

梵谷在寫這封信的時候，在心中無疑地已經有了之前提到的大幅人物素描畫系列的構想。他故意以法文來命名這些作品，希望能透過西奧賣出它們，同時也想到了要以一年的各個月份

---

15. 梵谷給凡·拉帕德的信，1885年9月（533/R58）。
16. 梵谷給西奧的信，1885年7月（522/418）。

來創作這個系列，像是一件被命名為《馬鈴薯園中的掘地者，二月》（*Digger in a potato field, February*）的作品。他所景仰的畫家，雷赫密特和米勒也曾經創作過類似以農人工作為主題的系列。這幅人物素描也是為了新的人物畫所作的準備，很可能是一個收成的場景。有一些描繪農場工人的油畫習作被保留了下來，當中有些和素描有關，但是梵谷並沒有完成任何一幅大件的油畫。

這幅大件的素描，清楚地顯示出梵谷已經掌握了人物素描的一些技巧，像是在紙上以透視法來縮小比例：《捆麥束的農婦》（*Peasant Woman Binding Wheat Sheaves*）、《拾穗農婦的正面》（*Peasant Woman Gleaning, Seen from the Front*）和《鋤地的農夫》（*Peasant with a Hoe*，頁191、186和184 [KM 120. 804, KM122. 483 and KM 126. 338 verso]）。這當中最後一幅素描裡，我們看到梵谷接受了西奧的建議，在素描中加上了更多「周遭的環境氛圍」（*entourage*）。西奧在8月到荷蘭探視家人，據他說，梵谷這樣做有助於銷售他的素描。那個時期傳世的6幅作品中，梵谷的確把他的人物放在一個清楚的環境中，在一片風景中，或是以農村為背景。

就在他的人物素描有所進展的同時，他的創作突然停滯了。1885年9月，梵谷被不實的指控說—他讓他的一個模特兒懷孕。同時也因為碰上收穫的季節，使得尋找模特兒對他來說變得額外困難。一名天主教神父甚至特別要求教居區民不要擔任梵谷的模特兒。因此，儘管他希望繼續創作人物油畫，他還是被迫尋找不同的主題，像是靜物和風景；他知道他在那個領域還有很多需要學習的地方。因此在11月底，梵谷決定動身前往安特衛普（Antwerp），參加當地學院的課程。

Van Gogh as Draughtsman: 1883-1885

Aukje Vergeest

Teio Meedendorp

The Nuenen years, 1883-1885

In this new drawing, I start the figures at the torso and it seems to me that this has made them fuller and broader. If 50 is not enough, I shall draw 100 and if that is not enough then I shall draw more, until I have solidly achieved what I want, namely that everything is round, as it were, and there is neither beginning nor end anywhere on the form, and yet it constitutes one harmonious living whole.

Vincent to Theo, ca. Jun 2nd 1885 (509/410)

With Van Gogh's return to the family home on December 4th 1883, after a two year stay in The Hague and Drenthe, the conflict with his parents seemed to have eased to some extent. Yet it soon became apparent that the relationships had been seriously upset, and would remain so. The characters of Van Gogh and his father were irreconcilable. Roughly a week after arriving, Vincent wrote to Theo: 'There is a similar reluctance to having me in the house as there would be to having a large rowdy dog in the house. He'll bring his wet paws into the room - and then, he is so unruly. He will get in everyone's way. **And his bark is so loud**. In short, it is a filthy beast'. [...] The dog only regrets that he did not stay away, because it was less lonely on the heath than it is in this house - despite all the kindness'.[1] Through letters, Theo played a kind of mediator's role between Vincent and his father and despite the difficult relations, Van Gogh still received support from his parents. He was allowed to use the mangle room for storage and a studio. In a letter to Theo, he gave an ironic description of this workroom, situated between the coal-shed and the dung-pit, with a sewer in front and behind. Compared to his studio in The Hague it was all a case of making do. In May 1884, however, he found two rooms en suite with Mr and Mrs Schafrat, whereby he no longer had to inconvenience his parents, except for meals and to sleep. A year later, after the death of his father, he would also move in there. The fact that Schafrat was the sexton of the Catholic Church made the situation in the minister's family no more amiable.

In his time in Nuenen, Van Gogh gained more confidence in his work and in its saleability in the long term. From now on, he wished to regard the monthly allowance that Theo had long been providing him as a payment for works that he sent to his brother. Moreover, he expected Theo, who ran his own department of the art-dealers Goupil & Cie on the Boulevard Montmartre in Paris, to actively try to sell his work.[2] This put Theo in a difficult position, because he could hardly bring his brother's work to the public's attention under the gaze of his superiors, even if he had wanted to, because in his day (1876), Vincent himself was discharged from the head office in Paris. Although he did occasionally show some work to his dealer friends, Theo probably made little effort further to accommodate Vincent's drawings and paintings elsewhere, which also led to a somewhat heated correspondence between the brothers.

Immediately on his arrival in the village in Brabant, the picturesque character of which had already once been described to him by his sister Willemien, Van Gogh began capturing the surrounding area and its inhabitants. His high expectations were not disappointed: the 'civilization' had not yet permeated through, which was an important plus for Van Gogh. He enjoyed being among the farmers and weavers, people who in his opinion were honest and simple, with an 'entirely different way of life than that of we,

---

1. Letter to Theo, ca. December 15th 1883 (415/346).
2. After the withdrawal of the Goupil family, from 1884 onward, the art-dealership was known by the name Boussod, Valadon & Cie, successeurs de Goupil & Cie.

Weaver in front of his room, 1884 May-June,
drawing, Kröller-Müller Museum, Otterlo [KM 121.558]

cultured people'. [3] Van Gogh became attached to the simplicity of the countryside, which was under threat from increasing industrialization at the end of the nineteenth century. With his depictions of country life, he wanted to give a new impulse to this rustic genre, following the painters of the Barbizon School. Jean-François Millet - whose very recent biography by Sensier he had read in The Hague - was his great example in this. Gradually he developed specific opinions on figure drawing, in which anatomical perfection was of minor importance, as long as the figures were 'alive', showed great expression and displayed character. Van Gogh was equally aware that this nevertheless required a great deal of study. However, the drawn studies were again, even more than previously, in the service of painting. His ambition to be an illustrator on a magazine had faded to the background, in favour of an all-round artistic practice. The materials he made ample use of in Nuenen were pen and ink (mainly for landscapes), pencil (for very precise drawings), black crayon (for a more expressive character and stronger contrasts between light and dark) and opaque watercolours, which he had also tested in The Hague (applied diluted and usually in combination with other materials).

In those days North Brabant had a large textile industry and despite the growing industrialization, there were a remarkable number of home weavers working in Nuenen and the surrounding area, around 400.[4] Van Gogh had previously encountered weavers in the Borinage and was fascinated by them on that occasion too. 'I would count myself lucky if I were one day permitted to draw them, as then these never, or almost never before published types would come to light', he wrote to Theo at the time.[5] Weavers were indeed seldom depicted. In the first three months in Nuenen, Van Gogh made about ten paintings and approximately sixteen drawings of this subject. 'These people are difficult to draw, because in their cramped accommodation one cannot stand at a sufficient distance to draw the loom, which I believe is the reason why drawing them is frequently destined to fail. I have, however, found a place where there are two looms & where it can be done'.[6] Together with his friend Anthon van Rappard, who visited Nuenen for around ten days, he went wandering around to capture 'weavers and all sorts of fine circumstances outside'.[7] *Weaver in front of his loom* ([KM 121.558]) is a pen drawing made after a painting *Loom with weaver* (p. 175 [KM 105.976]) which is preserved in the Kröller-Müller Museum.[8] The drawing is heavily worked with highlights, which makes it reminiscent of an etching or engraving. The fact that Van Gogh considered this a fully-fledged - and perhaps saleable - drawing is apparent from the clear signature in the bottom right-hand corner. Incidentally, there was originally an even larger signature in the bottom left-hand corner, but Van Gogh removed this probably because it made the composition unbalanced; the remains are still faintly visible.

In March/April 1884, Van Gogh focused on the landscape, which resulted in a series of around seven large pen drawings of exceptional quality within his Dutch oeuvre. It is conspicuous that, for this series, just as in The Hague with the commissions for his uncle Cor, he reverted to drawing with pen and ink, with which he more often achieved very impressive results. He once admitted to the artist Jan Hendrik Weissenbruch that he viewed his surroundings as if drawing them with a pen: 'Then you must draw with the

3. Letter to Theo, ca. April 30th 1885 (501/404).
4. C. van der Heijden, 'Een zeer armzalig volkje. Leef- en werkomstandigheden van de Nuenense wevers in de tweede helft van de negentiende eeuw', in: Van den Brink & Frijhof 1990, pp. 23-35.
5. Letter to Theo, September 24th 1880 (157/136).
6. Letter to Theo, ca. January 2nd 1884 (422/351).
7. Letter to Theo, late May 1884 (450/369).
8. Respectively, *Weaver* (F32/JH480) and *Loom with weaver* (F35/JH478).

pen', Weissenbruch replied. [9] The drawing entitled *The Kingfisher* (Van Gogh Museum) has, for example, a strong composition and is drawn with a wide variety of pen strokes. The bird, only just visible above the water of the pool, is of minor importance in this winter landscape with its bare bushes, hedges and trees. Van Gogh did not manage to sell these ambitious drawings, neither via Theo, nor via his friend and colleague Van Rappard, who he also involved. For a while after this disappointment, Van Gogh focused almost exclusively on painting, in which he still had a lot to learn. Fascinated by colour theories, he sought to master the various technical problems of painting by making as many studies as possible.

The potato eaters, April 1885, drawing, Kröller-Müller Museum, Otterlo [KM 126.726]

At the end of 1884, Van Gogh once again made a number of drawn studies, which often served as a sketch for a painting. It was now painting from a model in particular that demanded his attention. Fortunately (particularly in the winter months when there was little to do on the land), he found many villagers willing to pose for him, for a fee, 'a few pennies for an afternoon or morning'. [10] In his studio, Van Gogh had a collection of costumes, in which to clothe his models and, furthermore, rumour has it that he had a 'cupboard with at least thirty birds' nests, all sorts of moss and plants collected from the heath, a few stuffed birds, shuttle, spinning wheel, bedpan, every country tool, old caps and hats, foul ladies bonnets, clogs, etc. etc.'. [11] With the country tools mentioned, Van Gogh was able to stage various scenes indoors, although he also made sketches outside on the land to study certain poses. In the winter of 1884, Van Gogh made around 40 drawn studies of heads and hands, and a few figures half-body or head to toe. The sheet of sketches (p. 165 [KM 114.886]) shows a number of such studies: the head of a woman, to the left of which, possibly the same woman in a rough, highlighted version, and above that, a tiny head. In the bottom left-hand corner, Van Gogh drew a man on a path with a piece of wood on his shoulder and an axe in his right arm with a farm in the background.

More detailed studies of heads can be found in the collection of the Van Gogh Museum, including the large sheet *Head of a woman*, a profile study of a farmer's wife, executed in black crayon. Conspicuous is her ugliness, the furrowed worn-out face, or as H.P. Bremmer, the art 'pedagogue' and advisor to H. Kröller-Müller put it, a 'monstermensch'(monstrous person), with a 'brutish heavily portrayed' lower jaw. [12] Van Gogh set great store by physiology or rather physiognomy, the pseudo-scientific insights that date from late eighteenth century - and were highly popular at the end of the nineteenth century - which assumed that the character of a person could be determined from their features; this often involved making comparisons to animals.

Van Gogh usually chose very distinct types for his models, the most ugly according to his acquaintances. Their peasant faces and the resemblance to animals were a confirmation for him that these people stood close to nature. In his letters, he referred to these studies as 'koppen uit het volk', a direct reference to *Heads of the people*, a series of characteristic portraits of labourers from the journal *The Graphic*. Thus, in his studies of heads, it was not Van Gogh's intention to produce a painstaking portrait or a correct depiction. Theo occasionally tried to convince his brother to make more 'cheerful' work, but he continued to persevere

9. Letter to Theo, May 1st 1882 (221/195).

10. Letter to Theo, ca. October 10th 1882 (273/238).

11. A. Kerssemakers, 'Herinneringen aan Vincent van Gogh I', De Amsterdammer, April 1912, nr. 1816.

12. H.P. Bremmer, Moderne Kunstwerken. Schilderijen, teekeningen en beeldhouwwerken, 8 (1910) instalment 11, nr. 82.

The potato eaters, April 1885, oil on canvas, Kröller-Müller Museum, Otterlo [KM 109.982]

on the path he had taken.

In retrospect, the many drawn and painted studies from the first months of 1885 can be regarded as the preparations for a large figure piece that Van Gogh was hoping to make, and which eventually came to fruition in *The potato eaters*. It was his greatest desire to become a figure painter, which according to tradition was the most highly regarded genre of painting that an artist could practice. That winter, he painted and drew around one hundred heads in total. In addition, he also made interior studies of women doing needlework or peeling potatoes, in order to gain a better understanding of the incidence of light in the small huts - either by natural means, through the window, or artificial in the light from an oil lamp or hearth fire. (p. 170 [KM 113.109])

The potato eaters, Van Gogh's first - and last - large figure piece, was created in phases in April 1885. 'All winter long I have had the threads of this fabric in my hands and sought the definitive pattern', he wrote to Theo in the spring, and when the time came, his extensive preliminary work enabled him to construct the composition fairly easily: a painted study and a lithograph preceded the eventual pièce de résistance ([KM 126.762]). The criticism of the work that Van Gogh subsequently had to endure was, however, scathing. Theo found the figures rather flat and Van Rappard in particular, who had received a print of the litho by post, showed no mercy in a letter:

> You must agree that such work is not to be taken seriously. You can do better than this - thankfully; then why is everything observed and treated in an equally superficial manner? Now, they are posing. That coquettish little hand of the woman at the back, how unrealistic! And what is the relationship between the coffeepot, the table and the hand that sits on top of the handle? [...] And why must the man on the right have no knee and no belly and no lungs? Or are they behind him? [...] And why must the woman on the left have a pipe stem with a die on the end of it as a nose? And with such a manner of working, you dare invoke the names of Millet and Breton? Come now! It seems to me that art is too esteemed to be treated so nonchalantly.

In reply, a deeply offended Van Gogh returned the letter, with the words: 'I happened to receive your mail - to my surprise. I return it to you herewith. Regards, Vincent'. [13] He returned to this vicious letter in June and tried to explain how he regarded the painter's profession: 'My contention is simply this: that drawing an anatomically correct figure, or that an evenly reasoned brushstroke, has little - or at any rate less than is generally assumed - to do with the current demands, the urgent demands in the field of painting'. [14] The friendship with Van Rappard eventually disintegrated.

Despite everything, Van Gogh did take the criticism seriously and was himself certainly aware of the shortcomings in *The potato eaters*, particularly in the depiction of the figures. He thus continued tirelessly making figure studies. This kept him almost fully occupied from May through August: his production from that time consists of only a dozen paintings compared to over ninety drawings. As a result of reading the book *Causeries sur les artistes de mon temps* by Jean Gigoux, which includes a description of the

13. Letter from Van Rappard to Van Gogh, May 24th 1885 (507/R51a) and Van Gogh's reply, d.d. May 25th 1885 (508/R51). Because it was returned, this is the only letter from Van Rappard to Van Gogh that has been preserved. He himself was no diligent archivist of the correspondence he received.
14. Letter from Van Rappard, second half of June 1885 (513/R52).

working method of the famous French painter Eugène Delacroix, he now tried to draw more on the basis of volumes rather than contours. Theo had sent him this book and he quoted from it frequently throughout the summer months, particularly a certain passage in which a painter visited Delacroix with an antique bronze statue in order to ask him whether it was actually genuine: "'ce n'est pas de l'antique, c'est de la renaissance'", according to Delacroix, because: "' c'est très beau, mais c'est pris par la ligne, et les anciens prenaient par les milieux (par les masses, par noyaux)!" Then he added: "Look here," and drew a number of ovals on a piece of paper - he connected these ovals together with little lines, with virtually nothing, and thus created a prancing horse, full of life and movement. "Géricault and Gros", he says, "learned that from the Greeks, to first depict the masses (nearly always ovals), then to infer the contours and action from the position & proportion of these ovals." [...] I ask you, is that not a magnificent truth! However... is this taught to the plaster cast draughtsmen at the drawing academy? I think not. If it was taught thus, I would happily idolize the academy, but I know very well that this is not the case.' [15]

The Kröller-Müller Museum has a group of 22 small drawings, made predominantly with black crayon, from the period May-June 1885, all of which show small, thickset figures, women with a mourning mantilla, or with a pail, shovel or broom in their hands, farmers working on the land, or walking with their hands on their backs. In some drawings, it is clearly visible that Van Gogh has indeed attempted to build 'mass' out of ovals and ellipses, as Delacroix had recommended (p. 193 [KM 114.398 recto]). A total of 40 such drawings are known of.

In the same period, an unusual event drew Van Gogh's attention: the old tower in Nuenen was to be demolished. This old tower, with the graveyard where his father had recently been buried, stood in the middle of the fields and Van Gogh wanted to record the various stages of its demolition. In preparation for a watercolour drawing (p. 172 [KM 118.569 verso]), he made a number of sketches in situ of the public sale, where villagers gathered to bid for the wood, slate and old iron in an auction. On one of the sheets, he sketched the head of the village constable Johannes Biemans (in cap and uniform), who is depicted in the watercolour while watching over the crowd of people.

After the series of small figures, Van Gogh also began working from model in a large format, around fifty works of which have been handed down. Nineteen pieces are in the Kröller-Müller Museum, with the theme of harvest and other activities on the land. Nearly all are drawn in black crayon, whereby Van Gogh fixed the crayon in the same way as he had the pencil drawings in The Hague: with diluted milk. Usually, he did not fix the whole sheet, just the figure, thus a discolouration of the paper is often visible around the contours of the figures. As the large drips on some of the works suggest, Van Gogh sometimes hurled the liquid at the drawing (p. 186 [KM 122.483]). He sometimes worked with the brush in the fixative or with water in the drawing to obtain subtle grey tints, or he rubbed the figures with an eraser or breadcrumbs for stronger light/dark contrasts and, for instance, to better accentuate the drapes of the cloth.

Theo had shown his brother's work to some of his acquaintances in Paris - the art-dealer Alphonse Portier and the painter/lithographer Charles Serret - whose evaluation was not entirely unfavourable. Thus in a long letter to Theo, Vincent attempted once again to explain that he was not striving for technical perfection, but expressiveness:

> *Tell Serret that I would be despairing if my figures were good, tell him I do not want them to be anatomically correct, tell him what I mean is, that if one photographs a man digging, then he would certainly not be digging. Tell him that I find the figures of Michelangelo magnificent, although the legs are certainly too long - the hips and buttocks too broad. Tell him that in my view, Millet and Lhermitte are therefore the true painters, because they paint the things not as they are, retraced through dry analysis, but as they, Millet, Lhermitte, Michelangelo feel them to be. Tell him that my greatest desire is to reveal such inaccuracies, such deviations, revisions, alterations of reality, that they might be, well - lies, if one pleases - but truer than the literal truth.* [16]

When writing this letter, Van Gogh undoubtedly had the just-mentioned series of large figure drawings in mind. He deliberately gave some of the sheets a French title with an eye to a possible sale via Theo,

15. Letter to Van Rappard, September 1885 (533/R58).
16. Letter to Theo, July 1885 (522/418).

but also with the idea of making a series on the months of the year. For example, one work bears the title *Bêcheur dans un champ de pommes de terres, février (Digger in a potato field, February)*. The painters he so greatly admired, Léon Lhermitte and Jean-François Millet had made similar series of farmers working in the fields. The figure drawing was also further intended as preparation for a new large figure piece, which was very likely to have been a harvest scene. A few painted studies of agricultural workers have been preserved, some of which can also be connected to drawings, but a large painting was never produced.

The large drawing clearly shows that Van Gogh had gained more control over certain aspects of figure drawing, such as the perspective foreshortening in the sheets *Peasant woman binding wheat sheaves*, *Peasant woman gleaning*, seen from the front and *Peasant with a hoe* (pp. 191, 186 and 184 [KM 120.804, KM 122.483 and KM 126.338]). In the last drawing, we see that Van Gogh has taken Theo's advice to add more 'entourage' to his drawings. According to Theo, who visited his family in the Netherlands in August, this might have a positive effect on the saleability of Vincent's drawings. In around six surviving sheets from that period, Van Gogh has indeed placed his figures in a clear setting, in a landscape or with a farm in the background.

Just as he was making such progress in figure drawing, his production suddenly stagnated. In September 1885, Van Gogh was - wrongly - accused of making one of his models pregnant. It now became extra difficult for him to find models - all the more because it was also harvest time. One catholic priest in particular urged his parishioners to no longer pose for Van Gogh. Thus, he was forced to look for different subjects such as still lifes and landscapes, though he still wanted to continue with figure painting; he knew he had a lot to learn in that field. Therefore, at the end of November, Van Gogh decided to travel to Antwerp in order to take lessons at the academy there.

梵谷的素描：法國時期（1886－1890）

泰歐‧梅登多普
歐克耶‧斐黑斯特

> 素描總是需要快動作，而不論你是用筆刷或其他工具立刻去素描，例如沾水筆，你怎樣
> 素描永遠都嫌不夠。我現在試著誇張要點，而故意讓不重要的細節模糊不清。
>
> 梵谷給西奧的信，1888年5月26日（615/490）

安特衛普─巴黎─阿爾，1885年11月至1889年5月

1885年11月底，梵谷離開了努南前往比利時的安特衛普（Antwerp），他在那待了大約三個月並短暫地上了藝術學院的課程。晚上他參加了素描社團，在那裡他能夠畫（裸體）模特兒。在學院裡他素描石膏像，這樣的課程需要專注於輪廓線上，然而梵谷在努南的三個月裡，實際上已經專注於由量塊體積出發的素描上。他決定到藝術訓練機會更廣的巴黎去，他加入了法國歷史畫畫家柯爾蒙（Fernand Cormon）的工作室，但這位畫家也抱持著類似的學院派觀點，因此梵谷最終還是離開了。[1]在巴黎的第一年，他主要把心力放在油畫上，因為他發現自己的色彩跟他「現代的」同儕們，也就是印象派畫家比起來，陰暗了許多，在這裡他第一次看到印象派的作品。一直到1887年2月和那年夏天，梵谷又畫了幾幅素描，而在這些素描作品中色彩扮演了很重要的角色。一系列都市風景的水彩作品，顯示出了他在這個

《Roubine du Roi 運河的洗衣站》，約1888年7月15至17日，素描，庫勒穆勒美術館，奧特羅 [KM 112.856]

過渡時期的進步。梵谷熱心收集在當時的巴黎很流行的日本版畫，它們對他的影響也十分明顯：色彩和構圖都令人聯想到像是歌川廣重（Hiroshige）的版畫。[2]油畫在梵谷在巴黎的第二年也佔有主要的地位。梵谷對秀拉及席涅克等點描派的熟悉，讓他開始使用不同的油畫筆觸及用色。

由於對野外、陽光和鄉野的渴求，梵谷在1888年2月前往了南法的阿爾（Arles）。在那裡他

---

1. 梵谷跟著柯爾蒙學習的時期，參閱Marije Vellekoop和Sjraar van Heuhten，《文生‧梵谷，素描第3輯，安特衛普及巴黎 1885-1888》（Vincent van Gogh. Drawings. Volume 3. Antwerp & Paris 1885-1888. Van Gogh Museum），阿姆斯特丹，2001，頁18-23。
2. 梵谷對日本版畫藝術的欣賞，參閱Louis van Tilborgh，《梵谷和日本》（Van Gogh and Japan），阿姆斯特丹，2006。

（再次）發現了蘆葦筆來作為素描的工具，使他能夠用畫油畫的方式素描：不同粗細大小的線條、轉折和點。在阿爾，日本版畫繼續帶給他許多靈感，激發他創作出一系列小幅的風景素描，打算膠裝起來並且能夠像日本版畫一樣摺疊。儘管有些已經褪色，梵谷在阿爾的素描顯示出一種成熟、獨特的風格和動人之處。《Roubine du Roi 運河的洗衣站》（[KM 112. 856]）是流暢的墨水筆素描系列中的一幅，梵谷依照他之前的油畫完成這幅作品，並將它寄給他的藝術家朋友貝爾納（Emile Bernard），讓他知道他現階段的創作。

梵谷夢想在阿爾開創一個藝術家的社區，也就是他提及的「南方工作室」（Studio of the South），一種藝術家之間合作關係的體現。當高更（Paul Gauguin）在1888年來到阿爾與梵谷合作時，梵谷的素描創作就完全退居不重要的地位。這兩位固執的畫家共事的這9週收穫很多，但也使兩人精疲力竭：他們對於藝術不同的看法和同樣急躁的個性，使得彼此間的關係日益緊張，導致了12月23日的爭執，在這次爭執中梵谷割掉了他一部份的左耳，這也讓他被送到了當地的醫院。在接連著的兩次精神崩潰後，基於他「精神上的愚蠢或精神官能症或神經錯亂」，他自願進入位於阿爾西北28公里的聖雷米（Saint-Rémy-de-Provence）的聖保羅精神病療養院（Saint-Paul-de-Mausole）。[3]他在1889年5月8日星期三抵達療養院。

聖雷米時期，1889年5月至1890年5月

梵谷在這間前身是修道院的療養院有兩間房間：「我有一間小房間，裡頭有灰綠色的壁紙，兩片水綠色的窗簾，上頭有著淡粉紅色的裝飾，用血紅色的細條點綴。……雖然窗外有著鐵欄杆，我可以看見一片被圍起來的麥田，就像一幅Van Goyen的全景風景畫，每天早上我都可以從那裡看見充滿光輝的日出。而且因為有超過30間的空房，所以我多得到了另一間房間作為畫室。這裡的食物還算過得去。這裡聞起來自然就有霉味，就像身在一間巴黎髒亂的餐廳或是供膳食的宿舍裡。」[4]根據他的主治醫師培宏（Peyron）的說法，梵谷罹患的是癲癇的一種，常會有恐慌症發作，這類病人偶爾會傷害自己。「一旦你知道了這是什麼」，梵谷寫信給他的弟弟，「一旦你知道了你的狀況，知道了自己可能會發作，我想你自己就能夠針對這點做些什麼，來避免突然被恐懼侵襲。……我覺得自己很有希望能夠戰勝它。」[5]由於醫院有例行的觀察期，梵谷在前四個禮拜都不能夠走到戶外。但他被允許在男性病房後的院內，一座綠草蔓生的花園中作畫。

起初，梵谷完成了幾幅大的油畫，但是當油畫的工具，特別是亞麻畫布用盡時，他開始使用蘆葦筆和畫筆完成了許多素描，描繪花園的主題。跟隨著日本版畫家的腳步，他從非常接近的距離觀察他的主題，像是巨大的帝蛾和各式各樣的植物。這樣細微的觀察和素描「草的葉片、松樹的枝幹和玉米穗」[6]，是梵谷尋求自我平靜的一種方式。《療養院花園一隅》（Corner in the garden of the asylum, [KM 114. 435]）的日期註明，創作於他在聖雷米的前幾週，這件作品主要是由黑色蠟筆構圖，再用蘆葦筆和墨水畫在上面。蠟筆畫出環繞花園的牆，線條貫穿了畫面上的樹。《療養院花園中開花的玫瑰叢》（Flowering Rosebushes in the Asylum Garden，頁209 [KM 124. 948]）則是這個時期另一幅色彩更豐富的作品，這件素描是以紫色墨水和梵谷僅存的稀釋過的油畫顏料所完成。可惜的是，梵谷畫在玫瑰上的顏色，特別是紅色顏料，很明顯地隨著時間褪色，也使原本花朵與四周綠色的對比變得柔和。在畫中好幾個部份，花朵的形狀都只能靠著梵谷素描勾畫的藍色

3. 梵谷給高更的信，約1889年1月22日（743GAC VGPG）。
4. 梵谷給西奧的信，1889年5月22日（778/592）。
5. 同上。
6. 梵谷給威爾的信，1889年7月2日（788/W13）

輪廓線來辨認。

療養院前那片被圍起來的麥田，成為他許多油畫和素描的主題。他在收到西奧從巴黎寄給他的新的顏料和畫布之後，完成了一幅油畫《有山脈和白雲的麥田》（Wheat field with mountains and white clouds, NY Carlsberg Clyptotek, Copenhagen），這件作品和另一幅素描《有太陽和雲的麥田》（Wheat field with sun and clouds, [KM 125.482]）有關。在這幅油畫中，小麥

《療養院花園一隅》，1889年5月底至6月初，素描，庫勒穆勒美術館，奧特羅 [KM 114. 435]

被暴風雨給吹平，而在素描裡頭，太陽似乎正要從一大片雲後露臉。在這幅素描中，梵谷用夾雜著些許對角線的、細細的墨水筆的筆觸來表現出太陽的光芒，而殘留在這些地方的白色顏料，顯示出梵谷用畫筆在這些線條上，加上了一些不透明的白色水彩。

梵谷對於送來的顏料和畫布感到非常開心，他在一封6月9日的信中告知他弟弟，「因為我渴望能再次作畫，因此過去幾天我走到戶外，在這療養院的周圍作畫。」[7]那時他也得到了可以在戶外作畫的許可，從此，梵谷再一次全神貫注在油畫創作上；南方景色中的麥田、橄欖樹和柏樹，如同療養院後低矮的阿爾畢耶（Alpille）山脈，吸引了他的注意。為了讓西奧知道他正在創作的內容，他偶爾會畫出與油畫相同內容的素描寄到巴黎。這些作品最顯著的特徵，在於優雅描繪最重要部分的形體，以及對於流動線條的強調。關於這些作品，梵谷寫道：「我知道上次寄的那些有著扭曲線條的素描習作，並不一定非要這樣呈現，但是相信我，我會繼續嘗試用畫出內容物糾結的素描，替風景畫中的事物增添一份重量。」[8]為了尋找屬於自己的獨特風格，梵谷也在他的油畫中，用多變的筆法及緊張的線條和筆觸，發展出一種強而有力的視覺語彙，這些正是一幅「更陽剛及更有力的素描」的證明。[9]

梵谷在聖雷米前三個月的作品產量都很高，但大約在6月中，儘管療養院提供了「必要和治療性的隔離」，他又一次發病了。這發生在一個颶風的日子裡他正在作畫的時候，之後他寫信給西奧，並絕望地表示：「我再也看不見任何擁有勇氣和希望的機會了。」[10]直到9月他才能再著手作畫，但他痊癒的希望和對未來的信心均受到嚴重的打擊。「你看得出來我相當地鬱悶」，他告訴他的弟弟，「因為我的進展並不好。而且我覺得作畫要取得醫生許可是件很荒謬的事。如果早晚我恢復到了某個程度，你也可以認為這是因為作畫的幫助，它增強我的意志力，藉此我精神崩潰的機會就會減少了。」[11]培宏醫生在這封信後的加註指出梵谷有自殺傾向，也（仍然）為惡夢所

7. 梵谷給西奧的信，約1889年6月9日（781/594）。
8. 梵谷給西奧的信，約1889年11月2日（818/613）。
9. 同上。
10. 梵谷給西奧的信，1889年8月22日（798/601）。
11. 梵谷給西奧的信，1889年9月3日或4日（799/602和602a）。

《有太陽和雲的麥田》，1889年5至6月，素描，庫勒穆勒美術館，奧特羅
[KM 121.558]

苦。

在這次病發後的一段時期，梵谷都沒有勇氣在戶外作畫，即使是到花園也不敢。為了避免忘記人物畫的技巧，這段時間他畫了很多自畫像，和他週遭人物的畫像。另外他也臨摹了許多（黑白）版畫，或是他心中的典範米勒及德拉克洛瓦的作品的複製品。他稱這些臨摹作品為即興創作或是色彩詮釋：它們教育，同時也撫慰了梵谷的心靈。到了9月底他才敢再踏出戶外，10月初他開始致力描繪花園中秋天的景色，直到10月中旬顏料用罄為止。一組表現出療養院花園裡外

許多樹木的素描習作，可能就是這個時期的作品。這些速寫作品呈現出各式各樣不同的線條和急促的筆劃，給予了作品相當的活力。梵谷使用鉛筆、黑色蠟筆或是兩者共用，來實驗不同的素描風格。他試圖從很近或很遠的距離交替描繪他的主題（樹、牆、長椅或是植物）。在收到新的顏料及畫布之後，梵谷繼續臨摹米勒的作品，或者可以說對其版畫複製畫做「色彩詮釋」。而一直到那年年底，他都很少再素描了。

兩次密集發生在1889年12月底和1890年1月的精神崩潰，再加上寒冷的天氣，使梵谷無法到戶外作畫。儘管如此，他還是照著1889年的一幅油畫《柏樹與兩個人物》（*Cypresses with two figures*，頁215 [KM 115.638] 和頁217 [KM 103.931]），完成了一件素描作品。這件油畫內容原本只有柏樹，他加上兩個人物後把這件作品寄給了年輕詩人兼評論家奧赫耶（Albert Aurier）。1890年1月這位評論家曾經在《法蘭西信使》（*Mercure de France*）中發表了一篇很長的文章來讚揚梵谷。他寫信對奧赫耶說：「我發現你用文字作畫，無論如何，在你的文章中我看到了我的油畫，只是它比現實中的畫更好、更豐富，也更具意義。」接著梵谷謙虛地表示，像是高更或蒙地伽利（Monticelli）那樣的畫家更值得被讚揚，並在信後再一次地感謝奧赫耶：「在我下次寄給我弟弟的郵件中，我會附上一幅柏樹的習作，希望我有這個榮幸將它送給你，作為那篇文章的一件紀念品。我目前還沒畫完，因為我希望在這幅作品中加入另一個人物。」[12] 最後梵谷在畫中加入了兩個人物，他們的相對尺寸使得他們在這幅素描中的存在比在油畫中要來的顯眼。這兩件作品現在都被收藏在庫勒穆勒美術館中。

同時，從梵谷和他弟弟往來的信件，可以越來越清楚地看出梵谷想離開療養院，往北搬到巴黎近郊居住和創作。1月30日，西奧的妻子喬漢娜（Johanna）生下了一個男孩，他們以梵谷的名字替孩子命名為文生·威廉（Vincent Willem）。梵谷自然很希望能見見他的小姪子，但他還沒完全從之前的精神崩潰中恢復過來，又在2月22日面臨了一次嚴重的危機，而這帶給他的影響一直持續到了4月底。之後他寫信給西奧，提到他在生病期間，憑想像完成了一些作品，但他是多

---

12. 梵谷給奧赫耶的信，1890年2月10或11日（854/626a）。

麼希望能夠真正捕捉這些開花的樹木。「現在已經幾乎結束了，那些開花的樹，真的，我沒有任何運氣了。是的，我必須想辦法離開這裡，但能去哪呢？」[13] 在這段發病期間所完成的素描，主題都重複他在荷蘭時期的作品，都是他在南方很懷念的：耕作中的農夫、在爐邊、農舍及泥炭屋的人物，他甚至想要重畫一幅「燈光下晚餐的農人的油畫」，也就是《食薯者》（The Potato Eaters）。梵谷稱它做「北方的回憶」，這在他的恢復期中給他帶來了安慰。

　　梵谷在聖雷米的這一年，主要專注在油畫的創作上，因此有了很大的進展。在油畫工具用盡，或是他不被允許畫油畫的時候，他就改畫素描。有時在他精神崩潰後會被禁止使用油畫工具，以免他可能吃下顏料或是喝下顏料溶劑中毒。[14] 在一封信中，西奧向梵谷指出如果油畫顏料這麼危險，他最好還是素描就好，但梵谷回覆說：「現在這些油畫已經在我腦中完全成熟了，我很希望能在這幾個月裡把它們完成，為什麼我得要改變我表達的方式呢？」[15]

　　精神病院的生活終究還是變得令梵谷無法忍受，在與西奧討論過後，梵谷決定定居在奧維（Auvers-sur-Oise），一個位在巴黎西北的城鎮。這裡也是嘉舍醫生（Paul-Ferdinand Gachet）的家鄉，這位好幾個人推薦的醫生在與西奧會面後，答應要治療梵谷，或者說，「密切注意他。」5月16日梵谷離開了聖雷米前往巴黎與西奧重聚，也首次和喬漢娜及小文生見面，只是沒過幾天，他就動身前往奧維了。

奧維時期，1890年5至8月

　　在奧維，梵谷還是偏好使用油畫顏料作畫，他在這裡的素描作品主要是以鉛筆和黑色蠟筆畫成，有時候還會結合彩色粉筆，然而他在阿爾及聖雷米時期還使用了蘆葦筆和墨水來素描。他在奧維的70天裡，共有57幅素描和超過70幅的油畫傳世。這些素描主要是以蠟筆完成的風景、人物和肖像速寫，而這些素描中最引人注目的就是它們簡單的「圓滑」線條。儘管創作量極大，梵谷還是覺得他失敗了而鬱鬱寡歡。此外，西奧在成家後，為了負擔家計而考慮創業當一個獨立的畫商。梵谷一直以來對西奧的依賴、對未來經濟來源的不確定和伴隨而來的罪惡感，都沒有能改善此一狀況。7月27日，梵谷對著自己的胸口開槍自盡，兩天後，他在摯愛的弟弟西奧身邊離開了人世。

13. 梵谷給西奧的信，1890年4月29日或30日（864/629）。
14. 參照Marije Vellekoop和Roelie Zwikker，《文生梵谷，素描，第4輯第1及第2部份。阿爾、聖雷米及奧維 1888-1890年》，阿姆斯特丹，2007年，第1部份第26頁注釋131。（Vincent van Gogh. Drawings. Volume 4, part I and II. Arles, Saint-Rémy, & Auver-sur-Oise 1888-1890. Van Gogh Museum, Amsterdan 2007）這似乎是培宏醫生在Le grand register de l'asile de Saint-Rémy的每月札記中所表達的憂慮。
15. 西奧給梵谷的信，1890年1月3日（837/T23）和梵谷給西奧的信，1890年1月4日（838/622）。

Van Gogh as Draughtsman: 1886-1890

Aukje Vergeest

Teio Meedendorp

Drawing, this always involves hurrying, and whether you do it immediately with the brush or something else, the pen for instance, you can never draw enough. I am now trying to exaggerate the essential while keeping the minor details deliberately vague.

Vincent to Theo, May 26th 1888 (615/490)

Antwerp-Paris-Arles, November 1885-May 1889

At the end of November 1885, Van Gogh left Nuenen to head for Antwerp in Belgium, where he stayed for around three months and briefly took lessons at the art academy. In the evenings, he went to drawing clubs, where it was possible to work from a (nude) model. At the academy he drew from plaster models, whereby it was required to focus on the contours, while Van Gogh had actually been concentrating on drawing derived from volumes in his last three months in Nuenen. He decided to go to Paris, where the possibilities for artistic training were more extensive, and enrolled at the studio of the French historical painter Fernand Cormon, who, however, held similar academic points of view, and thus Van Gogh eventually left there too.[1] In his first year in Paris he focused mainly on painting, because he recognized that his pallet was very dark in comparison to his 'modern' colleagues, the impressionists, whose work he saw here for the first time. It was not until February 1887 and the following summer that Van Gogh made a few more drawings, in which colour played an important role. A series of cityscapes in watercolour show how he had progressed in the interim. The influence of Japanese prints, which were fashionable in Paris at the time and enthusiastically collected by Van Gogh, is clear: both the use of colour and the composition are highly reminiscent of prints by, for example, Hiroshige.[2] Painting also prevailed in his second year in Paris. Van Gogh's familiarization with the pointillism of Seurat and Signac enticed him to use a different brush technique and colour pallet.

Craving the open air, sun and countryside, in February 1888, Van Gogh left for Arles in Southern France. There he (re)discovered the reed pen as drawing instrument, which provided

Wash stands at the canal 'Roubine du Roi', ca. July 15th -17th 1888, drawing, Kröller-Müller Museum, Otterlo [KM 112.856]

---

1. For Van Gogh's study period with Cormon, see Marije Vellekoop and Sjraar van Heugten, *Vincent van Gogh. Drawings. Volume 3. Antwerp & Paris 1885-1888.* Van Gogh Museum, Amsterdam 2001, pp. 18-23.
2. For Van Gogh's appreciation of Japanese print art, see Louis van Tilborgh, *Van Gogh and Japan*, Amsterdam 2006.

him the opportunity to draw in a similar way to how he painted: with lines, twirls and dots of different thickness and size. In Arles, the Japanese prints continued to inspire him, which resulted in a series of small landscape drawings that were intended to have the sheets glued together so they could be folded out, as was also done with Japanese prints. Van Gogh's pen drawings from Arles reveal - although some discoloured and faded - a mature, distinctive style and great persuasiveness. *Wash stands at the canal 'La Roubine du Roi'*([KM 112.856]) belongs to a

Corner in the garden of the asylum, late May-early June 1889, drawing, Kröller-Müller Museum, Otterlo [KM 114.435]

series of fluent pen drawings that Van Gogh made after his own paintings and which he sent to his friend the artist Emile Bernard, to show him what he was working on.

Van Gogh dreamed of beginning an artists' colony in Arles, which is also referred to as the 'Studio of the South', a collaboration between artists. When Paul Gauguin came to Arles in 1888 to work with him, Van Gogh's drawing faded entirely to the background. The nine weeks that the two headstrong artists spent together were productive, but exhausting: their different artistic opinions and quick-tempered characters led to increasing tension, which reached a head in an argument on December 23rd, during which Van Gogh cut off a piece of his left ear, which landed him in the local hospital. After a further two mental breakdowns he decided, due to his 'mental foolishness or neurosis or madness' to voluntarily admit himself into the psychiatric hospital Saint-Paul-de-Mausole in Saint-Rémy-de-Provence, 28 kilometres to the north-west of Arles.[3] He arrived there on Wednesday May 8th 1889.

Saint-Rémy-de-Provence, May 1889-May 1890

Van Gogh was given two rooms in this former monastery: 'I have a small room with grey-green wallpaper and two water-green curtains with patterns in very pale tints of pink, enlivened with fine blood-red stripes. [...] Through the window with iron bars before it, I can see a walled cornfield, a panorama such as that of Van Goyen, above which I see the sunrise in all its glory in the mornings. Furthermore - because more than 30 rooms are empty - I have an extra room in which to work. The food is so-so. Naturally it smells a bit mouldy here, like in a Parisian cockroach restaurant or in a boarding house'.[4] According to the doctor who treated him, Peyron, Van Gogh was suffering from a form of epilepsy, which involved panic attacks, whereby the patient occasionally wounded himself. 'Once you know what it is', Vincent wrote to his brother, 'once you are aware of your condition and that you may have an attack, then I think that you are able to do something about it yourself, in order to avoid being seized by fear or dread' [...] 'I have every hope of getting on top of it'.[5] Due to a customary observation period, for the first four weeks Van Gogh was not

3. Letter to Paul Gauguin, ca. January 22nd 1889 (743/GAC VG/PG).
4. Letter to Theo, May 22nd 1889 (778/592).
5. Idem.

Wheat field woth sun and cloud, 1889 May-Jun., drawing, Kröller-Müller Museum, Otterlo [KM 125.482]

allowed outside the walls of the home. He was, however, permitted to work in the lush overgrown garden within the compound, behind the men's dormitory.

First, Van Gogh painted several large canvases, but when his painting materials - particularly the linen - were exhausted, he began making various drawings with reed pen and brush depicting garden motifs. Following the example of Japanese print artists, he observed some subjects from very nearby, such as a large emperor moth and various plants. This detailed observation and drawing of 'a blade of grass, a pine branch, an ear of corn'[6], was a way for Van Gogh to be at peace with himself. *Corner in the garden of the asylum* ([KM 114.435])dates from those first weeks in Saint-Rémy, and is laid-out in black crayon, on top of which Van Gogh worked in ink with a reed pen. The crayon lines of the wall that encircles the garden run straight through the trees. *Flowering rosebushes in the asylum garden* (p. 209 [KM 124.948]) is a more colourful work from the same period. This drawing is made with purple ink and thinned oil paint, the last remains of Van Gogh's supply. Unfortunately, the red paint in particular, with which Van Gogh painted the roses, has faded significantly in the course of time, softening the original contrast with the surrounding green. In various places, the form of the flowers only remains recognizable by the blue contours that Van Gogh drew around them.

The walled cornfield served as the theme for several paintings and drawings. The sheet *Wheat field with sun and clouds* ([KM 125.482]) can be linked to the painting *Wheat field with mountains and white cloud* (Ny Carlsberg Glyptotek, Copenhagen), which he made after receiving the fresh paint and linen that Theo had sent him from Paris. In this painting, the wheat has been flattened by a thunderstorm, while in the drawing, the sun actually seems to be emerging from behind a large cloud. In the drawing, Van Gogh suggests the sun's rays using fine pen strokes, with a few light diagonal lines in among them. The remains of white pigment that were found here indicate that Van Gogh applied these lines with a brush and a little white opaque watercolour.

Van Gogh was delighted with the consignment of paint and linen, he informed his brother in a letter around June 9th, 'because I was longing to work again. Hence, for the past few days, I have been going outside and working in the surrounding area'.[7] By then, he had also received permission to work outside the home and from that moment on, Van Gogh once again focused almost entirely on painting; the wheatfields, olive trees and cypresses in the southern landscape drew his attention, as did the low massif just behind the home, the Alpille. To give Theo an idea of what he was working on, he occasionally made drawings of his paintings and sent them to Paris. These works are characterized by an elegant treatment of the most important forms and an emphasis on flowing lines. He wrote of them: 'I do realize that the drawn studies with the crooked lines from the last delivery were not what it must become, but take my word for it, one will continue seeking to give the things weight in the landscape by means of a drawing that attempts to

6. Letter to Wil, July 2nd 1889 (788/W13).

7. Letter to Theo, ca. June 9th 1889 (781/594).

depict the entanglement of the components'. [8] In searching for an original style, Van Gogh also developed a powerful visual idiom in his painting, with capricious brushstrokes and nervous touches and lines, which were evidence of a 'more masculine and powerful drawing'. [9]

Van Gogh's production was high during those first three months in Saint-Rémy, but around mid June he suffered another attack, despite the 'necessary and curative isolation' that the institute offered him. It struck while he was painting on a windy day, he later wrote to Theo, and made him desperate: 'I no longer see any chance of having courage and good hope'. [10] He was unable to work again until September, but his hope of recovery and his faith in the future had taken a severe blow. 'You see that I am rather moody', he informed his brother, 'that is because it is not going well. Furthermore, I find it ridiculous to go and ask the doctor's permission to make paintings. If, incidentally, sooner or later I recover to a certain degree, then you may also assume that this has been through working, which strengthens the will and through which the chances of those mental breakdowns are reduced'. [11] A short addition to this letter by doctor Peyron indicated that Van Gogh had suicidal tendencies and (still) suffered from unpleasant dreams.

In the next period after the attack, Van Gogh did not feel strong enough to work outside, not even in the garden. In order not to lose sight of his figure painting, he now made a number of self-portraits and portraits of people in his immediate environment. In addition, he painted various copies from (black-and-white) prints of, or after the work of Jean-François Millet and Eugène Delacroix, his great examples. He called these copies improvisations or interpretations in colour: they were educational and comforted him. He did not dare venture outside again until late September, early October when he threw himself into painting autumn scenes in the garden, until his supply of paint ran out in mid October. A group of study drawings showing various trees in and outside the garden of the home probably dates from that period. These sketches display a large variety of lines and dashes, which impart the works with a great liveliness. Van Gogh experimented with different drawing styles in pencil, black crayon or a combination of both. He sought to depict his subjects (a tree, wall, bench, or vegetation) alternately from nearby and from further away. When a new consignment of paint and linen arrived, Van Gogh continued making copies, or rather 'interpretations in colour' from prints of Millet. Further, he drew very little until the end of the year.

The two breakdowns occurring shortly after each other, in late December and late January 1890, but also the cold weather, impeded him from working outside. He did, though, make a drawing after a painting from 1889, *Cypresses with two figures* (pp. 215 and 217 [KM 115.638] and [KM 103.931]). The painting originally contained only the cypresses. He added the two female figures because he gave the canvas to the young poet and critic Albert Aurier, who had written a long article in praising Van Gogh in the *Mercure de France* in January 1890. He told Aurier: 'I find that you paint with words; anyway, I recognize my paintings in your article, only better than they are in reality, richer, more meaningful.' Van Gogh then modestly wrote that artists such as Gaugin or Monticelli were far more deserving of praise than he, and ended by thanking Aurier once again: 'With the next consignment that I send my brother, I shall include a study of a cypress tree, I hope that you will give me the pleasure of accepting it as a memento of your article. I am still working on it at the moment, as I wish to include another figure'. [12] In the end, he added two figures, whose relative size makes their presence rather more emphatic in the drawing than in the painting. Both works are currently in the Kröller-Müller Museum.

Meanwhile, from the correspondence between Van Gogh and his brother it becomes increasingly clear that Van Gogh wants to leave the home and has plans to move to the north, towards Paris, in order to live and work in the vicinity. On January 30th, Theo's wife Johanna gave birth to a baby boy, who they named Vincent Willem after his uncle. Van Gogh naturally wanted to visit his little nephew, but barely recovered from the previous breakdown, he was felled by a new severe crisis on February 22nd, which lasted until the end of April. Later he wrote to Theo that during his illness he had made a few works from imagination, but that he would have so loved to actually capture the trees in blossom. 'Now it is already nearly over, the

8. Letter to Theo, ca. November 2nd 1889 (818/613).
9. Idem
10. Letter to Theo, August 22nd 1889 (798/601).
11. Letter to Theo, September 3rd or 4th 1889 (799/602 and 602a).
12. Letter to Albert Aurier, February 10th or 11th 1890 (854/626a).

blossoming trees, really, I am having no luck. Yes, I must try to get away from here, but where to?'[13] The drawings that were produced in this same crisis period were repeats of subjects that he had once worked on in the Netherlands and which he missed in the south: farmers working on the land, figures by the open hearth, farmhouses and huts, and he even thought about remaking 'the painting of the farmers at dinner, with lamplight effect' - in other words, *The potato eaters*. This 'memory of the North', as Van Gogh called it, offered him comfort during his convalescence.

Throughout the year that Van Gogh spent in Saint-Rémy, he focused primarily on painting, in which unsurprisingly he underwent a huge development. He drew at moments when his painting materials were used up or when he was not permitted to paint. He was sometimes prohibited from doing so after a breakdown, out of the fear that he might poison himself by eating the paint or drinking the white spirit.[14] In a letter, Theo pointed out to his brother that it might be better for him to draw, if working with paint was so dangerous, but Van Gogh replied: 'Currently the paintings are fully ripened in my head; I now see all the places that I still want to make in these months, why then should I change my means of expression?'[15]

Life in the psychiatric hospital eventually became unbearable. In consultation with Theo, he decided to settle in Auvers-sur-Oise, a town to the northwest of Paris. This was home to doctor Paul-Ferdinand Gachet, who had been recommended by various parties and who promised to treat Van Gogh, or rather 'keep an eye on him' after a meeting with Theo. On May 16th, Van Gogh left Saint-Rémy for Paris - where he was reunited with Theo and made his first personal acquaintance with Johanna and the little Vincent - only to travel on to Auvers a few days later.

Auvers-sur-Oise, May-July 1890

In Auvers, Van Gogh again preferred to work with oil paints. The drawings he produced here are almost exclusively in pencil or black crayon, sometimes in combination with coloured chalk, whereas in Arles and Saint-Rémy he was also fond of drawing with the reed pen and ink. From the seventy days he spent in Auvers, 57 drawings and over 70 paintings have been handed down. The drawings are predominantly quick crayon sketches of landscapes, figures and portraits, and are conspicuous for their simple 'round' line patterns. Despite his enormous production, Van Gogh felt he had failed and was sombre. Adding to that, Theo, who now also had a family to support, was considering setting himself up as an independent art-dealer. His continuous dependence on Theo, an uncertain financial future and attendant feeling of guilt, did not improve the situation. On July 27th, Van Gogh shot himself in the chest, and two days later he died, in the presence of his beloved brother Theo.

13. Letter to Theo, April 29th or 30th 1890 (864/629).
14. See Marije Vellekoop and Roelie Zwikker, *Vincent van Gogh. Drawings. Volume 4, part I and II. Arles, Saint-Rémy, & Auvers-sur-Oise 1888-1890*. Van Gogh Museum, Amsterdam 2007, part I, p. 26, note 131. It appears that this was feared from the 'notes mensuelles' of doctor Peyron in *Le grand registre de l' asile de Saint-Rémy*.
15. Letter from Theo to Vincent, January 3rd 1890, (837/T23) and letter to Theo, January 4th 1890 (838/622).

庫勒穆勒美術館及其館藏

埃弗特·范·斯達登

> 庫勒穆勒美術館館藏中的當代藝術，反映出一個獨特的、延展的，以及連結著歷史的整
> 體。這裡並非單獨地強調荷蘭當地的觀點，而是由來自多數歐洲國家卓越的藝術作品，
> 顯示出過去和未來所引領的新潮流的一致性。觀眾能直接體驗到這種發展的必要和它的
> 邏輯：從19世紀畫家之間的相互學習和競爭，到當代藝術中無可避免且刻意的顛覆。

這是德國藝術記者F.M. Huebner在1921年出版的一本關於荷蘭現代藝術私人收藏的書中，對庫勒穆勒的典藏所做的開場白。1913年起，這批持續增加的收藏中，有一部分固定地展示在海牙The Lange Voorhout穆勒公司的辦公室。

德國人海倫·穆勒（Helene Müller）於1869年出生於埃森附近的霍爾斯特（Horst）。她父親在當地擁有一間鑄造廠，不久又在杜塞爾多夫（Dusseldorf）成立了一間船運貿易公司，並在鹿特丹設有分公司。1888年，海倫嫁給了當時剛成爲鹿特丹分公司負責人的荷蘭人安東·庫勒（Anton Kröller）。海倫的父親在1889年過世，於是安東成爲這個家族企業的領袖。接下來幾年，他靠著船運、貿易和採礦作業的利益，將事業從荷蘭擴展至國際舞台。這些獲益成爲了後來購藏藝術作品的經濟來源。

1905年，海倫在女兒的建議之下，開始向一位具影響力的藝術鑑賞家布瑞默（H.P. Bremmer）學習。他打動了她的心：從那時起，她開始對現代藝術充滿熱情。從1907年到1925年，她委託布瑞默替她完成私人收藏。海倫的野心不只是要收集藝術品，而是要像她曾經在佛羅倫斯看過的梅第奇家族（Medici）的藝術遺產一樣，希望能藉此豐富那個時代的文化生活。她的收藏因爲龐大的購藏計畫，很快地就達到了博物館的規模，因此它們需要一個安置的地方，並讓這些藝術作品最終屬於整個社會。

在達到這個目標之前，海倫在1910年到1913年間，接連委託了L.J.Falkenburg、Peter Behrens、Ludwig Mies van der Rohe和H.P.Berlage，替Wassenaar附近的Ellenwoude莊園設計一間有藝術品陳列室的宅邸。Behrens和Mies van der Rohe在那裡用木頭和帆布製作出他們原寸大小的設計模型。兩人的競爭非常激烈，而布瑞默在這當中扮演了一個關鍵角色，他替Berlage的設計說情。但到最後他們都沒有獲得青睞，庫勒夫婦賣掉了那片土地，並買下一座現成的莊園，Wassenaar附近的Groot Haesebroek。

而在1909到1921年間，安東·庫勒在Gelderland省中心的扶鹿（Veluwe）買下了超過6000公頃尙未開發的圍獵場。現在的厚荷·扶鹿（De Hoge Veluwe）國家公園就曾經是這個地區的中心地帶。在1914年或1915年時，Berlage受委託在這裡建造一間庫勒家族的打獵小屋，於1920年完工。海倫覺得幾次到扶鹿的旅行都很愉快，於是她在1915年決定在這裡建造她的新家和博物館。她在1928年回顧這番經過寫道：「經過思考後，我們覺得現在距離不再是缺點，而對觀眾來說，在這片雄偉、未被污染的自然中，能讓他們用一種與在城市完全不同的方式來享受藝術，特別是館藏中那些複雜的抽象藝術，需要極大的專注力和安靜的沉思，來欣賞當中的精神內容。」

Berlage第一次的扶鹿博物館設計在1917至1918年間完成，但是因爲他與海倫個性極端不

海倫‧庫勒穆勒（1869-1939）及安東‧庫勒（1862-1941），結婚照，1888年（庫勒穆勒美術館典藏，奧特羅）

合，他的計畫完全沒有被採用。海倫與建築師A.J.Kropholler有過短暫合作，之後在1919年年底指定亨利‧文得菲爾德（Henry van de Velde）設計位於厚荷‧扶鹿的博物館。亨利在山腳下設計了一座華麗的建築 Franse Berg。還在1921年製作了許多草圖，在1922年安置了地基，但是經濟危機限制了財務來源，工程只得暫停，但他們還是希望日後能夠繼續完成這項工程。

然而這個希望終究還是徒勞一場。1928年這批典藏和莊園被移轉到一個獨立的基金會底下。這個由庫勒穆勒夫婦共同管理的基金會，將這批典藏移交給荷蘭政府，而政府答應會在厚荷‧扶鹿為這些收藏成立並經營一間博物館。至於莊園則被賣給了一個新成立的基金會，這個基金會至今依然管理著這個地區，也就是厚荷‧扶鹿國家公園。在1921年設計的工程會重啟的預期下，亨利‧文得菲爾德被要求先設計一間「過渡性的美術館」，這間博物館在1938年以庫勒穆勒國立美術館（Rijksmuseum Kröller-Müller）的名字開幕。這間「過渡性的美術館」在日後成為現在庫勒穆勒美術館的核心部份，而在Franse Berg的「華麗的美術館」（grand museum）則一直不曾完成。所以Henry Moore所完成的三件銅像旁邊那斷垣殘壁的地基，已變成當初庫勒家族希望成為現代的梅第奇的紀念碑。

二次大戰期間，文得菲爾德為了使這間「過渡性的美術館」成為一間「永久的博物館」，擬訂出一個擴建計畫，包括一間雕塑室、一間演講堂、一系列的畫廊和一間董事辦公室，而這個計畫一直到戰後的1953年才得以實現。它是一個簡樸的博物館複合體，其特色包括了室內傾瀉而下的日光，以藝術品為焦點，還有和周圍自然融合的雕塑室。

接著是1960年由J.T.P.Bijhouwer設計建造的雕塑公園。1955年Gerrit Rietveld在為Sonsbeek展覽設計的一座雕刻涼亭，於1965年重建在這座公園中。也因有此基礎，使得庫勒穆勒國立美術館成為一間具有權威性的當代雕塑博物館。

到了一九六〇年代，館藏的增加、策展的需求及視覺藝術形式的改變使得博物館需要擴建。擴建的工作被委任給了Wim Quist，而在七〇年代他完成了一座有講堂、辦公室、服務區和陳列展覽大型立體作品的新展廳。他擅長從空間內外相互呼應來捕捉該地的精神，而這也塑造出庫勒穆勒美術館的典型氣氛：一個比例單純、注重細節，服務藝術視覺的複合體。

在那個寫實主義和理想主義更迭的年代，海倫‧庫勒穆勒的收藏反映出她發展藝術的想法。她很早就相信她的收藏必須要具備理想，而且必須讓大眾共享，根據她自己的說法，她是「客觀且有目的」的收藏藝術。最初她希望能證明抽象藝術並非深不可測，也不代表與傳統藝術間一定有道鴻溝。藉著結合新舊藝術作品，她試圖證明現代藝術的正當性。當抽象藝術被接受時，她修改了收藏趨勢，專注在寫實主義及更多新古典主義。根據庫勒夫人的說法，這又是一個時機來證明抽象藝術不是唯一重要的藝術，而抽象藝術仍是以現實作為基礎。

她收藏中最重要的四個核心部份是用來說明寫實主義的發展，但主要是作為現代抽象藝術背景的傳統藝術作品，從大約1850年起，經歷了印象主義、新印象主義和立體派，主要以法國（或是在法國發展的作品）和荷蘭藝術家為基礎，其次是表現出寫實主義的藝術品。第三部份是一些抗拒時代發展趨勢的畫家，像是J.Thom Prikker, Jan Toorop, James Ensor, William Degouve de

Nunques或Odilon Redon的作品。最後，也是最重要的是，做為收藏重心的梵谷的作品。除此之外，她的收藏還包含了其他重要的內容，像是傳統大師的素描、雕塑、岱爾夫特陶器（delftware pottery）、中國藝術、古陶器和平面藝術。庫勒夫人的理念還包括了強調所有藝術一體。因此，同時展現出新與舊、東方與西方、歐洲與非歐洲的藝術，成為她收藏品的一個主題。這就是建立基本原則的方式：透過省略和個人好惡所達到的明晰原則，用戰後的說法，可以是阿波羅式（Apollonian）的，邏輯式的、理性的偏見。屬於迪奧尼索司的（直覺式的）則被擺在一邊或是予以省略。沒有馬諦斯，沒有野獸派，沒有德國的表現主義，沒有藍騎士（Blaue Reiter），康丁斯基和馬爾克（Wassily Kandinsky & Franz Marc），也沒有達達主義、超現實主義或是構成主義。廣泛來說，對於那些可能被稱為表現主義的任何事物，這無疑地是一種選擇上刻意的限制。

戰後，庫勒穆勒美術館決定不再擴充庫勒夫人的油畫收藏，除非是要做一些填補或是補充些小規模的作品。五○年代初期，當時的館長Bram Hammacher以在戶外展示為中心思考，繼續增加雕塑作品的收藏。1953年文得菲爾德建築中的雕塑室開始開放，而雕塑公園的第一區則在1961年開放。儘管資金和可能性都非常受限，大約自1850年起，雕塑藝術發展樣貌的收藏卻也逐漸累積出來了，那是一個與繪畫收藏一致的，經由一種類似的、非教條主義的、庫勒夫人風格的個人選擇而成的收藏。它包括了羅丹（Auguste Rodin）、亨利‧摩爾（Henry Moore）、黑普瓦絲（Barbara Hepworth）、瑪塔‧潘（Marta Pan）、Alicia Penalba、葛雷柯（Emilio Greco）和沃吐巴（Fritz Wotruba）及理普希茨（Chaim Lipchitz）等藝術家的重要作品。而由於雕塑收藏的擴充，該美術館在庫勒夫人所收集的275件雕塑作品上，增添了如馬約爾（Aristide Maillol）、孟德達科斯塔（Jozef Mendes da Costa）、Joseph Casaky和雷漢布魯克（Wilhelm Lehmbruck）等不同藝術家的傑出作品。

該館的另外一個特色，是收藏了一批雕塑家的素描。在素描領域上，庫勒夫人的收藏被視為無法公開的收藏，但該博物館針對這個限定的領域，持續收集與收藏雕塑有直接關係的素描作品。一直到今天，這些為了強調雕塑家的素描為一種獨立的藝術表達形式，一個將理念視覺化的殿堂，也就是雕塑的思維，因此而不再被具體化。

緩慢的起步之後，在五○年代後期，由於取得額外的基金，館藏品的收集有了爆炸性的加速，而一座作品充實均衡的雕塑公園得以在1961年開放。一些藝術家如瑪塔‧潘接受委託，在商議後針對選定的地點創作出適合的作品，這成了收藏政策中的一種獨特主題，一直延續到今天。在雕塑室中或是建築室內雕塑作品也成為一種特色。到了七○年代，在兩個方面發生了變化。一方面來說，這段時間以新的建設計畫為主，並在1977年完成工程；另一方面，雕塑藝術有了新的發展。一群較年輕，比較觀念取向，並常以脆弱材質創作的雕塑家，覺得他們不再需要將作品放在戶外，而是選擇將作品放在室內空間與建築互動。隨著杜布菲（Jean Dubuffet）和塞拉（Richard Serra）的大型計劃的完成，這個時期漸漸接近尾聲。就技術面來說，可能做到的都已經完成了。經過一段長時間的考慮之後，Matthias Goeritz、海扎（Michael Heizer）和諾曼（Bruce Nauman）的設計被認為不可實行而遭到擱置。此外，可供使用的地區的大小和土地種類，無法再負荷希望利用廣大空間、沙漠和獨立地區打造大規模作品的藝術家。儘管地景藝術（Land Art）和大地作品（Earth Works）能融入庫勒穆勒美術館的氣氛中，但除以文獻的方式之外，該館已無法再建置此類作品。

七○年代由Rudi Oxenaar館長領導的擴建計畫實現後，空間的問題得到了舒緩；從那時候起，一個嶄新且較大的空間，使得室內大件作品的陳列變得可能，就像一直以來室外的收藏一樣。庫勒穆勒美術館也得以思考更多更大件的作品與室內建築的關係，如同之前提到的，這正

是雕塑家需要的。這段時間庫勒穆勒的館藏有了相當的增加。由於購入第一批威塞（Visser）的收藏，使得美術館能夠塑造出一些重要的核心團體來發展出更清楚的特色。因此，在奧特羅（Otterlo）所呈現的是歐美或其他地方所沒有的極簡藝術（Robert Morris、Sol LeWitt、Donald Judd、Carl Andre和Dan Flavin），同樣重要的另一個核心則是，以貧窮藝術（Arte Povera）為主軸而聚集的作品（Mario Merz, Kuciano Fabro, Giovanni Anselmo, Jannis Kounellis，還有Joseph Beuys、Eva Hesse和Barry Flanagan）。以自然與建築的關係為主的重要新媒介—攝影—也開始展示，尤其是Jan Dibbets, Ger van Elk, Gilbert & George, Richard Long和Hamish Fulton的攝影作品。而一些重要的作品或是系列性作品，像是海扎（Heizer）、歐登柏格（Claes Oldenburg）、蘇維洛（Mark Di Suvero）、塞拉（Serra）、諾曼（Nauman）、Long、呂克里姆（Ulrich Rückriem）、克里斯托（Christo）、帕納馬仁珂（Panamarenko）、曼佐尼（Piero Manzoni）、威塞（Carel Visser）和布罕（Daniel Buren）等人所作，都成為庫勒穆勒美術館的館藏。

因此，雕塑作品及雕塑家的素描開始與館內最初的油畫收藏有相同的重要地位。在這大範圍的現代藝術中，作品的選擇必須盡量考量其目的。以提供整體概念為目的，以已有的典藏為特色，並突顯該館建築和土地所能提供的各種可能性。但這當中有很大的一部份被忽略了。像眼鏡蛇派、行動繪畫、巴黎畫派、普普藝術、新現實主義、超現實主義和抽象畫派幾乎或完全沒有展示出來。這是因為美術館的偏好，為了將館藏建構及限制在基本點上，為了選擇那些能夠替美術館特色加分的作品。

從1990年12月我接下了這個職位開始，我將美術館組織的強化及典藏品狀況的改善視為第一要務。這間美術館於1994年7月1日開始獨立經營，並冠上庫勒穆勒美術館這個名字。在政府資金的幫助下，2001年我們完成了一個全面性的計畫，來補強藏品狀況不足的部分。同年，隨著一座大型雕塑庫房的完工，庫房的狀況也得到了改善。為了使美術館能夠運作並能實現現代化政策，我總是將理想的便民性和館藏的最佳狀況做為首要條件。這並不是說收藏的方針從1990年開始就在原地踏步，相反地，藏品數量增加了，先前提到的許多空白也填補了起來。過去制定的方針已保留下來，為的是要再一次強調館藏歷史的延續性。

我視這些收藏猶如以原本館藏為中心的蜘蛛網：它是一個有連續性的整體，但從當中的一點要到另外一點需要經過許多的交叉點。然而，館藏中的藝術品不能有固定的、等級分明的位置。因此，庫勒穆勒美術館的任務是透過不同的安排來展示作品，使觀眾能夠有機會體驗到藝術品不斷改變的意義。

現在，庫勒穆勒美術館已經成為在自然中、在寧靜中，以及大片空間中體驗藝術的最重要美術館。它提供給觀眾一個機會，使他們能與精美的藝術作品面對面，並且思考這些存在的精神面。由於它的特性及位置，庫勒穆勒美術館誘發了細膩的思考、沉思及安靜的享受。

我們的收藏主要動機仍然是要展現出雕塑（立體作品）、油畫、建築與自然之間的多元關係。然而對藝術作品的特別關注複雜了它們之間的關係。海倫的收藏品提供了理念發展的契機，但雕塑公園已經成為了一個不可或缺的部份，再加上在厚荷·扶鹿國家公園中的位置，使得庫勒穆勒美術館成為國際間難得一有的獨特的美術館。

The Kröller-Müller Museum and its Collections

Evert van Straaten

"Als ein einziger und grosser, entwicklungsgeschichtlicher Zusammenhang spiegelt sich die Kunst der Gegenwart in der Sammlung Kröller-Müller wieder. Hier liegt der Akzent nicht so sehr auf örtlich-holländischer Einstellung. Massgebende Werke aus den meisten Ländern Europas legen die Einheit des neuen Strebens in der Breite nach rückwärts und nach vorwärts dar. Der Besucher wird unmittelbar gewahr, wie notwendig und folgerichtig alles verläuft: das Voneinander-Lernen und das gegenseitige Sich-Überbieten der Malergenerationen während des 19. Jahrhunderts und dann in unseren Tagen die unvermeidliche und trotzige Umkehr."

("In the Kröller-Müller collection, contemporary art is reflected as a unique, extensive and historically coherent whole. Here, the accent is not so much on a local, Dutch point of departure. Prominent works of art from most European countries reveal the uniformity of the new tendencies, broadly guided by the past and the future. The visitor can immediately experience the necessity and logic of the progression: from the mutual learning and bidding against each other of the generations of 19th century painters to the inevitable and wilful reversal in our time.")

This is how German art journalist F.M. Huebner opens the chapter on the Kröller-Müller collection in his book on modern art in Dutch private collections, which was published in 1921. Since 1913, a selection from this steadily growing collection had already been on constant display in the offices of the Müller company, on the Lange Voorhout in The Hague.

The German Helene Müller was born in Horst, near Essen in 1869. There, her father owned a small foundry and later established a shipping and trading company in Dusseldorf with a branch in Rotterdam. In 1888, Helene married the Dutchman Anton Kröller, who had recently become head of the company in Rotterdam. Helene's father died in 1889 and Anton became director of the family business. In the years that followed he expanded the business from the Netherlands into a powerful international concern with interests in shipping, trade and mining operations. The profits from this would form the basis for the subsequent acquisition of the art collection.

In 1905, on the advice of her daughter, Helene began taking lessons from the influential art connoisseur H.P. Bremmer. He struck a chord with her: from that moment on, her passion for modern art began to flourish. From 1907 to 1925, she contracted Bremmer to help build up a collection. Her ambition went further than simply putting together an art collection. Just as the Medici, whose artistic legacy she had seen in Florence, Helene wanted to enrich the culture of her time. The collection, which rapidly took on museum dimensions due to the extensive acquisition programme, would need to have a home of its own, which would ultimately belong to the community.

Before reaching that point, in the years 1910-1913 she gave a succession of commissions to L.J. Falkenburg, Peter Behrens, Ludwig Mies van der Rohe and H.P. Berlage to design a country residence with an art room for the rural estate Ellenwoude near Wassenaar. Life-size mock-ups of the designs by Behrens and Mies van der Rohe were produced on site in wood and canvas. The design by Mies van der Rohe came into direct competition with the design by Berlage. Bremmer played a key role in this by making an emotional plea for the realization of Berlage's design. In the end nobody won, as the Kröllers sold the land and bought an existing country estate, Groot Haesebroek near Wassenaar.

Meanwhile, between 1909 and 1921, Anton Kröller bought over 6,000 hectares of unbroken hunting and riding land on the Veluwe, in the middle of the province of Gelderland. The current De Hoge Veluwe National Park once formed the heart of this area. In 1914 or 1915, Berlage was commissioned to build a hunting lodge for the family there, which was completed in 1920. Helene found the trips to the Veluwe so agreeable that she decided, as early as 1915, to build her new home and museum there. Looking back on

Helene Kröller-Müller (1869-1939) and Anton Kröller (1862-1941), wedding portrait 1888 (Archive Kröller-Müller Museum, Otterlo)

this in 1928, she wrote: "We took this decision, on consideration, that nowadays distances are no longer a drawback and that the visitor, in this majestic, unspoilt nature, can enjoy art in an entirely different manner than in whichever city - and particularly the often complicated abstract art, which the collection includes, and which requires great dedication and quiet contemplation for its spiritual content."

Berlage's first designs for a museum in the Veluwe date from 1917-18, but due to the ultimately irreconcilable characters of Berlage and Helene, nothing came of his plan. After a short intermezzo with the architect A.J. Kropholler, she appointed Henry van de Velde in late 1919 for the museum house in De Hoge Veluwe. He designed a grand building at the foot of a hill, the Franse Berg. From 1921 on, a huge amount of drawings were produced and in 1922 the foundations were laid, but the economic crisis constrained the financial means and halted the progress of construction, although the hope was to resume it at a later date.

That hope proved to be in vain. In 1928 the collection and the country estate were put in to a separate foundation. This foundation, which was co-administered by the Kröller-Müllers, transferred the collection to the Dutch State, who promised to build and maintain a museum for the collection in De Hoge Veluwe. This foundation sold the country estate to a newly established foundation, which still manages the area today as the De Hoge Veluwe National Park. In anticipation of the resumption of building work on his 1921 design, Henry van de Velde was asked to design a 'transitional museum'. The museum opened to the public in 1938 as the Rijksmuseum Kröller-Müller. It is this 'transitional museum' that remains the core of the current Kröller-Müller Museum; the 'grand museum' under the Franse Berg was never built. The ruins of its foundations near the three large bronzes by Henry Moore have become monuments to the Kröller's ambitions to become modern-day Medici.

While still during the war years, Van de Velde designed an extension plan for the 'transitional museum' with a sculpture room, an auditorium, a number of galleries and a trustees' room, in order to make it into a 'permanent' museum. This extension was only realized after the war, in 1953. Thus, a modest museum complex was created, which was characterized by closed volumes with daylight pouring in from above, and with a focus on the works of art, and a sculpture room that opened onto the surrounding nature.

The construction of the sculpture garden followed in 1960, after a design by J.T.P. Bijhouwer. In 1965, the sculpture pavilion that Gerrit Rietveld had designed for the Sonsbeek exhibition in 1955 was rebuilt in this garden. With this, the foundations were laid to make the Rijksmuseum Kröller-Müller into an authoritative museum of modern and contemporary sculpture.

In the course of the nineteen sixties, the growth of the collection, the need to organize exhibitions and the changing form of visual art required an expansion of the museum. Wim Quist was commissioned for this and throughout the nineteen seventies he realized a new wing for exhibitions and large three-dimensional work, with an auditorium, offices and service areas. He was masterful in capturing the spirit of the place in a spectacular interplay of inside and outside spaces, which characterizes the typical atmosphere of the Kröller-Müller Museum: a complex of pure proportions, with great attention to detail, in the service of visual art.

The collection that Helene Kröller-Müller assembled reflected her ideas about a development in art, in which times of realism and idealism were alternating factors. From early on, she was convinced that her collection must have an idealistic tendency and must be placed at the disposal of the community: therefore, by her own account, she collected 'impersonally and purposefully'. Initially she wished to prove that abstract art was not that difficult to fathom and did not represent a total rift with the older art. By combining old and new works of art, she sought to substantiate the right of the new art. When, during her time, abstract art became fully recognized, she adjusted her acquisition policy by focusing on realistic, more neoclassical tendencies. It was time again, according to Mrs Kröller, to prove that abstract art is not the only art that counts and that it nonetheless has its basis in reality.

The four most important core components of her collection are old works of art, which illustrate the development of realism, but which were mainly intended to give background to the modern abstract pieces, and works of art that illustrated realism from ca. 1850, through the periods of impressionism, neo-impressionism and cubism, primarily on the basis of French (or those whose work developed in France) and Dutch artists. Thirdly are the groups of works by individuals who to some extent resisted the developments of their time, such as J. Thorn Prikker, Jan Toorop, James Ensor, William Degouve de Nunques or Odilon Redon, and last, but not least, the work of Vincent van Gogh, as the hub of the collection. In addition to this, her collection contained a few other important components, such as drawings by old masters, sculptures, delftware pottery, Chinese art, antique earthenware and graphic art. Mrs Kröller's ideal also included placing emphasis on the oneness of all art.

Thus, it became a theme in her collection to show old and new, Eastern and Western, European and non-European art in unity. This is how the basic principle was established; a principle of clarity through omission and clarity through a personal preference for art with what one might refer to, using a post-war term, as an Apollonian bias. The Dionysian was set aside or absent. No Matisse, no Fauvres, no German expressionists, no Blaue Reiter (Kandinsky, Marc), but neither any dadaists, surrealists or constructivists. To a large extent, certainly for everything that may be called expressionism, this was a conscious limitation of the selection.

After the war, it was decided not to extend Mrs Kröller's painting collection, unless it concerned the filling of gaps or small supplementations. In the early nineteen fifties, the then director Bram Hammacher took the initiative in continuing and extending the collection in the field of sculpture, with the central, inspiring idea of placing the pieces outside. In 1953, the sculpture room in the Van de Velde building became available and the first section of the sculpture garden opened in 1961. Despite the very limited means and possibilities, a collection gradually accumulated that was intended, in a concerted action with the paintings, to provide a parallel image of the development of sculptural art since ca. 1850, with a similar non-doctrinal, personal method of selecting pieces to that adopted by Mrs Kröller. In this way, important pieces were acquired by artists including Auguste Rodin, Henry Moore, Barbara Hepworth, Marta Pan, Alicia Penalba, Emilio Greco, Fritz Wotruba en Chaim Lipchitz. By choosing to extend the sculpture collection, the museum was, incidentally, building on the existing group of some 275 sculptures that Mrs Kröller had already amassed, with prominent works by diverse artists such as Aristide Maillol, Jozef Mendes da Costa, Joseph Csaky and Wilhelm Lehmbruck.

As a speciality a collection of sculptors' drawings has developed. In the field of drawing, Mrs Kröller's collection was indeed respected as a closed totality, but the museum continued collecting in this one limited area and in direct relation to the sculpture collection. The intention was, and has remained to this day, to place emphasis on the drawings by sculptors as an independent means of expression, as a sanctuary for visualizing ideas, which are sculptural thoughts, and hence, not necessarily required to be practical for realization.

After a slow start, in the late nineteen fifties, due in part to the allocation of extra funds, an explosive acceleration of acquisitions occurred, such that the sculpture garden was able to open in 1961 with a wide-ranging and balanced selection of sculptures. Commissions for artists, such as Martha Pan, to make an appropriate piece for a spot chosen in consultation with them, became a characteristic theme in the policy and remains so to this day. A stronger accent was also placed on sculpture inside, in the sculpture room and elsewhere in the building. The nineteen seventies offered an altered perspective in two directions. On the one hand, those years were dominated by plans for new construction, which reached completion in 1977; on the other, new developments were taking place in sculptural art. A younger generation of sculptors, more conceptually oriented and often working with fragile materials, no longer felt the need to place their work outdoors, opting instead for the interior space, for a relationship with architecture. With the large projects by Jean Dubuffet and Richard Serra, a period more or less drew to a close. In a technical sense, the limits of what was possible had been reached. After long consideration, designs by Matthias Goeritz, Michael Heizer and Bruce Nauman had to be set aside as impracticable. Moreover, the sort and size of the available terrain was often no longer suitable for the very large-scale ideas, in which artists dreamed of vast spaces, deserts, isolated regions. Land Art and Earth Works, much as they belong in the ambiance of the Kröller-Müller Museum, were difficult to accommodate, other than in documentary form.

The realisation of the extension in the seventies, on the initiative of director Rudi Oxenaar, brought relief: new and larger spaces made it possible, from that moment on, to collect larger works for the interior space as had previously been done for the exterior. The museum was able to consider more and larger work in an architectural context and, as already mentioned, that was exactly what sculptors required. The collection grew reasonably well during these years. Due in part to the acquisition of the first segment of the Visser collection, it became possible to form a number of important core groups, in order to develop clear specializations. Thus, Minimal Art (Robert Morris, Sol LeWitt, Donald Judd, Carl Andre, Dan Flavin) is now represented in Otterlo as virtually nowhere else in Europe or America, and an equally important core was assembled around the umbrella term Arte Povera (Mario Merz, Luciano Fabro, Giovanni Anselmo, Jannis Kounellis, but also Joseph Beuys, Eva Hesse, Barry Flanagan). The important new medium photography, concentrating on the relationships with nature and architecture, was broadly represented with works by Jan Dibbets, Ger van Elk, Gilbert & George, Richard Long and Hamish Fulton, among others. Important pieces or groups of pieces by artists including Heizer, Claes Oldenburg, Mark Di Suvero, Serra, Nauman, Long, Ulrich Rückriem, Christo, Panamarenko, Piero Manzoni, Carel Visser and Daniel Buren were acquired.

Thus, the collection of sculptures and sculptor's drawings started to become a counterpart of equal value to the original painting collection. Within the broad field of modern art, the selection of work was as goal-oriented as possible. With the goal of providing a general overview, but with specializations in keeping with what was already collected and geared towards the specific possibilities that the building and grounds had to offer. A great deal was omitted. Movements such as Cobra, action painting, Ecole de Paris, Pop Art, neo-realism, surrealism and abstract expressionism were barely represented, if at all. This occurred out of preference, out of the need for structure and restriction to the essential, out of the desire to select that which might gain an added value in the museum's particular ambiance.

Since taking up my post in December 1990, I have given priority to the strengthening of the museum's organization and the improvement of the condition of the collection. The museum became independent on July 1st 1994 and since then bears the name: Kröller-Müller Museum. With the help of extra government funding, a comprehensive programme was undertaken to make up lost ground in the condition of the collection, which was completed in 2001. In the same year, the depot situation was also improved with the construction of a large depot for sculpture. I have always considered optimal accessibility and the best possible condition of the collection to be prerequisites for allowing the museum to function and being able to effect a modernization of the policy. That is not to say that the collection policy has been marking time since 1990. On the contrary, additions have been made and gaps filled in many of the areas mentioned above. The line set out by our predecessors is deliberately continued in order to once again underline the continuity in the history of the collection.

I envisage the collection as a spider's web, with the original Kröller-Müller collec¬tion at its centre: it is one coherent whole, but to get from any given point to another sometimes requires crossing a great many intersections. Contrary to what this comparison might suggest, the overriding opinion is that the works of art in the collection must not have a fixed, hierarchical position. For that reason, the museum considers it its task to display the pieces in a constantly altering arrangement, to give the visitors to the museum every possible opportunity to experience the continuously changing significance of a work of art.

By now, the Kröller-Müller Museum has become the foremost museum to experience visual art in nature, in the midst of tranquillity and space. It offers its visitors the opportunity to come face to face with high quality works of art and to contemplate the immaterial side of existence. Due to its character and location, the Kröller-Müller Museum invites attentive consideration, reflection and quiet enjoyment.

The central motive for the acquisitions is still to display the multifarious relationships between sculpture (in the sense of three-dimensional work), painting, architecture and nature, but thereby paying particular attention to works of art that complicate the relations between them. The collection that Helene brought together provides the inspirational point of departure for this, but the sculpture garden has become an essential component, which, together with its location in the total complex in the De Hoge Veluwe National Park, makes the Kröller-Müller Museum into the internationally unique museum that it is.

波林納吉（Borinage）是比利時的礦區，位在蒙斯（Mons）的西南方。在1878年12月到1880年10月間，梵谷在這裡待了很長一段時間，也畫了很多素描。然而，此時的作品幾乎沒有留下來，[1] 而根據現有的記錄，這些作品的水準仍有許多改進的空間。[2]《雪地裡的礦工》完成於1880年9月，不久之前梵谷才下定決心要走上藝術這條道路，因此這幅作品乃是梵谷已知最早以獨立藝術家的心態所創作的作品。

　　在1880年8月20日一封寫給弟弟西奧（Theo）的信（155/134）中，我們第一次讀到這幅素描的主題：「我畫了一幅礦工及助手[3]（包括男孩與女孩）的塗鴉，他們在早晨穿過雪地前往礦井，路邊長著荊棘的樹叢：他們穿過陰影，在微光中若隱若現。背景是巨大的礦場建築與煤灰堆成的小丘，在天空隱約的襯托下更為顯著。我將這幅塗鴉寄給你，讓你看看它的樣子。」這幅塗鴉保存了下來。從兩封後來的書信中我們可以推論，梵谷這幅塗鴉是根據1879到1880年冬天之間所畫的一幅素描，而這也說明了為什麼他會在夏末畫冬季的景象。在信中他寫道：「可是我還是忍不住要用比較大尺寸的速寫來畫走向礦井的礦工，也就是我先前寄了幅塗鴉給你的那幅，不過我對人物的配置做了點修改。」（156/135，1880年9月7日）塗鴉與《雪地裡的礦工》的相似之處讓我們可以推測後者就是梵谷所提到的「速寫」。因此，兩幅作品都是根據範本而畫出的，不過和塗鴉裡像浮雕一樣線描的人物圖相比，梵谷在速寫裡做了更多改變。其中一項改變就是在前景的右方增加三個人物。整體的構圖看起來比較不那麼靜態，因為所有的人物都表現出行走的動作而且彼此交錯。在1881年早期，他畫了另一幅雪中礦工的素描，並且在信中對父母說：「它比去年冬天畫得好一點，更有個性，效果也更好。」（162/144，1881年2月16日）梵谷口中的「去年冬天」指的應該是塗鴉與速寫所根據的範本。那幅素描並沒有保存下來，而1881年早期的那一幅也沒有。[4]

　　《雪地裡的礦工》顯示出梵谷剛開始在人物素描上的笨拙。從他在人物輪廓上所做的許多修正，尤其是腿及相對較大的腳等部分，更可明顯看出這一點。儘管踏著堅決的步伐，但是這些礦工的構成都相當僵硬，而且幾乎沒有體積。其中有些穿著皮製頭盔，但是也可以看到其他典型的礦工特徵，包括燈、鶴嘴鋤、鏟子等。右方三個較小的人物之中，位居中央的人物以背影呈現，暗示通往礦坑的道路要向左轉。起初最右邊的兩個男性人物比較靠近邊緣，因此那裡還看得到一些他們後來被擦掉的痕跡。

　　畫紙的右邊以及左邊的小部分後來經過剪裁，亦即起初的構圖應較為空曠。[5]畫面中央的四個人物幾乎和小幅塗鴉上的完全一模一樣。這一組人物中，中間兩個是女性，其中左邊的女孩頭髮綁進髮網內，就像右邊三個較小的人物中最左邊的那一個。比起原有的塗鴉更重要的改進（因此或許也超越原有的範本）就是在最左邊結束整個畫面，背上背著籃子的女性。在整個畫面中，只有她的身體略微朝向觀者。她，就像拿著鏟子的男性，都有著凝重的表情，因此讓兩者的個性更為突出，看起來不像其他人物那麼呆板。這兩個人物的服裝都上了淺藍色及褐色的淡水彩，比起其他人物多了點顏色。

　　在畫面的背景，在一排覆蓋著白雪的房屋上方，我們可以看到一堆煤灰（Terril）也覆蓋著白雪，左右分別有礦場建築、橋樑、煙囪等。我們很難辨認畫作描繪的明確地點，但是左方較大的礦場建築有第二個較小的屋簷從主要的屋簷延伸出來，其下方還可以看到起重纜的大慣性輪，整體的描繪有點類似Fosse No 3 d'Hornu et Wasmes這個礦坑。[6]在塗鴉中，建築與長鐵橋所描繪的方式比起當時更貼近實際的狀況。就素描的版本而言，梵谷或許在為上半部收尾時遇到困難，因此一座橋直接跑進建築的屋頂，儘管實際上通常不會這樣。

　　畫紙本身經歷了許多滄桑。紙張變色的情形相當嚴重，許多地方都有嚴重的受損。在早期的一次修復中，畫紙的背後被塗上紙漿加以強化，但不幸這也遮蓋了題記的一部分。題記的筆跡相當近似收藏家Hidde Nijland的筆跡，而這幅素描原先也是屬於他的收藏。能夠辨識的字跡只有「Besteld」（預定）以及「1895年1月8日」這個日期，這或許是有關1895年2月至3月在Haagsche Kunstkring所舉行的一次展覽，其中展示了Nijland所收藏的超過80幅梵谷的素描。

---

1. 1888年梵谷寫信給Eugene Boch（書信696/335b），說他在波林納吉第一次依據自然而創作，但是「當然我很早以前都已經將它們全部毀掉了。」1879年夏天所創作的《波林納吉的煤礦坑》（Coal mine in the Borinage）（F1040）是少數留存下來的作品之一，目前是梵谷美術館的藏品之一（Van Heugten 1996，頁69-71）。

2. Pierard 1929，頁57-88。

3. 梵谷的用語是「scloneurs et scloneuses」，這通常指年輕的礦工（男孩與女孩）他們會協助「abatteur」（將煤礦敲鬆的礦工）將鬆了的材料搬開。

4. Lisbeth Heenk認為此處所引的話指的就是《雪地裡的礦工》並因此將這幅素描定為1881年2月，因為她認為塗鴉與素描的差異太大，不可能是根據同一個範本（Heenk 1995，頁18-19）。不這樣就很難理解梵谷在1880年9月7日的書信提到這幅速寫之後又繼續進一步的修飾。

5. 塗鴉裡明顯有更多空間，特別是右方。我們並不清楚是否是梵谷本人縮減了作品的尺寸。沒有一個角落是原來的，而且每一邊都經過剪裁。

6. 有關波林納吉部分礦場建築的老照片，請參閱http://mineshainaut.ibelgique.com與http://borain.be。在1879到1880年之間，梵谷花了很多時間待在(Petit-)Wasmes（Hulsker 1985，頁121-148）。

雪地裡的礦工　Miners in the Snow
1880年9月　1880 Sep.
鉛筆、彩色粉筆、水彩、織紋紙　pencil, colored chalk and watercolor on wove paper
44×55公分　44 x 55 cm
Collection Kröller-Müller Museum, Otterlo, The Netherlands

「如果我沒記錯，你一定還有米勒的那幅《田間勞動》（Les Travaux des Champs）。可不可以請你借給我一段時間，並且將它寄給我？我得告訴你，現在我正在用大型的素描來臨摹些米勒的作品〔……〕。寫這封信給你的時候我還正在素描，所以我趕著要回去繼續去畫。」梵谷寫這封信給西奧的時間是在1880年8月20日，是從波林納吉的Cuesmes所寄出，同時這也是目前所知在梵谷決心成為藝術家之後所寫的第一封信。（155/134）從這封以及後來的信中，我們知道梵谷給自己很大的時間壓力。當時他27歲，要開始藝術家的生涯不算年輕，要學的還有很多。他特別渴望要做人物素描的練習，而這些練習就包括臨摹他崇拜的藝術家的作品。米勒（Jean-Francois Millet, 1814-1875）是法國農民生活畫家，也是對梵谷最重要的模範。[1]目前已知他在1880年8月到1881年5月間臨摹米勒並畫了好幾十幅作品，其中除了此處所介紹的2幅之外只有少數留存下來。[2]

兩幅素描都可以相當肯定為1880年10月間所創作。在當月上旬，梵谷搬到了布魯塞爾，並且與Tobias Victor Schmidt聯絡。Schmidt是個畫商，負責古比藝廊（Goupil & Cie）在當地的分公司，當年梵谷還在古比工作時兩人就已認識。[3]梵谷希望Schmidt能夠幫他找個有畫室的畫家好讓他能上課。（書信158/137，1880年10月15日）見面的時候Schmidt借給梵谷兩張照片，這是根據11月1日的一封信（159/138）：「剛剛根據Braun的照片素描了米勒的《掘地者》。我從Schmidt那裡找到這幅照片，另外他還把《晚禱》也借給我。我將這兩幅素描都寄給爸，讓他知道我有在努

力。」最後這句話很重要，因為這或許解釋了為什麼這兩幅素描能留下來，而且指的就是此處介紹的這兩幅。兩件作品都沒有簽名，但是在標題之後都有同樣的筆跡用黑墨水寫的題詞：d'apres J. F. Millet〔仿米勒〕。我們幾乎可以確定這就是畫家的筆跡。這兩幅大型素描都畫得不錯，所以一定讓梵谷很有信心將它們寄給他的父親。[4]

Ad. Braun & Co這幅《掘地者》的照片內容是米勒於1857年所畫的一幅素描。[5]梵谷用鉛筆畫，但是有幾個地方他後來用黑色粉筆來增強色調，像是右邊的掘地者，右邊的石頭，還有前景的陰影部分。他相當忠實於原作，儘管他在右邊留了比較多空間，創造出一種較為延伸的構圖。掘地者在他的生涯中始終是個重要的主題。在臨摹米勒的一系列油畫作品中，有另一個版本的《掘地者》是在1889年在聖雷米所畫的。為了這幅畫，梵谷還特別請西奧將這幅素描的Braun照片寄給他。（書信806/607，1889年9月19日）[6]

畫著《掘地者》的畫紙受到相當的損害，邊緣有許多皺摺。充滿纖維的織紋紙因時間久遠而發黃。這或許指出紙張本身原來是染成藍色，同樣的，用來畫《晚禱》的紙張也已經變黃了。在《晚禱》中，就在那籃馬鈴薯的下方，還看得到一塊長方形的原來的淺藍色。[7]米勒這幅1855到1857年間的畫作描繪一位單純的女性在一天勞累的工作之後和丈夫在田野間進行晚禱。由於許多的複製畫讓這幅畫在19世紀末非常受到歡迎。在梵谷的這幅素描裡，他是根據這幅畫作的Braun照片來進行繪製，但是他在1876年已經在Durand-Ruel以每張一法郎的價格購買了三張這幅作品的蝕刻畫（書信

晚禱（仿米勒）　　L'Angelus du Soir (after Millet)
1880年10月　　1880 Oct.
黑色粉筆、鉛筆、暈染、紅色粉筆及　　black chalk, pencil, wash and red chalk heightened with white,
白色粉筆打亮、（原）藍灰直紋紙　　on (originally) grey-blue laid paper
46.8×62公分　　46.8 x 62 cm
Collection Kröller-Müller Museum, Otterlo, The Netherlands

72/58）。在購買這些畫作的兩年之前，他就曾說：「米勒的那幅畫，《晚禱》，『就是它』，的確如此，那真偉大，那就是詩。」（書信17/13，1874年1月）梵谷或許不知道，當他還在布魯塞爾繪製這幅素描時，米勒的原作剛好也在同一個城市裡。[8]

　　從技術觀點來看，《晚禱》比起《掘地者》有更細緻的構思。在這幅素描裡，梵谷主要使用的也是鉛筆和黑色粉筆，但是在天空上他用非常稀釋的白色不透明水彩塗了淡淡的一層顏色。天空以及沿著畫紙邊緣棕紅色粉筆的色調或許是用來強調暮色即將來臨，而且在畫紙仍是淡藍色的時候無疑地效果更好。現在則可以從梵谷加在草叉、籃子、以及人物身上延伸的陰影看出暮色的降臨。在原野的位置上，梵谷用畫筆刷上淡水彩，創造出灰色調的效果。某些地方他後來用擦子擦出較亮的色調，來強調寬闊的傍晚的光線效果。男性處在背光的位置，女性的圍裙及木屐則灑上最後的陽光，這樣的對比在米勒的原作上比較顯著，特別是中間區域比較明亮。但是

兩幅作品最大的差異在於比例：梵谷的仿作有較顯著的空間，因為他在左邊、右邊以及底部大量地擴展了構圖。由於距離邊緣較遠，他的人物看起來比較沒有巨大的雕像感。在米勒的原作裡，推車幾乎碰到構圖的邊緣，而整幅畫比較接近正方形。在梵谷的素描裡，草叉位置較遠，籃子和女性腳下的木屐有更多的空間。最後，在兩個人物之間，地平線較低，而女性人物交握的雙手則高過了地平線。[9]我們甚至可以看出，在擴大了構圖之後，梵谷不確定該怎麼運用額外的空間，因為在左右邊緣約10公分寬的地方他的筆觸比起其他部分更為遲疑且不精確。

　　米勒的原作比起梵谷的素描大不了多少，但是由於原作呈方形，人物較大，所以讓整幅畫看起來更沈重，更巨大，讓它成為虔誠鄉間生活的代表圖像。[10]梵谷的空間配置讓整幅素描更接近隨興的觀察，和《掘地者》相比，也比較不是忠實的臨摹，但是在其中米勒的原作當然仍是呼之欲出。

---

1. 有關梵谷與米勒的關係，請參見Van Tilborgh et al. 1988及Van Tilborgh et al. 1998。
2. 這幾幅包括《收割者（仿米勒）》（*Reaper (after Millet)*，F1674/JH2，私人收藏）；《播種者（仿米勒）》（*Sower (after Millet)*，F830/JH1，梵谷美術館）：兩幅均為1881年4月間所作。另一個版本的《掘地者》（F828/JHXII）也是在1880年10月間創作。
3. Schmidt大約在1875年間從Hendrik Vincent van Gogh，也就是文森與西奧口中的「伯父Hein」手中接管這間分公司（Stolwijk & Thomson 1999，頁24及193；Nonne 2000，頁40），當梵谷去拜訪的時候，他並不知道當時Schmidt因為要自己創業所以與家人處得並不好。但是梵谷還是受到熱誠的接待。（書信159/138）
4. 另一個版本的《掘地者》（F828）沒有題記，但是卻有簽名。我們並不清楚簽名是否是畫家本人所為。
5. 參見Chetham 1976，頁258。有關米勒《掘地者》，又稱為*Les deux becheurs*的不同版本，參見Herbert 1974，頁159-166，167及169。
6. 作品編號F648，Stedelijk Museum，Amsterdam。
7. 染成藍色的紙張有時很容易明顯地變黃。然而，上色的纖維殘餘並沒有在《掘地者》上發現。《晚禱》上之所以會出現紙張原來的顏色，可能的解釋是紙張背後對應的位置被覆蓋起來。（Hoefsloot 1987，頁8）沿著紙張邊緣也可以隱約看到藍色。紙張左下方的角落後來被撕去一角，暫時經過修復，但是在1980年代整張畫紙的背後以日本紙進行強化。
8. 此為John W. Wilson收藏的一部分（Herbert 1974，頁104，105）。此畫作原先的標題為*L'Angelus*，沒有*du soir*。Angelus意為奉告祈禱，一天共有三次，分別在清晨6點、中午12點、傍晚6點。
9. 女性人物的頭部原先的位置較高，這可從她的帽子周圍可見的修改痕跡看出。
10. 參見Herbert 1974，頁103至106。

掘地者（仿米勒）　Les Becheurs (after Millet)
1880年10月　1880 Oct.
鉛筆、黑色粉筆、織紋紙　pencil and black chalk on wove paper
37.5×61.5公分　37.5 x 61.5 cm
Collection Kröller-Müller Museum, Otterlo, The Netherlands

《背負重物的人們》這幅相當具有企圖心的素描描繪的是礦工的生活。梵谷是在布魯塞爾開始繪製，或許後來才在埃頓完成。和《雪地裡的礦工》相比，我們不禁許異於梵谷在半年的時間裡有了如此的進步。不僅是人物有了更多的質量感，比例也更有可信度，景物消失的透視畫法也相當標準。這幅素描當然不是沒有缺點，但是從它身上可以明顯看出，梵谷在自己所選擇的主題上有相當大的表現能力。素描裡所描繪的女性真的是被沈重的負擔壓得直不起身：她們從背景的煤丘收集了一袋袋尚堪使用的碎煤。除此之外，以灰色水彩寫在右下角的英文標題The Bearers of the Burden《肩負重擔的人》指出這些可憐的礦工太太們也該被視為具有象徵意義的形象。

在1881年4月12日即將出發到埃頓前由布魯塞爾所寄出的一封信中，梵谷也提到這個主題。當時西奧本來也要去埃頓，所以信中梵谷提到自己「非常期待那一刻，特別是因為我已經在拉帕德那裡畫了兩幅素描，分別是《提燈者》（The Lamp Bearer）與《背負重物的人們》，所以我想跟你談談它們該怎麼繼續下去。」（書信164/143）《提燈者》並沒有留存下來，但這個主題無疑和礦工也有關係。[1]這兩幅素描明顯還在草稿階段，或許是以鉛筆畫的初稿。《背負重物的人們》完全是以鉛筆畫草圖，然後用墨水筆繼續發展。梵谷用了兩種墨水，棕色以及黑色[2]。他用不同粗細的墨水筆，這一點從前景以及人物周圍的輪廓線可以明顯看出。透過筆觸的強力交錯，他建構出素描的節奏。女性人物所走的道路是用細陰影線及較寬的水平線來進行描繪。其後方區域主要是短的相連線條，構成上方的耕地之間「較亮」的間隔，而耕地主要是垂直線，朝向教堂附近地平線上的消失點。構圖結束於右方的一棵樹，樹上有個小小的神龕，裡面釘了一個十字架。十字架完全以鉛筆描繪，並沒有以墨水進一步勾勒。

在煤灰堆間拾取碎煤的女性稱為arracheuses或ramasseuses。在梵谷待在波林納吉的時候一定每天都看到她們典型這種彎腰負重的姿勢。帶頭的女性提著一個礦工使用的燈，似乎用它來照亮回家的路。[3]梵谷或許用這個方式來暗示著《提燈者》是這幅畫的連作。

在背景的村莊裡，梵谷用教堂來與礦坑對比，再加上十字架以及構圖右方的兩把鏟子，強調出當地居民的生活狀態，也就是基本上只有「祈禱及工作。」[4]梵谷對採礦的人有相當深的情感，這樣的情感在梵谷離開波林納吉之前的一封給西奧的信有了動人的表達：「礦工與織工還是一種和其他工人與匠師有點不同的一群人，我和他們相當有共鳴。如果有一天我能畫出他們，那麼我就會覺得自己很幸運了。因為這樣一來，這些仍不為人知，或者說幾乎不為人知的類型就會重見天日。來自深處的人，來自深淵的人，de profundis，這就是礦工。另一類人，他們看著遠方的視線，幾乎像作白日夢，幾乎像夢遊，這就是織工。現在我在他們之間生活已經將近2年，對他們特殊的性格有了點了解，特別是礦工。我總是覺得這些貧窮的、鬼魅一樣的勞動者有種動人、幾乎是可悲的成份。」（157/136，1880年9月24日）後來在海牙的時候，梵谷有一度還考慮要回去波林納吉一陣子。[5]

前面梵谷提到的拉帕德指的是凡・拉帕德（Anthon Gerard Alexander Ridder van Rappard, 1858-1892），一個他在布魯塞爾認識的荷蘭藝術家。雖然剛開始有點不順利，但是友誼還是在梵谷以及年輕卻受過完整訓練的凡・拉帕德之間開始成長。這段友誼將會持續四年半的時間。[6]大規模的墨水筆勾勒幾乎讓整張畫紙有了雕版畫或蝕刻畫的效果，這或許有部分是受到凡・拉帕德的影響，因為他在這個領域經驗較為豐富。但是梵谷會採用這個方式或許有另一個理由。大約在1881年1月間，梵谷除了臨摹之外也開始創作更多獨立素描，希望能擔任插畫家的工作。同時，他開始（或者，依照一封他給父母的書信，又繼續）收集木版畫，而他在接下來幾年會對這發展出越來越大的熱情。[7]從前引梵谷給西奧的書信中，我們可以知道梵谷本人覺得這兩幅畫或許適合複製：「我必須設法找到適合的模特兒來完成它們，那麼我相信結果一定會不錯，也就是說我就有幾張構圖可以給Smeeton Tilly或者L'Illustration之類〔出版社〕的人看了。」（164/143）L'Illustration是聲望卓著的法國期刊，而巴黎的雕版師Burne Smeeton與Auguste Tilly在當時為許多流行的刊物提供插圖。

---

1. 這告訴我們，梵谷很早就發展出連作或系列作品的創作方式。在這之前，他已經畫過礦工早晨上工、傍晚回家的聯作。
2. 也有可能是棕色墨水褪色為黑色。無論如何，兩者在構圖上都不相同。由於畫紙上的黑色墨水的黑色仍然相當良好，所以可能是印度墨水（Indian ink）。棕色或褪色的黑色或許來自較便宜的沒食子墨水（Gallnut ink）。有關梵谷素描褪色的問題，請參見Van Heugten 2005。
3. 這樣的燈通常是礦場的財產，在礦工早晨上工進入礦坑之前會分發給他們。梵谷所描繪的燈具可以辨認出是Meuseler類型的燈具（請參見http://mineshainaut.ibelgique.com）。
4. 有著典型屋頂的礦場建築以及鄰近的煙囪相當接近《雪地裡的礦工》背景的建築。但是，前景裡的小型建築被安排到其他地方，指出梵谷在背景的元素安排上相當自由，或許是根據先前在現場所作的速寫。煤堆左方那座高聳的橋樑切過天空，讓構圖充滿力量，似乎也並非忠於實際情況。
5. 參見書信264/R42。在1882年11月，梵谷畫了另一張關於arracheuses的水彩畫。過去礦工幾乎從未成為藝術創作的主題，一直要到比利時畫家Constantin Meunier（1831-1905）在1880年代，也就是正當梵谷要離開波林納吉的時間，注意到他們為止。梵谷相當推崇Meunier的作品。
6. 後面有更多關於凡・拉帕德的討論。有關他的生平及作品，請參見Brouwer et al. 1974。
7. 書信162/141，1881年2月16日。有關梵谷的版畫收藏，請參見Luijten 2003。

背負重物的人們　The Bearers of the Burden
1881年4月　1881 Apr.
鉛筆、黑色與褐色墨水筆、白色與灰色　pencil, pen in brown and black ink, white and grey opaque watercolor,
不透明水彩、（原）藍色直紋紙　on (originally) blue laid paper
47.5×63公分　47.5 x 63 cm
Collection Kröller-Müller Museum, Otterlo, The Netherlands

我們不能確定梵谷在埃頓的哪個地方畫下這幅充滿田園風味的《庭園一隅》。他或許是在牧師公館裡的庭院繪製的，但是佐證資料並不多。牧師公館在1905年拆除，四周的環境也經過劇烈的改變，讓人很難看出過去的風貌。[1]

　　這幅素描梵谷是先用鉛筆進行速寫，整幅畫面都還清楚看得到鉛筆的筆跡。背景的樹木描繪得有點倉促，因此也做了所有必要的修正。典型的特徵包括用尖銳的點與短線條用來暗示天空所襯托出的樹葉。在鉛筆素描之上，尤其是畫面的下半部，梵谷又用墨水筆加以修飾。棚架下的家具他畫得相當精準，用細緻的陰影線與隨意畫的筆觸交錯，讓它在背景間更為凸顯。幾個地方稍微上了色，用的是稀釋得很淡的紅棕色及綠色不透明水彩。至於牆上及棚架裡的樹葉，梵谷用非常特殊的方式來畫：像是有角的心與圈圈以及幻想式的星星。這非常接近後來他在阿爾以及聖雷米用蘆葦桿筆所畫的樹葉。[2]

　　在這張畫紙上，梵谷專注於要相當精確地描繪一個簡單、浪漫的場景：庭院裡的棚架，背景是長滿植物的石牆，有幾件家具但沒有人物。但還是有人的跡象：柳條編的籃子、格子布、兩者間有一顆球和一縷纖維，或許是一顆毛線球。由於這點，這幅畫似乎並非只是某個任意主題的習作。或許梵谷心裡想到了他的妹妹Willemien的離去。她在6月離開父母居住的地方，讓梵谷相當難捨。[3]

　　這幅素描讓庫勒穆勒女士感覺到一種「心靈的」空虛與感傷的氛圍。在1912年3月28日寫給摯友Salomon ("Sam") van Deventer的一封信裡，她以慣有的說教口吻如此寫道：「Salomon，現在你可對梵谷的畫有更深的了解？就是那幅有凳子、茶几、還有非常靜謐的小庭院的畫。你難道不能想像兩個人坐在那裡，剛剛才起身離開，他們沒有經驗到什麼，卻又經驗了這麼多，也發覺了這個庭院簡單卻偉大的美？在他們身後，房子成了庭院顯現的背景。再看一次這幅畫，它對我如此珍貴，也和梵谷其他畫作裡雄厚的情感形成如此的對比。」[4] 她和往常一樣，依照人的情境來觀看構圖。更精確地說，她在這裡所指的是位於Scheveningen的Kröller別墅裡Huize ten Vijver的庭院，在這裡她會與Van Deventer交談，有時會讀他所寫的信。

---

1. 可參見Van Uitert et al. 1987，頁196-197；Heenk 1995，頁32。梵谷在1876年為牧師公館正面所畫，兩幅素描，其中背景的右邊可以看見一棟建築，有點接近《庭園一隅》牆後的建築（Ven Heugten 1996，頁57-59）。在Daniel Gevers於1831年位牧師公館所畫的更為精確的素描中，兩者的相似度更高，但是還是很難提供一個更確定的答案（Rozemeyer et al. 2003，頁87及頁8附圖）。在該幅素描中可以清楚看見建築增建的部份，在《庭園一隅》也應該要能看的到。

2. 例如，可比較梵谷在聖雷米的療養院花園裡用墨水筆為長滿常春藤的樹木所做的素描：作品編號F1522及F1532（兩幅皆為梵谷美術館所藏）。

3. 參見書信167/146，1881年6月。這會讓《庭園一隅》成為《埃頓花園回憶》（Memory of the garden at Etten，F496）很好的對照。在這幅畫中，梵谷加入了兩位女性並肩行走，暗示著他的母親與Willemien。（書信725/W9，約1888年11月16日）

4. 那時23歲的Van Deventer在Wm. H. Müller & Co位於Bremen的辦公室工作。自從2005年起，庫勒穆勒女士給Sam van Deventer的許多書信就被收藏在庫勒穆勒美術館的S. van Deventer Archive內。在這封信寄出時，這幅素描仍是Hidde Nijland的收藏，但是它的照片卻已經出現在庫勒穆勒女士及Van Deventer都很熟悉的出版品中，例如Nijland 1905，pl. 46，Bremmer 1907， pl. 3與Bremmer 1911，pl. 9等。她的心理投射也受到Bremmer的影響，因為後者稱這個花園為「沉默的見證者」，看著兩個人進行最後的交談，從此再也不會相見（Bremmer 1911，頁75）。

庭園一隅　Corner of a Garden

1881年6月　1881 Jun.
鉛筆、黑色粉筆、墨水筆、墨水、灰色與　pencil, black chalk, pen, ink, grey and brown wash, opaque
褐色暈染、不透明水彩、直紋紙　watercolor on laid paper
44.5×56.7公分　44.5 x 56.7 cm
Collection Kröller-Müller Museum, Otterlo, The Netherlands

1880年8月，梵谷待在Cuesmes，當時他寫了封信給Hermanus Gijsbertus Tersteeg，他是法國畫商古比海牙分公司的經理，也是梵谷之前的老闆。在信中，梵谷向他商借巴爾格（Charles Bargue, 1826/27-1883）所編著的素描課本《學院術科準備炭筆寫生練習》。（1871）Tersteeg不只寄給梵谷這本課本，還寄了巴爾格的另一本教科書《素描畫法》（1868-1870），此外還有幾本有關透視法與解剖學的教科書。[1]巴爾格的著作是由古比在巴黎出版的，因此梵谷或許還記得這幾套書，因為他曾在1869至1876年之間在該公司工作。

　　在梵谷臨摹米勒與其他藝術家的同時，他也根據巴爾格的範本進行素描。在兩個星期之內，梵谷已經將《炭筆練習》的所有60幅範本都畫了一次。這些練習為男性裸體的輪廓素描。在一年之內還會再重複這麼做至少三次，後來他曾說：「仔細的學習並持續反覆臨摹巴爾格的炭筆練習讓我對人物素描有更清楚的認識。我學會測量、觀看、尋找整體的輪廓，所以，感謝上帝，以前我覺得完全不可能的事現在逐漸變得有可能了。」[2]

　　在Cuesmes的時候梵谷也臨摹了《素描畫法》的第一部分，也就是70幅以畫石膏像為範例的石版畫（Modèles d'après la bosse）。10月初的時候他搬到布魯塞爾，並開始進行第二部分課程的67幅畫，標題為《歷代及各派大師範例》。其中超過三分之一都是仿自霍爾班（Hans Holbein the Younger, 1497/98-1543）作品的石版畫。這些範例梵谷也在一年內臨摹了至少兩次，但他臨摹的確切頻率目前仍不清楚。目前已知他有四幅根據《素描畫法》的素描傳世，其中兩幅是根據同一個範例，也就是《雅各‧梅爾之女》。[3]巴爾格的石版畫所根據的是霍爾班大約在1526年以Basel市長的女兒安娜‧梅爾（Anna Meyer）為對象所畫的細緻彩色素描。巴爾格的畫品質相當好，相當精確地呈現出原作。[4]在臨摹時，梵谷也體認出這一

點，並在信中告訴弟弟說：「《大師範例》裡頭霍爾班的作品真是太棒了。現在我正在畫它們，所以感覺比以前更為深刻。但是我得跟你說，它們可不容易。」（159/138，1880年11月1日）

　　第二幅《雅各‧梅爾之女》在運筆及性格上都相當不同。梵谷首先使用鉛筆勾勒底圖，接著再用墨水筆進行細部繪製。在背景及臉部他主要使用較細的筆，因此創造出接近雕版的十字線網絡。輪廓線、頭髮以及某些細部則用較粗的筆來繪製。這幅素描也相當忠實地呈現原來的範例，除了頭部之外。這個頭部的描繪完全是自己的性格，和安娜‧梅爾幾乎沒有相似之處。梵谷省略了在範例中頸部左側可見的頭髮，讓下巴更明顯地突出在衣領上。鼻子比較不圓，比較長，它的輪廓線讓整個臉看起來有點粗獷，給了這個女孩一種鄉村質樸的表情。梵谷似乎有意不依循範例。作為一種典型，這幅臨摹甚至有點暗示了梵谷後來在海牙及努南所繪製的典型頭像。和先前臨摹的版本不同的是，梵谷沒有在構圖四周繪製框架，因此在右下方角落的背景陰影線上就遭遇困難，而此處也沒有用鉛筆繪製底圖。在霍爾班讓安娜‧梅爾的頭髮碰觸到素描邊緣的地方，梵谷留下了一點空間。

　　由於細緻的墨水筆畫表現出更有經驗的手法，因此也指出此作完成的時間較晚。這幅畫大約可以確定是在1881年夏天完成的。畫紙也指向這樣的方向。在1881年7月的一封信裡，梵谷說因為氣候溫暖，所以他留在室內「根據巴爾格來臨摹霍爾班的素描。」（168-147）目前已知只有三幅作品也使用帶著這樣的浮水印（H v I和面對左方，帶著軍刀及箭袋，人立的獅子）的直紋紙，而這三幅素描都是庫勒穆勒美術館的館藏，分別是《森林一隅》（View of a wood）、《庭院一隅》（Corner of a garden）與《Willlemina的肖像》（Portrait of Willlemina Jacoba ('Wil') van Gogh），都屬於1881年6、7月間的作品。

1. 書信155/134，1880年8月20日；書信156/135，1880年9月7日。其他的書或許是John Marshall的 *Esquisses anatomiques à l'usage des artistes* 以及Cassagne的著作之一（Van Heugten 1996，頁16-17）。

2. 書信171/150，約為1881年9月。在1881年1月，梵谷臨摹了第三次（書信161/140）。這些作品都沒有留存下來，或許是因為它們都只是練習，沒有理由留下來。1890年在奧維的時候，梵谷最後一次臨摹了《炭筆練習》，有幾張作品留存了下來（F1508 recto；F1609 verso，沒有F編號，全都是梵谷美術館的館藏。參見Van de Wolk 1986，頁267-268）。

3. 巴爾格圖版26，〔Bourgeois lady from Basel (after Holbein)〕的臨摹作品（F848）目前為私人收藏，之前被誤以為是依據圖版27，*A lady of the court of Henry VIII* 所做的（De la Faille 1970，頁316；Chetham 1976，頁258；Heenk 1995，頁25）。第四個例子，F849a（目前所在地不明）不被De la Faille（1970，頁318）認為是臨摹巴爾格的作品（Chetham 1976則沒有提到這幅作品），但它是根據圖版18，*Roman woman (head study)*，仿自Paul Dubois的原作而來。有關所有巴爾格範例的複製，請參見De Roberros & Smolizza 2005，頁127-137。

4. 霍爾班的畫作目前在Basel Art Museum（Müller 1988，頁197-198）。

雅各·梅爾之女　The Daughter of Jacob Meyer

（仿自巴爾格素描本中霍爾班的畫作）　(after Barque after Holbein)

1881年7月　1881 Jul.

鉛筆、墨水筆、黑色墨水、直紋紙　pencil, pen and black ink on laid paper

42×30公分　42 x 30 cm

Collection Kröller-Müller Museum, Otterlo, The Netherlands

八月下旬梵谷在海牙待了幾天，拜訪了Tersteeg與莫弗等人，之後在回家的途中他在多德勒克做了短暫的停留，因為正如他向西奧解釋的：「從火車上我看到一個地方就是我想畫的，有一排風車磨坊。雖然在下雨，但是我還是設法完成了，因此這段旅程至少還有個小小的紀念品。」（170/149，1881年8月26至28日）他很熟悉這個區域。1877年的1月至5月他曾在多德勒克的一間書局工作，開暇時間喜歡散步，「沿著堤防，一路上沿著軌道走，遠方只見到風車磨坊。」（106/92，1877年3月7日）他指的是城市西南方，沿著Papengat分布的Weeskinderendijk。1881年的時候至少還有10座風車磨坊仍在運作，多半都是鋸木場。

　　就《多德勒克的風車磨坊》這幅素描而言，梵谷是由Papengat的東邊朝西北的方向來觀看整個窪地。前景主要是一座簡單的白色圍欄封閉著溝渠的匯流處。在圍欄後方，一個小小的人物沿著小路穿過原野。在畫紙中央略為上方，灰色的天空襯托出磨坊。左方兩座大型的磨坊，Het Anker（錨）與De (Jonge) Ruiter（「年輕的」騎士），位在堤防的東側。南方的磨坊在兩者間清楚可見。上方及圍欄右側三座大型的磨坊分別是Willen I、De Kleine Noordsche boer（北地小農夫）與De Zwaan（天鵝），皆位於北側。

　　最右邊在地平線上可以看到另外兩座磨坊。儘管前述的磨坊都安置在足堪辨認的位置，彼此間的關係也相當適中，但是這兩座磨坊卻以簡略的筆法描繪，並且有點太大。那個方位在實際上並沒有磨坊。梵谷加入它們或許是為了讓構圖更為平衡。[1] 有趣的另一點是，他將它們的扇葉畫得好像面對不同的方向。

　　這幅素描透過不同媒材的細緻筆觸加以完成，這指出梵谷或許當場在雨中只能用鉛筆完成簡單的草圖。[2] 在繪製草圖時，他對地平線上的細節相當注意。磨坊間可以看見較小的建築，另外同樣清楚的還有Oude Maas上航行船隻的桅杆與帆。另外可以辨認的還有幾座蒸汽動力工廠的煙囪，這些工廠很快就會取代風車磨坊的工作。[3] 天空、原野及前景大範圍的區域用刷子及高度稀釋的水彩塗上棕色。用白色不透明水彩繪製的精細色調加到了天空、磨坊、還有前景的圍欄的許多部分，這裡梵谷用墨水筆來畫出陰影。他用綠色的粉筆及紅棕色的水彩為原野及背景的建築增添一點色彩。梵谷透過這種方式來創造出相當有說服力、具有傳統風格的陰天荷蘭風景。

　　在前往Papengat附近窪地的路上，距離車站不遠處，梵谷經過了名為「橙樹」的麵粉磨坊。在素描中，磨坊及外圍建築都相當詳細地描繪。一張1860年的照片從另一個角度呈現了整個景象。[4] 左方樹木的後方就是鐵軌，並不容易辨認出來，在遠方可以看見Weeskinderendijk的風車磨坊。在素描中，大部分的前景都被在此轉彎的河道的水流佔滿。水面反映出左側的一排樹以及右側的磨坊，強而有力地切割出構圖。河道尖銳的對角線以之字形流向遠方也創造出動態的視角。空間的效果有點類似梵谷1882年在海牙所繪製的素描，其中對角線也扮演重要的角色。[5]

　　從畫紙上可以看出匆忙的痕跡，因此似乎是在現場所繪製。相關證據包括樹木粗野的刮痕以及大部分的炭筆都有沾抹的痕跡。有些地方梵谷下筆太過用力，讓鉛筆劃破了畫紙。另外畫紙某些地方似乎也在繪製時沾濕了，尤其是畫紙的下方，讓這些地方更容易受損。這或許指出梵谷在多德勒克工作時的天氣狀況。

---

1. 這些已經被辨認出是多德勒克Kalkhaven地區的De Eikenboom（橡樹）與De Treurwilg（哭泣的柳樹），但是Kalkhaven是在梵谷的視野之外（Bouman 1989）。梵谷並不是隨便去移動它們，因為De Eikenboom已經在1878年拆除。Bouman指出另外三座當時已經不存在的風車磨坊。目前所做的辨認是藉由http://www.molendatabase.nl的協助，根據1866年從Oude Maas的另一邊所拍攝的Papengat的照片所完成，該照片刊登於Bakker 1998，頁226。請參見Meedendorp 2005b。
2. De la Faille 1970的編者指出，梵谷是根據沒有留存下來的習作初稿來進行繪製，這個可能性當然不能排除。
3. 在梵谷所描繪的所有風車磨坊之中，只有De (Jonge) Ruiter留存到20世紀。
4. Bouman 1990根據這張照片來辨認出素描裡的磨坊。然而，這張照片的日期較晚，而且就像Molendijk 1990一樣，Bouman相信帶著高帽的男性人物就是梵谷本人，但這一點的可能性相當低（參見Meedendorp 2005b）。
5. 可參見（Ditch along Schenkweg）。也因此，Heenk 1995，頁58-59將《「橙樹」風車磨坊，多德勒克》定為1882年4月下旬。但是，在那個時候，梵谷這類的構圖都使用「透視框」（perspective frame），但是畫紙上並沒有這類的痕跡。梵谷當時也不再大量使用炭筆作畫了。

「橙樹」風車磨坊，多德勒克　Windmill 'De Oranjeboom', Dordrecht
1881年8至9月　1881 Aug.-Sep.
炭筆、鉛筆、織紋紙　charcoal and pencil on wove paper
34.9×60公分　34.9 x 60 cm
Collection Kröller-Müller Museum, Otterlo, The Netherlands

多德勒克的風車磨坊
1881年8至9月
鉛筆、黑色與綠色粉筆、墨水筆、水彩筆、
墨水、不透明水彩、直紋紙
25.7×59.8公分

Windmills at Dordrecht (Weeskinderendijk)
1881 Aug.-Sep.
pencil, black and green chalk, pen and brush in ink and
opaque watercolor on laid paper
25.7 x 59.8 cm
Collection Kröller-Müller Museum, Otterlo, The Netherlands

73

在準備進行神學的學習時，梵谷曾經寫信告訴自己的弟弟說他想成為「神的話語的播種者」（112/93，1877年4月22日），此處的典故來自基督在聖經裡「將祂的福音像種子一樣灑在人群之間。」（馬太福音13章2-9節及18-23節）儘管身為藝術家的梵谷並未遵循自己父執輩的信仰，但是在他對農民生活的再現中，還是常見到宗教性的情懷（或者說自然宗教的暗示）。[1] 在他眼中，播種者、收割者、掘地者、以及其他努力勞動的農場勞工都在永恆的生命循環中佔有一席之地。舉例來說，在寫給貝爾納（Emile Bernard）的一封信中，梵谷認為播種者與麥穗象徵著永恆。（630/B7，約1888年6月18日）在他眼中，最了解這一點，最能描寫這一點的藝術家就是米勒。他在1850年透過《播種者》（Le Semeur）這幅畫描繪了一個年輕的農民透過強而有力的動作揮灑手中的一把種子，讓這幅畫成為一個在19世紀經常被臨摹的原型，象徵著艱困的鄉間生活。[2]

梵谷從未看過原作，不過他知道它的構圖，特別是因為他曾在波林納吉將它的複製蝕刻畫相當密集地臨摹了5次。梵谷的解釋是「我完全沉浸在這個人物之中。」（156/135，1880年9月7日）這幅蝕刻畫唯一留下來的臨摹作品的日期為1881年4月。（F830，梵谷美術館）有關這裡所討論的播種者，三幅全部都是根據模特兒來繪製，其中只有一幅依照米勒的範例畫的是側身像。儘管兩幅作品的動態無法相提並論，但是播種的動作仍然清楚地描繪出來。畫家仔細觀察人物，正在播種的右手臂較為困難的前縮透視也處理的相當有說服力，而衣服上的陰影效果而是如此。頭部和腿部都有許多修改的痕跡。畫家專注在描繪人物典型的姿態。之後，他以黑色粉筆強調出輪廓線，下筆相當用力，從紙的背面也能清楚看出線條。另外兩幅播種者被描繪在他們自然所處的環境中，但是他們缺少了米勒的原型那樣充滿能量的前傾動作。梵谷替兩幅素描都做了速寫，附在1881年9月初寫給西奧的信裡（171/150），所以兩幅畫的時間都可相當明確的定於當時。速寫完成時或許素描並未完成，因為兩者間有相當重要的差異，特別是背景描繪的方式。

在另一幅素描則指出了季節，亦即背景右方可清楚地看出一隻飛翔的燕子，這是在南方過冬的鳥。這隻燕子並沒有出現在給西奧的速寫上。速寫中所描繪的是其他的鳥類：那是烏鴉或鴿子，不像燕子那樣是以昆蟲為食物，而常見在剛犁過的農田左右。在這張畫紙上，梵谷主要是以鉛筆繪圖，有時塗擦得太過用力還劃破紙張。[3] 播種者這個人物或許也是以Schuitemaker為模特兒，全身上了棕色的淡水彩，然後再用白色不透明水彩襯托。背景的天空也稍微強化。原來藍色的紙張褪色相當嚴重，因為年代久遠已經變黃了。

儘管梵谷或許想讓這些播種者超越單純的人物習作，但是它們也必須以習作來看待。畫家知道在他能夠創造強而有力的獨立作品之前，還有很多需要努力的地方。從梵谷和凡・拉帕德的書信往返中，我們可以看出這一點。凡・拉帕德常常指出梵谷作品中的技術缺陷，而梵谷當然也都謹記在心。舉例來說，梵谷一幅播種者不僅寄給了西奧，也寄給了凡・拉帕德，要讓後者知道他自己在人體素描上的進展。[4] 針對凡・拉帕德所做的批評（並未留存下來），梵谷如此回應：「你說的沒錯，那個播種者的人物並不是在播種，而是擺出播種的姿勢。」但是接下來，梵谷又說：「可是，我將這些習作純粹視為人物的習作，它們也不想假裝是其他什麼。得要在一年或幾年之後，我才有能力描繪正在播種的播種者。這一點我和你意見相同。」（175/R2，1881年10月15日）六個月之前，梵谷已經向西奧解釋過，他的習作該被視為「種子，未來將會成長為素描。」（165/144，1881年4月30日）但是，當然梵谷偶爾也會非常仔細地描繪某個主題，此外透過這種溫和的回應，梵谷也是在保護自己免於進一步的批評。

---

1. 在Kodera 1987、Sund 1988、Kodera 1990中對這一點有進一步的探討。
2. 有關梵谷作品中的播種者及米勒的範本，請參見Van Tilborgh et al. 1988，頁156-162。
3. 在紙張的這些地方的背後已經做了修復。
4. 有趣的是，在速寫的背景中，梵谷也畫了麥捆堆（但是沒有燕子）。這幅速寫可在Van Crimpen & Berends-Albert 1990，頁401中看到，原來出於1881年10月15日的書信（175/R2）。然而在這封信裡，梵谷也提到凡・拉帕德對他播種者素描的批評，因此可能他寄出速寫的時間還要更早一點。10月12日書信編號172/R1指出梵谷將速寫寄給凡・拉帕德的時間是在這個日期之前。

播種者 Sower
1881年9月　1881 Sep.
鉛筆、黑色粉筆與暈染、　pencil, black chalk and wash, opaque
不透明水彩、藍灰直紋紙　watercolor on grey-blue laid paper
60.2×44.2公分　60.2 x 44.2 cm
Collection Kröller-Müller Museum,
Otterlo, The Netherlands

播種者 Sower
1881年9至10月　1881 Sep.-Oct.
炭筆、黑色粉筆、直紋紙　charcoal and black chalk on laid paper
55.9×33.2公分　55.9 x 33.2 cm
Collection Kröller-Müller Museum,
Otterlo, The Netherlands

削馬鈴薯的婦人　Woman Peeling Potatoes
1881年9月　1881 Sep.
黑色粉筆、灰色暈染、不透明水彩、直紋紙　black chalk, grey wash and opaque watercolor on laid paper
30×22.6公分　30 x 22.6 cm
Collection Kröller-Müller Museum, Otterlo, The Netherlands

在埃頓的時候，有個年輕人偶爾會造訪梵谷。這個年輕人也會素描與油畫，但是在梵谷的書信中卻沒有提到他。他是Jan Benjamin Kam（1860-1932），是鄰近的Leur鎮的牧師Jan Gerrit Kam（1833-1917）的長子。在1912年，Jan Benjamin Kam在一封給藝評家Albert Plasschaert的信中寫下許多他與梵谷交遊的有趣觀察。舉例來說，在一封給凡·拉帕德的信中，梵谷只寫到他已經「找到一群相當樂於擔任模特兒的人。」（172/R2，1881年10月12日）然而根據Kam親眼所見，梵谷其實是這麼做的：「他那時正在畫播種者，會跑進小屋裡去畫正在從事居家雜務的婦女。他強迫這些人為他擺好姿勢。他們很怕他，所以我陪著他不是很愉快。」[1]所以婦女在室內工作的素描，例如這些削馬鈴薯的婦女，或許不是在多愉快的情況下所完成的。

這兩張有許多共同點。[2]所使用的大部分材料都相同，婦女們擺出相同的姿勢，兩者都戴著薄紗帽。但是，第一幅並沒有畫到邊緣，格式與細節也有差異，例如窗外的景色、有沒有桶子、婦女臉上的表情等。在第一幅構圖中，畫家用白色粉筆畫框，大致上與另一幅的格式相當，框內的區域和第二幅完全對應。[3]所以，畫家並沒有沿著框剪裁畫紙，而是再畫了第二幅更仔細從事的版本。奇怪的是，他只在第一幅簽名，第二幅卻沒有。[4]在9月所寫的一封書信（171/150）裡，梵谷用墨水筆為第一個版本畫了一幅小的速寫，忠實呈現了白色框裡的構圖。然而，在左方，他寫了幾行字，這幾行字在大的素描的框外的相應位置也可看見。從窗外可以看見幾棵細瘦的小樹，在第二個版本裡則換成了幾棵砍斷樹梢的柳樹。同樣一排柳樹也出現在時間約為10月12日給西奧的信（173/151）中所

削馬鈴薯的婦人　Woman Peeling Potatoes
1881年9月　1881 Sep.
黑色粉筆、灰色暈染、不透明水彩、　black chalk, grey wash, opaque watercolor,
彩色與白色粉筆和鉛筆、直紋紙　colored and white chalk and pencil on laid paper
40.3×32.9公分　40.3 x 32.9 cm
　Collection Kröller-Müller Museum, Otterlo, The Netherlands

附的一張速寫。

　　這幾個女性人物最值得注意的就是她們過長的大腿。梵谷常常不能夠描繪出讓人信服的人體比例，一直要到他開始使用繪圖網格（drawing grid）以及透視框才克服這個問題。 他給莫弗看了幾張他的人物素描，而莫弗立即看出梵谷坐得離模特兒太近，所以「很多時候幾乎沒有辦法達成適當的比例。」（191/164，約1881年12月21日）但是，在實際上一定也很難保持距離，因為在他「強迫」模特兒擺出姿勢的房子通常都相當小，而Kam也指出了這一點。

1. 這封1912年6月12日的書信現藏於阿姆斯特丹的梵谷美術館，典藏編號inv. No. FR b3025。感謝該館的Hans Luijten為編者指出這封信的意義。
2. 參見Heenk 1995，頁38，認為這幅素描畫的是削洋蔥，但這並不太可能。在梵谷附上此一構圖的速寫的書信（171/150）裡，他也寫到自己畫了「戴著白色帽子的婦女在削馬鈴薯。」
3. 框的範圍大約為32×24公分。
4. 這或許代表梵谷將這個版本贈送給人，因此簽上名字。這兩幅素描是庫勒穆勒分別購入的。
5. 儘管梵谷或許已經由Cassagne的教科書中得知這類的素描工具，但是他或許一直到1882年3月之後才開始使用這些工具。

在臨摹巴爾格的圖例時，梵谷發展出一種在大張畫紙上素描的偏好。他後來如此解釋：「一般來說，就我自己的練習而言，我確實需要人物的比例大一點，這樣頭部、雙手、雙腳才不會太小，可以盡情地畫。也是因為這樣，我才將巴爾格的《炭筆練習》當成自學的範本，因為那個大小可以輕易地一眼就看清，而細節部分又不會太小。」（292/250，1882年12月2或3日）那樣的大小符合前者「大偏中」的紙張大小（47×62公分），而《篩種》就是畫在這樣還保留原有邊緣的紙張上。[1]

這裡的畫面常被誤認為簸穀。[2]簸穀是要將穀物放進通常是蘆葦桿編成的大型籃子裡搖晃，好讓較輕的穀殼被風吹走。這裡所描繪的篩子是農民用來清潔種子的，通常是用兩個平的漏杓緊緊疊在一起，中間張著一張穿孔的豬膀胱皮。[3]畫家用黑色粉筆在篩子上下方畫出點及線條，代表抖動的種子渣滓。老農夫站在穀倉門口，背後隱約可見樑下堆著乾草。其實在這個地方篩種頗為奇怪，除非

剛好有風吹過門口，讓灰塵不會吹近穀倉裡。也或許梵谷主要是想表現農民篩種的典型姿態，就像他著力去表現掘地者與播種者典型的姿態一樣。

由於畫的是人物的側面，所以畫家有技巧地避開了「前縮透視法」（foreshortening）的問題。梵谷主要使用的是鉛筆與黑色粉筆，後者是用以強調輪廓線。他用高度稀釋的淺藍色不透明水彩來為襯衫的袖子著色，過程中潑灑出一道顏料，從畫面中間門柱的附近流向左邊到畫紙的下方角落。和梵谷先前所畫的木匠一樣，這個老農夫—模特兒是Cornelis Schuitemaker（1813-1884）—姿態有點僵硬。他甚至看起來好像有點倚靠在門柱上。[4]然而，他的比例畫得比較好，只是左手臂有點過長。梵谷或許從開放的門上交錯的木板條上建立相對比例的支撐。[5]往後我們將會深入討論一封梵谷給西奧的信，信中便附上以這幅素描為基礎所畫的一幅速寫。

1. 參見http://members.chello.nl/j.nikkels/gen/papier/terminologie.html。直紋紙（laid paper）邊緣較粗，因此紙張大小通常與標準大小不同。除此之外，這張畫紙的上方及右邊經過裁剪。

2. 請參見Hulsker's catalogue raisonne (JH24)的不同版本：Van Uitert et al. 1987，頁134。Van Tilborgh et al. 1988，頁28指出這幅素描與米勒的《簸穀的人》（The winnower）的相似處：梵谷知道這幅畫的石版畫。

3. 相關資訊由阿姆斯特丹的Meettens Institute的Gerard Rooijakkers提供。

4. Schuitemaker與妻子住在埃頓附近的Heike（De Bruyn-Heeren 1992，頁160-171）。

5. 但我們不能因此認為（如同M. Trappeniers在Van Uitert et al. 1984，頁134-135所指出）在這幅素描中，梵谷運用了Cassagne有關透視法較複雜的課程，將主角投射在籠形結構（cage construction）中來更清楚了解前縮透視。梵谷的確知道Cassagne的著作，但只是選擇性地使用這些方式（參見Van Heugten 1996，頁17-19）。

篩種　Sieving
1881年9月　1881 Sep.
鉛筆、黑色粉筆、不透明水彩、直紋紙　pencil, black chalk and opaque watercolor on laid paper
62.7×47.3公分　62.7 x 47.3 cm
Collection Kröller-Müller Museum, Otterlo, The Netherlands

在1881年9月初，梵谷在一封給西奧的信中寫道：「現在我一定要畫掘地者、播種者、耕地的男人與女人，絕不停止：我一定要仔細研究並描繪鄉間生活的每一部分，就像過去與現在許多人所做的。我不再像以前那樣無助地面對自然了。」（171/150）。在這封信裡，梵谷還附上許多他正在創作的素描的速寫。他提到他自己的素描正在改變。這或許有部分是因為莫弗對他的讚美，有部分則是因為不停地臨摹巴爾格的範本讓他「學會衡量、觀看並尋找整體的輪廓。」現在他還找到適合的模特兒，所以他能寫信告訴西奧說：「我畫了一個帶著鏟子的男人，也就是五個不同姿勢的『掘地者』。」這個人物的大小與《炭筆練習》上的差不多。梵谷附上了第一幅《掘地者》（Digger）與《休息中的掘地者》的速寫。[1]第二幅《掘地者》與第一幅非常接近，應該是同時完成的。這兩幅素描都是根據同一個模特兒，也就是17歲的Piet Kaufmann，他是一個勞工同時也兼任梵谷牧師的園丁。[2]

這三幅素描大部分都是用同樣的材料繪製而成。梵谷從海牙帶回了黑色粉筆（conte crayons）、鉛筆及一些畫紙。在前面所引述的給西奧的信中，梵谷表示他也「開始將畫筆與擦筆」帶入自己的素描之中，並且使用「烏賊墨與黑墨水，偶爾再加上一點顏色。」在這三幅素描中，黑色粉筆都是主要的媒材。另外可以看出畫家謹慎地使用顏色，而顏色主要在第一幅《掘地者》中以稀釋或較濃稠的不透明水彩的形式廣泛使用。淡水彩是以畫筆加水或稀釋的墨水來製作。只有在《休息中的掘地者》才使用到鉛筆，是用以強調頭部的細節。另外還能略微看到炭筆的痕跡，這些或許是這幅素描初期草圖的殘餘。後來梵谷在一封給西奧的信中也描述了這個方式，儘管其脈絡完全不同：梵谷這裡的描述是用來當做比喻，用來解釋一個先前只是隱約提到的一件事。「我試著用長而直的炭筆線條來指出比例與空間；當我描出必要的輔助線條之後，就會用手帕將炭筆擦掉，並且開始仔細描繪細節。同樣的，比起之前的

信，這封信也會以更親近、較不嚴苛或充滿稜角的語調來書寫。」（178/154，1881年11月7日）從這個時期的幾幅人物素描中可以看出，梵谷似乎是在迅速畫出的炭筆草圖上進一步用黑色粉筆來進行繪製。

梵谷隨信附上的《休息中的掘地者》的速寫顯示，這個人物站立的區域圍繞著樹木與樹叢。在素描中仍然可以看出這樣的周遭環境，但是梵谷修剪了畫紙，將所有的注意力放在人物身上，而素描裡的人物與速寫比起來身體的姿態較為緊繃。畫紙的邊緣顯示素描原有的線條一定繼續向外發展，因而有突然切斷的痕跡。在左上方仍殘留著小樹的枝幹，而這棵小樹的全貌出現在信中所附的速寫裡。然而，這幅素描的構圖一直都不是水平發展，即使速寫的版本會讓人有這樣的聯想：在進行素描時，梵谷是讓畫紙保持垂直。[3]梵谷一定是自己裁剪了畫紙，這點可以從畫家在左下方鏟子的附近簽名以及他在裁剪之後才在畫紙塗上了淡水彩而看出。有幾個地方淡水彩一直塗到畫紙邊緣。在畫紙下方，水彩還塗到簽名中的nt兩個字母。

運用真人模特兒來進行素描對梵谷而言是額外的支出，因為他得付錢請人為他擺姿勢。[4]這些帳單都是由西奧來支付，而西奧也在經濟上提供支持梵谷（梵谷的父親起初也是如此）。梵谷希望能很快賣出自己的作品好補償西奧，因為他相信人物素描非常符合市場需要，尤其是對於任何「學會處理人物，持續在上頭努力，直到能安全地將人物畫到紙上的人而言。」（171/150）梵谷覺得自己進步很多。樂觀的他之所以有這麼強的自信，毫無疑問是因為他在海牙所得到的鼓勵，但是還有另一個原因。那年夏天梵谷愛上了自己的表姊凱（Kee Vos），她帶著年幼的兒子來到埃頓與梵谷的家人同住。在一封信中，梵谷第一次向西奧透露自己的感覺：「自從遇見她，我的畫作就進行得越來越好。」（177/153，1881年11月3日）

---

1. 信中還附上另一幅《掘地者》的速寫（F860，P.和N. de Boer Foundation, Amsterdam）。
2. 梵谷寫的是Kaufman。Stokvis 1926，頁19-21強調Kauffmann是正確的拼法，但其實正確的拼法為Kaufmann，參見Kerstens 1990。當這個模特兒已經60歲時，Stokvis前來與他訪談，那時Kaufmann表示他為梵谷擺姿勢的次數大約30到50次。有時候梵谷會給他一幅素描當禮物，但是這些都在Kaufmann搬家時遺失了。他也是《持鐮割草的男孩》所根據的對象。《休息中的掘地者》裡人物較為年長，看起來有點像Schuitemaker（參見《爐邊閱讀的人》）。
3. Heenk 1995，頁37指出信中的速寫是根據一幅現在已經遺失的大幅素描，而且《休息中的掘地者》也是根據這件作品。通常呈現水平的浮水印在這裡是垂直的：ED & Cie的橢圓型標誌位在左邊木展繪製的位置，而PL BAS這個戳記就位在人物頭部的位置。這代表畫家在右邊作了較多裁剪，總共裁剪了24公分（大約畫紙的一半長度）。畫紙的上下共裁剪了約8公分。
4. 他每天大約得花20到30分荷蘭盾當做給模特兒的酬勞（186/160，1881年11月19日）。

休息中的掘地者　Digger Resting
1881年9月　1881 Sep.
鉛筆、黑色粉筆、墨水筆、墨水、　pencil, black chalk, pen and ink, wash and
暈染、不透明水彩、直紋紙　opaque watercolor on laid paper
53.8×23公分　53.8 x 23 cm
Collection Kröller-Müller Museum, Otterlo, The Netherlands

梵谷曾抱怨他的模特兒有時候根本不知道該怎麼擺姿勢。在1881年8月初，他寫信給西奧說：「農民與村民對這都固執的不得了，很難讓他們在這一點上讓步：他們只願意穿著爲上教堂準備的最好的衣服過來，而服裝上都是難以處理的花邊〔……〕。」（169/148）但是在埃頓時期的人物習作中，大部分的男性模特兒所穿的其實都是普通的工作服：一條常有補釘的長褲、藍色的罩衫、短外套或無袖背心、帽子和木屐。第一眼看到，可能會覺得這裡正在種植的人好像穿著最好的衣服：一條有點長的外套、及膝馬褲、綁腿、鞋子及頂部有點圓的帽子。然而，這是典型布拉邦地區農民的服裝，儘管這已經過時了快20年了。或許是這個人堅持要穿

這樣的衣服，或許追求眞實的梵谷有意地選擇了這種服裝，要求這個還年輕的模特兒穿上這種衣服。[1]

　　梵谷非常注意黑色服裝上的陰影與皺摺。在某些地方，他也修正了這個人的體態。在帽子、頭部後方、左邊在外套與腳附近還可以看到擦去的線條，只是畫家企圖用白色水彩將它蓋過。雖然做了這些修正，但是梵谷還是沒有辦法讓比例看起來有說服力，即使這第一眼不容易注意到。就如同姿勢相近的《持鐮除草的男孩》一樣，梵谷似乎太靠近模特兒。跪著的人物本身看起來還算成功，但是如果針對肩膀與手臂注視得久一點，它們開始看來越來越像移植在身上的怪異觸手。

---

1. 這種過時的帽子還可以在《播種者》（F866a）上看到，只是那個人物戴的帽型有點不同。Heenk 1995，頁87，認爲這兩幅畫都是在德倫特（Drenthe）所畫，因爲梵谷寫說那邊的人都穿著短馬褲（389/324，約1883年9月15日）。然而，這個論點似乎站不住腳，而且Heenk並沒有提到，梵谷從埃頓時期之後在人物習作的技巧上有很大的進步。

種植者　Man Planting
1881年秋　1881 Autumn
黑色粉筆、炭筆、棕色暈染、　black chalk, charcoal, brown wash and
不透明水彩、直紋紙　opaque watercolor on laid paper
38.5×41.5公分　38.5 x 41.5 cm
Collection Kröller-Müller Museum, Otterlo, The Netherlands

《室內速寫》這幅素描是畫在《織襪的婦女》（*Woman Knitting Stockings*, F888r）的背面。梵谷為了畫後者而將畫紙略作裁剪，因此《室內速寫》的年份一定比較久。[1] 這是一幅用黑色粉筆所做的潦草速寫，畫的是有壁爐的室內景象。很大的煙囪稍微遮蔽了左側的窗戶。在那黑色充滿煤灰的火爐上，有個鉤子吊著一個鐵製湯鍋，就在柴薪架的上方。它的旁邊是一個簡單的暖足器，但是考慮到它的形狀相當簡單，也有可能是個劈柴火時所墊的木樁。

最值得注意的是前景的鍋子，以及它側放在牆壁上的蓋子。這種陶器幾乎只有在Bergen op Zoom這個地方製造。[2] 最後，畫面中還有一張椅子。我們會在其他大型的爐邊人物素描中發現這些元素。在這類素描中，通常在煙囪的鉤子上都會掛著一個鍋子，而柴薪架內都會有木頭在燃燒。在《爐邊的老人》裡，我們可以在背景看到一個陶鍋。所以這裡我們所看到的或許是Cornelis Schuitemaker位於het Heike的家。

---

1. 正面的水彩溢了出來，流過左側、底部及右側的邊緣；因此可以推斷，淡水彩與水彩上色是在這幅素描被剪裁之後。
2. 感謝隸屬於Meertens Institute, Amsterdam的Gerard Rooijakkers。

室內速寫　Sketch of an Interior
1881年10月　1881 Oct.
黑色粉筆、直紋紙　black chalk on laid paper
52.5×32公分　52.5 x 32 cm
Collection Kröller-Müller Museum, Otterlo, The Netherlands

在1881年10月底，凡‧拉帕德再次短暫地前往埃頓。他的目的地是布魯塞爾，因此梵谷敦請他順道一訪，有部分是因為他很好奇凡‧拉帕德在水彩畫上的進展程度。（175/R2，1881年10月15日）由於莫弗的建議，梵谷自己也開始多花時間在水彩畫上。[1]他的Cent伯父—畫商Vincent van Gogh（1820-1888）—送給他一盒水彩用具。（173/151，約為1881年10月12日）到目前為止，梵谷在水彩上的運用僅限於素描中的「上色」。他仍未掌握真正的水彩畫，亦即要幾乎完全使用畫筆及顏料，所以他一定迫不及待想知道受過完整技巧訓練的凡‧拉帕德有什麼進展。[2]在11月2日他寫信給凡‧拉帕德說他很高興「能看到你的水彩作品，你真的進步很多」，還說「今天我又畫了一張掘地者，而因為你的來訪，我也畫了一張拿著鐮刀割草的男孩。」（176/R3）他提到的一定就是這張素描，因此這幅素描最晚可以定為10月最後一個星期到11月1日之間。

梵谷首先畫了人物，主要用的是黑色粉筆，接著再用炭筆與粉筆畫出人物周遭的風景，畫法與《帶著掃帚的男人》（Man with Broom）一樣。前景黃綠色色調的水彩也可出現在那幅素描中。畫家關注的重點在於男孩割草時的姿勢。[3]從他穿著的某種拖鞋以及畫中的季節來看，他或許是在室內擺出這個姿勢。[4]顏色上得相當簡略，主要使用相當稀釋的不透明水彩：臉上及雙手有肌肉的色彩，袖子及褲子的淺藍色以及頭髮的淺棕色。梵谷在人物周遭刷上淡水彩，而炭筆的顆粒有時會在淡水彩的邊緣堆積。在上淡水彩的時候，鐮刀的刀身留白，因而顯示出紙張原有的顏色。天空上了相當厚的白色不透明水彩，有部分原因是為了遮掩先前用炭筆在地平線上畫的一排樹。[5]

《種植者》（Man Planting）已經顯示出梵谷在描繪蹲姿的側身像上所遭遇的困難。在這幅習作上裡，肩膀上奇怪的附加物也顯示出畫家同樣的掙扎。彎著的左腳的位置安排並不成功。一開始腳也許畫的太瘦弱，所以梵谷為了修飾，在膝蓋以下畫得寬一點，但是扁平的腳踝還是透露出腿部過瘦。另外不清楚的地方，就是手肘後方位在陰影中的褲管到底是屬於左腳或是右腳。整體來說，人物相當不穩定，上身太寬，特別是手臂佔據相當寬的位置，而收攏在一起的雙腳卻幾乎沒有什麼深度。

像這樣不對稱的比例或許很大的原因在於梵谷距離模特兒太近，所以沒有辦法得到清楚的整體印象。他會用眼睛掃視人物的一部分，然後在大張畫紙上進行素描，然而卻無法同時留意整體的比例。所幸他對輪廓的注意讓整體的形態最後仍能有良好的突顯。[6]無論如何，梵谷本人對這幅素描應該相當滿意，所以會在畫紙上簽名。在簽名的左方可以看到畫家沾上藍色水彩厚重的大拇指指紋。

這幅習作的模特兒還是Piet Kaufmann。Kaufmann一生都在埃頓及Leur之間度過。他是在1864年在埃頓出生，於1940年在Leur過世。[7]在1881年的秋天，他數度擔任梵谷的模特兒。梵谷早在8月初就曾寫信給西奧說：「我也希望能成功地找到好的模特兒，也就是Kaufmann，他是個勞工。但是我認為讓他拿起鏟子或犁擺姿勢的最好地方不是在這裡的家，而是在工廠（yard）、在他家裡、或是在田裡。」（169/148）梵谷信中提到的yard，或許指的是Kaufmann那個農舍兼旅舍的家（人稱「鐵爐」，Den IJzeren Pot）後頭的木屐工廠，位於Leursestraatje，而Kaufmann也在這裡學做木屐。[8]他也曾在梵谷牧師家的花園打工，根據他自己的說法，他也常常在週六在牧師公寓為梵谷擔任模特兒。他記得梵谷是個「奇怪的傢伙。」[9]梵谷的畫室就在牧師公寓旁的庫房，或許Kaufmann就在這個不怎麼大的空間裡為梵谷擺出姿勢。

---

1. 梵谷8月底來到海牙，要將自己用墨水筆所畫的素描給莫弗看，當時莫弗告訴他：「你該試試用炭筆、粉筆、畫筆、擦筆。」（198/169，1882年1月7日），另外又補充說：「色彩也是素描。」（174/152，1881年10月12-15日）梵谷明顯地接受了這個建議。
2. 凡‧拉帕德在1880-1881年間的水彩畫沒有多少留存下來，但是僅有的樣本顯示在這個媒材上，他的技巧遠比梵谷更為高明（Brouwer et al. 1974，編號31-35、39-42）。
3. 這個姿勢常被與米勒《田間勞動》系列畫中彎著腰的割草者相提並論。梵谷早期曾經臨摹過米勒的這系列畫作（Van Uitert et al. 1987，頁137）。
4. 參見Heenk 1996，頁40。
5. 如果將這幅素描對著光源，便可看到這排樹。白色的顏料有部分與炭筆混和，因此有些地方呈現較明顯的灰色。
6. 梵谷用黑色粉筆強化了輪廓線。庫勒穆勒美術館資深修復員Hoefsloot曾說：「畫家自己常常因為情緒性的素描方式在畫紙上留下損傷。」（Hoefsloot 1987，頁5）除此之外，畫紙的邊緣經過多年也有大量的損傷。
7. Kerstens 1990，頁21。
8. 同前書。
9. Stokvis 1926，頁20。

持鐮除草的男孩　Boy with a Sickle

1881年10至11月　1881 Oct.-Nov.

黑色粉筆、炭筆、灰色暈染、不透明水彩、直紋紙　black chalk, charcoal, grey wash and opaque watercolor on laid paper

46.6×60.4公分　46.6 x 60.4 cm

Collection Kröller-Müller Museum, Otterlo, The Netherlands

1881年夏天，梵谷前去拜訪他的畫家親戚—安東・莫弗（Anthon Mauve, 1838-1888）。這個經驗對他的作品有長遠的影響。[1]這代表梵谷不再狂熱地臨摹巴爾格、米勒與其他畫家。除此之外，他開始用不同的媒材、強調要根據模特兒來素描、並且更頻繁地使用色彩。莫弗甚至想讓梵谷開始畫油畫，但是最後他們協議讓梵谷在畫了更多習作之後再來拜訪他。[2]接下來這個秋天，梵谷有更多靈感。他幾乎等不及想讓莫弗看看他最新的進展，而10月及11月之間幾乎每封信梵谷都提到莫弗，有時甚至對他讚不絕口。在給凡・拉帕德的信中，梵谷說：「最近，在我最需要的時候，莫弗給了我信心。他真是個天才。」（175/R2，1881年10月15日）莫弗本來應該在秋天來到埃頓，但是因為許多原因，包括生病，讓這次的拜訪並沒有實現。

梵谷最需要的建議或許是有關色彩。如果梵谷想要創作賣得出去的作品，那麼他就得成為技巧更高的水彩畫家，原因很簡單：有顏色的素描賣得比較好。除了莫弗之外，西奧也向他強調這一點（201/172，1882年1月22日）：此外住在埃頓附近的Prinsenhage的伯父Cent，也就是退休的畫商Vincent van Gogh（1820-1888）也是這麼告訴梵谷。這位伯父「也說，如果什麼時候我畫了比今年夏天這些小一點的素描，而且有更多水彩成分，那麼我可以把作品寄給他，他會接受。」（203/174，1882年2月13日）我們可以從這三幅縫衣婦女的素描中看出，梵谷對水彩的使用僅限於為已經以鉛筆、粉筆或炭筆完全畫好細部的素描作品上色。他並沒有學會「真正的」水彩畫，也就是純粹使用水彩進行繪畫。一直要到這次拜訪過後三個月，梵谷才在海牙接受莫弗這方面的指導。

由於是自學起家，所以梵谷對其他人創作的方式相當好奇。10月底凡・拉帕德在前往布魯塞爾的途中順道來訪，當時梵谷特別要他帶幾張水彩畫過來。（175/R2，1881年10月15日）在這次短暫的聚會過後，梵谷寫信給西奧說：「拉帕德剛剛過來，帶了看來不錯的水彩畫。莫弗也很快會過來，希望如此，不然我就得去找他了。我畫了很多素描，而且我相信自己進步很多。我比以前更常用畫筆。最近天氣很冷，所以我幾乎都是在室內做素描，畫些縫衣婦人、編籃子的工人等等。」（177/153，1881年11月3日）這幾幅大型的縫衣婦人素描似乎與這有關，所以應該是凡・拉帕德來訪前後所完成的。其中兩幅畫的是一個較為年長的婦女，戴著喇叭型棕色的帽子，穿著鞋尖相當彎曲的木屐，而這樣的木屐也出現在許多其他的素描裡。[3]兩幅素描分別描繪她在同一張桌子的左右兩邊。透過窗外可以看到遠處的樹木與樹叢，兩者都清楚地呈現秋天的顏色。第三幅《縫衣婦人與貓》是畫得最仔細的一幅。與這個時期其他的人物習作比較，這幅的年輕女性以更柔和的筆觸來畫。這件作品有種其他作品沒有的魅力。在比例掌握上常見的缺陷在此處比較不明顯，或許有部分是因為用單純的色彩所做的完美上色以及畫家對細節的注意。唯一奇怪的比例在於椅子，因為右邊的椅腳好像長了一點，但左邊卻看不到椅腳，這顯示出模特兒的小腿可能有點

短。這位女性坐在火爐前，火爐上還有一大盆水。後方的牆上可以看到烤箱的門。她的受光相當平均，上半身在身後的牆壁右側投下一個陰影，創造出她與背景的距離感。左下方是畫家的簽名，而梵谷事後似乎又用黑色粉筆再簽了一次，顯示他自己對成品也相當滿意。

婦女從事縫紉工作是海牙派藝術家相當喜愛的主題，而梵谷也仿效他們的作法。舉例來說，我們可以注意，也正是在這個時期他在一封給凡・拉帕德的信中（175/R2，1881年10月15日）引用了Thomas Hood所做的《襯衫之歌》（The Song of the Shirt）這首詩。這首詩揭露了（英國）從事家庭手工的縫衣婦人可憐的工作及生活處境；她們工時很長，收入卻少的可憐。[4]我們可以質疑梵谷是否真的想用這些縫衣婦女的素描來達到相同的社會寫實主義。他所描繪的活動似乎只是鄉間居民平常家居的瑣事。無論如何，他並沒有試著在《縫衣婦人與貓》這幅作品裡避免某種居家的閑適感，特別是在作品中我們可以看到一隻（明顯地）相當心滿意足的貓窩在年輕女性的腳邊。這隻動物的前縮透視處理得相當不錯，是以正面略微俯視的角度來描繪。畫家在上淡水彩時刻意避開這隻貓，後來並且使用白色不透明水彩來加以強調。

儘管貓常常與從事縫衣工作的女性放在一起，但是在全部梵谷的作品中，這是唯一的例子，儘管梵谷畫了許多縫衣、編織的女性，但幾乎沒有畫任何寵物。[5]這隻貓運用了相當高超的寫實技法來描繪，讓人不禁懷疑梵谷是否有人幫忙，或是根據範本來描繪。在這裡，凡・拉帕德很有可能扮演了某種角色。在他所留下來的速寫本裡，發現了各種貓的鋼筆速寫，姿態與手法都相當接近梵谷的貓。事實上，速寫本該頁的左邊那隻較大的貓和梵谷素描裡的貓大小差不多（兩者都是大約17公分高）。梵谷的貓頭部轉向左邊，這更像凡・拉帕德速寫本裡面右上角那隻貓。所以，很有可能是凡・拉帕德在他於10月底拜訪梵谷時幫助他完成這幅素描，或許是為他在畫紙上畫那隻貓的速寫，也或許是將一份和自己速寫本裡類似的範例留給梵谷。但是速寫本確切的年份卻無法確定。大部分的速寫一定是在1880年代後期所完成的，但是也有許多張速寫是來自其他的時期，有些是來自1879年凡・拉帕德還在布魯塞爾的時候。其他幅有貓的速寫或許可定於1880年代早期。[6]

《縫衣婦人與貓》這幅素描作品之所以大致上是如此成功，或許也是因為技巧更為高明的凡・拉帕德，他無疑給了梵谷這位年齡較大的同行許多建議甚至直接的協助。無論如何，他這次的拜訪啟發梵谷繼續使用畫筆創作。稍後，當梵谷終於與莫弗開始學習繪畫，他告訴弟弟「示範教學」對他有多重要。充滿熱情的梵谷要西奧去跟隨身邊的藝術家：「如果你有機會看人畫畫或素描，你要注意，因為我相信，假如畫商真的知道畫是如何完成的，那麼他們將會對很多繪畫產生不同的看法。確實人可以靠直覺知道某些部分，但是我很確定的是，透過看人創作並且親自嘗試，我對許多事物有了更清楚的了解。」（204/175，1882年2月13日）

1. 1874年莫弗娶了梵谷的大表姊Arletta Sophia Jeanette ('Jet') Carbentus (1856-1894)，她是梵谷媽媽的弟弟Arie Carbentus的女兒。
2. 在10月中，莫弗寄給梵谷一盒繪畫工具，裡面有油彩、畫筆、調色刀等，但是我們不清楚梵谷有沒有立刻就試著使用（192/165，之前定為1881年12月22-24日）。
3. 感謝阿姆斯特丹Meertens Institute的Gerard Rooijmakers提供資訊。這種樣式的木屐通常都不是女性穿著的類型。女性的木屐通常較低，沒有上半部，通常會有綁帶。
4. Thomas Hood（1799-1845）的《襯衫之歌》於1843年首次出版，很快就透過不同的譯本而享譽國際。這首詩的前七行就足以顯示整首詩的調性：疲倦破皮的手指／沈重紅的眼睛／那女人坐著，裹著毫無女人味的破衣／針線來回穿梭／織呀織呀織／在貧困、飢餓、骯髒之中／仍用她那悲傷的音調／唱出「襯衫之歌」。
5. 在1881年夏天，梵谷參觀了在海牙由Hollandsche Teekenmaatschappij所舉辦的展覽，在裡面他欣賞了Jozef Israël著名的水彩畫Sewing School at Katwijk。（170/149，1881年8月27日）在那幅畫的前景清楚描繪了一隻貓。這幅水彩畫在1989年由阿姆斯特丹的梵谷美術館購入。
6. 這幾張畫紙或許是由之前的所有人，畫家及插畫家L.W.R. Wenckebach（1860-1937）所添入。他是凡・拉帕德的好友。畫紙編號11到17不屬於原來這本速寫本，而畫著貓的畫紙位在編號17的畫紙上（Brouwer et al. 1974，頁140-141）。

縫衣婦人　Woman Sewing
1881年10至11月　1881 Oct.-Nov.
黑色粉筆、灰色暈染、不透明水彩、直紋紙　black chalk, grey wash and opaque watercolor on laid paper
59.7×44.7公分　59.7 x 44.7 cm
Collection Kröller-Müller Museum, Otterlo, The Netherlands

縫衣婦人　Woman Sewing
1881年10至11月　1881 Oct.-Nov.
黑色粉筆、暈染、不透明水彩、直紋紙　black chalk, wash and opaque watercolor on laid paper
61.9×47.1公分　61.9 x 47.1 cm
Collection Kröller-Müller Museum, Otterlo, The Netherlands

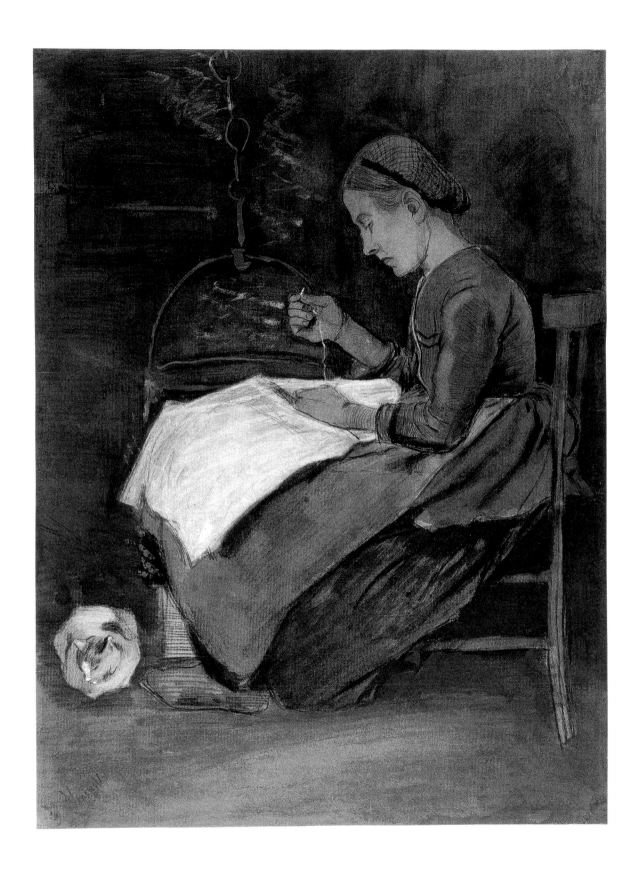

縫衣婦人與貓　Woman Sewing and Cat
1881年10至11月　1881 Oct.-Nov.
黑色粉筆、暈染、不透明水彩、白色粉筆、直紋紙　black chalk, wash, opaque watercolor and white chalk on laid paper
59.3×45.2公分　59.3 x 45.2 cm
Collection Kröller-Müller Museum, Otterlo, The Netherlands

梵谷在埃頓的農民住家裡所完成的素描有一部分是以火爐為背景。在16及17世紀，坐在火爐邊的年長男女通常是代表冬天的意象。到了19世紀，以Josef Israëls（1824-1911）為代表的藝術家也會描繪類似的景象，但是他們更著力去寫實地描繪一般人貧困的生活處境。[1] 梵谷也深受這一點吸引，而他也是Israëls忠實的愛好者之一。這一點的佐證，就在於梵谷第一幅描繪火爐邊的老人的素描。在埃頓時期的作品中，這一幅是少數梵谷下了（英文）標題的作品；其標題為Worn out，意為「筋疲力竭。」[2] 在1881年9月，梵谷寫信給西奧說他終於畫了「一個年老、患病的農人坐在火爐邊椅子上：他雙手抱頭，手肘抵在膝蓋上。」（171/150）他的標題是借用自Thomas Faed（1826-1900）一幅描繪疲倦工作者的油畫，這幅畫的複製版本梵谷曾經看過。

如同梵谷後來曾指出的，這個「年老、患病的農人」是根據Cornelis Schuitemaker（1813-1884）所畫的，而他或許也出現在《爐邊閱讀的人》及《爐邊的老人》內。[3] 火爐的細節也有很多相符之

處，不僅在這些素描中，在《火爐邊的女人》也是如此。很有可能，梵谷創作─或者開始創作─這些素描的地方就在Schuitemaker與他的妻子Johanna van Peer位於St. Willebrord的家中，那是埃頓西邊的一個小農舍，當時的人暱稱為het Heike，亦即「荒地」。從另一個資料，我們知道梵谷在那裡完成很多作品。在1930年，有封信寫給庫勒穆勒基金會的董事長，信件的作者是某位A. Mijs，他指出1929年7月20日的Wereldkroniek雜誌登出一幅《爐邊閱讀的人》的複製畫引起了他的注意，「因為我相信那個人物是我認得的一位Schuitemaker，他是het Heike唯一的一位新教徒，他當兵的時候曾經在1830到1839年之間住在那裏，娶了一位名為R. C.的女性。我的父親是埃頓的牧師，是梵谷牧師的繼任者，而後者是畫家梵谷的父親。所以Schuitemaker偶爾會來見我的父親，我曾聽他說過梵谷常常來畫他和他的妻子。我仍然可以認出他耳朵上灰色堅韌的頭髮，以及那大而偏圓的臉。」[4] 除了老人獨特的頭部之外，梵谷之所以常常用他當模特兒或許還有人道的考量，因為擺姿勢所換得的微薄

爐邊閱讀的人　Man Reading at the Fireside
1881年10至11月　1881 Oct.-Nov.
黑色粉筆、炭筆、灰色暈染、不透明水彩、直紋紙　black chalk, charcoal, grey wash and opaque watercolor on laid paper
45.7×56.1公分　45.7 x 56.1 cm
Collection Kröller-Müller Museum, Otterlo, The Netherlands

報酬對Schuitemaker相當有用：從1881年9月開始，這對夫妻就只靠埃頓、Hoeven與Oudenbosch教區所提供的貧民財務補助來生活。[5]

從《爐邊閱讀的人》我們可以相當清楚看到人物堅韌的灰色頭髮以及偏圓的臉。這幅素描或許是《火爐邊的女人》的姊妹作，而後者的女主角或許是Johanna van Peer。[6] 在一封凡・拉帕德於10月底來訪不久後所寫的信裡（176/R3，1881年11月2日），梵谷寫到自己畫了「一個男孩拿鐮刀割草」以及「一對男女坐在火爐邊」，或許指的就是這兩幅素描。然而，後者的描述或許也可能指的是一幅畫著一男一女的素描。

這兩幅素描一個重要的差異處在於完成的程度。比起《爐邊閱讀的人》，《火爐邊的女人》較沒有那樣完全上了水彩。只有女性人物的襪子以及圍裙下露出的裙子看得見上了色彩，分別是藍色及綠色（以及一點點紫色）。除此之外，鋪著淡淡的橘棕色地磚的地板在灰的背景下也相當突出。最讓人驚訝的是畫家用白色不透明水彩來暗示煙霧。壁爐與牆壁的交界是由背景那看來有點奇怪、

寬寬的一道白色顏料來指出的。相形之下，《爐邊閱讀的人》有較強的明暗對比，比起來完成的程度也較高。事實上，《火爐邊的女人》右下角的簽名很可能不是真的。[7]

在11月18日寫的一封信裡，梵谷提到了《爐邊的老人》：「我的素描寄到了嗎？我昨天又畫了一幅，一個農村男孩早晨在壁爐裡點火，上面還掛著一個水壺；我畫的另一幅是一個老人朝火中放著枯樹枝。」（183/158）這清楚地描繪出Schuitemaker在素描裡所做的動作，因此這幅素描可定於11月17日。就這幅素描而言，梵谷為自己找了一點麻煩，因為他選擇了一個在模特兒正前方的位置，因此得處理較困難的前縮透視。在這之前，他都選擇「簡單一點」的側面來觀看他的對象。想像的地平線放在畫紙中央，讓視線更容易朝向下方。拿著枯枝的那隻伸展的手臂以流暢的動作朝向下方的火焰前進。在左方邊緣的水壺則是有效的視覺引導（repoussoir）。在右側的地板上躺著一支掃帚以及用來將水壺掛在火上的三腳鐵架，兩者也強化了透視感。值得注意的是，梵谷在素描的大部分區域上

哺乳中的母與子　Nursing Mother with Child
1881年10至11月　1881 Oct.-Nov.
黑色粉筆、炭筆、暈染、不透明水彩、直紋紙　black chalk, charcoal, wash and opaque watercolor on laid paper
45.2×59.2公分　45.2 x 59.2 cm
Collection Kröller-Müller Museum, Otterlo, The Netherlands

了紅棕色的淡水彩，強化了從開放式火爐所透出的火光。[8]另外，他用橘紅色的粉筆強調了火焰。Schuitemaker的身上大部分都上了灰色的淡水彩。在不同顏色的淡水彩間，幾個沒有上到色的小區域一例如在木屐上一都透出紙張原有的色澤。

在梵谷埃頓時期所有的人物素描中，這一幅最具有動態感，因此畫家或許很快就將它寄給弟弟。事實上，他在11月18日寫了第二封信給西奧，信中他說：「現在，弟弟，如果你將『旅費』寄給我，那麼你就會立刻得到三張素描：《午餐休息》、《點火者》、《教區的男人》。」（184/159）《點火者》毫無疑問指的是現在已經遺失的那幅農村男孩早晨點火的素描。《教區的男人》很有可能就是《爐邊的老人》，因為Schuitemaker從教區領取貧困補助。[9]

這封信所提到的「旅費」指的是梵谷需要額外的錢才能前往阿姆斯特丹，這裡住著大他七歲的表姊一「凱」（Cornelia Adriana（"Kee"）Vos-Stricker）。在她當年夏天住在埃頓一陣子時，梵谷就深深地愛上了她。凱是梵谷母親的姊姊的女兒，寡居並有個兒子。[10]但是梵谷的愛並未得到回應。11月間兩兄弟的書信往返盡是有關梵谷迫切地想贏得凱的愛，然而這卻遭遇了包括梵谷及Stricker兩個家族強烈的反對，其中最反對的就是凱她自己。她毫不掩飾地說：「不，絕對不要」，清楚地讓表弟知道自己不想要這段關係。

在此之前，梵谷在埃頓的創作從未明確連結到自己對表姊的愛，唯一的例外是他妹妹Willemina的肖像畫，因為這幅畫偶爾被認為是凱的畫像。[11]然而在《哺乳中的母與子》中，或許真的有這樣的關聯。首先，就梵谷在埃頓的畫作而言，這幅畫的構圖相當不尋常。梵谷的人物習作通常畫的都是一個人（男人、女人或小孩），或許正在做某種手工藝或勞動。這裡描寫的卻是一個女人正在哺育母乳。在她的腳邊，一個年齡較大的孩子坐著，身前放著像是滿滿的一籃水果。這幅素描的主要關懷是母性或家庭生活，儘管

稜角分明，有點笨拙，但還是一幅感人的作品。[12]仔細檢視會發現女主角的眼睛有點心不在焉盯著前方的空間，似乎沒注意到自己在哺乳。她的五官有點嚴厲，嘴邊的表情相當嚴肅。除此之外，她的頭部大的不合比例。很有可能梵谷想強調貧困的年輕家庭所遭受的無助困境，但是他或許心中也想到自己和凱的關係。一幅凱的肖像照片顯示出她和這幅素描的女主角非常相似，都有強而有力的下巴、高聳而稜角分明的前額、髮線、以及鼻子與嘴唇間隱約可見的右臉頰。凱不可能也沒有道理當梵谷的模特兒，但是畫家或許是根據這張照片來畫。哺乳的母親毫無疑問是一位布拉邦的模特兒，地點就在一個年輕女性的簡樸小屋裡，但是梵谷將她的五官換成自己所愛的人。他或許想要用這幅畫面展現出自己所渴望的生活處境。

在11月9日或10日間，梵谷寫信給西奧說：「自從我真的戀愛以來，我的素描也有更多的真實，現在我在這間小屋裡寫信給你，屋裡滿滿都是het Heike的男人、女人、小孩的素描在我身邊。」（179/155）我們幾乎可以想像這幅素描也掛在牆上，或許《火爐邊的女孩》（Girl at the Fireside）也是。兩幅素描間都運用相似的技巧，也帶著類似的笨拙。[13]從梵谷的許多信件中，我們可以看出他需要女人的愛來讓他的創作更好。他寫給西奧說：「因為要繼續素描下去的最好方式就是繼續去愛人。」（181/157，1881年11月12日）除此之外，如果身邊有個女人，就可以讓他修正創作中可能的錯誤。因此有關《爐邊的老人》梵谷曾說：「讓我遺憾的是，我的素描還是有種堅硬而嚴厲，因此我覺得自己需要她，特別是她的影響，來變得柔軟。」（183/158，1881年11月18日）西奧終於還是將旅費寄給他，而梵谷也在11月24日左右啟程前往阿姆斯特丹。三天之後，由於任務失敗，梵谷繼續旅行，前往海牙。

---

1. 參見De Leeuw et al. 1983，頁193。

2. 這裡這幅素描曾經為凡‧拉帕德所擁有，另有一幅較大且同標題的素描並未留存下來。梵谷另外寄給凡‧拉帕德這幅素描較小的速寫（F864），也隨信（171/150）寄了一幅速寫給西奧。這些速寫與這裡這幅素描稍有差異：背景的右方是一把鏟子靠在牆上，水壺也不是掛在鍊子上，而是騎在火焰的灰爐上。

3. 當梵谷在1882年11月重新回到悲傷男人的主題時，他寫信給西奧說前一年他是以Schuitemaker為模特兒（288/247，1882年11月24日）。Schuitemaker另外還出現在F860、F860a、以及《帶著掃帚的男人》（Man with Broom）。

4. 這封來自Oostburg地區公證人A. Mijs的信，其時間為1930年1月6日，庫勒穆勒美術館檔案編號HA376740。Arend Mijs（1866-1934）的父親是Jacob Mijs，他在1883年5月接替T. van Gogh擔任埃頓地區的牧師，並且與家人搬到牧師公寓裡（Van Geertruy 2003，頁34）；6個月之前梵谷才被叫到努南。Schuitemaker在1884年10月過世，因此Arend認識他並沒有多久。

5. 參見De Bruyn-Heeren 1992，頁169-170。St. Willebrord隸屬於Oudenbosch的新教教會，但是Schuitemaker只在埃頓參與教會活動，因此也在當地受堅信禮。Schuitemaker每週分別由三個教會領取75分錢，直到他過世。之後他的（信奉天主教）妻子領取了一筆總數為5荷蘭盾的金錢，而協助便此為止。根據梵谷在1881年11月18日寫給西奧的信（185/160），他每天給模特兒的酬勞大約在20到30分荷蘭盾之間。

6. F883以及Woman Churning似乎是根據Johanna van Peer（1812-1887）所畫。

7. 可比較《爐邊閱讀的人》裡面真的簽名。姑且不論梵谷的偏好是在左下方簽名一除非它會造成構圖或美學的問題，否則梵谷不會不循這個慣例一可參見《坐在織布機前的織工》（Weaver in front of his loom）一這個簽名與梵谷在布魯塞爾、埃頓、以及海牙早期作品的簽名有許多相似之處。這些簽名全都是以鉛筆寫成（即使在該素描作品中沒有或僅有少數地方使用鉛筆，例如此幅作品）；V相當寬大，t則有交錯的一筆明確地轉了一圈並繞全名加上底線。這個簽名沒有出現在Nijland所收藏的許多埃頓時期的素描中，但是在Enthoven的收藏中（除了本幅素描之外還包括《多德勒克的風車磨坊》以及《縫衣婦人》）以及其他早期收藏者不明的作品（F860a、F930a、F1235、F1246、F1680）中卻可看到。

8. 這種淡水彩已經不再那麼顯著，因為時間久遠，紙張受損嚴重而且已經變黃（可參考紙面上產生的許多褐斑，尤其是在背景的左方）。這幅素描已經用日本紙加上襯裡（Hoefsloot 1987，頁9）。

9. 過去《爐邊的老人》並未與「教區的男人」聯想在一起。在第一封信裡，梵谷清楚指出在一幅素描正在點燃火焰，而在另一幅裡有個人「將乾的樹枝放進火裡」，所以不太可能說第二封信裡「點火的人」指的是《爐邊的老人》。在早先一封11月12日的信裡，梵谷將《午餐休息》這幅素描敘述給凡‧拉帕德知道：「一個勞工喝著咖啡、切著麵包。地上放著一支他從田裡帶回來的鏟子。」（182/R4）沒有一幅埃頓時期的素描符合這樣的描述，所以一定向《點火的人》一樣遺失了。

10. 有關這段關係詳盡的描述，請參見Hulsker 1986，頁168-180。

11. Soth 1994，頁106的確在廣義上將《縫衣婦人》居家的氛圍連結到梵谷對凱的愛。

12. 舉例來說，梵谷在處理搖籃背後那個角落的透視上遇到困難：這裡兩道牆應該要垂直，但是看起來卻好像連在一起。

13. 《火爐邊的女孩》所根據的對象也出現在《耙草的女孩》（Girl Raking, F884, Centraal Museum, Utrecht）。

爐邊的老人　Old Man at the Fireside
1881年11月　1881 Nov.
黑色粉筆、紅棕色與灰色暈染、橘紅色粉筆、　black chalk, reddish brown and grey wash, orange-red chalk and
不透明水彩、直紋紙　opaque watercolor on laid paper
55.8×44.5公分　55.8 x 44.5 cm
Collection Kröller-Müller Museum, Otterlo, The Netherlands

向阿姆斯特丹的表姊凱‧沃斯（Kee Vos）求婚被拒絕之後，梵谷以辛勤的工作來排遣心情。1881年11月底，他前往海牙向表姐夫安東‧莫弗（Anton Mauve）學習繪畫。梵谷的創作到當時為止都限於素描作品。莫弗是一位知名的風景畫家，也是農民畫的提倡者，梵谷深受這個主題吸引。莫弗教導梵谷油畫的技巧與用色的方法，也啟蒙梵谷的水彩畫創作。12月初時梵谷向西奧描述他最初的一些嘗試：「嗯，莫弗馬上讓我坐在有一對木屐與其他物品的靜物前，好讓我可以開始畫。」（189/162，1881年12月1、2或3日）

在海牙的數星期當中，梵谷創作了若干數量不明的畫作。大約在12月18日左右他告知西奧他已經畫了5幅習作：2件水彩畫與「一些塗鴉(scribbles)。」（190/163）這些習作為靜物，他在該封信中進一步說明並畫出了其中兩件，一件為《有包心菜與木屐的靜物》（F1），另外還有一尊戴著毛皮帽的孩童陶土頭像迄今仍下落不明。[1]《有木屐的靜物》與《有草帽的靜物》則為上述5幅習作中的兩幅。

在1946年之前，當Carlo Derkert認定這兩幅作品與梵谷向莫弗習畫有關係時，他推測它們是梵谷在努南時畫的。[2] 但是若與梵谷努南時期的靜物畫簡略的設計與厚塗的技法相較，《有木屐的靜物》與《有草帽的靜物》卻是相當注意細部，以少量的油彩平塗（除了《有木屐的靜物》中部份以厚塗增強亮度之處與畫布左方較粗略的前景）。這使得它們在風格上與《有包心菜與木屐的靜物》相近，該畫作據De le Faille在1928年認定，是梵谷在海牙向莫弗習畫時的作品。[3]

雖然《有包心菜與木屐的靜物》被認為是梵谷最早的油畫，其實《有木屐的靜物》是更明顯的選擇。在前者，包心菜是注意的焦點。那雙梵谷在給西奧的信中提到的，是他最初的繪畫母題的舊木屐，在構圖中的重要性不如庫勒穆勒美術館藏的靜物畫中的木屐。此外，《有木屐的靜物》畫在帆布上，《有包心菜與木屐的靜物》卻像《有草帽的靜物》一樣是畫在紙上。也許莫弗在梵谷初抵達時『款待』他一幅畫布，以便他有個好的開始，之後就讓他在較便宜的材料上練習。[4]

莫弗對梵谷的《有木屐的靜物》與《有草帽的靜物》的指導在於用色與質地的變化：帽子粗糙的磨舊的草質、瓶子透明發亮的玻璃、陶質的煙斗與白色的布料。其中的一個陶製的罐子—附有一個刷子與湯匙的，重覆出現在這二幅靜物畫之中。它們的構圖很簡單：一些在寬木板拼成的木桌子上的物品，放置成與畫面正好一致的角度。在第一幅靜物畫中有一雙木屐，半邊被陶罐遮蔽。左側有一個裝著些許液體的綠瓶子。梵谷用某種鈍物在桌面顏料上刮線條—可能是用畫筆的筆桿，來表示木板的邊緣。

在《有草帽的靜物》中，一些物品在粗糙的木桌上依著綁黑緞帶的草帽為中心排列，草帽前是一個陶質煙斗，後方是陶瓶，紅棕色的陶罐與一個栓著草提把的綠色薑罐。桌子邊緣有一盒火柴，後面有塊看似泥炭塊的東西，[5] 該處的色調很暗，所以幾乎很難從背景分辨出那件物品。梵谷以少量的顏料在淺色底的畫家用紙上畫這幅靜物，紙張的粒狀結構至今依然清晰可辨。只有增強亮度之處與淺色處稍微多用了一點顏料。這兩幅靜物畫在好幾個地方都可以看出底稿的痕跡，讓人得以窺見梵谷在上色前是怎樣用炭筆的粗寬線條打好物品的輪廓線。[6]

莫弗對梵谷最初的成果很驚喜：「我一直以為你是個非常令人生厭的人，現在我發現其實不是這樣。」梵谷在一封12月初的信中告訴西奧莫弗的反應，並寫著：「我可以向你擔保，莫弗這句簡單的話比大量的虛偽讚美還令我高興。」（189/162）他自己也對最初的油畫習作很滿意。雖然它們毋庸置疑的不會是甚麼「傑作」，「但我真的相信，無論如何，它們比迄今我做過的任何作品，自有其穩健與真實之處。因此我認為我現在正開始從事一件嚴肅的事情。因為我現在可以使用更多的技法，也就是說，顏料與畫筆，每件事看起來好像又是新鮮的了。」（191/164，c. 21，1881年12月21日）他將他的繪畫視為他藝術家生涯的起點：「因為，西奧，我真正的藝術家生涯隨著繪畫展開了。你不覺得我這麼想很對嗎？」(192/165，1881年12月22-24日)

梵谷可能將《有木屐的靜物》與《有草帽的靜物》留在自己身邊很長的一段時間：前者到1912年，後者到1920年為止，都下落不明。莫弗曾教他要將習作保存起來：「莫弗說我必須保存所有的習作」（189/162）；它們可供比較之用。依他在1881年大約12月21日寫給弟弟的信來看，可以合理的推論他將這兩幅畫帶到埃頓的父母家：「無論如何，我離開莫弗時帶了一些油畫習作和水彩畫。」（191/164）他在12月底回到海牙，打算停留久一點，他帶去了他(所有或部份的)習作。當他後來在1883年9月搬到德倫特省的Hoogeveen時，他的畫作起先被留在海牙，直到他在1883年12月，初搬去和遷居努南的父母居住時，才將這些畫作取回。兩年後他到安特衛普時，他把可能包括這兩件靜物的作品留在母親A.C. van Gogh-Carbentus（1819-1907）身邊，她後來在1886年遷居Breda時便帶著他的作品，交給一個名為Schrauwen的木匠貯藏。之後這些作品的去處不明。梵谷的母親有可能忘記這些作品了，據說Schrauwen並不明白它們的價值，在1902年將之整批賣給一位舊貨商J.C. Couvreur（1887-1961）。後者又將若干畫作（許多素描似乎立刻被毀壞了）轉賣給Breda的Kees Mouwen與Willem van Bakel，這些畫作在1903年鹿特丹Kunstzalen Oldenzeel的幾個拍賣展覽中出現。然而這些展覽展出不同來源的數批產物，《有木屐的靜物》的出處為何迄今不明。[7]

《有木屐的靜物》在1912年被庫勒穆勒夫人在阿姆斯特丹（可能透過藝術商Komter）購得；她在1920年在Enthoven 收藏的拍賣會以3,100基爾德購得《有草帽的靜物》。

---

1. 這件孩童頭像迄今下落不明。目前這個時期傳世的3件靜物畫作為F1、F62與F63。（在本圖錄中，F為 J.B. de la Faille 1970年版的梵谷作品目錄之縮寫，其後的數字則代表該件作品在De la Faille書中的編號）。
2. Carlo Derkert是第一個在1946年提出這兩幅作品與梵谷美術館的靜物畫有關的理論，但很多人不同意。1987-1988出版的 *Van Gogh in Brabant* 這本圖錄將這兩件靜物視為海牙時期的作品；1989和1996年的Hulsker的書則將之放於努南時期的那一章。有關這幾件作品的年代問題的文章可參考Van Tilborgh and Vellekoop 1999年的書，頁35，註釋19。
3. 該畫作因此成為De le Faille書中第一號的作品。
4. Louis van Tilborgh口述。
5. 庫勒家族在1920年從Enthoven Collection的拍賣買下這件作品的，當時的拍賣目錄中描述這件事物為「泥炭塊」。
6. 庫勒穆勒美術館2002年技術檢驗。
7. 參考Stokvis 1926，頁3-8；Van Tilborgh & Vellekop 1999，頁32-34，註釋14；關於梵谷作品的流傳經過資料，參考Op de Coul 2003.

有草帽的靜物　Still Life with Straw Hat
1881年11至12月　1881 Nov.-Dec.
紙本油彩裱於帆布　oil on paper mounted on canvas
36.5×53.6公分　36.5 x 53.6 cm
Collection Kröller-Müller Museum, Otterlo, The Netherlands

從1882年1月1日開始，梵谷在海牙的Schenkweg這裡租了一間附有凹室的房子。梵谷將這裡當成自己的畫室。他得找新的模特兒，其中有個不會太貴的「小老太太。」（202/173，1882年1月26日）這一幅《縫衣婦人》或許就是以她爲對象。[1] 過去學者對這幅素描的年份有許多不同的看法，但是它毫無疑問屬於海牙時期早期的人物習作，這時畫家仍未使用透視框與方板（squaring）來輔助。除此之外，這些素描仍透露出與埃頓時期有某種關係。[2] 舉例來說，以《縫衣婦人》爲例，我們可以注意人物較長的大腿以及暖爐和椅子之間的距離。除此之外，比例上還算相當讓人信服，而且梵谷也已經聽從莫弗的建議，和模特兒保持較遠的距離。稍後，上了棕色的前景與背景都再次用鉛筆進行描繪。前景所描繪的木質地板的對角線是最後用黑色粉筆與尺畫出來的。右手邊大約3公分處曾經摺了過來，因此還能清楚看到原來的褶痕變成一條白色的線。這個褶痕的一邊可以看到短的鉛筆直線，或許代表著畫紙要切割的部份，但後來並未割去。我們並不清楚這是不是梵谷本人留下的。裁減右手邊會造成窗戶，特別是背景有不正常的傾斜。

　　到了2月，水彩逐漸由墨水筆取代。其實墨水筆更適合梵谷，而他也認爲這讓他更有機會找到雜誌的工作。他希望成爲插畫家的想法當然還沒有消退，正如他在一封向西奧請求建議的信中所說的：「如果你找得到，請務必讓我知道什麼樣的素描可以賣給雜誌當做插畫。我覺得它們應該用得到以普通人爲對象的墨水筆素描，而且我真的想開始畫這樣的素描，畫些能夠被複製的畫。」（203/174，1882年2月13日）

---

1. 《編織的女人》（*Woman Knitting*）也是根據同樣的模特兒。（F910a，目前所在不明）
2. De la Faille 1928/1970、Vanbeselaere 1937與Hulsker 1977/1996將《縫衣婦人》的年份定爲1883。Hefting 1980，頁13，不確定《縫衣婦人》屬於1882或1883年。（前引書，頁30）Hammacher 1961，頁13將《縫衣婦人》定爲1882年1月到2月之間，或許是第一個將這幅畫定在這個年份的人。Heenk 1995，頁46及18、Dorn 1996，頁68都認爲這幅素描屬於這個時期。

縫衣婦人　Woman Sewing
1882年1至2月　1882 Jan.-Feb.
鉛筆、黑色與棕色粉筆、褐色與黑灰色暈染、　pencil, black and brown chalk, brown and black/grey wash, opaque
不透明與透明水彩、織紋紙　and transparent watercolor on wove paper
56.3×48.6公分　56.3 x 48.6
Collection Kröller-Müller Museum, Otterlo, The Netherlands

在1882年3月18日，梵谷寫信給西奧說：「如果你來，可不可以請你一定要記得帶些安格爾素描紙（Ingres paper）？特別是比較厚的那一種，因為我喜歡用這種紙來畫，而且我覺得這種紙也適合用來作水彩畫習作。」（209/180）雖然西奧後來沒有拜訪他，但是他確實從海牙寄了一包紙給梵谷。在4月初梵谷也回信向西奧致謝。從後來的書信中，我們可以得知梵谷要的那種較厚的素描紙並沒有包括在內。梵谷在5月又提到這件事：「我真的最喜歡的紙就像那種我用來畫身體向前彎曲的女性的那種畫紙，但是如果可能的話最好是那種纖維沒有經過漂白的。那種厚度的紙我都沒有了。我相信這種紙稱為雙層安格爾紙（double Ingres）。我在這裡買不到這種紙。如果你看看我怎麼畫素描的，你就會了解那麼薄的紙幾乎沒辦法支撐我的畫法。」（223/192，1882年5月3日至12日）梵谷所提到的那幅「身體向前彎曲的女性」非常可能就是由席恩當模特兒的兩幅標題為《坐著的婦人》的大型習作之一，畫中的女主角雙手抱頭，身體姿勢悲慘、駝背。

這兩幅習作，以及另外三幅大型的人物習作，所用的畫紙都是由兩張直紋紙貼在一起，紙張並帶有橢圓形、內含ED&Cie字樣及PL BAS的浮水印。[1] 這兩張紙是由經銷商或製造商黏合起來的，黏合的方式讓浮水印以及紙模的線條（在直紋紙上總是很容易看見）彼此間有點不一致。所以如果我們將這樣的畫紙對著光看，就很容易看出它有兩個浮水印及紙模線。梵谷在荷蘭時期常常使用這樣的畫紙「單張」來創作。四月初所寄給他的那包紙或許就是這種紙，因為他接受C.M. van Gogh的委託所繪製的大型市景圖全都是用有這種浮水印的直紋紙。[2] 1882年7月26日的一封信說明梵谷最後還是向Stam買到最後一批這種紙（252/220）；Stam指的是Stam-Liernur這位寡婦在Papestraat街上所開的文具店。我們很難明確肯定到底是什麼時候開始，但是至少從5月開始這種紙就已經用完了。[3]

有關透視框的使用，在《帶著孩子的婦人》（Woman with Child）這幅素描上，梵谷用的是5×5公分方格的透視框，而其他的素描則是使用6.5×6.5公分方格的透視框。梵谷一定有不少這樣的透視框（除了前述兩種之外，他還有一種3×3公分方格的透視框）。從梵谷1882年7月1日給西奧寫的一封信可以證實這一點：信中梵谷寫道「我那位過去幫了我許多忙的木匠朋友也幫我製作了透視的工具。」（241/209，1882年7月1日）這種運用透視框與方板的實驗指出，在這個時期梵谷非常重視提昇自己準確掌握透視法的能力，而這個能力對他而言並不是自然且容易的事。儘管透視框本來只是一種輔助工具，讓畫家能更快速而容易地臨摹一個主題，但是梵谷終其一生都持續使用透視框，甚至包括他的油畫作品。[4]

第一幅《坐著的婦人》描繪一位穿著黑衣、較年長的女性（或許是席恩的母親），另一幅《坐著的婦人》則描繪席恩坐在火爐前抽著雪茄，兩幅都沒有方板的痕跡。或許因為這樣，兩個人物的比例都不太能令人信服。

從5月用完最後一張畫紙之後，梵谷就花了很多時間在尋找「雙層的安格爾紙。」到了8月，他覺得他找到了。「昨天下午，我待在Laan〔海牙的一條街〕上的Smoulders紙張批發商的閣樓。在那裡我找到了一你猜猜是什麼一是雙層安格爾紙；它的名稱是Papier Torchon，纖維比你寄的還粗糙。我會寄一張樣本給你看看。那裡有很多這種紙，很舊、充滿時間的痕跡，非常好。現在我先買了半刀，但是以後隨時可以回去買。」（254/222，1882年8月5日）[5] 在1882年8月以及之後，梵谷有很多畫也是畫在印有DAMBRICOURT FRERES HALLINES 1877浮水印的厚水彩紙上；這種紙或許就是他在海牙所找到的紙，那其實是粗面水彩畫紙（Torchon paper）而不是安格爾或雙層安格爾紙。

---

1. 如前所述，梵谷口中的「安格爾紙」其實是通稱所有的直紋紙，有時也包含其他有粗糙表面的紙。事實與梵谷的用法完全相反：直紋紙才是通稱用法，而安格爾紙是一種直紋紙。在1881年12月，莫弗建議梵谷說直紋紙不適合用來畫水彩畫。（191/164，約1881年12月21日）
2. 梵谷在3月間為叔叔所繪製的小幅市景圖用了織紋紙與直紋紙。梵谷用的直紋紙上面有EDB的浮水印，代表Erven D. Blaauw，是位於Zaandam的製紙商。現在無法了解ED&Cie指的是哪一間法國的製紙商。
3. 在1881年夏天梵谷前往海牙時，也在Stam的店裡找到了厚的畫紙：「我在Stam那裏找到了些安格爾紙，比一般的紙厚了兩倍，所以可以盡情地使用。可惜的是，那是白色的。你想你可不可以找個機會幫我找顏色像未漂白的棉布或亞麻布的紙呢？」（170/149，1881年8月28日）這聽起來像是「雙層安格爾紙」的描述，不過至今仍沒有找到梵谷埃頓時期畫在雙層直紋紙上的素描。有關Stam-Liernur的資訊，請參閱Bert van Vliet在網路論壇www.vggallery.com上針對海牙顏料商Van Leurs所做的討論。
4. 除了劃分成方格外，梵谷也常常在畫油畫時使用有兩道垂直十字線的板子。
5. 一刀紙大約包含24或25張紙。

坐著的婦人　Woman Seated
1882年3月　1882 Mar.
鉛筆、墨水筆與畫筆、黑色（部分褐色）　pencil, pen and brush in black ink (partly browned),
墨水、直紋紙（雙層）　on laid paper (two sheets)
60.8×37.2公分　60.8 x 37.2 cm
Collection Kröller-Müller Museum, Otterlo, The Netherlands

坐著的婦人 Woman Seated
1882年4至5月　1882 Apr.-May
鉛筆、墨水筆與畫筆、稀釋墨水、　pencil, pen and brush in ink (diluted), wash, traces of squaring,
暈染、方板痕跡、直紋紙（雙層）　on laid paper (two sheets)
58×43公分　58 x 43 cm
Collection Kröller-Müller Museum, Otterlo, The Netherlands

縫衣婦人　Woman Sewing

1882年4至5月　1882 Apr.-May

鉛筆、灰色暈染、方板痕跡、直紋紙（雙層）　pencil, grey wash, traces of squaring, on ladi paper (two sheets)

58×45.4公分　58 x 45.4 cm

Collection Kröller-Müller Museum, Otterlo, The Netherlands

梵谷當然會嘗試畫能賣的畫作，儘管在他過世之後廣泛流傳著他對此毫不在意的神話。[1]然而梵谷的確不願意向市場屈服，而寧願希望讓市場為他做出調整。這種態度讓梵谷與古比的海牙分公司的主管H.G. Tersteeg及其他人產生衝突。一開始Tersteeg對梵谷並沒有惡意，偶爾會借錢給他，也向他買了一幅水彩畫。但是對梵谷表達興趣的同時，他也常指責梵谷在經濟上仰賴西奧，建議他該為自己的生活費打拼。除此之外，Tersteeg總是重複地說梵谷該畫小幅的水彩畫，因為這樣賣得最好，偏偏這正是梵谷做不到也不願屈服的一點。[2]梵谷對自己的能力相當嚴苛，覺得自己先要能對形態有較好的掌握，而只有孜孜不倦地素描才能做到這一點。另外，西奧對他某一小幅水彩的讚美也讓梵谷不是很高興：「你說那一小幅水彩是你所見過我的作品中最好的一嗯，這不對吧！因為你手中那些我的習作其實更好，而且今年夏天那些墨水筆的素描也比那更好；那一小幅畫沒有意義，至少我當初寄給你只是要讓你知道將來我也會用水彩創作。但是我有更多嚴肅的習作，在其他方面上有更好的完整性，即使它們剛開始看起來很難親近。」（206/177，1882年2月25日）在這一點上，梵谷倒是得到J.H. Weissenbruch（1824-1903）這位不輕易讚美別人的藝術家的支持。由於莫弗的請求，Weissenbruch參觀了梵谷的畫室，並且認為他的墨水筆素描特別好。（204/175，1882年2月13日）

像這樣的支持一定鼓勵了梵谷，讓他向自己的叔叔，也就是阿姆斯特丹的畫商Cornelis Marinus van Gogh（1824-1908，人們通常以他姓名的縮寫C.M.來稱呼他）描述了自己在海牙的經驗，並且邀請他前來拜訪。大約在3月11日左右，C.M.來到了梵谷的畫室。就在兩人的交談快要面紅耳赤的時刻，梵谷隨手拿起一本小的素描及習作來轉移注意力。「剛開始他不說話，直到我們看到一幅我和Breitner在午夜漫步時所作的素描，畫的是從Turfmarkt所看到的Paddemoes（也就是Nieuwe Kerk附近的猶太區）。我第二天早晨又用墨水筆再補強了一點。」（210/181，約1882年3月11日）C.M.非常喜歡，立即委託了梵谷繪製同樣的小型市景素描。梵谷為每幅作品定的價格是2.50荷蘭盾。如果這些作品令人滿意，他的叔叔答應會再委託12幅阿姆斯特丹的市景，並且會訂好價格；C.M.又說：「而且你會賺得多一點。」（210/181）確實有第二次的訂單，但是卻改成6幅典型的海牙市景。梵谷在兩個星期內就完成了第一次的訂單。《海牙一景》不僅是信中提到那幅讓C.M.決定下訂單的素描，最後也成為其中之一。這幅素描在1895年之前就由Hidde Nijland由C.M. van Gogh手中購得。

梵谷在1882年2月13日的一封信中首次提到George Hendrik Breitner（1857-1923）：「這些日子我常與Breitner去素描；Breitner是個年輕畫家，他認識Rochussen就像我認識莫弗一樣。他的素描相當得心應手，和我用的方式完全不同，我們也常常在施食處及候車室做人物的素描。他常常到我的畫室來看木刻版畫，我也常去他的畫室。」（203/174）我們可以從稍後的一封信推斷，梵谷和Breitner曾在3月2日傍晚進城想尋找作畫的對象。（207/178，1882年3月3日）[3]因此我們可以得知《海牙一景》的初稿是在午夜左右完成的。Paddemoes指的是海牙最古老也最貧困的一個區域；在17世紀中葉，這區很大一部分都被拆除，好興建Nieuwe Kerk這座教堂，儘管它並沒有出現在素描裡，但是它就在牆後區域的右側。梵谷所站的位置大約與教堂的入口等高，這裡也是Turfhaven及Turfmarkt與Spui會合的地點。在Turfhaven的另一邊是Houtmarkt：目前有一幅大約在1891年8月左右從這裡拍攝Nieuwe Kerk的照片。從照片中可以看出這座教堂獨特的圍牆，尤其是那三根厚實、方正的石柱就和素描裡一模一樣。另外左邊也可看到一排楊樹，在素描中它們坐落在背景的St. Jacobstraat屋子的前方，與照片中的位置完全呼應。

在《海牙一景》中，梵谷並沒有使用透視框或方板，而在3月14到18日之間所寫的信（211/182）中所提到的《沙丘上的工作者》也沒有，但除此之外其他受委託所繪製的素描都有這些輔助工具的痕跡。因此，梵谷最早使用輔助工具的時間應該就在這個時期。[4]

這幅素描以及應委託所作的其他素描多半在畫紙的背後都用鉛筆記下所描繪的場景；這個筆跡不屬於梵谷或是他的叔叔。我們不知道是誰或是在什麼時候留下這些筆跡。但是時間一定相當早，至少是在1895年Hidde Nijland買下《海牙一景》之前，很有可能早於1890年。那一年，Rijnspoorweg失去了特許權，由Maatschappij tot Exploitatie van Staatsspoorwegen取而代之，但是在《Schenkweg沿路的水溝》（Ditch along Schenkweg）後卻寫著「Rinjinspoor附近區域」。或許這是畫商C.M. van Gogh的員工所做的紀錄，可能還是根據畫家本人所提供的資訊。梵谷在城市的邊緣尋找他的主角，而這些地方都是潛在的買家較不熟悉的區域（而這些地方就像梵谷的家一樣）。

---

1. 參見Koldenhoff 2003，頁189-199。
2. 西奧拜託他的哥哥與Tersteeg保持好的關係，但是後者責備梵谷說「我很清楚你沒有畫家的料」當然讓這段關係不太容易保持。（208/179，約1882年3月5日到9日）梵谷與Tersteeg的關係在春天急遽惡化，因為當時人們知道梵谷與（已從良的）妓女席恩（Sien Hoornik）開始交往。
3. 有關Breitner與梵谷的關係，請參見Hefting 1970，頁59到69。
4. 參見《修路工與運貨車》（Road Worker with a Wagon）說明。

海牙一景　View of The Hague ('Paddemoes')

1882年3月　1882 Mar.

鉛筆、黑色墨水筆（部分褪爲褐色）、暈染、織紋紙　pencil, pen in black ink (faded to brown in parts), wash on wove paper

24.9×30.8公分　24.9 x 30.8 cm

Collection Kröller-Müller Museum, Otterlo, The Netherlands

這幅素描描繪三個人物操作著一具大型的軋乾機，主要是以鉛筆繪製，並且用墨水筆加強色調。相關文獻通常將這幅素描歸於1884年梵谷在努南所作，但通常也會表示存疑。[1] 會做這樣的歸類通常是因為它與織工素描的內景有些表面的相似，也或者是因為梵谷在努南的第一個畫室位在牧師公寓後方的軋乾室裡。這裡我們將它歸為1882年2月到3月間在海牙所作。這個時期梵谷開始大量使用墨水筆取代鉛筆來創作，因此也導致後來他叔叔C.M. van Gogh委託他繪製一系列的市景素描。除此之外，在Schenkweg這個地方，這幅素描的主題可以說就在梵谷的隔壁：在這裡，他一開始住在洗衣店隔壁，而這個洗衣店也被畫入《木工作坊與洗衣店》（Carpenter's Yard and Laundry）這幅素描裡。[2] 事實上，坐在軋乾機前，頭髮綁成圓髮髻的女性甚至看起來有點像該幅素描前景裡的人物。軋乾機的尺寸也指出它應為專業類型的機器。

在風格上，這幅素描有點不穩定，但是我們不能忘記這是幅粗略地完成、很快畫下的鉛筆速寫。舉例來說，軋乾機左邊的男性是以較短、遲疑的筆劃畫成，同時也沒有用墨水加強色調，所以看起來比其他兩個人物更「弱」。這種速寫的風格來自交替使用持續而摩擦的短線與強而有力的直線，常見於梵谷海牙時期的許多習作。舉例來說，這位男性人物的畫法相當類似《帶著掃帚的男人》（Man with a Broom，F979a，私人收藏），而後者一般歸於1882年秋天，但也可能於當年1月完成。原因在於，這幅畫也被用來當做1882年3月所畫的《沙丘上的工作者》（Sandworkers in the Dunes，F922，目前所在地不明）其中一個人物的範本。

1. 參見De la Faille 1928/1970；Hulsker 1977/1996；Hefting 1980，頁60；Heenk 1995，頁129。只有Vanbeselaere 1937，頁413，將這幅畫歸於更晚的巴黎時期。
2. 梵谷的鄰居Anna Maria Simonis-de Mol的工作是洗衣婦，在1882年4月20日過世，沒多久洗衣店就歇業了。（Visser 1973，頁42及65-66）

軋乾機與三個工人　Mangle with Three Figures
1882年2至3月　1882 Feb.-Mar.
鉛筆、黑色墨水筆、織紋紙　pencil, pen and black ink on wove paper
22.9×29.5公分　22.9 x 29.5 cm
Collection Kröller-Müller Museum, Otterlo, The Netherlands

這幅鉛筆習作，梵谷使用方板來繪製比例與運貨車的前縮透視。他將透視框放在畫紙上，沿著線畫出方格。接著他從一個固定的點透過透視框看著要畫的對象，然後就能較容易地將整體的輪廓畫進紙上的方格中。這裡他也描出透視框的幾個條板，尤其是在畫紙的底部及右側。由於這些條板大約為2.5公分寬，所以整個透視框的大小約為30×20公分，由40個方格（8×5）組成，每個方格大小為3×3公分。[1] 在梵谷接受叔叔C.M. van Gogh的委託所繪製的素描中，大部分都使用了這樣的透視框。

　　比起運貨車前面的人物，運貨車後方的人物畫得較不令人信服：他正對著一堆磚塊彎腰，或許剛才從運貨車上搬下一堆磚塊。在《海牙Noordstraat街上的修路》（*Road Works in Noordstraat, The Hague*）這幅較大的構圖裡，也有一個非常相似的勞工，就在街上正在挖的溝渠裡。但是他在那裡做什麼並不是很清楚；觀看者會覺得他的手上應該有把鏟子。

　　這幅素描的構圖看來有點紊亂，因為人物間的比例相差懸殊，或許全都基於不同的範本。彎腰的人物所根據的範本並沒有留存下來，但是或許梵谷這兩幅素描都是基於同一幅人物習作。

---

1. 有關梵谷使用透視框的狀況，請參閱Van Heugten 1996，頁21至25。梵谷通常喜歡在他的透視框上作畫，但是每個方格不見得都與這個透視框一樣全都大小相同，重點是只要比例相同即可。梵谷使用這些相對較小但易於攜帶的透視框（大約30x20公分）的時間似乎僅限於1882年3月到4月間在海牙完成的素描。

修路工與運貨車　Road Workers with a Wagon
1882年3至4月　1882 Mar.-Apr.
鉛筆、方板痕跡、織紋紙　pencil and traces of squaring on wove paper
21×34公分　21 x 34 cm
Collection Kröller-Müller Museum, Otterlo, The Netherlands

這幅簡單但相當有力的鉛筆素描是梵谷在1882年年初所畫的許多人物習作之一。除了當做練習之外，它們還是有多位人物的大型或小型構圖的可能範本。[1]梵谷在3月間正在努力完成他的叔叔所委託的素描，因此這幅素描所根據的一定是來自那些素描中的陪襯人物。

這位婦女的側身像和席恩相當接近，特別是鼻子部分清楚的隆起。梵谷曾向西奧介紹席恩與她家庭的其他成員（沒有提到她的名字）並且說明他們是他最近找到的模特兒時，當時他曾經提到：「那位年輕女性的臉孔並不美麗，因為她曾得過水痘，但是她的體態相當優雅，讓我深受吸引。他們也有很好的衣服，像是黑色的毛衣、形狀很漂亮的帽子、質料很好的圍巾等。」（207/178，1882年3月3日）在這幅素描中，隱約可以在婦女的外套下看見優雅光亮的黑色毛線套裝。在其他大型的人物素描中，席恩會穿著這種衣服（用美麗諾羊毛所製成）擺姿勢，很清楚表現出衣料的華美。

---

1. 參見Heenk 1995，頁50-51。De la Faille 1928/1970/1992；Vabveselaere 1937，頁90；Hefting 1980，頁56將這張畫定為1882年10月，而Hulsker 1977/1996則將它定為1882年5月。

行走的婦人　Woman Walking
1882年2至4月　1882 Feb.-Apr.
鉛筆、織紋紙　pencil on wove paper
32.5×15.6公分　32.5 x 15.6 cm
Collection Kröller-Müller Museum, Otterlo, The Netherlands

「C.M.的訂單眞是一線曙光！」梵谷在1882年3月11日給西奧的信中如此寫道：當時他們的叔叔C.M. van Gogh向梵谷訂製了12幅海牙的市景，每幅定價2.5荷蘭盾。（210/181）如果C.M.喜歡這些畫，就還會再向梵谷訂製12幅阿姆斯特丹的市景。在梵谷的想像中，只要一點練習，他就應該能夠每天畫一小幅素描，這些素描他應該可以輕鬆地以每幅「5法郎」的價格賣出。這樣就足夠他每天生活及模特兒的支出。「有漫長白日的光明季節即將來到」，在同一封信中梵谷高興地寫道，「我的『飯票』，也就是那些讓我吃飯、付模特兒酬勞的小幅素描，可以在白天或傍晚來畫，其他時候我可以嚴肅地做人物習作。」

梵谷在兩星期內就完成這次的委託並且在依照計畫完成之後將畫作寄出。C.M.過了一陣子才回覆，但是當酬勞在4月初寄到時，附帶了下一批的委託，只是內容有點不同：「C.M.給了我酬勞還有另一批委託，但是他要的不太一樣：他要6幅詳細且有明確根據的市景。然而，我會努力讓自己完成這些畫作，因爲根據我自己的了解，這6幅畫的酬勞將會和上次那12幅畫一樣。接著或許就會要我畫阿姆斯特丹了。」（213/184）從信的內容來看，我們可以推測他的叔叔不完全滿意第一批的作品。所謂的「詳細且有明確根據的市景」指的當然是要更有特色，更精確地描繪海牙的畫作。

在完成第二批委託畫的過程，梵谷遭遇了相當的困難。四月是個潮溼的月份，讓他無法在戶外工作。除此之外，人物素描佔據他越來越多時間。在5月中，他寫信給西奧，提到他已經爲這批畫做了不同的習作，但是覺得很難堅持把它們完成。（227/193）最後，梵谷在月底將7幅畫寄到阿姆斯特丹，比原來同意的多了一幅，或許是爲了時間上的耽誤向叔叔賠罪。寄出的這批畫包括了兩幅大的素描、四幅中型的素描、以及一幅小的素描（與上一批委託的畫同樣尺寸）。[1]《席凡寧根的晒鰈魚乾場》屬於中型尺寸的素描，依照梵谷的說法，大約是半張安格爾紙的大小。畫作寄出沒多久，梵谷就寫信給西奧說：「但是他會喜歡這些畫嗎？或許不會。在我眼中，這些素描不過是透視法的習作，這也是爲什麼它們對我而言主要是各種我練習的方式。即使我尊貴的叔叔不要這些畫，我也不會爲我的努力付出感到遺憾，因爲我自己會很高興將它們保留下來，以練習這些非常基本的技能：透視法與比例。」（229/200，約1882年5月23日）

《席凡寧根的晒鰈魚乾場》在用筆上更爲節制。白色不透明水彩用得不多，主要用在兩個婦女的服裝以及爲前景中的灘草加強色調。其他的地方主要是用墨水筆在鉛筆草圖上繪製。在這幅素描，梵谷也用了繪圖網格，並且從較高的視角，也就是在沙丘上，觀看整個景物。這幅構圖裡的不同視覺線非常有力。在左側，觀衆的視線被向上吸引，帶到從沙丘露出一點的燈塔上。在右側，視線則順著背景席凡寧根的Oude Kerk不停往下。[2]梵谷是在西南方的小村落最遠的邊緣來繪製，這個村落是個勞動階級的區域，居民主要的經濟來源是漁業。這幅素描所描繪的房屋與晒鰈魚乾場在前方連接著Citadel街，那原來是一條小街，在作畫的時間左右拓寬並改名爲Duinstraat。在背景右側中央的圍籬之間是Kolenwagenslag，其中有更多煙燻及晒魚乾的建築。[3]鰈魚是比目魚（plaice）的一種，一般會抹鹽、穿線、掛在竹竿上晒乾。在素描中，它們就是屋後架上掛著的菱形物。前景中有無數破損而且塡滿了沙的籐籃，它們是「用來預防沙丘的沙到處吹襲」；後來當梵谷在同樣的地點畫水彩畫時，曾經寫信給西奧解釋這些籐籃。（252/220，1882年7月26日）所以它們或許不像某些人所認爲的是屬於某個在此處開業的籐籃製造商。[4]

在1882年5月28日星期日的傍晚，梵谷寫了一封信給凡‧拉帕德，他才剛剛來拜訪梵谷，並且認爲梵谷爲叔叔畫的那些素描相當好。那時《席凡寧根的晒鰈魚乾場》這幅素描並不在其中，因爲從信中我們可以得知，他就在當天才完成這幅素描：「今天早上我起得很早，去沙丘那邊畫一個晒魚乾場，也像木匠那幅畫一樣是由上往下看的：現在是凌晨1點，但是這幅畫已經完成了，感謝老天，現在我終於敢正眼看我那恐怖的房東了。」（231/R8）的確，梵谷也在這個時期畫了另一幅晒鰈魚乾場的墨水筆速寫（F940，私人收藏），但是這幅速寫梵谷是在魚乾場的後方用較低的視角來畫的，所以信中所指的一定是這裡的這幅素描。當晚他就爲叔叔將這幅畫及其他6幅畫包好，但是在此之前，梵谷又在畫中增添一個兩臂交抱的男人以及其他的細節。在1980年代早期，發現了一幅有關這個人物的獨立的人物習作。（沒有F編號：JH add. 19，私人收藏）[5]這裡，梵谷直接用墨水筆在素描裡添上這個人物，另外還有他身邊那張椅子，兩者都沒有任何鉛筆畫的底圖。從梵谷寫給凡‧拉帕德的信中我們可以得知，梵谷由於凡‧拉帕德的建議，在某些畫作中做了些修改。

在完成委託之後沒多久，梵谷就生病了。他6月大部分的時間都待在醫院治療淋病。在入院前沒多久，C.M.寄給梵谷20荷蘭盾，但沒有附帶任何的字句，而且根據梵谷自己的說法，這比原先約定的還少了10荷蘭盾。他在6月3日寫信給西奧說：「目前我眞的不知道他會不會再委託我畫新的東西，甚至也不知道他喜不喜歡那些素描。」（235/205）他懷疑他的叔叔只喜歡水彩畫，很難欣賞其他種類的素描：「我承認，對只習慣於水彩畫的人而言，素描只是用墨水筆畫出來，或是用筆勾出光線，或是用不透明顏料上色，這些看來可能有點沈悶。但是也有些人，就像對健康的身體而言，在強風中散步感覺很愉悅、很令人振奮；在我心中，也有些熱情的人不害怕這樣的沈悶。舉例來說，Weissenbruch就不會認爲這兩幅素描不令人愉悅或沈悶。」但是C.M.的確寄了一封信，而且他的叔叔很明顯在信中寫說他對梵谷很感興趣，但是他很生氣梵谷對H.G. Tersteeg沒有感恩的表現：這一點可以從給西奧的一封信中看出。（237/206，1882年6月8日或9日）在一封給凡‧拉帕德的信中，梵谷對他的叔叔描述的更露骨：「我收到20荷蘭盾，配上一封責備我的信：『我眞的覺得這樣的素描有任何商業價值嗎？』」（236/R9，1882年6月4日或5日）

---

1. 一般相信除此之外，F923、F930、F941、F942與F946a也屬於第二批寄出的畫作。根據Van der Mast& Dumas 1990，頁173與Heenk 1995，頁57，這個版本的《木匠作坊與洗衣店》（*Carpenter's Yard and Laundry*）—F939—並不屬於委託的一部分，而是相關的另一幅素描F944（紐約私人收藏）。然而，這並不太可能，因爲F939的品質更好，細節更加清楚，以及Vincent的簽名前有「delt」（delineavit的縮寫），這個字樣只出現在這批委託畫作中的另外兩張（《席凡寧根的晒鰈魚乾場》與F942）。除此之外，F939是在1895年之前由Hidde Nijland向畫商C.M. van Gogh所購入，另外購入的還包括第一批畫作中的《海牙一景》與《席凡寧根的晒鰈魚乾場》（參見Ives et al. 2005，頁76）。F944或許是梵谷在1882年6月3日（235/205）隨著另一版本的晒鰈魚乾場素描而寄給西奧的版本。
2. 7月時梵谷也在這裡畫了一張水彩畫，但是那個時候他將自己的視線轉向右方，因而造成一個較爲平淡的構圖（F945，私人收藏）。
3. 有關的確切地點請參見Van der Mast& Dumas 1990，頁63、64、177。Visser 1973，頁95相信梵谷的主題其實是Kolenwagenslag本身。
4. Van der Mast & Dumas 1990，頁65。
5. 這幅習作在1983年Op de Coul首次出版。

席凡寧根的晒鰈魚乾場
1882年5月
鉛筆、黑色墨水筆與畫筆（部分褪爲褐色）、
白色不透明水彩、方板痕跡、直紋紙
29×45.4公分

Dab-drying Barn in Scheveningen
1882 May
pencil, pen and brush in black ink (faded to brown in parts),
white opaque watercolor, traces of squaring, on laid paper
29 x 45.4 cm
Collection Kröller-Müller Museum, Otterlo, The Netherlands

梵谷用《漫步海灘的人們》這幅鉛筆的習作來當做一幅大型水彩畫（F1038, Baltimore Museum of Art）的主題。這幅習作的年代可以定為1882年的秋天，那個時期梵谷正在練習群像的構圖。這種構圖最麻煩的一點在於，畫家首先得很快地畫下一群正在移動的人的印象，其中每個人都有自己的位置。之後在畫室裡，畫家可以用這樣的速寫來建構一個明確的構圖，將過去的人物習作用在畫面的每個人物上。根據這幅速寫所畫的水彩畫有很多地方和原來的速寫不同，同時在構圖上也留有更多的空間。梵谷在一封給西奧的信中詳細地描述了這樣的困難：「至於構圖，每個景象都會有人物，不管是市場、是船隻靠岸、救濟中心外的一群人、候車室、醫院、當舖、街上的人群、有的聊天、有的正在步行─描繪這些的原則就如同描繪一群羊的原則相同（因此才有moutonner這個字），而簡單

來說最重要的都是光、棕色、透視。我可以用不同的方式調整我的畫作，但是還是一直都有無數的方式來畫。」（265/231，1882年9月17日）

在同一封信中，梵谷提到另一幅相關的墨水筆速寫，描寫的是漁船靠岸時岸邊的一群人。像這樣的一群人，「有無限的可能，需要無數的個別的不同人物的習作與塗鴉，而你都得很快地在街頭上捕捉下這些畫面。這樣一來，你會逐漸地帶入個性與意義。我最近畫了一幅海灘上的男男女女的習作，每個人都朝各自的方向走動。」最後這句話有可能指的就是這一幅素描。梵谷在畫紙上簽了名字，這一點相當不尋常，尤其是對這樣匆促完成的習作而言。或許這是因為，這幅素描是梵谷給他的房東Michiel Anthonie de Zwart的一個禮物。

漫步海灘的人們　People Strolling on the Beach
1882年9月　1882 Sep.
鉛筆、織紋紙　pencil on wove paper
15.9×25.5公分　15.9 x 25.5 cm
Collection Kröller-Müller Museum, Otterlo, The Netherlands

在Bezuidenhout這幅素描的背面，可以看到梵谷在街頭上所畫的速寫，描繪驢子套著小車以及幾個人物。在車子以及左邊房屋的牆壁下方，可以看到之前鉛筆速寫的痕跡，但是看不清楚它們代表什麼。當這張畫紙因為正面的構圖而經過剪裁而變小，車子的上半部有一部分被切掉，只剩下（或許是）驢子的腿以及車輪的一部分。這個不完全的殘片相當接近《驢車與人物》（*Donkey Cart with Figures*）這幅畫，尤其是驢子表現出完全相當的姿勢。

街景　Street Scene
1882年9月　1882 Sep.
鉛筆、黑色墨水筆（部分褪為褐色）、水彩紙　pencil, pen in black ink (faded to brown in parts), on watercolor paper
19.1×20公分　19.1 x 20 cm
Collection Kröller-Müller Museum, Otterlo, The Netherlands

這三幅素描描繪席恩（Sien Hoornik）與她的兒子威廉（Willem），後者是在1882年7月2日出生於Leiden醫院。梵谷認識席恩的時候，她已經有7個月的身孕卻被男方拋棄；兒子出生的時候也有許多併發症。當席恩回到海牙的時候，她就前往與梵谷同居，而那時梵谷已經搬到Schenkweg附近住宅的頂樓。他特別為了席恩買了一張柳條編的大椅子，而這張椅子可以在其中一幅素描中看到。（245/213，1882年6月6日）第二幅素描，描繪席恩在為威廉哺乳。這幅畫中大量的垂直線條主要是因為梵谷所用的畫板太過粗糙。木板的紋理讓水平線皺折扭曲，造成有些地方比較暗，另外當梵谷將一個地方填滿水平線時，垂直線也自動出現。右上方可以清楚分辨木板紋理曲度更大的線條。

第三幅素描事實上和前兩幅一樣，都是相當概略的鉛筆素描，但是只有這幅後來加上了顏色。有趣的是，梵谷是用油彩來上色的。有幾個地方還可以看到清楚的鉛筆線，但是只要將這幅畫對著光看，就可以看到底圖詳盡的細節。從畫的背面可以看出油彩下方有大範圍的陰影線。我們的印象是，對梵谷而言這是個實驗，因此畫家隨便選擇一個現有的速寫來做。寶寶除了頭跟手塗了點肉色之外全部都留白。[1]

現存描繪席恩與威廉寶寶的畫非常少。幾乎每一幅都是基本的習作與速寫，幾乎所有都曾經屬於梵谷在海牙的房東M.A. de Zwart，就像這裡的前兩幅一樣。第三幅素描已知最早的所有者是Jan Dona（1870-1941），他是Bremmer圈子裡的藝術家，他與Bremmer最早從1890年就認識，並且有時會提供協助。[2]

---

1. 油彩經過高度的稀釋，塗了相當厚（例如席恩的帽子）。在紙背有大量的棕色，因為油墨滲透過紙背。阿姆斯特丹的梵谷美術館藏有另一幅試驗性的油畫畫作，畫中只有威廉寶寶（F912），但是並不是根據任何現有的鉛筆素描（Van Heugten 1996，頁94-96）。
2. Balk 2004，附錄"Kunstenaars rond H.P. Bremmer"（Bremmer身邊的藝術家）。Dona擁有另外兩幅梵谷早期的素描，分別是《背泥煤的人》（*Turf Carrier*, F964, National Gallery of Art, Washington）與《播種的農婦》（*Peasant Woman Sowing Seeds*，F883，私人收藏）。

坐著的母子　Seated Mother with Child
1882年秋　1882 Autumn
鉛筆、方板痕跡、水彩紙　pencil, traces of squaring, on watercolor paper
49.2×27公分　49.2 x 27 cm
Collection Kröller-Müller Museum, Otterlo, The Netherlands

哺乳的母親　Mother Suckling Her Child
1882年秋　1882 Autumn
鉛筆、方板痕跡、直紋紙　pencil, traces of squaring, on laid paper
43×26.4公分　43 x 26.4 cm
Collection Kröller-Müller Museum,
Otterlo, The Netherlands

母與子　Mother with Child
1882年秋　1882 Autumn
鉛筆、油彩、水彩紙　pencil, oils, on watercolor paper
41.1×24.5公分　41.1 x 24.5 cm
Collection Kröller-Müller Museum,
Otterlo, The Netherlands

1882年11月初，梵谷寫信給西奧說：「我又再度畫水彩畫，這次描寫的是礦工的妻子在雪地中背負著一袋袋的煤炭。不過我主要畫了大約12幅人物習作和3幅頭像，但我還沒有準備好。我想水彩會給我適當的效果，但是我不相信那對人物的性格而言有足夠的力量。現實，就像米勒的《拾穗者》一樣，是嚴苛的，所以你了解我不能將它變成一種雪景效果，那只會給人一種印象，而其存在的理由就不過像是一幅風景畫一樣。」（281/241，約1882年11月2日至3日）梵谷對人物畫與風景畫的區分相當典型：這幅畫的重點正是在於這些貧困而努力工作的婦女所展現出的性格與驕傲。四周環境必須能符合這個主題，不能凌駕主題之上。拾穗者英雄式的彎曲體態，這些貧困的拾穗者，從收割過的田地收集著剩餘的穀粒，而因為米勒1857年的畫（Musée d'Orsay, Paris）而永垂不朽，便成為閃耀的範本。

　　梵谷之前已經試著要在《負重的搬運工》裡達到類似的效果，在那幅畫裡他讓背景的礦坑襯托出婦女背負重擔走過田地。在這裡所討論的水彩畫裡，他也在遠處描繪了冒煙的煙囪來暗示這是個採礦的區域。人物是根據不同的習作來構思並置入此一構圖。在前方三個人物上，我們可明顯看出模特兒擺出的姿態。左側的那一位是以側身像表現，但是看起來好像她剛剛向畫家的方向轉身。其他兩個模特兒的身體都相當前傾，但是還是試著想從重擔下回頭。在繪製習作時，梵谷還不是很清楚這些婦女是如何將袋子背在頭上。1882年10月31日，梵谷寫信給凡·拉帕德說：「我花了一番功夫才發現波林納吉的礦工妻子是如何背袋子的。你或許記得，當我還在那裏的時候，我畫了一點有關的素描，但是它們不是真的。現在我畫了12幅同一個主題的習作。是像這樣的：袋子的開口先綁起來〔速寫〕然後往下提。底部的兩端連起來，就變成一種最迷人的僧侶斗篷〔……〕我常常請一位婦女帶著這樣的袋子當我的模特兒，但是總是感覺不對。有個在Rijnspoor鐵路場幫人裝煤炭的男人教了我正確姿勢。」（278/R6）從左側人物來看，我們可以清楚看出她的確將袋子像某種僧侶的斗篷一樣戴在頭上。

雪地裏背煤炭袋的婦女　Women Carrying Sacks of Coal in the Snow
1882年11月　1882 Nov.
炭筆 (?)、不透明水彩、畫筆、墨水、織紋紙　charcoal (?), opaque watercolor, brush and ink, on wove paper
31.9×50.1公分　31.9 x 50.1 cm
Collection Kröller-Müller Museum, Otterlo, The Netherlands

在1882年9月18或19日，梵谷寫信告訴凡‧拉帕德說：「最近我從救濟所找到一個人常常來當我的模特兒。」（267/R13）這封信所提到的這個模特兒可以在1882年秋天所畫的許多素描中看到。這個人住在「荷蘭改革宗老人之家」（Dutch Reformed Home for the Elderly），這裡的居民常被稱為diaconiemannetjes與diaconievrouwtjes，意思是「靠教區」過活的老人。梵谷常常稱這位模特兒為「孤單人」（Orphan Man），不過這個名詞其實指的是「羅馬天主教孤兒及老人之家」（Roman Catholic Home for Orphans and the Elderly）的居民。[1]梵谷覺得這個名字很動人，如同他不久之後在信中告訴凡‧拉帕德的那樣：「我最近忙著畫孤單人的素描；這些依靠教區而活的貧困老人都是這樣被稱呼的。你覺不覺得『孤單人』與『孤單女』（orphan woman）這樣的說法相當合適？要畫這些隨時在街上可以看到的人並不容易。」（269/R14，1882年9月22或23日）這封信另外附了一幅這位模特兒的速寫，畫面下方寫上No. 199，這個編號也繡在老人黑色長大衣的袖子上。這個編號讓我們後來能辨認出這個老人就是Adrianus Jacobus Zuyderland（1810-1897），他從1876年開始就住在荷蘭改革宗老人之家，而住在這裡的每個人都必須配戴一個可供辨認的註冊號碼。[2]梵谷可以從老人之家裡找到更多模特兒，包括婦女，但是Zuyderland是他的最愛。他告訴西奧說：「他有個很好的禿頭、大（又聾）的耳朵、以及白色的鬢角」（271/235，約1882年10月1日），而這些特徵都可以從許多的習作中看到。

這幾幅習作讓Zuyderland表現出許多姿勢，戴著高帽或扁帽，通常都穿著黑色的長大衣。老人之家的居民都有這樣的衣服，但是梵谷多年以來也收集了數量相當多的服裝，可供模特兒使用。在《拿著傘與懷錶的老人》這幅畫裡，Zuyderland的外衣翻領上別了一枚勳章，這或許是他在1830年代的比利時獨立戰爭中由於特殊的功績所獲頒的「鐵十字」勳章。[3]

這些習作很難精確的定出年份，因為梵谷從9月中一直到12月底畫了非常多這類的習作。在1882年夏天，他第一次專注地在畫油畫，之後他也回頭繼續畫水彩畫，發現很難具有說服力的描繪群像。因此，他覺得自己該更努力地畫人像。如同他在10月8日告訴西奧的：「像我一樣，你會立刻注意到，我需要做很多人物習作。我將全部的力量集中在這裡，幾乎每天都找模特兒來畫。我畫了更多孤單人的習作，而這個禮拜我希望能從救濟所找個婦女來畫。」（272/236）在一封11月22日的信中，他談到他的「許多孤單人的習作」。他說他的朋友，H.J. van der Weele這位藝術家，要他用這些習作來創作構圖，但是梵谷寫道：「我不覺得自己已經準備好了。」（287/246）

不管是不是準備好了，梵谷正在讓自己為未來做準備。在11月，他第一次實驗石版畫，希望能讓自己更有機會從事插畫家的工作。[4]他在那個月畫6幅石版畫，其中3幅是根據Zuyderland的習作。[5]

在8幅老人的鉛筆素描中，有5幅是畫在梵谷在8月底找到的那種粗糙較厚的水彩畫紙，而這種紙也較適合梵谷相當用力的素描習慣。梵谷用牛奶的溶液來為這5張畫紙固色，在人物周圍的褪色中還可以清楚看出這個痕跡。在《拿著帽子的老人》與《拿著傘與懷錶的老人》的背面，可以看到方格的痕跡，但是只在正面的人物輪廓線的範圍內。正反面的方格並不一致。這些方格是來自下方相連的一頁畫紙，上面梵谷原先已經畫了方格，而是在他用木工鉛筆用力繪製這些素描時從後方所「轉印」上去的。

---

1. 參見Van Heugten 1996，頁129。
2. 參見Visser 1973，頁62-65。羅馬天主教的收容人則沒有相關的規定。
3. 同前書，頁63-64。
4. 有關梵谷的圖像作品請參閱Van Heugten & Pabst 1995。
5. 作品編號分別為F1657、F1658、F1662。

拿著傘與懷錶的老人　Old Man with Umbrella and Watch
1882年9至12月　1882 Sep.-Dec.
鉛筆、方板痕跡、人物周圍上有已　pencil, traces of squaring, fixative discoloration around figure,
變色的固色劑、水彩紙　on watercolor paper
48×28.7公分　48 x 28.7 cm
Collection Kröller-Müller Museum, Otterlo, The Netherlands

拿著玻璃杯的老人　Old Man with a Glass

1882年9至12月　1882 Sep.-Dec.

鉛筆、方板痕跡、（原）紫藍織紋紙　pencil, traces of squaring, on (originally) bluish purple wove paper

49.1×24.7公分　49.1 x 24.7 cm

Collection Kröller-Müller Museum, Otterlo, The Netherlands

拿著帽子的老人　Old Man Holding His Hat

1882年9至12月　1882 Sep.-Dec.

鉛筆、方板痕跡、人物周圍上有　pencil, traces of squaring, fixative discoloration around figure,

變色固色劑、水彩紙　on watercolor paper

48.1×23.5公分　48.1 x 23.5 cm

Collection Kröller-Müller Museum, Otterlo, The Netherlands

梵谷在1882年12月31日至1883年1月2日之間寫給西奧的一封信中提到了這幅素描，並且也解釋了自己新的作畫方式。這部份的說明值得全部引述，因為其中清楚說明梵谷認為自己的問題何在：「我在畫石版畫時，突然發現石版畫蠟筆是一種相當舒服的材料，所以我覺得自己該用它來畫素描。但是，有個問題你一定了解－因為它很油，不能用一般的方式來擦掉－如果用它來畫在紙上，那麼甚至連唯一能將它從石版上擦掉的東西，也就是刮刀（Grattoir），都不能用，因為它無法以適當的力量用在紙上，因為這會將紙刮破。但是我想到了，可以先用木工鉛筆畫好素描，然後再用石版畫蠟筆繼續勾勒，這樣（因為材料本身又油又黏）就會讓鉛筆固定；這是一般粉筆做不到的－就算可以，效果也不好。（這樣畫了一張速寫之後，畫家就可以用穩定的筆觸在需要的地方使用石版畫蠟筆，不會遲疑也無須塗改。）所以我用鉛筆完成了相當不錯的素描，至少是在當時可能的情況下。接著我用牛奶將它固定並且讓筆跡變淡。接著我再用石版畫蠟筆再畫一次，然後在需要最深色調的地方，用畫筆或墨水筆沾上「燭黑」（noir de bougie）來畫上幾筆，在需要亮的地方則使用白色不透明水彩。這樣我就畫了一幅老人坐著閱讀，燭光照在他的禿頭、手和書上的畫。第二幅是一個受傷的人綁著繃帶的頭像。我的模特兒真的是一個頭部受傷的人，左眼也真的綁著繃帶。舉例來說，他就像從俄國撤退回來的年老守衛的士兵頭像。」（298/256）最後的描述說的正是《蒙著單眼的男子頭像》。儘管一開始不容易看出來，但是確實有繃帶從暗色布料下露出來。針對梵谷對自己的畫法的描述，另外可以補充的是，梵谷用墨水筆來畫沒有遮住的那隻眼睛。墨水的棕色在四周的黑色中相當突出。那支長長的陶製煙斗並沒有上色。這幅素描的明暗對比也相當標準：畫的左側背景是暗的，右側背景則是明亮的。帽子則出現在轉換的點上，而這裡畫家則以相反的方式來畫：左側是亮的，右側是暗的。因此，這幅成為梵谷一直想練習的明暗對比的很好範例。頭的形狀則是有點問題。眼睛的繃帶幾乎沒有綁好，讓整個臉的右側看起來有點平板。

蒙著單眼的男子頭像
1882年12月
鉛筆、黑色石版畫蠟筆、灰色暈染、黑色墨水筆
（部分褪為褐色）、方板痕跡、水彩紙
45×27.5公分

Head of a Man with an Eye-Bandage
1882 Dec.
pencil, black lithographic crayon, grey wash, pen in black ink
(faded to brown), traces of squaring, on watercolor paper
45 x 27.5 cm
Collection Kröller-Müller Museum, Otterlo, The Netherlands

這幅畫相當難斷定時間，或許是在1883年年初畫的，儘管畫的主題讓人想到梵谷在1882年秋初為席恩與她的兒子威廉所畫的鉛筆素描。這裡寶寶或許看起來大了點。除此之外，梵谷並未像平常一樣用鉛筆畫底圖，而是直接用黑色粉筆來作畫，因此這幅畫應該屬於較為後期的作品。或許因為這樣，構圖上有許多色點，因為較油的粉筆所造成的污痕相當難處理。人物身後背景的灰色水彩凸顯了人物的輪廓，不過上色的方式也相當隨便。寶寶白色帽子上的水彩也有溢出的痕跡。

母與子　Mother with Child
1883年1至2月　1883 Jan.-Feb.
黑色石版畫蠟筆、白色與灰色不透明水彩、直紋紙　black lithographic crayon, white and grey opaque watercolor, on laid paper
40.5×27公分　40.5 x 27 cm
Collection Kröller-Müller Museum, Otterlo, The Netherlands

對梵谷而言，《蒙著單眼的男子頭像》就像一個序曲，隨之而來的就是他在1883年頭幾個月間開始致力描繪的一個主體：頭像素描。他給這個主題起了一個英文名字—*Heads of the people*，亦即「人物頭像」；英國的插畫雜誌*The Graphic*也曾經在1870年代用這個標題出版了一系列粗獷的人物類型木刻畫，內容包括「英國流氓」、「海巡隊員」、「礦工」等。梵谷非常喜歡收集這類的木刻畫，從許多舊的英、美、法、德的雜誌中剪下這些插圖並收集在夾子裡，有些他則是裝裱在粗糙的紙張並且懸掛在畫室裡。凡‧拉帕德也是個收藏家，因此兩人常常交換彼此的收藏。[1]梵谷曾寫信給凡‧拉帕德說：「在我看來，這類畫面的收藏就像是藝術家的聖經一樣，讓他不時透過閱讀這些畫面而進入適當的情緒之中。我認為不僅要認識它們，更要讓它們成為畫室裡持久的存在。」（313/R25，約1883年2月9日）幾個星期之前，梵谷也告訴凡‧拉帕德說：「〔我一直在〕努力畫黑白的素描，我希望能從這些插畫雜誌中學到更多黑色與白色的力量。〔……〕最近我特別努力在畫的是頭像—就稱之為*Heads of the people*吧—其中包括戴著防雨帽的漁夫頭像等等。」（303/R2，約1883年1月15日）

很快他就畫了一系列的漁夫頭像，模特兒多半都是來自老人之家。這張素描所畫的有著嚴肅嘴唇的老人也出現在梵谷美術館收藏的兩幅素描中。（F1014與F1015）

梵谷所發展出的新的技巧—他所謂的「更有力量的過程」—結合了深淺不同的黑色，而透過這種方式，他希望能為自己的素描注入更多情感。他認為，在這個方面，未完成的習作通常更為強而有力，而非那些他花了太多時間在上面的作品。梵谷寫信告訴弟弟：「你會了解我的意思。真正的習作會有生命的某種部分在其中，而創作它的人不會想到自己，而是想到畫中的自然，因此他喜歡這幅習作的程度會勝過後來以它為基礎所創作出的畫作，除非有某種不同的事物最後從許多的習作中出現，也就是從許多「個體」（individual）中出現的「類型」（type）。這是藝術的最高層面，也就在這裡，藝術有時會超越自然—例如米勒的《播種者》，你在其中所發現的靈魂遠遠超過田野間一般的播種者。」（299/257，1883年1月3日）

---

1. 梵谷所收集的木板畫中，有很大一部分留存下來，現藏於梵谷美術館。有關梵谷與他的版畫收藏，請參見Pickvance 1974與Luijten 2003等。

戴防雨帽的漁夫頭像
1883年1至2月
鉛筆、黑色石版畫蠟筆、黑色墨水筆與畫筆、
白色、灰色與粉紅色不透明水彩、
頭部周圍上有變色固色劑、方板痕跡、水彩紙
42.9×25公分

Head of a Fisherman with a Sou'wester
1883 Jan.-Feb.
pencil, black lithographic crayon, brush and black ink,
white, grey and pink opaque watercolor,
fixative discoloration around head, traces of squaring,
on watercolor paper
42.9 x 25 cm
Collection Kröller-Müller Museum, Otterlo, The Netherlands

這幅構圖描繪一個老漁夫寧靜地坐在矮牆上抽著煙斗，下方還隱約可見模特兒Adrianus Zuyderland為梵谷擺姿勢時所坐的椅子。這裡梵谷將一幅簡單的鉛筆習作進一步畫成細節更豐富的景象。如果仔細檢視，還會發現Zuyderland其實並沒有握著煙斗，而只是用右手撐住頭。煙斗是後來用白色不透明水彩再畫上去的，或許同時梵谷也在矮牆上畫了那杯咖啡。

坐著的老漁夫 Old Fisherman Seated
1883年1至2月　1883 Jan.-Feb.
鉛筆、墨水筆與畫筆、烏賊墨與中性灰色暈染、pencil, pen and brush in ink, wash with sepia and
黑色石版畫蠟筆、白色、灰色與粉紅色不透明水彩、neutral tint, black lithographic crayon, white,
方板痕跡、織紋紙　grey and pink opaque watercolor, traces of
45.6×25.7公分　squaring, on wove paper
45.6 x 25.7 cm
Collection Kröller-Müller Museum, Otterlo, The Netherlands

這兩幅相當有力量的素描，畫中坐在籃子上的人物或許是席恩，和較潦草的《母與子》一樣，是直接用較油的黑色粉筆來繪製，而沒有先用鉛筆畫好詳細的草圖。這兩幅素描色澤較深也較銳利，由於只用黑色粉筆，所以深黑色相當凸顯。經過一個實驗階段之後，梵谷很明顯在這個時期有足夠的自信略過鉛筆速寫，但是此時的作品留存的不多。1883年2月3日，梵谷寫道：「我也用孔特粉筆（conte）畫了幾個人物，我覺得不錯。不只是因為用了孔特粉筆，而且將整個東西擦開，讓陰影流動，讓光線再次出現。」（308/263）這裡他用的是同樣的方式，只不過用的是黑色的石版畫蠟筆，這種筆比起孔特粉筆更油更黑。清出光線，就像梵谷如此吸引人地描述，是透過用白色與灰色的不透明水彩，以及運用尖銳的工具將粉筆刮開。在《縫衣婦人》這個作品裡，在右側的背景以及裙子的輪廓線處可以清楚看到這個方式。

　　至於《坐在籃子上哀痛的婦人》，梵谷又回到聚焦在單一人物來呈現貧困與無助的主題。在早期這類型的作品中，主要的人物通常是男性。一年之前，梵谷才剛畫過幾幅大型的人物素描，描寫席恩用手支撐頭部，表情相當悲傷。

　　有關這幅素描與梵谷自己的版畫收藏的關係，梵谷喜歡的版畫是呈現未經修飾、粗獷的日常生活，並且要能以各種可能的姿勢來表現悲傷的典型。梵谷所尋找的主要是整體的性格刻劃，一種悲傷人物的典型。他從自己收藏的版畫（其中這樣的人物通常處在人群之中）所找到的範本成為這種追尋的一個重要靈感來源。

坐在籃子上哀痛的婦人　Mourning Woman Seated on a Basket
1883年2至3月　1883 Feb.-Mar.
黑色石版畫蠟筆、灰色暈染、　black lithographic crayon, grey wash, white and grey opaque watercolor
白色與灰色不透明水彩、方板痕跡、水彩紙　traces of squaring, on watercolor paper
47.4×29.4公分　47.4 x 29.4 cm
Collection Kröller-Müller Museum, Otterlo, The Netherlands

縫衣婦人　Woman Sewing
1883年2至3月　1883 Feb.-Mar.
黑色石版畫蠟筆、灰色暈染、白色與灰色不透明水彩、　black lithographic crayon, grey wash, white and grey opaque watercolor,
方板痕跡（僅見水平線）、水彩紙　traces of squaring (only horizontal stripes visible), on watercolor paper
38.2×23.3公分　38.2 x 23.3 cm
Collection Kröller-Müller Museum, Otterlo, The Netherlands

在1882年12月中，梵谷寫信告訴西奧：「現在我又畫了兩幅素描，一幅是男人在閱讀聖經，另一幅是男人在做餐前禱告，晚餐就在桌上。兩個人畫的方式，你或許會說帶著老式的情調，他們就像雙手抱頭的那個小小老人一樣。我認為Benedicite是最好的，但是兩幅畫其實是互補的。其中一幅可以從窗外看到雪地裡的田野。」（295/253，約1882年12月12-18日）這兩幅素描的模特兒還是Zuyderland這位孤單人。在《閱讀聖經的人》（*Man Reading Bible*，F1683，私人收藏）裡，他正在閱讀聖經，而在另一幅梵谷稱為Benedicite的素描裡，他坐在簡單的桌上，雙手交握。同樣主題的另一幅，梵谷或許讓席恩坐在桌子的另一邊，而且坐在同一張板凳上。當兩幅畫擺在一起，甚至看起來像在吃同一餐。兩個人面前都有一個正在冒煙的碗，儘管這在席恩的版本裡沒有那麼明顯。

根據梵谷習慣的程序，這兩幅祈禱的素描首先用鉛筆畫好細節，然後用黑色石版畫蠟筆、淡水彩、墨水、不透明水彩來完成。

席恩這個版本最後色調變得較灰。舉例來說，梵谷上淡水彩的方式是先用海綿沾上粉筆。接著他在板凳周圍以及女性的裙子附近將輪廓線抹開。畫家用深灰色的不透明水彩來完成女性服裝、頭髮、桌子以及板凳上的高光，但是女性臉上有幾個地方可以看到白色的油彩。[1]左側的背景塗上厚厚一層黑色的油墨，所以儘管在較暗的構圖中，席恩背部尖銳的輪廓還是能夠分辨出來。梵谷在板凳上用了同樣的墨水，用它來強化女性的輪廓線。[2]他或許是在幾個月後的1883年4月來完成最後的補筆。就是在這個時期，梵谷發現印刷油墨（printer's ink）這種黑色的材料只要用不同比例的松節油來稀釋就可以產生不同層次的黑。（336/278，約1883年4月1日或2日）從這幅素描的背景中，梵谷似乎就是這麼做的，而且他在《閱讀聖經的人》裡面也做了類似的實驗。在本文開頭所引的書信中，梵谷提到可以從背景的窗戶中看到冬天的風景，但是他後來用厚厚的一層墨將這個部分蓋掉。

---

1. 畫紙的背面可以清楚看到油彩大約在女性頸部的位置滲過紙背，並且留下一個棕色的色點。
2. 畫家在女性耳朵附近將墨層擦開，所以這裡可以看見鉛筆的痕跡。

餐前的感恩禱告　Saying Grace
1882年12月至1883年4月　1882 Dec.-1883 Apr.
鉛筆、黑色石版畫蠟筆、灰色暈染、畫筆與印刷油墨、　pencil, black lithographic crayon, grey wash, brush and printer's ink,
白色油彩、灰色不透明水彩、水彩紙　white oils, grey opaque watercolor, on watercolor paper
62.3×39.6公分　62.3 x 39.6 cm
Collection Kröller-Müller Museum, Otterlo, The Netherlands

在梵谷全部的作品中，《臨終的婦人》是個相當特別的構圖。梵谷很少以死亡作為主題，而且他從未像這幅作品一樣直接描寫死亡。[1] 無論如此，在1883年4月間，梵谷有短暫的時間著迷於這個主題。四月初，他寫信給凡‧拉帕德說：「我正在用這個方式進行的素描畫是一個孤單人站在棺木附近，這個地方人們稱為『屍體巢穴』。」（337/R33，約1883年4月2-4日）所謂的「這個方式」，梵谷指的是用印刷油墨來畫素描，但是並沒有這樣的構圖留存下來。四月稍後，他寫信給西奧說：「這個星期我畫了幾幅躺著的人物；將來我需要屍體或者病人的人物，包括男性與女性。」（339/280，約1883年4月21日）在這封信裡，梵谷也提到了印刷油墨；他說這時幾乎每一張畫他都用了畫筆與印刷油墨。在《臨終的婦人》這幅具有銳利對比的黑暗構圖中，這種油墨是用在臨死婦人的頭髮與背景上。這種油墨在身體附近上得特別厚，目前還帶有某種光亮，其他地方則稀釋的較淡。

從前引給西奧的信中的隻字片語，我們不清楚梵谷要畫的是真正的屍體與病人，或只是需要用躺著的人物習作來用在包含了死者與病人的構圖內。梵谷的靈感或許來自他閱讀了雨果的作品，因而創作了躺著的席恩的習作。大約在4月11日，梵谷寫信給西奧說：「我正在讀《悲慘世界》（*Les Misérables*）的最後一部分。芳婷（Fantine）這個角色是個娼妓，她在我心中留下深刻的印象。」（338/279）芳婷當然讓梵谷想起席恩，因為兩個可憐的女性都為愛人懷孕之後被遺棄，只能獨自撫養孩子，除了賣淫之外沒有其他可能。雨果將芳婷描繪為社會的犧牲者，梵谷也正是如此看待席恩。芳婷在故事中可悲地死去，或許梵谷也希望能用素描來呈現這種悲劇情懷。

無論如何，席恩穿了屍衣來扮成屍體，但是她身體的位置看起來有點做作。即使在前景中加上打開的書與熄滅的蠟燭兩個靜物（傳統上死亡的象徵），也無法挽回。[2] 這個骨瘦如柴的憔悴肉體所缺少的，或許可稱為「死亡的表情」。要不是雙手在胸前交握，我們可能會誤以為她正在睡眠。除此之外，相較於短小的上身，腿部似乎太長。為了達成白色與較亮的效果，梵谷用了不透明水彩與油彩。書與蠟燭並未預先畫上草圖，都只是用灰色及白色的油彩一揮而就。女性的服裝及枕頭都是用白色不透明水彩來畫，只是枕頭摻了一點藍色。最後，陰影部分是用黑色粉筆畫在白色的顏料上。底部是用這種粉筆輕輕畫在紙上，所以紙張粗糙的紋理結構清楚可見。

---

1. 目前已知只有一幅關於死去女性的油畫的素描副本，畫成時間大約是在布魯塞爾時期（1880-1881）（F1026a，梵谷美術館，阿姆斯特丹）

2. 在努南時，梵谷畫了一幅《有聖經的靜物》（*Still Life with Bible*，F117，梵谷美術館，阿姆斯特丹），時間約為1885年10月，當時他在打開聖經旁放了一根熄滅的蠟燭，其許多的可能意義之一就代表了他在當年年初時過世的父親（參見Van Tilborgh & Vellekoop 1999，頁222、224、註9）。

臨終的婦人　Woman on Her Deathbed

1883年4月　1883 Apr.

鉛筆、黑色石版畫蠟筆、灰色暈染、畫筆與　pencil, black lithographic crayon, brush in (printer's) ink, white oils,

印刷油墨、白色油彩、灰色水彩、水彩紙　grey watercolor, on watercolor paper

35.3×63.2公分　35.3 x 63.2 cm

Collection Kröller-Müller Museum, Otterlo, The Netherlands

在1883年2月底，梵谷的畫室裝了新的遮陽板，因爲從三扇大窗戶照進來的光太亮也造成太強的反射。他之前爲了減低光照而掛在窗戶上的網子已經不夠用。現在，他可以分別遮蔽窗戶的上半部或下半部，根據光的強度及照入的角度做細微的調整。這對他的明暗習作特別有幫助：「讓我最難過的就是，當我看見一位在小房間裡閒逛的婦女，發現這個人物有著典型而神祕的特質，但是一旦她進來畫室之後，這些特質全都消失不見。舉例來說，孤單人在陰暗的樓梯間比起在我的畫室更讓人感動。」（322/269，約2月25-26日）

光線更好的照射角度在稍後特別有用，因爲梵谷這時開始實驗一種非常黑的材料，也就是印刷油墨。（336/278，1883年4月1日或2日）他在這種油膩而且很黏的墨水中加入一些松節油，讓墨水較容易散開。事實上，這種溶液可以做高度的稀釋，讓它可以作爲一種透明的黑色淡彩。松節油蒸發很快，不會在紙上留下痕跡，而梵谷也寫信向凡・拉帕德介紹這種方式，希望引起他的興趣。（337/R33，約1883年4月2-4日）梵谷也會將墨水與白色的顏料或白色的粉末混和以製造深灰色。在這幅素描中可以看到這樣的方法。[1]

由於梵谷在這些習作中專注處理明暗對比，因此主題有時候會看起來相當詭異，儘管或許一開始看不出來。

《坐著的婦人》的模特兒很明顯不是席恩。她戴著白色的帽子，在畫中心事重重地坐在凳子上。梵谷在帽子上用了點白色的油彩。沿著帽子的上緣可以看到一條細細的棕色線，這是因爲油的流動所造成的。在過去的某一段時間，畫紙的底部被切了一條，而上面原有的簽名Port. Vincent則被剪下來並貼到畫面的右下角。我們不清楚是誰做了這樣的處理，但是從這幅作品最早的複製品中就可以看到這一點。[2]

梵谷寫信告訴凡・拉帕德說，這種繪畫方式不適合用在每一種紙上：「我的經驗是，這種印刷油墨可以相當好的附著在某種這裡稱之爲papier torchon紙的粗糙紋理上（但是這絕對不是Whatman torchon）。」（337/R33）《坐著的婦女》就是畫在梵谷所謂的Whatman torchon這種紙上：這種紙是 J. Whatman公司所生產的水彩畫紙。這種紙相當堅韌，但是這裡墨水淡彩讓紙張本身產生許多皺摺。婦女的圍裙部位也有撕裂的痕跡，而且紙張吸收了非常多的墨水，以至於在畫紙的反面都可以清楚看見。

---

1. 參見《餐前的感恩禱告》與《臨終的婦人》。
2. 參見Nijland 1905，編號1。

坐著的婦人　Woman Seated
1883年4至5月　1883 Apr.-May
鉛筆、灰色暈染、畫筆與印刷油墨、　pencil, grey wash, brush and printer's ink, white oils,
白色油彩、方板痕跡、織紋紙　traces of squaring, on wove paper
56.3×43.9公分　56.3 x 43.9 cm
　Collection Kröller-Müller Museum, Otterlo, The Netherlands

在De la Faille起初於1928年將這幅素描歸於努南時期之後，有好長一段時間人們認爲這幅素描是在德倫特所繪製的。[1]到了1993年，再度有人提出《有白橋的風景》一定是在梵谷的努南時期所完成的，其根據在於他們相信畫中的風景與努南西南方大約七公里的Mierlo區域的Eindhoven運河有關。兩年之後，有明確的證據證明梵谷一定是在海牙完成這幅畫。當時，Martha Op de Coul與Annet Tellegen出版了一篇文章，文章中附了一張油畫的照片；這幅油畫的作者是Antoine Philippe ('Anton') Furnee（1861-1897），[2]作畫的地點與梵谷一樣。這位Furnee的專業是測量員，而他的父親Hendrik Jan Furnee則是梵谷在海牙的顏料供應商，同時他在Korte Poten也開了一個藥舖。在1883年春天，梵谷開始教年輕的Furnee素描及油畫，而且兩個人常常一起出門尋找題材。《有白橋的風景》就是在這樣的行程中完成的。這些作品只能概略地定出年份，因爲目前並無法確定兩人一同出遊的日期，只能說大約是5月的某幾天。（345/285，約1883年5月20日）

這幅素描於1980年進行修復，在此之前畫的背後有段Furnee手寫的筆跡：*Oude wasscherij by den Binckhorstweg vlak over het spoor v/d SS geschilderd door A.Ph. Furnee fec. met Vincent*（Binckhorstweg附近的舊洗衣店，就在SS鐵路上方，由A.Ph. Furnee fec.與梵谷所畫）。[3]這條路就從Rijnspoor火車站建築的後方開始。梵谷與Furnee背對著城市站著，眼前在Veen低地與Binckhorstweg（或Binckhorstlaan）的方向有座橫跨著Schenk的小橋，而Schenk是流經De Binckhorst郡區域並繼續往前到Voorburg附近的Vliet。他們

兩人身後的鐵路線連接著Hollands Spoor與Rijnspoor這兩座海牙的火車站。畫紙背面上的字跡一定是在1890年之後所寫下的，因爲就在那一年，Nederlandsche Rhijnspoorweg Maatschappij（荷蘭Rhijnspoorweg公司）爲Staatsspoor（SS）公司所併購。[4]

這幅構圖有種不穩定的特性，這是來自大量漫不經心塗上的白色與灰色不透明水彩曾經覆蓋著主要的前景與天空。顏料變得相當堅硬，時間一久有部分區域龜裂脫落。顏料的脫落讓整個構圖更加斑斑點點。帶點棕色的粉紅色紙原來是帶點淺藍的紫色，所以這幅作品現在給人的印象一定與原來大不相同。[5]特別是灰色，原來一定更爲柔和。

這幅畫在右下角簽了Vincent。過去人們將這詮釋爲梵谷（他幾乎從未在這類的習作上簽名）一定是將這幅畫送給了Furnee。[6]然而，這個簽名並不是梵谷本人所簽，儘管他的確有可能將這幅畫送給學生。這個簽名很接近一組相近的、較爲狹長的簽名；這類簽名只出現在20幅1885年夏天在努南完成的人物習作，而這些全都出自Nijland的收藏。Nijland本人並未做這樣的簽名，但是他的這些畫很有可能來自Furnee的父親。老Furnee也爲身在努南的梵谷提供顏料，所以當畫家在1885年夏天無法清償帳單時，很可能就寄給他一組素描代替。所以，可能是Hendrik Jan Furnee—或者是他的朋友—做了這些簽名。Hidde Nijland早在1895年就提供某些「簽了名」的努南時期習作在海牙展覽，所以Furnee可能是最早的所有人。《有白橋的風景》很可能是與努南時期的其他素描一起購入，也很有可能出現在1895年的展覽中，儘管沒有直接證據。[7]

---

1. Vanbeselaere 1937，頁238及421，是第一個將這幅畫定於德倫特，1883年10-11月。Trabaut 1959，頁24也接受德倫特的說法。Hamacher 1952，cat.no.55，第一次將這幅畫定在海牙，根據的是與《沙地上的樹根》（*Tree Roots in a Sandy Ground*）及《伐木者》（*Woodcutter*）某些技術上的相似點—這樣的組合確實有點奇怪。De la Faille 1970又將它連結到德倫特，而Hefting 1980，頁44，則是因爲它與《農場》（*Farm*）的相似處而將它歸於德倫特，這確實是較好的觀察。
2. Op de Coul & Tellegen 1995。這篇文章討論的是梵谷與他的學生Furnee的關係。另請參見Dijk & Van der Sluis 2001，頁259。
3. 引自Dijk & Van der Sluis 2001，頁259。
4. Hollands Spoor車站位在Rotterdam-Amsterdam鐵路線上；此線在不遠處橫切過Binckhorstlan。這條線屬於Hollandsche Ijzeren Spoorwegmaatschappij的一部分，而後者在1917年加入Staatsspoor。
5. 這張直紋紙會褪色是因爲它過去曾被鑲入以酸性紙板製成的鑲畫框內。如果用放大鏡檢視，仍可以看到紙張上有部分紅色與藍色的纖維。紙上的浮水印，Saint Mars，就已知的梵谷所有作品來看相當獨特。或許他是用Furnee所帶的紙來畫。Hefting 1980，頁44，曾提到S.C. Mars的浮水印，但這並不正確。Dijk & Van der Sluis 2001，頁258提到這一點，並且將這連結到《修路工人與運貨車》。但是後者並非畫在直紋紙上，而是畫在織紋紙上，紙上的浮水印爲S&C，和《有白橋的風景》並沒有關係。
6. 參見Dijk & Van der Sluis 2001，頁259。
7. 因爲當時的評論與圖錄通常僅冠以簡單的「風景」（landscape）一詞，更因爲畫作的數量實在太多，因此要辨認出這幅構圖相當困難。

有白橋的風景　Landscape with a White Bridge
1883年5至6月　1883 May-Jun.
黑色粉筆、白色與灰色不透明水彩、　black chalk, white and grey opaque watercolor,
（原）紫藍直紋紙　on (originally) bluish purple laid paper
29.9×43.7公分　29.9 x 43.7 cm
Collection Kröller-Müller Museum, Otterlo, The Netherlands

梵谷在1882年夏末主要致力於風景畫的習作。雖然他也嘗試人物畫的油畫創作，但對他來說，後者並不容易掌握。在天候不佳無法外出時，梵谷在他的工作室內試著畫一些人物畫。他在1882年8月19日給西奧的信中寫道：「我寄了兩幅『塗鴉』（"scribbles"）給你，我很喜歡畫人物畫，但是仍有待磨練。我必須更熟知技法—也就是所謂的『藝術的火候』。」（259/226）但梵谷這段時期的人物畫習作並未被保存，目前唯一傳世的梵谷海牙時期的人物習作，為之後的1883年夏天的《漁夫》、《漁夫之妻》與五個挖馬鈴薯的人。其間梵谷為了充分掌握人體構造，畫了一系列的人物素描。

這兩件習作的年代可以相當肯定的定在1883年的8月初。漁夫之妻穿著相當醒目的紅披肩；1883年六月初梵谷曾寫信告訴西奧，他得到一件類似的東西。（353/291）[1]如果西奧能給他一些額外的錢，他希望也買「一件漁夫穿的短袖、立領的外套……」（335/293，1883年6月13或14日）但一個月後，他從兩位跟他學素描的測量員那裡，收到一件意外的禮物。[2]在這件漁夫的習作中，模特兒身穿的就是這種外套。梵谷在一月已經獲得了一頂防雨帽。[3]起先他利用這些特徵物品在素描中，但是在7月下旬他以很合算的價錢買了很多油畫顏料之後，他又再度開始畫油畫。（372/307，1883年7月29與30日）在1883年大約8月2日信中，他詳細報告了他作為一名人物畫畫家的過程：

在過去數天內我深感焦慮。去年我反覆嘗試人物畫的習作，但結果總令我絕望。如今我再度嘗試，素描變得比去年容易多了，所以我的作品不再有什麼阻礙物。當時我繪畫時，只要素描的草稿變不清楚了就會很混亂；所以如果我只能有很短的時間來畫模特兒，結果就會變得很糟，因為我需要很長的時間來素描。但是現在，我不再在乎素描是否被塗掉了，我直接用油畫畫筆來創作，形體也夠清楚可辨。（373/308）

在同一封信中他提到，他先用前一年的方法畫了兩件習作：「先素描，再填色在輪廓裡」，他之稱為「乾方法。」如今他把程序顛倒過來：「另一個方法是一開始先定出色調，實際上使素描更持久……。」

《漁夫》與《漁夫之妻》很有可能是他當時創作，其中可看出這種先定出色調與粗略畫出大概色彩的方法。事實上，以紅外線反射儀檢查這些習作，並未顯示出這2幅油畫有素描底稿。在有些地方可以看見初步的油畫底稿，雖然它們在繪畫的過程被刷掉了。梵谷用相當大的畫筆畫背景，包括大約2到3公分寬的筆刷。他以流動的筆法畫人物周圍的海灘與海，人物則用較小的畫筆來畫。作品中大體上的色彩都很接近。如同梵谷在上述給西奧的信中說明的，他的用意是「不要太在意素描，而是先將大概的顏色定調，與漸漸的畫出形體和細部的顏色。」他首先著重在色調的明暗度，避開如手與臉部等複雜的細部。但是稍後他會用像他描述的一種更類似素描的方式，用黑色油彩來畫，例如說，漁夫外套的衣褶。

與其他較生硬的人物畫如《林中女子》相較，梵谷這兩件習作雖然身體結構的比例有些笨拙，但人物的塑造已比較有說服力。漁夫之妻的紅披肩與白帽子，在一片深灰綠與灰棕的背景前營造出適度的色調效果。另一方面，漁夫習作背景的輕軟灰色調較明亮。這顯示出它們是兩件不同的光線效果的習作，他後來在布拉邦會作更多這類的練習。很有可能當時和他同居的席恩是《漁夫之妻》的模特兒。頭大而身軀短的漁夫是個粗壯個子，但是梵谷有可能是以一位年輕人來當模特兒。就在畫這兩件習作之前，他給西奧的信中提到：「我有了一個模特兒——個住在這一帶的農場男孩，我已經向他提過這些習作的繪畫了。」無論如何，這件《漁夫》讓人聯想的，與其說是成人，更像是「捕魚的男孩」。

1. Hefting 1980，頁42； Vanbeselaere 1937， 頁III, 223-224, 413； Van der Mast & Dumas 1990，頁34。
2. 梵谷在1883年5月結識了Antoine Furnee，一位跟他一樣在戶外素描的測量員。(345/285, c. 20 May 1883).他的父親 Hendrik Jan Furnee 是海牙的一位化學師與顏料商，安東‧莫弗在他那裡買顏料，梵谷也在那裡買材料。參考Op de Coul &Tellegen 1995，頁95-96與Van Tilborgh &Vellekoop 1999，頁20-21。
3. Van Heugten 1996，頁197-200。

漁夫之妻 Fisherman's Wife
1883年8月初 1883 Early Aug.
紙本油彩裱於木板 oil on paper mounted on panel
51.6×33.9公分 51.6 x 33.9 cm
Collection Kröller-Müller Museum,
Otterlo, The Netherlands

漁夫 Fisherman
1883年8月初 1883 Early Aug.
紙本油彩裱於木板 oil on paper mounted on panel
51.1×32.8公分 51.1 x 32.8 cm
Collection Kröller-Müller Museum,
Otterlo, The Netherlands

梵谷在1882年的夏天畫了數幅森林風景，而這幅描繪森林邊緣的畫作也因此總是被判斷爲這一時期的作品。[1] 但經過研究，有幾個理由將這幅畫認定爲1883年夏天的作品。

首先這幅畫梵谷使用了帆布爲底，然而1882年夏天他是嘗試在紙上畫油彩的，稍後，有時是相當後期了，才再托裱在帆布或木板上。紙比帆布便宜的多，梵谷認爲使用比較昂貴、他財力又難以負擔的材料來進行初步的嘗試是種浪費。[2] 經過數個月的素描練習，梵谷在1883年7月再度作畫，他給西奧寫道：「今天我買了個寫生畫架和帆布。這畫架很不錯，因爲在戶外跪著工作總是弄得髒兮兮的。」（372/307，1883年7月29、30日）除了可以保持乾淨些，他也更容易以較高的角度作畫。一項對《森林邊緣》明顯的觀察是將之與1882年的森林風景習作比較，這幅畫的確是從較高的角度來作畫，這也表示梵谷非常可能就是在此使用了他新買的寫生畫架。雖然在信裡他告訴西奧他買了帆布，但是否將帆布使用於本畫還有待商確。技術檢驗顯示梵谷使用比較細緻的布料，也許是1平方公分的織物密度爲22×25的棉布，很有可能是由他自己打底的。[3] 他可能使用一般的布料碎片，如同他1883年9月4日給西奧的信裡寫道：「我把之前買來作爲我習作帆布的材料，剛給了她去做裙子……。」（384/319）此處的「她」是指席恩·霍爾尼克（Sien Hoornik），當時梵谷仍與她一起生活，但一週後梵谷便離開她到德倫特。也許他只取了部份布料給席恩，將剩下的布料用於畫作上。

就風格而言，這幅畫與較早的森林習作的相似處在於：圖樣簡單、前景帶模糊、重疊的筆觸；但其他的線索讓本幅作品更貼近德倫特時期，例如：梵谷上彩相當厚重卻也頗爲平均，而這種方式令人聯想到德倫特時期陰暗沉重的繪畫習作。後來他改變前景小路的途徑，在X光下，這條小路蜿蜒至左方的樹林中，還可看見左方前景的第二棵樹的樹幹，梵谷將蜿蜒小路改直，成爲更平靜的構圖。右方纖細的樹幹所呈現的沉穩條紋畫在天空枯淡的背景上，有點讓人想起柯洛（Jean-Baptiste-Camille Corot, 1796-1875），梵谷常在信中提起他。

1883年12月梵谷結束在德倫特爲期3個月的活動並準備與父母一起生活時，將畫作寄至努南，但當他1885年搬至安特衛普（Antwerp）時卻將畫留在努南的工作室。這幅畫放在其中一個衣櫥裡，和其他荷蘭時期的作品一起打包存放在梵谷家於布瑞達（Breda）的朋友—木匠史勞文（A. Schrauwen）先生處。梵谷牧師死後，1886年他的遺孀自寬敞的牧師住宅搬遷至較小的房子，部分的物品留在史勞文處。幾年後當她搬至列登（Leiden），除了裝滿畫作的衣櫥，其他存放的物品都取走了。或許這是故意的，因爲東西都被蛀蟲給蛀壞了，也或許就是忘記了。不論如何，梵谷頗爲大量的畫作留給了布瑞達的木匠，1902年他以1荷蘭盾將大部份的畫作賣給了當地作二手貨生意的庫弗爾（J.M. & J.C. Couvreur）兄弟。根據估算，他們手上一定有超過200幅梵谷的油畫和相等數量的素描。然而他們評估絕大部份的畫作一毛不值，並撕毀許多素描，不過也的確賣出了一些油畫和素描給廢物場和街市。這批「梵谷收藏」的殘餘部份，包括本幅《森林邊緣》，被二手商賣給了當地市民，一位名叫康奈利·毛文（Cornelis Mouwen）的裁縫師。此外，數幅油畫和素描則到了皇家軍事學院中尉威廉·梵貝寇（Willem van Bakel）的手上。毛文和梵貝寇都和鹿特丹（Rotterdam）的藝術經紀人歐典希爾（Oldenzeel）聯繫，他曾經在1903年主持過至少3次以梵谷畫作爲主的拍賣展。[4]

庫勒穆勒夫人最早爲人知的收藏清冊中，布瑞默在1915年曾註記著《森林邊緣》是「以110荷蘭盾購於1909年拜辛（Biesing）的拍賣會。」更有可能的是這幅作品購於1908年，因爲這是庫勒穆勒夫人第一幅購買的梵谷作品。至少根據一封1928年寫給住在卡爾斯盧何（Karlsruhe）的康斯勒（Kunsthalle）的費雪醫生（Dr. L. Fischel）信件，也許是由庫勒穆勒夫人的秘書所寫，解釋這批藏品是如何產生的。[5] 在這之前，總以爲《4朵結籽的向日葵》、《播種者（仿米勒）》與《有檸檬與瓶子的籃子》是最早的購藏畫作。[6]

1. De la Faille 看到與F8a的相似之處，並斷定這幅作品是1882年9月；Hulsker 1977與1996斷定爲1882年8月。

2. Van Tilborgh &Vellekoop 1999，頁19-20。

3. 技術性檢驗，庫勒穆勒美術館，2002年7月17日。「一般」的帆布通常是稍細緻的編織物：1平方公分的織物密度爲12-15×15-18。

4. Stokvis 1926，以及Op de Coul 2003。

5. 頁23，注釋4。

6. Van Deventer 1956，頁34-36。向日葵是1908年8月購得，其他2幅作品則是1909年3月。雖然購買的時間隔了半年，Van Deventer 稱這3幅作品是「首次購買」，並於1909年3月25日首次獲得購買畫作時，人尚在外旅行的庫勒先生的欣賞。或許他當時只看到《播種者（仿米勒）》與《有檸檬與瓶子的籃子》，這2幅的確才剛買到手。

森林邊緣　Edge of a Wood
1883年8至9月　1883 Aug.-Sep.
帆布油彩裱於木板　oil on canvas mounted on panel
33.8×48.5公分　33.8 x 48.5 cm
Collection Kröller-Müller Museum, Otterlo, The Netherlands

如同《耕地者》（Ploughman）這幅素描，《泥草屋（夜晚的泥炭小屋）》也可連結到一封書信裡的速寫。大約在1883年10月22日這一天所寫的一封信裡，梵谷為自己正在畫的兩幅油畫「塗鴉」，分別是《燒雜草》（Burning Weeds）與《泥草屋》，但是後者並未留存下來。[1]他寫信給西奧說：「這裡有兩幅傍晚的印象。我還在畫那幅燒雜草的人，就色調而言，它用油畫習作來畫會比我以前畫過的看起來好得多，所以它能更強烈地傳遞出平原與薄暮的逼近。而那個火焰，帶著點煙，是唯一的光點。我一次又一次在晚上去看，有個雨後泥濘的傍晚，我看到這間小屋，在它自然的環境下非常的美麗。」（399/335）《泥草屋（夜晚的泥炭小屋）》這幅墨水筆素描也應該是在這個脈絡下畫成的。[2]無論是在書信的速寫或是在素描本身，傍晚的印象都能清楚捕捉到。在素描裡，梵谷讓紙張原來的白色透過窗戶展現出來，也沒有在這個地方上任何淡彩，不像畫面的其他地方：看起來似乎房子裡正點燃著火光。這間小屋看起來像個泥草屋，也就是在泥煤田工作的人所住的簡單小屋。[3]

　　梵谷並沒有用鉛筆畫底圖。他直接用筆與黑墨水畫在直紋紙上，並且上了很多淡水彩。我們可以看到灰色與棕色的淡彩，但是或許梵谷並不是用兩種顏色的墨水來製造這種效果。棕色的淡彩看起來像是灰色淡彩褪色所造成的，而且也與使用的墨水多寡有關：比起鄰近畫得較疏鬆的區域（這裡主要是灰色的淡彩），在畫得較密的區域，淡水彩的棕色較為明顯。屋前的道路沒有墨水的線條，所以呈現為較一致的淺灰色；天空有較疏的交叉線，上了不平均的淡彩，因而有較深的灰色並帶有棕色色調。前景可以看到更多的變化。在沾滿墨水的區域，墨水線條本身是明顯的黑色，例如線條的尾端；但是較細的線條都已經褪色成棕色了。[4]在道路上，梵谷用尖銳的器具將紙刮開，或許不想讓顏色過於單調。黑色的人物是後來才畫的（小屋的線條穿過他的身上），而且因為下方代表陰影的線條與人物本身是分開的，所以人物看起來像是漂浮在小路上。

　　特別吸引著梵谷的，就是那些貧困的鄉間居民真正的、簡樸的居所，與這點相關的就是他偏好那種未受工業化所破壞的、真正的鄉間生活。在埃頓的時候，梵谷喜歡待在像het Heike這樣農民的小屋；在努南，他進入織工們的家；在法國南部海岸的聖瑪利德拉梅（Les-Saintes-Maries-de-la-Mer），梵谷的注意力放在那些老舊、漆成白色、帶著波浪屋頂的典型小屋。這些小屋甚至讓梵谷想起德倫特的泥草屋。（622/494，約1888年6月4日）[5]

---

1. 《燒雜草》的油畫習作留存了下來（F20，私人收藏）。
2. 儘管梵谷並沒有真的說小屋的速寫是根據一幅油畫習作，但是可能性相當高。如果不是這樣，他或許會指出一幅速寫是根據油畫，另一幅則是根據素描。
3. 整個德倫特地區都分佈著泥草屋，而這些小屋是用當地的材料（荒原的泥土、樹枝、蘆葦、粘土與泥煤塊）搭配木板、木條、（偶爾會用的）石頭所建成的。每間小屋都不一樣，有些會有石頭搭成的煙囪。儘管它們是泥煤田區域順應採泥煤季節而建造的臨時居所，但是通常人們會住在這裡很長一段時間（Van Tilborgh & Vellekoop 1999，頁43；Dijk & Van der Sluis 2001，頁101-111、207-209、及222-224）。
4. 畫的背面有清楚的墨水腐蝕的痕跡，據此可推斷梵谷在素描裡用的是鞣酸鐵墨水（iron gall ink）。
5. 梵谷來到德倫特沒多久就開始在Hoogeveen這裡畫泥草屋的素描及油畫，過程中發生了一件奇怪的事。梵谷說道：「在我坐著那間小屋的時候，有兩隻綿羊及一隻山羊走了過來，開始在小屋的屋頂上吃草。山羊沿著屋脊爬了上來，從煙囪往下看。有個婦女聽到屋頂上有聲音衝了出來，拿起掃帚往前述的山羊丟了過去，而山羊像羚羊那樣靈巧地跳了下來。」（389/324，約1883年9月15日）

泥草屋（夜晚的泥炭小屋）　Sod Hut (Peat Shed at Night)
1883年10月　1883 Oct.
黑色墨水筆（部分褪為褐色）、灰色暈染、直紋紙　pen in black ink (faded to brown in parts), grey wash, on laid paper
22.2×28.9公分　22.2 x 28.9 cm
Collection Kröller-Müller Museum, Otterlo, The Netherlands

在一封大約於1883年8月21日所寫的一封信中，梵谷第一次詳細地向西奧說明自己前往德倫特的計畫（381/316）。凡·拉帕德已經來拜訪他，讓他對拉帕德前往作畫的德倫特的鄉村非常渴望。一年前，凡·拉帕德曾在那個區域遊歷，那時梵谷曾寫信給他說：「你口中的德倫特讓我非常有興趣。我從未親自看過那個地方，而只是透過例如莫弗與ter Meulen從那裡帶回來的東西來認識那個地方。我想像那裏應該很像大約20年前我小時候所住過的Noord-Brabant。」（257/R11，1882年8月13日）[1] 人口稀少，相當貧困的德倫特在風景畫家之間相當受歡迎，因為它的廣大荒原與風景般的村落仍是未受破壞的風景。1882年，梵谷當時還沒有具體地想到要前往那個地方，但是到了1883年夏天，情況就不一樣了。現在梵谷決心要多花時間在成本較高的油畫上，所以他希望住在德倫特能夠讓他省錢，因為他覺得住在那裏應該會比住在海牙便宜。他也渴望鄉間生活：如同他告訴西奧的：「事實上，如果需要，我也可以在這裡找到便宜點的住所，而且我覺得這裡很美。即使如此，我還是想花點時間與自然獨處，離開城市。」（381/316）凡·拉帕德特別推薦德倫特的東南角，而梵谷快樂地說道：「等我到了那裡，我想我或許會永遠住在那荒原之間。有越來越多畫家去住在那裏，或許時間一久，某種畫家的群體就會出現。」最後，儘管有諸多計畫，梵谷還是只在那裏待了三個月。[2]

9月11日，梵谷搭火車前往Hoogeveen。三個星期之後，他搭乘渡輪沿著Verlengde Hoogeveense Vaart前往Nieuw-Amsterdam/Veenoord這個位於Emmen南方荒原的雙子村。

在這段漫長的航程中，梵谷畫了許多習作，並將其中四張習作畫在一張速寫的畫紙上，然後在抵達之後附在一封寫給西奧的信裡：梵谷在信中寫道：「在我畫的素描中，有一張畫的是渡輪上的一個小婦人，帽子上用別針別著黑紗，因為她正在哀悼中，另外還畫了一個帶著寶寶的媽媽，寶寶頭上還包著紫色的圍巾。」（395/330，約1883年10月3日）

《婦女頭像》很有可能也是在這次航行中完成的。這位婦女似乎是在相當近的距離被畫像的，畫紙幾乎容納不下，就好像畫家就坐在她的身邊，因而只有有限的空間。婦女的頭相當大，鼻樑很高很挺，幾乎帶著古典的風貌；她的雙眼很黑很空，嘴唇很寬而兩邊下垂。她的黑色帽子或許完全罩在黑紗裡，也或許是由黑色皺紗所製成的，暗示著她正處在哀悼之中，因此或許她的旅伴就是那位帽子上別著針的婦女。梵谷用墨水筆掌握住她沮喪、憂鬱的表情，因此這幅構圖或許不適合附在那張速寫畫紙裡。薄薄的織紋紙非常可能是用來畫速寫的那種信紙，兩者尺寸也幾乎相同。[3]

梵谷是直接用墨水筆畫在紙上，沒有先以鉛筆畫底圖，而且他或許畫的很快，在陰影部分的處理相當精準。他在某些細節上畫得特別用力，因此筆觸損壞了紙張（例如婦女的右眼部分）。在構圖的底部，漫不經心地塗上了點淡水彩。

Dijk與Van der Sluis相信這幅素描應該是梵谷前往Nieuw-Amsterdam不久之前在Hoogeveen所畫的。[4] 當地在9月28日舉辦了一場喪禮，梵谷也確實見證了這一點：「今天我在渡輪上見到一場喪禮，看起來很奇怪：有六位裹在斗篷裡的婦女坐在一艘船裡，男人則在運河岸邊拉著這艘船前進。」（394/329，1883年9月29日）按照兩位作者所說，如果他在喪禮前幾天的期間畫了這幅素描，那麼我們很難相信梵谷並未在信中提到這一點，尤其因為梵谷很難找到人當他的模特兒。[5] 畫家似乎也不可能應邀參加喪禮，就算應邀參加，也不應該只用信紙來畫。[6] 所以最可能的情況是，梵谷是在幾天之後在渡輪上遇到這位婦女（她很有可能也參加了喪禮），所以在船上他可以相對較不受打擾也未經允許地去畫這位婦女。

1. 在那個時候，Francois Pieter ter Meulen（1843-1927）與莫弗一樣都是著名的風景、牛群、特別是羊群畫家。
2. 梵谷本來想帶席恩一起去，但是最後決定讓兩人的關係告一段落（參見1883年8月18日到9月10日之間所寫的書信：378/313、382/317到387/322）。
3. 紙本身有相當多皺摺與毀損，或許是因為梵谷畫得很用力，而且早期它曾被貼在一張厚紙板上。Nijland的註解就是寫在這個紙板上，而目前這張紙板已經移除。紙的每個邊都有剪裁的痕跡，但是並不多，因為畫筆的線條幾乎都停留在邊緣上。Heenk 1995，頁90，認為這張紙是來自速寫本，但是可能性並不高。
4. Dijk & Van der Sluis 2001，頁123-127。
5. 從書信391/326到394/329之中，梵谷抱怨他在找模特兒上遇到的問題。在書信393/328中，他提到自己終於在農場裡找到一個模特兒，但是考慮到所用的紙，像《婦女頭像》這樣的墨水筆素描不可能是這樣的作品。
6. Dijk & Van der Sluis 2001，頁125-126指認出這位女性是某位Roelofje Faken（1857-1900）。但是他們的證據只不過是這個女性與死者住在同一條街上。

婦女頭像 Head of a Woman
1883年10月　1883 Oct.
黑色墨水筆（部分褪為褐色）、暈染、織紋紙　pen and black ink (faded to brown in parts), wash, on wove paper
21.1×13.5公分　21.1 x 13.5 cm
Collection Kröller-Müller Museum, Otterlo, The Netherlands

這幅墨水筆素描畫的是一個婦女在潮溼的路上推著獨輪車的小身影，背景是典型的德倫特的泥草屋或泥炭小屋，但是過去一直被歸爲努南時期的作品（1884年2月）。[1] 但是，不僅這背景的小屋是德倫特獨有的建築（而且這裡梵谷又把建築的正面畫錯了，把煙囪放到了屋頂的最前方），連獨輪車的樣式也都是傳統上在泥煤區域運送泥草使用，稱爲 *Slagkrooi*。[2] 另外，根據技巧與風格而言，這幅素描很明顯是在德倫特完成的。和其他德倫特的墨水素描（包括附在書信內的速寫）一樣，梵谷直接用筆畫在紙上。之後，在努南時期，梵谷又會重拾先用鉛筆打底圖的作法。除此之外，畫面上鬆散的交叉陰影線，以及塗鴉畫樹的方式都與其他德倫特時期的素描有許多共同點。[3] 下雨天或傍晚的效果（請注意婦女與獨輪車在溼地上的倒影）處理的非常不錯。

　　這幅素描或許是梵谷德倫特時期相當晚的作品，因爲他用的畫紙（一種較硬、充滿纖維、棕色的木質織紋紙）也是他在1883年12月間在努南畫素描所用的畫紙（梵谷在12月5日前往該地）。這些畫紙尺寸不一，來自兩本不同的速寫簿：大本的尺寸約爲20.5×28.5公分；小本的約爲15.9×25.4公分。[4] 目前很難斷定《推獨輪手推車的婦女》是來自那一本速寫簿，因爲畫紙的左側與下方都經過剪裁。只有上方與右側保留原來的邊緣，而右側還有帶著藍色顏料的殘膠痕跡，很可能是原來黏在速寫簿的邊緣。[5] 梵谷一定是在德倫特買到這種速寫簿，或是請人寄給他，然而書信中卻找不到相關的解釋。另外，目前已知的德倫特時期的素描中並沒有運用這種畫紙的同樣尺寸的畫作。

---

1. 例如De la Faille 1970、Hulsker 1977/1996（他認爲這可能是附在書信內的速寫）、庫勒穆勒美術館1980年之前的梵谷圖錄等。De la Faille 1928；Vanbeselaere 1937，頁237及410；Tralbaut 1959，頁215；Heenk 1995，頁91；Dijk & Van der Sluis 2001，頁245-247均將此幅素描歸於德倫特。
2. 參見Heenk 1995，頁91。
3. 可參見《泥草屋（夜晚的泥炭小屋）》。兩幅素描的背後都可以見到墨水腐蝕的痕跡，因此可推斷畫家用的是鞣酸鐵墨水。正面相對於墨水腐蝕位置處的墨水顏色較爲黯淡。
4. 參見Van Heugten 1997，頁31。
5. 梵谷美術館藏有8幅素描，用的是這兩本速寫簿上的畫紙（Van Heugten 1997，頁30-44；圖錄編號69-76）。這些畫紙邊緣都可以發現殘膠，有的是紅色的墨水痕跡，有的是藍色，據此可推斷畫紙的四邊都上了膠，而速寫簿的邊緣或許有藍色與紅色的大理石花紋（Van Heugten 1997，頁31）。《推獨輪手推車的婦女》除了右邊有藍色殘膠的痕跡之外，左上方也有些綠色的色點，但是目前並不清楚它們是否爲膠痕。

推獨輪手推車的婦人　Woman with Wheelbarrow
1883年11至12月　1883 Nov.-Dec.
黑色墨水筆（部分褪爲褐色）、織紋紙　pen in black ink (faded to brown in parts), on wove paper
21×13.1公分　21 x 13.1 cm
　　　Collection Kröller-Müller Museum, Otterlo, The Netherlands

1884年1月17日，梵谷當時64歲的母親在Helmond火車站下車時跌斷了大腿，傷在尷尬的部位，亦即恥骨附近。[1] 她被送上馬車載回努南。她復原得不錯但相當緩慢。大約在1月24日左右，梵谷寫信給弟弟說：「考慮到她現在的處境這麼困難，我很高興媽媽的精神相當平靜而滿足。」（429/355）在同一封信裡，梵谷也提到他為母親畫了一幅「大小樹叢所圍繞的教堂」的油畫，其中的教堂指的是位於努南的Papenvoort、建於1824年的教堂，梵谷的父親就是在這裡為一小群改革宗的教友講道。為了讓西奧清楚這幅畫的樣子，梵谷也隨信附上一幅油畫的小速寫。庫勒穆勒美術館所藏的素描非常可能就是這個主題最起初的速寫。[2]

　　梵谷先畫了一個基本的鉛筆素描，接著用墨水筆打了密實的陰影線。小小的教堂與前景部分上了淡水彩。天空的頂端還可以看見鉛筆的筆跡。前景的小型人物，一個肩上荷著鏟子的男人，並沒有先畫底圖或是留白，而是畫家後來添畫上去的。這個男性的人物並沒有出現在油畫裡，但這是因為梵谷後來將整個構圖改為教友走出教堂，因此他用顏料將這個男人蓋掉。透過X光可以看到他，但是位置較為偏左，是在教堂封起來的窗戶下方。在寄給西奧的那幅速寫中，他也是在那個位置。[3]

　　要添加這個荷著鏟子的人物無疑是受到米勒作品的影響。1875年，梵谷在巴黎的盧森堡博物館（Musee du Luxembourg）看到米勒於1871-1874年之間所畫的《格勒維爾的教堂》（*The Church at Greville*），當時他就大為讚賞。米勒的畫描寫一個肩上荷著鏟子的男性走過一個鄉村的、用石頭砌成的諾曼式鄉村教堂（36/29，1875年6月29日）。[4] 當梵谷在阿姆斯特丹準備研讀神學，曾經聽見教會傳來的歌聲中有一句「教會是奠基於岩石上（De Kerke Gods staat op een rots）」，立刻就讓他聯想到米勒的畫作。（136/116，1877年12月9日）當梵谷再一次在德倫特的Zweelo看到那間小小的教堂，又再次想起了那幅畫；儘管這時他看到的「不是荷著肩膀的農夫，而是一群綿羊在樹叢邊行走」，在信中他如此對西奧描述。（407/340，1883年11月2日）在畫這所教堂時，梵谷也畫了牧羊人與他的羊群（F877，私人收藏）。他將荷著鏟子的農人保留到給母親的畫，因為她暫時無法參與先生的教會禮拜。儘管努南的小小教堂不會直接讓梵谷聯想到米勒的畫，但是它就像格勒維爾的教堂一樣，是農民社群中的神之居所，而在畫中加入這個人物則會強調出這一點。

　　在1980年的修復過程中，我們發現素描的下方大約有4公分的範圍摺了進去並黏了起來。[5] 在這個區域有個坐著的男人的速寫。起初認為梵谷在這個地方畫了一個鐵匠，但是進一步思考顯示梵谷應該是畫了一個正在捲紗線的男人，[6] 所根據的是這個小型人物典型的姿態就和大型素描《捲紗線的男人》裡面人物的姿態非常類似。這裡的速寫並沒有將捲線軸畫出來，但是稍加努力就可以看出捲盤的頂部。這個男人用左手從捲盤的上方拉出紗線並用右手捲到小小的捲線軸上。

1. 參見書信424/352及425/353（兩封均為1884年1月17日）、426/353（1月18-19日）、427/R34（1月18-20日）。
2. 參見Van Tilborgh & Vellekoop 1999，頁61。
3. 相關X光照片請參見前引書。在庫勒穆勒美術館所藏的素描及油畫中，這個人物都在構圖的中央。在油畫裡，梵谷也將教堂放在畫面的中央，因次讓人物自然就位在封起來的窗戶下方。在隨信附上的速寫裡，這個人物站的位置偏向中央的左邊。
4. 米勒的這幅畫作現藏於奧賽美術館（Musée d'Orsay）。
5. Hoefsloot 1987，頁8-9。
6. Heenk 1994，頁39及1995，頁112相信這個人物是個鐵匠。

努南改革宗的教堂　The Reformed Church at Nuenen
1884年1月　1884 Jan.
鉛筆、墨水筆、黑色/褐色墨水、　pencil, pen and black/brown ink, light brown wash, on wove paper
淺褐色暈染、織紋紙　20.5 x 13 cm
20.5×13公分　Collection Kröller-Müller Museum, Otterlo, The Netherlands

1883年12月至1885年5月期間，梵谷以油畫、素描、水彩等媒材一共畫了35幅努南的塔樓。塔樓歷經歲月而頹圮不堪，1873年鎮議會考慮將其拆除。[1] 十餘年後，拆除工作於1885年5月開始進行。尖塔被拆卸下來，所有可再回收利用的建材則拍賣出售。「田間的舊塔樓正進行拆除」—梵谷在5月11日告訴他的弟弟，這天是廢棄建材的第一次公開拍賣，「這裡有個拍賣木材、石板、舊鐵，包括十字架的拍賣會。我用之前畫木材拍賣的風格再畫了幅水彩，我想，我畫得更好了。」[2]（505/408）到了1886年，塔樓便完全自地平線上消失。

《努南的舊塔樓》是梵谷最早以教堂塔樓為題材的油畫之一。這時拆除工作尚未開始，尖塔依然屹立。梵谷將之繪於沉重多雲的天空下。他以傳統風景畫的畫法—特別是梵雷斯達爾（Jacob van Ruisdael, 1628-1682）、康斯坦伯（John Constable, 1776-1837）與多比尼（Charles-François Daubigny, 1817-1878）的作品來描繪雲朵。還要再過幾年，他才會發展出自己的生動色彩詮釋天空。雖然塔樓是構圖上最主要的焦點，但它並不是唯一吸引觀眾注意力的地方。較不顯眼但持續出現的是有圍牆的墓園，牆頂有著突出的木十字架。

梵谷還住在海牙時，便深為這墓園所吸引。梵谷的父親於1882年8月初以改革宗的教會牧師身分搬至努南，其後於1885年3月30日葬於此。梵谷的父親與西奧曾告訴他有關墓園的事。[3]「我非常高興爸爸的來訪，並與他談天」，在1882年9月25日父親來訪後，他這麼告訴西奧—「我再度聽到許多有關努南的事，而且我總是想著那座有著老十字架的墓園。我希望在適當的時機能去看看並把它畫下來。」（270/234）塔樓和墓園對梵谷而言不只是個適合入畫的題材而已，對他個人而言也深具重要性。當他將新完成的畫作在1885年6月初寄到巴黎時，他給西奧寫道：「我略去了些細節，我

想要透過這廢墟表達的是，長久以來，農民便安息在他們終生耕植之處。我想要表達死亡與埋葬是多麼完美地簡單，就如同秋葉落下一樣的簡單：僅是一抔土、一個小木十字架。四周的田野是墓園草叢的止境，越過圍牆，形成一道地平線前的終線，就像海平線一樣。如今這廢墟告訴我，信仰和宗教如何地鏽蝕殆盡；雖然它們曾被紮實地建立下來，但農民的生與死則互古不變，如同墓地上茂盛的花草持續地萌芽與凋零。」（510/411）在這件1884年2月至3月的早期版本中，許多「細節」依然可見，像是位於田園中央、即將倒塌的牆面與停屍間就在塔樓的不遠處、左邊鋤地的農民代表田野的墾植。[4]

當梵谷完成《努南的舊塔樓》後，將畫作送給了43歲的瑪格特‧貝格門（Magot Begemann, 1841-1907），她住在教區牧師住宅旁的房子（Nune Ville）。梵谷與她在1884年1月發展出一段親密的情誼。[6] 喬‧梵谷—邦格（Johanna van Gogh-Bonger, 1862-1925）在她為1914年出版的，大伯的書信集中所寫的序言裡，描述瑪格特是「比梵谷年紀大的多，既不漂亮也沒有才華，但充滿活力且有顆易感的心。她和文生常常造訪村中貧困的人、也很常一起散步，很快地，她便從友誼墜入了情網。」[5] 他們在努南的情誼被瑪格特家人嚴密的監視。她甚至企圖自殺，並在一位醫生友人的照顧在烏特勒支住了6個月。梵谷在他後來的人生，一直對她懷有溫情。在聖雷米，當他計畫為母親和妹妹畫些習作的，他寫給妹妹薇兒「……我尤其想讓瑪格特‧貝格門有我的畫。但透過妳交給她似乎比我直接給她要來的謹慎些。」（814/W15，約1889年10月20至22日）。他可能忘了，當他還住在努南時曾經送過她2幅畫，以及幾幅水彩作品；比較可能的解釋是他想以較晚期的繪畫風格來紀念她。[7]

---

1. De Brouwer 2000，頁17。1800年左右教堂建物坍塌為廢墟，於19世紀初期淨空（同一出處，頁10-16）。

2. 梵谷所提「木材拍賣」指的是1884年1月的水彩作品《木材拍賣》（F1113）。

3. 西奧在8月中已告訴梵谷關於父母新居那座如畫般美麗的墓園。梵谷至少曾在1882年8月的信中回覆他：「我對於你說的父母新居的周圍環境非常感興趣。我迫不急待想親手畫畫如此悠久的教堂與有著沙地墳墓和老木十字架的墓園。我希望將來能有機會。」（259/226）

4. De Brouwer（2000，頁49）認為這個農民是Jacobus van Bakel，地籍圖上E區596號的所有人，該區毗鄰墓園。

5. Van Crimpen 1987，頁85。

6. Van Gogh-Bonger 1990，頁20。

7. 除了《努南的舊塔樓》以外，瑪格特‧貝格門也擁有油畫《有樹的小屋》和水彩作品《席凡寧根的縫衣婦人》、《漂白場》、《席凡寧根的婦人》。

努南的舊塔樓　The Old Tower at Nuenen
1884年2至3月　1884 Feb.-Mar.
油彩、帆布　oil on canvas
36×44.3公分　36 x 44.3 cm
Collection Kröller-Müller Museum, Otterlo, The Netherlands

梵谷以粗獷的筆觸來描繪這幅婦女頭像，他在奶油色基底上以濕畫法上彩，製作出不透明的表層以及些許的厚塗畫區（唇部及帽子），但可能因為搬運的關係，這些層次現在都已變平了。從梵谷的畫風考量，這件作品因其平滑的畫面反而更具特色。

婦人穿戴的綠色披肩以粗略的筆觸描繪，背景與披肩不同的綠色對比著帽子的溫暖大地色調。婦人的臉部僅局部完成，右眼幾不可見，只能從筆觸所呈現的弧狀起伏來察覺，左眼珠有特別增強亮度之處，給予婦人的臉部一種凝滯注視的表情。藉此他試圖描繪出具有表情特色的頭像。

梵谷在1884年12月至1885年1月間畫過此幅《婦人頭像》的素描，也因此為本幅畫作提供了創作年代的線索：1884年11月至1885年1月。[1]

最初畫布的尺寸是比較大的，但今四周尺寸皆被縮小了，所以原來的顏料塗層延伸出繃好的畫布邊緣外。

---

1. Van Heugten 1997，頁131。依此定年，這幅作品可能是3月31日或6月5或6日寄給西奧的第5或第6批作品中的一件：見Van Tilborgh & Vellekoop 1999，附錄頁238。

婦女頭像　Head of a Woman
1884年11月至1885年1月　1884 Nov.-1885 Jan.
油彩、帆布　oil on canvas
42.5×33.1公分　42.5 x 33.1 cm
Collection Kröller-Müller Museum, Otterlo, The Netherlands

梵谷在布拉邦所畫的所有素描中，有幾張畫紙在單張畫紙上畫了幾個獨立的速寫。庫勒穆勒美術館所藏的粉筆素描中有不同的人物習作、與1885年5月建築廢料拍賣相關的場景、以及其他單張的不同人物習作。從現存的梵谷努南時期的速寫簿中，有時候也會在單張畫紙上出現兩幅塗鴉，但是這裡所討論的這幅單張畫紙上的三幅（或者四幅）完全用墨水筆畫的小型素描（而且彼此間有點相互干擾）就梵谷所有作品而言仍然相當獨特。梵谷一定畫了更多這樣的墨水筆速寫，不過都沒有留存下來。

畫著這些速寫的畫紙原先應該稍微大一點，但是左右兩邊都經過剪裁，而且剪裁的位置相當逼近畫面本身，這點可從右側背景的淡彩以及左下角的小細線看得出來，兩邊都有相當粗糙的裁切痕跡。上下的邊緣都被撕開。然而，從殘存的浮水印可以看出，這張畫紙原來是從大約42x67公分大小的直紋紙中裁切出來的。這幅速寫的定年（1884年12月到1885年1月）主要是根據畫面上較大的婦人頭像，因為梵谷在1884年12月到1885年1月之間根據油畫的習作畫了一系列11幅速寫，為的是要讓西奧了解他當時的創作；從這系列速寫中，同樣的婦女出現了兩次（兩幅都在阿姆斯特丹的梵谷美術館）：一幅是她在暗的背景中（F1150r），另一幅則是在亮的背景中（沒有F編號：JH589）。後者畫在一張與本件作品相似但較小的直紋紙上，紙張上可以看到相同的浮水印。[1]目前很難確定本件素描上的女性頭像是否根據油畫畫作而來。這裡的女性頭像和前面所提到的兩幅有個很小但很重要的差異點。在三幅作品中的婦女都有垂到頸部、短而硬的頭髮，但是只有在梵谷美術館所藏的兩幅小型素描裡，她耳邊的頭髮才有較大的卷曲。除此之外，在本件作品裡，墨水流進她的眼睛。

畫面最上方的細小頭像似乎從下方頭像的腦部冒了出來，但其實它畫的時間更早一點。較大的速寫似乎是一種筆觸的實驗。模特兒明顯與短髮的女性頭像是同一人，但這次梵谷幾乎完全用垂直的影線來畫。這種畫法並沒有出現在梵谷其他的畫作裡，然而在某種程度上與他巴黎時期的兩幅鉛筆素描略微接近。

最後，在畫紙的最下方，梵谷畫了一個男人的背影：他沿著一條路前進，肩上擔著一塊木頭，右手則持著一把斧頭，斧頭的刃隱約可見。背景有個大型農場。梵谷將這個主題用許多線條框了起來，或許想先看看該用什麼樣的構圖來畫成大型的素描。然而，目前並沒有這樣的作品留存下來。[2]

1. Van Heugten 1997，圖錄編號108-118。在這兩幅墨水筆素描中，只有黑色背景的頭像所根據的油畫習作留存下來（F132，私人收藏）。
2. 參見帶著一捆樹枝的男人的小型粉筆素描（F1297，阿姆斯特丹的梵谷美術館）：兩幅作品有類似的框線。

速寫　Sketches
1884年12月至1885年1月　1884 Dec.-1885 Jan.
黑色墨水筆與畫筆、直紋紙　pen and brush in black ink on laid paper
17×10.7公分　17 x 10.7 cm
Collection Kröller-Müller Museum, Otterlo, The Netherlands

這幅《婦女頭像》是對背光效果的探索，強調的是突顯於背景的頭部形狀，至於臉部的造型與表情則完全被視爲次要。藍綠色的帽子融入深色的頭髮，分髮線的細緻線條下延至前額，帽子則以一筆帶過。背景是由不同色調的藍綠色組成，自婦人的右肩處漸次融入色調更深的區塊。這種似素描般筆法的明暗轉換，顯示梵谷意圖讓作品明確作爲明暗法效果的習作。

梵谷喜歡請努南的農民與織工穿戴日常服飾爲其作畫時的模特兒：「這裡的人似乎本能地穿著我所見過最美的藍色。他們以黑色與藍色爲經緯而編織成的粗亞麻布，製作出黑藍條紋的樣子。當顏色經過風雨洗刷而消褪後，變成令人無法置信的內斂細緻色調，更能突顯膚色。這種藍，藍得足以活化所有隱藏橘色元素的顏色，卻又消褪地剛好，不至於形成色調的不和諧。」（487/394，1885年2月）

婦女頭像　Head of a Woman
1885年3至4月　1885 Mar.-Apr.
油彩、帆布　oil on canvas
39.7×25.5公分　39.7 x 25.5 cm
Collection Kröller-Müller Museum, Otterlo, The Netherlands

1885年2月，西奧宣布他要試著讓他哥哥的一幅畫在即將來臨的沙龍展出，假如他有適合的作品的話。梵谷對此相當感激，但是手邊並沒有適合的作品，因此在信中寫道：「假如我在6個星期前就知道，我已經會試著為了這個目的寄點東西給你。現在我沒有什麼能夠寄給你的作品。你也知道，最近我幾乎都只是畫頭像，而且它們真的只是習作—也就是說，它們只適合待在畫室裡。」（488/395，約1885年3月1日）然而，西奧的畫確實讓梵谷開始思考要畫大型的構圖，最後催生出四月完成的《食薯者》（The Potato Eaters）。

　　在這個過程中，除了用油畫與素描進行頭像習作之外，梵谷也畫室內的勞動婦女，以增進自己對小房間內的光線掌握（而他的模特兒正是居住在這些小房間內）。這裡所討論的勞動婦女素描，包括兩幅《縫衣婦人》與一幅《爐邊削馬鈴薯的婦人》都與這個動機有關。

　　儘管梵谷在書信並未提到這些素描，但是在1885年3月，他提到了一幅室內人物的油畫習作，裡面他主要關注的則是背光的效果：「我正在想些更大、更細緻的事〔……〕也就是背向窗戶射進來的光的人物。我畫了這些人物的頭像習作，有的背光，有的面光，我也畫了幾次全身像：縫衣婦女捲著紗線或是削馬鈴薯的人物。有的是正面，有的是側面。這種效果很難，我不知道自己有沒有做好。」（489/396，1885年3月）在素描裡，縫衣婦女們並不是描繪在這樣的直接背光之下，而更接近側光的效果。

　　《爐邊削馬鈴薯的婦人》是梵谷努南時期全部畫作中已知最大型的素描。這幅大得不尋常的素描同樣有一幅較小的油畫版本，兩者在許多方面都有些差異。例如：在油畫中，火爐左邊有一把空的椅子，火堆上掛的是一把水壺而不是大湯鍋。在兩幅作品中，畫家似乎都專注在平均而陰暗的光源。在素描裡，他用粉筆的側邊掃在畫紙上，創造出背景的灰色調。在湯鍋背後的牆上沾滿煤灰的位置，畫家強化了黑色調。在他開始畫左側的人物之後沒多久，一定突然發現位置不夠，根本沒有空間容納那個人物，因為那裡幾乎連椅子都放不下。因此，現在坐在角落的這個戴著帽子的人物看起來似乎像個鬼魂。

縫衣婦人　Woman Sewing
1885年3至4月　1885 Mar.-Apr.
黑色粉筆、直紋紙　black chalk on laid paper
41.2×25.2公分　41.2 x 25.2 cm
Collection Kröller-Müller Museum, Otterlo, The Netherlands

爐邊削馬鈴薯的婦人　Woman Peeling Potatoes at the Fireside
1885年3至4月　1885 Mar.-Apr.
黑色粉筆、水彩紙　black chalk on watercolor paper
58.4×83.1公分　58.4 x 83.1 cm
Collection Kröller-Müller Museum, Otterlo, The Netherlands

縫衣婦人　Woman Sewing
1885年3至4月　1885 Mar.-Apr.
黑色粉筆、直紋紙　black chalk on laid paper
29.1×25.7公分　29.1 x 25.7 cm
Collection Kröller-Müller Museum, Otterlo, The Netherlands

大約在1885年5月11日左右，梵谷寫信告訴西奧：「最近這幾天，我都在努力畫素描。附近的居民正忙著拆除田野間的舊塔樓，所以也有一個公開的拍賣，要出售那些木頭、石板、還有舊的鐵器，包括十字架。我完成了一幅這個場景的水彩畫，用的是廢木拍賣的風格，但是畫得比較好一點，我是這麼覺得。」（504/408）不僅是這幅水彩畫留存了下來，在兩側所畫的三幅素描也可以直接連接到這次的拍賣。[1]

　　這次拍賣是在5月11日舉行，所賣的物品是拆除舊塔樓塔頂所剩下的建築材料。從留存下來的報告中可以得知市長Jan van Hombergh負責這次的拍賣，而他的助手有警官Johannes Biemans與木匠Theodorus de Vries。[2] 在第一幅素描的兩個地方可以清楚看到這位警官：在下方的群像中，他站在中央，並沒有像在水彩畫版本裡那麼突出於人群；在右上角，他正面向左方。從這裡我們可以推斷，梵谷是從另一邊來觀看整個場景。兩組群像之間夾著一個頭像的背影，脖子很細，戴著奇怪的領子與帽子。在下方群像的最左邊，有個戴著帽子的男人手上拿著一張紙，他很明顯不是市長，但或許是木匠De Vries。

　　在這組習作第二幅背面的下方，梵谷畫了舊墓園的一部分，其前景則堆著建築廢料。一個肩上荷著梯子的男人佔據這張畫紙的主要部分。透過留存下來的報告，我們知道這個人是誰。Francis van Engeland花了20分錢買下這座梯子。木匠De Vries則花了55分錢買下一扇門，然後這次拍賣就此結束。在1885年7月17日至1886年2月12日之間又再舉行了5次拍賣，但是就目前所知梵谷並沒有將它們記錄下來。[3]

---

1. 第三幅習作（F1231r/v）與這幅水彩畫目前都藏於梵谷美術館（Van Heugten 1997，頁185-191）。
2. 相關報告出版於De Brouwer 2000，頁75與78-79。
3. 參見De Brouwer 2000，頁79。

扛梯子的男人，人物群像，有木十字架的墓園
1885年
粉筆、紙
34.5×20.5公分

Man with Ladder, A Group of Figures and Cemetery with Wooden Crosses
1885
chalk on paper
34.5 x 20.5 cm
Collection Kröller-Müller Museum, Otterlo, The Netherland

建築廢料拍賣（習作）　Sale of Building Scrap (Studies)
1885年5月　1885 May
黑色粉筆、直紋紙　black chalk on laid paper
35×21公分　35 x 21 cm
Collection Kröller-Müller Museum,
Otterlo, The Netherlands

梵谷在1884年的6月底夏天畫了兩幅織工的油畫，包括這件《紡織機與織工》。他在給西奧的信中描述它：「是個開有三扇可以看見黃色草地的小窗戶的室內；黃色草地與織布機上的藍色布料，和另一種織工的工作服的藍色，形成對照。」(454／372，1884年7月初）這段敘述顯示了梵谷用畫家的眼光來觀察織工的程度。他當時對這間陰暗的工作室感興趣的是「林布蘭式」（Rembrandtesque）的明暗對比（chiaroscuro）。織工的服裝、織布機上的布匹與背景的風景一起形成種種不同的藍與綠色調子交錯的景色。梵谷稱爲「木頭怪物」的織布機則顯示出另一種棕色與黑色的豐富變化。光線與色彩的運用加強了室內與室外的對比。

　　在這幅畫作中梵谷以織工典型的姿態描寫了織工在織布機前的樣子：左臂前伸，用板條將緯線打進去，右臂稍微舉起，來回穿梭連著投梭帶的梭子。梵谷因爲畫人物畫的困難，描繪的織工很少

變化，可能也因爲他的財務困難－他必須節省顏料，而且他也請不起模特兒來畫較費時的人物習作。結果就是重覆描繪姿態類似的織工。

　　《紡織機與織工》大約作於1884年6月底或7月初，是梵谷織工油畫中較晚期的一例。他對這些技工的興趣產生了一系列重要的作品。當他在1883年底和1884年初開始畫織工時，他還很缺乏油畫創作的經驗。經由持續的練習，他顯然逐漸熟悉這項媒材的技巧潛能。他實驗色彩與色調的變化，也成功地在平面的畫布上描繪出複雜的立體的織布機。

　　梵谷有很長的時期對織工的題材充滿興趣，但在1884年上半年，他在努南充分地投入這個題材之後，就突然停止了。這大約發生在1884年盛夏，他突然將對家庭織工的興趣轉移到農夫的生活與工作上。

紡織機與織工　Loom with Weaver
1884年6至7月　1884 Jun.-Jul.
油彩、帆布　oil on canvas
61×93公分　61 x 93 cm
Collection Kröller-Müller Museum, Otterlo, The Netherlands

七月向來是收割小麥以及綑綁麥束的月份，也是這幅油畫所描繪的場景：大約是1885年的夏天時節，五、六捆的麥束彼此傾靠一起。

畫作的構圖區分為數個不同的平面：前景梵谷畫的是剛收割、留有短小殘梗的麥田；背景則是尚未收割的麥田，遠處是與之相連的森林邊緣與其上的天空。這些層次藉由麥束醒目而直立的元素予以襯托。梵谷主要的意圖似乎在於練習質地與筆觸。他運用頗為有力的筆觸，以油彩摹畫剛收割、留有殘梗的麥田，但卻以細筆細緻地描繪出麥束纖長的莖桿。他通常以細筆刷完成細節處，像是他所描繪的鳥巢便是如此。與常見的梵谷畫作不同，這幅畫作畫在淺色的底色上，他先畫好天空，才在空白處描繪麥束。

《麥束》因其主題：單獨的麥束堆，而在梵谷的所有作品中有其獨特的地位。麥束也出現在不同的素描中，但以田間成排或數排的方式呈現，通常還繪有綑綁麥束的人物於其中。後來在阿爾與聖雷米，梵谷的創作靈感依然受到金黃麥田的啟發，他畫了數十幅有著麥田或麥束的作品。成捆的麥束有時也出現在這些作品中，但多為風景中的一部份，而不是像此幅畫將之放置於前景中醒目顯著的地方。

麥束　Sheaves of Wheat
1885年7至8月　1885 Jul.-Aug.
油彩、帆布　oil on canvas
40.2×30公分　40.2 x 30 cm
Collection Kröller-Müller Museum, Otterlo, The Netherlands

這幅畫中所呈現的農民是梵谷喜歡的樣子：揮汗辛苦工作著，過著艱辛的農民生活。早些時候在埃頓和海牙時，掘地的農民是梵谷素描的主題，與縫衣服的人和織工成為他在荷蘭時期作品的主要題材。不過不像縫衣服的人和織工，梵谷並未將這農民置於鄉間的環境中。這裡梵谷主要專注於人物本身的重現—他也對此畫了素描—與他的服裝。2月時他告訴西奧他認為農民簡單的服裝能有多好看：「這裡的農民通常穿著藍色的衣服，那種藍，在成熟的麥田中，或倚著山毛櫸籬笆枯萎的落葉時，不同深淺藍色褪色的些許色差，透過金色調與紅棕色的對照，讓顏色活了起來，美麗非常，一開始便令我屏息。」（487/394）肩上的光線讓粗糙的藍綠色工作服布料與農民臉上、手上的暗紅膚色相互對照。

梵谷知道他並沒有依循學院教授的解剖比例規則來描繪人物。在1885年7月寫給西奧的長信中（522/418），他為此辯解，將他自己與學院派畫家亞歷山大・卡巴內爾（Alexandre Cabanel）與葛斯塔夫・傑奎特（Gustave Jacquet）所畫的人物相對照，他們的人物「總是以相同的方式表現手腳與身體結構：也許迷人、比例正確又符合人體結構。」但這不是梵谷想要的，他認為自己的理念從其他畫家的例子得到支持，像是喬瑟夫・依瑟列（Jozeg Israëls）、奧諾雷・杜米埃（Honoré Daumier）、里歐・雷赫密特（Léon Lhermitte）：「舉例來說，當依瑟列、杜米埃或雷赫密特畫人物時，你更能感受到身體的形態，但是一這正是我為何特別提及杜米埃一比例幾近獨斷，解剖與結構在學院派人士眼裡更是一無是處。但這種人物畫才有生命。」他敦促西奧挑戰畫家查爾斯・西瑞特（Charles Serret），此人曾向西奧表達對《食薯者》中人物的批評，梵谷認為西瑞特：

> 告訴西瑞特如果我的人物畫是好的，我會感到絕望，告訴他我並不想要他們是結構上正確的，告訴他我指的是，如果有人照相拍了一個掘地者，那麼那個人物就一定不會是在掘地。告訴他我覺得米開朗基羅的人物非常動人，儘管他們的腿太長，臀部太寬。告訴他在我看來，米勒和雷赫密特才是真正的畫家，因為他們不照著事物的模樣畫，不依循枯燥的分析作畫，而是照著他們，米勒、雷赫密特和米開朗基羅，對於這些對象的感覺來作畫。告訴他我最大的願望就是顯示這樣的不精確、這樣真實的偏差、修正和更改，這些可能都是，怎麼說呢，「謊言」，但卻比拘泥字義的事實還要真實。

梵谷想要重製「活動中的農民」：「農民必須真的是農民，正在掘地的人物必須真正掘地著。」他覺得那才是重製人物之獨特處所在，以及「現代的本質，現代藝術的核心，不是希臘、亦非文藝復興或傳統荷蘭畫派曾做到的。……農民或工人的人像開始是一種『繪畫』，但今天，在永遠的大師米勒的引導下，這已成為現代藝術的本質而且永遠會是如此。」

掘地者　Digger
1885年8月　1885 Aug.
油彩、帆布　oil on canvas
45.4×31.4公分　45.4 x 31.4 cm
Collection Kröller-Müller Museum, Otterlo, The Netherlands

經過多幅為了創作《食薯者》而畫的頭像與農家室內的人物習作，1885年夏秋時節，梵谷花了許多時間在戶外速寫田裡工作的農民。掘地是常見的主題，庫勒穆勒夫人也擁有數件以此為主題的作品，包括本幅描繪正在挖掘馬鈴薯的2名農婦。這件作品可能是根據1件較早的2名掘地農婦的速寫而畫的，這幅速寫也是庫勒穆勒美術館的藏品。

梵谷無疑地是借用米勒的畫題。早在1880年10月，他靠借來的照片臨摹米勒著名的《掘地的農民》（1856）。[1]他也曾讀過一段1881年由宋思爾（Alfred Sensiers）所寫的《米勒的一生與作品》（*La vie et l'oeuvre de J.-F. Millet*），並在信中提到：「在犁過的田裡，但有時也在很少犁過的區域，你看見以鏟子或尖鋤掘地的人們，這些人不時會直起身來以手背擦拭額頭。『你必汗流滿面才得糊口』。」[2]掘地者的辛勞喚起米勒特定的宗教聯想，在《創世紀》第3章第19篇：「你必汗流滿面才得糊口，直到你歸了土……」梵谷亦對掘地有著相同的聯想。[3]

在《挖掘馬鈴薯的二名農婦》中，梵谷盡其所能地描繪工作中的2名人物。「從我的速寫，你可以看到，我特意描繪她們是在活動之中，顯示她們正在做某件事」。梵谷告訴凡‧拉帕德，並在信中畫了這個場景的小素描來說明。凡‧拉帕德也讓他的畫中人物彎下腰來表現「活動」，他回信寫道：「至少你構圖中的其中一個人已經彎著腰，我認為這相當不錯。構圖中有相當多的垂直線條，這也許會讓工作正在進行的事實更難表達出來。」（529/R57，1885年8月下旬）對梵谷而言，訣竅在於讓掘地者真正在掘地。

---

1. 「我以米勒為範本畫了掘地者，我在施密特（Schmidt）家找到布勞恩（Braun）攝影的照片，並請他借給我，還包括《晚禱》」，梵谷在1880年11月1日從布魯塞爾寫給西奧的信中提到（159/138）。仿米勒《晚禱》的素描亦是庫勒穆勒美術館的館藏。
2. 譯自 Kōdera, 1978，頁60。
3. 見梵谷1883年3月30日與4月1日寫給西奧的信函（335/277）。

挖馬鈴薯的農婦　Peasant Women Digging Up Potatoes
1885年8月　1885 Aug.
油彩、帆布　oil on canvas
31.5×42.5公分　31.5 x 42.5 cm
Collection Kröller-Müller Museum, Otterlo, The Netherlands

由於《食薯者》受到嚴厲批評，梵谷開始畫許多小幅習作，努力給予人物更多體積與生命。接著在1885年夏天，他也開始創作大型的人物素描。這個時期留下了約50件作品，可以看成一組具有共通點的作品。[1] 其中有19幅作品現藏於庫勒穆勒美術館，而本文的討論會依據主題將它們分為兩組：以收穫為主題的習作（收割、捆麥束、拾穗、堆乾草等）和以其他活動為主題的素描。第一組也包括了一幅有收割者的小型素描以及兩幅收穫的構圖，因為它們主題相關並且完成於相同的時期。也因為同樣的原因，第二組也包括了一幅小型的人物習作《劈木柴的農婦》（Peasant Woman Chopping Wood）。

大致上，這些素描很難精確地定出創作時間。在6月21或22日，梵谷寫信給西奧：「每天我都認真地畫人物素描，但是我至少要畫一百張這樣的素描，甚至更多，然後才算完成〔……〕現在快到收穫的時間，所以我一定要畫收割和挖馬鈴薯這兩種活動。到那個時候，要找模特兒就更難了，但是這還是必須的。」（514/414）7月初的時候梵谷在信中寫到他畫了不少，其中包括一幅婦女「彎腰拾麥穗」的素描。（519/416）然而，他不太可能在那個時候的田間看到這種景象，因為麥穗的收割時間還要再晚一點。他的解決方法應該是在很長一段時間讓模特兒擺出各種與收穫相關的姿勢，但是等到這些活動本身已經開始，他就可以親自下田觀察。8月6日西奧到努南拜訪，梵谷留了一封信給西奧與母親，信中寫道：「人們在麥田裡收割，所以我今天很忙，因為你也知道，這個活動只會持續幾天，也是最美好的一件事之一。」（524/419）

從梵谷的書信中我們可以看到，他一直到9月都還在畫人物習作，因此這些畫作多半都概括為7月到9月間完成。在9月間，梵谷越來越難找到模特兒，因為「神職階級的可敬紳士們」覺得梵谷和他的模特兒們太過親近，因此建議他們不要再擔任他的模特兒。（532/423，1885年9月初）由於我們知道梵谷聽從了西奧在8月間來訪時所給予的建議（如果要讓這些素描有市場價值，就要畫「多一點周遭事物」），因此有幾幅作品可以稍微精確地確定為8月至9月，例如《鋤地的農夫》與《工作中的農夫》。

這裡所討論的人物習作全都是用黑色粉筆畫在織紋紙上，只有水平的《捆麥束的農婦》是畫在直紋紙上。梵谷塗在粉筆畫上的定色劑通常和他在海牙時期畫在鉛筆素描上的一樣，都是一種牛奶加水的溶液。[2] 他不會將這種溶液塗在整張畫紙上，通常只塗在人物的周圍，所以在收割者與其他田野的勞動者身體的輪廓線外圍通常會看到彎曲的紙張褪色痕跡。有一、二張畫可以看得出來畫家是把定色劑甩到畫紙上。梵谷偶爾也會用定色劑調成淡彩塗滿整張畫紙，等到乾了之後再用擦子或麵包屑來塗擦，以創造出更明顯的皺摺並且強化色調。在沒有使用定色劑的地方，他會用畫筆沾水塗在粉筆的筆觸上，創造出美麗的灰色調。那個夏天最後的結果就是創造出令人印象深刻的一系列農民工作者全部活動的人物素描，而這也正是他的意圖所在。在1885年7月寫給弟弟的一封長信裡，梵谷仔細地解釋了他的意圖（522/418）。在巴黎，西奧將梵谷的作品（主要是油畫）帶給畫商Alphonse Portier（1841-1902）及畫家兼石版畫家查爾斯·西瑞特（1824-1900）等人看，而他們的看法並不負面。梵谷立刻抓住這個機會要繼續說服兩人接受自己的觀念。梵谷寫信給西奧說：「當我寄給你與西瑞特幾幅掘地者或農婦除草、

拾麥穗等的素描時，那些是一系列田野間各種活動素描的起初幾幅作品，因此你和西瑞特或許會在其中發現缺點；我承認會有這些缺點，而知道他們對我也會很有幫助。」這些評語立刻讓我們想起梵谷曾經與凡·拉帕德針對他所畫的人物的扁平有過的討論；因為雖然梵谷在信中提到他願意承認這些錯誤，但是他同時也擔心在他試圖用自己的方式來達成某個目標時，其他人會用技術的好壞來評斷他。

在信中，梵谷一開始並不能夠精確地描述他的意圖為何。他不能夠，也不願意依照受過學院訓練的畫家如Alexandre Cabanel等人畫裸體的方式來畫農民，而為了替自己辯護，他援引了自己最愛的畫家，例如Leon Lhermitte、米勒、依瑟列、杜米埃等人的作法，而這些人所關心的並不在於比例正確上。梵谷說：「我這樣說還不夠清楚。告訴西瑞特如果我的人物畫是好的，我會感到絕望，告訴他我並不想要他們是結構上正確的，告訴他我指的是，如果有人照相拍了一個掘地者，那麼那個人物就一定不會是在掘地。告訴他我覺得米開朗基羅的人物非常動人，儘管他們的腿太長，臀部太寬。告訴他在我看來，米勒和雷赫密特才是真正的畫家，因為他們不照著事物的模樣畫，不依循枯燥的分析作畫，而是照著他們，米勒、雷赫密特和米開朗基羅，對於這些對象的感覺來作畫。告訴他我最大的願望就是顯示這樣的不精確、這樣真實的偏差、修正和更改，這些可能都是，怎麼說呢，『謊言』，但卻比拘泥字義的事實還要真實。」在他寫作這一段畫的時候，心裡一定想著那時他正在創作的這一系列人物習作。

從書信中我們也發現，梵谷一直希望能將這些大型的素描寄給西奧，希望透過他帶給西瑞特，但是他卻發現自己很難割捨這些作品。他寫道：「因為我正在畫其他的素描，需要它們來準備畫油畫。我將會需要它們來畫我的人物，而這些人物的大小終究不會超過一個指幅（span），可能會更小；所以畫中的一切都會更加集中。」（521/417，約1885年7月中旬）梵谷所說的「指幅」指的是成年男性手掌張開時拇指尖到小指尖的距離，大約是22公分。[3] 這些素描裡的人物通常是這個尺寸的兩倍大，所以畫家可以更用心來處理細節，這樣會有助於將來處理人物較多的構圖中較小的人物。

梵谷或許正在計畫要畫大型的油畫構圖以及規模較小的油畫，而他為此做準備的方式就是透過許多素描的習作，這不禁讓人想到當年較早的時候他處理《食薯者》的方式。[4] 就本文討論的作品來看，梵谷很明顯想要畫一個收穫的場景，因為他畫的這組習作中許多都是收割者、農婦綑綁麥束等等。

就《鋤地的農夫》與《工作中的農夫》這兩幅素描而言，梵谷在背景用兩座農舍填滿，但以描繪的細緻度來說是《鋤地的農夫》較高。在後者中，農人在做什麼也比較清楚。以畫家對細節的注意及畫作精確的完成度而言，這幅素描是這組作品中少數足堪視為成熟的素描而非僅僅是習作的作品。然而，梵谷並未在畫作上簽名。右下角的簽名並不是真的，就像這組畫作中絕大多數的簽名一樣〔均非梵谷本人所為〕。

在《堆乾草的農婦》美麗、直接、流動的構圖中，梵谷成功地也相當有說服力地描繪了拋擲乾草的活動。農婦專注地看著乾草，身體呈現出稍微扭曲的姿態，散發出相當大的能量。因此，我們不容易注意到木製耙子的下半部畫得有點笨拙且比例錯誤。

《工作中的農夫》背景右方的農舍，就像《鋤地的農夫》一

樣，可以連結到《掘地的農婦》（F89，私人收藏）裡的農舍，可以從側面看到其建築。

《有收割者與拾穗農婦的麥田》的這幅素描上，梵谷用了許多工具，其中他用海綿在構圖的大部分區域塗上淺灰色的淡水彩，接著再用黑色粉筆來勾勒，用擦子或其他尖銳的工具擦出較亮的色調。後者可以在兩個人物、右側的麥田、前景的麥束上看到他再次

用擦子將天空的某些部分擦開。而梵谷主要用的是一種非常黑的，或許是石版畫蠟筆來勾勒。

《捆麥束的農婦》底部的麥束原來更接近左側，超過農婦的木屐，但是梵谷修正了過來。右側他也先用畫筆及水在沾染了粉筆的地方塗上淡水彩，然後再塗上定色劑。定色劑只塗到左側麥束的下半部，而這個區域也先上過淡水彩了。

---

1. 參見Van Heugten 1997，頁222。
2. 這樣的技巧，梵谷是從Armand Cassagne於1873年所著的*Guide pratique pour les différents genres de dessin*這本教科書中學到的（參見Van Heugten 1997，頁239）。
3. 參見Van Heugten 1997，頁237。
4. 同前書，頁223。

有收割者與拾穗農婦的麥田　Wheat Field with a Reaper and a Peasant Woman Gleaning
1883至1885年　1883-1885
粉筆、油畫顏料、紙　chalk and paint on paper
24.5×34公分　24.5 x 34 cm
Collection Kröller-Müller Museum, Otterlo, The Netherlands

鋤地的農夫　Peasant with a Hoe
1885年7至9月　1885 Jul.-Sep.
粉筆、紙　chalk on paper
43.6×32.8公分　43.6 x 32.8 cm
Collection Kröller-Müller Museum, Otterlo, The Netherlands

堆乾草的農婦　Peasant Woman Making Hay
1883至1885年　1883-1885
粉筆、紙　chalk on paper
56.5×44.4公分　56.5 x 44.4 cm
Collection Kröller-Müller Museum, Otterlo, The Netherlands

拾穗農婦的正面　Peasant Woman Gleaning, Seen from the Front
1883至1885年　1883-1885
粉筆、紙　chalk on paper
52×37.7公分　52 x 37.7 cm
Collection Kröller-Müller Museum, Otterlo, The Netherlands

工作中的農夫　Peasant Working
1883至1885年　1883-1885
粉筆、紙　chalk on paper
44×33.1公分　44 x 33.1 cm
Collection Kröller-Müller Museum, Otterlo, The Netherlands

收割的農夫　Peasant Reaping
1883至1885年　1883-1885
粉筆、紙　chalk on paper
53.2×36.7公分　53.2 x 36.7 cm
Collection Kröller-Müller Museum, Otterlo, The Netherlands

擦洗鍋子的婦人　Woman Scouring Pots
1883至1885年　1883-1885
粉筆、紙　chalk on paper
54.5×43.7公分　54.5 x 43.7 cm
Collection Kröller-Müller Museum, Otterlo, The Netherlands

捆麥束的農婦　Peasant Woman, Binding a Sheaf of Grain
1885年　1885
粉筆、紙　chalk on paper
55.1×43.4公分　55.1 x 43.4 cm
Collection Kröller-Müller Museum, Otterlo, The Netherlands

捆麥束的農婦　Peasant Woman Binding Wheat Sheaves
1885年8月　1885 Aug.
粉筆（暈染）、紙　chalk (washed) on paper
44.7×58.5公分　44.7 x 58.5 cm
Collection Kröller-Müller Museum, Otterlo, The Netherlands

1885年4月，梵谷正忙著爲《食薯者》這幅畫做素描與習作當作準備，這時他讀到Jean Gigoux（1806-1894）所寫的《論時代藝術家》（Causeries sur les artistes de mon temps）這本書；這本書是在當年年初出版，由西奧所寄來。[1] 書中有段德拉克洛瓦（Delacroix）的話在梵谷心中留下深刻的印象，讓他在幾個月後又在信裡提到這段話，在9月一封給凡·拉帕德的信中詳盡地說明：「畫家Gigoux帶著一座古董的青銅雕像給德拉克洛瓦看，想問他覺得這座雕像是不是真的：『Ce n'est pas de l'antique, c'est de la renaissance』（這不是古典時期的，是文藝復興的）德拉克洛瓦這麼說。Gigoux問爲什麼，而他說：『Tenez, mon ami, c'est très beau, mais c'est pris par la ligne, et les anciens prenaient par les milieux (par les masses, par nouaux)！』（朋友，你看這裡，這是很美，但是它的起點是線，而對於古人而言，起點是中間（是質量、核心）。）而且他又補充說：『你看著』，然後再線上畫了幾個橢圓形，然後小小的、幾乎看不見的線條來連接這些橢圓，並且因此創造出一匹以後腿站立的馬，充滿生命與動態。他說：『傑利柯（Gericault）與格羅（Gros）從希臘人身上學到這一點，用來先表現質量（幾乎都是蛋形），從這些橢圓形的位置與比例來描寫輪廓線與動作。而我呢，』德拉克洛瓦說，『是從傑利柯那裡第一次聽到這個方法的。』現在我要問你，這難道不是個美好的真理嗎！但是……我們會從石膏像或是素描學校學到這些嗎？我想不會。如果先這麼教學生，那麼我會很高興地成爲學院熱情的崇拜者，但是我非常清楚事實並非如此。」（533/R58）

幾個月之前，凡·拉帕德嚴厲批評了梵谷《食薯者》這幅石版畫，覺得人物的處理太弱。儘管梵谷對凡·拉帕德無禮的批評相當憤怒，但是他當然也把他的論點謹記在心，因此德拉克洛瓦所說的，不要從線條（或者說輪廓線）開始畫，而是從體積開始畫，就成了梵谷新的座右銘。在大約4月13-17日寫給西奧的一封信裡，他甚至表現出自己已經這麼畫了一段時間，只是不知道該怎麼稱呼這種方式：「『les anciens prenaient par les milieux』意思是說從體積的圓或橢圓的基礎開始，而不是輪廓線。我在Gigoux的書中發現了這句話的原文，但是這個事實已經在我心中好長一段時間。」（497/401）無論實情如何，在完成《食薯者》這個計畫之後，梵谷就投身於人物素描，因爲連遠在巴黎的西奧收到梵谷寄去的話都曾指出人物太過扁平。大約在5月11日左右，梵谷寫信給西奧說：「這就是爲什麼我想到要用相當不同的方式來嘗試，例如從軀幹開始畫，而不是從頭部。」（505/408）在同一封信中，他提到：「這些日子我又再次忙著畫人物素描。」有爲數甚多的一組小型人物習作，包括本文討論的作品，都可以連結到梵谷的這句話，因此應該是在1885年5月到6月間完成的。[2]

就這些黑色粉筆所畫成的習作而言，梵谷通常用與過去不同的方式來畫，雖然它們當然不是由蛋形建構起來的，但是從許多人物的造型可以看出梵谷如何將德拉克洛瓦的話謹記在心。這裡面所有的人物最令人注意的特徵就是他們都相當矮壯，這當然代表畫家主要關心的是質感與體積。輪廓線通常較不重要，也有明顯的斷裂。《行走的農夫》、《行走的婦人》、《扛棍而行的農夫》這幾幅畫都清楚地顯示出梵谷是從蛋形開始畫，而從《扛棍而行的農夫》裡可以看到這有時會創造出奇怪的螺旋效果。梵谷希望透過這種新的素描方式來爲他的人物注入更多的活力：「目前，透過手掌與手臂的素描，我正努力實踐德拉克洛瓦針對素描所說過的話：『ne pas prendre par la ligne, mais par le milieu』（不由捕捉線條，而由捕捉中心體積而成）。這給我足夠的機會從蛋形開始。我努力要達成的不是畫出一隻手，而是畫出姿勢，不是一顆在數學上正確的頭顱，而是整體的表情。舉例來說，要畫出掘地者抬起頭聞聞吹過來的風或是說話。簡單來說，就是生命。」（505/408，約1885年5月11日）

1. 最早提到這點的是一封信：495/399，約1885年4月11日。
2. 這批素描的總數將近40幅，多半都在庫勒穆勒美術館與梵谷美術館（參見Van Heugten 1997，頁196-214）。這些素描都是畫在織紋紙上，紙上有VdL的浮水印或者（因爲梵谷通常會將大張的畫紙分成兩張來畫這些素描）是其副標誌，亦即畫有戴著皇冠的獅子、軍刀、及CONCORDIA RES PARVAE CRESCUNT這個字樣的紋章。

挂棍而行的農夫　Peasant Walking with Stick
1883至1885年　1883-1885
粉筆、紙　chalk on paper
34×19公分　34 x 19 cm
Collection Kröller-Müller Museum, Otterlo,
The Netherlands

行走的婦人　Woman Walking
1883至1885年　1883-1885
粉筆、紙　chalk on paper
34.5×21公分　34.5 x 21 cm
Collection Kröller-Müller Museum, Otterlo,
The Netherlands

農夫的人像習作　Three Figure Studies of a Peasant and a Head Seen from Behind
1883至1885年　1883-1885
粉筆、紙　chalk on paper
21×34.8公分　21 x 34.8 cm
Collection Kröller-Müller Museum, Otterlo, The Netherlands

行走的農夫　Peasant Walking
1883至1885年　1883-1885
粉筆、紙　chalk on paper
35×21公分　35 x 21 cm
Collection Kröller-Müller Museum,
Otterlo, The Netherlands

工作中的農夫　A Peasant Working
1883至1885年　1883-1885
粉筆、紙　chalk on paper
34.7×20.7公分　34.7 x 20.7 cm
Collection Kröller-Müller Museum,
Otterlo, The Netherlands

布瑞默（H.P. Bremmer）在1939年寫道：「梵谷無疑的將這幅畫作視爲一件自畫像。」他認爲這是梵谷最好的自畫像之一，可看出這位藝術家天才的力量：「我想說的是，他並非是爲了要畫一幅詳盡的、分析式的習作，才把自己當成畫題；相反的，他的目的是要將自己眼中的自己，作爲一個人的整體畫下來。」[1]梵谷在巴黎時期畫了大約25幅（大部份爲小尺寸）的自畫像，比任何其他時期還多，也有可能是因爲缺乏請模特兒的錢。最早的幾幅仍舊是以相當保守的寫實風格，或是浪漫寫實的風格畫的。他可能藉此展現他畫頭像的進步，也可能希望藉此得到畫肖像畫的委託。然而這個希望一旦破滅後，他開始利用自畫像進行更急進的風格實驗。

Hulsker估計，梵谷大約在1887年畫了22幅自畫像，他認爲這些作品可能在一年內相當短的間隔下畫的，而且「它們幾乎總是成對出現的。」他根據這項觀察將這些作品分爲八組，每一組包括2到3件作品：他把這幅四分之三側面的自畫像分類爲1887年4到6月的「柔和色調」的一組，依他的分類，這一組介於3月到4月的所謂的「優雅組」（F294，F295與F296），與春天到夏初的「點描派組」（F356與F345）之間。[2]Hulsker分類所依據的色彩，這幅畫作的確相當柔和：襯映著柔和的藍綠色斑紋背景的，是鑲灰綠邊的淡紫色外套，與淺藍色的領帶。雖然雙眼透露出些許的焦慮與憂鬱，但是臉部表情尙屬沉靜。臉部的筆觸顯示梵谷的技巧比畫前一組自畫像時更爲熟練，背景的輕快筆觸帶來空間的深度感，並使畫面整體更鮮活。下一系列的自畫像則是以較濃重色調的、典型的點描派的藍色與紅色的點爲特色。

這幅畫作曾經屬於德國最狂熱的梵谷崇拜者之一的卡爾·斯特恩（Carl Sternheim）。斯特恩可能在1908年，經由Meier-Graefe，注意到這位藝術家，從此他開始造訪歐洲眾多的畫廊與博物館，收集梵谷的作品與進行著述。[3]在1909年9月底斯特恩拜訪了在阿姆斯特丹的喬·梵谷—邦格（Jo van Gogh-Bonger）。根據他後來的記述，在那裏畫作被放在地板上，在陽光下靠在一起，有些甚至卡在一起，所以「當把它們分開時，有一件畫著兩個人物與柏樹的大幅風景畫上的月亮就掉了一片到地上。」[4]斯特恩是在誇大事實，就好像他說他這次拜訪喬一共買了六件作品一樣。事實上他買了四件，其中的一件就是這幅自畫像。[5]因爲他的妻子緹亞（Thea）是使他的收藏得以快速成長的出資人，所以她的名字一再出現在畫作的出處記錄中。對斯特恩，對德國，也許也是對他們1914年起定居的比利時而言，不幸的是，他們自1912年起，因財務困難被迫賣掉許多作品，賣剩下來的一包括7件梵谷以及數件高更、雷諾瓦與傑利柯（Géricault）的作品，都在1919年戰後拍賣掉了。海倫·庫勒穆勒就是在那時買下這幅自畫像，這是她從斯特恩收藏中買下的第二件梵谷（第一件是《開花的栗子樹》）。

1. Bremmer（1930），引自Van Gelder et al，1956，頁45。
2. Hulsker，1996，頁260-262與272。
3. 參考Bridgwater 1987，頁97-107。
4. 參考*Lutetia: Beriche uber europaische Politik, Kunst und Volksleben*, 1926；引自Bridgwater 1987，頁98。
5. Heijbroek & Wouthuysen 1993，頁194。

自畫像　Self-portrait
1887年4至6月　1887 Apr.-Jun.
油彩、木板　oil on cardboard
32.8×24公分　32.8 x 24 cm
Collection Kröller-Müller Museum, Otterlo, The Netherlands

與梵谷早先1886年夏天畫的花卉靜物相比，一年後畫的（冬季時沒有新鮮切花，梵谷無法畫這個題材）更爲歡樂愉悅。光線與色彩支配著畫面，在這幅花束中亦如此。畫中花瓶也出現在其他兩幅大約同時期的靜物畫—《有紫丁香、雛菊、秋牡丹的瓶花》（F322）、《有矢車菊、罌粟的瓶花》（F324）之中。從稍微側面的角度看去，放置在由結實的黃綠色筆觸畫成的桌面上，有光澤的淺藍瓶子裡插滿了白雛菊、黃色的春天向日葵、藍色紫丁香、豔紅的秋牡丹；右後方則有一大束百合與毛茛。[1]瓶子與花朵在藍色的點描派風格的背景前很突出，靠近畫面底部則漸漸變成灰與紫色調的組合。

　　梵谷在一張之前可能用來畫過一幅平坦的風景畫的帆布上畫這件靜物。原先的景物被刮掉，再重新打底在帆布上，至今炭筆或黑色鉛筆畫的素描底稿的痕跡仍可以看出來，顯露出瓶子和一些花的輪廓。

　　這件花卉靜物作爲題材來說，處理得相當保守，花瓶位置的安排幾乎是守舊的，構圖極端簡單整齊。顏料的堆砌以不規律的，或長或短的筆觸堆疊。另一方面，花束豔麗的用色，證實了梵谷日

益增長的技術與自信。他藉著花卉畫作，練習掌握強烈的色調與對比，目標於此可說是達成了，雖說有些顏色已經褪色或變暗了。實驗期結束了。梵谷最初經由密切的模仿來吸收的，印象派與新印象派的課題，如今已然學會與整合成一個高度個人化的、自然的、印象派的光與點描派的筆法的融合。

　　這幅畫充滿了梵谷只有在巴黎才能獲得的信念—相信自身的藝術創作力，與自由實驗的氣氛。在這裡比在荷蘭有更多創新的空間，有同儕藝術家提供他亟需的鼓勵。日後每當他需要解決某些創作的問題，他就會利用這個題材，例如描繪花朵的內部結構，或是運用同色系的數種不同色調，主要是黃色，例如阿爾時期著名的向日葵系列。

　　1892年初，大約2月左右，奧赫耶（Aurier）寫了一封信給他妹妹，叫她買一幅當時在巴黎的一個「舊貨商」那裡賣的，要價15法郎的梵谷的花卉靜物畫作。[3]Hammacher相信那一定就是這一幅《藍色瓶花》。他並未說明原因，但他的理由很可能會是，這是日後Williame收藏中唯一的一件靜物畫。[3]

---

1. 此爲修復師T.Oostendorp.所辨認。但是梵谷美術館的植物學者卻有不同的看法：藍色勿忘草，黃色春天向日葵，淺藍色與深藍色秋牡丹。
2. 參考梵谷美術館奧赫耶檔案中此信的副本。
3. Hammacher 1960，頁56。

藍色瓶花　Flowers in a Blue Vase
1887年6月　1887 Jun.
油彩、帆布　oil on canvas
61.5×38.5公分　61.5 x 38.5 cm
Collection Kröller-Müller Museum, Otterlo, The Netherlands

席涅克（Signac）對梵谷的影響，在他前往南法之後，於1887年的夏天達到最高點。這幅有著桌上花卉的《餐廳內》很可能是那年夏初畫的，是梵谷運用新印象派的原理畫出的作品之一。稀薄塗敷的點描主義筆觸以及互補色的對比（牆面的紅與綠，地板的黃與灰紫，以及橘黃的家具和藍色的桌布）是經過系統化的構思與繪製的。關於這件作品，Rosenblum與Jason認為梵谷嘗試建立一個全新的個人風格，為了探索顏色、筆法、透視法（這一點實際上因為後方牆面粉紅色的鑲板的位置而相當混淆）等客觀問題，畫家壓抑了所有主觀的表現。[1]

雖然梵谷後來提及，他不願意遵從點描主義的嚴格規則，而在這幅畫中他也並不像平常認知的那樣貫徹這些規則，Welsh-Ovcharov將這件作品歸類為「梵谷最正統的點描主義畫作之一。」[2] 然而，桌椅並非由點，而是由長形筆觸組成。畫面的好幾個地方可以看出靠透視框幫忙的鉛筆素描底稿。此外，用來表示陰影的色調濃淡，其實是比較寫實主義，而非點描主義的風格。因為梵谷這張畫是畫在一張舊畫布的反面，這表示它可能是一件實驗之作。X光照片顯示，夾在右方的一棟房子或小屋的屋頂，上方的工廠的邊界或圍籬之間的，是一個花園或一片草地，還可以看見幾棵樹，這很可能是蒙馬特的一個公有地花園。

無論如何，結果這是一件賞心悅目的點描主義風格作品，梵谷很可能藉此作表達對這新的藝術流派的敬意。據Welsh-Ovcharov觀察，「這是梵谷在1887年用來取悅他的朋友保羅‧席涅克，並表示自己與新印象派運動關係密切而畫的。」[3] 畫作的主題是一個典型中產階級的餐廳，是（新）印象派畫家們最喜歡的主題之一，雖然他們不太可能會畫一個全然沒有任何客人的歡樂室內。後世的迷思常常認為巴黎時期的梵谷以世界人或甚至紈跨子自居，其實相反的，梵谷從未對中產階級懷有太多的認同感。《餐廳內》是梵谷作

品相當罕見的一個描繪經典的印象派主題的例子。

畫中有一頂奇怪地高掛牆上的黑色高禮帽，很可能用來表示當時巴黎的前衛畫家常穿的（中產階級）服裝。[4] 最右側的草草畫出的海報或版畫，可能與藝術家自己對日本版畫的興趣有關，正中的畫作一已經被認出來是梵谷自己在1887年春天畫的《阿斯尼埃爾Voyer d'Argenson公園的小徑》（*Lane in Voyer d'Argenson Park at Asnières*, F276）一很可能暗指梵谷自己希望在新的藝術發展中扮演的角色。無論如何，點描主義在梵谷的藝術生涯中最終不過只是一條旁路，確然有助於解放他的用色與筆觸，但也很快被梵谷以太不個人化與太教條主義而摒棄。然而這幅畫作無疑地代表了他新印象派時期的高峰點。

畫中的餐廳無法確認是哪裏。幾乎所有梵谷在巴黎時期常去的餐廳都曾被點名：他與西奧常去的蒙馬特餐廳，例如Lepic街附近的Chez Bataille餐廳；他常常作畫的阿斯尼埃爾的De la Sirène餐廳（F312，F313與F1408）和Rispal餐廳（F355）；還有Gustave Coquiot提到的Clichy大道上的一個店家。[5] 其他可能包括Du Chalet或Le Tambourin一雖然後者的桌子是圓形的、鈴鼓狀的（F370），在1886到1887年的冬天梵谷曾在該處展出他的日本版畫收藏，並且後來又展出他自己與貝爾納（Bernard）和羅特列克的作品。

1895年7月3日喬‧梵谷一邦格（Jo van Gogh-Bonger）寄了一幅《餐廳的室內》給巴黎的畫商Vollard作為展售之用。然而並不清楚是否是這一幅或另外一幅。當J.H. de Bois仍然為C.M.梵谷工作的時期，他收到這件作品好幾次委託出售。1908年夏天他帶著這件作品參加蘇黎世的一個展覽。在那年年底，該作品在C.M.梵谷海牙與阿姆斯特丹的畫廊分店展示，1909年它又在海牙店的夏季展覽中展示。在中間的空檔期間則還給喬‧梵谷一邦格。在1908到1912年，開價從1300漲到5000基爾德。[6]

1. Rosenbium & Janson 1984，頁411。
2. Welsh-Ovcharov 1981，頁104。
3. 同上註。
4. Rewald 1956，頁153-154。在一張1886年的相片中，梵谷與貝納在Asnieres的塞納河岸區，他自己便戴著一頂摺邊的低帽子。（前引文，頁60。）
5. Welsh-Ovcharov 1976，頁234。
6. Heijbroek & Wonthnysen 1993，頁193。

餐廳內　Interior of a Restaurant
1887年夏　1887 Summer
油彩、帆布　oil on canvas
45.5×56公分　45.5 x 56 cm
Collection Kröller-Müller Museum, Otterlo, The Netherlands

1888年5月30日的清晨，梵谷花了5個小時從卡馬爾格（Camargue）到臨地中海邊的聖瑪莉德拉梅的漁村。聖瑪莉地區以其天主教的傳統著名，它以二位「聖瑪莉」遺跡而自豪。根據早期的基督教傳說，她們從猶太（Judea）搭船來此，在南法海岸神奇地靠岸，並進一步改變了整個普羅旺斯地區的信仰。對梵谷而言，這是一趟朝聖之旅。大海讓他想起在荷蘭海軍的尚叔叔（1817-1885），1877-78年間準備研究神學時，梵谷曾與叔叔一起住在阿姆斯特丹；漁村破舊的小房子也讓他想到了德倫特的房子（622/499，約1888年6月4日），海岸地區也再次讓他相信南法與日本的相似。「一陣子過後，你的眼光改變了：你以日本人的眼光來看事情，你對色彩的體驗也變得不一樣了。」6月3日晚上回到阿爾不久後，梵谷曾如此寫道。

　　與1年多以前的作品《阿爾的橋》所表現的強烈色調相較，此處梵谷的色調柔和多了，雖然淡紫色的薰衣草田原本一定是更偏紅的色調。梵谷寫道在聖瑪莉他希望他的素描技巧可以變成「更流暢、更誇張的」（620/495），而且在薰衣草田後方矗立的建築輪廓線的確清楚地以一種令人聯想起「圈線主義」（Cloisonism）和日本主義（Japonism）的畫法描繪。[1]這種方式畫出的馬賽克區塊，在受光面被填進橘色調，陰影面則是互補色的藍色調。區塊的建構與單純的顏色都讓人想起塞尚。梵谷稍後也在約6月12日表示欽佩塞尚的明亮用色，雖然他在談論中也提到德拉克洛瓦（Delacroix）：「也許有人會說，現在這裏每一處都有舊金色、青銅色、紅銅色、和晴朗天空的美妙碧藍色相映，和諧非凡，有著德拉克洛瓦的色調風格。（⋯⋯）如果帶著帆布回家我對自己說：『看，我已經有了塞尚老爹的色調！』我的意思是，就像左拉，塞

尚是如此熟悉鄉間，在其中悠遊自在，我們必須在腦中進行同樣的計算，才能達到一樣的色調。」（627/497）

　　梵谷從聖瑪莉寫給西奧說道，他已經畫了3幅油畫，2幅是海景、1幅是村莊景致。（622/499）此外，他還畫了至少9幅的素描，其中3幅當他一回到阿爾，使用來當作油畫的基礎。其中也還有一幅是這張《聖瑪莉德拉梅一景》的素描，不過根據他從聖瑪莉所寫的信件，這幅油畫不可能是他稍後在阿爾依據素描完成的畫作。素描和油畫很有可能都是在當地完成的，雖然還是不清楚到底哪一幅是先畫的，或是其中一幅是否作為另一幅的範本。油畫和素描的不同處只在於剪裁、細節、以及沒有眩目的太陽。

　　那3幅在聖瑪莉所畫的油畫後來經歷如何我們一無所知。梵谷仍在聖瑪莉時寫道：他得把畫作留下，「當然因為顏料未乾，所以不可能經得起5小時馬車車程的顛簸。」（622/499）他大概計畫下次去聖瑪莉時將畫作帶回，但卻再也沒回去（624/494、626/496、628/498、681/w7）。有可能他還是把畫帶走了，或讓它們在這個月中便送至阿爾，就像7月5日他寫給西奧的信中所建議的：「舉例而言，在聖瑪莉所畫的習作」還沒乾，因為他所用的慢乾的鋅白色顏料。（639/508）[2]

　　相關的紀錄無法回溯至比胡眞戴克（Hoojendijk）更早，不過大家知道胡眞戴克從傅勒（Vollard）處買了許多作品，而傅勒再向喬‧梵谷一邦格買畫（不過，在喬的帳目紀錄中沒有這幅畫），他也向梵谷的朋友買畫，這些友人透過贈送或交換取得了梵谷的畫（然而其中並沒有這幅畫的相關資料）。更甚者，1895到1897年間，傅勒請了位助手到阿爾，就為了到處尋取梵谷遺留當地的畫作。

---

1. Welsh-Ovcharov 1981，頁125-126。
2. 梵谷常讓被迫留下的作品寄回給他。

聖瑪莉德拉梅一景　View of Saintes-Maries-de-la-Mer
1888年6月1至3日　1888 1-3 Jun.
油彩、帆布　oil on canvas
64.2×53公分　64.2 x 53 cm
Collection Kröller-Müller Museum, Otterlo, The Netherlands

「自從我來到這裡，荒廢的花園給了我足夠的工作，園中有著巨大的松樹，樹下雜草高而亂，混著各式長春花，而我還沒到過外面去。」梵谷於住進聖保羅療養院二週後，在1889年5月22日這麼寫給弟弟。（778/592）他所謂的「外面」，指的是療養院外。當他住院後不久便在花園架起畫架，梵谷希望藉由畫畫能對病情帶來正面的影響。現在他住了院，在一群瘋子間緩和了對瘋狂的懼怕。他注意到有些病人像他一樣，發作時會聽到「奇怪的聲響」，而且「眼睛看到的東西也好像會變化」，不過，在同一封信他寫道：「一旦你知道這是疾病的一部分，你就比較容易接受了。」經過了5個月，他逐漸好轉，他希望再也不會像在阿爾時一樣有那麼嚴重的發作。根據他的說法，最大的危險在於「在這待段時間後，人會變得非常無力。嗯，我的創作某種程度地保護我免於陷入這情況。」

花園位於療養院的西側，提供他許多的作畫主題，大概一週後，他著手畫2幅大油畫，描繪鳶尾花和紫丁花。同時他在花園畫了數幅非常棒的素描與水彩，其中一幅現存於庫勒穆勒美術館。他以30號橫幅帆布尺寸畫鳶尾花和紫丁花。稍後他以2幅直幅的30號帆布畫了《聖雷米療養院的花園》與一幅長滿長春藤的樹幹。畫《聖雷米療養院的花園》時，梵谷把畫架放置與療養院北翼男子區平行，那裡的空房間讓他能有個工作室。大約1900年費德列克‧喬治（Frédéric George）從此處幾乎一模一樣的地點拍照，擷取叢生的雜草以及頗具特色、攀附在正面牆上的溢流水管。

雖然在上面所提的3幅畫作中，梵谷專注在植物上，在這幅作品他以療養院的建築物與成長茂盛的樹木作一對照。因為梵谷的畫架放在離正面很近的地方，所以景象後退的很明顯，製造出一種奇特的透視效果，這也是他常用在構圖上的方法。當他仍在荷蘭工作時，他從1867年出版，由查‧布朗（Charles Blanc）所著的《繪畫藝術的法規》學習如何適當使用透視法來表現。[1]首先，他以鉛筆或黑色粉筆來畫底圖，這在某些地方還可看見。[2]他畫樹用輕重不同的厚塗法，以及短而強有力的筆觸。反之建築物與前景以比較不那麼厚塗的方式上色。局部在已開花的樹梢部分，梵谷則以不斷的濕筆畫在未乾的顏色上形成變化多端的顏色。至於樹間可見的綠草地，他則以相對較平滑的筆觸，營造出一個讓眼睛可以在一堆鬆散筆觸之外稍事休息之處。大部分的通道是以濕筆畫法與他面前的主題一起完成，但在最後階段，此時帆布必定已經有相當程度的乾燥，他用軟的尖頭筆刷重點式畫上大量的透明深藍色與紅色顏料，這在整幅畫中清楚可見，不僅是可以平衡用色，也擴大了，例如說，開花樹枝的結構。最後他在帆布上簽名，如同他在其他3幅花園畫作上所簽的方式。那個簽名是值得注意的，因為當他在7月把畫作寄給西奧時，他只對《紫丁花》和《長春藤樹》這二件作品用「*tableaux*」這個名稱，亦即成熟的畫作。另外2幅，他說道：「與其說是畫作的題材，不如說是對大自然的研究。總是如此：你在達成一個有意義的整體之前，你必須有許多的嘗試。」（792/600，約1889年7月9日）梵谷對「研究」與「畫作」所作的區別是他信件不斷提及的主題，雖然他並沒有對此有非常清楚的定義，稱某些作品是研究，某些是畫作，但似乎在他眼中，一幅稱得上是成熟的作品一定是他滿意的主題，並且內蘊更深層的意涵。他相當確信在完成一幅滿意的作品前，大量的練習是必需的，這點是無庸置疑的。然而，畫作的形式在這過程就是次要的了。[3]

1. Van Uitert等人，1990，頁234。
2. 由庫勒穆勒美術館所做的技術檢驗，2002年7月29日。
3. 見Dorn 1990b，頁47。

聖雷米療養院的花園　The Garden of the Asylum at Saint-Rémy
1889年5月　1889 May
油彩、帆布　oil on canvas
91.5×72公分　91.5 x 72 cm
Collection Kröller-Müller Museum, Otterlo, The Netherlands

梵谷素描作品的高峰包括一組七幅彩色的畫作，而《療養院花園中開花的玫瑰叢》就是其中之一。這系列畫作是在1889年5月下旬梵谷在療養院的花園裡完成的。有很長一段時間，這些作品被認為是水彩畫，但是最近的研究已經確定梵谷所用的是稀釋的油彩加上紫色墨水。[1]這些畫作所完成的時間，正值梵谷沒有適當的材料來創作油畫。例如，5月22日，梵谷寫信告訴西奧：「我不得不再請你寄給我一些顏料，另外還要畫布。」（778/592）在下一封信裡，他又再要了畫布與新的畫筆。（780/593，1889年6月2日）正如在這系列的其他素描一樣，我們可以從這幅作品中看到某些筆劃的末段看來有點參差不齊，這或許是因為他用壞掉的畫筆來作畫。新的畫具大約在6月8日寄到，同時他也獲得了許可，因此可以離開療養院的範圍作畫。

儘管在這系列的其他素描作品中都可以看到基本的鉛筆或粉筆草圖，但是在這幅素描裡梵谷並沒有畫底圖。[2]他讓自己待在接近主要主題的位置，並且幾乎將整張畫紙都填滿了玫瑰花叢。由於藍色出現在這個構圖的每個地方，而且淺藍色與綠色仍然不尋常地清楚明亮，所以畫面的景深從第一眼很難判斷。[3]除此之外，玫瑰經過多年已經多半褪色了，無法像原來那樣提供更強的紅色與粉紅色

的色調。[4]有很多地方，玫瑰花朵漂浮在葉片間，好像是淡粉紅甚至是完全白色的污點，而且通常只能夠透過畫家有時在花朵外圍所的藍色輪廓線來便認出玫瑰花的位置。現在我們幾乎不會注意到這幅素描總共有超過30朵玫瑰花。梵谷將綠色主要保留給玫瑰花叢的葉片，所以它的確在背景間較為突出。

療養院的花園共有三層，由前往後逐漸升高。在左上方，可以看見部分的石頭矮牆，其後方則有亮紅色的花朵；而就在上方邊緣的下方，可以看到一條持續延伸、較黑的交叉陰影線代表著外牆，並且在幾個地方都與玫瑰花叢的枝幹交錯。[5]左側的地面是用水平的黃色、綠色、紫色筆觸畫成的。在畫面的底部，一連串較長的垂直筆觸代表樹叢自草叢間升起。整個構圖是由無數長度、厚度、方向不同的筆劃交錯而成的織錦。線條與筆觸幾乎不帶有任何描述性的意圖，除了幾個例外之處（像玫瑰花），其他都形成了不同群組的閃亮、抽象的記號，用以暗示概略的形態。在最後階段，梵谷添畫了深且暗的藍色筆劃，通常是有節奏地穿插在不同群組之間，讓整件作品帶著顯著的完成意味。在這個時期，梵谷用類似的方式在他主要的油畫中構成樹木與喬木叢。[6]

1. 參見Marije Vellekoop的文章，刊載於Ives et al. 2005，頁294-295與304-307，其中也包含了對這些畫作完成時間的討論。這系列畫作包含F1526、F1527、F1533、F1534、F1535、F1536、F1537。《療養院花園中開花的玫瑰叢》的背面有許多暗色的圈圈，這是因為油滲透過畫紙。在療養院所畫的一系列內景（F1528、F1529、F1530）也已經發現是以油彩而非水彩來畫成的（同前書，頁322-327），這代表梵谷在聖雷米完全沒有畫任何水彩畫。
2. F1526（私人收藏）也以同樣的盛開的玫瑰花叢為主題，也沒有任何底圖。這兩幅畫或許可以當成聯作。也可以將這系列的其他畫作結合起來看（Pickvance in Van der Wolk et al. 1990，頁284-285；Heenk 1995，頁185-186；Pickvance 2000，頁238與308）。
3. 要強化視覺的深度，可以讓較遠處的部份逐漸變得更藍，以便與綠色的前景與中央區分；在許多17世紀的風景畫中都可以看到這種方式。相反的，這裡清楚而不中斷的淺藍色有節奏地散佈在整個畫面，因此強化了畫面的扁平感。
4. 褪色的原因或許來自使用了不穩定的有機紅色顏料（參見Ban Heugten 2005，頁53）。
5. 背景的紅色之所以沒有褪色，不像前景的玫瑰花那樣，或許是因為梵谷在這個地方用了不同的顏料。
6. 相關的例子可參照5月初所畫的《百合花》（Lilacs，F579，Hermitage, St Petersburg）與《聖雷米療養院的花園》（The Garden of the Asylum at Saint-Remy）。

療養院花園中開花的玫瑰叢
1889年5月
畫筆、稀釋的油彩與墨水、織紋紙
61.3×46.7公分

Flowering Rosebushes in the Asylum Garden
1889 May
brush, diluted oils and ink, on wove paper
61.3 x 46.7 cm
Collection Kröller-Müller Museum, Otterlo, The Netherlands

「這裡有著非常漂亮的橄欖樹叢，灰色的、銀綠色的，像是修剪過的柳樹，這裡的藍天讓我百看不厭」，梵谷在1889年7月2日給母親的信中如此寫道。（787/598）這幾乎就是此幅《橄欖樹叢》的描繪，梵谷很有可能是在寫這封信時已完成這幅畫。同一時期他正在畫著《橄欖樹與背景的阿爾畢耶山》，在他的信中很明確地提到這幅作品，不像《橄欖樹叢》這件作品那樣並非在信中言明。橄欖樹叢成為他喜愛的畫題之一，雖然在阿爾時他什麼都畫，就是避開這主題。如同柏樹、麥田與山景，橄欖樹是普羅旺斯風景的一部分，在聖雷米，梵谷計畫以這些主題作畫，將它們發展為系列的畫作。1889年6月至12月間，他畫了約15幅的橄欖樹叢，大部分是秋天時節，其中11幅是他最喜歡的30號油畫尺寸。[1]

這幅寫生的習作，除了樹幹、樹枝、及輪廓部分是有著較長的畫筆筆觸，梵谷主要是使用短而彎曲的筆觸，透過無數筆觸從而營造出油彩脈動的畫面，並以濕筆畫法直接上彩，讓畫家作畫時的悶熱氣候幾乎是可觸及的。梵谷這時已習慣了悶熱，在前述同一封寫給母親的信中他還寫道：「我已經在一天裡最熱的時候在麥田作畫了一陣子了，不讓炎熱的天氣妨礙我。」稍後，當油彩夠乾，他用深藍色顏料來強調葉子，這裡一畫、那裡一筆地增加輪廓的厚重感，並以優雅的弧形，沿著彎曲的筆觸的方向，加上他的簽名。《橄欖樹叢》是聖雷米時期7幅有簽名的畫作之一，雖然有人質疑其中《黃昏的松樹》簽名的真實性。梵谷1889年5月所畫的4幅大型習作皆有簽名，包括《聖雷米療養院的花園》，如同《橄欖樹叢》，這幅畫也是帆布完全乾燥後，以深藍色的油彩簽名。約在7

月15日左右，梵谷將這4幅「五月習作」和其他在聖雷米與阿爾完成的作品一起寄給巴黎的西奧。這批畫作還包含了一幅很可能就是本幅畫作的《橄欖樹》。（720/600，約1889年7月9日）[2]

1912年4月13日庫勒穆勒夫人自巴黎畫商尤金・杜瑞（Eugène Druet）手中買下梵谷5幅畫作。「但最美麗的一幅是橄欖樹叢」，當晚她在旅館房內寫給她的年輕密友山姆・范・德凡特（Sam van Deventer），「如此溫柔、衷心，又這麼完整的大畫。我無法向你描述它，但在大多數人眼中，它會是最美的一幅，因為畫中沒有一處會令人不安。」[3]她還提及，與庫勒穆勒夫婦同行的布瑞默（Bremmer）談到一筆好買賣，只以開價的三分之一就買到了這5幅作品：「他走到外面顫抖如樹葉般，對到手的收穫高興極了。」這是可以理解的反應，除了非常棒的《橄欖樹叢》之外，這批「收穫」還包括了《蘋果籃》、《喬瑟夫—麥可・吉諾克斯肖像》、《峽谷》、《織布機與織工》。同一天，午餐過後不久，庫勒穆勒夫人再於柏恩翰・傑尤恩（Bernheim-Jeune）處買了2幅梵谷畫作《搖籃曲》與《有麥束與上昇的月亮的風景》、2幅梵谷素描《祈禱的婦人》與《撿拾麥穗的農婦》、以及秀拉的油畫《漢夫盧爾的堤防》。她提醒范德凡特，她如何早在數年前，便決定讓先生與家人「分享影響她至深的思想領域」。這裡暗指她當時的決定要請布瑞默每週來家裡，上一次實務美學以及如何收藏藝術品的課程。她在信件最後說道：「如果您今天愉快地以6萬荷蘭盾購買畫作，這不會是件深深令人感到滿足的事嗎？」

1. Pickvance 1986，頁98；頁16。
2. 同上，頁293-295。
3. 引用於Van Deventer 1956，頁54-56。

橄欖樹叢　Olive Grove
1889年6月　1889 Jun.
油彩、帆布　oil on canvas
72.4×91.9公分　72.4 x 91.9 cm
Collection Kröller-Müller Museum, Otterlo, The Netherlands

在1890年5月畫這件作品之前，幾乎是在8個月之前，梵谷就寫信告訴西奧：「我也要摹倣德拉克洛瓦的《好索馬利亞人》。」梵谷在他發病的夏天開始摹倣畫作，也完成了他自己對德拉克洛瓦的《聖殤圖》（Pieta）的仿作。他曾貫注在米勒等畫家的作品，但在1890年2月，他在信中再度提到他想畫《好索馬利亞人》，很有可能那時候他已經開始在進行了。後來他的精神狀況又變差，使他的畫作沒有進展，但到了5月，他就告訴西奧：「我也已經畫了德拉克洛瓦的《好索馬利亞人》。」這是他最後一次在信中提到這個畫題。

梵谷用他收藏很久的 J・Laurens的石版畫複製畫為摹本。他在阿爾的醫院病房就掛著德拉克洛瓦的《聖殤圖》和《好索馬利亞人》兩幅畫的複製畫。他並不認為摹倣他敬愛的大師是一種沒有獨創性的模仿行為；相反的，他希望藉此學習，並增加新的東西進去。他將自己比擬為一位以自己的方式詮釋世界名曲的音樂家。他在信中寫道，他「將黑白的複製畫放在眼前，然後我以色彩即興創作，但是當然並不只是發自我的想像，而是根據我對這些畫作的記憶 — 記憶，那模糊的色彩合聲，雖然不盡然全對，但至少有正確的感受，這就是我的詮釋。」當梵谷倣畫德拉克洛瓦時，這些「色彩的記憶」一定格外重要，比他學米勒時更重要。前者是以熱烈的色彩主義著稱，也使梵谷宣稱，在用色方面，德拉克洛瓦比印象派畫家「更完全」。在他跟西奧為他自己的一些有點造作的作品爭執時，梵谷為自己辯護時，把德拉克洛瓦引為「描繪各種要素的交互關聯」的藝術家典範。

色彩和素描正是梵谷在他的仿作中強調的兩個面向。線條有力的動感和人物扭曲的動作，加強了前景故事的戲劇張力。背景的山重複著起伏的筆觸，令人聯想起阿爾畢耶山(Alpilles)的風景。索馬利亞人的鮮紅色頭巾，和紫紅色衣服，反映了德拉克洛瓦的用色。聖經中，不信主的好索馬利亞人，在旅途中停下來，幫助遇劫的無助路人重新上馬的故事，無疑也影響了梵谷摹倣這件作品的決定。當梵谷在前一年9月，第一次想畫這幅畫時，他自己還未復原，在1890年5月時亦如是。當時他終於決定要永遠離開療養院了，所以這件作品也可能和他的弟弟西奧有關，因為他是梵谷個人的索馬利亞人，總是隨時準備好，要幫忙將梵谷扶回馬鞍上，然而，他的信中並未提到這一點。[1]

早先的《聖殤圖》，同時期的「改譯」自林布蘭同名的版畫複製畫的《拉撒路的復活》，和《好索馬利亞人》，是梵谷僅有的三件宗教畫作，而它們都是模仿的作品。高更和貝爾納也創作相似的題材，但並非仿作，而是另外獨立的構圖；但是梵谷一點也不喜歡這種方式。他覺得他們離現實太遠了，創作出全然抽象的東西。德拉克洛瓦和林布蘭的例子在梵谷看來是無可超越的—但是可以被詮釋。在《好索馬利亞人》這幅作品中，梵谷似乎用他有力的筆觸來與他大師朋友們平坦的形式作區別。

---

1. Homburg 1996，頁73-74。

好索瑪利亞人（仿德拉克洛瓦）
1890年5月
油彩、帆布
73×59.5公分

The Good Samaritan (after Delacroix)
1890 May
oil on canvas
73 x 59.5 cm
Collection Kröller-Müller Museum, Otterlo, The Netherlands

1890年1月，在《法蘭西信使》雜誌（*Mercure de France*）裡刊登了第一篇詳細讚賞梵谷的文章，作者是年輕的藝評家兼詩人奧赫耶（Gabriel-Albert Aurier, 1865-1892）。[1] 這篇文章讓梵谷非常高興，但是在他寫給奧赫耶的謝函裡也相當謙遜，提到像高更與Monticelli這樣的藝術家比他自己更值得這麼大的讚賞（854/626a，1980年2月10日或11日）。在同一封信裡，梵谷承諾要寄給奧赫耶一幅油畫習作：「如果你願意接受，那麼我將會畫一幅柏樹習作給你，並且附在下一批寄給我弟弟的畫作之中，以紀念你的這篇文章。現在我還在畫，因為我想加一個小小的人物在裡面。〔……〕我想畫給你的習作畫的是位在夏日麥田一角的一群柏樹，正吹來一陣〔乾冷的〕西北風。」那幅作品（現藏於庫勒穆勒美術館）梵谷其實早在1889年6月就完成了，但是在那之前都一直留在自己身邊。最後他為奧赫耶添加了不只一位，而是兩位女性人物。在將它寄到巴黎託西奧轉交給奧赫耶之前，梵谷首先為自己畫了他的摹本：一幅小型的油畫習作（F621，梵谷美術館）以及本文討論的這一幅素描。[2]

梵谷的這幅素描相當精準地臨摹了該幅油畫，但是在畫面的左側他留了多一點天空。在油畫中那樣充滿張力的旋轉雲朵，梵谷並未在素描中多加強調，而只是畫了幾筆較亮的線條。他用不同的墨水筆畫在用黑色粉筆畫的相當細的底圖上，某些地方有輕微的污漬。在最後階段，他用了較寬的蘆葦筆來勾勒柏樹的暗色調，而柏樹的其他部位則完全由逗點一樣的筆觸所組成。[3] 最特別的是，相對於油畫，素描上的人物大了許多，因此讓他們在整個構圖中較為突出。在油畫中可以清楚看到，兩個人物是後來加上去的。梵谷並沒有多花時間將顏料刮掉，而是直接將人物畫在原有已經相當厚塗的顏料層上。因此人物有點骯髒。在素描裡，人物在後方的柏樹襯托下相當明顯，因此較能讓人相信他們是四周環境的一部分。

梵谷是畫在有點次級的織紋紙上，經過多年畫紙已經明顯地變暗，或許是因為很長一段時間它被黏在酸性的紙板上。[4] 因此，整個畫面比起原來所希望的更加嚴肅。某些地方可以看到較亮的區域，在那些地方畫紙某種程度上仍保有原來的色澤。在最右邊的柏樹中，可以看到一些綠色、黃色、白色油彩混合的色點，另外還有一小點藍色的色點。從這裡可以推斷梵谷在畫小型油畫的摹本時，這幅素描就放在旁邊非常接近的位置。

在二次大戰時，德國佔領軍由庫勒穆勒美術館取走館藏中的3幅畫作並運往德國，之後該館自德國所獲得的補償金便用於購入這幅素描及《雨中墓園》（*Graveyard in the Rain*）。戰時的館長山姆·范·德凡特之所以知道有這幅素描，是因為藝術史學者J.G. van Gelder的提醒，後者在他1942年11月27日寫給山姆·范·德凡特的信中提到他已經向這幅素描的主人—來自Haagsche Kunsthandel的Jan Frequin—推薦了庫勒穆勒美術館。[5] 這幅素描自從喬·梵谷—邦格在1905的拍賣之後就從大眾的視線中消失，也未曾出現在文獻中：例如De la Faille在1928年出版的全集中就沒有這幅素描。Van Gelder以及後來的許多人都認為它是該幅油畫創作前的習作，因此兩幅作品應該一同典藏在庫勒穆勒美術館內。[6]

---

1. G-Albert Aurier, 'Les isolees: Vincent van Gogh', *Mercure de France* 1 (1890), 頁24-29.
2. 梵谷之前在1889年也根據這幅油畫作了一幅大型的墨水筆素描，其中並沒有人物（*Cypress*, F1524, Art Institute of Chicago）。
3. 例如可參見《柏樹與四個在田野間工作的人》（*Cypress with Four Figures Working in the Field*, F1539r, Folkwang Museum, Essen）：這幅黑色粉筆繪製的素描也是在1890年2月至3月間完成的，而畫中的柏樹也是以類似的方式畫成。
4. 這幅素描在1987年進行修復，並且在背面用日本紙加以裱褙，因為「畫紙〔……〕已經處在嚴重的腐朽狀態。」（Hoefsloot 1987，頁70）
5. 這幅油畫早在1914年就由庫勒穆勒女士向奧赫耶的後人購入，請參見Otterlo 2003，頁296-300及406-410。De la Faille 1970也認為這幅素描是準備階段的習作，因此將這幅素描定為1889年6月，儘管De Gruijter 1962，頁110-111早已指出這幅素描必定是梵谷在1890年2月為油畫進行增補之後才完成的。Hulsker 1977，頁439將這幅素描定為1890年2月。Hefting 1980，頁117注意到人物是在1890年2月才添加到油畫之中，但還是認為根據風格而言這幅素描較適合歸於1889年。
6. 儘管Van Gelder在信中也提到不需要因為購藏的價格而反對，但是他在信中並未說明該價格的實際數字（該信現藏於庫勒穆勒美術館檔案）。最後這幅素描購入的價格為2200荷蘭盾，但是館長A.M. Hammacher在1943年的購藏清冊（由Sam van Deventer於1944年4月11日編成，現藏於庫勒穆勒美術館檔案）的頁緣上註明這幅素描「根據van Gelder教授的說法，當初〔Jan Frequin〕向他開出的價格為800荷蘭盾」，兩個數字間的差距相當奇特。

柏樹　Cypresses
1889年　1889
墨水、粉筆、紙　ink and chalk on paper
31.9×23.7公分　31.9 x 23.7 cm
Collection Kröller-Müller Museum, Otterlo, The Netherlands

柏樹纖細黝暗，火焰般的身影是南方常見的景觀。柏樹是一種可以生長至高齡的常綠植物。在希臘羅馬的古典時期，柏樹是好幾個神祇的象徵，最重要的是克洛諾斯（Chronos），宙斯(朱比特)的父親，老人的保護神。柏樹象徵，例如長壽；在基督教中：來世的希望和死亡。塞帕里索斯（Cyparissus）意外誤殺他很寵愛的阿波羅送他的公鹿之後，被變成一棵樹，他的名字就是柏樹名稱的由來。柏樹是最好的喪禮之樹，至今在地中海國家的墓園一帶仍相當常見。十九世紀尤以德國藝術家Arnold Böcklin（1827-1901）在他的畫作《死之島》（Toteninsel）中，賦予柏樹有如神秘的哀弔巨人般的不朽形象。

然而這並無法確認梵谷在他的畫作中暗喻柏樹為死亡的象徵。如果考量他常常發作的極度憂鬱症，也許會有此推論；但是也許他對具撫慰性的繪畫創作的不斷追尋，使他不會選擇一個很顯然悲傷的主題；雖然他偶爾會含蓄的提到如此的主題。在阿爾時，他只有在一些畫作中畫有柏樹，例如《柏樹圍繞的果園》（Orchard Bordered Cypresses），但它們的功用只是用來當防風林。這個時期的其他畫作中，它們有時是用來替背景加上一個「黝暗的記號。」（692/541，約1888年9月27日）只有在聖雷米時期，梵谷將柏樹當成一個全然獨立的主題來畫，明顯地主要將它視為一個繪畫創作上的挑戰。在1889年6月25日他寫信給西奧：

我們已經有了幾天的好天氣，我開始畫更多的油畫，所以有希望可以完成12張三十號的油畫。有兩件柏樹的習作是以困難的酒瓶綠的色調來畫；我用厚厚的鉛白色的層次畫前景，給予地面厚實感。我認為Monticelli的作品很常是這樣打底的，然後再上別的顏色上去。但我不知道這些帆布是否足以勝任這樣的作法。（785/596）

他提到的這兩件習作，現在一件在紐約，一件《有兩個人物的柏樹》在庫勒穆勒美術館。這兩件作品和同時期開始畫的《有太陽和收割者的麥田》都屬於他最厚塗的作品，據Pickvance形容「幾乎像淺浮雕」一般的厚。[1] 在同一封信裡梵谷又進一步告訴西奧：

柏樹盤據著我的思維；我想要像向日葵的畫作一樣，畫一些柏樹的作品，因為我很訝異它們迄今尚未被以我所看到的形式畫出來。它們在線條和比例上像埃及的方尖碑一樣美麗。而它們的綠是如此獨特。它們是晴朗風景中的一抹黑記號，但是它是一個最有趣的黑記號之一，是我能看到的，最難捕捉在畫布上的東西之一。

如果梵谷在這裡是把柏樹視為是一象徵感謝、希望和友誼的向日葵的對照物，他現在似乎意指傳統中與柏樹聯想在一起的憂鬱和悲傷。他也可能是在技法上有些很個人的想法，類似他畫的向日葵，很可能他在醞釀一系列由柏樹構成的裝飾性作品。Druick和Zegers主張，梵谷在暗指柏樹的死亡的象徵，就好像他同時期的畫作《有太陽和收割者的麥田》中的收割者一樣。[2] 梵谷曾明白的將那幅畫作和永生中死亡的階段聯結在一起，但他並未明白地將那個時期的柏樹作此種解釋。當他在七個月之後不得不面對又一次的惡化病情，在1890年2月2日的信中梵谷提到向日葵這個畫題時更清楚的表示：「要創作出美麗的東西，你需要某種靈感，來自天上的光，某種身外之物。我畫完那些向日葵之後，我尋求與它們相反的，但對等的東西，然後我說：就是柏樹。」（851/625）

以上引述自梵谷針對在一本新發行的《法蘭西信使》雜誌（Mercure de France）的創刊號（1890年1月）上登載的，介紹梵谷本人的文章而寫的信。這篇文章〈孤立者：文生‧梵谷〉（"Les isolés: Vincent van Gogh"），是第一篇認真談論這位藝術家的文章，由年輕的詩人兼評論家艾伯特‧奧赫耶（Albert Aurier）所作。[3] 梵谷對這篇文章非常驚訝而並非十分開心。他認為奧赫耶對他過譽了，他覺得他的繪畫並未達到奧赫耶形容的那種程度，雖然他很希望有一天他能夠真的如此。奧赫耶興奮地描述梵谷的作品，將之比擬為寶石、礦物、金屬和水晶（詳述他的同儕詩人波特萊爾所謂的「對應」"correspondances"。）他稱讚這位畫家為一位作夢的寫實

柏樹與兩個人物　Cypresses with Two Figures
1889年6月至1890年2月　1889 Jun.-1890 Feb.
油彩、帆布　oil on canvas
91.6×72.4公分　91.6 x 72.4 cm
Collection Kröller-Müller Museum, Otterlo, The Netherlands

主義者，他隨意馴馭現實的能力無人所及。梵谷在給西奧的信中寫道：「作為一種藝術評論，這樣的文章自有其價值」，[4]「我認為該尊重它，而作者必然誇張他的語調……」奧赫耶也提及柏樹：「……這些柏樹矗立它們夢魘般的火焰側影，那是黑色的……」梵谷很贊同的寫著：「奧赫耶也有同感，所以他說，甚至黑色也是一種色彩，而它們有時候看起來像火焰。」在信末他請西奧向奧赫耶致謝：「我當然會寄給你一封給他的感謝箋和一幅習作。」

奧赫耶最後收到的，很適切的，就是這幅《柏樹與兩個人物》。在9月梵谷寄給西奧那幅現在在紐約的習作，奧赫耶可能在西奧那裡看過。梵谷自己保留了另一幅習作。[5]他在要給奧赫耶的這幅加了兩個女子，畫了一張尺寸稍小的版本自己留著，也畫了一張素描；然後在4月底將畫寄給西奧，後者再轉給奧赫耶。在2月10日或11日梵谷寫了一封信給奧赫耶，謝謝他並告訴他這件禮物：

> 我要給你的習作畫的是在一個颳西北風的夏日，麥田一隅的數棵柏樹。它因此是一抹黑記號，被包圍在氣流湧動的藍色之中，和罌粟的朱紅色形成對比。你可以發現它的顏色組合近似那些漂亮的蘇格蘭格子花紋，綠、藍、紅、黃、黑；我們曾經都很喜歡，但如今很悲哀的已不多見了。（854/626a）

在這段敘述中並無憂鬱的意味，雖然梵谷也寫道：「目前我尚未能完全捕捉到我對它們的感覺；觀賞自然時產生的強烈情感，驅使我瀕臨失去意識的邊緣，我因此兩個星期多都不能工作。」

梵谷自己的內在衝突使他時時懷疑自己的能力，這是一場現實與夢想之間的消耗性的拉鋸戰，最好的情況下，會創造出有靈感的畫作。大約在他寫信給奧赫耶的同時，文生給西奧的信中寫著：

> 如果我膽敢放任自己，膽敢將自己從現實中解放，膽敢用顏色創造色調的旋律，像Monticelli的某些畫作一樣，奧赫耶的文章就能激勵我。但是，對我而言，真實，甚至只是要作出一些真實的東西的奮鬥，是如此的可貴；最終我認為，我相信我寧願當鞋匠，勝於色彩的音樂家。（855/626，1890年2月10或11日）

梵谷有告訴奧赫耶該如何處理他的畫作，也因此讓世人得以略知他認為對自己的作品該怎樣處理：

> 當我送給你的習作完全乾了之後，包括厚塗的部份—這部份可能至少一年才會乾—你可以替它上一層凡尼斯，同時它必須用水洗好幾遍以便把油去掉。這幅習作是以深色的波斯藍色的畫的〔……〕，一旦這些波斯藍乾透了，我認為你替它上過凡尼斯之後，會得到全然的黑色調，它們可以襯托出數個不同的黑綠色調。（854/626a）

雖然梵谷形容柏樹猶如晴天風景中的一個黑記號，他幾乎不曾用過黑色顏料。像奧赫耶一樣，他認為黑色也是一個顏色，而他喜歡波斯藍勝於深暗的顏色。關於畫框，他建議用一個「非常簡單的鮮豔橘色平框」，會和藍色與黑綠色的色調最相稱，突顯出一個漂亮的蘇格蘭格子般的效果。奧赫耶是否有照梵谷的指示作並無從得知。現代科技的檢測顯示在柏樹和天空部份有一層骯髒的棕色凡尼斯漆的痕跡。[6]然而，因為深綠色調的關係，無法以紫外線測知上了幾層凡尼斯。

1. Pickvance 1986，頁110。
2. 同前引文：參考 Dorn 1990。
3. Druick & Zegers 2001，頁289。
4. 參考Mathews 1986與Pick vance 1986，頁310 315；；頁406 410。
5. Pickvance 1986，頁298。
6. 庫勒穆勒美術館2002年7月15日技術檢驗。這是梵谷唯一一次在信中提及為他作品上凡尼斯。

梵谷創作此畫時，正忙著準備永遠離開聖雷米的療養院。這極有可能是最後一幅他在聖雷米所做的油畫，大約是在1890年5月12至15日。大約一個月後他寫信給高更，信中首度仔細描述這幅畫的場景：

> 從那裡，我也畫了柏樹和一顆星星，這是最後一次的嘗試：有著暗月的夜空，鐮刀似的新月自土地黑暗陰影處昇起；一顆異常光亮的星星，如果你能想像的話，在有著浮雲的深藍色天空透著淡粉和綠色的光芒。下方是一條路，沿路有著高高的黃色蘆葦，在這後面，遠方的下緣是低低的藍色阿爾卑斯山脈；一幢窗戶透出桔色光線的舊農舍，和一棵非常高的柏樹，挺直而色深。路上有一輛由白馬拉著的黃色馬車，和二位徒步晚歸的路人。你可以說這非常浪漫，但我想也非常的普羅旺斯。（信稿893/643，約1890年6月17日）

似乎怕文字還不夠清楚，他還附上了速寫。然而，速寫和描述都有幾處和原先畫作明顯不同，可能是因為梵谷是在寫信的一週後，才收到從聖雷米寄來的畫作，所以不得不憑記憶來描述的。（896/644，1890年6月24或25日）例如：油畫中可見兩顆明亮的星星與兩棵柏樹，但在素描中只各見一個。速寫中柏樹是在假想中軸線的左方，但油畫中是置於右方，而這讓素描的畫面上有更多的空間給背景的小旅店。油畫中，前景徒步的路人很明顯是回家的工作者，其中一人肩上還扛著鏟子。

梵谷不僅是憑印象描述、速寫這場景，畫作本身其實也是想像的產物。這也是他給高更信中所指的一次「最後的嘗試」：最後一次努力從腦海裡，從純粹的幻想來創造。在阿爾時，在高更的指導下，他第一次試驗這種作法，在聖雷米他以3幅夜景來作再次的探索，也就是他最重要的成果：《星夜》、《有麥束與上昇月亮的風景》以及這幅《普羅旺斯夜間的鄉村路》。在他最近一次的發作期間，他憑記憶創作了5幅小尺寸的作品，這件畫作即與此有關。舉例而言，背景中的小旅館強烈喚起當時他所畫的被他稱作「北方的回憶」的有草屋頂的農舍。同時期他也畫了好幾幅馬車、荷鍬農民、徒步路人的素描，這些他稍後都應用於油畫中。

皮克文斯（Pickvance）曾主張速寫和油畫的歧異這麼大，一定是因為梵谷在奧維時曾經大幅度的修改畫作，不過他也承認這很難證明。[1] 事實上這似乎不太可能，因為最近的技術性檢驗顯示明顯的油畫底稿痕跡，在一開始，就已經定好了構圖。[2] 不過，也有證據顯示梵谷在抵達奧維後曾修改油畫，例如他更改了道路和其中一個人物。他可能也為畫布加了裡襯。[3] 新月的橘色是後來塗上的，一層薄薄的透明油彩覆在已經乾燥的表面。當然，無法確定這些改變究竟是梵谷自己做的，還是另有他人，還有是在哪個確切的時間點。在《黃昏的松樹》裡的太陽也曾以類似的手法補筆，而在《有麥束與上昇月亮的風景》好幾筆橘彩在油畫乾燥後才再畫上去。在《有麥束與上昇月亮的風景》與《普羅旺斯夜間的鄉村路》的畫作中這種橘黃色，比簡單的黃色，更能形成對比藍紫色為主的天空的較強的互補色對照效果，從這點看起來似乎是梵谷自己做的調整，因為他總是追求這種色彩效果。[4]

還有一個有趣、不過僅是推理的因素顯示大致的構圖早已確

普羅旺斯夜間的鄉村路　Country Road in Provence by Night
1890年5月　1890 May
油彩、帆布　oil on canvas
90.6×72公分　90.6 x 72 cm
Collection Kröller-Müller Museum, Otterlo, The Netherlands

立，至少天空與柏樹的位置是如此。在速寫中，有著光暈的明亮星星位於左方，鄰靠近畫紙的邊緣；但在油畫中，下方有第二顆光暈較柔和、較小的星星。兩顆星星與月亮，三者形成一道弓形。大約在他畫這幅畫的時期，法國天文學界宣布在1890年4月20日，新月的隔天，在晚上7點至8點20分之間，是觀察新月的特佳時機，而且月亮、金星與水星會連成一線。那個晚上，這3個天體將清楚可見排成一列5度的弧形。梵谷相當準確的描繪此星相，只是排列順序顛倒過來：事實上，月亮應該在金星的左方，水星在金星的右方。[5] 梵谷可能覺得這個自然現象很有趣而予以描繪，而在稍後幾週作畫時不是記錯排列方式，就是基於構圖的考量，故意將順序顛倒，如同在速寫中，他把柏樹放在假想中軸線的另一邊。

這「最後的嘗試」將梵谷聖雷米時期所有重要的主題匯聚一起。他所描述的沿路蘆葦也令人想起他所喜愛的成熟麥穗。他認為柏樹是個好主題，也是普羅旺斯的典型特徵，他所以希望能為其投注一系列的作品。結合左方背景他所喜愛黑藍色暗影的阿爾皮耶山，以及代表「北方回憶」的小旅店在右方，這裡他描繪他在地中海邊逗留的每一特色。就尋求風格而言，這幅作品完美保有他為了與高更和貝納的藝術競爭而創作的實驗作品。1889年秋天，他已告訴西奧他將帶回的作品，是要形成一個整體的「普羅旺斯印象」。（806/609，1889年10月5日）《普羅旺斯夜間的鄉村路》可說是這些印象的縮影。在寫給高更的信稿我們讀道：「我可能會把這所有普羅旺斯的回憶和其他的風景和主題作成蝕刻版畫，而且我非常高興給你一個我大約構思過的概略。」梵谷會在奧維發現新主題，聖雷米只是個回憶。蝕刻版畫從未製作，不過也許他有送給高更或貝納爾他承諾過的用畫的「概略」？

這幅作品最早的歷程並不清楚，但在1895年傅勒（Vollard）畫廊的展覽有這幅作品。目前我們所知，這幅作品從未在西奧遺孀的手上，也未曾透過將此畫賣給藝術商或私人收藏家。因此，就目前來看，無法有明確的定論。

---

1. Pickvance 1986，頁191。
2. 庫勒穆勒美術館的技術性檢驗，2002年7月31日。
3. J.J Susijn的技術報告，1983年1月（庫勒穆勒美術館檔案）。
4. 月亮可能因為一個非常不同的原因而補筆。在 *Lutetia*（1925）一書中，德國收藏家卡爾·史德翰（Carl Sternheim）描述一場「意外」：他記得發生於1909年，在一次拜訪阿姆斯特丹的喬·梵谷一柏格時，有好幾幅作品靠著牆上，完全曝曬於陽光下，而且是畫心對著畫心擺放著。史德翰寫道，由於熱度，畫作變成黏在一起，因此「當分開它們時，有片月亮從其中一幅有兩個人物與柏樹的大風景畫中鬆脫掉到地上。」史德翰喜歡誇大，至少根據他的傳記作者派崔克·布吉瓦特（Patrick Bridgewater）所言，但這絕對是一場奇怪的巧合。然而，喬從未擁有過收藏家所指《普羅旺斯夜間的鄉村路》，梵谷唯一一幅畫有柏樹、兩個人物還有月亮的畫。是否史德翰拜訪的是其他人（例如Amédée Schuffenecker或Wagram王子）？或者是他1912年或之後拜訪庫勒穆勒夫人？這奇特的意外或可解釋為何畫中的月亮是補筆的。現在也尚未有證據顯示史德翰拜訪海牙庫勒家。
5. Eijgenraam 1990，頁16。

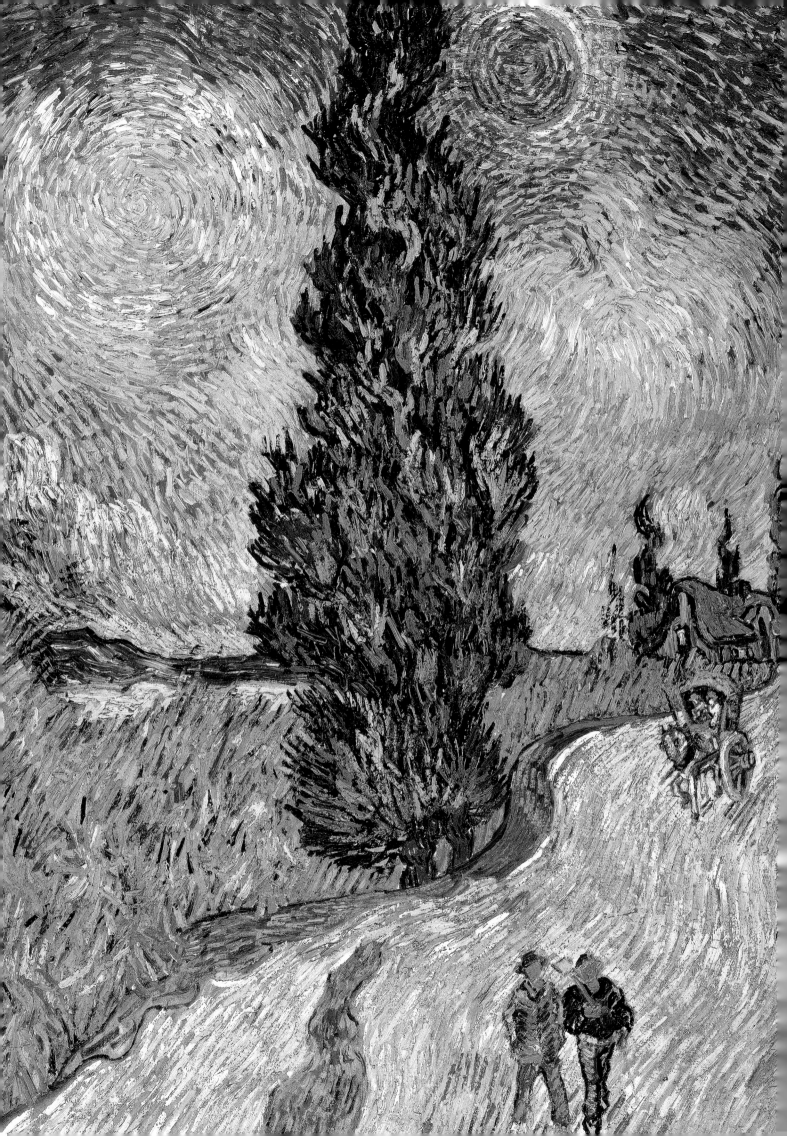

梵谷在離開聖雷米的精神病院後，在西奧巴黎的家待了幾天。他後來就搬到巴黎近郊的奧維舒瓦資（Auveres-Sur-Oise）這個美麗的小村莊，在那裡從1890年5月到7月，度過他生命中最後的2個月。透過西奧的介紹，一位熱愛藝術並在週日自己也作畫的精神科醫生—保羅‧嘉舍（Paul Gachet）負責照顧梵谷。靠著嘉舍的幫忙，梵谷在深受精神病發作所苦惱的情況下，繼續旺盛的創作。

這幅作品是梵谷以在嘉舍醫生家中發現的野花為題材，在1890年6月16日或17日所創作的幾幅靜物畫中的其中一幅。目前傳世的梵谷的畫，有薊花的野花靜物畫，只剩下這一幅以及一件私人收藏的《瓶中的野花和薊花》。雖然這兩幅畫中的花卉有異，但都被插在一張圓桌的同款式的花瓶中。因此這兩件作品被視為大約在同時

期畫的。

從桌子和花瓶的輪廓線上似乎可以觀察出梵谷在巴黎熱心收集的浮世繪的影響。

鋸齒狀的薊花葉子和麥穗彷彿擁抱花朵一樣向外展開。花瓶上接近同心圓的筆觸和淡青色背景上的垂直和水平交錯的筆觸，顯示梵谷仍然持續地探究線條、色彩和質地的效果。

梵谷於7月27日在一處麥田中舉槍自盡；他在兩天後過世。他的作品在他生前幾乎完全不受人賞識，但在他身後，崇拜他的野獸派和表現主義的畫家們都深受他的大膽用色和熱情筆觸的獨特表現所影響。

薊花　Flower Vase with Thistles
1890年6月16或17日　1890 16/17 Jun.
油彩、帆布　oil on canvas
40.8×33.6 cm　40.8 x 33.6 cm
POLA美術館　POLA Museum of Art (Pola Collection)

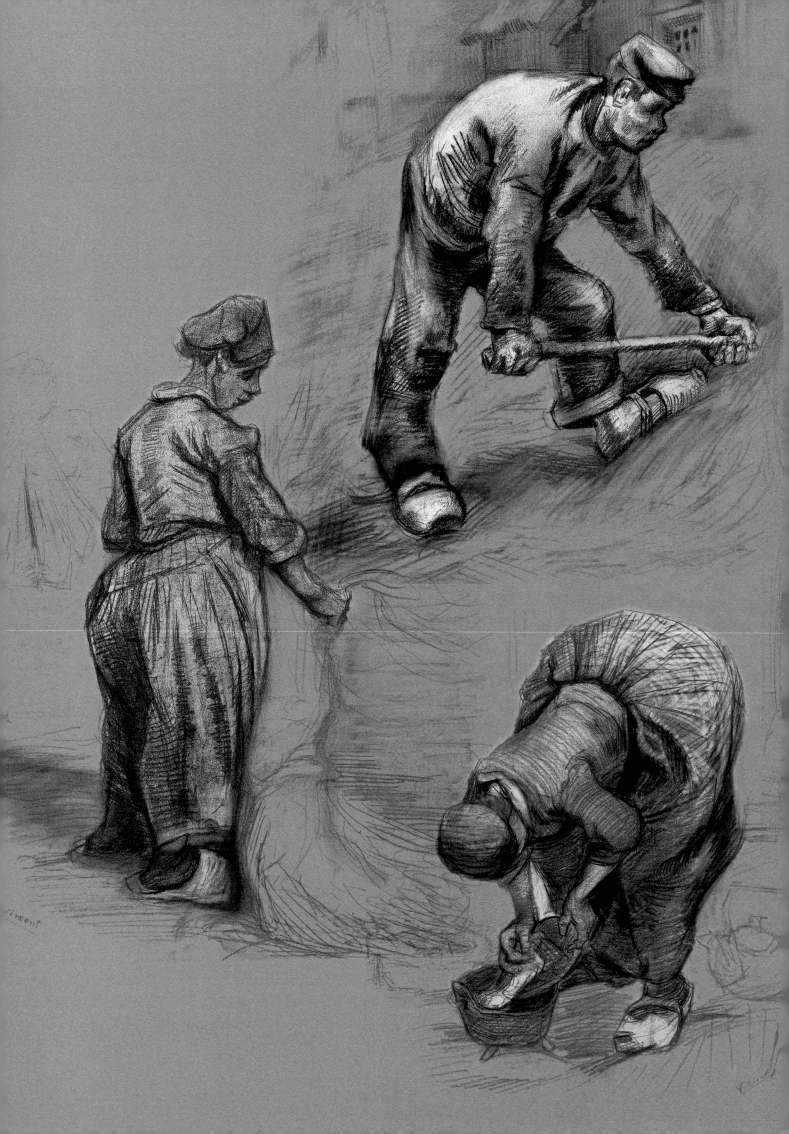

附録
Appendice

P. 59

Miners in the snow

September 1880
pencil, coloured chalk, watercolour, on wove paper
44 x 55 cm
no watermark
unsigned
F831/JH juv.11
KM 111.966

INSCRIPTIONS
verso, lower left: no 4 (pencil).
41 (black ink)
Verz : Hide Nijland (black ink)
lower centre: besteld [illegible] 8 Jan 1895 (black chalk).
upper left: diep groen of [illegible] (pencil).
KR 12 (blue chalk)

PROVENANCE
[probably A.C.W. Terhell coil., The Hague].
acquired by Hidde Nijland, Dordrecht, before 1895.
purchased from Hidde Nijland by AG. Kröller, The Hague,
July 1928.
donated to the Kröller Müller Foundation by A.G. Kröller,
December 1928

EXHIBITIONS
Dordrecht 1904, cat. no. 180.
Amsterdam 1924, cat. no. 14.
The Hague 1928, unnumbered.
Hamburg 1929, cat. no. 49.
Amsterdam 1930, cat. no. 1.
New York/Philadelphia/Boston and other cities, 1935-1936,
cat. no. 70.
Liège/Brussels/Mons 1946-1947, cat. no. a.
Paris 1947, cat. no. 2.
Geneva 1947, cat. no. 2.
Basel 1947, cat. no. 109.
London/Birmingham/Glasgow 1947-1948, cat. no. 100.
Paris 1952, cat. no. 333.
Saint Louis/Philadelphia/Toledo 1953 1954, cat. no. 1.
Nuremberg 1956, cat. no. 1.
Tokyo/Kyoto 1958, cat. no. 3.
Munich 1961, cat. no. 1.
London 1962, cat. no. 1.
Arnhem 1966, unnumbered.

Van Gogh did a great deal of drawing in the
Borinage, the Belgian mining district south-west
of Mons, where he stayed for long periods from
December 1878 to October 1880. Next to nothing
remains of this work, however,[1] and by all reports
the quality left much to be desired.[2] Miners in the

snow was made in September 1880, shortly after Van
Gogh had definitely decided to embark on the artistic
path, making it one of his earliest known works as an
independent artist.

In a letter to his brother Theo written on 20
August 1880 (155/134) we read about the subject for
the first time: 'I have made a hasty scribble of miners
and haulers [3] (both boys and girls) going to the shaft
in the morning through the snow, by a path along a
thorn hedge: passing shadows, dimly visible in the
twilight. In the background the large mine buildings
and the hill of cinders stand out vaguely against the
sky. I am sending you the scribble so you can see
what it is like.' That scribble has been preserved. It
can be deduced from two later letters that Van Gogh
based this scribble on an existing drawing made in
the winter of 1879-1880, which also explains why he
was working on a winter scene in the late summer.
He wrote, 'Yet I could not keep from sketching in a
rather large size the drawing of the miners going to
the shaft - which I sent you a scribble of-though I did
change the placement of the figures a little' (156/135,
7 September 1880).

The similarities between the scribble and
Miners in the snow make it quite likely that the latter
is the "sketch" to which Van Gogh referred. Both
were therefore drawn from a model, although he
made more changes in the sketch than in the frieze-
like line-up of figures. One of those changes was the
addition of three figures in the right foreground. The
entire composition looks less static because almost all
the figures are shown walking, and they also overlap
each other. In early 1881 he made another drawing
with miners in the snow 'which is somewhat better
than last winter's - there is more character and effect
in it," he wrote to his parents (162/144, 16 February
1881). By last winter's' Van Gogh will have meant the
model he used for the scribble and the sketch. That
drawing has not been preserved, nor has the one from
early 1881.[4]

Miners in the snow reveals Van Goghs initial
clumsiness when it came to figure drawing. This is
especially evident in the many corrections he made
in the outlines of the figures, especially in their legs
and relatively large feet. Despite their resolute gait
the miners are stiffly composed and have almost
no volume. A number of them are wearing leather
helmets, but other typical miners' attributes such
as a lamp, pickaxe and shovel can also be seen. The
middle figure of the three smaller figures on the right
is shown from the back, suggesting that the path to
the mine turns to the left. Originally the two male
figures furthest to the right were a bit closer to the
edge; erased traces of them are still slightly visible
there.

The sheet was later trimmed on the right
and to a lesser degree on the left, which means the
composition must have been more spacious at first.[5]"
The four central figures are an almost exact replica of
those in the small scribble. The two in the middle of
this group are girls; the girl on the left has her hair
tied up in a net, as has the leftmost of the three small
figures on the right. An important improvement over
the scribble (and therefore probably over the original
example as well] is the woman with the basket on

her back who terminates the picture on the far left.
She is the only figure whose body is turned slightly
towards the viewer. Like the man with the shovel, her
expression is rather grim, giving both of them more
character so they look less wooden than the other
figures. The clothing of these two has also been given
a bit of colour in the form of a light blue and brown
wash.

In the background above a row of snow-
covered houses a mound of cinders ('terril') can be
seen, also covered in snow, with mining buildings,
bridges, chimneys and the like to the left and right.
It is difficult to identify the exact location of the
work, but the larger mine building to the left, with
a second smaller roof extending from its main roof,
under which the large flywheels of the lift cables
can be seen, is somewhat reminiscent of the mining
pit 'Fosse No 3 d'Hornu et Wasmes'.[6] The way the
building and the long metal bridges in the scribble
are rendered is closer to the situation as it was at the
time. In the large drawing Van Gogh probably had
trouble bringing the upper part of the drawing to a
resolution, and as a result one bridge runs right under
the building's roof, which is not customary.

The sheet has suffered from considerable
ill treatment. The paper is badly discoloured and
seriously damaged in several places. During an early
restoration the sheet was reinforced on the back with
paper pulp, which unfortunately obliterated part of
an inscription The handwriting of the inscription
resembles that of the collector Hidde Nijland, from
whose collection the drawing was obtained. Only
the word 'besteld' (ordered) and the date '8 Jan 1895'
are still legible, which may have had to do with the
exhibition of more than So Van Gogh drawings from
Nijland's collection that were shown in February
Match 1895 at the Haagsche Kunstkring.

1. In 1888 Van Gogh wrote to Eugène Both (letter 696/335b)
that he had started working from nature for the first time
in the Borinage, but 'of course I destroyed it all a long time
ago'. Coal mine in the Borinage (F1040) from the summer
of 1879 is one of the rare works that have been preserved;
it is part of the collection of the Van Gogh Museum (Van
Heugten 1996, pp. 69-71).
2. Piérard 1929, pp. 57-88.
3. Van Gogh wrote 'sclôneurs et sclôneuses'; these were
usually young miners (boys and girls) who assisted the
'abatteur' the miner who hacked the coal looseby hauling
away the loosened material.
4. Liesbeth Heenk identifies Miners in the snow with this
quote and dates the drawing to February 1881 because she
regards the differences between the scribble and the sketch
as too great to have been based on the same model (Heenk
1995, pp. 18-19). it is otherwise not inconceivable that
Van Gogh continued working on the sketch after having
mentioned it in the letter of 7 September 1880.
5. There is clearly more space in the scribble, especially on
the right. It is not clear to what extent Van Gogh himself
was responsible for reducing the size of the work. None of
the edges is original and all the sides have been trimmed.
6. For old photographs of a number of mine buildings in the
Borinage, see http://mineshainaur.ibelgsque. com. and
http://borain.be. Van Gogh spent a great deal of time in
(Petit) Wasmes during the period 1879-1880 (Hulsker 1985,
pp. 111-148).

P. 61

L'Angélus du soir (after Millet)

October 1880
black chalk, pencil, wash, red chalk, heightened with white,
on(originally) grey-blue laid paper
46.8 x 61.9 cm
watermark: B a ST mars [maas?]
unsigned
F834/JH juv.i4
KM 115.117

INSCRIPTIONS
recto, lower left (by the artist):d'après J.F. Millet/L'Angélus du
soir(black ink).
lower right: ATEL: VINCENT (black chalk)
verso, lower left: No 36 (black ink).
lower right: 189 (pencil).
KR[illegible] (blue chalk)

PROVENANCE
acquired by Hidde Nijland, Dordrecht, before 1904.
purchased from Hidde Nijland by A.G. Kröller, The Hague,
July 1928.
donated to the Kröller-Müller Foundation by A.G. Kröller,
December 1928

EXHIBITIONS
Dordrecht 1904, cat. no. 189.
The Hague 1918, cat. no. 56.
Amsterdam 1924, cat. no. 15.
The Hague 1928, unnumbered.
Hamburg 1929. cat. no. 100.
Amsterdam 1930. cat. no. 3.
Nuremberg 1956 cat. no. 2.
Vienna 1958 cat. no. 4.
Tokyo/Kyoto 1958, cat. no. 4.
Munich 1961, cat. no. 2.
Brussels 1961, no cat.
Belgrade 1966, cat. no. 1.
Mons 1980, cat. no. 4.
Amsterdam 1980-1981, cat. no. 42.
Rome 1988, cat. no. 49.
Otterlo 1990, cat. no. 2.
Yokohama/Nagoya 1995-1996, cat. no. 1.
Tokyo/Fukuoka 1999-2000, cat. no. 2.

P. 63

Les bêheurs (after Millet)

October 1880
pencil, black chalk, on wove paper
37.5 x 61.5 cm
no watermark
unsigned
F829/JH C.B.
KM 119.703

INSCRIPTIONS
recto, lower left (by the artist): d'aprs J F Millet/Les Bêcheurs
(black ink)

PROVENANCE
acquired by Hidde Nijland, Dordrecht, before 1904.
purchased from Hidde Nijland by A.G. Kröller, The Hague,
July 1928.
donated to the Kröller-Müller Foundation by A.G. Kröller,
December 1928

EXHIBITIONS
Dordrecht 1904, cat. no. 178.
Amsterdam. 1924, cat. no. 16.
The Hague 1928, unnumbered.
Hamburg 1929, cat. no. 61.
Amsterdam 1930, cat. no. 4.
Munich 1956, cat. no. 3.
Cuesmes1960. Brussels 1961, no cat.
Warsaw 1962, cat. no. 5.
Tel Aviv/Haifa 1962-1963, cat. no. 4.
Belgrade 1966, cat. no. 3.
MOSCOW/Leningrad 1971, cat. no. 3.
Mons 1980, cat. no. 3.
Osaka 1986, cat. no. 10.
Rome 1988, cat. no. 48.

NOTE
A Since De la Faille 1928 it is often mistakenly noted that Les
bêcheurs is signed "Vincent' at the lower right.

'If I am not mistaken, you must still have "Les
Travaux des Champs" by Millet. Would you be so kind
as to lend it to me for a short time, and send it by
mail? I must tell you that I am working on some large
drawings after Millet [...]. I am writing to you while
I'm drawing, and I am in a hurry to go back to it.' Van
Gogh wrote this on 20 August 1880 from Cuesmes in
the Borinage to Theo in the first letter known to us
after he had decided to become an artist (155/134).
From this and later letters we learn of the time
constraints he put himself under. As a 27-year-old he
was not very young for a beginning artist and he still
had a lot to learn. He was especially eager to practise
figure drawing, and some of this practice consisted of
copying the work of artists he admired. Jean-François

Millet (1814-1875), the painter of French peasant life,
was far and away the most important example for Van
Gogh.[1] Of the dozens of copies he must have made
after Millet between August 1880 and May 1881 only
a few have been preserved in addition to the two
drawings being treated here.[2]

Both drawings can be dated with quite some
certainty to October 1880. Van Gogh had moved to
Brussels during the first half of that month. There
he had sought contact with Tobias Victor Schmidt,
an art dealer who had taken over the local branch of
Goupil & Cie and whom he still knew from the days
when he himself worked for Goupil.[3] He hoped that
Schmidt might be able to help him find an artist with
a studio where he could take lessons (letter 158/137,
15 October 1880). At that meeting Schmidt lent him
two photographs, as we discover from a letter dated 1
November (159/138): 'Have drawn "Les bêcheurs" by
Millet, from a Braun phot. which I found at Schmidt's
and which he lent me along with that of " L'angélus
du soir". I sent both these drawings to Pa so he might
see I am working.' That last comment is important
because it probably explains why the drawings were
preserved and can be identified with the works being
dealt with here. Both sheets are unsigned but bear
inscriptions in black ink made with the same hand:
'd'après J.F. Millet' followed by their title. It is almost
certainly the handwriting of the artist. These are two
large drawings that turned out well, which must have
made him feel confident enough to send them to his
father.[4]

The photograph of Les bêcheurs from Ad.
Braun & Co. refers to a shot of Millet's drawing from
c. 1857.[5] Van Gogh drew with pencil, but in several
places he later applied black chalk to add accents,
as in the digger on the right, the stones to the right
and the shadows in the foreground. He followed the
original fairly closely although he did leave more
space on the right, producing a more elongated
composition. Diggers were an important theme in the
course of his career, right up until the end. There is
another version of Les bcheurs in the series of painted
copies after Millet that he made in Saint-Rmy starting
in September 1889, for which he had explicitly asked
Theo to send him the Braun photo of the drawing
(letter 806/607,19 September 1889).[6]

The sheet of paper on which Les bêcheurs is
drawn has been rather damaged and is quite wrinkled,
especially along the edges.

The extremely fibrous wove paper has turned
brown over time. This may indicate that it was once
tinted blue, as was the paper used for L'Angélus du
soir, which also turned brown. On that drawing a
rectangular patch of the original light blue colour
is visible in the middle, right below the basket of
potatoes.[7] Millet's composition from 1885-1857 of a
simple peasant woman praying the angelus with her
husband in the fields after a hard day's work became
extremely popular at the end of the nineteenth
century thanks to all the reproductions that were
made. In this case Van Gogh worked from Braun's
photo of the work, but he had already bought three
copies of an etching of L'Angélus du soir from
Durand-Ruel in 1876 for one franc each (letter
72/58).

Two years before that he had confided, 'That painting by Millet, "L'Angélus du soir", "that's it", indeed - that's magnificent, that's poetry'(letter 17/13, January 1874). Van Gogh probably did not know that while he was in Brussels working on the drawing, the painting happened to be there in the very same city.8

L'Angélus du soir is more elaborately conceived from a technical point of view than Les bêcheurs. Here, too. Van Gogh used mainly pencil and black chalk, but in the sky he applied a light wash with highly diluted white opaque watercolour. The accents in brownish red chalk in the sky and along the upper edge were probably intended to emphasise the sense of the approaching night-fall and were doubtless more effective when the paper was still totally light blue. The low evening light is now suggested by the elongated shadows that Van Gogh added to the pitchfork, the basket and the figures. In the field he applied washes to the drawing in places with brush and water to create grey tonal effects. He later broke these areas open by rubbing in light accents with an eraser, thus reinforcing the effect of broad evening light. The contrast between the man, who is backlit, and the woman, who is catching the last rays of the sun on her apron and clogs, is stronger in Millet, where the middle area is much lighter. But the most striking difference is in the proportions: Van Gogh's copy is more spacious because he enlarged the composition considerably to the left and the right and at the bottom. Placed further from the edge, his figures appear less monumental. In Millet the wheelbarrow is almost touching the edge of the composition, which is more square as a whole. In Van Gogh the pitchfork is a bit further back and more room has been created between the basket and the woman's clogs. Finally, the horizon between the figures has been lowered and the woman's folded hands go over it.9 You can even see that in enlarging the composition Van Gogh was not entirely sure what to do with the extra space, because the strips to the left and the right (about ten centimetres in width) are drawn hesitantly and with less precision than the rest.

The actual painting is not much larger than the drawing, but because of the square format and the larger figures it looks heavier and more monumental, allowing it to grow into an icon of the deeply pious country life.10 Van Gogh's spatial plan tends more towards casual observation and is less a literal copy than, say, Les bêcheurs, although Millet's example is still emphatically present, of course.

1. For the relationship between Van Gogh and Millet, see Van Tilborgh et al. 1988 and Van Tilborgh et al. 1998.
2. These are: Reaper (after Millet) (F1674/JH2), privately owned, and Sower (after Millet) (F830/JH1), Van Gogh Museum, both dated April 1881. There is another version of Les bêcheurs (F828/JHXII), also dated October 1880.
3. Schmidt had taken over the branch in around 1875 from Hendrik Vincent van Gogh, Vincent and Theo's 'Uncle Hein' (Stolwijk & Thomson 1999, pp. 24 and 193; Nonne 2000, p. 40). when Van Gogh made his visit he did not know that Schmidt was having problems with the family at that moment because he had started out on his own. Van Gogh was warmly received nevertheless (letter 159/138).
4. The other version of Les bêcheurs (F828) has no inscription but it does have a signature; it is unclear

whether the signature was applied by the artist himself.
5. Chetham 1976, p. 258. See Herbert 1974, pp. 159-166, 167 and 169 for the various versions of Millet's Les bêcheurs, also referred to as Les deux bêcheurs.
6. F648, Stedelijk Museum, Amsterdam.
7. Blue tinted paper sometimes has the tendency to fade into an intense brown. Remnants of coloured fibres were not found in Les bêcheurs, however. The probable explanation for the area of original paper colour in L'Angélus du soir is that the back of the paper was covered in the same place (Hoefsloot 1987, p. 8.). The blue colour is also faintly visible along the edges. The lower left hand corner was torn away at some point and provisionally repaired, but in the 1980s it was reinforced when the entire sheet was backed with Japanese rice paper.
8. Part of the John W. Wilson collection (Herbert 1974, pp. 104-105). The painting is usually entitled L'Angélus without the addition of du soir. The angelus is a threepart prayer that is offered up at 6 a.m., 12 noon and 6 p.m.
9. The woman's head was initially positioned a bit higher, as can be seen from the visible corrections round her cap.
10. Herbert 1974, pp. 103-106.

P. 65

The bearers of the burden

April 1881
pencil, pen in brown and black ink, white and grey opaque warercolour
on (originally) blue laid paper
47.5 x 63 cm
watermark: ED & Cie (in cartouche) PL BAS
unsigned
F832r/JH C.B.
KM 122.865 RECTO

INSCRIPTIONS
recto: lower right (by the artist):
The Bearers of the Burden (white opaque watercolour)

PROVENANCE
acquired by Hidde Nijland, Dordrecht, before 1895
purchased from Hidde Nijland by A.G. Kröller, The Hague, July 1928.
donated to the Kröller Müller Foundation by A.G. Kröller, December 1928

EXHIBITIONS
The Hague 1895, no known cat.
Dordrecht 1897, no cat.
Dordrecht 1904, cat. no. 188.
The Hague 1918, cat. no. 74.
Amsterdam 1924, cat. no. 13.
The Hague 1928, unnumbered.
Hamburg 1929, cat. no. 91.
Amsterdam 1930, car. no. 2.
Liège/Brussels/Mons 1946-1947, cat. no. 3.
Paris 1947, cat. no. 3.
Geneva 1947, cat. no. 3.
Basel 1947, cat. no. 110.
London/Birmingham/Glasgow 1947-1948, cat. no. 101.
New York/Chicago 1949-1950, cat. no. 13.
Milan 1952, cat. no. 1.
The Hague 1953, cat. no. 1.
Otterlo/Amsterdam 1953, cat. no. 1.
Munich 1956, cat. no. 4.
Vienna 1958, cat. no. 3
Munich 1961, cat. no. 3
Mons 1980, cat. no. 5.
Amsterdam 1980-1981, cat. no. 44.
Paris/London/The Hague 1983, cat. no. 151.
Tokyo/Nagoya 1985-1986, cat. no. 1.
Osaka 1986, cat. no. 4.
Otterlo 1990, cat. no. 3
London 1992, cat. no. 15.
Yokohama/Nagoya 1995-1996, cat. no. 2.
Tokyo/Fukuoka 1999-2000, cat. no. 3.
Brussels 2000, unnumbered

The bearers of the burden is an ambitious drawing of the miner's life that Van Gogh started in Brussels and probably completed afterwards in Etten. Compared with Miners in the snow (p.17) it is striking how much he has progressed in a half year's time. Not only have the figures been given more volume but the proportions are more convincing and the perspective of the receding landscape is exemplary. Although certainly not free of imperfections, this drawing is the first evidence of Van Gogh's great expressiveness in a subject of his own choosing. The women depicted are literally weighed down by their heavy burdens: sacks full of usable scraps of coal gathered from the mound of cinders in the background. At the same time, the English title The bearers of the burden - written in the lower right in grey watercolour - indicates that these poor miners' wives should also be regarded as such in the figurative sense.

Van Gogh mentioned the subject in a letter of 12 April 1881, sent from Brussels when he was just about to leave for Etten. Theo was supposed to be going there as well, and Van Gogh wrote that he was 'looking forward to it very much, particularly because I have sketched two drawings at Rappard's, "The lamp bearers" and "The bearers of the burden," and should like to consult you about how to go on with them' (letter 164/143). The lamp bearers has not been preserved, but undoubtedly its subject also had something to do with miners.1 Apparently the drawings were still in the sketch phase, probably a first draft in pencil. The bearers of the burden is underdrawn entirely in pencil and is further developed in pen and ink. Van Gogh used two different kinds of ink, first brown and then black.2 He worked with pens of varying widths, which is clearly visible in the broader strokes in the foreground and the contours round the figures. By strongly alternating the pen strokes he built up the drawing rhythmically. The path on which the women are walking is rendered with fine crosshatchings and wider horizontal lines. The area behind that consists mainly of short adjacent stripes that form a 'light' intermezzo for the ploughed field above, where diagonal lines run towards the vanishing point on the horizon near the church. The composition is terminated at the right by a tree, on which a little shrine containing a crucifix has been nailed. The crucifix is executed entirely in pencil and has not been overdrawn in ink.

The women scouring the cinder mounds were called 'arracheuses' or 'ramasseuses'. Their typical bent over gait must have been a common sight for the artist during his stay in the Borinage. The first woman is carrying a miner's lamp, which she seems to be using to light her way back.[3] This may have been Van Gogh's way of referring to The lamp bearers as a companion piece. In the village in the background he contrasted the church with the mining plant. Along with the crucifix and the two spades to the right of the composition they emphasise the living conditions of the area inhabitants, which basically boiled down to 'pray and work'.[4] Van Gogh had developed a great affection for the mining folk, which he touchingly expressed in a letter to Theo shortly before his departure from the Borinage: 'The miners and the weavers still form a race somehow apart from other workers and artisans and I have much sympathy for them and I should consider myself fortunate if I could draw them one day, for then these as yet unknown, or virtually unknown, types would be brought out into the light of day. The man from the depths, from the abyss, "de profundis", that is the miner. The other, with the faraway look, almost daydreaming, almost a sleepwalker, that is the weaver. I have been living among them now for nearly two years and have learned a littleof their special character, in particular that of the miners. And I always find something touching and even pathetic in these poor and wraithlike workers' (157/136, 24 September 1880). Later in The Hague, Van Gogh briefly toyed with the idea of returning to the Borinage for a short time.[5]

The 'Rappard' mentioned by Van Gogh was Anthon Gerard Alexander Ridder van Rappard (1858-1892), a Dutch artist he had come to know in Brussels. After a rather difficult start a friendship grew between the younger Van Rappard, who had already been thoroughly trained, and Van Gogh, a friendship that was to last for four and a halfyears.[6] The extensive pen and ink overdrawing almost made the sheet of paper resemble an engraving or an etching and may have been influenced in part by Van Rappard, who was a bit more experienced in this area. But Van Gogh may have had another reason for taking this approach. In about January 1881 he began making more independent drawings in addition to copying in the hope of securing a position as an illustrator. At the same time, he started (or resumed, as he said in a letter to his parents) collecting wood engravings, for which he would develop an increasingly stronger passion in the coming years.[7] The fact that he thought The bearers of the burden and The lampbearers might be suitable for reproduction is suggested in the letter to Theo already quoted: 'I must somehow have the necessary models to finish them, and then I trust the result will be good, that is, I shall have a few compositions to show to Smeeron Tilly, or to the people at L'Illustration or the like' (164/143).

L'Illustration was a reputable French journal, and the engravers Burne Smeeton and Auguste Tilly, who were located in Paris, provided illustrations for a number of popular publications at that time.

---

1. This tells us that working with companion pieces or series was something Van Gogh had developed early on. Before this he had drawn companion pieces of miners going to work in the morning and coming home in the evening (see letter 155/134).
2. It is possible that the brown ink is faded black ink. In any case it was different in composition. Since the black ink on this sheet is still a good black, it maybe Indian ink. The brown or faded black is perhaps a cheaper gallnut ink. See Van Heugren 2005 on discoloration in the drawings of Van Gogh.
3. Such lamps were usually the property of the mine and were distributed to the miners in the morning before they went down in the mines. The lamp depicted by Van Gogh can be identified as the 'Mueseler' type (see http://mineshainaut.ibelgique.com).
4. The mine building with the typical roof and adjacent chimneys closely resembles the building in the background of Miners in the snow. The small houses in front are placed elsewhere, however, which suggests that Van Gogh freely combined the elements in hisbackground, possibly based on earlier sketches made on site. There also seems to be little realism in the tall bridge that cleaves the air to the left of the cinder mound and provides such compositional strength.
5. See letter 264/R42. In November 1882 he made another watercolour with 'arracheuses'. Miners were hardly ever chosen as attistic subjects until the Belgian artist Constantin Meunier (1831-1905) took notice of them in around 1880, just when Van Gogh was leaving the Borinage. Van Gogh greatly admired the work of Meunier.
6. Van Rappard will be discussed more frequently later on. See Brouwer et al. 1974 on his life and work.
7. Letter 162/141, 16 February 1881. See Luijten 2003 on Van Gogh's print collection.

P. 67

Corner of a garden

June 1881
pencil, black chalk, pen and ink, grey and brown wash
opaque watercolour, on laid paper
44.5 x 56.7 cm
watermark: H v I,
lion rampant facing left with sabre and sheaf of arrows
unsigned
F902/JH9
KM 115.487

INSCRIPTIONS
recto, lower left: Atelier/Vincent (pencil) 'Verz: Hidde Nijland (black ink)
verso, upper left: KR 46 (in frame) (blue chalk); Gekocht van den Kunstkooper/Oldenzeel te Rotterdam/teekening van Vincent van Gogh/Dordrecht Dec: 1892/Hidde Nijland (pencil)

PROVENANCE
A.C.W. Terhell coil., The Hague, ? 1892'
purchased by Hidde Nijland, Dordrecht, at Oldenzeel, art dealer, Rotterdam, December 1892 '
purchased from Hidde Nijland by A.G. Kröller, The Hague, July 1928 '
donated to the Kröller Müller Foundation by A.G. Kröller, December 1928

EXHIBITIONS
Rotterdam 1892, no cat.
The Hague 1895, no known cat.
Dordrecht 1897, no cat.
Dordrecht 1904, cat. no. 179.
The Hague 1918, cat. no. 68.
Amsterdam 1924, cat. no. 23.
The Hague 1928, unnumbered.
Hamburg 1929, cat. no. 77.
Amsterdam 1930, cat. no. 22.
Basel 1947, cat. no. 115.
's Hertogenbosch/Breda 1950.
Milan 1952, cat. no. 5.
The Hague 1953, cat. no. 2.
Otterlo/Amsterdam 1953, cat. no. 2.
Saint Louis/Philadelphia/Toledo 1953-1954, cat. no. 5.
Nuremberg 1956, cat. no. 4.
Munich 1956, cat. no. 8.
Vienna 1958, cat. no. 12.
Tokyo/Kyoto 1958, cat. no. 7.
Munich 1961, cat. no. 7.
London 1962, cat. no. 2.
Charleroi/Antwerp/Paris/Lyon 1971-1972, cat. no. 10.
's Hertogenbosch 1987-1988, cat. no. 65.
Otterlo 1990, cat. no. 5.
Tokyo/Fukuoka 1999-2000, cat. no. 10.
Seattle/Atlanta 2004-2005, cat. no. 13.

We do not know for certain where in Etten Van Gogh drew this idyllic Cornet of a garden. He probably worked in the garden of the parsonage, but reference material is scarce. The parsonage was pulled down in 1905, and the immediate surroundings have also undergone such drastic change that there is little recalling earlier times.[1]

Van Gogh sketched out the drawing in pencil, which is still clearly visible throughout. The trees in the background have been rendered in a rather helter skelter fashion, with all the requisite corrections. Typical features are the sharp dots and short stripes used to suggest the leaves of the trees against the sky. Van Gogh worked over the pencil drawing, especially the lower half, with pen and ink. He drew the furniture beneath the arbour with the utmost precision so it would stand out against the background, with its fine crosshatching alternating with more loosely executed work. Colour has been sparingly applied in several places in the form of strongly diluted brown red and green opaque watercolour. Van Gogh drew some of the leaves on the wall and in the arbour in a strikingly stylised way:

as angular hearts and circles as well as fanciful stars. This very much resembles the way he later would draw foliage with the reed pen in Arles and especially in Saint Rémy.[2]

On this sheet Van Gogh focused on a fairly precise rendition of a simple, romantic scene: an arbour in a garden against a stone wall overgrown with plants, with a few pieces of furniture but no people. Yet there are signs of human presence: the wicker basket, the chequered cloth, and between them a ball and a strand of fibre, probably a ball of yarn. Because of this, the sheet seems to transcend a study of some arbitrary motif. Perhaps Van Gogh intended to make a reference to the departure of his youngest sister Willemien, who had left their parents' home in June, much to his regret.[3]

Mrs Kröller Müller recognised a 'psychic' emptiness and a sentimental atmosphere in the drawing. In a letter dated 28 March 1912 she wrote to her confidant Salomon ('Sam') van Deventer in the instructive tone that was so characteristic of her writing: 'Salomon, do you now have a better understanding of Van Gogh's picture: the bench, the table and that very silent little garden. Can you not imagine two people having sat there and just recently having stood up, who had experienced nothing & yet so much, who also saw that garden in all its simple and great splendour? And behind them the house, which forms the backdrop to what the garden revealed. Look once again at the picture, which was always so dear to me & formed such a contrast to the robustness of feeling in Van Gogh's other works.'[4] As she often did, she saw the composition in terms of a personal situation. To be more precise, what she was alluding to here was a bench in the garden of Huize ten Vijver, the Kröller's villa in Scheveningen, where she had had conversations with Van Deventer and sometimes read his letters.

---

1. See for instance Van Uitert et al. 1987, pp. 196-197; Heenk 1995, p. 32. In two drawings that Van Gogh made of the front of the parsonage in 1876 (Juv. xxI and xxII) a building can be seen in the background to the right that vaguely corresponds to the house behind the wall in Corner of a garden (Van Heugten 1996, pp. 57-29) In a more precise and older drawing of the parsonage from 1831 by Daniel Gevers the similarities between the two are stronger, mainly in the roof and the chimneys, but it is still difficult to provide a definitive answer (Rozemeyer et al. 2003, p. 87, fig. p. 8). An annex can be clearly seen in that drawing, for example, that should also be visible in Corner of a garden.
2. Compare, for example, Van Gogh's pen drawings of the ivy coveted trees in the garden of the asylum at Saint Remy: F1522 and F1532 (both Van Gogh Museum, Amsterdam).
3. See letter 167/146, June 1881. This would make Corner of a garden a fine counterpart to Memory of the garden at Etten (F496), where Van Gogh includes two women walking together whom he associated with his mother and Willemien (letter 725/w9, c. 16 November 1888).
4. At that time the 23 year old Van Deventer worked in the office of Wm. H. Muller & Co in Bremen. Since 2005 the extensive collection of letters from Mrs Kröller Muller to Sam van Deventer has been kept in the Kröller-Müller Museum, Archive S. van Deventer. At the time this letter was sent the drawing was still the property of Hidde Nijland, but pictures of it appeared in Nijland 1905, pl. 46, Bremmer 1907, pl. 3 and Bremmer 1911, pl. 9, publications with which Mrs Kröller Müller and Van Deventer were

familiar. Her projection was also influenced by Bremmer, who called the garden 'a silent witness' to two people who had had their last conversation and would never see each other again (Bremmer 1911, p. 75).

P. 69

The daughter of Jacob Meyer (after Bargue after Holbein)

July 1881
pencil, pen and black ink, on laid paper
54 x 42.8 cm
watermark: H v I
lion rampant facing left with sabre and sheaf of arrows
unsigned
F833/JH13
KM 128.492

INSCRIPTIONS
verso: upper left: 80½-64½ (pencil).
upper centre: lijst 12 (pencil)

PROVENANCE
L.C. Enthoven coll., Voorburg.
sale Amsterdam (Frederik Muller & Cie), 18 May 1920 (Enthoven collection), lot 249: Capie d'après le dessin de Holbein représentant Anna
Meyer et se trouvant au Musée à Bâle.
purchased by H. Kröller Müller at sale Amsterdam (Frederik Muller & Cie), 20 June 1922,
lot 42: Copie d'après le dessin de Holbein représentant Anna Meyer et se trouvant au Musée à Bâle (190 guilders)

EXHIBITIONS
Basel/Bern/Brussels 1927, cat. no. 35.
Düsseldorf 1928, cat. no. 208.
Berlin 1928-1929, cat. no. 2.
Hamburg 1929, cat. no. 29.
Amsterdam 1930, cat. no. 6.
Basel 1947, cat. no. 111.
Milan 1952, cat. no. 3.
Munich 1956, cat. no. 5.
Vienna 1958, cat. no. 5.
Montreal/
Ottawa/Winnipeg/Toronto 1960-1961, cat. no. 83.
Warsaw 1962, cat. no. 6.
Tel Aviv/Haifa 1962-1963, cat. no. 5.
Yokohama/Nagoya 1995-1996, cat. no. 4.

Detroit/Boston/Philadelphia 2000-2001, unnumbered.
Amsterdam 2005, no cat.

In August 1880, while in Cuesmes, Van Gogh had written a letter to Hermanus Gijsbertus Tersteeg, the manager of the Hague branch of the French art dealers Goupil & Cie and Van Gogh's former boss, asking if he could borrow the drawing course entitled Exercices au fusain pour préparer à l'étude de l'académie d'après nature (1871) by Charles Bargue (1826/27 1883). Tersteeg sent him not only the course but also Bargue's other teaching method Cours de dessin (1868-1870), plus a few textbooks having to do with perspective and anatomy.[1] Bargue's works were published by Goupil in Paris, and Van Gogh probably still remembered them from when he had worked for the firm, from 1869 to 1876.

Drawing the examples from Bargue coincided with copying the work of Millet and other artists. Within two weeks Van Gogh had already drawn all 60 examples once from Exercices au fusain 'exercises with charcoal' that consisted of outline drawings of the male nude. He would do the same at least three more times over the space of a year, later commenting, 'Careful study and the constant and repeated copying of Bargue's Exercices au fusain have given me better insight into figure drawing. I have learned to measure and to see and to look for the broad outlines, so that, thank God, what seemed utterly impossible to me before is gradually becoming possible now.'[2]

In Cuesmes he also copied the first part of the Cours de dessin, 70 lithos based on plaster models (Modèles d'après la bosse). When he moved to Brussels in early October he started on the 67 sheets of part two of the course entitled Modèles d'après les maîtres de toutes les époques et de toutes les écoles. More than a third of these were lithos after the work of Hans Holbein the Younger (1497/98 1543). Van Gogh also copied these examples at least twice over the course of a year; exactly how often he did so is still unclear. A total of four drawings by him after the Cours de dessin are known. Three of these are after Holbein, two of which are based on the same example, The daughter of Jacob Meyer.[3] Bargue's litho of Holbein's delicately coloured drawing from about 1526 of Anna Meyer, the daughter of the mayor of Basel, is of fine quality and renders the original with great precision (fig.).[4] Van Gogh himself recognised this while he was working, when he wrote to his brother: 'Those Holbeins in the Modèles d'après les Maîtres are splendid. Now that I am drawing them, I feel it even more strongly than before. But I assure you, they are not easy.' (159/138, 1 November 1880)

The second copy of The daughter of Jacob Meyer is different in execution and character. Van Gogh started with a schematic pencil underdrawing, which he worked over extensively in pen and ink. He used a fine pen mainly in the background and face, resulting in networks of crosshatchings as in an engraving. Contours, hair and some of the details were drawn with a broader pen. Here, too, the example is followed quite precisely, except for the head. This head has a character all its own and bears little resemblance to Anna Meyer. Van Gogh omitted the hair that in the example is visible to the left of the neck, so that the chin projects more emphatically over the collar. The nose is less rounded, longer, and its contour makes the face look rather coarse, giving the girl a more rustic expression. The artist seems to have departed from the example quite intentionally. As a type, this copy even hints a bit at the distinctive heads he later would make in The Hague and Nuenen. Unlike the earlier copy, Van Gogh did not draw a frame around the composition. This is why he had trouble with the background hatching which is not underdrawn in pencil in the lower right hand corner. Where Holbein let Anna Meyer's hair touch the edge of the drawing there is now a bit of remaining space.

The subtle pen and ink work reveals a more experienced hand and suggests a somewhat later date, which can be placed with quite some certainty in the summer of 1881. The paper points in this direction as well. In a letter from July 1881, Van Gogh said that because of the warmth he was working indoors, 'copying the drawings by Holbein from the Bargues' (168/147). The only other known works using the laid paper bearing the same watermark (H v I and a lion rampant facing left with sabre and sheaf of arrows) are three drawings that are also part of the Kröller-Müller collection, View of a wood, Corner of a garden and Portrait of Willemina Jacoba ('Wil') van Gogh (pp. 35, 37, 41), all to be dated to June/July 1881.[7]

1. Letters 155/134, 20 August 1880, and 156/135,7 September 1880. The other books were probably John Marshall, Esquisses anatomiques l'usage des artistes, and one of the works by Cassagne (Van Heugten 1996, pp. 16-17).
2. Letter 171/150, c. September 1881. In January 1881 he copied them for the third time (letter 161/040). None of these have been preserved, probably because they were only exercises and there was little reason to save them for a longer period. In 1890 in Anverssur Oise Van Gogh copied the Exercices one last time, a few sheets of which have survived (F1508 recto, F1609 verso, without F number, all Van Gogh Museum, Amsterdam; Van der Wolk 1986, pp. 267-268).
3. A copy of plate 26, Bourgeois lady from Basel (after Holbein) (F848), now privately owned and formerly incorrectly identified as made after plate 27, A lady of the court ofHenry VIII (De la Faille 1970, p. 316; Chetham 1976, P. 258; Heenk 1995, p. 25). The fourth example, F849a(present location unknown) is not recognised by Dela Faille (1970, p. 318) as a copy after Bargue (Chetham 1976 does not mention it) but was made after plate 18,Roman woman (head study) after an original by Paul Dubois.See De Robertis & Smolizza 2005, pp. 127-137 for reproductions of all Bargue examples.
4. Holbein's drawing is now at the Basel Art Museum (Müller 1988, 197-198).
5. Which may explain why it was among the few that were preserved. It is not known exactly when and from whom H.P. Bremmer acquired the sheet. It is not listed in his earliest known inventory from 1911 1915, but it does appear in his second inventory from 1920 1922 (Balk 2004, Bijlage Verzameling H.P. Bremmer, p. 19).The name 'Van Gogh' was more frequently misspelled in the past, certainly in France. Indeed, the artist was more widely known by his first name, Vincent.
7 See pp. 427-428.

P. 71

Windmill 'De Oranjeboom', Dordrecht

August September 1881
charcoal, pencil, on wove paper
34.8 x 59.9 cm
watermark: B (fragment?) A
unsigned
F843/JH6
KM 122.956

INSCRIPTIONS
recto, lower right: AT VINCENT (pencil)

PROVENANCE
acquired by Hidde Nijland, Dordrecht, before 1904'
purchased from Hidde Nijland by A.G. Kröller, The Hague, July 1928'
donated to the Kröller Müller Foundation by A.G. Kröller, December 1928

EXHIBITIONS
Dordrecht 1904, cat. no. ?.
The Hague 1918, cat. no. ?.
Amsterdam 1924, cat. no. 12
The Hague 1928, unnumbered.
Hamburg 1929, cat. no. 118
Amsterdam 1930, cat. no. 7.
Vienna 1958, cat. no. 6.
Tokyo/Kyoto 1958, cat. no. 6.
Warsaw 1962, cat. no. 7
Tel Aviv/Haifa 1962-1963, cat. no. 6.
Belgrade 1966, cat. no. 4.
Yokohama/Nagoya 1995-1996, cat. no. 5.
Dordrecht 2005, unnumbered

NOTE
A Wharman's watercolour paper has a watermark featuring a separate letter 'B' (see Woman grinding coffee, p. 103). The 'B' in this watermark is in a different typeface and is in a position where, if it were from Whatman, more of that watermark would have to be visible.

P. 72

Windmills at Dordrecht (Weeskinderendijk)

August September 1881

pencil, black and green chalk, pen and brush in ink
opaque watercolour, on laid paper
25.7 x 59.8 cm
watermark: ED & Cie (in cartouche),
PLBAS signed lower right (not by the artist): Vincent (pencil)
A F850/JHI5
KM 126.249

INSCRIPTIONS
verso, centre left: goud (pencil)

PROVENANCE
L.C. Enthoven coll., Voorburg.
purchased by H. Kröller Müller at sale Amsterdam (Frederik Muller & Cie), 18 May 1920 (Enthoven collection), lot 256: Les Moulins (1,000 guilders)

EXHIBITIONS
Basel/Bern/Brussels 1927, cat. no. 34.
Düsseldorf 1928, cat. no. 100.
Karlsruhe 1928, cat. no. 35.
Berlin 1928-1929, cat. no. 5.
Hamburg 1929, cat. no. 139.
Amsterdam 1930, cat. no. 155.
New York/Philadelphia/Boston and other cities, 1935-1936, cat. no. 73.
Nuremberg 1956, cat. no. 12.
Munich 1956, cat. no. 9.
Essen 1957, cat. no. 130.
Vienna 1958, cat. no. 8.
Tokyo/Kyoto 1958, cat. no. 16.
Montreal/Ottawa/Winnipeg/Toronto 1960-1961, cat. no. 80
Warsaw 1962, cat. no. 13.
Tel Aviv/Haifa 1962-1963, cat. no. 12.
Belgrade 1966, cat. no. 10.
Moscow/Leningrad 1971, cat. no. 9.
New York/Chicago/Ottawa and ocher cities, 1973-1974, cat. no. 22.
London/Newcastle upon Tyne 1974, cat. no. 12.
Otterlo 1990, cat. no. 15.
Yokohama/Nagoya 1995-1996, cat. no. 6.
Tokyo/Fukuoka 1999-2000, cat. no. 1.
Seattle/Atlanta 2004-2005, cat. no. 14.
Amsterdam/New York 2005, cat. no. 2.

NOTE
A For this type of signature see
Woman sewing

After Van Gogh had spent a few days in late August in The Hague, where those he visited included Tersteeg and Mauve, he made a stop in Dordrecht on the way back because, as he explained to Theo, 'from the train I had seen a spot I wanted to draw a row of windmills. Though it was raining, I managed to finish it, and so at least I have a souvenir from my little trip' (170/149, 26 28 August 1881). He knew the area well. He had worked in a bookshop in Dordrecht from January to May 1877 and enjoyed taking walks during his free hours 'along the dike, where the mills are that one sees in the distance as one walks along the tracks' (106/92,7 March 1877). He was referring to the Weeskinderendijk southwest of the city that runs around the Papengat. There were still ten active mills there in 1881, mostly sawmills.

For Windmills at Dordrecht Van Gogh viewed the polder from the east of the Papengat looking northwest. The foreground is dominated by a simple white fence closing off a ditch crossing. Behind the fence, walking along the path through the field, is a small figure. Slightly above the middle of the sheet are the mills, outlined against the grey sky. The two large mills to the left, Her Anker (The Anchor) and De (Jonge) Ruiter (The [Young] Horseman) are on the east side of the dike; the mills on the south side are visible between them. The three large mills above and to the right of the fence, the Willem I, De Kleine Noordsche boer (The Little Northern Farmer) and De Zwaan (The Swan) are on the north side.

Two other mills are visible on the horizon to the far right. While the other windmills have been placed in an identifiable location and in proper relation to each other, these two are shown more schematically and are a bit too large. Actually there were no mills there. Van Gogh probably added them to give the composition more balance.[1] Also interesting is that he drew their blades facing in a somewhat different direction.

The detailed finishing touches in a variety of media suggest that Van Gogh was probably only able to make a basic pencil sketch at the site in the rain.[2] He paid close attention to the details on the horizon while making the sketch. Smaller buildings are visible between the windmills, as are the masts and sails of ships on the Oude Maas. Also recognisable are a few chimneys from the steam powered factories, which would soon take over the work being performed by the windmills.[3] Large areas of the sky, the field and the foreground have been given a brown tint with brush and highly diluted watercolour. Subtle accents made with white opaque watercolour have been added to the sky, the windmills, and more extensively in the fence in the foreground, where Van Gogh used pen and ink for the shadows. He gave the field and the buildings in the background a bit of colour with green chalk and reddish brown watercolour. In this way he produced a convincing and rather traditional looking Dutch panorama on a cloudy day.

On the way to the polder near the Papengat, not far from the station, Van Gogh passed the flourmill known as 'De Oranjeboom' - the Orange Tree. The mill and outbuildings are rendered in quite some detail in the drawing.

A photograph from 1860 shows the scene from another perspective.[4] Directly behind the trees to the left is the railway, difficult to recognise as such, and in the distance the Weeskinderendijk windmills can be seen. In the drawing most of the foreground is taken up by the water of a canal, which takes a turn. Reflected in this water is the row of trees on the left and the mill on the right, strongly dividing the composition. The sharp diagonals of the canal as it zigzags into the distance also serve to create a dynamic perspective. The spatial effect is somewhat similar to the drawings Van Gogh would make in early 1882 in The Hague, in which diagonals also play an important role.[5]

This sheet shows traces of haste and therefore does seem to have been drawn on site. Among the indications of this are the wild scratches in the trees and the way much of the charcoal is smudged. In some places Van Gogh pressed so hard with the pencil that tears were left in the paper. It also seems as if the paper had become damp in certain places

while he was working on it, especially at the bottom, making it especially vulnerable to damage. This may be an indication of the kind of weather in which Van Gogh was working in Dordrecht.

1. They have been identified as De Eikenboom (The Oak Tree) and De Treurwilg (The Weeping Willow) on the Kalkhaven in Dordrecht, but the Kalkhaven was outside Van Gogh's field of vision (Bouman 1989). Van Gogh did not wilfully move them, since De Eikenboom had already been taken down in 1878. Bouman mentions three other windmills that were no longer standing at that time. The present identification is based on an 1866 photograph of the Papengat from the other side of the Dude Maas, published in Bakker 1998, p. 226, and with the assistance of http://www.molendatabase.nl. Also see Meedendorp 2005b.
2. The editors of De la Faille 1970 note that Van Gogh worked from a preliminary study that has not been preserved, which certainly should not be ruled out.
3. Of all the mills rendered by Van Gogh only De (Jonge) Ruiter survived into the twentieth century.
4. The mill in the drawing was identified by Bouman 1990 with the help of this photograph. The photo is dated later, however, and following Molendijk 1990 Bouman believes the figure with the top hat to be that of Van Gogh, which is extremely unlikely (see Meedendorp 2005b).
5. See for example Ditch along Schenkweg, p. 113. For this reason Heenk 1995, pp. 58-59, dates Windmill 'De Oranjeboom', Dordrecht later, in April 1882. At that time, however, Van Gogh used a perspective frame for such compositions, and no trace of that is evident on this sheet. Van Gogh had also given up the extensive use of charcoal by then.

P. 75

Sower

September 1881
pencil, black chalk, wash, opaque watercolour,
on grey-blue laid paper
60.2 x 44.2 cm
watermark: E M THIERS [fragment?]
unsigned
F862/JH31
KM 113.257

INSCRIPTIONS

verso, centre left: 2 (pencil).
205 (pencil).
upper left: KR 14 [in frame] (blue chalk).
upper right: VII (blue chalk)

PROVENANCE
acquired by Hidde Nijland, Dordrecht, before 1895.
purchased from Hidde Nijland by A.G. Kröller, The Hague, July 1928.
donated to the Kröller-Müller Foundation by A.G. Kröller, December 1928

EXHIBITIONS
The Hague 1895, no. known cat.
Dordrecht 1897, no. cat.
Dordrecht 1904, cat. no. ?.
The Hague 1918, cat. no. ?.
Amsterdam 1924, cat. no. 93.
The Hague 1928, unnumbered.
Hamburg 1929, cat. no. 51.
Amsterdam 1930, cat. no. 14.
New York/Chicago/Ottawa and other cities, 1973-1974, cat. no. 21.
London/Newcastle-upon-Tyne 1974, cat. no. 11.
Rome 1988, cat. no. 50.
Amsterdam 1988-1989, cat. no. 68.

P. 75

Sower

September October 1881
charcoal, black chalk, on laid paper
55.9 x 33.2 cm watermark: M[ICHALLET]A
unsigned
F856/JH17
KM 117.520

INSCRIPTIONS
recto, lower left: Port Vincent (black chalk)
verso, centre left: Port: Vincent/Hidde Nijland (black ink)
lower left: 26 (blue chalk)
upper left: KR 8 [in frame] (blue chalk).
lower right: 38 (blue chalk)

PROVENANCE
acquired by Hidde Nijland, Dordrecht, before 1895.
purchased from Hidde Nijland by A.G. Kröller, The Hague, July 1928.
donated to the Kröller-Müller Foundation by A.G. Kröller, December 1928

EXHIBITIONS
The Hague 1895, no. known cat.
Dordrecht 1897, no. cat.
Dordrecht 1904, cat. no. ?.
The Hague 1918, cat. no. ?.
Amsterdam 1924, cat. no. 84.
The Hague 1928, unnumbered.
Hamburg 1929, cat. no. 45.
Amsterdam 1930, cat. no. 13.
Amsterdam 1988 1989, cat. no. 66.
Yokohama/Nagoya 1995 1996, cat. no. 7.
Tokyo/Fukuoka 1999-2000, cat. no. 4.

NOTE
A Only a fragment of the 'M' from the watermark
MICHALLET can be seen, in reverse, in the upper right.
So far this type of paper has been found in only two other
drawings, which date to October/November 1881

When Van Gogh was preparing himself for
theological study, he wrote to his brother that he
wanted to become a sower of the Word' (112/93,
22 April 1877), an allusion to the biblical parable of
Christ, who scatters his gospel among people like
seeds (Matthew 13:2-9, 18-23). Although as an artist
Van Gogh would leave the faith of his fathers, there
is often a religious undertone (or hints of natural
religion) in his representations of the peasant life.[1]
In his vision, sowers, reapers, digger sand other hard-
working farm laborers all had a place in the eternal
life cycle. In a letter to Emile Bernard, for example,
he called the sower and the sheaf of wheat symbols
of the eternal (630/B7, C. 18 June 1888). In his
opinion, the artist who understood and depicted
this best of all was Jean-François Millet (1814-1875).
His rendering of a young farmer hurling a handful of
grain with a powerful, supple motion in the painting
Le semeur from 1850 became a prototype and a
frequently copied pose in the nineteenth century, an
icon ofgruelling country life.[2]
       Van Gogh had never seen the painting but he
knew the composition, especially from a reproduction
etching he had copied five times in rapid succession
in the Borinagewith the explanation 'I am so entirely
absorbed in that figure' (156/135,7 September 1880).
The only surviving copy made of this etching dates
from April 1881 (F830, Van Gogh Museum). Of
the three sowers being dealt with here, all of which
were drawn from models, only the one showing
the figure from the side follows Millet's example.
Although the two cannot be compared in terms of
dynamism, the act of sowing is clearly rendered in
any case. The figure has been carefully observed, and
the troublesome foreshortening of the right arm in
the act of sowing is also convincingly done, as is the
shadow effect in the clothing. Various corrections are
visible in the head as well as in the legs. The artist
concentrated on the typical attitude of the figure.
Afterwards he emphasised the outlines with black
chalk, pressing so firmly that the lines can clearly be
seen on the other side of the sheet. The two other
sowers are shown in their natural setting but they lack
the energetic forward motion of Millet's archetype.
Van Gogh made sketches of both sheets in a letter to
Theo of early September 1881 (171/150), so they can
be dated to that month with quite some certainty.

The sketches were probably made before the drawings
were finished since there are important differences,
especially in the way the backgrounds are worked out.
       A comparable seasonal reference can be seen
in the other sheet, where a flying swallow – a bird
that winters in the south – can clearly be recognised
in the background to the right. This swallow does
not appear in the sketch in the letter to Theo, where
other birds are depicted: crows or doves that, unlike
an insect eater like the swallow, are often seen flying
just above the surface of a ploughed field. In this
sheet Van Gogh drew mainly with pencil, sometimes
scraping and pressing so hard that he penetrated the
paper.[3] The figure of the sower himself for which
old Schuitemaker was probably the model is largely
covered in a brown wash and then heightened with
white opaque watercolour. The sky in the background
is also slightly heightened. The original blue paper
has badly faded and turned brown over the years.
       Even though Van Gogh may have intended
to surpass the level of a simple model study with
these last two sowers, they, too, must be regarded
primarily as studies. The artist knew he still had
a lot of practising to do in order to produce
powerful independent work. This is evident in his
correspondence with Van Rappard, who frequently
brought up his friend's technical shortcomings.
Van Gogh certainly took this criticism to heart. For
example, he sent sketches of the sower with the sling
not only to Theo but to Van Rappard as well, to give
him an idea of the progress he was making in model
drawing?[4] 'Your remark about the figure of the sower
- that he is not a man who is sowing but one who is
posing as a sower - is very true,' he wrote in reaction
to Van Rappard's criticism, which has not survived.
But he went on to comment, 'However, I look upon
my present studies purely as studies after the model,
they have no pretension to being anything else. Only
after a year or a couple of years shall I have gained the
ability to do a sower who is sowing; there I agree with
you' (175/R2, 15 October 1881). Six months earlier
he had already explained to Theo that his studies were
to be regarded as 'the seed which must later produce
the drawings' (165/144, 30 April 1881). But of course
there was nothing stopping him from working out
a subject in greater detail every now and then, and
in his meek response Van Gogh will also have been
safeguarding himself against further criticism.

1. This is discussed in more detail by such authors as Kōdera
   1987, Sund 1988 and Kōdera 1990.
2. See Van Tilborgh et al. 1988, pp. 156-192, about the sower
   in the oeuvre of Van Gogh and the example of Millet.
3. The sheet has been restored in these places on the back.
4. It is interesting that Van Gogh also drew sheaves of wheat
   in the background of that sketch (and no swallow). It is
   shown in Van Crimpen & Berends-Albert 1990, p. 401,
   as belonging to letter 175/R2 of 15 October 1881. But
   in this letter Van Gogh takes up Van Rappard's criticism
   of his drawing of the sower, so it is more likely that he
   sent the sketch at some earlier time. Letter 172/R1 of 12
   October suggests that he had sent sketches to Van Rappard
   before that date. Jean-François Millet, The sower, c. 1852,
   lithograph, probably printed posthumously. Kröller-Müller
   Museum, Otterlo

P. 76

Woman peeling potatoes

September 1881
black chalk, grey wash, opaque watercolour
on laid paper
30.1 x 22.8 cm
watermark: ED&Cie (in cartouche) [fragment of cartouche],
[PL BAS]
unsigned
F1213/JH23
KM 116.218

INSCRIPTIONS
verso, upper left: 43½ 55 (pencil).
9 (pencil)

PROVENANCE
purchased by H. Kröller-Müller at sale The Hague (Oldenzeel,
art dealer), 26-27 June 1917, lot 41: Brabantsch oud vrouwtje
(550 guilders)

EXHIBITIONS
Basel/Bern/Brussels 1927, cat. no. 70.
Düsseldorf 1928, cat. no. 136.
Karlsruhe 1928, cat. no. 71.
Berlin 1928-1929, cat. no. 65.
Hamburg 1929, cat. no. 33.
Amsterdam 1930, cat. no. 134.

P. 77

Woman peeling potatoes

September 1881
black chalk, grey wash, opaque watercolor,
colored and white chalk, pencil
on laid paper
40.4 x 32.9 cm
watermark: [ED]&cie (in cartouche),
PL [BAS]
signed lower left (by the artist):
Vincent (black chalk)
F12097 JH22
KM 120.486

INSCRIPTIONS
recto, lower right: Verz:
Hidde Nijland (black ink)

PROVENANCE
acquired by Hidde Nijland, Dordrecht, before 1904'
purchased from Hidde Nijland by A.G. Kröller, The Hague,
July 1928
donated to the Kröller-Müller Foundation by A.G. Kröller,
December 1928

EXHIBITIONS
Dordrecht 1904, cat. no. 174.
The Hague 1918, cat. no. 78?.
Amsterdam 1924, cat. no. 120.
The Hague 1928, unnumbered.
Hamburg 1929, cat. no. 74.
Amsterdam 1930, cat. no. 138.
Vienna 1958, cat. no. 9.

In Etten Van Gogh was sometimes visited by
a young man who drew and also painted but who is
not mentioned in Van Gogh's letters. His name was
Jan Benjamin Kam (1860-1932) the oldest son of
the Reverend Jan Gerrit Kam (1833-1917) from the
neighbouring town of Leur. In 1912 Jan Benjamin
Kam wrote a number of interesting observations
about his association with Van Gogh in a letter to
the art critic Albert Plasschaert. In a letter to Van
Rappard, for example, Van Gogh had only written
that he had 'found a number of models who are
willing enough' (172/R2, 12 October 1881). As an
eyewitness, Kam reveals how he actually accomplished
this: 'He was drawing sowers at that time and would
enter the small houses to draw the woman as she
was engaged in some domestic chores. He forced

the people to pose for him. They were afraid of him
and it was not pleasant to accompany him.'[1] So the
drawings of women working indoors, such as these
women peeling potatoes, may have been made under
less than congenial conditions.

The first two sheets have a great deal in
common.[2] Most of the materials used are the same,
the women are posed in the same way and both are
wearing gauze bonnets. The first sheet is not worked
out to the edges, however, and there are differences
in the format and details, such as the view from the
window, the presence or absence of a bucket and the
facial features of the women. In the first composition
the artist drew a frame with white chalk that is
approximately as large as the format of the other
sheet, and the framed area corresponds exactly to
that second composition.[3] So rather than trim the
drawing along this frame, the artist made a second,
more carefully considered version. Oddly enough,
he signed the first but not the second.[4] In letter
171/150, written in September, Van Gogh made a
small pen sketch of the first version, adhering to the
composition within the white frame. On the left,
however, he scribbled a few lines that are also visible
in the large drawing at the same place outside the
frame. Through the window a few scrawny trees can
be seen that were replaced in the second version by
a few bare pollard willows. The same row of willows
appears in a sketch in letter 173/151 to Theo of c. 12
October.[5]

All these figures are striking for their
enormously long upper legs. Van Gogh often had
problems rendering the proportions of his figures
convincingly, certainly before he began using a
drawing grid and a perspective frame.[7] He showed
a number of his figure drawings to Mauve, who
immediately saw that he was sitting too close to his
models so that 'in many cases it's virtually impossible
to achieve the proper proportions' (191/164, c.
21 December 1881). It must have been physically
difficult to take distance, however, because the houses
in which he 'forced' his models to pose were usually
quite small, as Kam already noted.

---

1. The letter, dated 12 June 1912, is now at the Van Gogh
   Museum, Amsterdam, inv. no. FR b3o25. Thanks to Hans
   Luijten of the Van Gogh Museum for bringing this letter to
   my attention.
2. Heenk 1995, p. 38, is of the opinion that onions are being
   peeled in this drawing, which is not very likely. In the same
   letter in which he included a pen sketch of the composition
   (171/150) Van Gogh wrote that he had made a drawing
   of'a woman in a white cap peeling potatoes'.
3. The frame measures c. 32 x 24 cm.
4. This might indicate that Van Gogh gave this version away
   and signed it on that occasion. The drawings were acquired
   separately by H. Kröller-Müller.
5. In October Van Gogh made a great many drawings in
   the area around Leursestraatje, which was surrounded by
   willow trees.
6. Livestro-Nieuwenhuis 1986, pp. 55 and 83-84.
7. Although he already must have known about such drawing
   aids from the instruction books by Cassagne, Van Gogh
   probably did not begin using them until March 1882.

P. 79

Sieving

September 1881
pencil, black chalk, opaque watercolour
on laid paper
62.8 x 47.5 cm
watermark: En & Cie (in cartouche), PL BAS
unsigned
F891/JH24
KM 122.479

INSCRIPTIONS
verso, lower right: KM 247 (pencil)

PROVENANCE
acquired by Hidde Nijland, Dordrechc, before 1904.
purchased from Hidde Nijland by A.G. Kröller, The Hague,
July 1928
donated to the Kröller Müller Foundation by A.G. Kröller,
December 1928

EXHIBITIONS
Dordrechc 1904, cat. no. 201.
The Hague 1918, cat. no. 79.
Amsterdam 1924, cat. no. 85.
The Hague 1928, unnumbered.
Hamburg 1929, cat. no. 50.
Amsterdam 1930, cat. no. 24.
Warsaw 1962, cat. no. 9.
Tel Aviv/Haifa 1962-1963, cat. no. 21a.
s Hertogenbosch 1987-1988, cat. no. 3.

In copying Bargue's loose example pages, Van
Gogh developed a preference for drawing on large
sheets of paper. As he later explained,'in general for
my own study I definitely need the figure to have
rather large proportions so that the head, hands and
feet will not be too small and can be drawn vigorously.
That is why I took the size of Exercices au fusain by
Bargue as an example for my own study, because the
size can easily be taken in with one glance and yet the
details are not too small' (292/250, 2 or 3 December
1882). That size corresponds with the former 'large-
medium' paper size – 47 x 62 centimetres – on which
the drawing Sieving was made, a sheet that still has its
original edges.[1]

The scene shown here is often taken for
winnowing.[2] Winnowing involves shaking grain in a

large basket, usually reed, so the lighter chaff can be blown away by the wind. The sieve shown here, which the farmer is using to clean his seeds, consists of two flat skimmers fit tightly inside each other, probably with a perforated pig bladder stretched in between.[3] The whirling remains of the seeds are shown above and below the sieve rendered with black chalk as dots and stripes. The old farmer is standing in the doorway of a barn in which a supply of hay appears to be stored under the beams. This would actually have been an odd place to separate seeds unless a convenient air current was blowing through the doorway to prevent the dust from going into the barn. But perhaps Van Gogh was mainly interested in the typical pose of the farmer with his sieve, just as he would concentrate on the characteristic poses of diggers and sowers.

By showing the figure in profile the artist cleverly avoided the problem of foreshortening. He worked mainly with pencil and black chalk, using the latter to sharply reinforce the contours. He coloured the sleeves of the shirt with highly diluted light blue opaque watercolour and in doing so spilled a strip of paint, which runs left from the middle near the door post to the lower edge of the sheet. Like the carpenter in the previous drawing, the old farmer for whom Cornelis Schuitemaker (1813 1884) was the model   is shown stiffly posed: he even appears to be leaning back a bit against the door posr.[4] He is better proportioned, however, although the left arm is exceptionally long. Van Gogh may have sought support for the relative proportions in the lines of the cross laths in the open door.[5] In a letter to Theo to be discussed in more detail in the next drawing he made a small sketch based on this sheet.

---

1. See: hrrp://members.chello.nl/j.nikkels/gen/papier/ terminologie.html. A sheet of laid paper has rough edges, so the sizes usually deviate somewhat from the standard size. In addition, this sheet had been trimmed along the top and on the right.
2. See for instance the various editions of Hulsker's catalogue raisonné (JH24); Van Uitert et al. 1987, p. 134. Van Tilborgh et al. 1988, p. 28, refers to the affinity with Miller's The winnower (Le Vanneur), the litho of which was known by Van Gogh.
3. Information from Gerard Rooijakkers, Meertens Institute, Amsterdam.
4. Schuitemaker and his wife lived near Etten at 't Heike (De Bruyn Heeren 1992, pp. 160-171).
5. It is going too far to suggest (as M. Trappeniers does in van Uitert et al. 1984, pp. 134-135) that here Van Gogh is using one of the more complicated lessons in perspective from Cassagne, in which the subject is projected in a cage construction for a better understanding of foreshortening. Van Gogh knew the works of Cassagne but made selective use of them (see Van Heugren 1996, pp. 17-19).

P. 81

Digger Resting

September 1881
pencil, black chalk, pen and ink, wash, opaque watercolour on laid paper
54.2 x 23.2 cm
watermark: ED&cie (in cartouche), PL BAS
signed lower left (by the artist): Vincent (black chalk)
861/JH40
KM 125.820

INSCRIPTIONS

PROVENANCE
acquired by Hidde Nijland, Dordrecht, before 1895'
purchased from Hidde Nijland by A.G. Kröller, The Hague, July 1928'
donated to the Kröller-Müller Foundation by A.G. Kröller, December 1928

EXHIBITIONS
Rotterdam 1892, no cat.
The Hague 1895, no known cat.
Dordrecht 1897, no cat.
Dordrecht 1904, cat. no. 191.
The Hague 1918, cat. no. 60.
Amsterdam 1924, cat. no. 43.
The Hague 1928, unnumbered.
Hamburg 1929, cat. no. 88.
Amsterdam 1930, cat. no. 17.
Munich 1956, cat. no. 11.

'Now I must draw diggers, sowers, men & women at the plough, without cease,' Van Gogh wrote to Theo in early September 1881, 'scrutinize and draw everything that is part of country life, just as many others have done and are doing. I no longer stand helpless before nature as I used to' (171/150). He illustrated his letter with a great many sketches of the drawings he was working on at the time. A change had taken place in his drawing, he wrote. Mauve, with his laudatory remarks, had had something to do with this, and by endlessly copying the examples in Bargue he had 'learned to measure and to see and to look for the broad outlines'. Now that he had also found suitable models, he was able to write to Theo that 'I have drawn a man with a spade, that is "un bêcheur" five times over in a variety of poses [...]. The size of

the figures is about the same as that of an Exercice au fusain. He enclosed sketches of the first Digger and of Digger resting.[1] The second Digger is very much like the first and will have been made at the same time. Van Gogh worked with the same model for both drawings, the seventeen year old Piet Kaufmann, a laborer who also served as the Reverend Van Gogh's gardener.[2]

The three drawings are executed in the same materials for the most part. Van Gogh had brought conté crayons (black chalk), pencils and a supply of paper with him from The Hague. In the letter to his brother quoted above he writes that he had 'also started to introduce the brush and the stump' in his drawings, and to work 'with a little sepia and India ink, and now and then with a little color'. In these three sheets black chalk is the dominant medium. The cautious use of color is also quite evident and is used most extensively in the first Digger in the form of opaque watercolor, both highly diluted and somewhat thicker. The washes are made with brush and water or diluted ink. Only in Digger resting did he also work in pencil, to emphasize the details of the head. The charcoal, of which only traces can sometimes be seen, is probably a residue from the drawing's preliminary sketch. In a later letter to Theo he described this method, although in an entirely different context: as a kind of metaphor for explaining a matter that he had first alluded to with more general hints. 'I tried to indicate the proportions and planes with long, straight charcoal strokes; when the necessary auxiliary lines have been traced, then we brush off the charcoal with a handkerchief or a wing and begin to draw the more intimate details. So this letter will be written in a more intimate, less harsh and angular tone than the former' (178/154, 7 November 1881). In several of the figure drawings from this period, Van Gogh seems to have worked with black chalk over a hastily made charcoal sketch.

The sketch in the letter of the digger resting shows that figure standing in an area thickly surrounded by trees and bushes. Those surroundings are also still visible in the drawing itself, although Van Gogh trimmed the sheet and focused all the attention on the figure, who has assumed a more relaxed pose than in the sketch. The edges of the sheet show that originally the lines in the drawing must have continued outward and were abruptly cut. In the upper left are the remains of the branches of the little tree that is shown in its entirety in the letter sketch. The composition was never horizontal, however, which the sketch actually implies; when making the drawing Van Gogh kept the paper upright.[3] He must have been responsible for trimming the sheet himself, as is evidenced by the position of the signature on the lower left near the spade and the fact that he applied washes to the sheet after trimming it. The washes run right up to the edge in several places. At the bottom some of the washes run over the 'nt' in the signature.

Using live models for his drawings was an additional expense for Van Gogh because he paid people to pose for him.[4] All these bills were paid by Theo, who supported him financially (as did their father, too, at first). Van Gogh hoped to compensate for this soon by selling his work, since he believed figure drawings were very suitable for selling, certainly by anyone 'who has learned to tackle a figure and hang on to it until it is safely down on paper' (171/150). He thought he had made considerable progress. The optimistic artist undoubtedly derived his self-confidence from the stimulating comments he had heard in The Hague, but there was another factor involved. That summer he had fallen in love with his older cousin Kee Vos, who had stayed with the Van Gogh family in Etten along with her young son. 'Ever since meeting her I have been getting on much better with my work,' he wrote in a letter in which he revealed his feelings to Theo for the first time (177/153, 3 November 1881).

---

1. A sketch of Digger (F860; P. and N. de Boer Foundation, Amsterdam) is also included in the letter.
2. Van Gogh wrote 'Kaufman'. Stokvis 1926, pp. 19-21, stressed 'Kauffmann' as the correct spelling, but it is 'Kaufmann', see Kerstens 1990. Kaufmann told Stokvis, who had come to talk to him when the model was 60 years old, that he had posed for Van Gogh between 30 and 50 times. Sometimes he was given a drawing as a gift, but all these had gone missing when Kaufmann moved house. He also posed for Boy with a sickle. The older model for Digger resting looks a bit like Schuitemaker.
3. Heenk 1995, p. 37, suggests that the sketch in the letter was of a now lost large drawing, and that Digger resting was also based on this work. The watermark, which is usually horizontal, is vertical here; the cartouche with ED&Cie is located where the left clog is drawn, and the counter-mark PL BAS where the man's head is. This means that the artist reduced the sheet -on the right more than the left - by a total of about 24 centimetres (that is, by half). About 8 centimetres were removed from the top and bottom.
4. He spent about 20 to 30 guilder cents a day on models (185/160, 19 November 1881).

P. 83

Man planting

autumn 1881
black chalk, charcoal, brown wash, opaque watercolour, on laid paper
38.5 x 41.5 cm
watermark: [E]D & Cie (in cartouche), PL [BAS]
unsigned
F879/JH62
KM 114.869

INSCRIPTIONS
verso, lower right: Art: Vincent/Verz: Hidde Nijland (black

---

ink).
upper right: 202 (black chalk)
upper left: KR 49 [in frame] (blue chalk)

PROVENANCE
acquired by Hidde Nijland,Dordrecht, before 1904.
purchased from Hidde Nijland by A.G. Kröller, The Hague, July 1928.
donated to the Kröller-Müller Foundation by A.G. Kröller, December 1928

EXHIBITIONS
Dordrecht 1904, cat. no. 202.
The Hague 1918, cat. no. 57.
Amsterdam 1924, cat. no. 101.
The Hague 1928, unnumbered.
Hamburg 1929, cat. no. 148.
Amsterdam 1930, cat. no. 19.
Vienna 1958, cat. no. 14.

Van Gogh complained that his models sometimes knew nothing about posing. In early August 1881 he wrote to Theo, 'Both peasants and villagers are desperately obstinate about it, and it is hard to make them yield on this point: they only want to pose in their Sunday best, with impossible folds [...]' (169/148). Yet most of the male models in the Etten figure studies wear what was then considered common work clothing: a pair of long and often patched trousers, a blue smock, a short jacket or sleeveless vest, a cap and clogs. At first glance the man shown planting here does look as if he is wearing his 'Sunday' best: a somewhat longer jacket, knee breeches, gaiters, shoes and a hat with a slightly rounded crown. Yet this is typical Brabant farmers' attire, albeit an older style that had been out of fashion for about twenty years. Perhaps the man insisted on wearing these clothes, or perhaps Van Gogh, in his penchant for authenticity, consciously chose this historical costume and asked the model, who looks like he is still a young man, to put it on.[1]

Van Gogh focused a great deal of attention on the shadows and folds in the dark suit. In some places he corrected the man's attitude. Erased lines are still quite visible near the hat, the back of the head and to the left near the jacket and the foot, despite attempts to cover them up with white water colour. Despite his corrections he was still not able to keep the proportions from looking rather strange, although this is not immediately noticeable. As in Boy with a sickle, where the figure is bent in a similar way, Van Gogh seems to have sat very close to his model. The kneeling figure is fairly successful as a closed form, but if you study the shoulders and arms too long they begin looking more and more like bizarre implanted tentacles.

---

1. There is a second drawing in which we encounter this outdated clothing, Sower (F866a), although the hat worn there is a bit different. Heenk 1995, p. 87, places both drawings in Drenthe because Van Gogh wrote that the men there wore short breeches (389/324, c. 15 September 1883). This does not seem to be a very strong argument, however, and Heenk says not a word about the remarkable technical progress Van Gogh had made in his figure studies since Etten.

P. 85

Sketch of an interior

October 1881
black chalk on laid paper
32 x 30 cm
no watermark
unsigned
F888v/JH65
KM 117.368 VERSO

INSCRIPTIONS
verso, lower right: Art: Vincent/Verz: Hidde Nijland (black ink).
upper right: 202 (black chalk)
upper left: KR 49 [in frame] (blue chalk)

PROVENANCE
acquired by Hidde Nijland,Dordrecht, before 1904.
purchased from Hidde Nijland by A.G. Kröller, The Hague, July 1928.
donated to the Kröller-Müller Foundation by A.G. Kröller, December 1928

EXHIBITIONS
Dorfrecht 1904, cat. no. 187.
The Hague 1918, cat. no. 59.
Amsterdam 1924, cat. no. 115.
The Hague 1928, unnumbered.
Hamburg 1929, cat. no. 152.
Amsterdam 1930, cat. no. 151.

On the back of the sheet there is a fairly large fragment of a drawing which was reduced in size when Van Gogh drew on the other side, and which must therefore be a little older.[1] It is a rough sketch in black chalk of an interior with a fireplace. The large chimney piece partly obscures the view of the window on the left. In the black, soot-covered hearth hangs a chimney crook holding a metal cooking pot above a firedog. Next to it is a simple foot-warmer or possibly, given the very rudimentary nature of the cube, a wooden block on which to chop firewood. The most striking feature is the pot in the foreground and the wooden lid belonging to it that rests against the wall. This is a mixing crock in red-firing earthenware of a kind made almost exclusively in Bergen op Zoom.[2] Lastly, there is also a chair. We find all these elements in other large drawings of figures by the fire. In them a kettle usually hangs from the chimney crook and wood burns on the firedog. The mixing crock is seen in the background of old man at the fireside. So perhaps what we see here is the home of Cornelis Schuitemaker in het Heike.

---

1. The water colour on the recto has run in and over the

edges on the left, the bottom and the right: so the wash
and water colour were applied after the drawing had been
trimmed.
2. With thanks to Gerard Rooijakkers, Meertens institute,
   Amsterdam.

P. 87

Boy with a sickle

last week of October 1881 -1 November 1881
black chalk, charcoal, wash, opaque watercolor
on laid paper
46.6 x 60.4 cm
watermark: ED & Cie (in cartouche), PL BAS
signed lower left (by the artist): Vincent (black chalk)
F851/JH61
KM 111.847

INSCRIPTIONS
recto, lower left: no 4 Verz. Hidde Nijland (black ink faded to
brown) verso, lower left: no. 27 (pencil)

PROVENANCE
[probably A.C.W. Terhell coll., The Hague]
acquired by Hidde Nijland, Dordrecht, before 1895.
purchased from Hidde Nijland by A.G. Kröller, The Hague,
July 1928.
donated to the Kröller-Müller Foundation by A.G. Kröller,
December 1928

EXHIBITIONS
The Hague 1895, no known cat.
Dordrecht 1897, no cat.
Dordrecht 1904, cat. no. 173.
The Hague 1918, cat. no. 75.
Amsterdam 1924, cat. no. 96.
The Hague 1928, unnumbered'
Hamburg 1929, cat. no. 80.
Amsterdam 1930, cat. no. 15.
Liège/Brussels/Mons 1946-1947, cat. no. 4.
Paris 1947, cat. no. 4.
Geneva 1947, cat. no. 4.
Basel 1947, cat. no. 113.
London/Birmingham/Glasgow 1947-1948, cat. no. 102.
New York/Chicago 1949-1950, cat. no. 14.
Milan 1952, cat. no. 8.
The Hague 1953, cat. no. 3.
Otterlo/Amsterdam 1953, cat. no. 3.
Saint Louis/Philadelphia/Toledo 1953-1954, cat. no. 6.
Nuremberg 1956, cat. no. 10.
Munich 1956, cat. no. 12.
Essen 1957, cat. no. 131.
Tokyo/Kyoto 1958, cat. no. 14.
Munich 1961, cat. no. 8.
New York/Chicago/Ottawa and other cities, 1973-1974, cat.

no. 23
London/Newcastle-upon-Tyne 1974, cat. no. 13.
s-Hertogenbosch 1987-1988, cat. no. 6.
Rome 1988, cat. no. 53.
Otterlo 1990, cat. no. 12.
Tokyo/Fukuoka 1999-2000, cat. no. 9.
Seattle/Atlanta 2004-2005, cat. no. 15.
Amsterdam/New York 2005, cat. no. 3.

At the end of October 1881 Anthon van
Rappard again paid a (short) visit to Etten. He was
on his way to Brussels and Van Gogh had urged
him to come by, partly because he was curious about
Van Rappard's progress in watercoloring (175/R2,
15 October 1881). On Mauve's recommendation, he
himself had also begun to work more in watercolour.[1]
His 'Uncle Cent' - the art dealer Vincent van Gogh
(1820-1888) - had given him a watercolor box (173/151,
C. 12 October 1881). So far his use of watercolor had
been limited to 'coloring in' drawings. He had not
yet mastered true watercoloring, in which brush and
paint are used almost exclusively, and so he must have
been eager to learn how Van Rappard, who was better
trained technically, had got on.[2] On 2 November he
wrote to Van Rappard that he was glad 'to have seen
your watercolors, you have made good progress', and
'today I drew another digger & since your visit a boy
cutting grass with a sickle as well' (176/R3). He was
undoubtedly referring to this drawing, which can thus
be dated to the last week of October or 1 November
at the latest.
　　Van Gogh first drew the figure, principally
in black chalk, and then the landscape round it in
charcoal and chalk, as he had also done with Man
with broom. The yellowish green accents in watercolor
in the foreground are also seen in that drawing. He
was chiefly concerned with the pose of the boy as he
cut.[3] In view of his footwear, slippers of some kind,
and the time of year, he probably posed indoors.[4]
Color was added in a fairly cursory fashion using
much diluted, opaque watercolor: flesh tints for the
face and hands, light blue in the sleeves and socks,
light brown for the hair. Van Gogh used wash mainly
in the areas around the figure, and grains of charcoal
sometimes accumulated at the edges of the wash. The
blade of the sickle was left blank when the wash was
applied and shows the original color of the paper.
The rather thickly applied white opaque watercolor in
the sky was in part intended to conceal a row of trees
on the horizon drawn earlier in charcoal.[5]
　　Man planting has already shown how difficult
the artist found it to depict a squatting figure in a
side view convincingly. The peculiar attachment of
the shoulder in this study reveals a similar struggle.
The positioning of the bent left leg is also not very
successful. The leg probably came out too puny at
first, and Van Gogh tried to correct this by making
it slightly broader from the knee down, but the flat
heel still suggests a much thinner leg. It is also unclear
whether the part of the trouser leg in shadow on the
left behind the elbow belongs to the left or the right
leg. The figure as a whole looks shaky: the upper body
is extremely broad, as seen in the wide positioning of
the arms, whereas the legs pulled close together have
hardly any depth.

　　These lopsided proportions can very probably
be attributed to a large extent to Van Gogh's being
too close to his model, so that he could not get a
good overall impression. With his eyes he would scan
a part of the figure and draw that on the large sheet
of paper, without being able to keep an eye on the
proportions. The emphasis he put on the outlines
ensured that the form stands up reasonably well after
all.[6] At any rate he himself was sufficiently pleased to
sign the sheet. To the left of the signature the artist's
thick thumbprint in blue watercolor is visible.
　　The model for this study was again Piet
Kaufmann. Kaufmann spent his entire life in Etten-
Leur, where he was born in 1864 on the Etten side
and where he died in 1940 on the Leur side.[7] In
the autumn of 1881 he posed many times for Van
Gogh, who wrote to Theo as early as the beginning of
August: 'I also hope to be successful in finding a good
model, e.g. Piet Kaufman[n], the laborer, but I think it
will be better to have him pose with a spade or plough
or something not here at home but at the yard, or
at his home or in the fields' (169/148). By the 'yard'
Van Gogh probably meant the clog-makers located
behind the Kaufmann family's combined farmhouse
and inn (called 'Den IJzeren Pot'- The Iron Cauldron)
in Leursestraatje, where Piet trained as a clog-maker.[8]
He also worked in the Reverend Van Gogh's garden,
and by his own account he posed for Van Gogh in
the parsonage, usually on Saturdays. He remembered
the artist as 'a funny little chap'.[9] Van Gogh had his
studio in an outhouse next to the parsonage and
Kaufmann probably posed for this drawing in that
none too large space.

1. Mauve had told Van Gogh, when the latter came to The
   Hague at the end of August to show him his pen and ink
   drawings: 'you should have a try with charcoal & chalk &
   brush & stump (198/169,7 January 1882), adding 'colour
   is drawing too' (174/152, 12-15 October 1881). Van Gogh
   clearly followed this advice.
2. Not many watercolours by Van Rappard from the period
   1880-1881 have survived; what there is shows that he was
   more skilled than Van Gogh in this medium (Brouwer et
   al. 1974, nos. 31-35, 39-42).
3. This pose has been compared with the stooping mower in
   Millet's series Les travaux des champs, which Van Gogh
   copied at an early stage (Van Uitert et al., 1987, p. 137).
4. Heenk 1996, p. 40.
5. This row of trees becomes visible if the sheet is held
   against the light. The white paint has partly mixed with the
   charcoal and is locally a little greyer as a result.
6. Van Gogh strengthened the outlines considerably with
   black chalk, leading Kröller-Müller Museum restorer
   Hoefsloot to remark: 'The artist himself has inflicted
   damage on the paper through his rather temperamental
   drawing manner' (Hoefsloot 1987, p. 5). In addition, the
   edges of the sheet have suffered considerable damage over
   the years.
7. Kerstens 1990, p. 21.
8. Ibid.
9. Stokvis 1926, p. 20.

P. 89

Woman sewing

October-November 1881
black chalk, grey wash, opaque watercolour
on laid paper
59.7 x 44.8 cm
watermark: ED & Cie (in cartouche), PL BAS
signed lower left (by the artist):
Vincent (black chalk)
F885/JH71
KM 115.250

INSCRIPTIONS
recto, lower right: Verz:
Hidde Nijland (black chalk)

PROVENANCE
acquired by Hidde Nijland,Dordrecht, before 1904
purchased from Hidde Nijland by A.G. Kröller, The Hague,
July 1928
donated to the Kröller-Müller Foundation by A.G. Kröller,
December 1928

EXHIBITIONS
Dordrecht 1904, cat. no. 194.
The Hague 1918, cat no. 83.
Amsterdam 1924, cat. no. 46.
The Hague 1928, unnumbered.
Hamburg 1929, cat. no. 153.
Amsterdam 1930, cat no. 144.
Paris 1947, cat. no. 6.
Basel 1947, cat. no. 114.
London/Birmingham/Glasgow 1947-1948, cat. no. 103.
Montreal/Ottawa/Winnipeg/Toronto 1960-1961, cat. no. 84.
Rome 1988, cat. no. 54.

P. 90

Woman sewing

October-November 1881
black chalk, wash, opaque watercolour
on laid paper
62 x 47.2 cm
watermark: MICHALLET
signed lower left (not by the artist): Vincent (pencil)
F1221/JH70
KM 122.653

INSCRIPTIONS

PROVENANCE
L.C. Enthoven coll., Voorburg. purchased by H. Kröller-
Müller at sale Amsterdam (Frederik Muller & Cie), 18
May 1920 (Enthoven collection), lot 250: Vieille paysanne
racommodant une chemise d'homme (800 guilders)

EXHIBITIONS
Basel/Bern/Brussels 1927, cat. no. 71.
Düsseldorf 1928, cat. no. 137.
Karlsruhe 1928, cat. no. 72.
Berlin 1928-1929, cat. no. 66.
Hamburg 1929, cat. no. 140.
Amsterdam 1930, cat. no. 148.
New York/Philadelphia/Boston and other cities, 1935-1936,
cat. no. 99.
Liège/Brussels/Mons 1946-1947, cat. no. 5.
Paris 1947, cat. no. 5.
Geneva 1947, cat. no. 5.
's-Hertogenbosch/Breda 1950
Nuremberg 1956, cat. no. 5.
Munich 1956, cat. no. 18.
Tokyo/Kyoto 1958, cat. no. 9.
Munich 1961, cat. no. 10.
Warsaw 1962,cat. no. 10.
Tel Aviv/Haifa 1962-1963, cat. no. 9.
Moscow/Leningrad 1971, cat. no. 4.
New York/Chicago/Ottawa and other cities, 1973-1974, cat.
no. 29.
London/Newcastle-upon-Tyne 1974, cat. no. 19.
Hertogenbosch 1987-1988, cat. no. 7.
Otterlo 1990, cat. no. 8.
Yokohama/Nagoya 1995-1996, cat. no. 10.
Tokyo/Fukuoka 1999-2000, cat. no. 8.
Amsterdam/New York 2005, cat. no. 4.

P. 91

Woman sewing and cat

October-November 1881,
black chalk, wash, opaquewatercolour, white chalk
on laid paper
59.3 x 45.2 cm
watermark: ER, left and tightof a caduceus (in cartouche)
signed lower left (by the artist): Vincent (twice, one on top of
theother: first brown watercolour, then black chalk)
F887/JH73
KM 127.980

INSCRIPTIONS
recto, lower left: 2 or 3 fingerprints lower right: Vera: Hidde
Nijland (black ink)
verso, centre: Hidde Nijland (black ink)

PROVENANCE
acquired by Hidde Nijland, Dordrecht, before 1904.
purchased from Hidde Nijland by A.G. Kröller, The
Hague,July 1928 '
donated to the Kröller-Müller Foundation by A.G. Kröller,
December 1928

EXHIBITIONS
Dordrecht 1904, cat. no. 190[?].
The Hague 1918, cat. no. 83.
Amsterdam 1924, cat. no. 37.
The Hague 1928, unnumbered.
Hamburg 1929, cat. no. 141.
Amsterdam 1930, cat. no. 149.
Paris 1947, cat. no. 5.
s-Hertogenbosch/Breda 1950.
Warsaw 1962, cat. no. 11.
Tel Aviv/Haifa 1962-1963, cat. no. 10

Van Gogh's visit to his cousin by marriage,
the artist Anton Mauve (1838-1888), in the summer
of 1881 had far-reaching consequences for his work.[1]
It marked the end of his passion for copying Bargue,
Miller and others. In addition, he used different
materials, gave priority to drawing from the model
and worked more with colour. Mauve even wanted to
get him painting in oils, and they agreed that when
Van Gogh had enough new studies he would call
again.[2] Van Gogh was given fresh inspiration for the
autumn. He could hardly wait to show his most recent
progress to Mauve, who is quoted in nearly every
letter from October and November and sometimes

praised to the skies. 'Mauve gave me heart when I needed it recently,' he wrote to Van Rappard, 'he is a man of genius' (175/R2,15 October 1881). Mauve was supposed to come to Etten in the autumn, but for various reasons, including illness, the visit did not take place.

The most important advice that Van Gogh needed probably related to colour. If he wanted to produce saleable work, he had to become a more skilled watercolourist, because the simple fact was that coloured drawings sold better. Not only Mauve, but Theo too impressed this upon him (201/172, 22 January 1882), as did Uncle 'Cent, the retired art dealer Vincent van Gogh (1820-1888), who lived not far from Etten at Prinsenhage. This uncle had 'also said that if at some point I had a drawing a little smaller than those of this summer and more watercolour, I should send it and he would take it from me' (203/174, 13 February 1882). As may be seen in these three drawings of women sewing and in the previous sheets as well, Van Gogh's use of watercolour was mainly limited to colouring in a drawing that had first been laid down in detail in pencil, chalk or charcoal. He was not to learn 'true' watercolour, in which watercolour was used almost exclusively, until he was taught by Mauve in The Hague, three months after his first visit.

Being self-taught, Van Gogh was curious about how others worked. When Van Rappard dropped by on his way to Brussels in late October, Van Gogh explicitly asked him to bring some watercolours (175/ R2, 15 October 1881). After this brief visit he wrote to Theo: 'Rappard was here, brought watercolours that are getting to be good. Mauve is coming soon I hope, otherwise I'll go to him. I'm drawing a lot and believe it is getting better. I'm working in brush much more than in the past. Now it's so cold that almost all I do is figure drawing indoors, seamstress, basketweaver etc' (177/153, 3 November 1881). The large drawings of women sewing seem to be related to this, and would have been done around the time of Van Rappard's visit. Two of them show an older woman with a brown double cap of the 'cornet' type and clogs with strikingly curled tips, which are also seen in various other drawings.[3] She is portrayed to the left and right of the same table in turn. The trees and bushes visible through the window in the distance clearly show autumnal colours. The third sheet, Woman sewing and cat, is the most carefully worked up. Compared with other figure studies from this period, the young woman depicted here is drawn much more softly. The piece has a charm that is lacking in other sheets. The usual imperfections in the proportions are slightly less noticeable here, partly because of the excellent finishing in simple colours and the close attention to detail. Only the odd proportions of the chair, whose right leg is rather long whereas on the left no leg can be seen, betray the fact that the lower legs of the model are somewhat short. The woman sits in front of a fireplace with a large pot hanging above it. In the wall behind it an oven door is visible. She is evenly lit and her upper body casts a shadow to the right on the wall behind her, thus detaching her from the background. The signature at the lower left, which on second thoughts Van Gogh went over again in black

chalk, indicates that he too was satisfied with the final result.

Women doing needlework was a popular subject among the artists of the Hague School, and Van Gogh followed their lead. It is noteworthy, for example, that precisely in this period he quoted the poem The Song of the Shirt by Thomas Hood in a letter to Van Rappard (175/R2, 15 October 1881). It denounces the wretched working and living conditions of the (English) home-based seamstresses; they laboured for long hours for a pittance.[4] It is open to question whether Van Gogh was aiming at a similar social realism with his drawings of women sewing. The activities he depicted seem to be the normal household chores of the rural population. At all events he did not try to avoid a certain cosiness in Woman sewing and cat, in which an - apparently - contented, purring cat lies at the feet of the young woman. The foreshortening of the animal is exceptionally well done, frontally and from slightly above. It was left blank when the wash was applied and heightened with white opaque watercolour.

Although cats were regularly shown in combination with women doing needlework, this is the only example in Van Gogh's oeuvre, which includes many sewing and knitting women, but hardly any pets.[5] The accomplished illusionistic rendering of the cat makes one suspect that Van Gogh had help or worked from an example. Van Rappard very likely played a part here. One of his surviving sketchbooks contains various pen sketches of cats which bear a close resemblance both in pose and execution to Van Gogh's cat. The big cat on the left of the sketchbook sheet is even roughly the same size in reality as the cat in Van Gogh's drawing (both are about seven centimetres high). The latter has its head turned to the left, which is more like the cat at top right on Van Rappard's sketchbook sheet. So it is not unlikely that Van Rappard helped him with this drawing during his visit at the end of October, either by himself sketching the cat on the sheet or by leaving an example behind comparable to the one on the sketchbook sheet illustrated here. The date of the sketchbook is, however, uncertain. Most of the sketches must date from the second half of the 1880s, but various sheets from other periods have been added, some from 1879, when Van Rappard was in Brussels. Other sheets with cats may date from the early 1880s.[6]

The fact that Woman sewing and cat is otherwise such a successful drawing may also be due to the technically more experienced Van Rappard, who doubtless gave his older colleague advice or even direct help. At any rate the visit inspired Van Gogh to work with the brush still more. Some time later, when he had finally had his first lessons from Mauve, he let his brother know how important 'teaching by demonstration' was for him. In his enthusiasm he advised Theo to follow an artist from close by: 'If you have an opportunity to see painting or drawing, pay attention, for I believe many an art buyer would think differently about many paintings &c. if he really knew how they were made. It's true that one can understand to some extent by instinct, but I am sure of this, that I have got a clearer idea of various things by seeing the work and giving it a try myself' (204/175, 13 February

1882).

1. In 1874 Mauve married Van Gogh's first cousin Ariëtta Sophia Jeanette ('Jet') Carbentus (1856-1894), a daughter of Arie Carbentus, the brother of Van Gogh's mother.
2. In the middle of October Mauve sent him a painter's box with oils, brushes, a palette knife and so on, but it is not known whether Van Gogh immediately set to work with it (192/165, previously dated 22-24 December 1881, seep. 86).
3. With thanks to Gerard Rooijmakers, Meertens Institute, Amsterdam. Clogs like this were not normally women's clogs, which were generally lower, without an upper section, and often with bands.
4. The Song of the Shirt by Thomas Hood (1799-1845) was first published in 1843, and soon became internationally known through various translations. The first of the eleven verses of this poem give an idea of the tenor: 'With fingers weary and worn,/With eyelids heavy and red,/A woman sat, in un-womanly rags,/Plying her needle and thread-/Stitch! stitch! stitch!/In poverty, hunger, and dirt,/And still with a voice of dolorous pitch/She sang the "Song of the Shirt."
5. In the summer of 1881 Van Gogh attended an exhibition put on by the Hollandsche Teekenmaat-schappij in The Hague, where he admired such works as the watercolour Sewing school at Katwijk by Jozef Israëls (170/149, 27 August 1881). A cat is depicted quite prominently in the foreground. The water-colour was acquired by the Van Gogh Museum, Amsterdam in 1989.
6. These sheets may have been added by the former owner, the artist and illustrator L.W.R. Wenckebach (1860-1937), a good friend of Van Rappard. Sheets 11 to 17 do not belong to the original sections of the sketchbook, and the cats illustrated here are on sheet 17 (Brouwer et al. 1974, pp. 140-141).

P. 93

Man reading at the fireside

October-early November 1881
black chalk, charcoal, grey wash, opaque watercolour, on laid paper
45.7 x 56.1 cm
watermark: MICHALLET
signed lower left (by the artist):
Vincent (brush in black
watercolour)
F897/JH63
KM 128.322

INSCRIPTIONS

PROVENANCE

[probably A.C.W. Terhell coll., The Hague].
acquired by Hidde Nijland, Dordrecht, before 1895.
purchased from Hidde Nijland by A.G. Kröller, The Hague,
July 1928
donated to the Kröller-Müller Foundation by A.G. Kröller,
December 1928

EXHIBITIONS
The Hague 1895, no known cat.'
Dordrecht 1897, no cat.
Dordrecht 1904, cat. no. 198.
The Hague 1918, cat. no. 63.
Amsterdam 1924, cat. no. 97.
The Hague 1928, unnumbered.
Hamburg 1929, cat. no. 154.
Amsterdam 1930, cat. no. 141.
New York/Philadelphia/Boston and other cities, 1935-1936,
cat. no. 75.
Hertogenbosch/Breda 1950' Milan 1952, cat. no. 7.
Saint Louis/Philadelphia/Toledo 1953-1954, cat. no. 4.
Eindhoven 1956, cat. no. 3.
Munich 1956, cat. no. 13.
Essen 1957, cat. no. 126.
Vienna 1958, cat. no. 13.
Tokyo/Kyoto 1958, cat. no. 12
Moscow/Leningrad 1971, cat. no. 8.
New York/chicago/ottawa and other cities, 1973-1974, cat.
no. 25.
London/Newcastle-upon-Tyne 1974, cat. no. 15.
Yokohama/Nagoya 1995-1996, cat. no. 11.
Tokyo/Fukuoka 1999-2000, cat. no. 6.
Detroit/Boston/Philadelphia 2000-2001, unnumbered

P. 93

Nursing mother with child

October-November 1881
black chalk, charcoal, wash, opaque watercolour
on laid paper
45.2 x 59.2 cm
no watermark
unsigned
F1070/JH74
KM 128.395

INSCRIPTIONS
recto, lower left: Atelier/Vincent (black chalk) ' lower right:
Verz: Hidde Nijland (black ink)
verso, upper centre: Door mij gekocht van den Kunstkooper
Oldenzeel Rotterdam, December 1892/Hidde
Nijland (pencil) upper left: KR97 (blue chalk) lower right:
KM 102 (pencil)

PROVENANCE
A.C.W. Terhell coll., The Hague ?-1892 '
purchased by Hidde Nijland, Dordrecht at Oldenzeel, art

dealer, Rotterdam, December 1892 '
purchased from Hidde Nijland by A.G. Kröller, The Hague,
July 1928 -
donated to the Kröller-Muller Foundation by A.G. Kröller,
December 1928

EXHIBITIONS
Rotterdam 1892, no cat.
The Hague 1895, no known cat.
Dordrecht 1897, no cat.
Dordrecht 1904, cat. no. 181.
The Hague 1918, cat. no. 77.
Amsterdam 1924, cat. no. 45.
The Hague 1928, unnumbered.
Hamburg 1929, cat. no. 159.
Amsterdam 1930, cat. no. 143.
Milan 1952, cat. no. 6.

Cornelia Adriana ('Kee') Vos-Stricker (1846-1918], c.1880,
photo. Van Gogh Museum, Amsterdam
(Vincent van Gogh Foundation)

P. 95

Old man at the fireside

17 November 1881
black chalk, reddish brown and grey wash, orange-red chalk,
opaque watercolour, on laid paper
55.8 x 44.5 cm
no watermark
unsigned
F868/JH80
KM 120.849

INSCRIPTIONS
recto, lower right: Atelier/VINCENT (black chalk) Vincent.
Verz Hidde Nijland (black ink)

PROVENANCE
A.C.W. Terhell coll., The Hague ?-c. 1893
acquired by Hidde Nijland, Dordrecht, c. 1893.
purchased from Hidde Nijland by A.G. Kröller, The Hague,
July 1928
donated to the Kröller-Müller Foundation by A.G. Kröller,
December 1928

EXHIBITIONS
Rotterdam 1892, no cat.
The Hague 1895, no known cat.
Dordrecht 1897, No cat.
Dordrecht 1904, cat. no. 126.
The Hague 1918, cat. no. 6.
Amsterdam 1924, cat. no. 68.
The Hague 1928, unnumbered.

Hamburg 1929, cat. no. 158.
Amsterdam 1930, cat. no. 135.
Nuremberg 1956, cat. no. 7.
Munich 1956, cat. no. 15.
Essen 1957, cat. no. 132.
Montreal/Ottawa/Winnipeg/Toronto1960-1961, cat. no. 82.
Belgrade 1966, cat. no. 8.
New York/Chicago/Ottawa and other cities, 1973-1974, cat.
no. 28.
London/Newcastle-upon-Tyne 1974, cat. no. 18.
Amsterdam 1980-1981, cat. no. 40.
Tokyo/Nagoya 1985-1986, cat. no. 26.
Osaka 1986, cat. no. 21.
's-Hertogenbosch 1987-1988, cat. no. 8.
Otterlo 1990, cat. no. 7.
Yokohama/Nagoya 1995-1996, cat. no. 12.
Tokyo/Fukuoka 1999-2000, cat. no. 7.
Amsterdam/New York 2005, cat. no. 5.

The drawings Van Gogh did inside the
peasants' houses in Etten are in part set by the
fireplace. In the sixteenth and seventeenth centuries
an old man or woman seated by the fire was often an
image of winter. In the nineteenth century artists like
Jozef Israëls (1824-1911) painted similar scenes, but
they were more concerned to depict realistically the
poverty-stricken existence of the common people.[1]
This had an enormous appeal for Van Gogh too, who
was a great admirer of lsraëls, as is evident from his
first depiction of an old man at the fireside, one of
the few works from Etten to which he gave an (English)
title, Worn out.[2] In September 1881 he wrote to
Theo that he had finally drawn 'an old, ill peasant
on a chair by the fire with his head in his hands and
his elbows on his knees' (171/150). He borrowed
the title from a painting of an exhausted worker by
Thomas Faed (1826-1900), which he knew from a
reproduction.

As Van Gogh later indicated, the model
for the 'old, ill peasant' was Cornelis Schuitemaker
(1813-1884), who may also be identified in man
reading at the fireside and old man at the fireside.[3]
There was considerable correspond-ence among the
details around the fireplace as well, both in these
three drawings and in Woman at the fireside. This
makes it likely that Van Gogh made or began these
works in the home of Schuitemaker and his wife
Johanna van Peer in St. Willebrord, a hamlet just to
the west of Etten that was often known as 'het Heike'
(the Heath) at that time. We know from another
source that he did a lot of work there. In 1930, in a
letter addressed to the director of the Kröller-Müller
Foundation, a certain A. Mijs wrote that his attention
had been caught by a reproduction of Man reading
at the fireside in the Wereldkroniek magazine of
20 July 1929, 'because I believed I recognised one
Schuitemaker, the only Protestant living in het Heike
[......], who as a soldier had stayed on there in 1830
and 1839 and had married an R.C. woman. My father
was the minister at Etten, after the Rev. v. Gogh, the
father of Vincent van Gogh. So Schuitemaker came
to see my father now and then, and I heard him tell
how Vincent van Gogh often came to draw him,
Schuitemaker, and his wife [...]. I can still see the grey,
wiry hair above the ears, and the large, slightly round
face.[4] Besides the old man's distinctive head, Van

Gogh may have had more philanthropic reasons for frequently using him as his model, for Schuitemaker could make good use of the small amount he received for posing: from the beginning of September 1881 the couple depended on financial support from the poor relief provided by the parishes of Etten, Hoeven and Oudenbosch.[5]

The wiry grey hair and slightly rounded face are quite visible in Man reading at the fireside. The drawing could be a pendant to Woman at the fireside, which might depict Johanna van Peer.[6] Van Gogh may have been referring to both drawings in a letter to Van Rappard written shortly after his visit at the end of October when he said that he had drawn a 'boy cutting grass with a sickle as well' and 'then a man & woman sitting by the fire' (176/R3, 2 November 1881). But the last description could also refer to a single drawing of a man and woman together.

One important difference between the two drawings is the degree of finishing. Woman at the fireside is less fully painted in watercolour than man reading at the fireside. Only the woman's socks and the few places where the skirt under her apron is visible are coloured, in blue and green respectively (and a little bit of purple). Apart from that, the light orange brown tiled floor stands out from the greyish background. The most striking aspect is the use of white opaque watercolour, particularly to suggest smoke. The transition between the hearth and the wall is indicated in the background by a curious-looking, broad band of white paint. Compared with Man reading at the fireside, in which the light-dark contrasts are also stronger, the work seems unfinished. Indeed, the signature at the lower right is very unlikely to be genuine.[7]

Old man at the fireside is mentioned in a letter of 18 November in which Van Gogh writes: 'Have my drawings arrived? I did another one yesterday, a peasant boy lighting the fire in the hearth where the kettle hangs in the morning, and another one, an old man putting dry twigs on the fire' (183/158). This clearly describes Schuitemaker's actions in the drawing, which can therefore be dated to 17 November. For this drawing Van Gogh made things a little more difficult for himself than previously by choosing a position directly in front of his model, which made the foreshortening tricky. Up to then he had usually viewed his models from the 'easier' sideways position. The imaginary horizon is placed in about the middle of the sheet, so that the eye is drawn downwards more strongly. The extended arm with the twigs runs in a fluent movement towards the fire at the bottom. The kettle, on the left edge, acts as an effective repoussoir. The broom lying on the floor on the right and a metal hanging trivet, a device for hanging pots over the fire, also provide perspective accents. It is noteworthy that Van Gogh has put a reddish brown wash on a large part of the drawing, thus reinforcing the glow from the open fire.[8] He accentuated the flames themselves with orange-red chalk. The figure of Schuitemaker has a grey wash for the most part. At the transitions between the washes small areas of blank paper are sometimes visible, such as by the clogs.

This is one of the most dynamic of all his figure drawings from Etten and Van Gogh was probably quick to send it to his brother. It is a fact that on 18 November he wrote a second letter to Theo in which he said: 'Now, brother, if you send me "travel money", then you'll immediately get 3 drawings: "Lunch break", "the fire lighter" and a "man on the parish" (184/159). The 'fire lighter' no doubt refers to the (now lost) drawing of the peasant boy lighting the fire in the morning. The 'man on the parish' may very well be old man at the fireside, because Schuitemaker received poor relief.[9]

The 'travel money' mentioned in the letter refers to the extra money Van Gogh needed for a visit to Amsterdam, the home of a cousin seven years his senior. She was Cornelia Adriana ('Kee') Vos-Stricker, and he had fallen deeply in love with her when she spent some time in Etten in the summer. Kee was the daughter of the sister of Vincent's mother; she was a widow and had a son.[10] But Vincent's love was unrequited. The correspondence between the two brothers in November was almost entirely concerned with Vincent's desperate attempts to win Kee over, which encountered strong opposition from both the Van Gogh and Stricker families, and especially from Kee herself. With her unambiguous 'No. never ever', she had made it clear to her cousin that she did not want a relationship.

Until now work by Van Gogh from Etten has never really been explicitly linked to his love for his cousin, apart from the portrait of his sister Willemina, which was sometimes thought to be of Kee.[11] Yet in the case of Nursing mother with child there may be such a connection. In the first place the composition is unusual in Van Gogh's work done in Etten. His figure studies generally show a single person (man, woman or child), whether or not occupied in some handwork or task. Here a woman is depicted as she breastfeeds her baby. At her feet an older child sits next to what appears to be a basket full of fruit. The drawing makes motherhood or family life the central concern, and in all its rather angular awkwardness it is a touching piece.[12] On closer inspection it is noticeable that the woman stares into space somewhat absently and hardly seems to be aware that she is feeding her baby. Her features are a little severe and she has a grim expression about her mouth. In addition, her head has come out disproportionately large. It is quite possible that Van Gogh wanted to emphasise the hopeless plight of a poor young family, but he may have had Kee and himself in mind as well. A portrait photo of Kee Vos shows a striking resemblance to the head of the woman in this drawing, with the same forceful chin, high, angular forehead, hairline, mouth, and right cheek, which is just visible beside the nose and mouth. It is both impossible and inconceivable that Kee herself posed, but Van Gogh may have used a print of the photo shown here. The nursing mother is no doubt drawn from a Brabant model, inside a young woman's humble cottage, but Van Gogh replaced her features by those of his beloved. He may have wanted this scene to show a situation that he aspired to himself.

'Since I've been really in love,' wrote Van Gogh to Theo on 9 or 10 November, 'there has also been more reality in my drawings, and I am now writing to you in the small room with a whole collection of men, women and children from her Heike etc. around me' (179/155). It is tempting to think that this drawing too hung on the wall, and perhaps also Girl at the fireside, which is quite similar in technique and in a certain awkwardness in the drawing to Nursing mother with child.[13] The idea that he needed the love of a woman in order to make his work better is found in several letters. 'For the best way to dessiner encore is aimer encore', he wrote to Theo (181/157, 12 November 1881). Moreover, possible faults in his work could be corrected if only he had a woman at his side. Thus he remarked in connection with old man at the fireside: 'To my regret there is still something hard and severe in my drawings, and I think that she, specifically her influence, will be needed to soften that' (183/158, 18 November 1881). Theo eventually sent him the travel money and Van Gogh left for Amsterdam around 24 November. Three days later, having failed in his mission, he travelled on to The Hague.

---

1. De Leeuw et al., 1983, p. 193.
2. The drawing shown here was once owned by Anthon van Rappard and is a variation of a larger drawing with the same title that has not survived. Van Gogh had also sent Van Rappard a smaller sketch of it (F864) and Theo a sketch in letter 171/150. These sketches differ slightly from the drawing illustrated here: in the background on the right there is a shovel against the wall, and the kettle is not hanging from the chain but lying in the embers of the fire.
3. When Van Gogh returned to the theme of a sorrowful man at the end of November 1882, he wrote to Theo that in the previous year Schuitemaker had been the model (288/247, 24 November 1882); Schuitemaker can also be identified in F860, F860a and man with broom.
4. Letter from A. Mijs, notary of Oostburg, dated 6 January 1930, Kröller-Müller Museum archives, HA376740. Arend Mijs (1866-1934) was a son of Jacob Mijs, who succeeded T. van Gogh as minister at Etten in May 1883 - six months after Van Gogh was called to Nuenen - and moved into the parsonage with his family (Van Geertruy 2003, p. 34). Schuitemaker died in October 1884, so Arend did not know him for long.
5. De Bruyn-Heeren 1992, pp. 169-170. St. Willebrord came under the Reformed congregation of Oudenbosch, but Schuitemaker always went to church in Etten and had also been confirmed there. The three congregations each gave 75 cents per week for Schuitemaker, until his death. After that his (Catholic) wife received a one time sum of 5 guilders and the assistance ended. Models cost Van Gogh between 20 and 30 cents per day, he told Theo in a letter of 18 November 1881 (185/160).
6. Johanna van Peer (1812-1887) also appears to have been the model for F883 and Woman churning.
7. Compare the genuine signature on man reading at the fireside. Even apart from the fact that Van Gogh liked to sign works at the lower left, a practice he deviated from only if it presented compositional or aesthetic problems, the signature shows similarities with a number of others on drawings from Brussels, Etten and early on in The Hague. They are all done in pencil (even when that material is not used or only rarely - as here - in the drawing), have a large, broad 'V' and a cross stroke on the 't' which comes out of the ascender in a distinctive loop and underlines the name. This signature is not seen on any of the numerous Etten drawings from the Nijland collection, but it is found on those from the Enthoven collection (apart from this sheet, Windmills at Dordrecht (Weeskinderendijk), and Woman sewing, and other collections whose earliest provenance is

often unclear (F860a, F930a, F1235, F1246, F1680).

8. This wash is no longer all that striking because over time the paper has suffered considerable damage and turned brown (see also the many spots, known as 'foxing', that occur all over the sheet, especially on the left in the background). The drawing has been lined with Japanese paper (Hoefsloot 1987, p.9).

9. Old man at the fireside has not previously been linked to 'man on the parish'. Van Gogh clearly indicated in his first letter that in the one drawing a fire is being lit and in the other a man 'puts dry twigs on the fire', so it is not likely that the 'fire lighter' in his second letter refers to Old man at the fireside. The drawing 'lunch break' is described in an earlier letter of 12 November to Van Rappard as 'a worker drinking coffee and cutting a slice of bread. On the ground a spade that he has brought from the field' (182/R4). It cannot be linked to any known Etten drawing and must have been lost just like 'fire lighter' (see also p. 390, note A).

10. See Hulsker 1985, pp. 168-180, for a detailed account of the relationship.

11. In a more general sense Soth 1994, p. 106, did relate the homely atmosphere of Woman sewing to Van Gogh's love for Kee.

12. Van Gogh had difficulty, for example, with the perspective of the corner behind the cradle: where the two walls ought to be at right angles, they appear to continue as one wall.

13. The model for Girl at the fireside is the same as for Girl raking (F884, Centraal Museum, Utrecht).

P. 97

Still life with straw hat

Late November - mid-December 1881
Oil on paper on canvas
36.5 x 53.6 cm
F62/JH922
KM 109.323

SIGNATURE/INSCRIPTIONS/LABELS -

PROVENANCE
A.C. van Gogh-Carbentus, Nuenen/Breda, November 1885/April 1886. A. Schrauwen, Breda, 1886. J.C. and J.M. Couvreur, Breda. W. van Bakel and C. Mouwen, Breda, 1902. Oldenzeel, art dealer, Rotterdam, 1903. L.C. Enthoven coil., Voorburg.
purchased by H. Kröller-Müller at Enthoven sale, Amsterdam (Frederik Muller), 18 May 1920, lot 222: Nature morte (f3,100)

EXHIBITIONS
Rotterdam 1903 (a), no. 12.
Basle/Bern 1927, no. 52.
Brussels 1927, no. 52.
Dusseldorf 1928, no. 118.

Karlsruhe 1928, no. 53.
Berlin 1928-1929, no. 50.
Hamburg 1929, no. 19.
Amsterdam 1930, no. 188.
New York/Philadelphia/Boston and other cities 1935-1936, no. 6.
Basle 1947, no. 13.
New York/Chicago 1949-1950, no. 5.
Milan 1952, no. 58. The Hague 1953, no. 32.
Otterlo/Amsterdam 1953, no. 29.
Saint Louis/philadelphia/Toledo 1953-1954, no. 32.
's-Hertogenbosch 1987-1988, no. 92
Vienna 1996, no. 2

After his proposal of marriage to his cousin Kee Vos in Amsterdam was rejected, Van Gogh sought diversion in hard work. In late November 1881 he went to The Hague to take a few painting lessons from Anton Mauve, his cousin by marriage. Up until then his efforts had been limited to drawings. Mauve was a well-known landscape painter and exponent of the peasant genre, a theme that also appealed to Van Gogh. Mauve gave him lessons in oil painting technique and in the use of colour. He also introduced him to watercolours. In early December, Van Gogh informed Theo of his first attempts: 'Well, Mauve at once sat me down before a still life with a pair of old wooden shoes and some other objects, so I could set to work' (189/162, I, 2 or 3 December 1881).

During his weeks in The Hague, Van Gogh produced an unknown number of works. On around 18 December he let Theo know that he had painted five studies: two watercolours and 'a few more scribbles' (190/163). The painted studies were still lifes, he says further on in the letter, and he included sketches of two of them: one of Still life with cabbage and clogs (FI) and one of a terracotta head of a child with a fur cap that so far has remained untraced.[1] Still life with clogs and Still life with straw hat are also among the five oil studies mentioned.

Before 1946, when Carlo Derkert made the link between these two paintings and Van Gogh's apprenticeship with Mauve, it was assumed that he had painted them in Nuenen.[2] But unlike the Nuenen still lifes, with their sketchy design and rough, impasto technique, Still life with clogs and Still life with straw hat are quite detailed, with a small amount of paint smoothly applied (apart from the impastoed highlights and the more roughly painted left foreground of the canvas in Still life with clogs).

This connects them stylistically with Still life with cabbage and clogs, which De la Faille in 1928 placed during Van Gogh's apprenticeship with Mauve in The Hague.[3] Although Still life with cabbage and clogs is regarded as Van Gogh's first painting, Still life with clogs is the more obvious choice. In the former, the cabbage is the focus of attention. The old clogs, which Van Gogh mentions in his letter to Theo of early December as the motif of his first painting, is a less important part of the composition here than the clogs in the still life in the Kröller-Müller collection. In addition, Still life with clogs is painted on canvas, whereas Still life with cabbage and clogs, like Still life with straw hat, is painted on paper. Perhaps Mauve

'treated' the enthusiastic Van Gogh to a real canvas upon his arrival to give him a good start, and then had him practice on cheaper material.[4]

Mauve's main lesson for Van Gogh in Still life with clogs and Still life with straw hat was variation in colour and texture: the tough, worn straw of the hat, the transparent and gleaming glass of the bottle, the clay pipe and the white cloth. The earthenware pot - with a brush or a spoon inside - appears in both still lifes. The compositions are simple: a few objects lying on the same wooden table made with broad boards, placed at exactly the same angle in the picture plane. In the first still life is a pair of clogs, half hidden behind an earthenware pot. To the left is a green bottle containing a small amount of liquid. Van Gogh scratched lines in the paint of the table top with a blunt object - probably the shaft of his brush - to indicate the edges of the boards.

In Still life with straw hat, the objects on the rough wooden table are arranged round a straw hat with a black ribbon. In front of the hat is a clay pipe. A bit further back are a clay bottle, the red-brown pot and a green ginger pot with fibre hangers. Lying at the edge of the table is a box of matches with something behind it that looks like a block of peat.[5] The painting is quite dark in that spot and the object can hardly be discerned from the background. Van Gogh painted this still life with a small amount of paint on artists' paper with a light-coloured, rolled ground, the granular structure of which is still quite visible. Only in the highlights and the light colours did he use a bit more paint. The underdrawing can be seen in several spots in both still lifes, showing how Van Gogh put down the contours of the objects with broad, rough lines in charcoal before painting them,[6] Mauve was pleasantly surprised by the first results: 'I have always thought you a dreadful bore, but now I see this is not the case,' Van Gogh passed this reaction on to Theo in his letter of early December, commenting, 'I can assure you that this simple sentence of M.'s pleased me more than a cartload of Jesuitical compliments would have.' (189/162) He himself was also satisfied with his first oil studies. It goes without saying that these were no 'masterpieces', 'yet I really believe that there is some soundness and truth in them, more at any rate than what I've done up to now. And so I reckon that I am now at the beginning of doing something serious. And because I can now call on more technical resources, that is to say, paint and brush, everything seems fresh again, as it were. (191/164, c. 21 December 1881) He regarded his paintings as the starting point of his artistic career: 'For, Theo, with painting my real career begins. Don't you think I am right to consider it so.' (192/165, 22-24 December 1881)

Van Gogh probably kept Still life with clogs and Still life with straw hat for a long time; their whereabouts up to 1912 and 1920 respectively are unknown. Mauve had advised him to save his studies: 'M. says I must keep all my studies' (189/162); they were to serve as comparative material. Going by the letter he wrote to his brother around 21 December 1881, it is reasonable to presume that the two still lifes were among the works he took with him to his parents in Etten: Anyway, I came away from him [Mauve] with some painted studies and a few watercolours.' (191/164) In late December he returned to The Hague, planning to stay longer, and he took his studies (or some of them) with him. When he subsequently moved on to Hoogeveen in Drenthe in September 1883 he left his work in The Hague, sending for it in early December 1883 when he moved in with his parents, who in the meantime had moved to Nuenen. Two years later when he departed for Antwerp he left his work, which probably included the two still lifes, with his mother, A.C. van Gogh-Carbentus (1819-1907). She took it with her when she moved to Breda in 1886. There she had it stored with a carpenter named Schrauwen. After that the history of the works' whereabouts is unclear. Van Gogh's mother may have forgotten about them, and according to reports, Schrauwen -unaware of the value of the work - sold the entire lot to a second-hand dealer, J.C. Couvreur (1877-1961) in 1902. Couvreur in turn sold some of the paintings (many of the drawings seem to have been immediately destroyed) to Kees Mouwen and Willem van Bakel of Breda, and in 1903 they turned up in Rotterdam at various sales exhibitions at Kunstzalen Oldenzeel. These exhibitions featured work from several estates, however, so exactly where Still life with clogs came from is still unclear.[7]

Still life with clogs was acquired by Mrs Kröller-Muller in 1912 at a sale in Amsterdam (possibly through art dealer Komter); she bought Still life with straw hat in 1920 for 3,100 guilders at the sale of the Enthoven collection.
AV

1. Nothing is known of the child's head, F1, F62 and F63 are the three still lifes from this period that have been preserved.
2. In 1946 Carlo Derkert was the first to make a link between these two works and the still lifes in the Van Gogh Museum, but his observations are far from unanimously accepted. While the catalogue Van Gogh in Brabant, published in 1987-1988, also places the two still lifes in the Hague period, in Hulsker 1989 and 1996 they are both in the Nuenen chapter. For a detailed study of the literature on the dating of these works see Van Tilborgh and Vellekoop 1999, p. 35, note 19.
3. This still life was therefore given the Faille number 1,
4. Oral communication from Louis van Tilborgh.
5. In the catalogue at the sale of the Enthoven collection in 1920, where this work was purchased by the Krollers, this object is described as 'peat'.
6. Technical examination, Kröller-Müller Museum, 2002.
7. See Stokvis 1926, pp. 3-8, and Van Tilborgh & Vellekoop 1999, pp. 32-34, note 14; more information on the peregrinations of Van Gogh's work in: Op de Coul 2003.

P. 99

Woman sewing

January-February 1882
pencil, black and brown chalk, brown and black/grey wash, opaque and transparent watercolour, on wove paper
56.5 x 48.6 cm
watermark: J WHATMAN 1881 B
unsigned
F1033/JH353
KM 129.246

INSCRIPTIONS
verso, lower left: k m. 197 (pencil)

PROVENANCE
Theo van Gogh, Paris, 1890-1891. Jo van Gogh-Bonger, Bussum/Amsterdam, 1891 S. Moulijn, Laren, after 1905. purchased by H. Kröller-Müller at Miedema, art dealer, Rotterdam, 18 December 1916 (500 guilders)

EXHIBITIONS
Amsterdam 1905, cat. no. 254.
Basel/Bern/Brussels 1927, cat. no. 12.
Düsseldorf 1928, cat. no. 79.
Karlsruhe 1928, cat. no. 14.
Berlin 1928-1929, cat. no. 36.
Hamburg 1929, cat. no. 137.
Amsterdam 1930, cat. no. 140.
Vienna 1996, cat. no. 4.

From 1 January 1882 Van Gogh rented a room and alcove in The Hague in Schenkweg, where he set up his studio. He had to seek out new models and among others found a 'little old lady' who was not too expensive (202/173, 26 January 1882). She probably posed for Woman sewing and Woman grinding coffee.[1] In the past these two drawings were given widely varying dates, but they belong unmistakably to the early model studies from The Hague which were not yet done with the aid of a perspective frame and squaring. Moreover, they still show some relation to the work from Etten.[2] This can be seen in Woman sewing, for example, in the model's elongated upper legs and in the distance between foot-warmer and chair. Otherwise the proportions are reasonably convincing, and Van Gogh has clearly got further back from his model, as Mauve recommended. Later on the foreground and background, both colored brown, were gone over thoroughly in pencil. The diagonal lines in the foreground which depict the

wooden floorboards were subsequently drawn in black chalk using a ruler. On the right-hand side about three centimeters were once folded over. The fold is still clearly visible as a white line. Slightly to one side of this fold short straight pencil strokes can be seen, probably marking a cut that was never made. It is not clear whether the artist himself was responsible for this. Trimming the right-hand side would have led to a curious lopping of the window in the background in particular.

In February watercolor gradually gave way to pen and ink. The latter actually suited Van Gogh better and he thought it would also improve his chances of getting work for magazines. His desire to be an illustrator had certainly not diminished, as appears when he asked his brother for advice: 'If you can find out, you must let me know what sort of drawings one could sell to the illustrated magazines. It seems to me that they would be able to use pen drawings of ordinary people & I would so like to start work on them to make something suitable for reproduction' (203/174,13 February 1882).

1. The same model was also used for Woman knitting (F910a, present whereabouts unknown).
2. De la Faille 1928/1970, Vanbeselaere 1937 and Hulsker 1997/1996 dated Woman sewing in the spring of 1883 and grouped Woman grinding coffee under Etten 1881. Hefting 1980, p. 13, also located the latter in Etten, but Woman sewing was given the uncertain date of '1882 or 1883' (ibid., p. 30). Hammacher 1961, p. 13, dated Woman sewing to January-February 1882, and was probably the first to do so. Heenk 1995, pp. 46 and 48, and Dorn 1996, p. 68, placed both drawings in this period.

P. 101

Woman seated

March-April 1882
pencil, pen and brush in black ink (partly browned), on laid paper (two sheen)
60.9 x 37.3 cm
watermark: ED&Cie (in cartouche), PLBAS
unsigned
F936/JH140
KM 128.630

INSCRIPTIONS

verso, lower right: Vincent v. G./
Verz: Hidde Nijland (black ink)

PROVENANCE
acquired by Hidde Nijland, Dordrecht, before 1904
purchased from Hidde Nijland by A.G. Kröller, The Hague,
July 1928
donated to the Kröller-Müller Foundation by A.G. Kröller,
December 1928

EXHIBITIONS
Dordrecht 1904, cat. no. ?.
The Hague 1918, cat. no. 9.
Amsterdam 1924, cat. no. 11.
The Hague 1928, unnumbered.
Hamburg 1929, cat. no. 55.
Amsterdam 1930, cat. no. 41.
Vienna 1958, cat. no. 17.
Munich 1961, cat. no. 15.
London 1962, cat. no. 6.
Moscow/Leningrad 1971, cat. no. 13.
The Hague 1990, unnumbered.
Detroit/Boston/Philadelphia 2000-2001, unnumbered.

P. 102

Woman seated

April-May 1882
pencil, pen and brush in ink (diluted), wash,
traces of squaring, on laid paper (two sheets)
58.2 x 43.5 cm
watermark: ED & Cie (in cartouche),
PL BAS unsigned
F937r/JH144
KM 128.135 RECTO

INSCRIPTIONS
verso, upper left: KR96(pencil).
5 [scratched out] (pencil). lower
centre: plgr/platgroen (pencil).
lower right: 42 (black ink)
RVKM (red stamp). 23 (pencil)

PROVENANCE
acquired by Hidde Nijland, Dordrecht, before 1895.
purchased from Hidde Nijland by A.G. Kröller, The Hague,
July 1928
donated to the Kröller-Müller Foundation by A.G. Kröller,
December 1928

EXHIBITIONS

The Hague 1895, no known cat.
Dordrecht 1897, no cat.
Dordrecht 1904, cat. no. 114 or 140.
The Hague 1918, cat. no. 1?.
Amsterdam 1924, cat. no. 28.
The Hague 1928, unnumbered.
Hamburg 1929, cat. no. 117.
Amsterdam 1930, cat. no. 39.
New York/Chicago 1949-1950, cat. no. 15.
Essen 1957, cat. no. 137.
New York/Chicago/Ottawa and other cities, 1973-1974, cat.
no. 32.
London/Newcastle-upon-Tyne 1974, cat. no. 22.
Moos 1980, cat. no. 7.
The Hague 1990, unnumbered.
Detroit/Boston/Philadelphia 2000-2201 unnumbered.

P. 103

Woman sewing

April-May 1882
pencil, grey wash, traces of squaring,
on laid paper (two sheets)
58 x 45.5 cm
watermark: ED&Cie (in cartouche), PL BAS
unsigned
F932/JH145
KM 123.444

INSCRIPTIONS
verso, lower left:
Port: Vincent/Hidde Nijland/NO 38 (black ink).
25 (blue chalk).
lower right: 158 (pencil) centre: 60 (blue chalk)
43 [scratched our] (blue chalk)
upper left: KR 48 (blue chalk)

PROVENANCE
acquired by Hidde Nijland, Dordrecht, before 1904
purchased from Hidde Nijland by A.G. Kröller, The Hague,
July 1928 -
donated to the Kröller-Müller Foundation by A.G. Kröller,
December 1928

EXHIBITIONS
Dordrecht 1904, cat. no. ?.
The Hague 1918, cat. no. ?.
Amsterdam 1924, cat. no. 27.
The Hague 1928, unnumbered.
Hamburg 1929, cat. no. 79.
Amsterdam 1930, cat. no. 33.

Antwerp 1952, cat. no. 37a.
Montreal/Ottawa/Winnipeg/Toronto 1960-1961, cat. no. 86.
Detroit/Boston/Philadelphia 2000-2001, unnumbered.

'If you come, would you above all remember
to bring some Ingres paper?', wrote Van Gogh to his
brother on 18 March 1882. 'It is especially the thick
variety that I like to work on and that, so it seems
to me, would even be suited for watercolour studies'
(209/180). Although Theo did not pay a visit, he did
send a package of paper from The Hague, for which
Van Gogh thanked him at the beginning of April
(213/184). From the later correspondence it emerges
that the thick paper asked for was not included. Van
Gogh returned to the subject in May: 'The paper
that I would actually like most is the kind used for
the drawing of the female figure bending forward,
but if possible in an unbleached linen tone. I have
none left of that thickness I believe it is called double
Ingres. I cannot get any more of it here. If you see
how the drawing is made, you will understand that
the thin paper can hardly support it' (223/192, 3-12
May 1882). Van Gogh's reference to the 'female figure
bending forward' is in all probability one of the two
large studies entitled Woman seated for which Sien
posed, in a dejected, hunched position, head in
hands.

These two studies, together with three of the
large figure studies illustrated here, are drawn on a
sheet that consists of two pieces of laid paper pressed
together and bearing the watermark ED&Cie (in
cartouche), PL BAS.[1] The two sheets of paper were
pasted together by the dealer or the papermaker in
such a way that the watermarks and the lines of the
mould which are always easy to see on laid paper - are
slightly out of alignment with respect to each other.
So when a sheet like this is held up to the light it can
be easily recognised because of its double watermark
and mould. Van Gogh often used the 'single' sheets of
this type of paper in his Dutch period. The package
of paper sent to him in early April probably consisted
of this type, because the large city views which he
made in April and May on commission from C.M.
van Gogh are almost all on laid paper with that
watermark.[2] A letter from 26 July 1882 suggests that
he had indeed managed to acquire the last batch
of that paper from 'Stam' (252/220), by which he
meant the shop owned by the widow Stam-Liernur
on Papestraat. It is difficult to say precisely when this
occurred, but by the beginning of May that supply was
clearly used up.[3]

For Woman with child Van Gogh used a
perspective frame with squares measuring 5 x 5 cm.
For a few other sheets he used a frame with larger
squares measuring c. 6.5 x 6.5 cm. He must have
had several of these frames (apart from these two, he
also had one with squares measuring 3 x 3 cm, see p.
116); this is confirmed in a letter to Theo from 1 July
1882, in which he writes of 'my friend the carpenter
who has helped me on many occasions assisting
me in making perspective instruments' (241/209, 1
July 1882). This experimentation using perspective
frames and squaring indicates the importance that
Van Gogh attached in this period to improving his

ability to reproduce perspective accurately-something which he was not naturally very good at. Although the perspective frame was partly intended as an aid so that later the artist could copy a subject more rapidly and with greater ease, Van Gogh continued to use it throughout his career, and also in his paintings.[4]

There are no traces of squaring on the first two drawings showing a somewhat older woman in a black dress (possibly Sien's mother) and Sien sitting in front of the stove smoking a cigar. Probably for this reason the proportions of both figures are not as convincing as on the other sheets. Van Gogh was a long time searching for the 'double Ingres' paper after he had used his last sheet in May. In August he thought he had found it. 'Yesterday afternoon I was in the attic of the wholesale paper dealers Smulders on the Laan [street in The Hague]. There I found— can you guess? – the double Ingres under the name of Papier Torchon, the grain is even coarser than yours. I'll send you a sample so you can see. There's a whole stock of it, old and already seasoned, very good. Now I've only taken half a quire but I can always go back later' (254/222,5 August 1882).[5] In the autumn of 1882 and also after that, Van Gogh did a lot of work on a heavy watercolour paper with the watermark DAMBRICOURT FRERES HALLINES 1877; this is probably the paper he had found in The Hague-indeed a Torchon paper and not Ingres or double Ingres.

---

1. As has been noted before, Van Gogh used the term 'Ingres paper' as a collective name for all types of laid paper and sometimes also for other paper with a coarse surface. In fact it should be exactly the reverse: laid is the collective name and Ingres paper is a type of laid paper. In December 1881 Mauve had advised him that laid paper was not suited for watercolour painting (191/164, C. 21 December 1881).
2. The small city views which he made for his uncle in March were drawn on both wove and laid paper. The latter paper has the watermark EDB, which stands for 'Erven D. Blaauw', paper manufacturers of Zaandam. It was not possible to discover which French papermaker the letters 'ED&Cie' refer to.
3. During a visit to The Hague in the summer of 1881 Van Gogh had also found thicker paper at Stam's: 'I found some Ingres paper at Stam's, twice as thick as the ordinary kind, you can use it more intensively. Unfortunately, it's white. Do you think you might find the opportunity to send me some of the sort that has a colour something like unbleached cotton or linen?' (170/149, 2 8 August 1881). This sounds like a description of the 'double Ingres', but until now no drawings made on a double sheet of laid paper are known from his Etten period. Information about Stam-Liernur, see contribution by Bert van Vliet on The Hague paint dealer Van Leurs on the online forum of www.vggallery.com.
4. Besides the division into squares he often used a frame with two diagonal crossed lines when he was painting.
5. A quire consists of 24 or 25 sheets of paper.

P. 105

View of The Hague ('Paddemoes')

early March 1882
pencil, pen in black ink (faded to brown in parts),
wash, on wove paper
24.9 x 30.8 cm
no watermark
signed lower left (by the artist):
Vincent (black ink)
F918/JH111
KM 118.997

INSCRIPTIONS
verso, lower right: Paddemoes
Jodenbuurt (pencil) ' lower left:
Vincent. Verz:/Hidde Nijland
(black ink) RVKM (red stamp)

PROVENANCE
C.M. van Gogh, art dealer, Amsterdam, 1882'
acquired by Hidde Nijland, Dordrecht, before 1895
purchased from Hidde Nijland by A.G. Kröller, The Hague, July 1928 '
donated to the Kröller-Müller Foundation by A.G. Kröller, December 1928

EXHIBITIONS
The Hague 1895, no known cat.
Dordrechc 1897, no cat.
Dordrecht 1904, cat. no. 112?.
The Hague 1918, cat. no. 15.
Amsterdam 1924, cat. no. 22.
The Hague 1928, unnumbered
Hamburg 1929, cat. no. 46.
Amsterdam 1930, car. no. 61.
Basel 1947, cat. no. 116.
New York/Chicago 1949-1950, cat. no. 16.
Milan 1952, cat. no. 11.
The Hague 1953, cat. no. 5.
Otterlo/Amsterdam 1953, cat. no. 8.
Saint Louis/Philadelphia/Toledo 1953-1954, cat. no. 9.
Nuremberg 1956, cat. no. 13.
Munich 1956, cat. no. 21.
Tokyo/Kyoro 1958, cat. no. 18.
Munich 1961, cat. no. 13.
London 1962, cat. no. 11
Arnhem 1966, unnumbered.
Belgrade 1966, cat. no. 11.
Moscow/Leningrad 1971, cat. no. 12.
New York/Chicago/Ottawa and other cities, 1973-1974, cat. no. 30.
London/Newcastle-upon-Tyne 1974, cat. no. 20.
Amsterdam 1980-1981, cat. no. 68.
Otterlo 1990, cat. no. 19.

Yokohama/Nagoya 1995-1996, cat. no. 13.
Tokyo/Fukuoka 1999-2000, cat. no. 12.
Seattle/Atlanta 2004-2005, cat. no. 19.

Van Gogh certainly made attempts to produce saleable work, although after his death the myth that he didn't care about this was widely believed.[1] Yet he was little inclined to give in to the market; he would rather that the market adapted to him. This attitude led to a conflict with among others H.G. Tersteeg, the head of the Hague branch of the dealers Goupil & Cie. Tersteeg was not ill-disposed towards him at first, lent him money now and then, and also bought a watercolour from him. But his interest was often accompanied byreproaches about Van Gogh's financial dependence on Theo and suggestions that he should earn his own living. Moreover, Tersteeg kept repeating that he should make small watercolours because they sold best, which was exactly what Van Gogh could not and would not give in to.[2] Critical as ever about his abilities, Van Gogh felt that he first needed a better grasp of form, which could only be achieved through assiduous drawing. Theo's praise of a small watercolour did not really please him either: 'You say that small watercolour is the best you have seen by me -well, that is not right, because my studies that you have are much better, and the pen drawings from this summer are better too, for that small drawing means nothing, at least I only sent it to you to show that it was not impossible that in time I would work in watercolour. But there is much more serious study and more thoroughness in the other things, even if they do have a green soap look' (206/177, 25 February 1882). In this he was supported by the artist J.H. Weissenbruch (1824-1903), who was known to be highly critical. At Mauve's request he had visited Van Gogh in his studio and thought his pen drawings particularly good (204/175, 13 February 1882).

Support like this must have encouraged Van Gogh to describe his experiences in The Hague to his uncle Cor, the Amsterdam art dealer Gornelis Marinus van Gogh (1824-1908),usually known by his initials 'C.M.', and to invite him for a visit. Around 11 March C.M. came to his studio. When the conversation threatened to take a disagreeable turn, Van Gogh picked up a portfolio of smaller studies and sketches as a distraction. 'At first he said no more - until we came to a drawing that I sketched once at midnight while strolling with Breitner, namely Paddemoes (that Jewish neighbourhood near the Nieuwe Kerk), seen from Turfmarkt. I worked on it again in pen next morning' (210/181, c. 11 March 1882). C.M. was so enthusiastic that he commissioned twelve small city views of the same kind from his nephew. The artist fixed the price at 2.50 guilders each. If they were satisfactory, his uncle promised to place a new order for twelve views of Amsterdam, for which he would fix the price: 'then you'll earn a bit more', said C.M. (210/181). A second order was indeed placed, but it was changed to six typical views of The Hague. Van Gogh completed the first commission within two weeks. View of The Hague ('Paddemoes') was not only the drawing referred to in the letter that led to the commission, but in the end also formed part of it. It was acquired before 1895 by Hidde Nijland from the dealer C.M. van Gogh.

George Hendrik Breitner (1857-1923) was first mentioned by Van Gogh in a letter of 13 February 1882: 'These days I often go drawing with Breitner, a young painter who is acquainted with Rochussen, as I am with Mauve. He draws very handily and entirely differently from the way I do, and we often do characters in the soup kitchen or the waiting room etc. together. He comes to my studio quite often to see wood engravings and I go to him too' (203/174). As may be deduced from a later letter, Van Gogh and Breitner went into town on the evening of 2 March in search of models (207/178, 3 March 1882).[3] It is conceivable that the first sketch for view of the Hague ('Paddemoes') was done then around midnight. Paddemoes was the name of one of the oldest and poorest neighbourhoods in The Hague; in the middle of the seventeenth century much of it had been pulled down to make way for the building of the Nieuwe Kerk. This church, not shown in the drawing, is to the right in the area behind the wall. Van Gogh stood about level with the entrance to the church, where Turfhaven and Turfmarkt joined Spui. On the other side of Turfhaven was Houtmarkt: a photo was taken of the Nieuwe Kerk from that side around August 1891. In it the distinctive fence can be seen, with three sturdy, square stone pillars, the same as the back three in the drawing. Also just visible on the left is the row of poplars shown in the background of the drawing parallel to the picture plane, in front of the houses in St. Jacobstraat.

Van Gogh made no use of a perspective frame or squaring for view of The Hague (Paddemoes'). Nor did he for Sandworkers in the dunes (F922, present whereabouts unknown), mentioned in letter 211/182 of 14-18 March, but all the other drawings from the commission bear traces of squaring. So Van Gogh's earliest use of this aid must date from around this time.[4]

These two drawings and most of the others in the commission have an inscription in pencil on the back giving the location depicted; the handwriting is not that of Van Gogh or his uncle. It is not known who added these inscriptions or when it was done. But it must have been quite early on, in any case before 1895, when View of The Hague ('Paddemoes') came into the possession of Hidde Nijland, and very probably prior to 1890. In that year Rijnspoorweg lost its concession, which was taken over by the Maatschappij tot Exploitatie van Staatsspoorwegen, but the words 'Grounds close to Rijnspoor' are written on the back of Ditch along Schenkweg. The locations may well have been put on by a member of staff at the dealer's C.M. van Gogh, possibly according to information from the artist himself, who had looked for his subjects on the periphery of the city, with which potential buyers were less familiar (although for him it was close to home).

1. See Koldehoff 2003, pp. 189-199.
2. Theo urged his brother to maintain good relations with Tersteeg, but his reproach 'It is clear to me that you are no artist' naturally made this difficult (208/179, c. 5-9 March 1882). Relations with Tersreeg worsened dramatically in

the spring, when it became known that Van Gogh had entered into a relationship with the (former) prostitute Sien Hoornik.
3. On Breitner and Van Gogh, see also Hefting 1970, pp. 59-69.
4. See p. 116.

P. 107

Mangle with three figures

February-March 1882
pencil, pen and black ink, on wove paper
23 x 29.6 cm
no watermark
unsigned
F1337 JH5o6
KM 120.703

INSCRIPTIONS
verso, lower right: Verz: Hidde Nijland (black ink)
upper right: 17 (blue chalk)
lower left: No 73(pencil).
on rape: KR 23 (blue chalk). km. 457 (pencil)

PROVENANCE
acquired by Hidde Nijland, Dordrecht, before 1904.
purchased from Hidde Nijland by A.G. Kröller, The Hague, July 1928 -
donated to the Kröller-Müller Foundation by A.G. Kröller, December 1928

EXHIBITIONS
Dordrecht 1904, cat. no. ?.
The Hague 1918, cat. no. ?.
Amsterdam 1924, cat. no. 76.
The Hague 1928, unnumbered.
Hamburg 1929, cat. no. 60.
Amsterdam 1930, cat. no. 23.

This pencil drawing with accents in pen and ink showing three figures operating a large mangle has usually been placed in the literature under Nuenen 1884, though generally with a question mark.[1] This was probably suggested by a superficial resemblance to interiors with weavers, or by the fact that Van Gogh's first studio in Nuenen was in the mangle room behind the parsonage. Here we opt for The Hague and February-March 1882, a period in which Van Gogh began to work more in pen and ink over pencil, which resulted in among other things a series of city views commissioned by his uncle C.M. van Gogh.

Moreover, in Schenkweg this subject was literally next door: here he initially lived next to a laundry, which is shown in Carpenter's yard and laundry.[2] The woman sitting at the mangle, with her hair in a bun, even looks a little like the figure in the foreground of that drawing. The size of the mangle also indicates a professional version.

Stylistically, the drawing is rather variable, but it should not be forgotten that this is a cursorily finished, quickly drawn pencil sketch. The man to the left of the mangle is done partly in short, hesitant scrawls, for example, and he is the only one not to be gone over in ink, so that he appears 'weaker' than the other two figures. This style of sketching, with searching, frayed lines alternating with vigorous, straight strokes is characteristic of various studies from The Hague by Van Gogh. The execution of the man is somewhat reminiscent, for example, of the figure study Man with broom (F979a, private collection), which is generally dated to the autumn of 1882, but must also be placed in the first months of that year. The reason is that this sheet was used as an example for one of the figures in Sandworkers in the dunes (F922, present whereabouts unknown) of March 1882.

1. De la Faille 1928/1970, Hulsker 1977/1996, Hefting 1980, p. 6o, Heenk 1995, p. 129. Only Vanbeaelaere 1937, p. 413, dared the sheer even later, in the Paris period.
2. Van Gogh's neighbour Anna Maria Simonis-de Mol, washerwoman by occupation, died on 20 April 1882. The laundry closed shortly afterwards (Visser 1973, pp. 42, 65-66).

P. 109

Road workers with a wagon

March-April 1882
pencil, traces of squaring, on wove paper
21.1 x 34cm
watermark: S & C unsigned
F1078/JH134
KM 119.381

INSCRIPTIONS

PROVENANCE
M.A. de Zwart, Voorburg, C. 1883 H.P. Baron van Tuyl1 van Serooskerken coll., Voorburg/Katwijk' purchased by H. Kröller-Müller at sale Amsterdam (Frederik Muller & Cie), 25-26 November 1913, lot 138: Deux homes déchargeantune charette de briques (160 guilders)

EXHIBITIONS
Basel/Bern/Brussels 1927, cat. no. 23.
Düsseldorf 1928, cat. no. 89.
Karlsruhe 1928, cat. no. 24.
Berlin 1928-1929, cat. no. 28.
Hamburg 1929, cat. no. 19.
Amsterdam 1930, cat. no. 29.

For this pencil study Van Gogh made use of squaring for the proportions and the foreshortening of the wagon. He put his perspective frame on the sheet and drew the squares along the strings. Then he looked at the subject through the perspective frame from a fixed point, and he was able to represent the main outlines within the grid on his paper fairly easily. Here he has also outlined several slats of the frame itself, which is particularly evident at the bottom and on the right. Since these slats were about 2.5 cm wide, the outer dimensions of the perspective frame must have been about 30 x 20 cm, with 40 squares (8 x 5) each measuring 3 x 3 cm.[1] He used this perspective frame for most of the drawings from the commission for his uncle C.M. van Gogh.

The figure behind the wagon is less convincingly portrayed than the man in front of it, who is bending over a stack of bricks and has probably just added some more from the wagon. A very similar labourer features in the large composition Road works in Noordstraat, The Hague, just right of the trench being dug in the street. But what he is doing there remains unclear; one would expect to see him with a spade in his hands.

The composition of the drawing looks rather messy because of the huge differences in dimensions between the figures, which were all based on separate examples. The example for the bent figure has not survived, but it is probable that Van Gogh used the same model study for both drawings.

1. On Van Gogh's use of the perspective frame, see van Heugren 1996, pp. 21-25. Van Gogh generally preferred to 'draw over' his perspective frame, but the squares of a grid need not necessarily have the same dimensions as those of the perspective frame, as long as the proportions are the same. His use of the relatively small but handy perspective frame measuring about 30 X 20 cm seems to have been limited to the Hague drawings from March and April 1882.

P. 111

Woman walking

February-April 1882
pencil on wove paper
32.5 x 15.7 cm
no watermark
unsigned
F1050/JH149
KM 126.075

INSCRIPTIONS
verso, upper centre: 4633 II8
(black chalk) [refers to 1913 Muller sale]

PROVENANCE
MA. de Zwart, Voorburg, c. 1883 H.P. Baron van Tuyll van Serooskerken coll., Voorburg/Katwijk.
purchased by H. Kröller-Müller at sale Amsterdam (Frederik Muller & Cie), 25-26 November 1913, lot 137: Femme vêtue d'un long manteau,Merchant vers la gauche (155 guilders)

EXHIBITIONS
Basel/Bern/Brussels 1927, cat. no. 16.
Düsseldorf 1928, cat. no. 83.
Karlsruhe 1928, cat. no. 18.
Berlin 1928-1929, cat. no. 23.
Hamburg 1929, cat. no. 12.
Amsterdam 1930, cat. no. 48.
Nuremberg 1956, cat. no. 18.
Munich 1956, cat. no. 31.
Tokyo/Kyoto 1958, cat. no. 24.

This simple but quite vigorous pencil drawing is one of the many figure studies by Van Gogh from the first months of 1882; as well as being exercises, they served as potential examples for large or small compositions with several figures.[1] He must have drawn mainly from this supply for the staffage in the drawings commissioned by his uncle on which he was working in March.

The woman's profile bears some resemblance to that of Sien Hoornik, because of the noticeable bump on her nose. When - without mentioning her name - Van Gogh introduced her and some other members of her family in a letter to Theo as recently discovered models, he wrote: 'The younger woman is not beautiful in her face, because she has had smallpox, but her figure is very graceful and to me has

charm. They have good clothes too, black merinos and nicely shaped caps and a fine shawl etc.' (207/178, 3 March 1882). In this drawing the elegantly finished black merino dress is just visible under the woman's coat. In the large figure drawings for which Sien posed this type of dress - made from the wool of merino sheep can be seen in all its glory.

1. See Heenk 1995, pp. 50-51. De la Faille 1928/1970/1992, Vanbeselaere 1937, p. 90, and Hefting 1980, p.56,dated the sheet to October 1882, Hulsker 1977/1996 to May 1882.

P. 114

Dab-drying barn in Scheveningen

late May 1882
pencil, pen and brush in black ink (faded to brown in pacts), white opaque wateccolour, traces of squaring, on laid paper
29 x 45.4 cm
watermark: En&Cie (in cartouche), (PL BAS]
signed lower left (by the artist): Vincent del' (black ink)
F938! JH152
KM 122.835

INSCRIPTIONS
recto, lower left (by the artist):
Scharrendroogerij te Scheveningen (black ink)
verso, lower tight: RVKM (red stamp)
lower left: RVKM (red stamp)

PROVENANCE
C.M. van Gogh, art dealer, Amsterdam, 1882.
acquired by Hidde Nijland, Dordrecht, before 1895.
purchased from Hidde Nijland by A.G. Kröller, The Hague, July 1928
donated to the Kröller-Müller Foundation by A.G. Kröller, December 1928

EXHIBITIONS
The Hague 1895, no known cat.
Dordrecht 1897, no rat.
Dordrecht 1904, cat. no.
The Hague 1918, cat. no. 18.
Amsterdam 1924, cat. no. 24.
The Hague 1928, unnumbered.
Hamburg 1929, cat. no. 97.
Amsterdam 1930, cat. no. 59.
New York/Chicago 1949-1950, cat. no. 18
Milan 1952, cat. no. 13.
Saint Louis/Philadelphia/Toledo 1953-1954, cat. no. 12.
Munich 1956, cat. no. 25.
Essen 1957, cat. no. 139.
Vienna 1958, cat. no. 19.
Schiedam 1958-1959, no known cat.

'C.M's order is a ray of light!', wrote Van Gogh to Theo on 11 Match 1882, after their uncle C.M. van Gogh had ordered twelve Hague city views for two and a half guilders each (210/181). If they were to his uncle's liking, he could expect a new commission for twelve Amsterdam scenes. He could just imagine it; with a little bit of practice he should certainly be able to do a small drawing every day, which he would then have little trouble selling for about '5 francs'. That would pay for his daily bread and model. 'The beautiful season with long days is about to begin; he wrote cheerfully in the same letter. 'I do the "soup ticker", i.e. the small bread-&-model drawing either in the morning or evening and during the day I seriously do model studies'.

He finished the commission within a fortnight and dispatched the work, having completed what he had planned. It was some time before C.M. responded, but when the money arrived in early April, accompanied by the next commission, the content was somewhat different: 'C.M. has paid me and given me a new commission, but one which is rather difficult: 6 detailed specific city views. However, I shall see to it that I do them because, as I understand it, I will receive as much for the six as I did for the first twelve. And then perhaps there will be sketches of Amsterdam' (213/184). It can be surmised from this that his uncle was not entirely satisfied with the first commission. He undoubtedly meant by 'derailed, specific city views' more characteristic and more accurately drawn pictures of The Hague.

Van Gogh completed the second commission with difficulty. April was a wet month, which prevented him from going outdoors to work. Moreover, the figure drawing took up increasingly more of his time. In mid-May he wrote to Theo that he had already made various studies for the commission but that he found it hard to persevere with the work (227/193). in the end he succeeded in sending seven drawings to Amsterdam by the end of the month, one more than had actually been agreed, probably to placate his uncle for the delay. The consignment comprised two large, four medium-sized and one small drawing (the size of the preceding commission).[1] Carpenter's yard and laundry and Dab-drying barn in Scheveningen are two medium-sized sheets, each about half an Ingres sheet in Van Gogh's terminology. 'But will he like them?' he had written to Theo shortly before he dispatched them, 'Perhaps not. I cannot see such drawings as anything other than studies in perspective - which is why for me they are primarily ways of practicing. Even if his lordship does not want them, I am not sorry for the trouble I rook

over them, because I am happy to keep them myself and practice the skill on which so very much depends: perspective and proportion' (229/200, C. 23 May 1882).

Dab-drying barn in Scheveningen by comparison is of more restrained execution. White opaque watercolor was used only sparingly, such as in the clothing of the two women and for accents in the marram grass in the foreground. Otherwise it is ink on pencil. Here, too, Van Gogh worked with a drawing grid and viewed the scene from a higher viewpoint, this time from a dune. The different sight lines in this composition are powerful. To the left the gaze is drawn upwards, to the lighthouse, just emerging above a dune. To the right the gaze flows downwards with the Oude Kerk of Scheveningen in the background.[2] Van Gogh was working on the far perimeter of the village to the southwest, a working class district where people lived mainly from fishing. The houses and dab-drying barn depicted here gave onto the Citadel at the front, a short street that was extended around this time and renamed Duinstraat. Between the fencing in the centre of the background on the right is Kolenwagenslag, where even more fish smoking and drying establishments were located.[3] The dab, a type of plaice, were salted and threaded onto sticks to dry in the sun. In the drawing they are hanging like lozenges in the racks behind the house. The numerous battered cane baskets, heavy with sand in the foreground, 'serve to prevent the sand of the dunes from blowing about, Van Gogh wrote later in a letter to Theo when he was working on a watercolor in that spot (252/220, 26 July 1882). So they probably did not belong to a basket maker who had his business there, as some have assumed.[4]

On a Sunday evening, 28 May 1882, Van Gogh wrote a letter to Van Rappard, who shortly before had dropped in on him and said that he thought the drawings for his uncle were very good. Dab-drying barn was at the time not among them, since it can be gathered from the letter that he had produced this drawing on that very day: 'I was up early today, [...] and went into the dunes to draw a fish-drying barn, also viewed from above, like the carpenter's yard & now it is one o'clock at night, but the job has been done thank goodness and I can look my frightful landlord in the eye' (231/R8). It is true that Van Gogh made a second pen sketch of the dab-drying barn around this time (F940, private collection), but for this he positioned himself right behind the barn from a low viewpoint, so the letter must be referring to the present sheet. He parcelled it up the same night for his uncle, together with the other six sheets, but not before he had first added the small man with the folded arms and a few other details. In the early 1980s a separate figure study was discovered of this small man (no F-number, JH add. 19, private collection).[5] Here, he was inserted in the drawing directly in ink, just like the chair to his right, with no pencil underdrawing. It also emerges from the letter to Van Rappard that Van Gogh, in response to comments made by his friend, introduced changes in some sheets.

Shortly after completing the commission Van Gogh became ill. He spent a good deal of June in

hospital being treated for gonorrhoea. Shortly before his admission G.M. sent him twenty guilders without any further accompanying note, ten guilders less than had been agreed, according to Van Gogh. 'Whether he will commission me to do something new, or whether he likes the drawings, for the time being I have absolutely no idea', he told Theo on June (235/205). He suspected that his uncle had confined his interest to watercolors and had difficulty appreciating any other kind of drawing: 'I admit for an eye that is solely used to watercolors, drawings scratched with a pen and lights scratched out again or put in with opaque paint may have something barren about them. But there are also people who, just as it can sometimes be pleasant and exhilarating for a healthy body to take a walk when the wind blows hard, there are also enthusiasts, to my mind, who are not afraid of that barrenness. Weissenbruch for instance would not think these two drawings are unpleasant or dull.' But a note did arrive from C.M. after all and apparently his uncle must have written that he was interested in him, but that he resented his nephew having behaved ungratefully towards H.G. Tersteeg, this much being deduced from a letter to Theo (237/206, 8 or 9 June 1882). In a letter to Van Rappard Van Gogh was a little more explicit about his uncle: 'I received twenty guilders with a kind of scolding to boot: "did I really think that such drawings had any commercial value whatsoever" (236/R9, 4 or 5 June 1 882).

1. It is generally assumed that in addition F923, F930,F94s, F942 and F946a were in the second consignment. According to Van der Mast & Dumas 1990, p. 173, and Heenk 1995, p. 57, it wasn't this version of Carpenter's yard and laundry -F939 - that was part of the commission, but the related drawing F944 (private collection, New York). However, this is improbable given the higher quality and more detailed execution of F939,and the signature 'Vincent' followed by 'delt (short for 'delineavit'), which otherwise only appears on two other drawings from this commission (Dab-drying barn in Scheveningen and F942). Moreover F939 was acquired before 1895 by Hidde Nijland from C.M. van Gogh, art dealer, where he also acquired View of The Hague ('Paddemoes') from the first commission (p.111) and Dab-drying barn in Scheveningen (see also Ives et al. 2005, p.76). F944 is probably the version that he sent to Theo on 3 June 1882 (235/205), together with a variant Of the dab-drying barn (F940).
2. Van Gogh also made a watercolour on this spot in July, but then directed his gaze more to the right, which produced a much less exciting composition (F945, private collection).
3. See for the exact location Van der Mast & Dumas 1990, pp. 63, 64 and 177. Visser 1973, p. 95, believed that Van Gogh found his subject on Kolenwagenslag itself.
4. Van der Mast & Dumas 1990, p.65; see also note 3.
5. The study was published for the first time in op de Coul 1983.

P. 117

People strolling on the beach

September 1882
pencil on wove paper
15.9 x 25.4 cm
no watermark
signed lower left (by the artist):
Vincent (pencil)
F980/JH204
KM 122.381

INSCRIPTIONS

PROVENANCE
M.A. de Zwart, Voorburg, c. 1883'
H.P. Baron van Tuyll van Serooskerken coll., Voorburg/
Katwijk'
purchased by H. Kröller-Müller at sale Amsterdam (Frederik
Muller & Cie), 25-26 November 1913, lot 138: Promeneurs
sur lu plage (200 guilders)

EXHIBITIONS
Basel/Bern/Brussels 1927, cat. no. 19.
Düsseldorf 1928, cat. no. 86.
Karlsruhe 1928, cat. no. 21.
Berlin 1928-1929, car. no. 27.
Hamburg 1929, car. no. 15.
Amsterdam 1930, car. no. 28.
Munich 1961, cat. no. 23.
The Hague 1990, unnumbered.

Van Gogh used the pencil study People strolling on the beach as the subject of a large watercolour (F1038, Baltimore Museum of Art). The study dates from a period in the autumn of 1882 when he was practising group compositions. The awkward thing about this type of composition was that he first had to draw a quick impression of a moving group of people in which each figure had a place of its own. Later on in his studio he could use such a sketch to build up a definitive composition, incorporating earlier figure studies for the individual figures. The watercolour made after this sketch also differs considerably in several points from the original and contains far more space in its composition. Van Gogh describes this difficulty in detail in a letter to Theo: 'As regards composition, every scene containing figures whether it be a market, the arrival of a boat, a crowd of people at a soup kitchen, in the waiting room, the hospital, a pawnbroker's shop, the groups in a street, chatting or walking along - is based on the same principle as the flock of sheep (and that's where the word "moutonner" must come from) and it all boils down to the same questions of light and brown

and perspective [...] I can vary my work in differing ways and there are and continue to be so infinitely many things to draw' (265/231, 17 September 1882).
In the same letter Van Gogh refers to an accompanying pen sketch showing a group of people on the shore as one of the fishing boats comes in. A group of people like this 'is infinitely varied and requires countless separate studies and scribbles of different figures, which you have to capture in flight, as it were, in the street. In this manner you gradually introduce character and meaning. I recently drew a study of gentlemen and ladies on the beach ambling along every which way.' It is possible that this last remark refers to the drawing under discussion. He signed the sheer, which was unusual for him, certainly in the case of such a quick study. It may be because the drawing was a present for its first owner, his landlord Michiel Anthonie de Zwart.

P. 119

Street scene (sketch)

September 1882
pencil, pen in black ink (faded tobrown in parts)
on watercolour paper
19.3 x 18.8 cm
no watermark
unsigned
F952v/JH193
KM 127.758 VERSO

INSCRIPTIONS and PROVENANCE
see KM 127.758 RECTO

On the back of the drawing of Bezuidenhout there are some sketches Van Gogh made in the street showing donkeys hitched to carts and a few figures. Below the carts and the house wall on the left, traces of an older pencil sketch are visible; however, it is not clear what they represent. When the sheet was made smaller on account of the composition on the front the upper cart was partly cut off, all that remain are the legs of (presumably) a donkey and part of a cartwheel. This incomplete fragment is strongly reminiscent of the sheet Donkey cart with figures,

in which the donkey appears in an almost identical position.

P. 121

Seated mother with child

autumn 1882
pencil, traces of squaring, on watercolour paper
49.2 x 27.4 cm
no watermark
unsigned
F1063/JH218
KM 112.211

INSCRIPTIONS
verso, lower centre: 48- 26 (pencil)

PROVENANCE
M.A. de Zwart, Voorburg, c. 1883'
H.P. Baron van Tuyll van Serooskerken coil., Voorburg/
Katwijk. sale Amsterdam (Frederik Muller & Cie), 25-26
November 1913, lot 128: Mère assise avec son enfant (300
guilders) Jac. de Vries, art dealer, Arnhem'
purchased by H. Kröller-Müller at sale Amsterdam (Frederik
Muller & Cie), 3 December 1918, lot 123: Mère assise avec
son enfant (190 guilders; with Carpenter, p. 47)

EXHIBITIONS
Basel/Bern/Brussels 1927, car. no. 29.
Düsseldorf 1928, cat. no. 95.
Karlsruhe 1928, cat. no. 30.
Berlin 1928-1929, cat. no. 7.
Hamburg 1929, cat. no. 25.
Amsterdam 1930, cat. no. 44.
New York/Philadelphia/Boston and other cities, 1935-1936,
cat. no. 86.
Hamburg 1963, cat. no. 87.

P.122

Mother suckling her child

autumn 1882
pencil, traces of squaring, on laid paper
43 x 26.6 cm
watermark: ED&Cie (in cartouche), [PL BAS]
unsigned
F1062/JH216
KM 113.983

INSCRIPTIONS
verso, upper left: 4633 113 (black chalk) [refers to 1913 Muller sale]

PROVENANCE
M.A. de Zwart, Voorburg, c. 1883
H.P. Baron van Tuyll van Serooskerken coll., Voorburg/ Katwijk.
sale Amsterdam (Frederik Muller & Cie), 25-26 November 1913, lot 136: Mère allaitant son enfant (280 guilders) Jac. de Vries, art dealer, Arnhem.
sale Amsterdam (Frederik Muller & Cie), 3 December 1918, lot 125: Mère allaitant enfant, purchased by H. Kröller-Müller at sale The Hague (Kleykamp), 11 November 1919, lot 58 (50 guilders)

EXHIBITIONS
Basel/Bern/Brussels 1927, cat. no. 32.
Düsseldorf 1928, cat. no. 98.
Karlsruhe 1928, cat. no. 33.
Berlin 1928-1929, cat. no. 11.
Hamburg 1929, cat. no. 28.
Amsterdam 1930, cat. no. 42.
Antwerp 1952, cat. no. 37f.
London 1962, cat. no. 7.
The Hague 2005, unnumbered.

REMARKS
On the verso is a small sketch in black chalk that is probably a small figure.

P.123

Mother with child

autumn 1882
pencil, oils, on watercolour paper
41 x 24.6 cm
watermark: DAMBRICOURT FRERES
unsigned
F1061/JH220
KM 112.180

INSCRIPTIONS

PROVENANCE
J. Dona coll., The Hague, 1908.
A.J.G. Verster coll., Hilversum.
sale Amsterdam (A. Mak),9 March 1920, lot 23 purchased by H. Kröller-Müller at Huinck, art dealer, Utrecht, 19 March 1920 (900 guilders)

EXHIBITIONS
Basel/Bern/Brussels 1927, cat. no. 33.
Düsseldorf 1928, cat. no. 99.
Karlsruhe 1928, cat. no. 34.
Berlin 1928-1929, cat. no. 12.
Hamburg 1929, cat. no. 138.
Amsterdam 1930, cat. no. 131.
New York/Philadelphia/Boston and other cities, 1935-1936, cat. no. 8.
Otterlo 1990, cat. no. 54.
Tokyo/Fukuoka 1999-2000, cat. no. 18.

These three drawings show Sien Hoornik with her son Willem, who was born on 2 July 1882 in a Leiden hospital. When Van Gogh got to know her she was several months pregnant by a man who had deserted her; the birth was not without complications. On her return to The Hague she went to live with Van Gogh, who by now had moved to the top floor of an adjacent dwelling on Schenkweg. He had bought a large wicker chair especially for her, which can be seen in the first drawing (245/213,6 July 1882). She is portrayed on the second sheet breast feeding Willem. The many vertical streaks in this picture are largely due to the rough drawing board which Van Gogh must have used as base. The graining in the wood cockled the horizontal lines, making them darker in certain places, and when Van Gogh filled an area with horizontal lines, vertical ones also appeared

automatically. Above right a more curving pattern of graining in the wood can be distinguished fairly clearly.

The third drawing is in fact a fairly rough pencil drawing, like the other two, but it is the only one of the three to which colour was later added. Interestingly, Van Gogh did this with oil paint. The pencil lines can be clearly distinguished in various places, but the great amount of detail in the underdrawing was revealed when the sheet was held up to the light; from the verso large sections of hatching could be detected beneath the layers of paint. One has the impression that this was an experiment, for which the artist selected an existing sketch. The baby was left entirely blank apart from his hands and face, which were given a flesh tint.[1]

Very few drawings have survived showing Sien with baby Willem. In almost every case these are rudimentary studies or sketches and almost all of them were once in the possession of Van Gogh's landlord in The Hague, M.A. de Zwart, as were the first two of these drawings. The earliest known owner of the third sheer is Jan Dona (1870-1941), an artist from the circle of Bremmer, whom he knew from 1890 onwards and sometimes assisted.[2]

1. The oil paint is both highly diluted and fairly thickly applied (see for instance Sien's cap). There is considerable brown efflorescence on the verso side of the sheer due to the oil which has seeped through. The Van Gogh Museum, Amsterdam has another experimental drawing with oil paint showing only baby Willem (F912), but it was not based on an existing pencil sketch (Van Heugren 1996, pp. 94-96).
2. Balk 2004, appendix 'Kunstenaars rond H.P. Bremmer' (Artists around H.P. Bremmer). Dona owned two other early drawings by Van Gogh, Turfcarrier (F964, National Gallery of Art, Washington) and Peasant woman sowing seeds (F883, private collection).

P.125

Women carrying sacks of coal in the snow

November 1882
charcoal (?), opaque watercolor
brush and ink, on wove paper
32.1 x 50.1 cm
no watermark
unsigned
F994/JH253

KM 121.745

INSCRIPTIONS
verso, lower right: Vincent van Gogh/Verz: Hidde Nijland
(black ink).Invent. K.M. 959 (pencil). lower left:
13-56 (pencil). upper left: KR 25 (blue chalk). lower centre:
XXVI
(green chalk).No 1 (pencil)

PROVENANCE
acquired by Hidde Nijland, Dordrecht, before 1895
purchased from Hidde Nijland by A.G. Kröller, The Hague,
July 1928.
donated to the Kröller-Müller Foundation by A.G. Kröller,
December 1928

EXHIBITIONS
The Hague 1895, no known cat.
Dordrecht 1897, no cat.
Dordrecht 1904, cat. no. 132.
The Hague 1918, cat. no. 10.
Amsterdam 1924, cat. no. 89.
The Hague 1928, unnumbered.
Hamburg 1929, cat. no. 145.
Amsterdam 1930, cat. no. 130.
Milan 1952, cat. no. 2.
Paris 1955, cat. no. 157.
Eindhoven 1956,cat. no. 8.
Munich 1956, cat. no. 32.
Essen 1957, cat. no. 152.
Vienna 1958, cat. no. 25.
Tokyo/Kyoto 1958, cat. no. 23.
Montreal/Ottawa/Winnipeg/Toronto 1960-1961, cat. no. 93.
Warsaw 1962, cat. no. 4.
Tel Aviv/Haifa 1962-1963, cat. no. 18
Hamburg 1963, cat. no. 85.
Belgrade 1966, cat. no. 2.
Moscow/Leningrad 1971, cat. no. 19.
New York/Chicago/Ottawa and other cities, 1973-1974, cat.
no. 38.
London/Newcastle-upon-Tyne 1974, cat. no. 27.
Amsterdam 1980-1981, cat. no. 52.
Otterlo 1990, cat. no. 64.
Aarhus 1991, unnumbered.
Yokohama/Nagoya 1995-1996, cat. no. 19.
Tokyo/Fukuoka 1999-2000, cat. no. 24.
The Hague 2005, unnumbered.

'Worked again on a watercolour of miners'
wives carrying sacks of coal in the snow,' Van Gogh
wrote to Theo in early November 1882. 'But mainly I
drew about 12 studies of figures for it and heads and
I'm still not ready. I think watercolour gives me the
proper effect, but I don't believe that one is strong
enough as far as character is concerned. The reality is
something like Millet's Les glaneuses - severe so you
understand that one mustn't turn it into an "effet de
neige", which would merely give an impression and
would only then have its raison d'être if it were done
as a landscape' (281/241, C. 2-3 November 1882).
Van Gogh's emphasis on the distinction between
landscape and figure is typical: the character and pride
of these poor, hard working women is what the work
is all about. The surroundings must be made to serve
this theme and must not be allowed to dominate. The
heroic, bent forms of the glaneuses, the poor gleaners
who gather the leftover grain from a harvested field
and whom Millet had immortalised in his painting
of 1857 (Musée d'Orsay, Paris), served as a shining

example.
Van Gogh had already tried to achieve the
same effect in The bearers of the burden,where the
sombre figures of the women carrying sacks past a
field are shown against the background of the mines.
In the watercolour under discussion he also depicted
smoking chimneys in the distance to suggest a mining
region. The figures were conceived on the basis of
separate studies and then placed in the composition.
The posing of the model or models is somewhat
obvious in the foremost three figures. The left one is
shown in profile but looks as if she has just turned
in the direction of the artist. The other two women,
both bent far over, are still trying to look backwards
from under their burdens. While working on the
studies Van Gogh remained puzzled as to exactly how
the women held those sacks on their heads. Writing
to Van Rappard on c. 31 October 1882, he said, 'Not
without some trouble I have at last discovered how
the miners' wives in the Borinage carry their sacks.
You may remember that when I was there I did some
drawings of it - but they were not yet the real thing.
Now I have made 12 studies of the same subject. It's
like this: the opening of the sack is tied up [sketch]
and hangs down. The points at the bottom are joined
together, producing the most charming sort of monk's
hood. [...] I often had a woman with such a sack pose
for me, but it never turned out right. A man who was
loading coal in the Rijnspoor railway yard has shown
me' (278/R16). From the left figure it is especially easy
to see that she does indeed hold the sack over her
head like a kind of monk's hood.

P. 127

Old man with umbrella and watch

September-December 1882
pencil, traces of squaring,
fixative discoloration around figure,
on watercolour paper
48 x 28.8 cm
watermark: HALLINES 1877
unsigned
F978/JH238
KM 113.952

INSCRIPTIONS
verso, lower right: 8 (pencil) lower left: small illegible scribble
in pencil

PROVENANCE
[possibly sent by the artist to art dealer C.M. van Gogh,
Amsterdam, c. 1883]
purchased by H. Kröller-Müller at C.M. van Gogh, art dealer,
Amsterdam, 25 November 1911 (150 guilders)

EXHIBITIONS
Cologne 1912, cat. no. 115.
The Hague 1913, cat. no. 56.
Basel/Bern/Brussels 1927, cat. no. 10.
Düsseldorf 1928, cat. no. 77.
Karlsruhe 1928, cat. no. 12.
Berlin 1928-1929, cat. no. 20.
Hamburg 1929, cat. no. 7.
Amsterdam1930, cat. no. a.
Nuremberg 1956, cat. no. 26.
Munich 1956, cat. no. 29.
Vienna 1958, cat. no. 23.
Tokyo/Kyoto 1958, cat. no. 27.
Arnhem 1966, unnumbered.
Charleroi/Antwerp/Paris/Lyon 1971-1972, cat. no. 13.
Yokohama/Nagoya 1995-1996, cat. no. 23.
Tokyo/Fukuoka 1999-2000, cat. no. 22.
Detroit/Boston/Philadelphia 2000-2001, unnumbered.

P. 128

Old man with a glass

September-December 1882
pencil, traces of squaring,
on (originally) bluish purple wove paper
49.2 x 24.6 cm
no watermark
unsigned
F959/JH244
KM 118.619

INSCRIPTIONS
recto, lower left: Port: Vincent (pencil) verso, lower centre:
Port. Vincent/Hidde Nijland (black ink). lower right: No 68
(scratched our] (pencil). lower right: 10 (pencil) upper left: KR
104 (pencil)

PROVENANCE

[possibly sent by the artist to art dealer G.M. van Gogh,
Amsterdam, c. 1883]
acquired by Hidde Nijland, Dordrecht, before 1895
purchased from Hidde Nijland by A.G. Kröller, The Hague,
July 1928
donated to the Kröller-Müller Foundation by A.G. Kröller,
December 1928

EXHIBITIONS
The Hague 1895, no known cat.
Dordrecht 1897, no cat.
Dordrecht 1904, cat. no. 143.
The Hague 1918, cat. no. 29.
Amsterdam 1924, cat. no. 21.
The Hague 1928, unnumbered.
Hamburg 1929, cat. no. 123.
Amsterdam 1930, cat. no. 53.

P. 129

Old man holding his hat

September-December 1882
pencil, traces of squaring, fixative discoloration
around figure on watercolour paper
48.1 x 23.5 cm
watermark: HALLINE5 1877
(largely cut away by the top edge)
[D]AMBRICOURT PRERE5
unsigned
F973/JH236
KM 123.042

INSCRIPTIONS

PROVENANCE
[possibly sent by the artist to art dealer G.M. van Gogh,
Amsterdam, c. 1883]
purchased by H. Kröller-Müller at G.M. van Gogh, art dealer,
Amsterdam, 25 November 1911 (150 guilders)

EXHIBITIONS
Cologne 1912, cat. no. 117.
The Hague 1913, cat. no. 61.
Basel/Bern/Brussels 1927, cat. no. a6.
Düsseldorf 1928, cat. no. 92.
Karlsruhe 1928, cat. no. 27.
Berlin 1928-1929, car. no. s6.
Hamburg 1929, cat. no. 22.
Amsterdam 1930, cat. no. 50.

Liège/Brussels/Mons 1946-1947, cat. no. 9.
Paris 1947, cat. no. 9.
Geneva 1947, cat. no. 9.
Basel 1947, cat. no. 9
London/Birmingham/Glasgow 1947-1948, cat. no. so6.
Gouda 1949, no cat.
Nuremberg 1956, cat. no. 24.
Munich 1956, cat. no. 27.
Essen 1957, cat. no. 151.
Vienna 1958, cat. no. 24.
London 1962, cat. no. 14.
The Hague 1990, unnumbered.
Yokohama/Nagoya 1995-1996, cat. no. 21.
Tokyo/Fukuoka 1999-2000, cat. no. 23.

'Recently I've had a man from the almshouse
come pose for me quite often,' Van Gogh wrote
to Van Rappard on 18 or 19 September 1882
(267/R13). With this he introduced a model who
can be recognised in a great many drawings from
the autumn of 1882. The man lived in the Dutch
Reformed Home for the Elderly, where the residents
were usually known as 'diaconiemannetjes' and
'diaconievrouwtjes' - old people living 'on the parish'.
Van Gogh usually referred to his model as an orphan
man, which actually was the designation for the
residents of the Roman Catholic Home for Orphans
and the Elderly.[1] He found the name touching, as
he wrote shortly thereafter, again to Van Rappard:
'I am very busy working on drawings of an orphan
man, as these poor old fellows living on the parish are
popularly called here. Don't you find the expressions
"orphan man" and "orphan woman" apt? It's not easy
to draw those characters one is always meeting in
the streets. (269/R14,22 or 23 September 1882). He
sent a sketch of his model along with this letter and
wrote 'No 199' beneath it, which was also sewn on
the sleeve of the man's long black coat. This made
it possible to identify the man later on as Adrianus
Jacobus Zuyderland (1810-1897), who since 1876 had
been living in the Dutch Reformed Home for the
Elderly, where every-one was required to wear a visible
registration number.[2] Van Gogh would have obtained
more models from the home, including women, but
Zuyderland was his favourite. 'He has a nice bald
head, large (deaf) ears and white sidewhiskers,' he told
Theo (271/235, c. 1 October 1882), which can be
clearly seen in many of the studies.

The figure studies grouped here show
Zuyderland in several poses, with a top hat or a cap,
and usually in a long black coat. The residents of the
home had dark clothing like this, but Van Gogh had
also accumulated a nice collection of garments over
the years in which he had his models pose. On old
man with umbrella and watch Zuyderland is wearing
a decoration on his lapel, presumably the 'metal cross'
for special merit that he received for military action at
the time of the Belgian Revolt of 1830.[3]

The studies are difficult to date with any
precision by and large because Van Gogh made
so many of them from mid-September to deep
into December. In the summer of 1882 he had
concentrated on painting in oils for the first time
and afterwards he returned to watercolours as well,
discovering how difficult it was to render groups of

figures convincingly. For this reason he felt compelled
to tackle the human figure with even more intensity,
as he wrote to Theo on 8 October: 'What you would
notice at once, as I do, is that I need to make lots of
figure studies. I am putting all my strength into this
and work with a model almost every day. I have made
even more studies of the orphan man, and this week
I hope to get a woman from the almshouse as well'
(z72/z36). In a letter dated 22 November he spoke
about his 'numerous studies of orphan Men'. He said
his friend, the artist H.J. van der Weele, wanted him
to 'make a composition' with them, but, Van Gogh
wrote, 'I didn't think I was ready' (287/246).

Ready or not, Van Gogh was preparing himself
for the future. In November he experimented with
lithography for the first time, hoping to increase his
chances of getting work as an illustrator.[4] He made six
lithographs that month, three of them after studies of
Zuyderland.[5] One of the lithographs shows an orphan
man seated on a simple chair and drinking coffee
(F1657); the drawn study for this work (F1682) is in
the Van Gogh Museum. Old man drinking coffee
shows the figure in a somewhat different position,
more bent over and with the cup of coffee at his
lips. The study will have been made during the same
modelling session. Most of the studies show only the
model and nothing of the surroundings, although
in one case Van Gogh put Zuyderland in front of
the stove. The shadows are often absent as well. In
December he would further develop his studies and
provide them with backgrounds.

Five of the eight pencil drawings of the old
man were made on the coarse, thick watercolour
paper that Van Gogh had discovered at the end of
the summer and that proved highly suitable for his
vigorous drawing style. He fixed these five sheets
with a milk solution, which is still quite visible in the
discoloration around the figures. In old man with an
umbrella there are a few uncovered places to the right
of the figure, such as the point of the elbow, the flap
at the bottom of the long dark coat and the toe of the
shoe.

There the pencil has retained its original grey
colour while the rest of the composition has darkened
because of the fixative. On the versos of old man
holding his hat, old man with an umbrella and old
man with umbrella and watch part of a squaring grid
is visible, but only within the contours of the figure
on the recto. Theses squares do not coincide with
those on the recto; they came from an adjacent sheet
lying underneath on which Van Gogh already had
placed a grid and were 'transferred' when he pressed
hard with his carpenter's pencil while working on the
drawing.

1. Van Heugten 1996, D. 129.
2. Visser 1973, pp. 62-65. The Roman Catholic variant did
   not make this obligatory. For Zuyderland also see. p 150.
3. Ibid., pp. 63-64.
4. See Van Heugten & Pabst 1995 on Van Gogh's graphic
   work.
5. F1657, F1658 and F1662.

P.131

Head of a man with an eye-bandage

late December 1882
pencil, black lithographic crayon, grey wash,
pen in black ink (faded to brown), traces of squaring
on watercolor paper
45 x 27.6 cm
watermark: HALLINE5 1877
unsigned
F1004/JH289
KM 124.545

INSCRIPTIONS
verso, lower left: 7 (pencil).
50(black chalk).
73-59 (pencil). lower right: k.m. 207 (pencil)

PROVENANCE
[possibly sent by the artist to art dealer C.M. van Gogh,
Amsterdam, c. 1883].
purchased by H. Kröller-Müller at C.M. van Gogh, art dealer,
Amsterdam, 25 November 1911 (150 guilders)

EXHIBITIONS
Cologne 1912, cat. no. 121.
The Hague 1913, cat. no. 58.
Basel/Bern/Brussels 1927, cat. no. 22.
Düsseldorf 1928, cat. no. 88.
Karlsruhe 1928, cat. no. 23.
Berlin 1928-1929, cat. no. 26.
Hamburg 1929, cat. no. 18.
Amsterdam 1930, cat. no. 38.
Nuremberg 1956, cat. no. 27.
Tokyo/Kyoto 1958, cat. no. 29.
Munich 1961, cat. no. 25.
Warsaw 1962, cat. no. 25.
Tel Aviv/Haifa 1962-1963, cat. no. 26.
New York/Chicago/Ottawa and other cities, 1973-1974, cat.
no. 40.
Rome 1988, cat. no. 61.

This drawing is mentioned in a letter to Theo dated 31 December 1882 - 2January 1883, in which Van Gogh explains his new way of working. It is worthwhile quoting this passage at length because it clearly reveals the problems he saw himself facing: 'When I made the lithographs, it struck me that the lithographic crayon was very pleasant material, and I thought, I'll make drawings with it. However, there is one drawback which you will understand - because it is greasy, it cannot be erased in the usual way - working with it on paper, one even forfeits for the most part the only thing that can be used to erase on the stone itself, namely the grattoir [scraper, TM], which cannot be used with sufficient pressure on the paper because it curs right through it. But it occurred to me to make a drawing first with carpenter's pencil and then to work in and over it with lithographic crayon, which [because of the greasiness of the material] fixes the pencil, a thing ordinary chalk does not do - or it does, but only very badly. (After doing a sketch in this way, one can, with a firm hand, use the lithographic crayon where it is necessary, without much hesitation or erasing.) So I finished my drawings pretty well in pencil, at least as much as was the least bit possible. Then I fixed them and dulled them with milk. And then I worked it up again with lithographic crayon, and where the deepest tones were, retouched them here & there with a brush or pen, with noir de bougie [lampblack, TM], and worked in the lighter parts with white opaque paint. In this way I made a drawing of an old man sitting reading, with the light falling on his bald head, on his hand and the book. And a second one, the bandaged head of an injured man. The model who sat for this really had a head injury and a bandage over his left eye. Just like a head of a soldier of the old guard in the retreat from Russia, for instance' (298/256).

This last description is an apt characterisation of Head of a man with an eye-bandage. Although it is not immediately noticeable, a piece of bandage does stick out from under the dark cloth. An additional comment that can be added to Van Gogh's description of his method is that he worked with pen and ink in the eye that is not covered. The brown of the ink stands out sharply against all the black. He left the long clay pipe blank. He set the light and dark passages against each other in an exemplary fashion: he made the background dark on the left and light on the right. At the point of transition the hat occurs, and here he does just the reverse: light on the left, dark on the right, making this sheer a good example of the light-dark studies that Van Gogh wanted to practise. He did have a few problems with the plasticity of the head itself. The eye-bandage is barely rounded, making the right half of the face appear rather flat.

P.133

Mother with child

January-February 1883
black lithographic crayon, white and grey opaque watercolor,
on laid paper
40.7 x 27 cm
watermark: ED&Cie (in cartouche) [PL BAS]
unsigned
F1066/JH322
KM 113.774

INSCRIPTIONS
verso, upper left: 4633 115 (pencil)
[refers to 1913 Muller sale]

PROVENANCE
M.A. de Zwart, Voorburg, c. 1883.
H.P. Baron van Tuyll van
Serooskerken coll., Voorburg/Katwijk purchased by H.
Kröller-Müller at sale Amsterdam
(Frederik Muller & Cie), 25-26 November 1913, lot 134:
Mère tenant son enfant sur ses genoux
(330 guilders)

EXHIBITIONS
Basel/Bern/Brussels 1927, cat. no. 24.
Düsseldorf 1928, cat. no. 90.
Karlsruhe 1928, cat. no. 25.
Berlin 1928-1929, cat. no. 29.
Hamburg 1929, cat. no. 20.
Amsterdam 1930, cat. no. 40.

This sheet, which is rather difficult to date,was probably drawn in the first months of 1883, although the subject is reminiscent of the pencil drawings Van Gogh made in early autumn 1882 of Sien and her son Willem. Here the baby already looks a bit older. In addition, Van Gogh did not make a pencil underdrawing for this sheet as he usually did; instead he drew directly with the black chalk, which would suggest a somewhat later date. That is partly why the composition has become so spotted, since smudging is difficult in greasy chalk. The grey watercolour in the background around the figure works as an outline, but it is also carelessly applied. The watercolour in the baby's white cap has run as well.

P. 135

Head of a fisherman with sou'wester

January-February 1883
pencil, black lithographic crayon, brush in black ink,
white, grey and pink opaque watercolor,
fixative discoloration around head, traces of squaring
on watercolour paper
42.9 x 25.1 cm
watermark: DAMBKICOURT FRERES
unsigned
F1011/JH309
KM 125.319

INSCRIPTIONS
verso, lower left: 4 [?] 50 (pencil) lower left: 9 (pencil)

PROVENANCE
possibly sent by the artist to art dealer C.M. van Gogh,
Amsterdam, c. 1883)
purchased by H. Kröller-Müller at C.M. van Gogh, arc dealer,
Amsterdam, 25 November 1911 (150 guilders)

EXHIBITIONS
The Hague 1913, cat. no. 37.
Basel/Bern/Brussels 1927, cat. no. 13.
Düsseldorf 1928, cat. no. 80.
Karlsruhe 1928, cat. no. 15.
Berlin 1928-1929, cat. no. 34.
Hamburg 1929, cat. no. 9.
Amsterdam 1930, cat. no. 36.
Munich 1956, cat. no. 34.
Vienna 1958, cat. no. 28.
Tokyo/Kyoto 1958, cat. no. 30.
Rome 1988, cat. no. 62.
The Hague 1990, unnumbered.
Yokohama/Nagoya 1995-1996, cat. no. 26.
Detroit/Boston/Philadelphia 2000-2001, unnumbered.
The Hague 2005, unnumbered.

For Van Gogh the Head of a man with an
eye-bandage was a kind of prelude to a project that
he seriously began working on in the first months of
1883: the drawing of heads. He gave it the English
name Heads of the people, the title under which
the English illustrated magazine The Graphic had
published a series of wood engravings in the 1870s
of gnarled physical types such as 'The British rough',
'The Coast Guardsman' and 'The Miner'. Van Gogh
was a passionate collector of such wood engravings,
most of which he clipped our of old issues of English

and French magazines - but also American and Dutch
- and saved in folders. Some he mounted on coarse
pieces of paper to hang in his studio. Van Rappard
was a collector, too, and the two of them frequently
traded clippings.[1] 'A collection of sheets like these
becomes, in my opinion, a kind of Bıble to an artist,'
Van Gogh wrote to Van Rappard, 'which he reads
from time to time to get in the proper mood. I think
it's not only a good thing to know them but also
to make them a permanent presence in the studio'
(313/R25, c. 9 February 1883). A few weeks earlier he
had told him, '[I have been] working hard on Black
& White drawings, and I hope to learn a few more
things about the forces of black and white from these
Graphics. [...] What I've been working especially hard
at of late is heads -Heads of the people - fishermen's
heads with sou'westers, among other things' (303/
R22, c. 15 January 1883).

Soon he had a series of fishermen's heads
ready, having obtained his models from the Home for
the Elderly. The aged man on the sheet shown here,
with the grimly set mouth, can also be recognised on
two drawings in the Van Gogh Museum (F1014 and
F1015).

With his newly developed technique of
combining various shades of black - a 'more powerful
process' as he called it - Van Gogh hoped to inject
more sentiment into his drawings. In that respect
the more unfinished studies were often stronger, he
thought, than if he spent too much time on them.
'You will understand what I mean,' he wrote to his
brother. 'In real studies there is something of life
itself, and the person who makes them will not think
of himself but of nature in them, and so prefer the
study to what he may perhaps make of it later, unless
something quite different should finally result from
the many studies, namely the type distilled from many
individuals That's the highest thing in art, and there
art sometimes rises above

P. 137

Old fisherman seated

January-February 1883
pencil, pen and brush in ink, wash with sepia and neutral tint

black lithographic crayon, white, grey and pink opaque
watercolor, traces of squaring
on wove paper
45.6 x 25.7 cm,
no watermark
signed lower left (by the artist):Vincent (black chalk)
F10100/JH306
KM 127.393

INSCRIPTIONS
-

PROVENANCE
Dr F.J. Michelsen coil., Amsterdam.
purchased by H. Kröller-Müller at sale Amsterdam (Frederik
Muller & Cie), 3 December 1918 (Michelsen collection), lot
306 (160 guilders)

EXHIBITIONS
Basel/Bern/Brussels 1927, cat. no. 31.
Düsseldorf 1928, cat. no. 97.
Karlsruhe 1928, cat. no. 32.
Berlin 1928-1929, cat. no. 35.
Hamburg 1929, cat. no. 27.
Amsterdam 1930, cat. no. 145.
Milan 1952, cat. no. 20.
Eindhoven 1956, cat. no. 7.
Washington/New York/Minneapolis and other cities,
1958-1959, cat. no. 144.
Sao Paulo 1959, cat. no. 8.
Montreal/Ottawa/Winnipeg/Toronto 1960-1961, cat. no. 94.
New York/Chicago/Ottawa and other cities, 1973-1974, cat.
510. 43.
London/Newcastle-upon-Tyne 1974, cat. no. 31.
Paris/London/The Hague 1983, cat. no. 153.
Tokyo/Nagoya 1985-1986, cat. no. 16.
Osaka 1986, cat. no. 22.
Rome 1988, cat. no. 63.
Amsterdam 1990, no cat.
Tokyo/Fukuoka 1999-2000, cat. no. 27.
Detroit/Boston/Philadelphia 2000-2001, unnumbered.

Still visible beneath this composition of an
old fisherman, peacefully sitting on a low wall and
smoking his pipe, is the chair on which the model
- Adrianus Zuyderland - posed for the artist. Here
Van Gogh worked a simple pencil study into a more
detailed scene. Upon closer inspection it appears
that Zuyderland is not holding his pipe but simply
supporting his head with his right hand. The pipe
was painted over the hand later on with white opaque
watercolour. The cup of coffee was probably given its
place on the wall at the same time.

P. 138

Mourning woman seated on a basket

February-March 1883
black lithographic crayon, grey wash,
white and grey opaque watercolor, traces of squaring,
on watercolor paper
47.4 x 29.5 cm
watermark: HALLINES 1877
unsigned
F1060/JH326
KM 123.495

INSCRIPTIONS
verso, lower left: 6 (pencil)

PROVENANCE
[possibly sent by the artist to
art dealer C.M. van Gogh,
Amsterdam, c. 1883
purchased by H. Kröller-Müller at C.M. van
Gogh, art dealer, Amsterdam,
25 November 1911 (150 guilders)

EXHIBITIONS
Cologne 1912, cat.no. 110.
Basel/Bern/Brussels 1927, cat. no. 25.
Düsseldorf 1928, cat. no. 91.
Karlsruhe 1928, cat. no. 26.
Berlin 1928-1929, cat. no. 30.
Hamburg 1929, cat. no. 21.
Amsterdam 1930, cat. no. 32.
Milan 1952, cat. no. 16.
Saint Louis/Philadelphia/Toledo 1953-1954, cat. no. 16.
Munich 1956, cat. no. 37.
Warsaw 1962, cat. no. 19.
Tel Aviv/Haifa 1962-1963, cat. no. 20.
Belgrade 1966, cat. no. 15.
Moscow/Leningrad 1971, cat. no. 23.
New York/Chicago/Ottawa and other cities, 1973-1974, cat.
no. 42.
London/Newcastle-upon-Tyne 1974, cat. no. 30.
London 1992, cat. no. 20.
Amsterdam 1995, unnumbered.
Amsterdam/New York 2oo5, cat. no. 14.

P.139

Woman sewing

February-March 1883
black lithographic crayon, grey wash,
white and grey opaque watercolor,
traces of squaring (only horizontal stripes visible)
on watercolor paper
38.2 x 23.2 cm
watermark: HALLINES [1877]
unsigned
F1294/JH321
KM 124.943

INSCRIPTIONS
verso, centre right: 13 (blue chalk)

PROVENANCE
H.P. Bremmer Coll., The Hague.
N.E. Kröller Coll., The Hague.
acquired by H. Kröller-Müller from the estate of N.E. Kröller,
The Hague, early 1924

EXHIBITIONS
Basel/Bern/Brussels 1927, cat. no. 7.
Düsseldorf 1928, cat. no. 71.
Karlsruhe 1928, cat. no. 7.
Berlin 1928-1929, cat. no. 72.
Hamburg 1929, cat. no. 5.
Amsterdam 1930, cat. no. 30.
Tokyo/Kyoto 1958, cat. no. 31.

These two extremely powerful drawings of
(probably) Sien seated on a basket were, like the
more sketchy Mother with child, drawn directly with
greasy black chalk without first having been carefully
planned out in pencil. In comparison with that work
these two drawings are sharper and darker, the deep
blacks emerging more strongly because of the sole use
of black chalk. Apparently Van Gogh was confident
enough to omit the pencil sketch after a period of
experimentation, although not many such examples
have survived from this period. On 3 February 1883
he wrote, 'I also drew a few figures with conté which
I think are better. Not just with conté, but the whole
thing sponged, letting the shadows flow and with
the lights cleared out once more' (308/263). He
used the same procedure here, except with black
lithographic crayon, which was greasier and darker

than conté sticks. Clearing out the lights, as Van
Gogh so charmingly describes it, was accomplished by
applying white and grey opaque watercolour and also
by scratching the chalk open in places with a sharp
instrument. In woman sewing this is especially evident
in the background to the right and along the outline
of the skirt.

For Mourning woman Van Gogh fell back on
the theme of poverty and hopelessness concentrated
in a single figure. In earlier variants the main figure
was usually male. Only a year before he had made
large drawings of Sien in which she also supports her
head with one hand while looking rather sad.

Van Gogh had a preference for prints that
showed the unvarnished roughness of daily life
and that feature various melancholy types in every
possible pose. Van Gogh was mainly searching for a
general characterisation, for a type of sorrowful figure.
The examples he found in his collection of wood
engravings - where such figures are usually part of a
group - were an important source of inspiration in
this search.

P. 141

Saying grace

December 1882/April 1883
pencil, black lithographic crayon, grey wash,
brush and printer's ink, white oils,
grey opaque watercolor, on watercolor paper
62.4 x 39.8 cm
no watermark
unsigned
F1053/JH357
KM 113.046

INSCRIPTIONS
verso, lower right: 6 (pencil)
km 208 (pencil) lower centre:
95 x 14 cm (pencil) upper left:
23 [underlined] (pencil)

PROVENANCE
purchased by H. Kröller-Müller at Bernheim-Jeune, art dealer,
Paris, April 1912 (700 guilders)

EXHIBITIONS
Cologne 1912, cat. no. 109.
The Hague 1913, cat. no. 63.
Basel/Bern/Brussels 1927, cat. no. 18.
Düsseldorf 1928, cat. no. 85.
Karlsruhe 1928, cat. no. 20.
Berlin 1928-1929, cat. no. 14.
Hamburg 1929, cat. no. 14.
Amsterdam 1930, cat. no. 43.
New York/Philadelphia/Boston and other cities, 1935-1936,
cat. no. 82.
Nuremberg 1956, cat. no. 19.
Munich 1956, cat. no. 35.
Vienna 1958, cat. no. 30.
So Paulo 1959, cat. no. 7.
Warsaw 1962, cat. no. 18.
Tel Aviv/Haifa 1962-1963, cat. no. 19.
Belgrade 1966, cat. no. 14.
Otterlo 1990, cat. no. 38.
Vienna 1996, cat. no. 36.
Tokyo/Fukuoka 1999-2000, cat. no. 26.
The Hague 2005, unnumbered.

'I have another two drawings now,' Van Gogh wrote to his brother in mid-December 1882, 'one of a man reading the Bible and the other of a man saying grace before his dinner, which is on the table. Both are certainly done in what you might call an old-fashioned sentiment - they are figures like the little old man with his head in his hands. I think the Bénédicité is the best, but they complement each other. In one there is a view of the snowy fields seen through the window' (295/253, c. 12-18 December 1882). The model for both drawings was the orphan man Zuyderland once again. In the one, Man reading the Bible (F1683, private collection), he is reading the Bible while standing, and in the other, which Van Gogh called ' Bénédicité (grace before meals), he is shown seated at a simple table with his hands folded For this female version of the same subject Van Gogh probably had Sien take her place on the other side of the table and sit on the same bench. When the sheets are placed side by side they even seem to be sharing the same meal. Both have a steaming bowl in front of them, although this is less visible in the version with Sien.

In accordance with Van Gogh's customary procedure, the two drawings of the prayer were first set down in detail in pencil and then finished with black lithographic crayon, washes, ink and opaque watercolour. The variant with Sien turned out much greyer and more tonal. For instance, Van Gogh applied the washes by daubing a sponge in the chalk. He then rubbed open the contours slightly around the bench and the woman's skirt. The highlights in her clothing, her hair, on the table and on the benches were achieved with dark grey opaque watercolour, but white oil paint can be seen in her face in several spots.[1] The background to the left is daubed completely black with a thick greasy layer of ink, so that despite the general duskiness of the composition the sharp contour of Sien's back can still be distinguished. Van Gogh worked the same ink into the bench and used it to accentuate the woman's contours.[2] He probably carried out these finishing touches a few months later on, in April 1883. It was then that he discovered printer's ink as a deep black

material that he could apply in countless gradations by mixing it with turpentine in different proportions 336/278, c. 1 or 2 April 1883). This is what he seems to have done here in the background, and he did something similar in Man reading the Bible. He wrote (see above) that on that sheet a winter landscape could be seen in the background through the window, but he obliterated this later on under a thick layer of ink.

1. On the verso there is clear evidence that the oil paint has seeped through the paper on the plate corresponding to the woman's neck and has left a brown spot.
2. He scratched the ink open near the woman's ear, making the pencil visible once more.

P. 143

Woman on her deathbed

April 1883
pencil, black lithographic crayon, brush in (printer's) ink, white oils, grey watercolor, on watercolor paper
35.42 x 63.2 cm
watermark: unclear
unsigned
F841/JH359
KM 115.817

INSCRIPTIONS
recto, lower left: Atelier Vincent (black chalk)
verso, lower tight: Door mij gekocht
v/d kunstk. Oldenzeel dec. 1892 Hidde Nijland (pencil).
on removed cardboard backing, lower left:
Hidden Nijland (black ink)
left: KR [......] [illegible] (blue chalk)
No 37 [crossed out] (pencil) lower
right: 192 (pencil)

PROVENANCE
A.C.W. Terhell coll., The Hague, ?-1892.
purchased by Hidde Nijland, Dordrecht at Oldenzeel, art dealer, Rotterdam, December 1892.
purchased from Hidde Nijland by A.G. Kröller, The Hague, July 1928.
donated to the Kröller-Müller Foundation by A.G. Kröller, December 1928.

EXHIBITIONS
Rotterdam 1892, no cat.
The Hague 1895, no known cat.
Dordrecht 1897, no cat.
Dordrecht 1904, cat. no. 192.
The Hague 1918, cat. no. 73.
Amsterdam 1924, cat. no. 132.
The Hague 1928, unnumbered.
Hamburg 1929, cat. no. 149.
Amsterdam 1930, cat. no. 142.
New York/Philadelphia/Boston and other cities, 1935-1936, cat. no. 71.
Liège/Brussele/Mons 1946-1947, cat. no. 12.
Paris 1947, cat. no. 12.
Geneva 1947, cat. no. 12.
Basel 1947, cat. no. 129.
London/Birmingham/Glasgow 1947-1948, cat. no. 112.
Gouda 1949, no cat.
Milan 1952, cat. no. 23.
Mons 1980, cat. no. 9.
Otterlo 1990, cat. no. 56.
Tokyo/Osaka/Nagoya 2005, cat. no. 6.

Woman on her deathbed is a rather remarkable composition in Van Gogh's oeuvre. Death is a rare theme in his work, and he certainly never depicted it as directly as he does here.[1] In any case it was a subject that preoccupied him for a short time in April of 1883. In the beginning of the month he wrote to Van Rappard, 'The drawing I am working on now with this method is that of an orphan man standing near a coffin - in what they call the 'corpses' den" (337/R33, c. 2-4 April 1883). By 'this method' Van Gogh was referring to drawing with printer's ink, but no such composition has survived. Later in April he told Theo, 'This week I drew a few reclining figures; at some point I shall need figures of corpses or of sick people, men as well as women' (339/280, c. 21 April 1883). In this letter he also speaks of printer's ink: Van Gogh wrote that almost none of the drawings he was then working on were made without brush and printer's ink. On Woman on her deathbed, a dark composition with sharp contrasts, this greasy ink is used in the hair of the dead woman and in the background. The ink is applied especially thickly close to the body and it still has a certain shine; in other spots it is more diluted.[2]

It is not completely clear from the fragment of the letter to Theo quoted above whether Van Gogh was planning to draw real corpses and sick people, or whether he needed the studies of reclining figures for compositions containing dead and sick people. It may be that he got the idea for the woman on her deathbed from reading Victor Hugo, and refashioned a study of a reclining Sien. 'I am reading the last part of Les misérables,' he wrote to Theo on c. 11 April. 'The figure of Fantine, a prostitute, made a deep impression on me' [338/279]. Fantine undoubtedly made him think of Sien, for both poor women were made pregnant and then abandoned by their lovers, had to raise their children alone and were doomed to prostitution. Hugo depicts Fantine as an innocent victim of society, and that is exactly how Van Gogh saw Sien. Famine died miserably in the story, and perhaps Van Gogh wanted to capture something of the sentiment of this tragic event in a drawing.

In any case, Sien wore a shroud when she modelled for the corpse, but the position of her body comes across as rather posed. Even the addition of the still life in the foreground - an open book and an extinguished candle, a traditional reference to death - could not remedy that.[3] Absent from the scrawny, emaciated figure is what might be called an 'expression of death'. If it were not for the hands folded on the breast she could be someone sleeping. In addition, the legs are a bit on the long side in proportion to the stocky upper body. For the white and lighter effects Van Gogh used both opaque watercolour and oil paint. There is no underdrawing for the book and candle, which were put down all at once in grey-white oils. The woman's garment as well as the pillow were rendered with white opaque watercolour, with a bit of blue mixed in for the pillow. Finally, for the shadows he worked with black chalk over the white paint. At the bottom he applied this chalk lightly across the paper, so that the structure of the coarse grain is clearly visible.

1. Only a drawn copy of a painting of a dead woman by Van Gogh is known, dating from the time he worked in Brussels (1880-1881) (F1026a, Van Gogh Museum, Amsterdam).
2. See the discussion of Woman seated on working with printer's ink.
3. In Nuenen Van Gogh painted Still life with Bible (F117,Van Gogh Museum, Amsterdam) in October 1885, in which he placed an extinguished candle beside an open Bible, referring, among other things, to his father, who had died earlier that year (see Van Tilborgh & Vellekoop 1999, pp. 222, 224, n. 16).

P. 145

Woman seated

April-May 1883
pencil, grey wash, brush and printer's ink, white olis, traces of squaring, on wove paper
56.3 x 44.1 cm
watermark: J WHATMAN TURKEY MILL [fragment]
unsigned
F1056/JH365
KM 117.634

INSCRIPTIONS
recto, lower right: cur from
original lower edge and pasted on: Port Vincent (black chalk)
lower right: Verz: Hidde Nijland (black ink) verso, centre:
Port Vincent/Hidde Nijland (black ink). centre left: KR1(blue chalk)
lower right: km935 (pencil)

PROVENANCE
acquired by Hidde Nijland, Dordrecht, before 1895.
purchased from Hidde Nijland by A.G. Kröller, The Hague,

July 1928
donated to the Kröller-Müller Foundation by A.G. Kröller, December 1928

EXHIBITIONS
The Hague 1895, no known cat.
Dordrecht 1897, no cat.
Dordrecht 1904, cat. no. ?.
The Hague 1918, cat. no. 64.
Amsterdam 1924, cat. no. 92.
The Hague 1928,unnumbered.
Hamburg 1929, cat. no. 39.
Amsterdam 1930, cat. no. 10.
New York/Philadelphia/Boston and other cities, 1935-1936, cat. no. 83.
Liège/Brussels/Mons 1946-1947, cat. no. 6.
Paris 1947, cat.no. 6.
Geneva 1947,cat.no. 6.
Nuremberg 1956, cat. no. 20.
Munich 1956, cat. no. 36.

In late February 1883 Van Gogh had new indoor shutters installed in his studio because the light, which came in through three large windows, was too bright and too reflective. The netting that he had previously stretched across the windows to soften the light was not adequate. Now he could block the upper and lower sections of the windows independently and make finer adjustments to the light's intensity and angle of incidence. It will have been especially helpful in his light-and-dark studies: 'It often made me desperate when I would see a woman puttering around a small room, for instance, and find something typical and mysterious in the figure, only to have it all disappear when I had the same woman in the studio. The orphan man, for instance, was also much more striking in a dark hallway than in my studio' (322/269, c. 25-26 February).

The light's improved angle of incidence was especially helpful a little later on when Van Gogh began to work with an extra dark material, printer's ink (336/278, 1 or 2 April 1883). He mixed this greasy, sticky ink with a bit of turpentine, making it easier to spread. In fact, the solution could be so highly diluted that it could be used as a transparent grey wash. The turpentine evaporated quickly and left no spots on the paper, he wrote to Van Rappard, whom he was trying to interest in his new-found procedure (337/R33, c. 2-4 April 1883). He also mixed the ink with white oil paint or white powder to produce deep greys. These various methods are quite evident in the three large figure studies assembled here.[1]

Because of Van Gogh's focus on the light-dark contrasts in these studies the subjects can seem rather strange, although this may not be immediately apparent. The same model probably posed for Woman seared, and apparently this was not Sien. She is wearing the same clothing and white head-dress, but here she is sitting somewhat forlornly on a bench. Van Gogh used a bit of oil paint once again for this headdress. Along the upper edge of the cap a thin brown line can be seen which was produced by the running oil. At some point in the distant past a strip was trimmed off the bottom where the original inscription 'Port. Vincent' was once located. The inscription was then cut from the strip and pasted on

the lower right of the drawing. It is not known who was responsible for this, but it can even be seen on the earliest known reproduction of the work.[2]

Van Gogh wrote to Van Rappard that this way of working did not lend itself equally well to every type of paper: 'It is my experience that this printer's ink clings very nicely to the rough grain of a certain paper which is called papier torchon here (but which is absolutely not a Whatman torchon)' (337/R33). By 'the rough grain of a certain paper' he was referring to the type of coarse watercolour paper on which Sower is drawn,[3] The other two sheets are smoother. The sheet on which the seated woman was drawn is a 'Whatman torchon as Van Gogh called it: watercolour paper from the J. Whatman company. That paper was quite sturdy, but here the ink washes have caused it to cockle a great deal. There is also a tear in the woman's apron, and the paper has absorbed so much ink that it is visible on the verso of both sheets.

1. Also see Saying grace and Woman on her deathbed.
2. Nijland 1905, no. 1.
3. Also see Woman on her deathbed, which was drawn on the same coarse watercolour paper.

P. 147

Landscape with a white bridge

May-July 1883
black chalk, white and grey opaque watercolor, on (originally) bluish purple laid paper
30 x 43.8 cm
watermark: Saint Mars
signed lower right (nor by the artist): Vincent (black chalk)
F1347/JH408
KM 123.060

INSCRIPTIONS
verso, lower left: Vincent Verz:/
Hidde Nijland (black ink). No 41
(pencil) centre: 58 (pencil) upper left: KR 25 (blue chalk)

PROVENANCE
A,Ph. Furnée or H.J. Furnée, The Hague (?).
acquired by Hidde Nijland, Dordrecht, before 1904.
purchased from Hidde Nijland by AG. Kröller, The Hague, July 1928
donated to the Kröller-Müller Foundation by A.G. Kröller, December 1928

EXHIBITIONS
Dordrecht 1904, cat. no. ?.
The Hague 1918, cat. no. ?.

Amsterdam 1924, cat. no. 62.
The Hague 1928, unnumbered.
Hamburg 1929, cat. no. 57.
Amsterdam 1930, cat. no. 68.
Basel 1947, cat. no. 135.
Vienna 1958, cat. no. 33.
Montreal/Ottawa/Winnipeg/Toronto 1960-1961, cat. no. 97.

It has long been assumed that this drawing was produced in Drenthe, after De la Faille had initially grouped it with the Nuenen work in 1928.[1] In 1993 the idea was once again put forward that Landscape with a white bridge must have been made in Van Gogh's Nuenen period based on a supposed connection with the landscape near the Eindhoven Canal in the area around Mierlo, about seven kilometres southeast of Nuenen. Two years later, however, it was proven beyond the shadow of a doubt that Van Gogh must have made the drawing in The Hague. At that time Martha Op de Coul and Annet Tellegen published an article in which they reproduced a photograph of an oil painting that Antoine Philippe ['Anton'] Furnée [1861-1897] made at the same location.[2] This Furnée had been trained as a surveyor and was the son of one of Van Gogh's paint suppliers in The Hague, Hendrik Jan Furnée, who was also a chemist with a shop on Korte Poten. In the spring of 1883, Van Gogh began giving Furnée lessons in drawing and painting, and they often went out together looking for subjects. It was during one of these sessions that the drawing and the painting Landscape with a white bridge were made. The works are rather broadly dated since it is not known exactly when the two went out together, apart from a few days in May (345/285, c. 20 May 1883).

Until a restoration conducted in 1980 there was a handwritten text on the back of the painting by Furnée: 'Oude wasscherij by den Binckhorstweg vlak over het spoor v/d SS geschilderd door A.Ph. Furnée fec. met Vincent' (Old laundry near Binckhorstweg just over the SS railway painted by A.Ph. Furnée fec. with Vincent).[3] This road began just behind the Rijnspoor depot complex. Van Gogh and Furnée stood with their backs to the city and looked towards the little bridge over the Schenk in the direction of the Veen polder and Binckhorstweg (or Binckhorstlaan), which ran past De Binckhorst country estate and on to Vliet near Voorburg. Right behind them was the line linking two Hague railway stations, Hollands Spoor and Rijnspoor. The text on the back of the painting must have been put there after 1890, since that was the year the 'Nederlandsche Rhijnspoorweg Maatschappij' (Netherlands Rhijnspoorweg Company) was taken over by the Staatsspoor (SS).[4]

The composition has a rather indeterminate quality on account of the profuse and carelessly applied white and grey opaque watercolour used to cover mainly the foreground and the sky. The paint has become so hardened that it has crumbled away somewhat over the years. This loss of paint has made the composition even more spotted. The brownish pink paper was originally a soft bluish purple, so that the total impression made by the work must have been quite different in the past.[5] The grey in particular will have been less jarring.

The sheet is signed 'Vincent' at the lower right. This has been interpreted as an indication that Van Gogh, who hardly ever signed these kinds of studies, must have given the sheet to Furnée.[6] The signature is not original, however, although it is still quite possible that he gave the sheet to his pupil. The signature has a great deal in common with a group of characteristic, rather elongated signatures that can only be found on twenty large Nuenen figure studies from the summer of 1885, all of which came from the Nijland collection. Nijland himself cannot be held responsible for this signature, but he may have acquired the drawings via Furnée's father. The elder Furnée also supplied paint to Van Gogh in Nuenen, and when the artist fell behind in paying his bills in the summer of 1885 he probably sent Furnée a group of drawings. So perhaps Hendrik Jan Furnée - or one of his acquaintances. - was responsible for the signature. Hidde Nijland had already put some 'signed' Nuenen studies out on loan for an exhibition in The Hague in 1895, making Furnée a possible source for the earlier provenance of these works. Landscape with a white bmiel8e may have been acquired along with the Nuenen drawings and may have hung in the 1895 exhibition as well, although there is no direct proof that it did.[7]

1. Vanbeselaere 1937, pp. 238 and 413, was first to date the drawing to Drenthe, October-November 1883. Tralbaut 1959, p. 24, also opted for Dtenthe. Hammacher 1952, cat.no. 55, placed the sheet forthe first time in The Hague because of its technical similarities with Tree roots in a sandy ground ('Les racines') and Woodcutters (p. 247) - admittedly a rather strange combination. De la Faille 1970 connected it to Drenthe again, and Hefting 1980, p. 44, also placed it there on account of its technical resemblance to Farms, a better observation.
2. Op de Coul & Tellegen 1995. The article has to do with the relationship between Van Gogh and his pupil Furnee. Also see Dijk & Van det Sluis 2001, pp. 255-259.
3. Quoted from Dijk & Van der Sluis 2001, p.259.
4. The Hollands Spoor station was located on the Rotterdam-Amsterdam line, which crossed Binckhorstlaan some distance further on. The line was part of the Hollandsche IJzeren Spoorwegmaatschappij, which joined with the Staatsspoor in 1917.
5. The laid paper is discoloured owing to an earlier passe-partout frame in which an acidic cardboard was used. Various red and blue fibres are still quite visible on the paper when examined under a loupe. The watermark 'Saint Mars' is unique in Van Gogh's oeuvre, as far as we know. Perhaps he worked on paper that Furnée had brought along. In Hefting 1980, p. 44, the watermark 'S.C. Mars' is mentioned, which is incorrect. This was picked up by Dijk & Van det Sluis 2001, p. 258, who connected it with the paper used in the drawing Road workers with a wagon. The latter was not drawn on laid paper, however, but on wove paper, with the watermark 's&c', and has nothing to do with the paper used in Landscape with a white bridge.
6. Dijk & Van det Sims 2001, p. 259.
7. Because reviews and catalogues often limit themselves to the simple designation 'landscape', and because there are usually so many of them, it is difficult to identify such a composition.

P. 149

Fisherman's wife

Early August 1883
Oil on paper on panel
51.6 x 33.9 cm
F6/JH189
KM 108.683

SIGNATURE/INSCRIPTIONS/LABELS-

PROVENANCE
A.C. van Gogh-Carbentus, Nuenen/Breda, November 1885/April 1886. A. Schrauwen, Breda, 1886. J.C. and J.M. Couvreur Breda. W. van Bakel and C. Mouwen, Breda, 1902. Oldenzeel, art dealer, Rotterdam, 1903. purchased by H.P Bremmer at sale Rotterdam (Oldenzeel, art dealer), 10 December 1918, no. 44. purchased by H. Kröller-Müller from H.P. Bremmer, The Hague, 1920 (f 750)

EXHIBITIONS
Rotterdam 1903(a), no. 422.
Basle/Bern 1927, no. 6.
Brussels 1927, no. 6.
Dusseldorf 1928, no. 72.
Karlsruhe 1928, no. 7.
Berlin 1928-1929, no. 10.
Hamburg 1929, no. 2.
Amsterdam 1930, no. 156.
New York/Philadelphia/Boston and other cities 1935-1936, no. 1.
Milan 1952, no. 29.
Munich 1956.no. 42.
Montreal/Ottawa/Winnipeg/Toronto 1960-1961, no. 2.

P.149

Fisherman

Early August 1883
Oil on paper on panel
51.1 x 32.8 cm
F5/JH188
KM 104.318

SIGNATURE/INSCRIPTIONS/LABELS-

PROVENANCE
A.C. van Gogh-Carbentus, Nuenen/Breda, November 1885/April 1886. A. Schrauwen, Breda, 1886. J.C. and J.M. Couvreur, Breda. W van Bakel and C. Mouwen, Breda, 1902. Oldenzeel, art dealer, Rotterdam, 1903. purchased by H.P. Bremmer at sale Rotterdam (Oldenzeel, art dealer), 10 December 1918, no. 43. purchased by H. Koller-Muller from H.P. Bremmer, The Hague,1920 (f 750)

EXHIBITIONS
Rotterdam 1903(a), no. 411.
Basle/Bern 1927, no. 5.
Brussels 1927, no. 5.
Dusseldorf 1928, no. 70.
Karlsruhe 1928, no. 5.
Berlin 1928-1929, no. 9.
Hamburg 1929, no. 1.
Amsterdam 1930, no. 158.
New York/Chicago 1949-1950, no. 1.
Saint Louis/Philadelphia/Toledo 1953-1954, no. 7.
Antwerp 1955 (b), no. 11.
Eindhoven 1956, no. 11.
Vienna 1958, no. 36.
.Tokyo/Kyoto 1958, no. 34.
Warsaw 1962, no. 28.
Tel Aviv/Haifa 1962-1963, no. 28.
Belgrade 1966, no. 43.
Moscow/Leningrad 1971, no. 11.

In the late summer of 1882 Van Gogh directed his attention chiefly to painting landscape studies. He also tried his hand at figure painting, which didn't come easily to him. He had made some attempts in his studio during a few days of bad weather. 'I'm sending you two scribbles,' he wrote Theo on 19 August 1882. 'Painting the figure appeals to me very much, but it must ripen. I must get to know the technique better - what is sometimes called "la cuisine

de l'art".' (259/226) Not a single painted figure study is known from these months. The only figure studies of which we are aware from Van Gogh's Hague period are Fisherman and Fisherman's wife, and a painting of Five potato diggers (F9), which he painted a year later in the summer of 1883. In the intervening period he had made a whole series of figure drawings in order to familiarise himself more fully with reproducing the human anatomy.

Both studies can be dated with a fairly high degree of confidence to early August 1883. The fisherman's wife wears a rather striking red cape; in early June 1883 Van Gogh had written to Theo that he had managed to get hold of a similar object (353/291) [1]. He also hoped to pick up 'a fisherman's jacket with a stand-up collar and short sleeves [...]' -if Theo would send him the extra money (355/293, 13 or 14 June 1883 But a month later he received an unexpected gift from two surveyors to whom he was giving drawing lessons. [2] In the study of the fisherman the model is wearing this kind of jacket. Van Gogh had already acquired the sou'wester in January.[3] At first he used these attributes for his drawings, but in the second half of July he started painting again, prompted by the acquisition of a large amount of paint bought at very good prices (372/307, 29 and 30 July 1883). In a letter of about 2 August 1883 he made a detailed report of his progress as a figure painter: 'A very heavy source of anxiety has fallen from my shoulders in the past few days. Last year I repeatedly tried painting figure studies, but the way they turned out drove me to despair. Now I've begun again, and there's no longer anything standing in the way of my work because drawing comes so much more easily than last year. At that time I got all mixed up whenever I lost track of my drawn sketch while painting; it took me a long time to make that sketch, so that if I could only have the model for a little while the whole thing would turn out very badly. But now I don't give a damn if the drawing is obliterated, and I just do it directly with the brush, and the form stands out enough to make it usable anyway.' (373/308) In the same letter he wrote that he had first made two studies following the technique of the previous year: 'first draw and then fill in the outline.' He called this 'the dry method.' Now he had turned the process around: 'The other way is actually to make the drawing last and to begin work by searching for the tones [...].'

This process of searching for tones and sweeping the colors through each other can easily be seen in Fisherman and Fisherman's wife which in all probability he was working on at the time. Indeed, infrared reflectography applied to the studies reveals no under-drawing for either one. In a few places the outlines of a rudimentary underpainting are visible, but they were brushed out in the painting process. Van Gogh used a rather large brush for the background, including one that was 2 to 3 cm wide. Working with flowing movements, he used this brush to paint the beach and sea around his figures, which he painted with somewhat smaller brushes. In general the colors lie close together. Clearly Van Gogh's intention, as he explained to Theo in the letter quoted above, was to proceed 'without bothering too much

about the drawing, just by trying to put the tones roughly in place and gradually to define the form and the subdivisions of the colors.' He concentrated first of all on the tonal values and avoided the complicated details such as hands and faces. But afterwards he painted, say, the pleats of the fisherman's jacket with black paint in a more drawing-like way, which closely coincides with the working method he described.

Compared with the somewhat stiff figure in Girl in a wood, the artist in these studies manages to model his figures more convincingly, although the anatomical pro-portions still seem a bit clumsy. Against the overwhelmingly dark grey-green and grey-brown background, the red cape and white cap of the fisherman's wife creates a modest tonal effect. The background of the study of the fisherman, on the other hand, is much lighter, with soft grey tints. This is a clear indication that the works are two different kinds of studies in light effects, which he would later make in greater numbers in Brabant. It is quite possible that the woman with whom he was living, Sien Hoornik, modelled for the Fisherman's wife. The fisherman, with his large head and short body, is a rather stocky figure, but Van Gogh may have made use of a youthful model here. Shortly before making these two studies he wrote to Theo, 'I have a model-a farm boy who lives here in the neighborhood - with whom I've already spoken about the painting of studies.' (372/307, 29 and 30 July 1883) The fisherman, in any case, is more suggestive of a 'fishing boy' than of an adult.

1. Hefting 1980, p. 42. Also see: Vanbeselaere 1937, pp. III, 223-224, 413, and Van der Mast & Dumas 1990, p. 34.
2. In May 1883, Van Gogh became acquainted with Antoine Furnee, a young surveyor who was doing some drawing outdoors, as was Van Gogh (345/285, c. 20 May 1883). His father, Hendrik Jan Furnee, was a chemist and paint dealer in The Hague, where Anton Mauve obtained his paint and where Van Gogh would also buy his materials. See: Op de Coul &Tellegen 1995, pp. 95-96, and Van Tilborgh &Vellekoop 1999, pp. 20-21
3. See Van Heugten 1996, pp. 197-200.

P.151

Edge of a wood

August -September 1883
Oil on canvas on panel
33.8 x 48.5 cm
F192/JH184

KM 109.023

SIGNATURE/INSCRIPTIONS/LABELS-

PROVENANCE
A.C. van Gogh-Carbentus, Nuenen/
Breda, November 1885/April 1886.
A. Schrauwen,
Breda, 1886. J.C. and J.M. Couvreur, Breda.
W, van Bakel and C, Mouwen, Breda, 1902.
Oldenzeel, art dealer, Rotterdam, 1903.
sale
Mouwen coil., Amsterdam (Frederik Muller), 3 May
1904, lot 10 (not sold).
Oldenzeel, art dealer,
Rotterdam. purchased by H. Kröller-Müller at sale
The Hague (J. Biesing), before August 1908 (f 110)

EXHIBITIONS
Rotterdam 1903 (c), no. 37.
Cologne 1912, no. 2.
The Hague 1913, no. 9.
Basle/Bern 1927, no. 39.
Brussels 1927, no. 39.
Dusseldorf 1928, no. 105.
Karlsruhe 1928, no. 40.
Berlin 1928-1929, no. 62.
Hamburg 1929, no. 6.
Amsterdam 1930 no. 179.
Antwerp 1955 (b), no. 12.
Vienna 1958, no. 35.

In the summer of 1882 Van Gogh painted a
number of woodland scenes, and this depiction of the
edge of a wood has always been dated to that period
as well. [1] But there are several more reasons for dating
this painted study to the summer of 1883.

In the first place Van Gogh used canvas for
this painting, whereas his experiments with oil paint
during the summer of 1882 had been done on paper
that was later - sometimes much later - transferred
to canvas or panel. Paper was much cheaper than
canvas, and he thought it wasteful to make his first
attempts on the more expensive material, for which
he hardly had enough money. [2] When Van Gogh
took up painting again in July 1883, after months of
drawing, he wrote to Theo: 'Today I bought a field
easel and canvas. The easel is nice because you get
so dirty when working out of doors on your knees.'
(372/307, 29 and 30 July 1883) Not only did he get
less dirty, but now he could more easily paint from a
higher angle. One striking aspect of Edge of a wood is
that compared with the woodland studies of 1882 it
is indeed painted from a higher angle, which means
it is very likely that Van Gogh used his new field
easel here. Although he told Theo in his letter that
he had bought canvas, it is doubtful that he used it
for this work. Technical examination has shown that
Van Gogh used rather fine fabric, perhaps cotton,
at 22X25 threads per square centimetre, and that he
probably applied the ground himself. [3] He may have
used an ordinary scrap of fabric, something he did on
other occasions as we read from a letter to Theo of
around 4 September 1883: 'I had just bought a piece
of material to make canvases for my studies, and have
now given it to her to make shirts [...]' (384/319). The
'her' is Sien Hoornik, the woman with whom he was
still living at the time but whom he left a week later

when he moved to Drenthe. Perhaps he only gave her
part of the piece and used the remaining fabric for his
paintings.

Stylistically there are similarities with earlier
woodland studies - the simplicity of the motif,
the somewhat muddy, overlapping strokes in the
foreground - but there are other indications that place
the work closer to his Drenthe period. Van Gogh
applied the paint quite thickly, for example, but also
rather evenly. This way of working is reminiscent of
the dark, heavily painted studies from Drenthe.

Afterwards he changed the course of the path
in the foreground. In the x-ray the path winds to the
left between the trees, and the trunk of a second tree
is visible in the left foreground. He changed this to a
more peaceful composition by straightening the path.
The confident streaks with which the thin tree on the
right is painted on the dry background of the sky are
somewhat reminiscent of Jean-Baptiste-Camille Corot
(1796-1875), whom Van Gogh mentions frequently in
his letters.

Van Gogh had the painting sent to Nuenen
after completing his three-month campaign in
Drenthe in December 1883 and going to live with
his parents, but when he moved to Antwerp in 1885
he left it there in his studio. The work was placed
in one of the chests that had been packed with his
work from the Netherlands period and stored with
Mr A. Schrauwen in Breda, a carpenter and friend of
the Van Gogh family. After the Reverend Van Gogh
died his widow moved from the spacious parsonage
to a smaller home in 1886, and part of her effects
remained with Schrauwen. When she moved to
Leiden a couple of years later the stored property
was collected except for the chests full of paintings.
Perhaps they were intentionally left behind because
they were infested with wood-worm, but they may
also have been forgotten. In any case, a considerable
amount of Van Gogh's work was left with the Breda
carpenter, who in 1902 sold the majority for one
guilder to J.M. and J.C. Couvreur, brothers living in
Breda who dealt in second hand goods. According
to estimates they must have had more than 200
paintings and the same number of drawings by Van
Gogh in their possession. They deemed most of the
work worthless, however, and tore up many of the
drawings, yet they did manage to sell various paintings
and drawings to a rubbish warehouse and in the street
market. The rest of this 'Van Gogh collection', which
included Edge of a wood, was sold by the second-hand
merchants to their fellow-citizen and tailor, Cornelis
Mouwen. Besides, several paintings and drawings
came into the hands of Willerm van Bakel, lieutenant
at the Royal Military Academy in Breda. Mouwen and
Van Bakel both contacted the Rotterdam art dealer
Oldenzeel, who organised no less than three sales
exhibitions in 1903 at which the work was featured. [4]

In his earliest known inventory of the
collection of Mrs Kröller-Müller, dating about 1915,
H.P. Bremmer noted that Edge of a wood was 'bought
at a sale at Biesing in about 1909 for 110 guilders.' It
is more likely that the work was purchased in 1908,
since it is the first painting that Helene Kröller-Müller
acquired by Vincent van Gogh. At least so it would
appear from a letter written in 1928 to Dr L. Fischel

of the Kunsthalle in Karisruhe, in which the writer,
probably Mrs Kröller-Müller's secretary, explains how
the collection came into being. [5] Before this it was
always assumed that Four sunflowers gone to seed,
The sower (after Millet) and Basket of lemons and
bottle were the first purchases. [6]

1. De la Faille 1970 sees an affinity with F8a and places the
   work in September 1882; Hulsker 1977 and 1996 date it to
   August 1882.
2. See Van Tilborgh & Vellekoop 1999, pp. 19-20.
3. Technical examination, Kröller-Müller Museum, 17 July
   2002. 'Normal' canvas is usually of a somewhat finer weave:
   12-15x15-18 per cm2.
4. See: Stokvis 1926. See also Op de Coul 2003.
5. See p. 23, note 4.
6. Van Deventer 1956, pp. 34-36. The sunflowers were
   acquired in August 1908, and the other two works in
   March 1909. Despite the six-month interval between
   these purchases, Van Deventer calls these three works 'the
   first purchase', which were first admired as a group on 25
   March 1909 by Mr Kroller, who had been away on a trip.
   Probably he only saw The sower (after Millet) and Basket
   with lemons and a bottle on that occasion, paintings which
   indeed had just been acquired.

P. 153

Sod hut (Peat shed at night)

October 1883
pen in black ink (faded to brown in parts), grey wash,
on laid paper
22.1 x 28.8 cm
no watermark unsigned
F1097/JH418
KM 121.207

INSCRIPTIONS
verso, lower left: At: Vincent/Hidde Nijland (black ink).
upper left: No 2 [crossed Out] 3 (pencil).
KR 2 (blue chalk). lower right: invent. km 936 (pencil)

PROVENANCE
acquired by Hidde Nijland, Dordrecht, before 1904
purchased from Hidde Nijland by A.G. Kröller, The Hague,
July 1928
donated to the Kröller-Müller Foundation by A.G. Kröller,
December 1928

EXHIBITIONS
Dordrechc 1904, cat. no. ?.
The Hague 1918, cat. no. ?.
Amsterdam 1924, cat. no. 35.

The Hague 1928, unnumbered.
Hamburg 1929, cat. no. 40.
Amsterdam 1930, cat. no. 67.
Meppel 1948, no cat.
Milan 1952, cat. no. 30.
Saint Louis/Philadelphia! Toledo 1953-1954, cat. no. 24.
Nuremberg 1956, cat. no. 28.
Munich 1956, cat. no. 43.
Tokyo/Kyoto 1958, cat. no. 35.
Munich 1961, cat. no. 32.
Arnhem 1966, unnumbered.
New York/Chicago/Ottawa and other cities, 1973-1974, cat.
no. 44.
London/Newcastle-upon-Tyne 1974, cat. no. 32.
Amsterdam 1980-1981, cat. no. 103.
Rome 1988, cat. no. 2.

Sod hut (Peat shed at night), like the drawing
Ploughman, can be related to a letter sketch. In a letter
of around 22 October 1883, Van Gogh made two
scribbles of oil studies he was working on, Burning
weeds and Sod hut, but the latter has not survived. [1]
'Here are a couple of evening impressions,' he wrote to
Theo. 'I am still working on that weed burner, which
in a painted study is better as fat as tone is concerned
than what I did earlier, so that it more strongly
conveys the immensity of the plain and the gathering
twilight. And the fire, with a bit of smoke, is the only
point of light. I went again and again to look at it at
night, and one muddy evening after the rain I found
this hut, which was tremendously beautiful in its
natural setting' (399/355). The pen drawing Sod hut
(Peat shed at night) will also have come about in this
context. [2] The evening impression is easy to recognise
in both the letter sketch and the drawing. In the
drawing Van Gogh let the white of the paper show
through in the windows and did not use washes there
as he did in the rest of the drawing, making it seem as
if a light was burning inside. The hut looks like a peat
shed, the humble dwelling of those who worked in
the peat bogs. [3]

Van Gogh did not make a pencil
underdrawing. He worked directly with pen and
black ink on laid paper, with extensive use of washes.
Both grey and brown washes can be seen, but he
probably did not use two different kinds of ink to
produce them. The brown washes seem rather like
a discoloration of the grey and are related to the
amount of ink that was used: in the more densely
drawn passages the wash is much browner than in the
adjacent lightly drawn areas, which are dominated by
the grey. The path in front of the hut, which has no
ink lines running through it, has a rather uniform
light grey tint, while the sky, which is lightly hatched
and unevenly washed, is a somewhat darker grey with
hints of brown. More intensive variations can be seen
in the foreground. The ink lines themselves are solid
black in the saturated areas - at the end of a stripe, for
example - but the thinner ones have faded to brown. [4]
In the path Van Gogh scratched the paper open a bit
with a sharp instrument, probably to break through
the uniform tint. The very dark figure was added
later on (the lines of the hut run right through it) and
seems to be floating above the path, owing to the two
curled shadows beneath it that are separate from the
figure.

Van Gogh was always especially drawn to the
authentic, modest dwellings of the poor country
folk, which was bound up with his preference for
the untouched country life that had not yet been
spoiled by the advance of industrialisation. In Etten
he enjoyed being in the peasant hovels at 'het Heike',
and in Nuenen he entered the weavers' homes. In the
town of Les-Saintes-Maries-de-la-Mer on the southern
French coast his attention was also drawn to the old,
characteristic, whitewashed huts with their wavy reed
roofs. They even made him think of the sod huts of
Drenthe (622/494, C. 4 June 1888). [5]

1. The painted study of Burning weeds has been preserved
   (F20, private collection).
2. Although Van Gogh does not say in so many words that
   the sketch of the hut is based on an oil study, it seems
   likely that that is the case; otherwise he probably would
   have noted that the one sketch was based on a painting
   and the other on a drawing
3. Sod huts were scattered all over Drenthe and were built
   with local materials such as heath sods, branches, reeds,
   clay and blocks of peat, in combination with boards,
   beams and (sometimes) scones. No two huts were the
   same and some had a stone chimney. Although they
   served as temporary accommodations in the peat areas, in
   connection with the seasonal aspect of pear cutting, they
   were often inhabited for longer periods (Van Tilborgh
   & Vellekoop 1999, p.43; Dijk& Van der Sluis 2001, pp.
   109-111, 203-207, 222-224).
4. On the verso there are clear traces of ink corrosion,
   indicating that Van Gogh used an iron gall ink in his
   drawing.
5. No sooner had he arrived in Drenthe than he began
   drawing and painting sod huts in the area of Hoogeveen,
   during which a curious incident occurred that he thus
   described: 'As I sat painting that hut, two sheep and a
   goat came and started to graze on the roof of the house.
   The goat climbed up on to the ridge and looked down
   the chimney. The woman, who had heard something on
   the roof, rushed outside and flung her broom at the said
   goat, which leapt down like a chamois' (389/324, c. 15
   September 1883).

P.155

Head of a woman

early October 1883
pen and black ink (faded to brown in parts), wash,
on wove paper
21.1 x 13.5 cm
watermark: unclear unsigned
F1073/JH404
KM 128.378

INSCRIPTIONS
verso, on removed cardboard
backing, lower right: Vincent Vert.
Hidde Nijland (black ink). upper centre: KR 88A (blue chalk)

PROVENANCE
acquired by Hidde Nijland, Dordrecht, before 1895.
purchased from Hidde Nijland by A.G. Kröller, The Hague,
July 1928
donated to the Kröller-Müller Foundation by A.G. Kröller,
December 1928

EXHIBITIONS
The Hague 1895, no known cat.
Dordrecht 1897, no cat.
Dordrecht 1904, cat. no. 166 or 172.
The Hague 1918, cat. no. 52 or 53.
Amsterdam 1924, cat. no. 33.
The Hague 1928, unnumbered.
Hamburg 1929, cat. no. 110.
Amsterdam 1930, cat. no. 123.
New York/Philadelphia/Boston and other cities, 1935-1936,
car. no. 93.
's-Hertogenbosch/Breda 1950.
Nuremberg 1956, cat. no. 49.
Munich 1956, cat. no. 47.
Montreal/Ottawa/Winnipeg/Toronto 1960-1961, cat. no.
108.

In a letter of around 21 August 1883, Van
Gogh wrote to Theo at length for the first time about
his plan to go to Drenthe (381/316). Van Rappard
had been to visit him and had aroused his enthusiasm
in the Drenthe countryside, where he himself had
gone to work. One year earlier Van Rappard had
travelled around that region, whereupon Van Gogh
had written him, 'What you say about Drenthe
interests me. I do not know it at all from my own
observation, but I do through the things Mauve &
ter Meulen have brought from there, for example.
I imagine it is something like Noord-Brabant when
I was young - say, some 20 years ago' (257/R11, 13
Augustus 1882). [1] The thinly populated and rather
impoverished Drenthe enjoyed modest popularity
among landscape painters because of the unspoiled
landscape with its vast heaths and picturesque villages.
In 1882 Van Gogh had not yet begun thinking in
concrete terms about going there, but in the summer
of 1883 things were different.

Now that he had decided to devote himself
more to painting, which was more expensive, he
expected to be able to save money in Dren- the
because he thought living there would be quite a bit
cheaper than in The Hague. He also longed for the
countryside, as he told Theo: 'Actually I can also look
for cheaper accommodations here if need be, and I
think it is beautiful here, too. Even so -I would like
to be alone with nature for a time - minus the city'
(381/316). Van Rappard had especially recommended
the southeast corner of Drenthe, and, continued

Van Gogh in a buoyant mood, 'Once there, I think I might stay in that country of heath and moorland for good. More and more painters are going there to live, and perhaps, in time, a kind of colony of painters might spring up.' In the end he only stayed there three months, despite all his plans.[2]

On 11 September Van Gogh travelled by train to Hoogeveen. Three weeks later he went by canal barge down the Verlengde Hooge-veense Vaart to the twin village of Nieuw-Amsterdam/Veenoord, located in the moor-land south of Emmen.

During that long journey by boat he drew several studies, four of which he worked into a sheet with sketches that he sent to Theo in a letter shortly after his arrival and of which he wrote, 'I drew, amongst others, a little woman on the barge wearing crepe round her cap brooches because she was in mourning, and later a mother with a baby - the latter had a purple shawl round its head' (395/330, c.3 October 1883).

In all probability, Head of woman was also made during the journey on the canal barge. The woman seems to have been drawn from quite close up and barely fits on the sheet, as if the artist had been sitting right next to her and his space was rather limited. She has a robust head with a strong straight, almost classical nose, large empty black eyes and a wide mouth with drooping corners. Her dark cap, probably entirely shrouded in or made of crepe, indicates that she is in mourning, so perhaps she was travelling with the woman with the cap brooches. Van Gogh managed to capture in ink her dejected, melancholy expression, because of which the composition may have been less suitable to include in the sheer with sketches. This makes it the only drawing made on the barge that has survived, since the others are only known from the sketch sheet. The thin wove paper is quite probably the same type of stationery that the sketches were made on and has approximately the same dimensions.[3]

Van Gogh worked directly on the paper with ink without making a pencil underdrawing, and he probably drew rather quickly, with great precision in his shading. He worked more intensively on certain details so that the pen strokes damaged the paper (as in the woman's right eye). At the bottom of the composition a bit of wash has been carelessly applied.

Dijk and Van der Sluis believe the drawing would have been made shortly before Van Gogh's departure to Nieuw-Amsterdam in Hoogeveen.[4] A funeral took place there on 28 September of which Van Gogh was indeed a witness: 'today J saw a funeral on a barge that was very curious - six women wrapped in cloaks in the boat, which the men pulled along the canal through the heath' (394/329, 29 September 1883). If he had made the drawing a few days before the funeral, during the condolence period, as the author's claim, it is striking that he did not refer to it further here, especially because he was so unsuccessful in finding people to pose for him.[5] It also seems out of the question that the artist would have been admitted to a funeral at all, and if he had been, he certainly would have drawn on something other than stationery.[6] This makes it all the more likely that he came across the woman (who, incidentally, could very well have attended the funeral) a few days later on the barge, where he could have drawn her relatively undisturbed and in fact unsolicited.

---

1. At that time François Pieter ter Meulen (1843-1927)- like Mauve - was a well-known painter of landscapes and cattle, especially sheep.
2. Van Gogh played with the idea of taking Sien with him but finally decided to bring their relationship to a close (see letters 378/313 and 382/317 through 387/322, written between 18 August and so September 1883).
3. The paper is rather wrinkled and damaged, partly because Van Gogh pressed so hard with the pen, and it was pasted to a piece of cardboard backing at an early stage. Nijland's annotation was on this cardboard, which has now been removed. The paper was trimmed on all sides, but not much, which can be deduced from the fact that most of the drawn lines end just at the edges. Heenk 1995, p. 90, thinks the paper was from a sketchbook, but that does not seem likely.
4. Dijk & Van der Sluis 2001, pp. 123-527.
5. In the letters 391/326 through 394/329, written between c.22. and 27 September 1883, Van Gogh complained about his problems with models. In letter 393/328 he wrote that he had finally had a model, in the barn, but a pen sketch like Head of a woman cannot have been part of this work in view of the paper used.
6. Dijk & Van der Sluis 2001, pp. 125-126, identified the woman as a certain Roelofje Faken (1857-1900). Their conclusion is supported by little more factual information than that this woman lived in the same street as the deceased.

P. 157

Woman with wheelbarrow

late November - early
December 1883
pen in black ink (faded to brown in parts), on wove paper
21 x 13.1 cm
no watermark unsigned
F1106/JF1460
KM 114.728

INSCRIPTIONS
verso, centre: No 6 (crossed out] 15 (pencil) lower left: Port. Vincent/ Hidde Nijland (black ink faded to grey)

PROVENANCE
acquired by Hidde Nijland, Dordrecht, before 1904
purchased from Hidde Nijland by A.G. Kröller, The Hague, July 1928 donated to the Kröller-Müller Foundation by A.G. Kröller, December 1928

EXHIBITIONS
Dordrecht 1904, cat, no. 157 or 171.
The Hague 1918, cat. no. 46 or 55.
Amsterdam 1924, cat, no. 57.
The Hague 1928, unnumbered.
Hamburg 1929, cat, no. 102.
Amsterdam 1930, cat, no. 126.
's-Hertogenbosch/Breda 195.
Munich 1961, cat, no. 33.
Moscow/Leningrad 1971, cat, no. 41.

This pen drawing of a small female figure behind a wheelbarrow on a wet road, with the characteristic shape of a Drenthe sod hut or peat shed discernible in the background, has repeatedly been dated to Nuenen (February 1884).[1] Not only is the hut typical of Drenthe, however - in which Van Gogh once again got the design of the façade wrong with respect to the placement of the chimney at the front of the roof -, but the shape of the wheelbarrow is also characteristic of the type used in the peat areas for moving sods, a so-called 'slagkrooi'.[2] In a very similar way Van Gogh depicted a man behind a 'slagkrooi' in a letter sketch, standing in front of a high stack of pear sods (399/335, c. 22 October 1883). Also with respect to technique and style it is clear that the drawing was made in Drenthe. As in most of the Drenthe ink drawings (including the letter sketches) Van Gogh worked directly with pen on paper. Later on, in Nuenen, he would resume the practice of first making a pencil underdrawing of the motif in addition, the loose hatching style and the way the trees were scribbled in has a great deal in common with other Drenthe pen drawings.[3] The effect of a drizzly day or evening-note the reflection of the woman and her wheelbarrow on the wet road - is rendered extremely well.

This drawing was probably made quite late in Van Gogh's Drenthe period, since the type of paper - a stiff, fibrous, woody brown wove paper - is what he also used for a number of drawings in Nuenen in December 1883, where he moved on 5 December. These are sheets of various dimensions taken from two different sketch blocks: a large block of around 20.5 x 28.5 cm and a smaller block of 15.9 x 25.4 cm.[4] Woman with a dung fork in a snowy landscape, for instance, was drawn on a sheet taken from the large block. It is difficult to determine which of the two blocks was used for Woman with wheelbarrow because the sheet was trimmed on the left and along the bottom. Only the top and right sides are original, and on the right edge there is still glue residue with a strip of blue pigment, the remains of having been glued into the sketch block.[5] Van Gogh must have acquired this sketch block in Drenthe or had it sent to him - the letters provide no explanation. There are also no other known drawings of these dimensions from Drenthe that are made on this type of paper.

1. in De la Faille 1970, Hulsker 1977/1996 - who suggested the possibility of a letter sketch - and in the Kröller-Müller Museum's Van Gogh catalogues up to and including 1980, among other sources. De la Faille 1928, Vanbeselaere 1937, pp. 237, 410, Tralbaut 1959, p. 215, Heenk 1995, p.91, and Dijk & Van det Sluis 2001, pp. 245-247, all dated the sheer to Drenthe.
2. Heenk 1995, p.91..
3. See for example Sod hut (Peat shed at night), p. 227. On the verso of Woman with wheelbarrow, as well as on that sheet, there are slight traces of ink corrosion, indicating the use of an iron gall ink. On the corresponding places on the recto the black ink is duller.
4. Van Heugten 1997, P.31.
5. The Van Gogh Museum has eight drawings that were made on paper from both sketch blocks (Van Heugten 1997, pp. 30-44, cat. nos. 69-76]. Glue residue was found on most of the side edges of these sheets, sometimes containing red pigment and sometimes blue, which indicates that they were glued on all four sides and that the sides of the drawing block were probably marbled blue and red (Van Heugren 1997, p. 31). In addition to the scant remains of blue on the right side of Woman with wheelbarrow there are also a number of green spots visible on the upper left. Whether these had anything to do with gluing is not yet clear.

P. 159

The Reformed Church at Nuenen

January 1884
pencil, pen and black/brown ink, light brown wash, on wove paper
20.5 x 13 cm
no watermark unsigned
F1117/JH446
KM 125.492

INSCRIPTIONS
verso, upper right: Port. Vincent/Hidde Nijland (black ink)
upper centre: No 14 (pencil) lower right NO 82 (pencil)

PROVENANCE
acquired by Hidde Nijland, Dordrecht/The Hague, before 1918. purchased from Hidde Nijland by AG. Kröller, The Hague, July 1928. donated to the Kröller-Müller Foundation by A.G. Kröller, December 1928

EXHIBITIONS
The Hague 1918, cat. no. 51.
Amsterdam 1924, cat. no. 118.
The Hague 1928, unnumbered.
Hamburg 1929, cat. no. 125.
Amsterdam 1930, cat. no. 98.
New York/Philadelphia/Boston and other cities, 1935-1936, cat. no. 94.
Vienna 1958, cat. no. 38.
Tokyo/Kyoto 1958, cat. no. 66.
London 1962, cat. no. 36.
Belgrade 1966, cat. no. 37.
Moscow/Leningrad 1971, cat. no. 40.
Amsterdam 1980-1981, cat. no. 141.
Yokohama/Nagoya 1995-1996, cat. no. 30.

REMARKS
On the verso is a small pencil sketch of a seated man in a cap in the same pose as the small figure at the bottom of the recto.
Vincent van Gogh, Congregation leaving the Reformed church in Nuenen, January-February 1884 and Autumn 1885 (F25), oil on canvas, 41.3 x 32.1 cm. Van Gogh Museum, Amsterdam (Vincent van Gogh Foundation)

On 17 January 1884 Van Gogh's 64-year-old mother broke her thigh in an awkward place, close to the pelvis, as she stepped from the train at Helmond station.[1] She was driven back to Nuenen in a coach. She recovered well, but slowly. 'Taking her difficult situation into consideration, I am glad to say Mother's spirits are very even and content', Van Gogh wrote to his brother at some time around 24 January (429/355). In the same letter he also wrote that he had painted 'the little church with the hedge and the trees' for her, meaning the small church dating from 1824 on the Papenvoort in Nuenen, where Van Gogh's father preached to his small Reformed congregation. To give his brother an idea of what it looked like, he also made a small sketch of the painting in the letter. The drawing in the Kröller-Müller Museum is in all likelihood an initial sketch of the subject.[2]

Van Gogh first made a rudimentary pencil drawing, which he then worked up with dense hatching in pen and ink. The small church and the foreground were given a light wash. The pencil is still clearly visible at the top in the sky. The small figure in the foreground, a man with a spade over his shoulder, is not underdrawn or left open but was inserted by him afterwards. This male figure cannot be seen in the painting, but that is because Van Gogh later reworked the composition into a scene of a congregation leaving the church, at which time he painted over the man. He can be seen in an x-ray, but slightly further to the left, under the blocked window of the church. He is also under that window in the sketch in the letter to Theo.[3]

The idea of adding a man with a spade was undoubtedly inspired by a work by Jean-François Millet. In Millet's painting The Church at Gréville from 1871-1874, which Van Gogh had greatly admired since seeing it at the Musée du Luxembourg in Paris in 1875, a man with a spade over his shoulder is shown walking by a rustic, stone Norman village

church (36/29, 29 June 1875) [4]. When Van Gogh was preparing to study theology in Amsterdam he had heard the stanza 'De Kerke Gods staat op een rots' (The Church is built upon a rock) during the singing in church, which had instinctively caused him to think of Millet's painting (136/116, 9 December 1877). And he was again reminded of it when he saw the small church in Zweelo in Drenthe, although here 'instead of the small peasant with the spade there was a shepherd with a flock of sheep walking along the hedge', he wrote to Theo (407/340,2 November 1883). In his drawing of this church he also depicted the Shepherd with his sheep (F877, private collection). He saved the man with the spade for the painting for his mother, who would have to forgo her husband's church services for the time being. Although the small church in Nuenen will not have reminded Van Gogh directly of Millet's example it was, like the Church in Gréville, a house of God for the peasant community and that is something he will have wanted to stress with the addition of the figure.

During restoration in 1980 it emerged that at the bottom of the drawing a strip of just over four centimetres had been folded back and glued.[5] On this strip there is a small sketch of a seated male figure. It was originally believed that Van Gogh had drawn a blacksmith here, but further consideration shows that he had almost certainly drawn a person reeling yarn.[6] This can be concluded from the typical posture of the small man, for example, who displays striking similarities to the figure in the large drawing Man reeling yarn. The bobbin winder itself is not reproduced in the sketch, but with a bit of effort it is possible to make out a reel crown. The man is using his left hand to feed the yarn from the reel crown to a small bobbin or spindle on the winder, which he is moving with his right arm.

1. Letters 424/352 and 425/353, both 17 January 1884, 426/353, 18-19 January and 427/R34, 18-20 January.
2. Van Tilborgh & Vellekoop 1999, p. 61.
3. Ibid. for the x-ray photo. In both the painting and the drawing in the Kröller-Müller Museum the figure is in the centre of the composition. In the painting Van Gogh also placed the church more centrally in the picture plane so that the man was automatically positioned under the blocked window. In the letter sketch he is standing slightly to the left of centre.
4. Millet's painting is currently in the Musée d'Orsay in Paris.
5. Hoefsloot 1987, pp. 8-9.
6. Heenk 1994, p. 39, and 1995, p.112 believed it was a blacksmith.

P. 161

The old tower at Nuenen

February - March 1884
Oil on canvas
36 x 44.3 cm
F34/JH459
KM 105.115

SIGNATURE/INSCRIPTONS/LABELS Recto, lower left:
Vincent

PROVENANCE
Gift of the artist to Margot Begemann, Nuenen, 1884.
purchased by H. Kröller-Müller from
Mrs Begemann-Elbing, Nuenen, between 1921 and 1925

EXHIBITIONS
Basle/Bern 1927, no. 37.
Brussels 1927, no. 37.
Dusseldorf 1928, no. 102.
Karlsruhe 1928, no. 37.
Berlin 1928-1929, no. 38.
Hamburg 1929, no. 4.
Amsterdam 1930, no. 177.
Basle 1947, no. 4.
s-Hertogenbosch/Breda 1950, no cat.
Milan 195 no. 62.
Munich 1956, no. 73.
Warsaw 1962, no. 52.
Tel Aviv/Haifa 1962-1963, no. 53.
Moscow/Leningrad 1971, no. 26.
's-Hertogenbosch 1987-1988, no. 69.
Yokohama/Nagoya 1995-1996, no. 37

From December 1883 through May 1885, Van Gogh rendered the tower at Nuenen in paintings, drawings and watercolors: a total of 35 works. The tower had become so dilapidated over the years that in 1873 the town council considered having it demolished.' More than ten years later, in May 1885, the demolition was begun. The steeple was taken down and any salvageable materials were auctioned off. 'The old tower in the fields is being torn down,' Van Gogh told his brother on 11 May, the day of the first public sale of building scrap. 'There was an auction of lumber and slate and old iron, including the cross. I finished a watercolour of it in the style of the lumber sale, but better, I think,[2] (505/408) By 1886 this imposing structure had completely disappeared from the landscape.

The old tower at Nuenen is one of the first painted versions of the church tower. The dismantling has not yet begun, and the steeple is still standing. Van Gogh painted the structure under a heavily clouded sky. For the clouds he resorted to traditional landscape painting, particularly the work of Jacob van Ruisdael (1628-1682), John Constable (1776-1837) and Charles-Francois Daubigny (1817-1878). It would be a few years yet before he developed his own vision of the sky in all its dynamic colour. Although the tower is the most dominant feature of the composition, it is not the only motif to which Van Gogh draws the viewer's attention. Less prominent, but insistently present, is the walled cemetery whose wooden crosses project beyond the top of the wall.

Van Gogh had become fascinated by this cemetery when he still lived in The Hague. His father had moved to Nuenen in early August 1882 as minister of the Reformed congregation and would be buried there on 30 March 1885, and he and Theo had told him about it.[3] 'It really gave me great pleasure to see Pa & talk with him,' he told Theo on 25 September 1882 after his father's visit. 'I heard a great deal about Nuenen once again, and I can't get that cemetery with the old crosses out of my mind. I hope that in due time I will be able to come and paint it.' (270/234) The tower and the cemetery were not just a picturesque motif for Van Gogh. He attached personal significance to them as well. When he sent his last painted version to Paris in early June 1885, he wrote to Theo, 'I have omitted some details - what I wanted to express is how the ruins show that for ages the peasants have been laid to rest in the very fields in which they spend their lives rooting around. I wanted to express how perfectly simple death & burial are, as easy as the falling of an autumn leaf - nothing but a bit of dug-up earth, a small wooden cross. The surrounding fields - where the grass of the cemetery ends, beyond the wall, they form a final line against the horizon like a horizon of a sea. And now those ruins tell me how a faith and a religion rotted away - firmly established though they were - but how the life & death of the peasants remains the same forever, constantly budding and withering like the grass and flowers that thrive there in the cemetery earth.' (510/411) In this early version of February-March 1884, where so many 'details' can still be seen such as the location in the middle of the fields, the tumble-down wall and the mortuary set a slight distance from the tower, the ploughing peasant on the left represents the burrowing of the field.[4]

When Van Gogh had completed The old tower at Nuenen, he gave the painting to Margot Begemann (1841-1907), a 43-year-old woman living in Nune Ville, the house next to the parsonage. Van Gogh began a close friendship with her in January 1884. Johanna van Gogh-Bonger (1862-1925), in her introduction to the 1914 edition of her brother-in-law's letters, described Margot as 'much older than he and neither beautiful nor talented, but she had a lively mind and a sensitive heart. She and Vincent frequently visited the poor of the village and took many walks together, and from her side the friendship quickly turned into love.'[6] Their friendship in Nuenen was kept under critical surveillance by Margot's family. She even attempted suicide, and spent six months under the care of a doctor friend in Utrecht. Later in his life Van Gogh continued to entertain warm feelings for her. In Saint-Remy, when he conceived the plan to make small studies for his mother and sisters, he wrote to Wil, '[...] I should especially like Margot Begemann to have one of my pictures. But giving it to her through you would seem more discreet than sending it to her directly.' (814/w15, C. 20-22 October 1889). He may have forgotten that he had already given her two paintings and a few watercolours when he was still in Nuenen; the more likely explanation is that he wanted to remember her with a sample of his later style.[7]
RV

1. De Brouwer 2000, p, 17. The church building had fallen into ruin in around 1800 and was vacated in the early nineteenth century (ibid., pp. 10-16).
2. By 'the lumber sale' Van Gogh is referring to the watercolour Lumber sale of January 1884 (F1113).
3. Theo had already told his brother in mid-August about the picturesque cemetery in their parents' new place of residence. Van Gogh answered him in at least one letter, dated 19 August 1882: 'What you tell me about their new surroundings interests me enormously. I would be only too glad to try my hand at painting such an old church & cemetery, with its sandy graves and old wooden crosses. I hope I have the chance some day.' (259/226)
4. De Brouwer (2000, p. 49) identified this peasant as Jacobus van Bakel, owner of the cadastral plot section E, no 596, which was adjacent to the cemetery.
5. Van Crimpen 1987, p. 85.
6. Van Gogh-Bonger 1990, p. 20.
7. Besides The old tower at Nuenen, Margot Begemann also had in her possession the painting Cottage with trees (F92) and the watercolours Scheveningen woman sewing, Bleaching ground, and Scheveningen woman (F869, F946r and F946v respectively).

P. 163

Head of a woman

November 1884 - January 1885
Oil on canvas
42.5 x 33.1 cm
F154/JH608
KM 105.591

PROVENANCE
A. Aurier coll., Pads. S.Williame - Aurier coll., Chateauroux,
5 October 1892.
purchased by H.P. Bremmer from J.Williame,
Chateauroux,June 1914. purchased by H. Kroller -Muller
from H.P. Bremmer,The Hague, 11 April 1917 (f 800)

EXHIBITIONS
Basle/Bern 1927, no. 41.
Brussels 1927, no. 41.
Dusseldorf 1928, no. 107.
Karlsruhe 1928, no. 42.
Berlin 1928-1929, no. 58.
Hamburg 1929, no. 8.
Amsterdam 1930, no. 187.
Milan 1952, no. 49.
Munich 1956, no. 86.
Vienna 1958, no. 63.
ToKyo/Kyoto 1958, no. 73.
Belgrade 1966, no. 48e.
London 1992, no. 25.
Amsterdam 1993, no. 16.
YoKohama/Nagoya 1995-1996, no. 39.

Working with broad brushstrokes Van Gogh
rendered this head of a woman. He painted wet-in-wet
on a cream-coloured ground, producing an opaque
surface with a few impasto areas (such as the lips and
the cap) that now are flattened - presumably through
transport. Considering Van Gogh's style, the work is
even more striking for being smoothly painted.

The woman is wearing a green shawl rendered
with rough brushstrokes. The various greens of the
background and the shawl contrast with the cap's
warm earth tones. The woman's face has been only
partially completed. Her right eye is barely visible, a
curve in the paint can only be detected in relief, and a
highlight has been placed in the left eye that gives her
face a rather deathly, staring expression. For all this he
managed to depict a head with characteristic features.

Van Gogh made a sketch of this painting,
Head of a woman (F1177), which is dated December
1884-January 1885, thus providing a clue for the
dating of the painting: November 1884-January 1885,[1]
Initially the measurements of the canvas were larger. It
has been shortened on all sides, so the original paint
layer now runs over the edges of the stretched canvas.

1. See Van Heugten 1997, p. 131, With this dating the work
   may have been part of shipment 5 or 6 to Theo on 31
   March and or 6 June 1885 respectively; see Van Tilborgh &
   Vellekoop 1999, appendix p. 238.

P. 165

Sketches

December 1884-January 1885
pen and brush in black ink on laid paper
17 x 10.8 cm
watermark: [roar of arms with
crowned lion rampant with sabre
and legend CONCORDIA RES]
PARVAE CRES[CUNT]
unsigned
F1151/JH576 KM 114.886

INSCRIPTIONS
verso, lower right: No 85 (pencil) [5 is somewhat unclear].
on removed cardboard barking: Afb. 6 (pencil).
6(pencil)

PROVENANCE
acquired by Hidde Nijland, Dordrecht, before 1904
purchased from Hidde Nijland by A.G. Kröller, The Hague,
July 1928 - donated to the Kröller-Müller Foundation by A.G.
Kröller, December 1928

EXHIBITIONS
Dordrecht 1904, cat. no. 168 (d) '
The Hague 1918, cat. no. 39 (d).
Amsterdam 1924, cat. no. 111 (d).
The Hague 1928, unnumbered.
Hamburg 1929, cat. no. 131.
Amsterdam 1930, cat. no. 124c.
Nuremberg 1956, cat. no. 49.
Munich 1956, cat. no. 49.
Tokyo/Kyoto 1958, cat. no. 6o.
Munich 1961, cat. no. 39.
Moscow/Leningrad 1971, cat. no. 44.

In Van Gogh's oeuvre of Brabant drawings
there are various sheets with several separate sketches
on a single sheet. The Kröller-Müller Museum has
chalk drawings with various studies of figures and
situations connected with the public sale of scrap
materials from the old tower in May 1885, and
other studies of several figures on a sheet. In Van
Gogh's surviving sketchbook from Nuenen there are
sometimes two scribbles on a single page as well, but
the three (or actually four) small drawings on the
sheet discussed here, done entirely in pen and ink

and all slightly in each other's way are fairly unique
in his oeuvre. Van Gogh will undoubtedly have made
many more such pen jottings that have not survived.

The sheet with sketches was once slightly larger
and was tightly trimmed on both the right and left, as
can clearly be seen in the washed background on the
right and the small lines at the lower left, both crudely
cropped. The top and bottom edges have been torn
off. However, the fragment of the watermark shows
that the sheet was once taken from a large sheet of laid
paper measuring approximately 42 x 67 cm. The date
given for the sketches - December 1884/January 1885
-is primarily based on the larger sketch of the woman's
head, since Van Gogh made a series of eleven small
sketches after painted studies in December 1884 and
January 1885 to give Theo an impression of his recent
work, and the same woman can be seen in two of
them (both in the Van Gogh Museum, Amsterdam),
in one against a darker background (F1150r) and in
the other against a light background (no F-number,
JH589). The latter is drawn on a similar but slightly
smaller piece of laid paper with a fragment of the
same watermark.[1] Whether the head on the sheet of
sketches discussed here was also based on a painting
is difficult to say. It differs in one small but distinctive
aspect from the other two heads. In all three works
the woman has stiff, wiry hair that curls into her
neck, but only in the two small drawings in the Van
Gogh Museum does she have a large curl under her
ear. In addition, here ink has run into her eye.

The tiny head at the top seems to sprout from
the brain of the head beneath it in a curious fashion,
but it was drawn earlier. The larger sketch is probably
an experiment in executing pen strokes. The model
is apparently the same woman with the wiry hair, but
this time Van Gogh drew her head almost entirely
with diagonal hatches. This method of working,
which is not found elsewhere in his oeuvre, is to a
certain extent similar to two pencil drawings from his
Paris period.

Finally, at the bottom of the sheet of sketches
Van Gogh drew a man seen from the back walking
along a road and carrying a piece of wood over his
shoulder. With his right arm he is grasping an axe,
the blade of which is just visible. In the background
there is a large farm. Van Gogh framed the motif
with several lines, perhaps to see which composition
he preferred before finally working it out on a larger
scale. No such work has survived however.[2]

The pen and ink sketch Head of a woman
is a facile study in which Van Gogh also applied a
wash at the bottom with a brush. He rendered her
profile and bonnet with very broad contours and
in doing so pressed so hard with the pen that he
pushed the two points of the nib apart, causing two
sharp indentations on either side of the contour line
of the bonnet. The area of this sheet that is drawn
on is approximately 14 x 9 cm and is located in the
upper left corner of the thin, fibrous and originally
fairly white wove paper. In that corner, however, the
paper has faded badly to brown. The rest of the sheet
is significantly less discoloured because it was once
covered by a frame which placed the head at the
centre of the picture plane.

1. Ibid., cat. nos. 108-118. Of the two examples of these pen drawings only the painted study of the head against a darker background has survived (F132, privately owned).
2. See for example the small chalk drawing of a man carrying a bundle of twigs (F1297v, Van Gogh Museum, Amsterdam), which was framed in a similar way.

Van Gogh intended the work explicitly as a study of the chiaroscuro effects.

Van Gogh preferred the Nuenen peasants and weavers to pose for him wearing their everyday clothes: 'The people here seem instinctively to wear to the most beautiful blue I've ever seen. It's a rough kind of linen they weave, the warp is black and the weft blue, so that a kind of black and blue stripe is created. When that fades and discolours in the rain and wind, it becomes an unbelievably quiet and delicate shade that heightens the flesh tones. It is blue enough to activate all the colours with hidden elements of orange and bleached out enough not to clash.' (487/394, February 1885)

P. 170

Woman peeling potatoes at the fireside

March-April 1885
black chalk on watercolour paper
58.4 x 83.2 cm
no watermark unsigned
F1211 /JH791 KM 113.109

INSCRIPTIONS
verso, on removed cardboard
backing, upper left: 1 a (material
unclear) .F1211 (material unclear)
centre left: boven de deur (pencil?)
centre tight: 59,5 x 83,5 (materialunclear).
lower left: Cat '53 125
[125 underlined] (material unclear)

PROVENANCE
A.C. van Gogh-Carbentus, Nuenen/Breda, 1885-1889.
A. Schrauwen, Breda, 1889-1902'
J.C. Couvreur, Breda, 1902' C. Mouwen and W. van
Bakel, Breda, 1902-1903 'Oldenzeel, art dealer, Rotterdam,
19o3(b), lot 65: Vrouw bij het vuur. A. Muller-Abeken coll.,
Scheveningen.
purchased by H. Kröller-Muller at sale Amsterdam (Frederik
Muller & Cie), 19 May 1920 (Mrs A. Müller-Abeken
collection, Scheveningen), lot 88: Paysanne pelant des
pommes de terre(725 guilders)

EXHIBITIONS
Rotterdam 1903(b), cat. no. 65.
Basel/Bern/Brussels 1927, cat. no. 74.
Düsseldorf 1928, cat. no. 140.
Karlsruhe 1928, cat. no. 75.
Berlin 1928-1929, cat. no. 64.
Hamburg 1929, cat. no. 35.
Amsterdam 1930, cat. no. 117.
's-Hertogenbosch/ Breda 1950.
Vienna 1958, cat. no. 54.
Montreal/Ottawa/ Winnipeg/Toronto 1960-1961, cat. no.
sot.
Warsaw 1962, cat. no. 36.
Tel Aviv/Haifa 1962-1963, cat. no. 36.

P. 167

Head of a woman

March - April 1885
Oil on canvas
39.7 x 25.5 cm
F150/JH650
KM 110.977

SIGNATURE/INSCRIPTIONS/LABELS -

PROVENANCE
L.C. Enthoven coll.,Voorburg . purchased by H. Kröller-
Müller at Enthoven sale, Amsterdam (Frederik Muller), 18
May1920, lot 227: Tete de jeune paysanne (f 1,000)

EXHIBITIONS
Basle/Bern 1927, no. 58.
Brussels 1927, no. 58.
Dusseldorf 1928, no. 124.
Karlsruhe 1928, no. 59.
Berlin 1928-1929, no. 52.
Hamburg 1929, no. 25.
Amsterdam 1930, no. 174.

In this Head of a woman the plasticity and expressivity of the face have been entirely subordinated to an exploration of the backlit effect: the emphasis lies on the shape of the head, which stands out sharply against the background. The blue-green cap blends into the figure's dark hair. The fine line forming the boundary between the hair falling over her forehead and the cap has been drawn in one stroke. The background is made up of various tones of greenish blue, which shade off into a darker area beside the woman's right shoulder. This sketchily executed transition from light to dark indicates that

P. 169

Woman sewing

March-April 1885
black chalk on laid paper
41.3 x 25.3 cm
watermark: [ED & cie (in cartouche)], PL BAS
signed lower left (by the artist): Vincent (black chalk)
F1203 /JH710
KM 112.189

INSCRIPTIONS
verso, lower right: No 11 (pencil). Vincent v. Gogh / Verz:
Hidde Nijland (black ink) ' upper left: KR 35
(blue chalk)

PROVENANCE
acquired by Hidde Nijland,
Dordrecht, before 1904.
purchased from Hidde Nijland
by A.G. Kröller, The Hague,
July 1928 donated to the Kröller-Müller Foundation
by A.G. Kröller, December 1928

EXHIBITIONS
Dordrecht 1904, cat. no. ?.
The Hague 1918, cat. no. ?.
Amsterdam 1924, cat. no. 105.
The Hague 1928, unnumbered.
Hamburg 1929, cat. no. 69.
Amsterdam 1930, cat. no. 116.
Munich 1961, cat. no. 40.

P. 171

Woman sewing

March-April 1885
black chalk on laid paper
29.2 x 25.8 cm
watermark: [ED & Cie (in cartouche)], PL BAS
signed lower right (nor by the
artist): Vincent (black chalk)
F1206 / JH705
KM 127.514

INSCRIPTIONS
verso, lower left: Hidde Nijland /
Port: Vincent (faded black ink).
lower centre: No 19 [crossed out]
11 (pencil) upper left: KR 21
(blue chalk) upper left: 68 br
[rest illegible] (blue chalk)

PROVENANCE
acquired by Hidde Nijland, Dordrecht, before 1904
purchased from Hidde Nijland by A.G. Kröller, The Hague,
July 1928 . donated to the Kröller-Müller Foundation by A.G.
Kröller, December 1928

EXHIBITIONS
Dordrecht 1904, cat. no. ?.
The Hague 1918, cat. no. ?.
Amsterdam 1924, cat. no. 44.
The Hague 1928, unnumbered.
Hamburg 1929, cat. no. 58.
Amsterdam 1930, cat. no. 115.
's-Hertogenbosch/Breda 1950.
Tokyo/Kyoto 1958, cat. no. 64.
are scarcely visible. In the drawings the women
who are sewing are not depicted in this direct
backlight but are lighted more from the side.

NOTES
1 There are similar sheets with seamstresses at the window in
the same room in the Van Gogh Museum (see Van Heugten
1997, pp. 164-175).
2 The same cornet in the interior can be seen in the small
painted study woman sewing (F157, private collection).

In February 1885 Theo announced that he
would try to get a painting by his brother placed
at the upcoming Salon, at least if he had anything
suitable. Vincent was very grateful for this, but had
nothing ready and wrote: 'Had I known it 6 weeks
ago, I would have tried to send you something for
this purpose. Now I have nothing that I would care

to send in. Lately I have, as you know, painted heads
almost exclusively, and they are studies in the real
sense of the word - that is to say, they are meant for
the studio' (488/395, c. 1 March 1885). However, it
did set him to thinking of a large composition, which
would ultimately result in April in The Potato Eaters.

In the meantime, apart from painted and
sketched studies of heads Van Gogh was also working
on interiors with working women in order to improve
his mastery of light in the small rooms where his
models lived. Four of the group of drawings of
working women in an interior assembled here can be
linked to this: the first three Woman sewing studies
and the large drawing Woman peeling potatoes at the
fireside.

Although Van Gogh did not mention any of
these drawings in his correspondence, in March 1885
he did refer to painted studies of figures indoors in
which he was mainly concerned with backlighting
effects: 'I am thinking about a couple of larger, more
elaborate things [...] namely figures against the light
of a window. I have studies of heads for them, against
the light as well as turned towards the light, and I
have worked several times already on the complete
figure: seamstress reeling yarn or a figure peeling
potatoes. Full face and in profile. It is a difficult
effect, so whether I'll manage it I don't know' (489/396
March 1885). In the drawings the women who are
sewing are not depicted in this direct backlight but
are lighted more from the side.

P. 172

Man with ladder, a group of figures and cemetery with wooden crosses

1885
black chalk on laid paper
34.5 x 20.5 cm
watermark: coat of arms with
crowned lion rampant with
sabre and legend CONCOROIA
RES PARS/AR CRESCUNT
unsigned
F1336r / JH767 KM 118.569 VERSO

INSCRIPTIONS
verso, lower left: V.v.G: Vera: Hidde
Nijland (black ink). lower right:
No 53 dubbel (pencil). 13 (blue chalk)

PROVENANCE
acquired by Hidde Nijland,
Dordrecht, before 1904
purchased from Hidde Nijland
by A.G. Kröller, The Hague,
July 1928. donated to the
Kröller-Müller Foundation
by A.G. Kröller, December 1928

EXHIBITIONS
Dordrecht 1904, cat. no. 150 (c).
The Hague 1918, cat. no.?
Amsterdam 1924, cat. no. 80.
The Hague 1928, unnumbered.
Hamburg 1929, eat. no. 106.
Amsterdam 1930, cat. no. 72.
New York/Chicago 1949-1950,
cat. no. 44 Milan 1952, cat. no. 42.
Nuremberg 1956, cat. no. 44.
Munich 1956, cat. no. 51.
Vienna 1958, cat. no. 41.
Moscow/ Leningrad 1971, cat. no. 47.
's-Hertogenbosch 1987-1988, cat. no. 44.
Otterlo 1990, cat. no. 100.
Tokyo/Fukuoka 1999-2000, cat. no. 42.

P. 173

Sale of building scrap (studies)

May 1885 black chalk on laid paper
35 x 21 cm
watermark: VdL
unsigned F112r / JH768
KM 124.979 RECTO

INSCRIPTIONS
verso, lower right: No 32 dubbel (pencil). Vincent Vera: HN.
(black ink)

PROVENANCE
acquired by Hidde Nijland, Dordrecht, before 1904.
purchased from Hidde Nijland by A.G. Kröller, The Hague,
July 1928 . donated to the Kröller-Müller Foundation by A.G.

Kröller, December 1928

'These last few days I have been working hard on drawings', Van Gogh wrote to Theo around 11 May 1885. 'They are busy pulling down the old tower in the fields. So there was a public sale of lumber and slates and old iron, including the cross. I have finished a watercolor of it, in the style of the lumber auction, but better I think' (505/408). Not only has the watercolor survived but three sheets drawn on both sides can also be linked directly to that auction.[1]

The auction took place on 11 May and involved the sale of materials from the demolition of the spire of the old tower. From a surviving report it is known that Mayor Jan van Hombergh was in charge of the sale and was assisted by constable Johannes Biemans and carpenter Theodorus de Vries.[2] The constable can be seen twice on the recto of the first sheet of studies: in the group sketch beneath he stands out less prominently above the crowd than in the watercolor, and in the upper right he is looking to the left. From this it can be concluded that Van Gogh was viewing the situation from the other side. The sketch of the back of a head between the two group scenes, on a thin neck and with a curious collar and cap. At the extreme left of the group there is a man with a hat and a piece of paper in his hands. This is apparently not the mayor but perhaps the carpenter De Vries.

At the bottom on the verso of the second sheet of studies Van Gogh drew part of the old churchyard with some scrap materials in the foreground. A man with a ladder over his shoulder figures prominently in this sheet. Thanks to the surviving report we know who it is. Francis van Engeland paid 20 cents for the ladder. The carpenter De Vries then bought the door for 55 cents and the auction was over. Five more auctions were held between 17 July 1885 and 12 February 1886, but as far as is known Van Gogh did not record them.[3]

1. Like the watercolor, the third sheet (F123ir/v) is in the Van Gogh Museum (Van Heugren 1997, pp. 185-191).
2. Published in De Brouwer 2000, pp. 75 and 78-79.
3. De Brouwer 2000, p. 79.

P. 175

Loom with weaver

June -July 1884
Oil on canvas
61 x 93 cm
F37/JH501
KM 105.976

SIGNATURE/INSCRIPTIONS/LABELS -

In late June 1884, Van Gogh was working on two paintings of weavers, including this Loom with weaver. In a letter to Theo he described it as 'an interior with three little windows looking out on the yellowish green, which contrasts with the blue of the fabric being woven on the loom and the smock of the weaver, which is yet another blue.' (454/372, early July 1884) This description shows the extent to which Van Gogh looked at the weavers with a painter's eye. What was interesting about the dusky workshop for him at this time was the 'Rembrandtesque' chiaroscuro. The weaver's clothing, the woven cloth on the loom and the landscape in the background constitute an alternating spectacle of varying tints of blue and green. The 'wooden monster', as Van Gogh called the loom, reveals another rich diversity of browns and blacks. The contrast between indoors and outdoors is reinforced here by the use of light and color.

In this painting, Van Gogh depicts the weaver at his loom in a typical weaver's attitude: left arm outstretched in order to beat the weft in with the batten and the right arm raised slightly to pass the shuttle back and forth with the picking band, Van Gogh varied little in his rendering of weavers because he still had difficulty painting figures, and probably because of his financial problems as well - he had to be sparing with his paint and couldn't afford models for prolonged figure studies. The result is a repeated depiction of weavers in similar physical attitudes.

Loom with weaver dates from late June/early July 1884, making it one of the later examples of Van Gogh's weaver paintings. His interest in these craftsmen had resulted in an important group of works. When he began work on the weavers at the end of 1883 and the beginning of 1884, he still had little experience in painting with oils. With constant practice he clearly became increasingly familiar with the technical possibilities of the medium. He experimented with differences in color and tone, and he managed to render convincingly the complex three-dimensional looms on the two-dimensional canvas.

The motif of the weaver occupied him for a long time, but after having fully abandoned himself to the subject in Nuenen during the first half of 1884 he rather abruptly let it go. It was the height of summer when he quickly shifted his interest from the craft of the home weaver to the life and work of the peasant.

1. Op de Coul 2003, p. 117.

the paint itself, rendering the stubble with rather powerful strokes. By contrast, he painted the slender stalks of the sheaves with very fine strokes using a thin brush. He often finished off details with a narrow brush, as in his birds' nests. The scene is painted on a light ground in which Van Gogh, contrary to his usual practice, first painted the sky and then rendered the sheaves in the blank space.

Sheaves of wheat occupies a special place in Van Gogh's oeuvre because of its subject: a single bundle of sheaves. The motif of the sheaves of wheat also appears in various drawings, but then in a whole row or even several rows in a field, often with a figure who is binding up the sheaves.' Later on, in Arles and Saint-Remy, Van Gogh continued to be inspired by the golden wheat; he painted dozens of works with fields or sheaves of wheat as their motif. Bundled sheaves sometimes figured in these works as well, but more as elements in. the landscape and not placed so emphatically in the foreground as they are here.

---

1. Examples include F 1319v, F1321, and F1339-1342·

EXHIBITIONS
Rotterdam 1903 (c), no. 5.
Basle/Bern 1927. no. 61.
Brussels 1927, no. 61.
Dusseldorf 1928, no. 127.
Karlsruhe 1928, no. 62.
Berlin 1928-1929, no. 57.
Hamburg 1929, no. 28.
Amsterdam 1930, no. 168.
New York 1940, no. 1.
Baltimore/Worchester 1942, no. 1.
Indianapolis/Cincinnati/Ottawa/Fortwayne 1943-1944, no. 1.
Basle 1947, no. 14.
Milan 1952, no. 54.
Vienna 1958, no. 67.
Warsaw 1962, no. 47.
Tel Aviv/Haifa 1962-1963, no. 48.

Van Gogh shows the peasant in this painting as he liked to see him: toiling and sweating, living his hard peasant existence. The peasant digging is a motif he had worked out in drawings earlier in Etten and The Hague, and it became one of the main subjects of his Dutch period, along with the sewer and the weaver. But unlike these others, Van Gogh did not locate this peasant in his country surroundings. Here Van Gogh concentrated mainly on reproducing the figure itself - of which he had also made a sketch - and his clothing. In February he told Theo how lovely he thought the simple peasant clothing could be: 'The peasant figures here are blue as a rule. That blue, placed in the ripe wheat or against the withered leaves of a beech hedge - so that the faded nuances of darker and lighter blue are brought back to life & made to speak by contrast with the gold tones or the reddish-brown - is very beautiful and has struck me here from the very first.' (487/394) The light on the shoulder causes the blue-green of the rough overalls fabric to contrast with the dark red flesh tone of the peasant's face and hand.

Van Gogh was aware that he was not rendering the human figure according to the system of anatomical proportions taught at the academy. He defended his rendering in a long letter to Theo in July 1885 (522/418), contrasting himself with academic painters such as Alexandre Cabanel and Gustave Jacquet. Their figures 'will always convey the limbs and the structure of the body in the same way: charming perhaps, accurate in proportion and anatomical detail.' But that was not what Van Gogh was after, and he felt him-self supported by painters like Jozef Israels, Honore Daumier and Leon Lhermitte: 'when Israels or, for instance, Daumier or Lhermitte draws a figure, you are much more able to feel the form of the body, and yet - and this is precisely why I'm mentioning Daumier - the proportions will be almost arbitrary, the anatomy and structure anything but good in the eyes of the academicians. But it will live.' And he urged his brother to challenge the painter Charles Serret., who had voiced his criticism of the figures in The potato eaters to Theo and from whom Van Gogh expected more of the same: 'Tell Serret that I should be in despair if my figures were good, tell him that I don't want them to be academically correct, that if one were to photograph a peasant digging,

P. 177

Sheaves of wheat

July - August 188
Oil on canvas
40.2 x 30 cm
F19/JH914
KM 102.692

SIGNATURE/INSCRIPTIONS/LABELS -

PROVENANCE
L.C. Enthoven coli., Voorburg. purchased by H. Kroller-Muller at Enthoven sale, Amsterdam (Frederik Muller), 18 May 1920, lot 207: Les gerbes de ble (f 675)

EXHIBITIONS
Basle/Bern 1927, no. 46.
Brussels 1927, no. 46.
Dusseldorf 1928, no. 112.
Karlsruhe 1928, no. 147
Berlin 1928-1929, no. 59.
Hamburg 1929, no. 13.
Amsterdam 1930, no. 180.
's-Hertogen-bosch/Breda 1950, no cat.
Tokyo/Kyoto 1958, no. 80·
Montreal/Ottawa/Winnipeg/Toronto 1960-1961, no. 6.
's-Hertogenbosch 1987-1988, no. 57.

July has traditionally been the month for mowing and gathering wheat and binding it up into sheaves. So it was that this painting of five or six sheaves of wheat, inclining towards each other, came about in the summer of 1885.

The composition is divided in different planes. In the foreground Van Gogh painted a short stubble field: the freshly mown wheat. In the background is the still unmown part of the wheat field, rimmed in the distance by the edge of a forest with the sky above. These are set off by the bundle of sheaves, contrasting the planes as a distinctly vertical element. Van Gogh seems to have been mainly intent on practising texture and touch. He modelled the stubble field in

P. 179

Digger

August 1885
Oil on canvas
45.4 x 31.4Cm
F166/JH850
KM 102.175

SIGNATURE/INSCRIPTIONS/LABELS -

PROVENANCE
A.C. van Gogh-Carbentus, Nuenen/Breda, November 1885/April 1886. A. Schrauwen,Breda, 1886. J.C. and J.M. Couvreur, Breda. W. van Bakel and C, Mouwen, Breda, 1902. Oldenzeel, art dealer, Rotterdam, 1903. L.C. Enthoven coll,, Voorburg. purchased by H. Kroller-Muller at Enthoven sale, Amsterdam (Frederik Muller), 18 May 1920, lot 226: Paysan bechant

he would certainly not be digging. Tell him I think Michelangelo's figures are splendid, although the legs are too long, the hips and buttocks too broad. Tell him that this is why to my mind Millet and Lhermitte are the true artists, because they do not paint things as they are, examined in a dry analytical way, but as they - Millet, Lhermitte, Michelangelo - feel them. Tell him that my great desire is to learn how to produce such inaccuracies, such aberrations, reworkings, transformations of reality, so that it might turn it into, well - a lie, if you like - but truer than the literal truth.'

He wanted to reproduce 'the peasant figure in action': 'the peasant must be a peasant, the digging figure must dig.' That, he felt, was what was distinctive about reproducing a figure and was 'essentially modern, the heart of modern art itself, that which neither the Greeks, nor the Renaissance, nor the old Dutch school have done. {...} The peasant's and workman's figure was begun as a "genre" ? but nowadays, with Millet in the lead as perennial master, it has become the very essence of modern art and will remain so.'

---

1 Op de Coul 2003, p. 115.

P. 181

Peasant women digging up potatoes

August 1885
Oil on canvas
31.5 x 42.5 cm
F97/JH876
KM 106.520

SIGNATURE/INSCRIPTONS/LABELS -

PROVENANCE
A.C. van Gogh-Carbentus, Nuenen/Breda, November 1885/April 1886 A. Schrauwen, Breda, 1886 J.C. and J.M. Couvreur, Breda W. van Bakel and C. Mouwen, Breda, 1902. Oldenzeel, art dealer, Rotterdam, 1903 . J. Smit Coll., Kinderdijk, 1905. purchased by H. Kröller-Müller at J. Smit sale, Amsterdam (Mak) 10 February 1919, lot 32 (f 3,500)

EXHIBITIONS
Rotterdam 1903 (c), no. 15.
Basle/Bern 1927, no. 77.
Brussels 1927, no. 77.
Dusseldorf 1928, no. 103.
Karlsruhe 1928, no. 38.
Berlin 1928-1929, no. 71.
Hamburg 1929, no. 35.

Amsterdam 1930, no. 173.
Liege/Brussels/Mons 1946-1947, no. 32.
Paris 1947, no. 32.
Geneva 1947, no. 32.
Basle 1947, no. 20.
Milan 1952, no. 52.
The Hague 1953, no. 37.
Otterlo/Amsterdam 1953, no. 23.
Munich 1956, no. 89.
Montreal/Ottawa/Winnipeg/Toronto 1960 -1961, no. 7.
's-Hertogenbosch 1987-1988, no. 62.
Yokohama/Nagoya 1995-1996, no. 41.

After his many studies of heads and figures made in peasant interiors and resulting in The potato eaters (F82), Van Gogh spent a great deal of time outdoors during the summer and autumn of 1885 in order to sketch the peasants working on the land. A frequently recurring motif was digging. Mrs Kröller-Müller also owned several works based on this theme, including this one featuring two peasant women digging up potatoes. It is probably based on an earlier sketch of two women digging that is part of the Kröller-Müller Museum collection as well.

Van Gogh had undoubtedly borrowed the motif from Jean-Francois Millet, As early as October 1880 he copied Millet's famous Digging farmers (1856) from a borrowed photograph.[2] He had also read a particular passage in Alfred Sensiers's biography La vie et l'oeuvre de J.- F. Millet, written in 1881, which was part of a letter from the admired painter: 'Dans les endroits laboures, quoique, quelquefois, dans certains pays peu labourables, vous voyez des figures bechant, piochant. Vous en voyez une de temps en temps se redressant les reins, comme on dit, et essuyant le front avec le revers de la main. "Tu mangera ton pain a la sueur de ton front".' (In the ploughed fields, but sometimes also in areas that scarcely yield to the plough, you see figures digging with spades or pickaxes. One of them will straighten up now and then and wipe his forehead with the back of his hand, "In the sweat of thy face shalt thou eat bread.")[3] The drudgery of human digging evoked specific religious associations for Millet, in this case from Genesis 3:19: 'In the sweat of thy face shalt thou eat bread, till thou return unto the ground......' Digging evoked the same association for Van Gogh.[4]

In Two peasant women digging up potatoes Van Gogh did his best to depict two figures in action. 'From my sketch you will see that I go to quite a bit of trouble to get action - work - into my little figures, to show them doing something,' he told Anthon van Rappard, and to demonstrate what he meant he illustrated his letter with a small drawing of this scene. Having his figures bend over was a way of suggesting 'action' that Van Rappard also utilized: 'I think it's good that at least one figure in your composition is already bending over - a great many vertical lines in the composition might make it more difficult to express the fact that work is actually in progress.' (529/R57, second half of August 1885) For Van Gogh the trick was having the digger actually dig.

---

1. Op de Coul 2003, p. 115.
2. I have drawn The Diggers by Millet, from a photograph by Braun that I found at Schmidt's and that he lent

me, together with that of The Evening Angelus, 'Van Gogh wrote to Theo on 1 November 1880 from Brussels (159/138). The drawing after Millet's Angelus (F834) is also part of the Kröller-Müller Museum collection.
3. Translated from Kōdera 1978, p.60.
4. Van Gogh in a letter to Theo, 30 March and 1 April 1883 (335/277)

P. 183

Wheat field with a reaper and a peasant woman gleaning

August 1885
black chalk, grey wash, traces of fixative
on wove paper 27.2 x 38.3 cm
watermark: Ts [& Z)
signed lower right (not by the artist): Vincent (black chalk)
E1301r/JH917
KM 128.894 RECTO

INSCRIPTIONS
verso, lower left: [Ve] rz: Hidde Nijland (black ink) upper right: No21 (pencil)

PROVENANCE
acquired by Hidde Nijland, Dordrecht, before 1904.
purchased from Hidde Nijland by A.G. Kröller, The Hague, July 1928.
donated to the Kröller-Müller Foundation by A.G. Kröller, December 1928

EXHIBITIONS
Dordrecht 1904, cat. no. ?.
The Hague 1918, cat. no. ?.
Amsterdam 1924, cat. no. 78.
The Hague 1928, unnumbered.
Hamburg 1929, cat. no. 62.
Amsterdam 1930, cat. no. 110.
New York/Philadelphia/Boston and other cities, 1935-1936, cat. no. 110.
's-Hertogenbosch/Breda 1950,
Warsaw 1962, cat. no. 33.
Tel Aviv/Haifa r9621963, cat. no. 33.
Osaka 1986, cat. no. 6.
Otterlo 1990, cat. no. 103.
Yokohama/Nagoya 1995-1996, cat. no. 31.

For this sheet Van Gogh used a sponge, among other things, to apply a light grey wash over a large part of the composition, which he then touched up again with black chalk, adding lightly scratched out accents with a scraper or other sharp object. The latter can be clearly seen in the two figures, the wheat on the right and the sheaves in the foreground. He partially opened the sky again with an eraser. For the touching up Van Gogh used a very black, possibly lithographic, crayon.

For this and the following drawing Van Gogh fleshed out the backgrounds with two farms, but he did so with slightly more exactitude in Peasant with a hoe. In this sheet it is also more obvious what the peasant is doing. In his attention to detail and precision in finishing this work, it seems to be one of the few in this group to be a mature drawing rather than a study. However, Van Gogh did not sign it himself. the signature in the lower right is not authentic, as is the case in almost all of these sheets.

rake is drawn somewhat clumsily and with incorrect perspective.

P. 184

Peasant with a hoe

August-September 1885 black chalk, traces of squaring, on wove paper
43.6 x 31.8 cm
watermark: T5 & z signed lower right (not by the artist): Vincent (black chalk)
F1315/JH903
KM 126.338

INSCRIPTIONS
verso, lower left: Vincent. Verz:/Hidde Nijland (black ink) ('Hidde Nijland' very faded] 'lower right:
No 10 (pencil). upper left: 54 (pencil). KR43 (blue chalk) [over '54']. upper right: 62.988 (pencil)
[9' unclear]

PROVENANCE
acquired by Hidde Nijland, Dordrecht, before 1904'
purchased from Hidde Nijland by A.G. Kröller, The Hague, July 1928 donated to the Kröller-Müller Foundation by A.G. Kröller, December 1928

EXHIBITIONS
Dordrecht 1904, cat. no. ?.
The Hague 1918, cat. no. 11 or 38?.
Amsterdam 1924, cat. no. 83.
The Hague 1928, unnumbered.
Hamburg 1929, cat. no. 76.
Amsterdam 1930, cat. no. 108.
Leiden/Enschede/Groningen/Leeuwarden 1950-1951, cat. no. 59.
Milan 1952, cat. no. 38.
Eindhoven 1956, cat. no. 16.
Munich 1956, cat. no. 69.
Vienna 1958, cat. no. 49.
São Paulo 1959, cat. no. 11.
Belgrade 1966, cat. no. 32.
Moscow/Leningrad 1971, cat. no. 59.
Amsterdam 1980-1981, cat. no. 154.
's-Hertogenbosch 1987-1988, cat. no. 51.
Otterlo 1990, cat. no. 105.
Yokohama/Nagoya 1995-1996, cat. no. 36.
Tokyo/Fukuoka 1999-2000, cat. no. 41.

P. 185

Peasant woman haying

July-August 1885
black chalk on wove paper
6.8 x 44.4 cm

watermark: TO & Z
unsigned F1260/ JH884 KM 116.889
INSCRIPTIONS
verso, lower right: No 24 (pencil)
Vincmtv. G.:/Verz: Hidde Nijland
(black ink) upper right: V [N] 2
(pencil)

PROVENANCE
acquired by Hidde Nijland, Dordrecht, before 1904'
purchased from Hidde Nijland by A.G. Kröllee, The Hague, July 1928 donated to the Kröller-Müller Foundation by A.G. Kröller, December 1928

EXHIBITIONS
Dordrecht 1904, cat. no. 119, 146 01 152.
The Hague 1918, cat. no. 4 or 20.
Amsterdam 1924, cat. no. 70.
The Hague 1928, unnumbered.
Hamburg 1929, cat. no. 44.
Amsterdam 1930, cat. no. 73.
Basel 1947, cat. no. 134.
Eindhoven 1956, cat. no. 15.
Tokyo/Kyoto1958, cat. no. 44.
Belgrade 1966, car. no. 27.
Vienna 1996, car. no. 72.
The Hague 2005, unnumbered.

In this beautiful, direct and fluidly drawn composition Van Gogh succeeded in depicting the activity of tossing hay very convincingly. The peasant woman is looking with concentration at her take and is presented in a slightly twisted posture that exudes a great deal of energy. Consequently, it is scarcely noticeable that the lower half of the wooden

P. 186

Peasant Woman gleaning

July-August 1885
black chalk, grey wash, traces of fixative, on wove paper
52.5 x 37.9 cm
watermark: Ta & z [fragment]
unsigned
P1265 / JH833
KM 122.483

INSCRIPTIONS
verso, lower centre: 79½ x 39 (pencil)

PROVENANCE
Theo van Gogh, Paris, 1890-1891'
Jo van Gogh-Bonger, Bussum,
1891-1896. A. Vollard, art dealer,
Paris, 1896. purchased by
C. Hoogendijk, The Hague,
at A. Vollard, art dealer, Paris,
between 1896 and 1899.
purchased by H. Kröller-Müller
at sale Amsterdam (Frederik Muller & Cie), 21-22 May 1912
(Hoogendijk collection), lot 112: Paysanne glanant du blé
(687.50 guilders)

EXHIBITIONS
Paris 1896, no known cat. '
Basel/Bern/Brussels 1927, cat. no. 67.
Düsseldorf 1928, cat. no. 133.
Karlsruhe 1928, cat. no. 68.
Berlin 1928-1929, cat. no. 37.
Hamburg 1929, cat. no. 30.
Amsterdam 1930, cat. no. 79.
Antwerp 1952, cat. no. 37 d.
Munich 1956, cat. no. 58.
Vienna 1958, cat. no. 47.
Tokyo/Kyoto 1958, cat. no. 50.
Yokohama/Nagoya 1995-1996, cat. no. 33.

P. 187

Peasant working

August-September 1885
black chalk, traces of fixative, on wove paper
44.1 x 33.2 cm
watermark: TS & z
signed lower right (nor by the artist): Vincent (black chalk)
F1326/JH904
KM 122.62

INSCRIPTIONS
verso, lower centre: No 47 (pencil)
centre: Vincent V Gogh/Hidde Nijland
(pencil) upper left: KR 101(pencil)

PROVENANCE
acquired by Hidde Nijland, Dordrecht/The Hague, before
1918 purchased from Hidde Nijland by A.G. Kröller, The
Hague, July 1928 - donated to the Kröller-Müller Foundation
by A.G. Kröller, December 1928

EXHIBITIONS
The Hague 1918, cat. no. 11 or 38?.
Amsterdam 1924, cat. no. 113.
The Hague 1928, unnumbered.
Hamburg 1929, cat. no. 120.
Amsterdam 1930, cat. no. 95.
's-Hertogenbosch/Breda 1950.
Saint Louis/Philadelphia/Toledo 1953-1954, cat. no. 45.
Nuremberg 1956, cat. no. 40.
Munich 1956, cat. no. 68.
Geneva 1957, cat. no. 130.
Tokyo/Kyoto 1958, cat. no. 53.
Amsterdam/New York 2005, cat. no. 30.

The farm on the right in the background - like
the one in the previous sheet - can possibly be linked
with the farm in Cottage with peasant woman digging
(F89, private collection), in which the building can be
seen from the side.

P. 188

Peasant reaping

July-August 1885
black chalk, grey wash, traces of fixative, on wove paper
53.3 x 36.7 cm
watermark. TS & Z
signed lower left (by the artist?): Vincent (pencil) signed lower
right (nor by the artist): Vincent (black chalk)
F1323 /JH862
KM 126.880

INSCRIPTIONS
verso, lower right: Vincent v. G.: /
Verz: Hidde Nijland (black ink).
No 80 (pencil) 9 (pencil, on a removed strip of light yellow
paper). upper left: s [underlined] (blue chalk) KR 47 (pencil,
on a removed strip of fight yellow paper)

PROVENANCE
acquired by Hidde Nijland,
Dordrecht, before 1904'
purchased from Hidde Nijland by AG. Kröller, The Hague,
July 1928 - donated to the Kröller-Müller Foundation by A.G.
Kröller, December 1928

EXHIBITIONS
Dordrecht 1904, cat. no. ?.
The Hague 1918, cat. no. ?.
Amsterdam 1924, cat. f0. 59.
The Hague 1928, unnumbered.
Hamburg 1929, cat. no. 78.
Amsterdam 1930, cat. no. 71.
Tokyo/Kyoto 1958, cat. no. 46.
Otterlo 1990, cat. no. 110.

Woman scouring pots

July-August 1885
black chalk, traces of fixative (splashed on), on wove paper

54.5 X43.8 cm
watermark: TS & Z
signed lower right (not by the artist): Vincent (black chalk)
E1282 / H906
KM 117.859

INSCRIPTIONS
verse, upper tight: 12 (pencil).
lower right: No 13 (pencil)

PROVENANCE
acquired by Hidde Nijland,Dordrecht, before 1904.
purchased from Hidde Nijland by A.G. Kröller, The Hague,
July 1928 donated to the Kröller-Müller Foundation
By A.G. Kröller, December 1928

EXHIBITIONS
Dordrecht 1904, cat. no. 148?.
Amsterdam 1924, cat. no. 29.
The Hague 1928, unnumbered.
Hamburg 1929, cat. no. 82.
Amsterdam 1930, cat. no. 102.
Easel 1947, cat. no. 139.
London/Birmingham/Glasgow 1947-1948, cat. no 112.
New York/Chicago 1949-1950, cat. no. 42
Milan 1952, cat. no. 40.
Saint Louis/Philadelphia/Toledo 1953-1954, cat. no. 50.
Nuremberg 1956, cat. no. 42.
Munich 1956, cat. no. 55.
Vienna 1958, cat. no. 50.
Tokyo/Kyoto 1958, cat. no. 55.
Montreal/Ottawa/Winnipeg/Toronto 1960-1961, cat. no.
104.
Belgrade 1966, cat. no. 33.
Moscow/Leningrad 1971, cat. no. 50.
Vienna 1996, cat. no. 70.
The Hague 2005, unnumbered.

P. 190

Peasant woman, binding a sheaf of grain

July-August 1885
black chalk, grey wash,traces of fixative
on wove paper
55.4 x 43.4 cm
watermark: TS & Z
signed lower left (by the artist?):
Vincent (pencil, two signatures on top of each other)

signed lower right (nor by the artist): Vincent (black chalk)
F1263/JH871
KM 115.212

INSCRIPTIONS
verso, lower left: Vincent. Verz:/Hidde Nijland. (black ink) '
lower right: NO 33 (pencil) centre left:
55 (blue chalk) upper left:KR 53 (blue chalk) ' upper right: I [or
J underlined] (blue chalk)

PROVENANCE
acquired by Hidde Nijland, Dordrecht, before 1904.
purchased from Hidde Nijland by A.G. Kröller, The
Hague,July 1928'
donated to the Kröller-Müller Foundation by A.G. Kröller,
December 1928

EXHIBITIONS
Dordrecht 1904, cat. no. 107, 133 or 161.
The Hague 1918, cat. no. 22, 28 or 37.
Amsterdam 1924, cat. no. 69.
The Hague 1928, unnumbered.
Hamburg 1929, cat. no. 84.
Amsterdam 1930, cat. no. 75.
Basel 1947, cat. no. 143.
London/Birmingham/Glasgow 1947-1948, cat. no. 121.
Vienna 1958, cat. no. 46.
Tokyo/Kyoto 1958, cat. no. 47.
Belgrade 1966, cat. no. 28.
Moscow/Leningrad 1971, cat. no. 55.
Otterlo 1990, cat. no. 111
Yokohama/Nagoya 1995-1996, cat. no. 32.
Tokyo/Fukuoka 1999-2000, cat. no. 38

REMARKS
On the verso is a sketch in black chalk made by the artist of a
woman binding wheat sheaves,
seen diagonally from the back.

The sheaf of wheat at the bottom originally
bent more to the left over the peasant woman's clog,
but Van Gogh corrected this. To the right here he also
first applied a wash with brush and water over the
smudged chalk before throwing a fixative over it. That
fixative only covers the lower half of the wheat sheaf
on the left, which was also first washed with a brush.

P. 191

72

Peasant woman binding wheat sheaves

July-August 1885
black chalk, grey wash, white opaque watercolour, traces of
fixative, on laid paper
44.8 x 58.4 cm

watermark: HFDC, coat of arms
with fleur-de-lis
signed lower right (nor by the artist): Vincent (black chalk)
F1262 / JH831
KM 120.804

INSCRIPTIONS
verso, lower right: Vincent v. G:
Verz: Hidde Nijland. (black ink).
centre left: NO 44 (pencil).
upper left: 18 (pencil)

PROVENANCE
acquired by Hidde Nijland, Dordrecht, before 1904.
purchased from Hidde Nijland by A.G. Kröller, The Hague,
July 1928 . donated to the Kröller-Müller Foundation by A.G.
Kröller, December 1928

EXHIBITIONS
Dordrecht 1904, cat. no. 107, 133 or 161.
The Hague 1918, cat. no. 22, 28 or 37.
Amsterdam 1924, cat. no. 72
The Hague 1928, unnumbered.
Hamburg 1929, cat. no. 98.
Amsterdam 1930, cat. no. 100.
New York/Philadelphia/Boston and other cities, 1935-1936,
cat. no. 100.
Wormerveer 1955, unnumbered.
Eindhoven 1956, cat. no. 14.
Vienna 1958, cat. no. 43
Charleroi/Antwerp/Paris/Lyon 1971-1972, cat. no. 16.
New York/Chicago/Ottawa and other cities, 1973-1974, cat.
no. 48.
London/Newcastle-upon-Tyne 1974, cat. no. 35.

In the wake of the criticism levelled at The
potato eaters Van Gogh started drawing a great many
smaller studies to give more volume and life to his
figures. Then in the summer of 1885 he began to
work on large.-scale model drawings as well. Around
fifty have survived from this period and can be seen
as a cohesive group.[1] Nineteen of them are in the
Kröller-Müller Museum, and they have been divided
here into two groups for thematic reasons: studies
whose subject is the harvest (reaping, binding sheaves,
gleaning, haying), and drawings that show other
activities. The first group also includes a smaller
drawing of a reaper and two harvest compositions
which are closely related to the subject and were
produced in the same period. For the same reason,
the second group also includes a smaller figure study,
Peasant woman chopping wood.

By and large it is difficult to date these
drawings precisely. 'Every day I work hard on drawing
figures,' Van Gogh wrote to Theo on 21 or 2 8 June,
'but I must have at least a hundred of them, even
more, before I am through [...] And it is about harvest
time -and then I must make a campaign both of
wheat reaping and potato digging. It is twice as hard
to get models then, yet it is necessary' (514/414). At
the beginning of July he wrote that he had, among
other things, a drawing of a woman 'bending to glean
the ears of wheat' (519/416). He can scarcely have
observed this in the fields at that time, however, since
the wheat would not be reaped until later on. His
solution will have been to have his models to pose for
the various aspects of the harvest over a longer period,

but when the activities themselves actually took place
he could be found out in the fields. On 6 August,
when Theo dropped by at Nuenen, he left a letter
for him with their mother with the message, 'They
are reaping the wheat in the fields which means I am
rather busy today, for, as you know, this lasts only
a few days and is one of the most beautiful things'
(525/419).

His correspondence also shows that van Gogh
continued to draw figure studies until September,
which is why most of these sheets are toughly dated
to between July and September. During September it
became increasingly difficult for him to find models
as the 'reverend gentlemen of the clergy' felt that he
was being too familiar with his models and therefore
advised them to stop posing for him (532/423, early
September 1885). Since we know that Van Gogh
followed the recommendation his brother made
during his visit in August - to incorporate 'more
entourage' around his figures if these drawings were
to have a certain marketability - several sheets can
be dated slightly more accurately to August and
September, i.e. Peasant with a hoe, Peasant working
and Woman digging.

All the studies of figures collected here were
drawn with black chalk on wove paper, except for
Peasant woman carrying wheat in her apron and the
horizontal Peasant woman binding wheat sheaves,
which were drawn on laid paper. Van Gogh usually
used the same fixative for the chalk as he had used
for his pencil drawings in The Hague: a solution of
water and milk [2] He did not apply this solution to
the whole sheet but generally only to the figure, so
that a curved discolouring of the paper is often visible
around the reapers and the other field labourers
which follows the contour of the figure. In one or two
cases the fixative was clearly flung onto the sheet. Van
Gogh also occasionally used the fixative as a wash in
the drawing, and after it dried he would sometimes
rub it with an eraser or bread-crumbs to make creases
more distinctive and to highlight accents. Where he
did not use fixative he applied a wash of water to the
chalk with a brush, creating beautiful grey effects.
The ultimate result of that summer was an impressive
series of powerful drawings of figures showing the
peasant labourer in full motion, which had indeed
been his intention.

In a long letter to his brother in July 1885
he explained his motives in detail (522/418). In
Paris, Theo had shown his work - mainly paintings -
to the art dealer Alphonse Portier (1841-1902) and
the somewhat older painter/lithographer Charles
Setter (1824-1900), and their opinions were not
unfavourable. Van Gogh immediately seized on this
to further convince the two men of his ideas. 'When I
send you & Setter a few studies of diggers or peasant
women weeding, gleaning wheat &c. as the first of a
whole series on all kinds of work in the fields, either
you or Serret may discover flaws in them, which it will
be helpful to me to know about and which I shall in
all probability acknowledge,' Van Gogh wrote to his
brother. These comments once again resound with
the discussion he had had with Van Rappard about
the flatness of his figures, since although he wrote
that he was willing to admit his errors, he was at the

same time fearful of being judged on technical finesse when he was trying to achieve something else with his methods.

In his letter Van Gogh was initially unable to precisely express what his intentions were. He could not and would not paint a peasant in the way academically trained painters like Alexandre Cabanel painted a nude, and in his defence he invoked his beloved examples Léon Lhermitte, Jean-François Millet and Jozef Israëls as well as Honoré Daumier, who were not so concerned with such things as correct proportions 'It still isn't well put,' he went on. 'Tell Setter that I should be in despair if my figures were good tell him that I don't want them to be academically correct, tell him that what I'm trying to say is that if one were to photograph a digger, he would certainly not be digging then Tell him that I think Michelangelo's figures are splendid, although the legs are unquestionably too long, the hips and buttocks too wide. Tell him that, to my mind, Millet and Lhermitte are the true artists, because they do not paint things as they are, examined in a dry, analytical manner, but as they, Millet, Lhermitte, Michelangelo, feel them to be. Tell him that I long most of all to learn to produce those very inaccuracies, those very aberrations, reworkings, transformations of reality, as may turn it into, well, a lie if you like, but truer than the literal truth.' He must have had the series of figure studies that he was working on at the time in mind as he wrote this passage.

From the letters it also emerges that Van Gogh repeatedly intended sending these large studies to Theo, and through him to Serret, but found it difficult to part with them. He wrote, 'For I am going to add others which I need for painting. I shall want them for figures that ultimately are not larger than, say, a span or even less - so that everything in it will become even more concentrated' (521/417, c.mid-July 1885). By span he meant the distance between the tips of the outstretched little finger and thumb of a male adult's hand, around 22 centimetres.[3] The figures in these drawings are generally more than twice that size, so that he could devote more attention to details that would help later on if he were to draw the figure smaller in a composition with a number of figures.

Van Gogh was probably planning to create large painted compositions as well as smaller oil paintings, and the way he prepared for this with numerous drawn studies recalls his project with The potato eaters earlier that year.[4] In this case, he obviously had a harvest scene in mind given the large number of studies of reapers, peasant women binding sheaves and the like in this group.

Eight drawings on the subject of the wheat harvest in general have survived and probably served as a draft for possible paintings. Two of them are in the Kröller-Müller Museum: Reaper, a drawing in which a reaper is depicted against a background of trees and cottages, and Grain harvest, with a more detailed composition of a reaper and a peasant woman binding sheaves of grain.[5] Both sheets were 'framed' by Van Gogh, Grain harvest more clearly than Reaper. In the latter, the vertical lines to the far right and left seem to run down and hence suggest not trees in the background but a framing of the

composition. These sheets can be dated with quite some certainty to August, when Van Gogh observed the actual harvest from close by. For both works he used a sheet on which he had already drawn. For Grain harvest he halved a study of a peasant with a pitchfork, the top half of which is in the Van Gogh Museum. On the recto of that sheet there is also a composition of the wheat harvest (F1321r).

---

1. Van Heugten 1997, p. 222.
2. Van Gogh derived this technique from the textbook Guide pratique pour les différents genres de dessin by Armand Cassagne, 1873 (see Van Heugten 1997, p. 239).
3. Van Heugten 1997, p. 237.
4. Ibid., p. 223.
5. The other six are in the Van Gogh Museum (see Van Heugten 1997, pp. 255-162). In four of them there are in fact no figures and only the sheaves of wheat in the field are depicted. The oil study Sheaves of wheat (F193,Kröller-Müller Museum, Otterlo), at the centre of which are about five sheaves of wheat leaning against each other, is the only painting that can be associated with these drawings (Van Heugten 1997, p. 255,and Otterlo 2003, p. 115).

P.193

Peasant walking with stick

May-June 1885
black chalk
on laid paper
34 x 19 cm
watermark: coat of arms with crowned lion rampant with sabre and legend CONCORDIA
RES PARVAE CRESCUNT
unsigned
F133or/JH780
KM 114.398 RECTO

INSCRIPTIONS
recto, lower right: No75 [70?] dubbel (pencil, very faint)
verso, lower left: 15 (blue chalk). verz. H.N. (black ink) [over the blue chalk]

PROVENANCE
acquired by Hidde Nijland, Dordrecht, before 1904.
purchased from Hidde Nijland by A.G. Kröller, The Hague, July 1928.donated to the Kröller-Müller Foundation

by A.G. Kröller, December 1928

EXHIBITIONS
Dordrecht 1904, cat. no. ?.
Amsterdam 1924, cat. no. 104.
The Hague 1928, unnumbered.
Hamburg 1929, cat. no. 68.
Amsterdam 1930, cat. no. 103.
Basel 1947, cat. no. 142.
London/Birmingham/Glasgow 1947-1948, cat. no. 128.
Milan 1952, cat. no. 39.
Saint Louis/Philadelphia/Toledo 1953-1954, cat. no. 46.
Nuremberg 1956, cat. no. 41.
Munich 1956, cat. no. 70.
Montreal/Ottawa/Winnipeg/Toronto 1960-1961, cat. no. 105.
Arnhem 1966, unnumbered.
Moscow/Leningrad 1971, cat. no. 48.
Mons 1980, cat. no. 16.
Amsterdam 1980-1981, cat. no. 159.
's-Hertogenbosch 1987-1988, cat. no. 47.

P.193

Woman walking

Woman with a mourning mantle - KM 122.078 Woman with a mourning mantle - KM 119.858 RECTO Woman with a mourning mantle - KM 119.858 VERSO Woman with a bucket - KM 124.401 RECTO
Woman with a broom - KM 124.401 VERSO Woman with a broom - KM 111.966 Woman with a shovel - KM 123.604 Woman walking - KM 127.894 RECTO Woman standing - KM 127.894 VERSO Man with his hand in his pocket - KM 116.693 RECTO Studies of a man - KM 116.693 VERSO Two figure studies - KM 125.260 RECTO Two figure studies - KM 125.260 verso Man walking - KM 122.498 RECTO
Three figure studies - KM 122.498 VERSO Man with a stick - KM 114.398 RECTO Man seen from the back and studies of hands - KM 114.398 VERSO Digger - KM 122.987

P. 194

Three figure studies of a peasant and a head seen from behind

May-June 1885
black chalk, traces of squaring around middle figure, on laid paper
21 x 34.8 cm
watermark: VdL
unsigned
F1328V / JF757
KM 116.693 VERSO

INSCRIPTIONS
verse, lower left: Vincent v. G.
verz: Hidde Nijland (black ink)
12 (blue chalk) . lower right:
No 67dubbel (pencil) centre:
39 (blue chalk)

PROVENANCE
acquired by Hidde Nijland,
Dordrecht, before 1904.
purchased from Hidde Nijland
by A.G. Kröller, The Hague,
July 1928 donated to the
Kröller-Müller Foundation
by A.G. Kröller, December 1928

EXHIBITIONS
Dordrecht 1904, cat. no. ?.
Amsterdam 1924, cat. no. 40.
The Hague 1928, unnumbered.
Hamburg 1929, cat. no. 87.
Amsterdam 1930, cat. no. 101.
Eindhoven 1956, cat. no. 17.
Munich 1956, cat. no. 71.
Essen 1957, cat. no. sys.
Hamburg 1963, cat. no. 90.

P. 195

Peasant walking

May-June 1885
black chalk on laid paper
35 x 21 cm
watermark: VdL
unsigned
F1329r/JH756 KM 122.498 RECTO

INSCRIPTIONS
recto, lower right: No79 dubbel (pencil, faint)
verso, lower left: Verz: Hidde Nijland
(black ink) 'vervalt (pencil)
upper left: 11 (blue chalk)

PROVENANCE
acquired by Hidde Nijland,
Dordrecht, before 1904.
purchased from Hidde Nijland ,
by A.G. Kröller, The Hague,
July 1928 - donated to the
Kröller-Müller Foundation
by A.G. Kröller, December 1928

EXHIBITIONS
Dordrecht 1904, cat. no. ?.
Amsterdam 1924, cat no. 102.
The Hague 1928, unnumbered.
Hamburg 1929, cat. no. 47.
Amsterdam 1930, cat. no. 90.
Monteal/Ottawa/Winnipeg/Toronto 1960-1961, cat. no. 106.
Warsaw 1962, cat. no. 38.
Charleroi/Antwerp/Paris/Lyon 1971-1972, cat. no. 18.

P. 195

A peasant working

May-June 1885
black chalk on laid paper
34.8 x 20.7 cm
watermark: coat of arms with crowned lion rampant with sabre and legend CORCIA.
RE5 PARVAE CRE5CUNT
unsigned F1311/JH848 KM 122.987

INSCRIPTIONS
verso, lower right: No 52 (pencil)
upper right: 14 (blue chalk)

PROVENANCE
acquired by Hidde Nijland,
Dordrecht, before 1904.

purchased from Hidde Nijland by A.G. Kröller, The Hague,
July 1928 - donated to the Kröller-Müller Foundation by A.G.
Kröller, December 1928

EXHIBITIONS
Dordrecht 1904, cat. no. ?.
Amsterdam 1924, cat. no. 66.
The Hague 1928, unnumbered.
Hamburg 1929, cat. no. 94.
Amsterdam 1930, cat. no. 88.
Antwerp 1952, cat. no. 37e.
Tokyo/Kyoto 1958, cat. no. 54.
Montreal/Ottawa/Winnipeg/Toronto 1960-1961, cat. no. 103

82 Woman walking
May-June 1885
black chalk on laid paper 34.5 x 21 cm
watermark: coat of arms with crowned lion rampant with sabre and legend CONCOROIA
RES PARVAE CRESCUNT
unsigned F5289r/ JH814 KM 127. 894 RECTO

INSCRIPTIONS
recto, lower right: No 8e dubbel
(pencil) verso, lower left: Vera: Hidde Nijland (black ink)
[pencil scribbles below this, damaged by former adhesive
edge; most likely this was: vervalt] upper left: 11 (blue chalk)

PROVENANCE
acquired by Hidde Nijland, Dordrecht, before 1904
purchased from Hidde Nijland by A.C. Kröller, The Hague,
July 1928 donated to the Kröller-Müller Foundation by A.G.
Kröller, December 1928

EXHIBITIONS
Dordrecht 1904, cat. no. ?.
Amsterdam 1924, cat. no. 36.
The Hague 1928, unnumbered.
Hamburg 1929, tat. no. 99.
Amsterdam 1930, cat. no. 78.
Basel 1947, cat. no. 140.
London/Birmingham/Glasgow 1947-1948, cat. no. 124.
Milan 1952, cat. no. 43.
Saint Louis/ Philadelphia/Toledo 1953-1954, cat. no. 47.
Tokyo/Kyoto 1958, cat, no. 58

In early April 1885, while he was busy making sketches and studies in preparation for The potato eaters, Van Gogh read the book Causeries sur les artistes de mon temps by Jean Gigoux (1806-1894] which had been published earlier that year and sent to him by Theo.[1] The book contained a comment by Delacroix that made such a huge impression on Van Gogh that he returned to it for months in his correspondence, most extensively in a letter to Van Rappard in September: 'the painter Gigoux comes to Delacroix with an antique bronze and asks his opinion about its authenticity: "Ce n'est pas de l'antique, c'est de la renaissance," [it is not from antiquity, it is from the renaissance] says D. Gigoux asks him why he thinks this. "Tenez, mon ami, c'est très beau, mais c'est pris parla ligne, et les anciens prenaient par les milieux (parles masses, par noyaux]!"

[Look here, my friend, it is very beautiful but its starting point is the line, and for the ancients the starting point was the middle (the mass, the core).] And he adds, "Look here," and draws a few ovals on a piece of paper, and connects these ovals by means of little lines, hardly anything at all and out of this creates a rearing horse full of life and movement. "Ge'ricault and Gros," he says, "have learned this from the Greeks, to express the masses (almost always egg-shaped) first, tracing the contours and the action from the position & the proportions of these oval shapes. And I," says Delacroix, "was first told of this by Géricault." Now I ask you, is this nota wonderful truth! But... does one learn it from the plaster-of-Paris artists or at the drawing academy I think not. If it were taught in this way, I should be pleased to be an enthusiastic admirer of the academy, but I know only too well that such is not the case' (533/R58].

A few months earlier Van Rappard had severely criticised lithograph The potato eaters for the feeble execution of the figures. Despite his anger at Van Rappard's curt comments, Van Gogh certainly took note of the criticism, and Delacroix's comment about not drawing from the line - or rather the contour - but from volumes, became his new motto. In a letter to Theo around 13-17 April he even gave the impression that he had been doing this for some time and simply did not really know what to call it: "les anciens ne prenaient pas par la ligne mais par les milieux," that means starting with the circle or elliptical bases of the masses instead of the contour. I found the exact words for the latter in Gigoux's book - but the fact itself has already preoccupied me a long time' (497/401). Whatever the case may be, after the completion of his Potato eaters project Van Gogh threw himself into figure drawing, since even Theo, when he was sent the painting in Paris, had criticised the flatness of the figures. 'That's why I've thought of trying it in quite a different way,' he wrote to Theo around 11 May, 'for instance starting with the torso instead of the head' (505/408).In the same letter he wrote: 'I am once again very busy these days drawing figures.' A large group of smaller figure studies, including the examples collected here, can be linked to this comment and will have been produced in the period May to June 1885.[2]

For these studies in black chalk Van Gogh generally used a different method of drawing than he had in the past, and although they are certainly not all constructed from ovals, a number of them show fairly clearly how he had taken Delacroix's comment to heart. A striking feature of all the figures is their stockiness, which does indeed indicate that the artist was primarily concerned with volumes and masses. The contour is generally of less importance and often conspicuously broken. The sheets Woman walking, Man walking and Man with a stick and the figures on the versos of each of them, Woman standing, Three figure studies and Man seen from the bock and Studies of hands, most clearly show his working from ovals which, as in Man with a stick, sometimes produced a curious spiral effect. The studies of hands even seem to refer directly to a passage in the letter dared c.11 May, which also shows that Van Gogh intended to instil greater liveliness in his figures with his new style of drawing: 'At present I am busy putting into practice, on the drawing of a hand and an arm, what Delacroix said about drawing: "ne pas prendre par la ligne, mais par le milieu." That gives me opportunity enough to start from ovals. And what

I try to achieve is not to draw a hand but the gesture, not a mathematically correct head, but the general expression For instance, when a digger looks up and sniffs the wind or speaks. In short, life.' (505/408).

1. The earliest reference is in letter 495/399, c. is April 1885.
2. There are neatly 40 drawings in all, most of them in the Kröller-Müller Museum and the Van Gogh Museum (see Van Heugten 1997, pp. 596-214). They are all drawn on wove paper with the watermark VdLor - because Van Gogh divided a large sheet of paper in two for these drawings - the counter-mark of a coat of arms with crowned lion with sabre and the legend CONCORDIA RES PARVAE CRESCUNT.

P. 197

Self-portrait

April - June 1887
Oil on cardboard
32.8 x 24 cm
F380/JH1225
KM 105.833

SIGNATURE/INSCRIPTIONSILABELS
Verso, on cardboard: G. Hennequin/Couleurs Fines,Toiles & Pinceaux/11 Avenue de Clichy (Paris) (stamp paint-dealer). Kunsthandel C.M. van Gogh/Sternheim (stamps)

PROVENANCE
Jo van Gogh-Bonger, Amsterdam. C.M. van Gogh (J.H. de Bois), art dealer, Amsterdam, 13 November 1909. C. Sternheim, Munich, 13 November 1909 (c. f6oo; together with F410, F420 and F752 for f 4,523.60). Mrs Th. Sternheim coll., La Hulpe-les-Bruxelles. purchased by H. Kröller-Müller at Th. Sternheim sale, Amsterdam (FrederiK Muller), 11 February 1919, lot 5: Portrait de lui-meme (f 6,500)

EXHIBITIONS
Basle/Bern 1927, no. 95.
Brussels 1927, no. 95.

Dusseldorf 1928, no. 158.
Karlsruhe 1928, no. 93.
Berlin 1928-1929, no. 89.
Hamburg 1929, no. 52.
Amsterdam 1930, no. 196.
Liege/Brussels/Mans 1946-1947, no. 74.
Paris 1947, no. 76.
Geneva 1947, no. 76.
Basle 1947, no. 45.
Milan 1952, no. 68.
The Hague 1953, no. 93.
Otterlo/Amsterdam 1953, no. 67.
Eindhoven 1956, no. 29.
Munich 1956, no. 102.
Vienna 1958, no. 72.
Tokyo/Kyoto 1958, no. 86.
London 1960, no. 7.
Paris 1960 (b), no. 44
Warsaw 1962, no. 95.
Tel Aviv/Haifa 1962-1963, no. 63.
Delft/Antwerp 1964-1965, no. 53.
Belgrade 1966, no. 54.
Moscow/Leningrad 1971, no. 66.
Hamburg 1995, cat. without nos..
Yokohama/Nagoya 1995-1996, no. 48.
Tokyo/Fukuoka 1999-2000, no. 47

REMARKS
Recorded in the account book of Theo van Gogh and Jo van Gogh-Banger (Stolwijk & Veenenbos 2002, p. 170)

'There can be no doubt that Vincent saw this painting as a self-portrait,' wrote H.P. Bremmer in 1939. He regarded it as one of Van Gogh's best self-portraits, recognising in it the power of the artist's genius: 'What I mean to say is that he did not take himself as his subject in order to create a detailed analytical study; instead, his aim was to render his whole being as a man, as he appeared to himself." During his Paris period Van Gogh painted around 25 - mostly small self-portraits, more than at any other time and probably because he lacked money for other models. The earliest of these are still painted in a rather conservative realist or romantic-realist style, which the artist probably adopted in order to demonstrate the progress he had made in depicting faces and perhaps in the hope of gaining portrait commissions. Once this hope had vanished, however, he began to use his self-portraits for ever more radical stylistic experiments.

Hulsker has counted 22 self-portraits dating to 1887, remarking that these were likely painted at relatively short intervals over the course of the entire year and 'that they nearly always appear in pairs.' Based on this observation he distinguishes eight groups, consisting of two or three works each, classifying the present three-quarters profile among the 'soft-coloured' group of April-June 1887. This he placed between the so-called 'elegant group' (F294, F295 and F296) of March-April, and the 'pointillist group' (F356 and F345) of the spring and early summer.[3] And, indeed, the colours on which Hulsker bases his taxonomy are rather subdued: mauve for the jacket with its grey-green piping and a light blue for the necktie, all set against a soft blue-green speckled background. The facial expression is relatively calm, although one can read a certain anxiety or melancholia in the eyes. The brushwork of the face reveals a much greater technical mastery than found in the previous group, while the quick strokes used for the background create a sense of depth and enliven the whole. The next series is characterised by the typical pointillist swarm of dots in harder shades of blue and red.

This painting was once in the collection of Carl Sternheim, one of Germany's most fervent Van Gogh admirers. The artist was probably brought to his attention by Meier-Graefe in 1908, and from that point onward he began visiting numerous exhibitions and galleries throughout Europe, to collect the painter's work, and to write about him.[4] In late September 1909 Sternheim paid a visit to Jo van Gogh-Bonger in Amsterdam, where, he would later write, the paintings lay on the floor, stood against each other in the full sun and in some cases were even stuck together, so that 'when taking them apart a piece of the moon in one of the large landscapes with two figures and cypresses became loose and fell to the ground." Sternheim was exaggerating, just as he exaggerated when he claimed to have bought six works from Jo on the same visit. In fact it was four, among them this self-portrait.[5] The fact that his wife Thea provided the funds for his fast-growing collection explains why her name appears repeatedly in the provenance. Unfortunately for the Sternheims, and for Germany - or Belgium, where the couple moved in 1914 - their financial situation was such that from 1912 they were forced to sell off a variety of works, while what was then left - seven Van Goghs as well as several works by Gauguin, Renoir and Gericault - was auctioned after the war, in 1919. It was at this time that Helene Kröller-Müller acquired the self-portrait, her second Van Gogh from the Sternheim collection (the other being Blossoming chestnut trees).

1. Bremmer (1939), in Van Gelder et al. 1956, p. 45.
2. Hulsker 1996, pp. 260-262 and 272.
3. See Bridgwater 1987, pp. 97-107.
4. In Lutetia: Berichte fiber europaische Politik, Kunst und Volksleben, 1926; quoted in Bridgwater 1987, p. 98.
5. Heijbroek & Wouthuysen 1993, p.194.

P. 199

Flowers in a blue vase

C. June 1887
Oil on canvas
61.5 x 38.5 cm
F323/JH1295
KM 107055

SIGNATURE/INSCRIPTIONS/LABELS Recto, lower right: Vincent

PROVENANCE
A,Aurier coll., Paris (?).
S.Williame-Aurier coll., Chateauroux, 5 October 1892.
purchased for H. Kroller Mulier by H.P. Bremmer from J. Williame, Chateauroux,June 1914 (f 5,000)

EXHIBITIONS
Basle/Bern 1927, no. 82.
Brussels 1927, no. 82.
Dusseldorf 1928, no. 143.
Karlsruhe 1928, no. 78.
Berlin 1928 1929, no. 80.
Hamburg 1929, no. 39.
Amsterdam 1930, no. 201.
Rotterdam 1935-1936, no. 60.
The Hague 1945, no. 29.
Liege/Brussels/Mons 1946-1947, no. 61.
Paris 1947, no. 56
Geneva 1947, no. 57.
Basle 1947, no. 37.
London/Birmingham/Glasgow 1947-1948, no. 22.
Milan 1952, no. 71.
Saint Louis/Philadelphia/Toledo 1953-1954, no. 79.
Eindhoven 1956, no. 31.
Sao Paulo 1959, no. 5.
Warsaw 1962, no. 58.
Tel Aviv/Haifa 1962-1963, no. 67.
Hamburg 1963, no. 75.
Belgrade 1966, no. 56.
Moscow/Leningrad 1971, no. 67.
Yokohama/Nagoya1995 1996, no. 49.

In comparison to Van Gogh's early Paris

flower still lifes, from the summer of 1886, those executed a year later - as there were no cut flowers he abandoned the subject during the winter months - are festive and cheerful. Light and color dominate, in this bouquet as well. The vase appears in two other still lifes, Vase with lilacs, daisies and anemones (F322) and Vase with cornflowers and poppies (F324), which were probably painted around the same time. Set on a table composed of sturdy yellow green touches, seen at a slight angle, the shiny light blue vase is filled with white daisies, yellow spring sunflowers, blue lilacs, a few bright red anemones and, at the back right, a thick bunch of Liliaceae or Ranunculaceae.[1] The vase and flowers stand out sharply against the blue pointillistic background, which towards the bottom shades off into a combination of grey and purple.

Van Gogh painted this still life on a previously used, horizontal canvas, probably a depiction of a rather flat landscape. This scene was scraped off and the canvas covered with a new ground, on which traces of an underdrawing in charcoal or black pencil can be found, showing the contours of the vase and some of the flowers.

As a motif, the flower still life is treated rather traditionally, with an almost old fashioned placing of the vase in an extremely simple and orderly composition. The modelling of the paint in non systematic touches, alternating between short and longer strokes, and the brilliant coloration of the bouquet, on the other hand, testify to Van Gogh's increasing technical command and self confidence. His goal of mastering the use of intense colors and color contrasts with the help of such flower pieces can herewith be regarded as fulfilled, despite the fact that some of the colors have faded or darkened. The period of experimentation was over. The lessons of impressionism and neo impressionism, which he had initially sought to make his own through rather close imitation, had now been learned and integrated into a highly personal, unaffected blend of impressionist light and pointillist touch.

The painting is suffused with a belief in his artistic powers that Van Gogh only attained in Paris, in an atmosphere where he could freely experiment, where there was more room for innovation than in the Netherlands, and where the example of and discussions with his fellow - artists provided him with much needed encouragement. Whenever he would turn to flower still lifes in the coming years it would be in order to solve certain artistic problems, such as the rendering of the internal structure of the blooms or the application of various tones of the same color, mainly yellow, as in the famous series of sunflowers painted in Arles

In early 1892, probably around February, Aurier wrote a letter to his sister in which he advised her to purchase a flower still life by Van Gogh then for sale for 15 francs at a Paris 'marchand de bric a brac.'[2] Hammacher believed this must have been Flowers in a blue vase.[3] He does not say why, but his reason was probably that it was the only still life to have later come from the Williame collection.

1. Identified as such by restorer T. Oostendorp. The botanist of the Van Gogh Museum, however, has identified the

flowers somewhat differently, as blue myosotis, yellow
spring sunflowers, pale blue and dark blue anemones,
2. See a copy of the letter in the Aurier file at the Van Gogh
Museum.
3. Hammacher 1960, p. 56.

P. 201

Interior of a restaurant

Summer 1887
Oil on canvas
45.5 x 56 cm
F342/JH1256
KM 110.328

SIGNATURE/INSCRIPTIONS/LABELS
Verso, stretcher: No 1 (black chalk).
CK (blue chalk)

PROVENANCE
Jo van Gogh-Bonger, Amsterdam. C.M. van Gogh (J.H. de
Bois), art dealer, Amsterdam, March 1909 (f 3,000).
Artz & De Bois, art dealer,The Hague. purchased by H.
Kröller-Müller at Artz & De Bois, art deale,The Hague,
November 1912 (f 6,000)

EXHIBITIONS
Rotterdam 1892, no. 43.
Amsterdam 1905, no. 50.
Paris 1908 (b), no. 20.
Munich 1908 (b) no. 7.
Dresden 1908, no. 7.
Frankfurt 1908, no. 10.
Zurich 1908, no. 5.
Amsterdam 1908, no. 14.
Munich/Frankfurt/Dresden/Chemnitz 1909-1910, no. 4
(unverkauflich/not for sale).
Amsterdam 1911, no. 21.
Hamburg 1911-1912, no. 4.
The Hague 1913, no. 82.
Basle/Bern 1927, no. 91.
Brussels 1927, no. 91 ?E.
Dusseldorf 1928, no. 154.
Karlsruhe 1928, no. 89.
Berlin 1928-1929, no. 86.
Hamburg 1929, no. 48.
Amsterdam 1930, no. 207.
New York/Philadelphia/Boston and other cities 1935-1936,
no. 19.
Liege/Brussels/Mons 1946-1947, no. 60.
Paris 1947, no. 63.
Geneva 1947, no. 64. Basle 1947,no. 40.
London/Birmingham/Glasgow 1947-1948, no. 19.

Milan 1952, no. 72.
The Hague 1953, no. 64.
Otterlo/Amsterdam 1953, no. 83.
Saint Louis/Philadelphia/Toledo 1953-1954, no. 71.
Eindhoven 1956, no. 32.
Munich 1956, no. 103.
Essen 1957, no. 244.
Vienna 1958, no. 73.
Tokyo/Kyoto 1958no. 90.
Montreal/Ottawa/Winnipeg/Toronto 1960-1961, no. 24.
Warsaw 1962, no. 59.
Tel Aviv/Haifa 1962-1963, no. 68.
Mons 1980, no. 35.
Toronto/Amsterdam 1981, no. 5.
Paris 1988, no. 41.
Amsterdam 1990, no. 24.
Tokyo/Fukuoka 1999-2000, no. 49.

REMARKS
Recorded in the account book of Theo van Gogh and Jo van
Gogh-Bonger (Stolwijk & Veenenbos 2002, p. 169) Photo
Druet no. 7219: Salle de restaurant

Signac's influence on Van Gogh was strongest
in the summer of 1887, after the former had left for
the south of France. This Interior of a restaurant,
which, given the flowers on the tables, must have
been painted in the (early) summer, is one of
Van Gogh's most consequent applications of neo-
impressionist principles. The thinly applied pointillist
brushwork and the complementary color contrasts
(red and green for the walls, yellow and grayish purple
for the floor, and yellow-orange for the furnishings
with blue in the tablecloths) are systematically
thought through and executed. Regarding this
work, Rosenblum and Janson speak of an attempt
to make an entirely new style his own, in which the
painter repressed all subjective expression in favor of
exploring the objective problems of color, brushwork
and perspective (which is, in fact, rather confused due
to the placement of the pinkish red panels against the
rear wall).[1]

Welsh-Ovcharov classifies it 'among the most
orthodox Pointillist-style paintings in Vincent's
oeuvre', despite the fact that Van Gogh would later
write (e.g. 673/528, c. 27 August 1888) of his refusal
to conform to the strict rules of the style, and the fact
that he has applied them here much less consistently
than has often been thought.[2] The tables and chairs,
for example, are made up not of dots, but rather of
long strokes. The pencil under-drawing was made
with the help of a perspective frame, and is visible
in several places on the painting's surface. Moreover,
gradations in tone are used to suggest shadow, a realist
practice that has nothing to do with pointillism. That
the picture was a kind of experiment is suggested by
the fact that Van Gogh used the reverse of an older
canvas. X-ray photographs show a garden or patch of
grass, confined at the right by the roof of a house or
shed and at the top by a plant border or hedge, above
which several trees can be seen - possibly an allotment
garden on Montmartre.

Nonetheless, the result is a delightful example
of pointillism, one which Van Gogh may well have
intended as a kind of homage to the new art. 'This is
the kind of painting with which in 1887 he was most

likely to please his friend Paul Signac and suggest his
affinity to the Neo-Impressionist movement,' observed
Welsh-Ovcharov.[3] The subject, a typical middle-
class restaurant, was one of the (neo-) impressionists'
favorite motifs, although it would have been highly
unusual for them to have painted such a festive
interior entirely empty of guests. Despite the fact
that Van Gogh never felt much affinity with the
bourgeoisie, contrary to later myths while in Paris he
occasionally presented himself as a cosmopolitan or
even dandy. Still, Interior of a restaurant remains one
of the relatively rare examples of a classic impressionist
motif in his oeuvre.

The black top hat, hanging oddly high on the
wall, may also be a reference to the (bourgeois) attire
preferred by the Parisian avantgarde at the time.[4]
The sketchily rendered poster or 'crepon' at the far
right could relate to the artist's interest in Japanese
prints, and the painting in the centre - which has
been identified as his own Lane in Voyer d'Argenson
Park at Asnieres (F276) painted in the spring of 1887
- might be an allusion to the role Van Gogh himself
hoped to play in the development of the new art.
Nonetheless, pointillism would eventually turn out
to be but a sideroad in his artistic career, one that
liberated his palette and brushwork to be sure, but
which he quickly rejected as too impersonal and
dogmatic. There can be no doubt, however, that
this painting represents the high-point of his neo-
impressionist phase.

The restaurant depicted cannot be identified
with any certainty. Almost all the restaurants Van
Gogh frequented during his Paris period have been
cited in this context: the ones in Montmartre where
he often went with Theo, such as Chez Bataille, near
rue Lepic; restaurants like De la Sirene (F312, F313
and F1408) and Rispal (F355) in Asnieres, where
he also painted; and an establishment on avenue de
Clichy mentioned by Gustave Coquiot in this regard.[5]
Other possibilities are Du Chalet or Le Tambourin
- although the latter had round, tambourine-shaped
tables (see F370), where in the winter of 18 86-1887
he exhibited his collection of Japanese woodcuts and,
later, his own work, together with that of Bernard and
Lautrec.

On 3 July 1895. Jo van Gogh-Bonger sent a
'salle d'un restaurant' to the Paris art dealer Vollard
for an exhibition of works for sale. It is not clear,
however, whether it was this painting or another one.
In the period when J.H. de Bois was still working for
the gallery of C.M. van Gogh, he received this work
several times to sell on commission. In the summer of
1908 he took it with him to a show in Zurich. Later
that year it was put on display at both the Hague and
Amsterdam branches of C.M. van Gogh, and in 1909
it was once again included in the gallery's summer
show in The Hague. In the interims it was returned
to Jo van Gogh-Bonger. Between 1908 and 1912 the
asking price rose from 1,300 guilders to 5,000.[6]

1. Rosenbium & Janson 1984, p.411.
2. Welsh-Ovcharov 1981, p. 104.
3. Ibid.
4. Rewald 1956, pp. 153-154. In an 1886 photograph
   showing van Gogh and Bernard on the banks of the Seine

at Asnieres, he himself wears a somewhat lower hat with a bent-down brim (ibid., p. 60).
5. Welsh-Ovcharov 1976, p. 234.
6. Heijbroek & Wonthnysen 1993, p.193.

P. 205

View of Saintes-Maries-de-la-Mer

1/3 June 1888
Oil on canvas
64.2 x 53 cm
F416/JH1447
KM 106.327

SIGNATURE/INSCRIPTIONS/LABELS
Verso, stretcher:
837 (label)

PROVENANCE
C. Hoogendijk coll., The Hague (probably purchased between late August 1897 and early December 1899).
purchased by H. Kröller-Müller at C. Hoogendijk sale, Amsterdam (Frederik Muller), 21 May 1912, lot 25: Aries (f 8,000)

EXHIBITIONS
Brussels 1913, no. 272 (Vue d'Avignon)The Hague 1913, no. 114.
Antwerp 1914, no. 29.
Basle/Bern 1927, no. 108.
Brussels 1927, no. 108.
Dusseldorf 1928, no. 176.
Karlsruhe 1928, no. 111.
Berlin 1928-1929, no. 98.
Hamburg 1929, no. 64.
Amsterdam 1930, no. 214.
Liege/Brussels/Mons 1946-1947, no. 107.
Paris 1947, no. 107.
Geneva 1947, no. 107.
Basle 1947, no. 59.
London/Birmingham/Glasgow 1947-1948, no. 42.
New York/Chicago1949-1950, no. 75.
Milan 1952, no. 79.
The Hague1953, no. 124.
Otterlo/Amsterdam 1953, no. 103.

Saint Louis/Philadelphia/Toledo 1953-1954, no. 99.
Essen 1957, no. 281.
Vienna 1958, no. 80.
Tokyo/Kyoto 1958, no. 98.
Aixen-Provence 1959, no. 12
Montreal Ottawa/Winnipeg/Toronto 1960-1961, no. 38.
Warsaw 1962, no. 61.
Tel Aviv/Haifa1962-1963, no. 71.
Belgrade 1966, no. 60.
Moscow/Leningrad 1971, no. 73.
Toronto/Amsterdam 1981, no. 17.
Copenhagen 1984-1985, no. 62a.
Rome 1988, no. 30.
Melbourne/Brisbane 1993-1994, no. 38.
Yokohama/Nagoya 1995-1996, no. 53.
Tokyo/Fukuoka 1999-2000, no. 54.

In the early morning of 30 May 1888 Van Gogh took the diligence for a five-hour journey through the Camargue to the fishing village of Saintes-Maries-de-la-Mer on the Mediterranean Sea. Saintes-Maries was famous for its Catholic traditions - it could boast the relics of two 'saint Marys', who according to an early Christian legend came by boat from Judea, made a miraculous landing on the southern coast of France, and proceeded to convert the whole of Provence. The excursion was a kind of pilgrimage for him. The sea made him think of his Uncle Jan (1817-1885) of the Dutch navy, with whom he had lived in 1877-1878 in Amsterdam when he was preparing for theological studies, while the shabby little houses reminded him of those in Drenthe (622/499, c. 4 June 1888), and the coastal region convinced him once again that the south of France resembled Japan. 'After a while one's sight changes: you see things with more of a Japanese eye, you experience colours differently', he wrote shortly after returning to Arles late in the evening on 3 June (623/500).

Compared with the harsh colours of his Bridge at Aries of more than a year before, here Van Gogh's palette is much more subdued, even though the mauve field of lavender must originally have been more reddish in tone. Van Gogh wrote that in Saintes-Maries he hoped to develop his drawing technique into something 'more spontaneous, more exaggerated' (620/495), and the contours of the buildings rising up behind the lavender field are indeed well-defined in a way that recalls 'cloisonism' and Japonism.[1] The mosaic of fields this gave rise to is filled in with orangey tones for the sunny facades and a complementary blue for those in shadow. Both the build-up of fields and the simple palette are reminiscent of Cezanne, whose bright colors Van Gogh also professed to admire somewhat later, around 12 June, even though he also referred in this context to Delacroix: 'Everywhere now there is old gold, bronze, copper, one might say, and this with the green azure of the white-hot sky: a delicious color, extraordinarily harmonious, with the blended tones of Delacroix. [...]. If coming home with my canvas I say to myself, "Look, I've got the very tones of pere Cezanne!" I only mean that Cezanne, like Zola, is so much at home in the countryside and knows it so intimately that we must make the same calculations in our head to arrive at the same tones' (627/497).

Van Gogh wrote Theo from Saintes-Maries that he had already painted three canvases there, two seascapes (F415 and F417) and a view of the village (622/499). In addition, he made at least nine drawings, three of which he used as the basis of paintings as soon as he returned to Arles (F413 after F1428, F419 after F1438, and F420 after F1434). There is also a drawing of this View of Saintes-Maries-de-la-Mer, but because of the reference to the canvas in his letter written from Saintes-Maries it is unlikely that the canvas was made later in Aries on the basis of the drawing (F1439). Both the drawing and the painting were probably made on the spot, even though it remains unclear which of the two was made first and whether one served as an example for the other. The painting differs from the drawing only in its cropping, the degree of detail, and the absence of the dazzling sun.

Just what happened to the three canvases from Saintes-Maries immediately after they were made is not known. Van Gogh wrote, while still there, that he would have to leave them behind, 'for of course they are not dry enough to be subjected to five hours of jolting in a carriage' (622/499). He probably intended to collect them on a second excursion to Saintes-Maries, though nothing ever came of this trip (624/494, 626/496, 628/498 and 68I/w7). It is possible that he took them along anyway, or else had them sent within the month to Arles, as suggested by a letter of 5 July, in which he wrote Theo that 'for instance the studies made at Stes-Maries' were not yet dry, owing to the slow-drying zinc white he had used (639/508).[2]

The provenance cannot be traced further back than Hoogendijk, but it is known that Hoogendijk acquired many works from Vollard and that Vollard in turn bought work from Jo van Gogh-Bonger (who, however, had no record of this canvas in her accounts), as well as from friends of Van Gogh who had acquired his work through gifts or exchanges (though nothing of the kind has been linked to this work). Moreover, from 1895 to 1897 Vollard had an assistant in Arles whom he employed for the express purpose of picking up works here and there which Van Gogh had left behind.

1. Seep. 206 and Welsh-Ovcharov 1981, pp. 125-126.
2. Van Gogh often had works sent to him which he had been forced to leave behind).

P. 207

The garden of the asylum at Saint-Rémy

May 1889
Oil on canvas
91.5 x 72 cm
F734/JH1698
KM 110.508

SIGNATURE/INSCRIPTIONS/LABELS
Recto, lower right: Vincent
Verso: cat. 141 (blue chalk) [= exhib. Paris 1947]

PROVENANCE
L.C. Enthoven coll.,Voorburg (R 1904)1.
purchased by H. Kröller-Müller at Enthoven sale, Amsterdam
(Frederik Muller), 18 May 1920, lot 247:Jardin de l'hopital a
Arles, (f 18,000)

EXHIBITIONS
Basle/Bern 1927, no. 125.
Brussels 1927, no. 125.
Dusseldorf 1928, no. 193.
Karlsruhe 1928, no. 128.
Berlin 1928-1929, no. 137.
Hamburg 1929, no. 80.
Amsterdam 1930, no. 238.
The Hague 1945 no. 36.
Liege/Brussels/Mons 1946-1947, no. 141.
Paris 1947, no. 142.
Geneva 1947, no. 142.
Basle 1947, no. 83.
London/Birmingham/Glasgow 1947-1948, no. 68.
New York/Chicago 1949-1950, no. 111.
The Hague 1953, no. 153.
Otterlo/Amsterdam 1953, no. 141.
Munich 1956, no. 141.
Vienna 1958, no. 93.
Tokyo/Kyoto 1958, no. 114.
Aix-en-Provence 1959, no. 37.
Montreal/Ottawa/Winnipeg/Toronto 1960-1961, no. 59.
Warsaw 1962, no. 72.
Tel Aviv/Haifa 1962-1963, no. 82.
Belgrad 1966, no. 70.
Tokyo/Fukuoka 1999-2000, no. 61.
Bremen 2002-2003, no. 2.

'Since I've been here, the neglected garden with large pine trees, beneath which the grass grows tall and unkempt, mixed with all sorts of periwinkle, has given me enough work, and I haven't gone outside yet,' wrote Van Gogh on 22 May 1889 to his brother, two weeks after arriving at the Saint-Paul-de-Mausole asylum (778/592). When he said 'outside', he meant outside the walls of the asylum. Having unfolded his easel in the garden shortly after his arrival, Van Gogh hoped, by painting, to exert a positive influence on his clinical picture. Now that he had ended up in an institution, in the midst of lunatics, the fear of madness abated. He noticed that a number of patients had, like himself, heard 'strange sounds and voices' during attacks, and that 'in their eyes, too, things seemed to be changing', but, he wrote in the same letter, 'once you know that it is part of the disease, you take it like anything else'. For five months he had been improving gradually, and he hoped never again to experience an attack as violent as the one he had had in Aries. According to him, the greatest danger lay in the 'extreme lethargy suffered by those who have been here for some years already. Well, my work will protect me from this to a certain extent.'

The garden, situated on the west side of the asylum, provided him with plenty of subject matter, and around a week later he was working on two large canvases depicting irises and lilacs (F608 and F579). At the same time he made several superb drawings and watercolours in the garden, one of which is preserved in the Kröller-Müller Museum. He painted the irises and lilacs on size 30 canvases in horizontal format. A short while later he took two size 30 canvases in a vertical format for The garden of the asylum at Saint-Remy and a painting of tree trunks overgrown with ivy (F609). For The garden of the asylum Van Gogh placed his easel parallel to the north wing of the men's quarters, where vacant rooms made it possible for him to have a studio. Around 1900 Frederic George took a photograph from almost the same spot, capturing the weeds, which had lost none of their luxuriance, as well as the characteristic overflow-pipes halfway up the facade.

Whereas in the three paintings mentioned above Van Gogh had concentrated completely on the vegetation, in this work he contrasted the profuse growth of trees with the architecture of the asylum. Because he had set his easel close to the facade, it recedes sharply, producing a somewhat peculiar perspective, one which he often employed in his compositions (F659). When he was still working in the Netherlands, Van Gogh had learned the proper use of perspective as a means of expression from the handbook Grammaire des arts du dessin by Charles Blanc, published in 1867.[2] First he made an underdrawing in pencil or black chalk, which is still visible in places.[3] He painted the trees with both heavy and light impasto and short, nervous brushstrokes, whereas the architecture and the foreground are painted in a slightly less pastose manner. He painted the tree tops, some of them in blossom, with huge variations in colour, largely the result of working endlessly wet-in-wet. For the field of green grass

visible between the trees he used rather smooth, flat brushwork, thereby creating a place where the eye can rest from the jumble of loose brushstrokes. Most of the passages were worked out wet-in-wet with the subject in front of him, but during a last session, by which time the canvas must have been reasonably dry, he used a soft, pointed brush to apply scores of accents with transparent dark blue and red paint, which are clearly visible over the whole of the picture, serving not only to balance the colour scheme but also to enhance the structure of, for example, the blossoming branches. Finally, he signed the canvas, just as he signed the other three works painted in the garden in a some-what comparable manner (F579, F608, F609). That signature is remarkable, because when he sent the canvases to Theo in July, he described only the Lilacs (F608) and the Trees with ivy (F609) as 'tableaux', meaning full-fledged paintings. The other two, he said, were 'more studies from nature than subjects for pictures. It's always like that: you must make several before you have one whole that amounts to anything' (792/600, C. 9 July 1889). The distinction that Van Gogh made between a study (etude) and a painting (tableau) is an ever-recurring theme in the correspondence. Although he does not define the concepts very precisely, calling some paintings etude and tableau alternately, it seems that in his eyes a work could only be called a full-fledged painting when he was satisfied with the subject and had tapped some deeper layer of meaning. He made quite sure there was no mistaking his need to make a lot of studies before arriving at a satisfactory result. The painting's format, however, played a subordinate role in this process.[4]

---

1. The painting, titled Fardin de couvent, appears under number 26 in Bremmer 1904,as being in the possession of Mr Enthoven in Voorburg. It is not known when and from whom he acquired it (see pp. 424-427).
2. Van Uitert et ai. 1990, p. 234.
3. Technical examination carried out at the Kröller-Müller Museum, 29 July 2002.
4. See Dorn 1990b, p. 47.

P. 209

Flowering rosebushes in the asylum garden

late May - early June 1889 brush, diluted oils and ink,
on wove paper
61.4 x 46.7cm
no watermark
unsigned
F1527/JH1708
KM 124.948

INSCRIPTIONS
verso, upper right: geteekend door/
Vincent Van Gogh/1890 Wed. Th. Van Gogh/Bonger (brown ink)

PROVENANCE
Theo van Gogh, Paris, 1890-1891. Jo van Gogh-Bonger, Bussum, 1891-1893. purchased by Thorvald Isaachsen, Bergen (Norway), 1893 (50 guilders)A sale Amsterdam (Frederik Muller & Cie), 29 April 1914, lot 406. purchased by H. Kröller-Müller at sale Amsterdam (Frederik Muller & Cie), 6 July 1915 (Isaachsen collection), lot 54 (1,150 guilders)

EXHIBITIONS
Basel/Bern/Brussels 1927, cat. no. 102.
Düsseldorf 1928, cat. no. 169.
Karlsruhe 1928, cat. no. 104.
Berlin 1928-1929, cat. no. 131.
Hamburg 1929, cat. no. 143.
Amsterdam 1930, cat. no. 129.
New York/Philadelphia/Boston and other cities, 1935-1936, cat. no. 121.
Basel 1947, cat. no. 165.
Leiden/Enschede/Groningen/Leeuwarden 1950-1951, cat. no. 60.
Milan 1952, cat. no. 95.
The Hague 1953, cat. no. 119.
Otterlo/Amsterdam 1953, cat. no. 136.
Saint Louis/Philadelphia/Toledo 1953-1954, cat. no. 159.
Munich 1956, cat. no. 139.
Essen 1957, cat. no. 332.
Vienna 1958, cat. no. 106.
Tokyo/Kyoto 1958, cat. no. 111.

Aix-en-Provence 1959, cat. no. 52.
Munich 1961, cat. no. 69.
Warsaw 1962, cat. no. 69.
Tel Aviv/Haifa 1962-1963, cat. no. 97.
Arnhem 1966, unnumbered.
Belgrade 1966, cat. no. 39.
Charleroi/Antwerp/Paris/Lyon 1971-1972, cat. no. 20.
Munich 1972-1973, cat. no. 308.
New York/Chicago/Ottawa and other cities, 1973-1974, cat. no. 53.
London/Newcastle-upon-Tyne 1974, cat. no. 40.
Otterlo 1990, cat. no. 217.
Yokohama/Nagoya 1995-1996, cat. no. 61.
Tokyo/Fukuoka 1999-2000, cat. no. 62.
Bremen/Toledo 2002-2003, cat. no. 4.

NOTE
A In Match 1892, about a year before he bought this drawing, the Norwegian clergyman Thorvald Isaachsen (1862-1933), together with his Dutch Fiancée Valborg Dudok van Heel (1868-1932), visited Johanna van Gogh Bonger in Bussum to see the collection (Stolwijk & Veenenbos 2002, pp. 141 en 198). He or his wife may perhaps have been responsible for the annotation with the incorrect date on the verso. Isaachsen's mother was Dutch and one of his postings was as chaplain to the Norwegian Seamen's Mission in Amsterdam (http://www.nederland.no/norske-spor/nsia, click on St. Olofskapel).

Among the high points of Van Gogh's drawn oeuvre is a series of seven colourful sheets - one of which is Blooming rose bushes - which he made in late May, early June 1889 in the garden of the asylum. For a long time it was assumed that they were done in watercolour, but recent study has established that Van Gogh used diluted oil paint combined with purple ink.[1] They were produced at a time when Van Gogh lacked the materials to paint properly. 'I am forced to ask you again for some paints and especially for canvas', he wrote to Theo for instance on 22 May (778/592), and in a subsequent letter he asked for more canvas and new brushes as well (780/593, June 1889). As in other drawings from the series, one can see here, too, that some of the ends of the paint strokes look somewhat ragged, which might be a sign that he had used worn brushes. The new materials arrived around 8 June and he began to paint mainly beyond the walls of the asylum, having meanwhile been given permission to do so.

While a rudimentary pencil or chalk sketch is visible in most of the other drawings in the series, Van Gogh managed without it here.[2] He placed himself close to the main subject and filled almost the entire picture plane with the bushes. Because the colour blue occurs throughout the composition and the light blue and green tones are still uncommonly clear and bright, the depth is initially difficult to gauge.[3] Moreover, the roses have for the most part faded over the years, though originally they must have provided stronger red and pink accents.[4] In many places they now float among the leaves like pale pink or even completely white blotches and their shape is often only recognisable from the surrounding blue contour that Van Gogh sometimes painted around them. Now one barely notices that there were altogether more than thirty roses. Van Gogh reserved the colour green largely for the leaves of the rose bush, so that this does

stand out a little from the background.

The asylum garden had three levels, rising to the rear. The roses here were in the central part. To the upper left, part of a low stone wall is visible, and behind that are other bright red flowers, while just below the upper edge the outer wall is just discernible in a continuous strip of darker crosshatching intersected here and there by a branch of the rose bush.[5] The ground to the left is done in horizontal yellow, green and purple strokes. At the bottom the bushes rise out of the grass in a series of longer vertical strokes. The entire composition is a woven tapestry of brush strokes of endlessly varying length, thickness and direction. The lines and strokes were made with scarcely any descriptive intent, but, with a few exceptions (such as the roses), were mainly grouped as shimmering, abstract signs suggesting general shapes. The deep, dark blue strokes Van Gogh added in a final phase, often rhythmically adjacent in ordered groups, lend the work a salient graphic finishing touch. He structured trees and bushes in a similar way in a number of his major paintings in this period.[6]

1. See the contributions of Marije Vellekoop in Ives et al. 2005, pp. 294-295 and 304-307, also for the dating of the sheets. The series comprises F1526, F1527, F1533, F1534, F1535, F1536 and F1537. Blooming rose bushes in she garden of the asylum is covered in dark rings on the verso from the oil soaking through the paper. The series of three interior scenes in the asylum (F1528, F1529, F1530) were also found to have been done in oil and not in watercolour (ibid., pp. 322-327), which means that Van Gogh made no watercolours at all in Saint-Rémy.

2. F1526 (private collection), with the same blooming rose bush as the main subject, has no underdrawing either. They may have been thought of as a pair. Combinations of the other sheets in the series are also conceivable (Pickvance in Van der Wolk et al. 1990, pp. 284-285, Heenk 1995, pp. 185-186 and Pickvance 2000, pp. 238 and 308).

3. Optically depth is accentuated by making parts that are further away gradually more blue to distinguish them from a green foreground and central plane, as can be seen in many seventeenth-century landscapes. The clear, unbroken light blue spread rhythmically over the entire plane conversely emphasises the flatness.

4. The fading can probably be attributed to the use of an unstable organic red pigment (see Van Heugren 2005, p. 53).

5. The fact that the flowers in the background have retained their colour, in contrast with the roses, is probably because Van Gogh used a different pigment here.

6. For example Lilacs (F579, Hermitage, St Petersburg) and The garden of the asylum as Saint-Rémy (F734, Kröller-Müller Museum, Otterlo) done in the first weeks of May.

P. 211

Olive grove

June 1889
Oil on canvas
72.4 x 91.9 cm
F585/JH1758
KM 104.278

SIGNATURE/INSCRIPTIONS/LABELS
Recto, lower left: Vincent
Verso, stretcher: Galerie Druet/No 6890/Gogh van! Les
oliviers verts/toile 73 x 92 (label). 4174 (blue chalk)

PROVENANCE
Jo van Gogh-Bonger, Amsterdam. purchased by A.
Schuffenecker, Meudon, April 1906. Prince of Wagram coll.,
Paris. art dealer Eugene Druet, Paris. purchased by H. Kröller-
Müller at Druet, art dealer, 13 April 1912 (f10,000)

EXHIBITIONS
Cologne 1912, no. 98.
The Hague 1913, no. 143.
Basle/Bern 1927, no. 104.
Brussels 1927, no. 104.
Dusseldorf 1928, no. 171.
Karlsruhe 1928, no. 106.
Berlin 1928-1929, no. 60.
Hamburg 1929, no. 60.
Amsterdam 1930, no. 243.
Paris no. 148.
Geneva 1947, no. 148.
Basle 1947, no. 87.
London/Birmingham/Glasgow 1947-1948, no. 74.
Amsterdam 1948, cat. without nos..
New York/Chicago 1949-1950, no. 120.
Milan 1952, no. 108.
The Hague 1953, no. 160.
Otterlo/Amsterdam 1953, no. 148.
Saint Louis/Philadelphia/Toledo 1953-1954, no. 137.
Eindhoven 1956, no. 41.
Munich 1956, no. 144.
Vienna 1958, no. 95.
Tokyo/Kyoto 1958, no. 115.
Paris 1960 (b), no. 204.
Moscow/Leningrad 1971, no. 97.
New York 1986-1987, no. 11.
Rome 1988, no. 37.
Yokohama/Nagoya 1995-1996, no. 67

REMARKS
Recorded in the account book of Theo van Gogh and Jo van
Gogh-Bonger (Stolwijk & Veenenbos 2002, p. 180 Photo
Druet no. 6334: Les oliviers verts

'Here there are very beautiful fields with olive

trees, which are grey and silvery green, like pollard
willows. And I never get tired of the blue sky,' wrote
Van Gogh on 2 July 1889 to his mother (787/598).
This is nearly an exact description of this Olive grove,
and Van Gogh had very likely finished the painting
by the time he wrote this letter. In the same period he
was working on Olive trees with Les Al-pilles in the
background, a canvas which is mentioned explicitly
in his letters, unlike this Olive grove. Olive groves
became one of the artist's favourite subjects, though
it was a theme he had all but avoided in Arles. They
belonged to the landscape of Provence, just like the
cypresses, the wheat fields and the mountainous
landscape, and in Saint-Remy Van Gogh conceived
a plan to work on these subjects, turning them into
series of paintings. Between June and December
1889 he painted around fifteen olive groves, most of
them in the autumn and eleven of them on size 30
canvases, his favourite format.[1]

In this study from nature Van Gogh used - in
addition to several longer brushstrokes for the tree
trunks, branches and contours - mainly short, curved
brushstrokes, thus creating a vibrant skin of paint
composed of countless brushstrokes, applied wet-in-
wet, which render almost palpable the sweltering heat
the painter was working in. Van Gogh had meanwhile become used to this, for in the letter to his
mother cited above he also wrote: 'I've been painting
in the wheat fields during the hottest part of the
day, without being much hampered by it.' At a later
stage, when the paint had dried enough, he used dark
blue paint to apply accents to the foliage, thicken the
contours here and there, and add his signature, which
follows in an elegant arc the direction of the curved
brushstrokes below it. Olive grove is one of the seven
signed paintings from the Saint-Remy period, though
doubt has been cast on the authenticity of one of
the signatures (Pine trees at sunset). The four large
studies Van Gogh painted in May 1889 are all signed,
including The garden of the asylum at Saint-Remy,
which, like the Olive grove, was signed with dark blue
paint when the canvas was sufficiently dry. Around
15 July Van Gogh sent these four 'May studies' - along
with other works, made in Saint-Remy as well as in
Arles - to Theo in Paris. This shipment also included
a work called 'Olives', which was very likely this Olive
grove (792/600, c.9July 1889).[2]

On 13 April 1912 Mrs Kröller-Müller bought
five paintings by Van Gogh in Paris from the art
dealer Eugene Druet. 'But the most beautiful is an
olive grove,' she wrote that evening in her hotel room
to her young confidant Sam van Deventer, 'so tender
and heartfelt and such a complete, large painting.
I can't describe it to you, but in the eyes of most it
will be the most beautiful painting of all, because it
contains absolutely nothing which is disturbing.'[3] She
also reports that Bremmer, who had travelled along
with her and her husband, had struck a very good
bargain by acquiring the five works for a third of the
asking price: 'He went outside trembling like a leaf,
he was so happy about his haul.' An understandable
reaction, considering that, in addition to the truly
magnificent Olive grove, the 'haul' also included
Basket of apples, Portrait of Joseph-Michel Ginoux,
The ravine (Les Peirouiets) and Loom with weaver

The same day, shortly after lunch, she bought two
more paintings by Van Gogh at Bernheim-Jeune's
(La Berceuse, and Landscape with wheat sheaves and
rising moon) and two drawings by Van Gogh (Woman
praying, F1053, and Peasant woman gleaning, F1269),
as well as a painting by Seurat (Fetty at Honfleur). She
reminded Van Deventer how she had decided several
years earlier to let her husband and her family 'share
in the realm of thought that affected her so much'.
This was an allusion to her decision at that time to
have Bremmer come to their house once a week to
give them lessons in practical aesthetics, as well as
to guide them in making a serious start at collecting
works of art. And she closes her letter by saying, 'Is
it not a source of deep satisfaction if today Monsieur
happily buys paintings for 60,000 guilders?'

1. Pickvance 1986, p.98; see also p.16
2. Ibid., pp. 293-295.
3. Cited in Van Deventer 1956, pp. 54-56.

P. 213

The good Samaritan (after Delacroix)

Early May 1890
Oil on canvas
713 x 59.5 cm
F633/JH1974
KM 104.010

SIGNATURE/INSCRIPTIONS/LABELS

PROVENANCE
Jo van Gogh Bonger in storage with Tanguy, Paris. Willy
Gretor (W.R.J. Petersen), Paris, 1891. P. Goldmann coll.,
Paris. Ambroise Vollard, art dealer, Paris, December 1895. E.
Schuffenecker, Paris, December 1895. Prince of Wagram coll.,
Paris. Barbazanges, art dealer, Paris. purchased for H. Kröller
Müller by Leonard in Paris, May July 1912 (f17,500)[1]

EXHIBITIONS
Paris 1901, no. 51 (Le bon Samaritain, app. E. Schuffenecker).
Paris 1909, no. 50 (Le bon Samaritain).

Cologne1912, not in cat. 2.
The Hague 1913, no. 145. Antwerp 1914, no. 42.
Basle/Bern 1927, no. 135.
Brussels 1927, no. 135.
Dusseldorf 1928, no. 200.
Karlsruhe 1928, no. 135.
Berlin 1928 1929, no. 133.
Hamburg 1929, no. go.
Amsterdam 1930, no. 239.
New York/Philadelphia/Boston and other cities 1935-1936, no. 54.
The Hague 1945, no. 38.
Liege/Brussels/Mons 1946-1947, no. 162.
Paris 1947, no. 163. Geneva 1947, no. 163.
Basle 1947, no. 101.
London/Birmingham/Glasgow 1947-1948, no. 85.
Paris 1950-1951, no. 20.
Milan 1952, no. 119.
The Hague 1953, no. 174.
Otterlo/Amsterdam 1953, no. 166.
Saint Louis/Philadelphia/Toledo 1953-1954, no. 149.
Munich 1956, no. 155.
Essen 1957, no. 361.
Vienna 1958, no. 105.
Tokyo/Kyoto 1958, no. 126.
Sao Paulo 1959, no. 11.
Warsaw 1962, no. 84.
Tel Aviv/Haifa 1962-1963, no. 94.
Belgrade 1966, no. 81.
Tokyo/Nagoya 1985-1986, no. 90.
Osaka1986, no. 18.

REMARKS

Recorded in the account book of Theo van Gogh and Jo van Gogh Bonger (Stolwijk & Veenenbos 2002, p. 182) Photo Druet no. 7304: L'enlevement

'I'm also going to copy Delacroix's Good Samaritan,' Van Gogh wrote to his brother Theo not, however, in May 1890, when the painting was actually executed, but almost eight months earlier (806/607, 19 September 1889). Van Gogh had begun making copies following his breakdown of the summer, and had already completed his own version of Delacroix's Pieta (F630). For some time, he remained preoccupied with Millet and others, but in February 1890 he wrote once again that he wanted to take up the Good Samaritan, and it seems possible he may at that time have already begun on it (855/626, 10 or 11 February 1890). A renewed crisis prevented further progress, but in May he was able to announce to Theo: 'I've also tried to make a copy of Delacroix's Good Samaritan' (867/632, 3 May 1890). This was the last time the subject would be mentioned in the correspondence.

Van Gogh had long owned the model on which this picture is based, a lithograph after the original by J. Laurens. Reproductions of both Delacroix's Pieta and The Good Samaritan decorated his room in the hospital at Aries (771/590, 3 May 1889). He regarded the copying of his favourite masters not as slavish imitation; rather, he sought to learn from them and to add something to their work, comparing himself to a musician giving his own interpretation to a well known composition. He set up the black and white reproduction in front of him, 'and then,' he wrote, 'I improvise on it with color, but of course not simply out of my imagination, but

seeking memories of their paintings the memory, the vague harmony of colors that may not be completely right but nonetheless have the right feeling, that is my own interpretation' (806/607, 19 September 1889). These 'memories of color' must have been particularly important when working after Delacroix, much more so than in the case of Millet. The former's reputation as a fervent colorist had already led Van Gogh to claim that as far as the use of color was concerned, Delacroix was 'more complete' than the impressionists (771/590, May 1889). And in the period of his squabbles with Theo regarding his own somewhat stylised works, he defended himself by praising Delacroix as the model of an artist who had also sought to 'render the interwovenness of the various components' (818/613, c. 2 November 1889).

It is precisely these two aspects — color and drawing - that Van Gogh emphasises in his copy. The powerful movement of the lines and the twisting movements of the figures strengthen the drama of the scene in the foreground. The undulating brushwork is repeated in the mountains in the background, which brings to mind the landscape of the Alpilles. The Samaritan's bright red turban and the purple blue clothing echo Delacroix's own palette. The biblical tale of the (non believing) Samaritan, who halts his journey to help the defenseless victim of a robbery remount his horse, undoubtedly also played a role in Van Gogh's decision to make a copy after this particular work. In September, when he first toyed with the idea, he himself needed to regain his footing, and the same was true in May 1890. At that time he had finally decided to leave the asylum for good, and it is not impossible that the painting also makes reference to his brother Theo, his personal Samaritan, who was always ready and willing to help him back into the saddle. There is, however, no mention of this aspect in the letters.'

The earlier Pieta, the contemporaneous 'translation' of The raising of Lazarus after an etching by Rembrandt and the Good Samaritan are Van Gogh's only three religious works, and they are all copies. The manner in which Gauguin and Bernard had tackled similar themes — not as copies but as independent compositions — did not appeal to Van Gogh in the least. He felt they had left reality too far behind and had created something overly abstract. The examples of Delacroix and Rembrandt were, in his opinion, unsurpassable, but they could be interpreted, and in The Good Samaritan Van Gogh appears to have used his strong brushwork to differentiate himself from the flattened forms employed by his friends.

1. Note by H.P. Bremmer in the inventory of c. 1915: 'Gekocht door Leonard te Parijs in 1912. Waarschijnlijk uit de verz. van den Prins y. Wagram.' ('Purchased by Leonard in Paris in 1912. Probably from the collection of the Prince of Wagram.')
2. The painting was added in August together with seven other works; documented by photographs, see Feilchenfeldt 1988, p. 149.
3. Homburg 1996, pp. 73-74.

P. 215

Cypresses

February 1890
black chalk, pen and reed pen in black ink, on wove paper
31.9 x 23.7 cm
no watermark unsigned F1525a/JH1887 KM 115.638

INSCRIPTIONS
verso, lower left: v. Gogh
tentoonstelling/no422 (black ink)
No 237 [crossed out] (black ink]'

PROVENANCE
Theo van Gogh, Paris, 1890-1891' Jo van Gogh-Bonger, Bussum/Amsterdam, 1891-1905 'purchased by Miss J.A. van Hasselt, Amsterdam, October 1905 (150 guilders)' purchased by the Rijksmuseum Kröller-Müller at the Haagsche Kunsthandel, The Hague, 21 January 1943 (2200 guilders)

EXHIBITIONS
Leiden 1893, no cat.
Amsterdam 1905, cat. no. 422.
Basel 1947, cat. no. 163.
Milan 1952, cat. no. 122.
Nuremberg 1956, car. no. 67.
Munich 1956, cat. no. 140.
Vienna 1958, car. no. 108.
Tokyo/Kyoto 1958, cat. no. 112.
Sao Paulo 1959, cat. no. 3.
Munich 1961, car. no. 70.
London 1962, cat. no. 61.
Warsaw 1962, car. no. 86.
Tel Aviv/Haifa 1962-1963, cat. no. 96.
Kassel 1964, unnumbered.
Arnhem 1966, unnumbered.
Moscow/Leningrad 1971, car. no. 98.
New York/Chicago/Ottawa and other cities, 1973-1974, car. no. 54.
London/Newcastle-upon-Tyne 1974, cat. no. 41.
Yokohama/Nagoya 1995-1996, cat. no. 64.
Tokyo/Fukuoka 1999-2000, cat. no. 65.
Sapporo/Kobe 2002, car. no. 44.
Seattle/Atlanta 2004-2005, car. no. 21.

NOTE
A In late 1890 Andries Bonger, the brother of Johanna van Gogh-Bonger, compiled a list of the Van Gogh paintings in Theo's collection, the so-called AR list, comprising 364 numbers and titles. No such list exists of the drawings, but Johanna herself did number some of the drawings on the back (Stolwijk & Veenenbos, pp. 23-24, 26-27). These can sometimes be traced back to exhibition and sale lists. The

crossed out number '237' on this drawing can, for example, be linked to an exhibition of drawings of Vincent van Gogh in 1893 in De Lakenhal in Leiden organised by Cees Verster. A handwritten list of the drawings exhibited there with Johanna's numbers and titles includes: '237 Populieren' (Poplars] (Wintgens Hötte & De Jongh-Vermeulen 1999, pp. 97-99). Cypresses and poplars at that time were often confused. The number was replaced in 1905 by 422, a reference to the catalogue of the major Van Gogh exhibition mounted that year in the Amsterdam Stedelijk Museum, where the title was 'Cypresses with female figures' (Amsterdam 1905, p. 40).

January 1890 saw the publication in the Mercure de France of the first detailed appreciative article about Vincent van Gogh written by the young critic and poet Gabriel-Albert Aurier [1865-1892].[1] Van Gogh was extremely pleased with the article but also proved modest in a thank you letter to Aurier, suggesting that artists like Gauguin and Monticelli actually deserved greater praise than he did (854/626a, 10 or 11 February 1890). In the same letter he promised to send Aurier a painted study: 'If you will do me the pleasure of accepting it, I shall include a study of a cypress for you in the next batch I send to my brother, in remembrance of your article. I am still working on it at the moment, as I want to put a small figure into it. [...] The study that I intend for you represents a group of cypresses in the corner of a wheat field on a summer day during a mistral: He had already painted that work, which is now also in the Kröller-Müller Museum, in June 1889, and held onto it up to then. In the end he inserted not one but two female figures for Aurier. Before sending it to Aurier in Paris by way of Theo he first made copies of it for himself. a small painted study (F621, Van Gogh Museum, Amsterdam) and this drawing.[2]

Van Gogh copied the painting fairly precisely, but in the left of the drawing he included a little more sky. He also placed less emphasis on the intensely spiralling banks of clouds shown in the painting and confined himself to a few light lines. He worked with various pens and ink on a fairly detailed underdrawing in black chalk which he smudged lightly in places. In a last phase he used a somewhat broader reed pen for the darker accents in the cypresses, which are otherwise entirely made up of comma-like strokes.[3] Most singularly, the figures are larger, relatively speaking, than in the painting, so that they become a more explicit part of the entire composition. One can clearly see in the painting that the figures were added later on. Van Gogh did not take the trouble to scrape off the paint but painted them directly onto the original, heavily impastoed layer. As a result the figures are a little messy. In the drawing they stand our more from the cypresses behind them and are a more convincing part of the surroundings.

Van Gogh worked on wove paper of rather sub-standard quality which has become considerably darker over the years, presumably because it was glued for a long time to an acidic cardboard.[4] Consequently the picture is now more somber than was originally intended. In a number of places light patches are visible where the paper has retained its original shade to some extent. In the cypresses to the extreme right a number of green/yellow/white mixed oil paint spots are visible and a minute speck of blue. This could indicate that Van Gogh had the drawing close by while he was working on the small copy in oil.

The sheet, like Graveyard in the rain (La fosse commune'), was acquired by the museum during the war with money that the German occupiers had made available as compensation for three paintings that had been removed from the collection and transported to Germany. The director during the war, Sam van Deventer, was alerted to the drawing by the art historian J.G. van Gelder, who wrote to him on 27 November 1942 that he had referred the owner, Jan Frequin of the Haagsche Kunsthandel, who had offered him the drawing, to the Kröller-Müller Museum.[5] The sheet had completely disappeared from public view after the sale in 1905 by Johanna van Gogh-Bonger and was not known in the literature: it is absent for example from De la Faille's 1928 catalogue raisonné. Van Gelder -and many others after him - believed it was a preliminary study and consequently thought it was entirely appropriate to keep it in the museum with the painting.[6]

1. G.-Albert Aurier, 'Les isolées: Vincent van gogh', Mercure de France 1 (1890) 1, pp. 24-29.
2. Van Gogh had also made a large pen drawing after the painting earlier in June 1889 without the figures (Cypresses, F1524, Art institute of Chicago).
3. Compare for example Cypresses with four figures working in the field (F1539r, Folkwang Museum, Essen), a drawing in black chalk that was also made around February/March 1890 and on which the cypresses are drawn in a similar way.
4. The drawing was restored in 1987 and backed with Japanese paper because 'the paper [...] was already in an advanced state of decay' (Hoefsloot 1987, p. 70).
5. The painting had been acquired already in 1914 by Mrs Kröller-Müller from Aurier's heirs, see Otterlo 2003, pp. 296-300 and 406-410. De la Faille 1970 also took it to be a preliminary study and dared the sheet June 1889, although De Gruijter 1962, pp. 110-111, had already pointed our that the drawing must have originated after the amended painting in February 1890. Hulsker 1977, p. 439, dated it to February 1890. Hefting 1980, p. 117, recognised the insertion of the figures on the painting in February 1890, but nevertheless was of the view that stylistically the drawing was better placed in 1889.
6. Although Van Gelder also wrote that the purchase price need not be an objection, he did not mention it (the letter is in the Kröller-Müller Museum Archives). In the end the drawing was acquired for 2200 guilders, but the director, A.M. Hammacher, noted after the war in the margin of a typed list of the acquisitions of 1943 (complied by Sam van Deventer on 11 April 1944, Kröller-Müller Museum Archives) that the drawing 'according to Professor van Gelder was offered to him for sale for around 800 guilders', a singular discrepancy (see also Graveyard in the rain ('Fosse commune'), p. 349, note 1).

P. 217

Cypresses with two figures

June 1889 (completed February 1890)
Oil on canvas
91.6 x 72.4 cm
F620/JH1748
KM 103.931

SIGNATURE/INSCRIPTIONS/LABELS
Verso, stretcher: 35 (blue chalk).
37 (blue chalk)

PROVENANCE
Gift of the artist to A. Aurier, Paris, 1890. S. Williame-Aurier coll,, Chateauroux, 5 October 1892. purchased for H. Kröller-Müller by H.P. Bremmer from J.Williame, Chateauroux, June 1914

EXHIBITIONS
Paris 1891 (b), no. 75 (Peupliers d'Italie) 1.
Paris 1895 (Peupliers d'Italie) 2.
Baste/Bern 1927, no. 131.
Brussels 1927, no. 131.
Dusseldorf 1928, no. 196.
Karlsruhe 1928, no. 131.
Berlin 1928-1929, no. 122.
Hamburg 1929, no. 86.
Amsterdam 1930, no. 237.
New York/Philadelphia/Boston and other cities 1935-1936, no. 49.
Liege/Brussels/Mons 1946-1947, no. 143.
Paris 1947, no. 144.
Geneva 1947, no. 144.
Basle 1947, no. 85.
London/Birmingham/Glasgow 1947-1948, no. 69.
New York/Chicago 1949-1950, no. 113.
The Hague 1953, no. 154.
Otterlo/Amsterdam 1953, no. 159.
Saint Louis/Philadelphia/Toledo 1953-1954, no. 132.
Munich 1956, no. 142.
Essen 1957, no. 35.
Vienna 1958, no. 94.
Tokyo/Kyoto 1958, no. 119.
Aix-en-Provence 1959, no. 39.
Amsterdam 1990, no. 91.
Essen/Amsterdam 1990-1991, no. 42.
Saint Louis/Frankfurt 2001, cat. without nos.

In southern regions the slender, dark and flaming silhouette of the cypress is a common sight. The tree - an evergreen - can grow very old. In classical antiquity the cypress functioned as the attribute of various deities, the most important of whom was Chronos (Saturn), the father of Zeus (Jupiter) and the tutelary deity of old men. The cypress, for example, is symbolic both of longevity - and, in Christianity, of the hope for an afterlife - and of death. Tradition has it that Cyparissus was changed into this tree after accidentally killing a pet stag that had been a gift from Apollo, giving rise to the name cypress. The funereal tree par excellence, it is still commonly found in and around cemeteries in Medi-terranean countries. In the nineteenth century it was the German artist Arnold Böcklin (1827-1901) in particular who so graphically immortalised these mysterious, mournful giants in his paintings of Toteninsel.

It is by no means certain, however, that Van Gogh was alluding in his paintings to the cypress as a symbol of death. One would expect it, considering his fits of extreme melancholy, but perhaps his endless search for consolatory painting prevented him from choosing a subject that was too overtly sad, although he sometimes referred to such themes implicitly. In Arles he included cypresses in only a couple of paintings, but only in their capacity as windbreaks, such as in Orchard bordered by cypresses. In other paintings dating from this period they sometimes lend a 'sombre note' to the background (692/541, C. 27 September 1888). Only in Saint-Rémy did he paint the cypress as a completely independent subject, apparently taking it up primarily as a painterly challenge. On 25 June 1889 he wrote to Theo:

We have had some glorious days and I have made a start on yet more canvases, so that there are twelve size 30 canvases in prospect. Two studies of cypresses of that difficult bottle-green hue; I have worked up their foregrounds with thick layers of lead white, which gives firmness to the ground. I think that the Monticellis were very often prepared in this way. You then put other colors over it. But I don't know if the canvases are strong enough for this work (785/596).

The two studies he mentions are the painting now in New York and Cypresses with two figures in the Kröller-Müller Museum. Together with Wheat field with reaper and sun, which he started at the same time, they belong to his most pastose works, painted, according to Pickvance, in 'near bas-relief', as it were.[3]

Further on in the same letter Vincent told Theo: 'The cypresses are always occupying my thoughts; I should like to make something of them like the canvases of the sunflowers, because it astonishes me that they have not yet been done as I see them. They are as beautiful as an Egyptian obelisk in line and proportion. And the green is so unique. It is a black spot in a sunny landscape, but it is one of the most interesting black notes, one of the most difficult to capture on canvas as far as I can tell.' If by this Van Gogh meant that he saw the cypress

as the counterpart of his sunflowers - symbols of gratitude, hope and friendship - he seems now to be referring to the melancholy and sorrow traditionally associated with the cypress. He may also have had something in mind in the way of a very personal technical execution, akin to what he had done with the sunflowers, and perhaps he was playing with the idea of a decorative programme consisting of a series of cypresses.[4] Druick and Zegers argue that Van Gogh was alluding to the cypress as a symbol of death, as he had done with the reaper in his contemporaneous Wheat field with reaper and sun.[5] Van Gogh had expressly connected that painting to death as a phase in the eternal life cycle, something he did not do explicitly with the cypresses of that period. Seven months later, when he was forced to cope with a new setback to his health, he expressed himself more clearly when on 2 February 1890 he again raised the subject of the sunflowers: 'To make beautiful things you need a certain dose of inspiration, a beam from above, something we do not have in us. When I had done those sunflowers, I sought their opposite, yet all the same their equal, and I said: it's the cypress, (851/625).

That quotation was taken from a letter containing Van Gogh's reaction to an article about him that had appeared in the first issue (January 1890) of the new magazine Mercure de France. The article, "Les isolés: Vincent van Gogh", considered to be the first serious piece of writing about the artist, was written by the young poet and critic Albert Aurier.[6] Van Gogh was very much surprised and not completely happy about it. He thought that Aurier had done him too much honour, and that he was not nearly so far with his painting as the critic made one think, though he hoped one day he would be. Aurier gave a breathtaking description of Van Gogh's work, which he compared with precious stones, minerals, metals and crystals (elaborating on the 'correspondances' of his fellow poet Baudelaire). He praised the painter as a dreaming realist whose ability to bend reality to his will was unrivalled. 'An article like that has its own value as a form of art criticism,' wrote Vincent to Theo, 'as such I think it is to be respected, and the writer must inflate the tone...' Aurier also mentioned the cypresses: '...these are cypresses holding up their nightmarish silhouettes of flames, which would be black...'. Vincent wrote approvingly: 'Aurier feels it too when he says that even black is a colour and that they somehow resemble flames.' At the end of his letter he asks Theo to thank Aurier: 'I shall of course send you a note for him, and a study as well.'

The study that Aurier was eventually to receive was, appropriately enough, this picture of Cypresses with two figures. In September Van Gogh had sent the study that is now in New York to Theo, where Aurier had probably seen it. Van Gogh kept the other study.[7] He added two female figures to the study intended for Aurier, made a copy for himself in a smaller format, as well as a drawing, and, at the end of April, sent the painting to Theo, who in turn gave it to Aurier. On 10 or 11 February Van Gogh wrote a letter to Aurier, in which he thanked him and told him about his present: 'The study that I mean to give

you represents a group of cypresses in the corner of a wheat field on a summer's day when the mistral is blowing. It is therefore a kind of black note wrapped in blue that is being moved by great air currents, and the vermilion of the poppies forms a contrast to the black note. You will see that it is nearly the same color combination seen in those pretty scottish tartans, green, blue, red, yellow, black, which both you and I used to like so much and which you hardly ever see nowadays, sad to say' (854/626a). No melancholy chord is struck in this description, though Van Gogh also wrote: 'So far I have not been able to do them as I feel them; the emotions that seize me when I behold nature drive me to the brink of unconsciousness, with the result that I am unable to work for a fortnight or so.'

It is the painter's inner strife which makes him doubt his own ability time after time, an exhausting battle between reality and dream which, at the best of times, could produce an inspired painting. At about the same time that he wrote to Aurier, Vincent wrote to Theo: 'Aurier's article would encourage me if I dared to let myself go and dared more to free myself from reality and dared to use color to make a melody of tones, as is the case with some of Monticelli's paintings. But the truth, even the striving to make something true, is so dear to me; in the end I think, I believe that I would rather be a shoemaker than a musician with colors' (855/626, 10 or 11 February 1890).

Van Gogh gave Aurier instructions on what to do with the painting, thereby raising the tip of the veil with respect to his own thoughts on the subject of how his work should be treated: 'When the study that I am going to send you is completely dry, also in the impastos — this will not be the case for at least a year — I think you would do well to give it a good coat of varnish. And in the meantime it must be washed a number of times with a lot of water in order to get all the oil out. This study is painted in deep Prussian blue [...]. As soon as these Prussian blue hues are quite dry, I think that after varnishing it you will get the thoroughly black tones which are necessary to bring out the various dark green hues' (854/626a). Although Van Gogh described the cypress as a black note in an otherwise sunny landscape, he hardly ever used black paint. Like Aurier, he thought that black was also a color, and he preferred Prussian blue for deep, dark colors. With respect to the frame, he suggested that a 'very simple flat frame in vivid orange lead' would go best with the blues and the black green hues, heightening the effect of a pretty Scottish tartan. Whether Aurier followed his instructions is not entirely clear. Technical examination has revealed traces in the cypresses and the sky of a dirty brown layer of varnish that could be authentic.[8] Because of the dark greens, however, it is not possible to determine the number of layers of varnish by means of ultraviolet light.

---

1. Aurier sent the painting, together with Terrace of a café at night and Wheat stack under a cloudy sky in December 1891 to Le Barc de Boutteville in Paris for the Ière Exposition des Peintres Impressionnistes et Symbolistes, where it was hung under the misleading title Peupliers

d'Italie (Italian poplars). Scarcely any notice was taken of this exhibition in the Van Gogh literature (see Dorn et al. 1990, p.136), and even though there were only three works by Van Gogh in the exhibition, it was the third time since his death that his work had been displayed in a Paris exhibition (the other two took place at the Artistes Independants in 1890 and 1891), Three months later, in April 1892, Emile Bernard mounted an exhibition of works by Van Gogh at Le Barc de Boutteville. Aurier died in the autumn of 1892 and his collection of presumably twelve Van Goghs remained together until 1914, when Mrs Kröller Müller acquired most of the Aurier estate, which had largely disappeared from view. Only in 1895 did his sister Suzanne send an unknown number of works to Vollard for an exhibition.

2. See Den Dulk 1895
3. Pickvance 1986, p.110.
4. Ibid.; see also Dom 1990.
5. Druick & Zegers 2001, p. 289.
6. See Mathews 1986 and Pickvance 1986, pp. 310-315; see also pp. 406-410.
7. Pickvance 1986, p. 298.
8. Technical examination carried out at the Kröller Müller Museum, 15 July 2002. This is the only time that Van Gogh refers in a letter to the varnishing of his work.

P. 221

Country road in Provence by night

C. 12-15 May 1890
Oil on canvas
90.6 x 72 cm
F683/JH1982
KM 108.488

SIGNATURE/INSCRIPTIONS/LABELS
Verso, stretcher: van Gogh/No 10205/La Route de Provence (label Paul Cassirer, art dealer, Berlin).
Berlin No 19 [14?] (blue chalk) [exhib. Berlin 1910?].
41 (blue chalk) 35 (blue chalk).
3442 (blue chalk).
No 4 (blue chalk)

PROVENANCE

A. Schuffenecker coll., Meudon (acquired before 1901). Paul Cassirer, art dealer, Berlin1. Prince of WagraColl., Paris. purchased for H. Kröller Müller by Leonard in Paris, May July 1912 (f10,000)2

EXHIBITIONS
Paris 1895, no cat.3.
Paris 1901, no. 38 (La route de Provence, app. A. Schuffenecker).
Paris 1905, no. 36 (La route de Provence, nuit etoilee, Coll. A. Schuffenecker).
Paris 1909, no. 4S (Paysage provencal).
Berlin 1910, no. 22 (Landstrasse in der Provence).
Cologne 1912, not in cat. 4.
The Hague 1913, no. 126.
Antwerp 1914, no. 43.
Basle/Bern 1927, no. 136.
Brussels 1927, no. 136.
Dusseldorf 1928, no. 201.
Karlsruhe 1928, no. 136. Berlin 1928-1929, no. 138.
Hamburg 1929, no. 91.
Amsterdam 1930, no. 236.
New York/Philadelphia/Boston and other cities 1935-1936, no. 59.
The Hague 1945, no. 37.
Liege/Brussels/Mons 1946 1947, no. 161.
Paris1947, no. 162.
Geneva 1947, no. 162.
Basle 1947, no. 99.
London/Birmingham/Glasgow 1947-1948, no. 83.
New York/Chicago 1949-1950, no. 131.
Milan 1952, no. 114.
The Hague 1953, no. 176.
Otterlo/Amsterdam 1953, no. 155.
Saint Louis/Philadelphia/Toledo 1953-1954, no. 151.
Eindhoven 1956, no. 48.
Munich 1956, no. 158.
Vienna 1958, no. 104.
TokyoKyoto 1958, no. 124.
Aix en Provence1959, no. 51.
Montreal/Ottawa/Winnipeg/Toronto 1960-1961, no. 68.
Warsaw 1962, no. 78.
Tel Aviv/Haifa 1962-1963, no. 88.
New York 1986-1987, no. 55.
Amsterdam 1990, no. 117.
Yokohama/Nagoya 1995-1996, no. 69.
Chicago/Amsterdam 2001-2002, no. 135.

REMARKS
Photo Druet no. 2405: Route de Provence

During the time he worked on this painting Van Gogh was busy preparing to leave the asylum in Saint Remy for good. It is very likely the last canvas he executed there, painted between 12 and 15 May 1890. Around one month later he gave an initial, highly detailed description of the scene in a letter to Gauguin: 'From down there, too, I also have a cypress with a star, a last attempt a night sky with a lustreless moon, nothing more than a thin sickle rising up out of the dark shadow of the earth; a star with an exaggerated glow, if you will, a pale pink and green light in the ultramarine sky with scudding clouds. Below is a road, with tall yellow reeds alongside, behind which, in the distance lie the low, blue Alpines; an old cottage with orange lit windows and a very tall cypress, bolt upright and very dark. On the road is a yellow carriage, drawn by a white horse, and two late wayfarers. Very romantic, if you like, but also

Provencal, I think' (draft letter 893/643, c. 17 June 1890). As if this was not enough, he also enclosed a sketch. Both this and the description, however, differ in several important points from the actual painting, probably a result of the fact that Van Gogh only received the work from Saint Remy a week after writing and had to describe it from memory (896/644, 24 or 25 June 1890). For example, two bright stars and two cypresses can be recognised in the canvas, while the drawing shows only one of each. In the sketch the cypress is placed to the left of the imaginary central axis; in the painting they are on the right. This makes for more room in the drawing for the inn in the background. In the painting, the wayfarers in the foreground are clearly workmen returning home. One of them carries a spade over his shoulder.

Van Gogh not only described and sketched the scene from memory, the painting itself is also a product of his imagination. This is what he meant when in his letter to Gauguin he referred to it as a 'last attempt,' that is: a final effort to create out of his head, purely from fancy. While under Gauguin's tutelage in Arles he had made his first experiments in this manner, and in Saint Remy he ventured it anew, with, as the most important results, the three night and evening landscapes The starry night (F612), Landscape with wheat sheaves and rising moon (p. 306) and this Country road in Provence. During his most recent breakdown, too, he had created five small works from memory, to which this picture is related. The inn in the background, for example, strongly recalls the thatchedroof farmhouses painted at the time and which he referred to as 'Reminiscences of the north'. He also made a number of drawings of horse drawn wagons, land labourers with spades and wayfarers in this period, which he then used for the painting.

Pickvance has argued that the discrepancies between the sketch and the painting are so great that Van Gogh must have considerably reworked the canvas while in Auvers, although he admits that this is difficult to prove.5 And indeed, it seems unlikely, given that a recent technical examination has shown clear traces of a painted underdrawing, which must have fixed the composition already at an early stage.6 There is, however, some evidence that Van Gogh did rework the canvas once he had arrived in Auvers; for example, he appears to have altered the road and one of the figures. It is also possible that he lined the canvas as well.7 The orange in the crescent moon, too, was applied later a layer of thin, transparent paint laid over the now dry surface. Of course, it is impossible to say whether these changes were made by Van Gogh himself or by someone else, and at exactly what date. In Pine trees at sunset the sun has been retouched in a similar manner, and in Landscape with wheat sheaves and rising moon several strokes of orange were applied to the moon after the paint had dried. In both the latter and Country road in Provence this yellow orange creates a stronger complementary contrast to the predominantly purple blue sky than would a simple yellow, making it seem probable that Van Gogh, who was always in search of such color effects, made the modifications himself.8

There is another interesting, although

somewhat speculative, factor that may indicate that the general layout of the composition was firmly established from the very beginning, at least as far as the sky and the placement of the cypresses is concerned. In the sketch, the bright star with its radiant halo is placed at the left, close to the edge of the paper; in the painting, however, there is a second, smaller star, with a more modest halo, just below it. Together with the moon, the three elements form a kind of bow. Around the time of painting, an announcement was made in French astronomic circles that on 20 April 1890, a day after the new moon, between 7 and 8:20 p.m., circumstances would be particularly favorable to a study of the crescent moon, as well as the conjunction between the moon, Venus and Mercury. On that evening, the three celestial bodies would be visible next to one another and clearly distinguishable in an arc of five degrees. Van Gogh has rendered this constellation quite exactly, only in reverse order: in reality, the moon was to the left of Venus, and Mercury to the right, and the arc went from left to right.[9] The artist probably found this natural phenomenon interesting enough to depict, and during the painting process several weeks later either remembered it this way or, on compositional grounds, consciously transposed it just as in the sketch he placed the cypresses on the other side of the imaginary central axis.

This 'last attempt' brings together all the important motifs of Van Gogh's Saint Remy period. What he describes as reeds along the side of the road is also reminiscent of the ripe wheat of which he was so fond. He felt cypresses were a wonderful subject and so typical of Provence that he hoped to devote an entire series to them. Combined with the dark blue silhouette of his much loved Alpilles in the left background, and the inn as a 'memory of the north' at the right, he here depicts the very essence of his sojourn in the Midi. In terms of the search for style, this picture is perfectly in keeping with the other experimental works he created in artistic competition with Gauguin and Bernard. Already in the autumn of 1889 he had written to Theo that the works he would bring back with him were to form a kind of whole, 'Impressions of Provence,' as he called them (809/609, 5 October 1889). Country road in Provence is a kind of summary of these impressions. In the draft letter to Gauguin we read: 'I will probably make etchings of these and the other landscapes and motifs, all memories of Provence, and it would give me great pleasure to present you with a summary that is more or less felt through and thought out.' Van Gogh's new motifs were to be found in Auvers; Saint Remy was but a memory. The etchings were never produced, but did he perhaps send Gauguin or Bernard the promised painted 'summary'? Our painting's earliest provenance is unclear, but in 1895 it was included in an exhibition at Vollard's. As far as we know, the work was never in the hands of Theo's widow and she was not responsible for its sale to either an art dealer or private collector. For the time being, then, no definitive conclusion can be drawn.

1. An old label is pasted onto the stretcher; written in a delicate script are the words: 'van Gogh No 10205/La

Route de Provence'. A similar label can be found on Sorrowing old man, with, in the same handwriting: '[van] Gogh No 11563/Alter Mann'. The label appears again on Still life with a plate of onions, with the inscription: 'van Gogh No 1570/Le paquet de tabac'; and on the Portrait of Joseph Roulin: 'van Gogh No 10204/Le Postier'. The label is (dirty) white with two rows of dotted lines; only the word 'No' is printed. These labels must have come from Paul Cassirer's gallery in Berlin. Cassirer, however, is mentioned neither in the provenance history of Country road in Provence by night nor in that of the Portrait of Joseph Roulin, although it is known that Sorrowing old man and Still life with a plate of onions passed through his hands; the former was sold to Mr Kröller in 1912, the latter to Marczell de Nemes in 1910.This may be an indication that sometime after 1905 Amedee Schuffenecker sold the picture to Cassirer, who in turn sold it to the Prince of Wagram, one of his regular clients. The same may be true for the Roulin portrait, which in 1905 also still belonged to Amedee Schuffenecker.
2. Note by H.P. Bremmer in the inventory Of c. 1915: 'Gekocht door Leonard te Paris in 1912 a f 10.000 Waarschijnlijk uit de verz. van den Prins van Wagram.' ('Purchased by Leonard in Paris in 1912 for 10,000 guilders. Probably from the collection of the Prince of Wagram.')
3. In June 1995 the painting was included in an exhibition at the gallery of Ambroise Vollard, 39, rue Laffitte, Paris. Of the 20 or so works on display, ten had come from Jo van Gogh Bonger (Feilchenfeldt 1990, p.19). A critic for Kunstwereld, E. den Dulk, wrote a review of the show in which the work is described in detail (Kunstwereld, 24 June 1895). It remains unclear whether at the time it belonged to Vollard himself, a French collector or to Jo. It is not mentioned in her account book.
4. The painting was very likely added in August, together with seven other works. See Feilchenfeldt 1988, p.149.
5. Pickvance 1986, p.191.
6. Technical examination at the Kröller Müller Museum, 31 July 2002.
7. Technical report by J.J. Susijn, January 1983 (Kröller Müller Museum archive).
8. The moon may have been retouched for a quite different reason. In Lutetia (1925), the German collector Carl Sternheim describes an 'accident' he remembers that occurred in 1909 during one of his visits to Jo van Gogh Bonger in Amsterdam. Leaning against the wall, in full sunlight, were a number of pictures, with their painted sides facing one another. Due to the heat,Sternheim writes, they had become stuck together, so that 'when taking them apart a piece of the moon in one of the large landscapes with two figures and cypresses became loose and fell to the ground.' Sternheim liked to exaggerate, at least according to his biographer Patrick Bridgwater (1987, p.98), but this is certainly a strange coincidence. However, Jo never owned the painting the collector appears to be referring to namely Country road in Provence by night, the only Van Gogh painting with cypresses, two figures and a moon. Was Sternheim perhaps paying a call to someone else (Amedee Schuffenecker or the Prince of Wagram, for example), or did he visit Mrs KrollerMuller in or after 1912? This bizarre incident could perhaps explain why the moon in the painting was reworked. There is (as yet) no evidence of a Sternheim visit to the Krollers in The Hague.
9. Eijgenraam 1990, p. 16.

P. 227

Flower Vase with Thistles

1890
oil on canvas
40.8 x 33.6 cm
acc. no. :P04-0024

After leaving the mental hospital at Saint-Rémy, Van Gogh spent a few days at his brother Theo's house in Paris. He then moved to the beautiful village of Auvers-sur-Oise on the outskirts of Paris, where he would spend the last two months of his life, from May to July 1890. There, through Theo's introduction, Van Gogh was placed under the care of Paul Gachet, a psychiatrist who was an enthusiastic art lover and a Sunday painter himself. With Gachet's help, Van Gogh continued to work energetically even while suffering from attacks of mental illness.

This work is one of the several still lifes that Van Gogh painted on either June 16 or 17, 1890, depicting some wild flowers that he had found at Gachet's house. The only surviving still lifes by Van Gogh of wild flowers that include thistles are this work and Wild Flowers and Thistles in a Vase in a private collection. While different flowers are featured in the two paintings, they have been arranged in the same vase on a round table in both cases. The two works are therefore thought to have been painted around the same time.

In the outlines that define the table and the vase, one can perceive the influence of the ukiyo-e print Van Gogh collected so enthusiastically in Paris. The serrated thistle leaves and the heads of wheat extend outward as if embracing the flowers. The nearly concentric brushstrokes of the vase and the intersecting vertical and horizontal strokes of the pale blue background reveal that Van Gogh was still continuing persistently to explore the effects of line, color, and texture.

On July 27, Van Gogh shot himself in a wheat field; he died two days later. His art was almost totally unappreciated in his lifetime, but after his death, his unique expression of bold colors and passionate brushstrokes greatly influenced admiring Fauvist and Expressionist painters.

Literature

Alauzen, A.M. & P. Ripert, *Monticelli. Sa vie et son oeuvre*, Paris 1969.

Amsterdam, Catalogus der tentoonstelling van schilderijen en teekeningen door Vincent van Gogh, Amsterdam (Stedelijk Museum), 1905.

d'Argencourt, Louise & Roger Diederen, coll. cat. *European Paintings of the 19th Century. The Cleveland Museum of Art, Catalogue of Paintings, part 4, vol. 1*, Cleveland 1999.

Ariëns Volker, M., *Dirk Nijland 1881-1955*, Assen 1993.

Arnold, Matthias, *Vincent van Gogh*, Munich 1993.

Arnold, Matthias, *Vincent van Gogh. Werk und Wirkung*, Munich 1995.

Atema, 'Voorwoord', in *De Muze van Hindeloopen. 40 jaar Hidde Nijland Stichting*, Hindeloopen 1959, n.p.

Auping, J.W. jr., coll. cat. *Vincent van Gogh*, Otterlo (Rijksmuseum Kröller-Müller) 1939.

Aurier, G. Albert, *Oeuvres posthumes*, Paris 1893.

Bailey, Martin, Deborah Silverman, *Van Gogh in England. Portrait of the Artist as a Young Man*, exh. cat. London (Barbican Art Gallery), London 1992.

Bailey, Martin, 'At least forty five Van Goghs may well be fakes', *The Art Newspaper 8* (1997) 72, pp. 21-24.

Bailey, Martin, 'The Van Gogh fakes scandal: the tally one year later', *The Art Newspaper 9* (1998) 83, p. 15.

Bakker, Rudolf, *Provence & Côte d'Azur*, Amsterdam 1999 (1995).

Bakker, J.S., 'Dordt-voordat de heidenen kwamen', *Molenwereld 1* (1998) 11, pp. 226-232.

Balk, Hildelies, De kunstpaus. H.P. Bremmer 1871-1956, Diss. Vrije Universiteit Amsterdam, 2004.

Balk, Hildelies, 'De freule, de professor, de koop man en zijn vrouw. Het publiek van H.P. Bremmer', *Fong Holland 9* (1993) 2, pp. 4-24.

Balk, Hildelies, 'H.P. Bremmer en Leiden', in: Doris Wintgens Hotte and Ankie de Jongh Vermeulen(ed.), exhib. cat. *Dageraad van de Moderne Kunst. Leiden en omgeving 1890 1940*, Zwolle/Leiden 1999, pp. 41-70.

Balk, Hildelies, *Het netwerk van H.P. Bremmer. Kunstenaars, verzamelaars en de markt voor moderne kunst*, Heino/Wijhe (Hannema de Stuers Foundation) 2001.

Beeldende Kunst (ed. H.P. Bremmer), 24 volumes, 1913-1938.

Berge, Jos Ten, 'No longer in the Kröller-Müller collection in Otterlo 2003, pp. 387-402.

Berge, Jos Ten, 'The acquisitive Cornelis Hoogendijk', in Otterlo 2003, pp. 420-423.

Bernard, Emile (ed.), Lettres de Vincent van Gogh á Emile Bernard, Paris 1911.

Blanc, Charles, *Grammaire des arts du dessin, architecture, sculpture, peinture*, Paris 1867.

Blanc, Charles, *Les artistes de mon temps*, Paris 1876.

Blotkamp, Carel, 'Kunstenaars als critici. Kunstkritiek in Nederland, 1880-1895', in: Richard Bionda and Carel Blotkamp (ed.), exhib. cat. *De schilders van Tachtig. Nederlandse schiiderkunst 1880-1895*, Zwolle/Amsterdam

1991, pp. 75-87.

Blühm, Andreas & Louise Lippincott, exhib. cat. *Light! The Industrial Age, 1750-1900 Art and science, technology and society*, Amsterdam (Van Gogh Museum)/Pittsburgh (Carnegie Museum of Art) 2000.

Bodt, Saskia de & Maartje de Haan, exhib. cat. *Bloemstillevens uit Nederland en Belgie 1870-1940*, Rotterdam (Kunsthal) 1998.

Bonnet, Marcel, Saint Rémy de Provence. *Chronique photographique de Frédéric George* (1868-1933), [s.l.] 1992.

Bouillon, Jean Paul, 'La correspondance de Felix Bracquemond. Une source inédite pour l'histoire de l'art français dans la seconde moitié du xlxe siècle', *Gazette des Beaux Arts* 115 (1973) 82, pp. 150-181.

Bouman, Jaap, 'Van Gogh en Dordt: het ongelijk van Lamers (2)', *De Dordtenaar*, 3 October 1989.

Bouman, Jaap, 'Van Gogh maakte nog 'n tekening', *De Dordtenaar*, 17 July 1990.

Bremmer, H.P., *Vincent van Gogh. Vier-en-twintig teekeningen uit zijn Hollandsche Periode -Verzameling Hidde Nijland*, Amsterdam 1907.

Bremmer, H.P., *Vincent van Gogh. Inleidende Beschouwingen*, Amsterdam 1911.

Bremmer, H.P., *Vincent van Gogh. 40 Photocollo graphies d'après ses tableaux et dessins*, Amsterdam 1904.

Bremmer, H.P., *Vincent van Gogh, 100 tekeningen uit de verzameling Hidde Nijland in het Museum te Dordrecht*, Amsterdam 1905.

Bremmer, H.P., *Een inleiding tot het zien van beeldende kunst*, Amsterdam 1906.

Bremmer, H.P., *Vincent van Gogh, 24 teekeningen uit zijn 'Hollandse Periode'. Verzameling Hidde Nijland*, Amsterdam 1907.

Bremmer, H.P., *Practisch aesthetische studies*, Amsterdam 1909.

Bremmer, H.P., *Vincent van Gogh. Inleidende beschouwingen*, Amsterdam 1911.

Bremmer, H.P., coll, cat. *Catalogus van de schilderijen verzameling van Mevrouw H. Kröller-Müller*, The Hague 1917.

Bremmer, H.P., coll, cat. *Vincent van Gogh: reproducties naar zijn werken in de verzameling van Mevrouw H. Kröller-Müller*, Utrecht 1919 (limited edition, not for sale).

Bremmer, H.P., coll, cat. *Catalogus van de schilderijen verzameling van Mevrouw H. Kröller-Müller*, The Hague 1921.

Bremmer, H.P., coll. cat. *Catalogus van de schilderijen verzameling van Mevrouw H. Kröller-Müller [deel] III. Van Van Gogh, Fransche Periode, tot Huszar*, The Hague 1925 (unpublished).

Bremmer, H.P., *Catalogus van de schilderijen verzameling van Mevrouw H. Kröller-Müller* (tweede deel), The Hague 1928.

Bremmer, H.P., *Vincent van Gogh*, met Hollandse Inleiding van H.P. Bremmer, Hoenderloo [1932] (limited edition of 100 copies). German edition: 'aus dem hollandischen frei ubertragen von Dr. Erhard Gopel', Hoenderloo 1942 (limited edition of 100 copies).

Bremmer Beekhuis, A.M., *H. P. Bremmer. Dienaar*

der kunst, unpublished manuscript [1937-1941] (with additions until 1943), Municipal Archive The Hague, Bremmer Archive.

Bridgwater, Patrick, *The expressionist generation and Van Gogh*, Hull 1987.

Brink, G.J.M. van den & W.Th.M. Frijhoff (ed.), exhib. cat. *De wevers en Vincent van Gogh* Tilburg (Nederlands Textielmuseum) 1990.

Brink, Gabriel van den, Willem Frijhoff, Cor van der Heijden, Gerard Rooijakkers, Monica Junega, Teio Meedendorp, Linda Nochlin, Anna Verkade-Bruining, Andrea Gasten, Ad van Kempen, De wevers en, *Vincent van Gogh*, Zwolle 1990.

Brooks, David, *Vincent van Gogh. The Complete Works*, CD rom 2002.

Brouwer, Jaap, Jan Laurens Siesling, Jacques Vis, Anthon van Rappard. *Companion & correspondent of Vincent van Gogh. His life & all his works*, Amsterdam / Maarssen 1974.

Brouwer, Ton de, *Van Gogh en Nuenen*, Venlo/ Antwerp 1998 (1984).

Brouwer, Ton de, *De oude toren en Van Gogh in Nuenen*, Venlo 2000.

Bruyn-Heeren, C. de, 'Ook Van Gogh hield van St. Willebrord: Cornelis Schuitemaker, een protestante Willebrorder als model voor Vincent van Gogh', Jaarboek Heemkundekring Willebrord, 1992, 160-73.

Buchmann, Mark, *Die Farbe bei Vincent van Gogh*, Zürich 1948.

Cachin, Françoise, *Paul Signac*, Paris 1971.

Cate, Phillip Dennis & Mary Shaw (ed.), *The spirit of Montmartre. Cabarets, humor, and the avantgarde, 1875-1905*, Rutgers 1996, published on the occasion of the exhibition of the same name, Rutgers (Jane Voorhees Zimmerli Museum)/Palm Beach (The Society of the Four Arts) /Gainsville (Samuel P. Harn Museum) 1996.

Chetham, Charles, *The Role of Vincent van Gogh's Copies in the Development of His Art*, New York/ London 1976.

Childs, Elizabeth C., 'Auf der Suche nach dem Atelier des Südens. Van Gogh, Gauguin und die Identität des Avantgardekünstlers', in: Homburg 2001(a), pp. 115-154.

Cooper, Douglas, *Van Gogh en Provence*, Aix-en-Provence 1959.

Cooper, Douglas, *Paul Gauguin. 45 Lettres à Vincent, Théo et Fo van Gogh*, The Hague/Lausanne 1983.

Coquiot, Gustave, *Vincent van Gogh*, Paris 1923.

Crimpen, Han van, 'De familie Van Gogh in Babant' in *Van Uitert et al.* 1987, pp. 72-91.

Crimpen, Han van, 'Friends remember Vincent in 1912', paper on Vincent van Gogh. International Symposium Tokyo - October 17-19, 1985, published in Haruo Arikawa, Han van Crimpen et al., Vincent van Gogh Exhibition, Tokyo 1988, pp. 73-90.

Crimpen, Han van, Berends-Albert, Monique (ed.), *De brieven van Vincent van Gogh*, 4 vols., The Hague 1990.

Crimpen, Han van, 'A newly discovered painted study

from Van Gogh's time in Paris', *Van Gogh Bulletin 6* (1991) 1, p. 12.

Crimpen, Han van, 'Inleiding', in: *Jansen & Robert* 1999, pp. 9-60.

Crimpen, Han van & Monique Berends Albert (ed.), *De brieven van Vincent van Gogh*, 4 vols., The Hague 1990.

Dantzig, M.M. van, *Vincent? A new method of identifying the artist and his work and of unmasking the forger and his products*, Amsterdam [1953].

Derkert, Carlo, 'Theory and practice in Van Gogh's Dutch painting', *Konsthistorisk Tidskrift* 15 (1946) 3/4, pp. 97-120.

Derkert, Carlo, Hans Ekiund & Oscar Reutersvärd, 'Van Gogh's landscape with corn shocks', *Konsthistorisk Tidskrift* 15 (1946) 3/4, pp. 121-130.

Destremau, Frédéric, 'L'Atelier Cormon(1882 1887)', *Bulletin de la Société de l'Histoire de l'Art Français 1996*, Paris 1997, pp. 171-184.

Deventer, Salomon van, *Kröller-Müller: de geschiedenis van een levenswerk*, Haarlem 1956.

Dijk, Wout J and Van der Sluis, Meent W., *De Drentse tijd van Vincent van Gogh. Een onderbe-lichte periode nader onderzocht*, Groningen 2001.

Dirven, Ron, 'Verloren vondsten', in Dirven & Wouters 2003, pp. 93-172.

Dirven, Ron, Wouters, Kees, Nelemans, Rebecca, and Sprangers, Hans, Vincent van Gogh: verloren vondsten. Het mysterie van de Bredase kisten, Breda 2003.

Distel, Anne & Susan Alyson Stein, exhib. cat. *Cezanne to Van Gogh. The collection of Doctor Gachet*, Paris (Grand Palais) / Amsterdam (Van Gogh Museum) /New York (The Metropolitan Museum of Art) 1999.

Dooren, Elmyra van, 'Van Gogh. Illness and creativity', in: Kōdera & Rosenberg 1993, pp. 325-345.

Dorn, Roland, Albrecht, Klaus Schroder and Sillevis, John, Van Gogh und die Haager Schule, exh. cat. Vienna (Bank Austria Kunstforum), Milan 1996.

Dorn, Roland, *Décoration. Vincent van Goghs Werk reihe für das Gelbe Haus in Arles*, Hildesheim/ Zurich/ New York 1990 (a).

Dorn, Roland (ed.), exhib. cat.*Vincent van Gogh en de moderne kunst 1890-1914*, Essen (Museum Folkwang)/Amsterdam (Rijksmuseum Vincent van Gogh) 1990 (b).

Dorn, Roland, "Refiler à Saintes Maries"? Pick vance and Hulsker revisited', *Van Gogh Museum Fournal 1997-1998*, Amsterdam/Zwolle 1998, pp. 14-25.

Dorn, Roland, 'Van Gogh's "Sunflowers" series. The fifth "toile de 30", *Van Gogh Museum Journal 1999*, Amsterdam/Zwolle 1999, pp. 42-61.

Dorn, Roland, 'Zur Malerei Van Goghs, 1884-1886', *Georges Bloch Fahrbuch des Kunsthistorischen Instituts der Universität Zürich 7* (2000), pp. 157-177.

Dorn, Roland & Walter Feilchenfeldt, 'Genuine or fake? On the history and problems of Van Gogh connoisseurship', in: Kōdera & Rosenberg 1993, pp. 263-307.

Dorra, Henri, *Symbolist art theories. A critical anthology*, Berkeley/Los Angeles/London 1994.

[Druet], coll. cat. *Catalogue Galerie E. Druet*, Paris s.a.

Druick, Douglas & Peter Kort Zegers, *Van Gogh and Gauguin: The Studio of the South, exh. cat. Chicago* (The Art Institute of Chicago)/ Amsterdam (Van Gogh Museum), New York 2001.

Druick, Douglas & Peter Kort Zegers, exhib. cat. *Van Gogh and Gauguin: The Studio of the South, Chicago* (The Art Institute of Chicago)/ Amsterdam (Van Gogh Museum) 2001.

Dulk, E. den, 'Tentoonstelling werken Vincent van Gogh', *De Kunstwereld 2* (1895) 24, p. 384.

Duret, Théodore, *Van Gogh, Vincent*, Paris 1916 (reprint 1924).

Eijgenraam, Felix, 'Cypres met maan en planeten', *NRC Handelsblad* 16 april 1990, p. 16.

Elgar, Frank, *Le Pont de l'Anglois. Van Gogh*, Paris 1948.

Enthoven, Paul Henri, *Kroniek van het geslacht Enthoven*, Zutphen 1991.

Faille, Jacob Baart de la, *L'Oeuvre de Vincent van Gogh. Catalogue raisonne* (4 vols.), Paris/ Brussels 1928.

Faille, Jacob Baart de la, *Les faux Van Gogh*, Paris/ Brussels 1930.

Faille, Jacob Baart de la, *Vincent van Gogh*, Paris 1939.

Faille, Jacob Baart de la, *The works of Vincent van Gogh*. His paintings and drawings, New York 1970.

Faille, Jacob Baart de la, Vincent van Gogh. *The complete works on paper*, 2 vols., San Francisco 1992.

Fechter, Paul, *Der Expressionismus*, Munich 1914.

Feilchenfeldt, Walter, Vincent van Gogh & Paul Cassirer, Berlin. T*he reception of Van Gogh in Germany from 1901 to 1914* (Cahier Vincent 4), Amsterdam/ Zwolle 1988.

Feilchenfeldt, Walter, 'Van Gogh fakes. The Wacker affair', *Simiolus* 19 (1989) 4, pp. 289-316.

Feilchenfeldt, Walter, 'Vincent van Gogh. Verhandeld en verzameld', in: Dorn 1990(b), pp. 16-23.

Feliciano, Hector, *The lost museum: The Nazi conspiracy to steal the world's greatest works of art*, New York 1997.

Ferretti Bocquillon, Marina, Anne Distel, Susan Alyson Stein & John Leighton, exhib. cat. *Signac 1863-1935*, New York (The Metropolitan Museum of Art)/Amsterdam (Van Gogh Museum) 2001.

Gachet, Paul (fils), *Souvenirs de Cézanne et de Van Gogh à Auvers*, Paris 1928.

Gachet, Paul (fils), *Lettres impressionnistes*, Paris 1957.

Gachet, Paul (fils), *Les 70 jours de Van Gogh à Auvers. Essai d'éphéméride dans le décor de l'époque (20 mai 30 juillet 1890,) d'après les lettres, documents, souvenirs et déductions Auvers sur Oise 1959* (with comments by Alain Mothe), Valhermeil 1994.

Gans, Louis, 'Vincent van Gogh en de schilders van de "Petit Boulevard", *Museumjournaal* 4 (1958) 5/6, pp. 85-93.

Gans, Louis, 'Twee onbekende tekeningen uit van Goghs Hollandse periode', *Museumjournaal* 7 (1961/1962), pp. 33-34.

Gauguin, Paul, *Avant et Après*, Paris 1989 (manuscript 1903).

Gauzi, François, *Lautrec et son temps*, Paris 1954.

Geertruy, Anieta van, 'De familie Van Gogh te Etten (1875-1881)', in Rozemeyer et al. 2003, pp. 16-36.

Gelder, Hendrik Enno van et al., *Herdenking Dr. H.P Bremmer*, Rotterdam 1956.

Gelder, Jan G. van, 'Vincent's begin', *De tafelronde* 2 (1958)8-9, pp. 23-28.

Gelder, Jan G. van, 'Juvenilia', in De la Faille 1970, pp. 600-609.

Gestel, Dimmen, 'Vincent van Gogh en eenige persoonlijke herinneringen aan hem', *Eindhovensch Dagblad*, 10 October 1930 (see also Verzamelde brieven 1973, vol. 3, pp. 90-91).

Giersbergen, Wilma van, 'De kunst is geheel en al bijzaak.' De moeizame carriere van C.C. Huijsmans (1810-1886), tekenmeester in Brabant, Tilburg 2003.

Gogh Bonger, Johanna van, *Verzamelde brieven van Vincent van Gogh*, Amsterdam/Antwerp 1952-1954.

Gogh Bonger, Johanna van, 'Inleiding' (1914), in: Van Crimpen and Berends Albert 1990, vol. I, pp. 1-42.

Groot, Irene M. de, A.A.E. Vels Heijn, C.J. de Bruyn Kops & j.W. Niemeijer, André Bonger en zijn kunstenaarsvrienden, Amsterdam (Rijksmuseum) 1972.

Groot, Reindert and Vries, Sjoerd de, *Vincent van Gogh in Amsterdam*, Amsterdam 1990

Grossvogel, Jill Elyse, 'The Van Gogh fakes: new revelations', *The Art Newspaper* 8 (1997) 73, pp. 4-5.

Grossvogel, Jill Elyse, *Claude Emile Schuffenecker. Catalogue raisonné, part I*, San Francisco 2000.

Gruijter, W. Jos. de, *Tekeningen van Vincent van Gogh*, n.p., n.d, [1962].

Gruyter, W. Jos de, 'Echt of vals', *Elsevier's Geïllustreerd Maandschrift* 40, vol. 80 (1930), pp. 65-67.

Gulik, Willem van & Fred Orton, *Japanese prints collected by Vincent van Gogh*, Amsterdam (Rijksmuseum Vincent van Gogh) 1978.

Haard, Miep de, 'Brabantse kleding in de negentiende en twintigste eeuw. Deel 1, Mutsen en poffers', *De Drijehornickels* 5 (1996) 2, pp. 42-46.

Haard, Miep de, 'Brabantse kleding in de negentiende en twintigste eeuw. Deel 2, Onder en bovenkleding van vrouwen', *De Drijehornickels* 6 (1997) 1, pp. 12-14.

Hammacher, A.H., Catalogue of 270 paintings and drawings of Vincent van Gogh belonging to the collection of the State Museum Kröller-Müller, Otterlo 1952.

Hammacher, A.H., Catalogus van 272 werken

van Vincent van Gogh behorende tot de verzameling van het Rijksmuseum Kröller-Müller Otterlo 1961.

Hammacher, A.M., 'De beteekenis van Fantin Latour', *Elsevier's Geïllustreerd Maandschrift*, 38, vol 75 (1928), pp. 153-169.

Hammacher, A.M., coll. cat. *Catalogus van 264 werken van Vincent van Gogh behorende tot de verzameling van het Rijksmuseum Kröller Müller*, Otterlo 1949.

Hammacher, A.M., exhib. cat. *Les amis de Van Gogh*, Paris (Institut Neerlandais) 1960.

Hammacher, A.M., exhib. cat. *Van Gogh's life in his drawings. Van Gogh 's relationship with Signac*, London (Marlborough Fine Art) 1962.

Hannema, D., *Flitsen uit mijn leven als verzamelaar en museumdirecteur*, Rotterdam 1973.

Hansen, Dorothee, Herzogenrath, Wulf, Dorn, Roland and Strobl, Barbara Nierhoff Andreas, Van Gogh: Felder. Das 'Mohnfeld' und der Kunstlerstreit, exh. cat. Bremen (Kunsthalle), Bremen 2002.

Hanzák, J. & P. Pospísil, *Nesten en eieren van beken de Europese vogels*, Amsterdam 1973 (Prague 1971).

Harrevelt, Loes van, 'Van Gogh en de hersenen van een mol. De herkomstgeschiedenis van het negatievenarchief Tutein Nolthenius', Nieuwsbrief Nederlands Fotogenootschap (NFg), December 1999, pp. 4-7.

Hartrick, A.S., *A painter's pilgrimage through fifty years*, Cambridge 1939.

Haverman, H.J., 'Vincent op het Buitenhof (Collectie Hidde Nijland)', De Kroniek 1 (1895) 10, pp. 75-76.

Hedström, Per & Britta Nilsson, 'Genuine and false Van Goghs in the Nationalmuseum', *Art Bulletin of Nationalmuseum Stockholm 7* (2000), pp. 98-101.

Heenk, Elisabeth, *Vincent van Gogh 's drawings. An analysis of their production and uses*, (diss.) University of London, 1995.

Heenk, Liesbeth, 'Van Gogh's drawings. A closer look', Apollo 140 (1994) 393, pp. 37-40.

Heenk, Liesbeth, Vincent van Gogh's drawings. An analysis of their production and uses, Diss. Courtauld Institute of Art (University of London), 1995.

Hefting, Paul (ed.), coll. cat. *Vincent van Gogh. A detailed catalogue of the paintings and drawings by Vincent van Gogh in the collection of the Kröller-Müller National Museum*, Otterlo 1980.

Hefting, Paul & Frank Gribling, coll. cat. *Teke-ningen uit de 19de en 20ste eeuw*, Rijksmuseum Kröller-Müller, Otterlo 1968.

Hefting, P.H., *G.H. Breitner in zijn Haagse tijd*, Utrecht 1970.

Hefting, P.H., *Brieven van G.H Breitner aan A.P. van Stolk*, Utrecht 1970.

Hefting, P. (ed.), *Vincent van Gogh. A detailed catalogue of the paintings and drawings by Vincent van Gogh in the collection of the Kröller-Müller National Museum*, Otterlo 1980.

Hefting, P., 'Breitner en het Panorama Mesdag'

in: Y. van Eekelen (ed.), Magisch panorama. Panorama Mesdag, een belevenis in ruimte en tijd, Zwolle/The Hague 1996, pp. 135-141.

Heijbroek, Freek, 'Het Rijksmuseum voor Moderne Kunst van Willem Steenhoff. Werkelijkheid of utopie?', *Bulletin van het Rijksmuseum* 39 (1991) 2, pp. 163-231.

Heijbroek, Freek & Ester Wouthuysen, *Kunst, kennis en commercie. De kunsthandelaar J. H. de Bois (1878-1946)*, Amsterdam/Antwerp 1993.

Heijbroek, J.F., Vis, A.A.M., *Verlaine in Nederland. Het bezoek van 1892 in woord en beeld*, Amsterdam 1985.

Heijbroek, J.F., Wouthuysen, E.L., *Kunst, kennis en commercie. De kunsthandelaar J.H. de Bois (1878-1946)*, Amsterdam/Antwerp 1993.

Heijbroek, J.F., Wouthuysen, E.L., Portret van een kunsthandel. De firma Van Wisselingh en zijn compagnons, 1838-heden, Zwolle /Amsterdam 1999.

Heijden, Cor van der, 'Nuenen omstreeks 1880', in: Van Uitert 1987-1988, pp. 102-127.

Heijden, Cor van der, 'Nuenen omstreeks 1880', in Van Uitert et al. 1987, pp. 102-127.

Heijden, Cor van der, 'Een zeer armzalig volkje. Leef- en werkomstandigheden van de Nuenense wevers in de tweede helft van de negentiende eeuw', in Van den Brink & Frijhoff 1990, pp. 23-35.

Heijden, Cor van der, Rooijakkers, Gerard, Kempische boeren en Vlaamse vissers. Kunstenaars en volkscultuur omstreeks 1885: *Victor de Buck and Joseph Gindra*, Eindhoven 1993.

Henkels, Herbert, 'Cézanne en Van Gogh in het Rijksmuseum voor Moderne Kunst in Amsterdam. De collectie van Cornelis Hoogendijk(1866 1911)', *Bulletin van het Rijksmuseum 41* (1993) 3/4, pp. 155-287.

Herbert, Robert L., Jean-Francois Millet, exh. cat. Paris (Grand Palais), Paris 1975.

Herzogenrath, Wulf & Dorothee Hansen (ed.), exhib. cat. *Van Gogh: Felder. Das 'Mohnfeld' und der Künstlerstreit*, Bremen (Bremer Kunsthalle), 2002.

Heugten, Sjraar van, 'Radiographic images of Vincent van Gogh's paintings in the collection of the Van Gogh Museum', *Van Gogh Museum Journal 1995*, Amsterdam/Zwolle 1995, pp. 62-85.

Heugten, Sjraar van, coll. cat. *Vincent van Gogh. Tekeningen 1. Vroege jaren 1880-1883*, Amsterdam (Van Gogh Museum) 1996.

Heugten, Sjraar van, coll. cat. *Vincent van Gogh. Tekeningen 2. Nuenen 1883-1885*, Amsterdam (Van Gogh Museum) 1997.

Heugten, Sjraar van & Fieke Pabst, *The Graphic Work of Vincent van Gogh* (Cahier Vincent 6), Amsterdam/Zwolle 1995.

Heugten, Sjraar van, Vincent van Gogh. Drawings I. Early Years 1880-1883, coll, cat. Amsterdam (Van Gogh Museum), Amsterdam/Bussum 1996.

Heugten, Sjraar van, Vincent van Gogh. Drawings II. Nuenen 1883-1885, coll. cat. Amsterdam (Van

Gogh Museum), Amsterdam/Bussum 1997.

Heugten, Sjraar van, 'Metamorphoses: Van Gogh's Drawings Then and Now in Ives et al. 2005, pp. 41-55.

Heugten, Sjraar van, Stolwijk, Chris (ed.), Van Gogh Museum. A Decade of Collecting. Acquisitions 1997-2006, Amsterdam 2006.

Hoefsloot, R.M.J.M., Restauratierapporten Vincent van Gogh [restorations of drawings carried out between 1978-1987], typescript Kröller-Müller Museum, Otterlo, 1987.

Hoek, Jack van, 'Voorstel tot correcties op benaming en datering van enkele werken van Vincent van Gogh', *De Drijehornickeis 4* (1996) 4, pp. 10-15.

Hoek, Jack van, 'Vincent van Goghs "Kerkhofbij regen" 't Gruun Buukske 22 (1993) 2, pp. 69-73.

Hoek, Jack van, 'Tekende Vincent van Gogh ook in Mierlo?, *Myerlese Koerier 7* (1993) 2.

Hoek, Jack van, 'Het zingend boerke', in Rob Verhallen et al., Ik yoel mij thuis daar. Opstellen over het leven en werk van Vincent van Gogh in Nuenen, Nuenen 2003, pp. 88-93.

Hoermann Lister, Kristin, 'Tracing a transformation. Madame Roulin into La berceuse', *Van Gogh Museum Journal 2001*, Amsterdam/Zwolle 2001, pp. 62-83.

Homburg, Cornelia, The copy turns original. *Vincent van Gogh and a new approach to traditional art practice*, Amsterdam/Philadelphia 1996.

Homburg, Cornelia (ed.), exhib. cat. *Vincent van Gogh and the painters of the Petit Boulevard*, Saint Louis (Art Museum)/Frankfurt (Städelsches Kunstinstitut) 2001 (a).

Homburg, Cornelia, 'Vincent van Gogh's avantgarde strategies', in: *Homburg 2001 (a)*, pp. 25-60 (b).

Horsman, P.J., 'Het Zuid Afrikaansch Museum te Dordrecht', *Kwartaal & Teken 3* (1977) 3/4, pp. 6-9.

Huebner, Friedrich Markus, Moderne Kunst in *den Privatsamntlungen Europas. Band I*: Holland, Leipzig 1922.

Hulsker, Jan, 'Van Gogh's first and only commission as an artist Bulletin of the Rijksmuseum Vincent van Gogh 4 (1976) 4, pp. 5-19.

Hulsker, Jan, 'What Theo really thought of Vincent', *Bulletin of the Rijksmuseum Vincent van Gogh 3* (1974) 2, pp. 2-28 (a).

Hulsker, Jan, 'The poet's garden', *Bulletin of the Rijksmuseum Vincent van Gogh 3* (1974) 1, pp. 22-32 (b).

Hulsker, Jan, *Lotgenoten. Het leven van Vincent en Theo van Gogh*, Weesp 1985.

Hulsker, Jan, *Van Gogh en zijn weg. Het complete werk*, Amsterdam 1989 (Irst edition 1977).

Hulsker, Jan, *Van Gogh in close up*, Amsterdam 1993.

Hulsker, Jan, *The new complete Van Gogh. Paintings, drawings, sketches*, Amsterdam/Philadelphia 1996.

Hulsker, Jan, 'De paradox van de publicatie. De nooit verzonden brieven van Vincent van Gogh', *Jong Holland 14* (1998) 4, pp. 42-52.

Hulsker, Jan, 'Facts instead of suppositions. Roland

Dorn revisited', *Van Gogh Museum Journal* 1999, Amsterdam/Zwolle 1999, pp. 25-28.

Hummelen, IJsbrand & Cornelia Peres, 'De schildertechniek van de aardappeleters', in: Van Tilborgh *et al.* 1993, pp. 58-69.

Ives, Colta, Stein, Susan Alyson, Heugten, Sjraar van, Vellekoop, Marije, Vincent van Gogh, The Drawings, exh. cat. Amsterdam (Van Gogh Museum)/ New York (The Metropolitan Museum of Art), New Haven/London 2005.

Jansen, Guido, 'Catalogus', in: exhib. cat. *Meesterlijk vee. Nederlandse veeschilders 1600-1900*, Dordrecht (Dordrechts Museum)/Leeuwarden (Fries Museum) 1988-1989, pp. 101-265.

Jansen, Leo & Jan Robert (ed.), *Kort geluk. De briefwisseling tussen Theo van Gogh en Jo van Gogh-Bonger* (Cahier Vincent 7), Amsterdam/ Zwolle 1999.

Johnson, Ron, 'Vincent van Gogh and the vernacular. The poet's garden', *Arts Magazine* 53 (1979) 6, pp. 98-104.

Joosten, Ellen, 'Het rijke begrip "invloed", *Museumjournaal 5* (1959) 4, pp. 73-76.

Joosten, Ellen, 'Bloemstilleven, Vincent van Gogh, 1853-1890', *Vereniging Rembrandt, verslag over 1974*, pp. 46-48.

Joosten, Joop M., 'Van Gogh publicaties' (9-11), *Museumjournaal* 14 (1969), pp. 154-157, 216 219, 269-273.

Joosten, Joop M., 'Van Gogh publicaties' (12-15), *Museumjournaal* 15 (1970), pp. 47-49, 100-103, 154-158.

Joosten, Joop M. (ed.), De Brieven van/Johan Thorn Prikker aan Henri Borel en anderen, 1892-1904, Nieuwkoop 1980.

Jullian, René, 'Van Gogh et le "Pont de 1'Anglois", *Bulletin de la Société de l'Histoire de l'Art Français 1977*, Paris 1979, pp. 313-321.

Kalmthout, A.B.G.M. van, Muzentempels. Multidisciplinaire kunstkringen in Nederland tussen 1880 en 1914, Hilversum 1998.

Kerssemakers, Anton, 'Herinneringen aan Vincent van Gogh', *De Amsterdammer* (1912) 1816, p. 6, en 1817, pp. 6-7.

Kerstens, Cor, 'Piet Kaufmann, Van Gogh's model', d'Huskes 11 (1990) 19, pp. 1-36.

Kōdera, Tsukasa, '"In het zweet uws aanschijns". Spitters in Van Goghs oeuvre', in: Van Uitert 1987 1988, pp. 59-71.

Kōdera, Tsukasa & Y. Rosenberg (ed.), *The Mythology of Vincent van Gogh*, Tokyo 1993.

Kōdera, Tsukasa, *Vincent van Gogh: Christianity versus Nature*, Amsterdam 1990.

Koldehoff, Stefan, *Van Gogh. Mythos und Wirklichkeit*, Cologne 2003.

Koldehoff, Stefan, 'Ein aufschlussreicher Brief. Ein Schreiben von Paul Gachet an Ludovico Rodo Pissarro liefert neue Erkenntnisse zur Druckpraxis bei van Goghs einziger Radierung', Weltkunst 76 (2005) 11, pp. 82-85.

Kröller Müller, *Helene, Beschouwingen over problemen in de ontwikkeling der moderne schilderkunst*, Hoenderloo 1925.

Lecaldano, Paolo, *Tout l'oeuvre peint de Van Gogh*, vol. 1 (1881-1888), Paris 1971.

Leeman, Fred, 'Van Goghs postume roem in de Lage Landen', in: Dorn 1990 (b), pp. 162-181.

Leeman, Fred, Sillevis, John, De Haagse School en de jonge Van Gogh, exh. cat. The Hague (Gemeentemuseum The Hague), Zwolle 2005.

Leeuw, Ronald de, 'Eerste afdeling: schilderen beeldhouwkunst. Van de Bock tot Berserik', in Haagse Kunstkring: werk verzameld, exh. cat. The Hague (Gemeentemuseum), The Hague 1977, pp. 7-50.

Leeuw, Ronald de, , John Sillevis, Charles Dumas, Hans Kraan, Charles S. Moffet, Herbert Henkels, De Haagse School. Hollandse meesters van de 19de eeuw, exh. cat. Paris (Grand Palais)/London (Royal Academy)/The Hague (Gemeentemuseum), The Hague 1983.

Lenssen, L., 'Boerderijen op de tekening van Vincent van Gogh', Myerlese Koerier 7 (1993) 2

Leprohon, Pierre, *Tel fut Van Gogh*, Paris 1964.

Leprohon, Pierre, *Vincent van Gogh*, Paris 19722.

Ligthart, Arnold, 'Vincent van Gogh & Thophile de Bock', Jong Holland 6 (1990) 6, pp. 18-34

Lindert, Juleke van, 'Scènes uit het alledaagse volksleven', in: Van der Mast & Dumas 1990, pp. 118-145.

Livestro Nieuwenhuis, Fea, '...die jakken en rokken dragen.' Brabantse klederdrachten en streeksieraden, exh. cat. 's Hertogenbosch (Noordbrabants Museum), 1986.

Luijten, Hans, 'Scharrelen in de houtsneden. Vincent van Gogh en de prentkunst', in Stolwijk et al. 2003, pp. 99-113.

Mac Coll, D.S., 'Vincent van Gogh. Further letters and a portrait', Artwork 22 (1930), pp. 135-141.

Marius, G.H., 'Vincent van Gogh', De Nederlandsche Spectator 40 (1895) 8, 23 February.

Mast, Michiel van der, Charles Dumas, Juleke van Lindert, John Sillevis, Martha Op de Coul, Van Gogh en Den Haag, Zwolle 1990.

Mathews, Patricia Townley, 'Aurier and Van Gogh. Criticism and response', Art Bulletin 68 (1986), pp. 94-104.

Meedendorp, Teio, 'Schetsen en studies; over het dateren van Van Goghs vroege tekenwerk', in Leeman & Sillevis 2005, pp. 170-178.

Meedendorp, Teio, 'Vincent van Gogh en Dordrecht', in M. Peters et al., Dromen van Dordrecht. Buitenlandse kunstenaars schilderen Dordrecht, 1850-1920, exh. cat. Dordrecht (Dordrechts Museum), Bussum 2005, pp. 54-55, 162.

Meedendorp, Teio, '"Dat zwarte gevaarte van goor geworden eikehout". De rol van de wevers in de ontwikkeling van Vincent van Gogh', in: Van den Brink & Frijhoff 1990, pp. 67-77.

Meier Graefe, Julius, *Vincent van Gogh. Der Zeichner*, Berlijn 1928.

Mendgen, Eva, Edwin Becker & Isabella Cahn, exhib. cat. *In perfect harmony. Picture + frame 1850-1920*, Amsterdam (Van Gogh Museum)/ Vienna (Kunstforum) 1995.

Merlhès, Victor (ed.), *Correspondance de Paul Gauguin. Documents, témoignages*, Paris 1984.

Michelet, Jules, *L'Oiseau*, Paris 1861 (1856).

Mitterand, Henri, 'Notice', in Zola 1983, pp. 424-448.

Moderne Kunstwerken. Schilderijen, Teekeningen en Beeldhouwwerken (ed. H.P. Bremmer), 8 volumes, 1903-1910.

Molendijk, Ad, 'De hoge hoed van Van Gogh', Kwartaal&Teken 16 (1990) 3, pp. 9-13.

Momeret, Jean, *Catalogue raisonné du Salon des Independants 1884-2000. Les Indépendants dans l'histoire de l'art*, Paris 2000.

Mongan, Agnes, Memorial Exhibition: Works of Art from the Collection of Paul J. Sachs, exh. cat. Cambridge (Fogg Art Museum), 1965.

Mothe, Alain, *Vincent van Gogh à Auvers sur Oise*, Paris 1987.

Müller, Eelke (ed.), *Museale Verwervingen 1940-1948. Rapport van de commissie Museale Verwervingen 1940-1948*, Amsterdam 1999.

Müller, Christian, Hans Holbein d.J.. Zeichnungen aus dem Kupferstichkabinett der offenlichen Kunstsammlung Basel, coll. cat.Basel (Kunstmuseum Basel), 1988.

Müller, Eelke & Helen Schretlen, *Betwist bezit. De Stichting Nederlands Kunstbezit en de teruggave van roofkunst na 1945*, Zwolle 2002.

Munching, L.L. von, De geschiedenis van de Batavier Lijn. Nederlands oudste stoomvaartlijn, 1830-1958, Franeker 1994.

Nelemans 2003. Rebecca Nelemans, 'Een zwervende portefeuille. De herkomst van de collectie Hidde Nijland', in Dirven & Wouters 2003, pp. 72-84.

Nijhof 2006. Wim H. Nijhof, Anton & Helene Kröller-Müller. Miljoenen, macht en meesterwerken, Apeldoorn 2006.

Nijland 1905. Vincent van Gogh - 100 Teekeningen uit de Verzameling Hidde Nijland in het Museum te Dordrecht, Amsterdam 1905

Nonne 2000. Monique Nonne, 'Theo van Gogh: his clients and suppliers', Van Gogh Museum journal 2000, pp. 38-51

Nordenfalk, Carl, 'Van Gogh Literature', *Journal of the Warburg and Courtauld Institute 10* (1947), pp. 132-147.

Novotny 1963. Fritz Novotny, 'Die Zeichnungen van Goghs in der Albertina', Albertina Studien 1 (1963), pp. 15-20.

Op de Coul, Martha, 'Van Gogh publicaties (7). Een onbekend stadsgezicht van Vincent van Gogh', Museumjournaal 14 (1969), pp. 42-44.

Op de Coul, Martha, 'Een mannenfiguur, in 1882 door Vincent van Gogh getekend', Oud Holland 97 (1983) 3/4, pp. 336-40.

Op de Coul, Martha, 'In search of Van Gogh's Nuenen studio. The Oldenzeel exhibitions of 1903', *Van Gogh Museum Journal* 2002, Amsterdam/Zwolle 2003, pp. 104-119.

Op de Coul, Martha & Annet Tellegen, 'Vincent van Gogh en Antoine Furnee', *Oud Holland* 109 (1995) 1/2, pp. 95-100.

Otterlo, Schilderijen van het Rijksmuseum Kröller-Müller, coll. cat. Otterlo (Kröller-Müller Museum), 1970.

Otterlo, Jos ten Berge, Teio Meedendorp, Aukje Vergeest, Robert Verhoogt, The paintings of Vincent van Gogh in the collection of the Kröller-Müller Museum, Otterlo 2003.

Oxenaar, R.W.D. (introduction), coll, cat. *Schilde rijen van het Rijksmuseum Kröller-Müller*, Otterlo (Rijksmuseum Kröller-Müller) 1970.

Oxenaar, R.WD., A.M. Hammacher, Johannes van der Wolk, Toos van Kooten, Jaap Bremer & Marianne Brouwer, *Kröller-Müller. Honderd jaar bouwen en verzamelen*, Haarlem 1988.

Pey, E.B.F., 'Krijt met de kleur van omgeploegd land op een zomeravond', in Van der Wolk et al. 1990, pp. 28-41.

Pickvance, Ronald, *English influences on Vincent van Gogh*, Nottingham 1974.

Pickvance, Ronald, exhib. cat. *Van Gogh in Aries*, New York (The Metropolitan Museum of Art) 1984.

Pickvance, Ronald, exhib. cat. *Van Gogh in Saint - Rémy and Auvers*, New York (The Metropolitan Museum of Art) 1986.

Pickvance, Ronald, exhib. cat. *Van Gogh et Aries, Exposition du Centenaire*, Arles (Ancien Hopital Van Gogh) 1989.

Pickvance, Ronald, Van Gogh, exh. cat. Martigny (Fondation Pierre Gianadda), 2000.

Pierard, Louis, Vincent. Een kunstenaarsleven, Arnhem 1929 (trans. La vie tragique de Vincent van Gogh, Paris 1924).

Plasschaert, A., 'Vincent van Gogh. (Oldenzeel)', *De Kroniek* 7 November 1903, p. 355.

Quesne van Gogh, Elisabeth H. du, *Vincent van Gogh. Persoonlijke herinneringen aangaande een kunstenaar*, Baarn 1910.

Rappard-Boon, Charlotte van, Willem van Gulik & Keiko van Bremen Ito, coll, cat. *Catalogue of the Van Gogh Museum's collection of Japanese prints*, Amsterdam/Zwolle 1991.

Rewald, John, *Post-Impressionism from Van Gogh to Gauguin*, New York 1956.

Rewald, John, 'Theo van Gogh, Goupil, and the Impressionists'. *Gazette des Beaux Arts* 6 (1973) 81, pp. 1-108.

Rewald, John, 'Theo van Gogh as art dealer', in: John Rewald, *Studies in Post-Impressionism*, London 1986, pp. 7-115.

Richard, Pierre, 'Vincent van Gogh's Montmartre', *Jong Holland* 4 (1988) 1, pp. 16-21.

Rioux, Jean Paul, 'The dislocation of Pinks and Purples in Van Gogh's Paintings from Auvers', in: Distel & Stein 1999, pp. 104-114.

Robertis, Antonio de, Matteo Smolizza, Vincent van Gogh. Le opere dispersi. Oltre 1000 disegni e dipinti citati dall'artista e introvabili, Nuoro 2005.

Roepers, Nicole, 'De strijd der deskundigen. H. P. Bremmer en het Wackerproces', *Jong Holland* 9 (1993) 2, pp. 25-36.

Rooijakkers, Gerard, 'De beeldenmakelaar. Vincent van Gogh en de materiele cultuur van Nuenense wevers en boeren', in Van den Brink & Frijhoff(ed.) 1990, pp. 37-53.

Rosenbium, Robert & H.W. Janson, *Art of the nineteenth century. Painting and sculpture*, London 1984.

Roskill, Mark, *Van Gogh, Gauguin and French painting of the 1880 's. A catalogue raisonné of key works*, Ann Arbor, Michigan 1970 (a).

Roskill, Mark, *Van Gogh, Gauguin and the impressionist circle*, London 1970 (b).

Rossiter, Henry P., 'Albertina for Boston?', Apollo 96 (1972) 8, pp. 135-137.

Rotonchamp, Jean de, Paul Gauguin 1848-1903, Paris 1925.

Rozemeyer, J.A., A. van Geertruy, R. Wols, Van Gogh in Etten, exh. cat. Etten-Leur (Van Gogh-centrum), 2003.

Ruiter, Peter de, *A.M. Hammacher. Kunst als levensessentie*, Baarn 2000.

Rummens, M., 'Van Goghs expressieve onhandigheid', *Jong Holland* 10 (1994) 4, pp. 27-39.

Saltzman, Cynthia, *Portrait of Dr Gachet. The story of a Van Gogh masterpiece, money, politics, collectors, greed, and Loss*, New York 1998.

Shelley, Marjorie, Silvia A. Centeno, 'Technical Studies: Observations on the Drawing Materials Used by Van Gogh in Provence', in Ives et al. 2006, pp. 348-356.

Sheon, Aaron, 'Monticelli and Van Gogh', Apollo 85 (1967) 6, pp. 444-448.

Sheon, Aaron, exhib. cat. *Monticelli. His contemporaries, his influence*, Pittsburgh (Museum of Art, Carnegie Institute) 1978.

Sheon, Aaron, 'Theo van Gogh, publisher. The Monticelli album', Van Gogh Museum Journal 2000, Amsterdam/Zwolle 2000, pp. 53-62.

Silverman, Debora, 'Pilgrim's Progress and Vincent van Gogh's métier', in: Martin Bailey (ed.), exhib. cat. *Van Gogh. Portrait of the artist as a young man in England*, London (Barbican Art Gallery) 1992, pp. 95-115.

Silverman, Debora, *Van Gogh and Gauguin. The search for the sacred*, New York 2000.

Silverman, Debora, 'Framing art and sacred realism. Van Gogh's ways of seeing Aries', *Van Gogh Museum Journal* 2001, Amsterdam/Zwolle 2001, pp. 45-63.

Soth, Lauren, 'Van Gogh's images of Women Sewing', Zeitschrift fur Kunstgeschichte 57 (1994) 1, pp. 105-110.

Stegeman, Elly, 'Bremmer, Van Gogh en de praktische esthetica', *Jong Holland* 9 (1993) 2, pp. 37-48.

Stein, Susan Alyson, Van Gogh, A Retrospective, New York 1986.

Stokvis, Benno, *Nasporingen omtrent Vincent van Gogh in Brabant*, Amsterdam 1926.

Stokvis; Benno, 'Nieuwe nasporingen omtrent Vincent van Gogh in Brabant', *Opgang* 7 (1927) 307, pp. 11-14.

Stolwijk, Chris & Richard Thomson, exhib. cat. *Theo van Gogh, 1857-1891, art dealer, collector, and brother of Vincent*, Amsterdam (Van Gogh Museum) 1999.

Stolwijk, Chris & Han Veenenbos, *The account book of Theo van Gogh and Jo van Gogh-Bonger*, Amsterdam/Leiden 2002.

Stolwijk, Chris, Uit de schilderswereld. Nederlandse kunstschilders in de tweede helft van de negentiende eeuw, Leiden 1998.

Stolwijk, Chris, Richard Thomson, Theo van Gogh, 1857-1891. Art dealer, collector and brother of Vincent, exh. cat. Amsterdam (Van Gogh Museum), Amsterdam/ Zwolle 1999.

Stolwijk, Chris, Sjraar van Heugten, Leo Jansen, Andreas Bluhm (ed.), Vincent's choice, The Musee imaginaire of Van Gogh, exh. cat. Amsterdam (Van Gogh Museum), Amsterdam/ Antwerp 2003.

Sund, Judy, 'The sower and the sheaf. Biblicalmetaphor in the art of Vincent van Gogh', *Art. Bulletin* 70 (1988) 4, pp. 660-676.

Sund, Judy, *True to temperament. Van Gogh and French Naturalist literature*, Cambridge 1992.

Szymanska, Anna, Unbekannte jugend-zeichnungen Vincent van Goghs und das Schaffen des Kunstlers in denJahren 1870-1880, Berlin 1968.

Tellegen, Annet, 'Vincent en Gauguin. Schilderijenruil in Paris', *Museumjournaal* 11 (1966) 1/2, p. 42.

Tellegen, Annet, 'De Populiereniaan bij Nuenen van Vincent van Gogh', *Bulletin Museum Boymans van Beuningen* 18 (1967), pp. 8-15.

Tellegen, Annet, 'Vincent van Goghs appelboomgaard te Zweeloo', Bulletin Museum Boymans-van Beuningen 18 (1967) 1, pp. 2-7.

Tellegen, Annet, 'De Vincent van Gogh tentoonstellingen bij de kunsthandels Buffa in Amsterdam en Oldenzeel in Rotterdam in februari maart 1892', *Museumjournaal* 14 (1969) 4, pp. 216-219.

Tilborgh, Louis van (ed.), exhib. cat. *Van Gogh & Millet*, Amsterdam (Rijksmuseum Vincent van Gogh) 1988.

Tilborgh, Louis van, The potato eaters by Vincent van Gogh /De aardappeleters van Vincent van Gogh, Zwolle 1993.

Tilborgh, Louis van, 'Framing Van Gogh 1880-1990', in: *Mendgen* et al. 1995, pp. 163-180.

Tilborgh, Louis van, 'Les quatre saisons', in: Van Tilborgh *et al.* 1998, pp. 68-79.

Tilborgh, Louis van & Ella Hendriks, 'Van Gogh's "Garden of the asylum". Genuine or fake?', *The Burlington Magazine* 142 (2001) 1176, pp. 145-156 (a).

Tilborgh, Louis van & Ella Hendriks, 'The Tokyo sunflowers. A genuine repetition by Van Gogh or a Schuffenecker forgery?', *The Van Gogh Museum Journal* 2001, Amsterdam/Zwolle 2001, pp. 16-43 (b).

Tilborgh, Louis van & Marije Vellekoop, 'Van Gogh in Utrecht. The collection of Geriach Ribbius Peletier (1856-1930)' *Van Gogh Museum Journal* 1997-1998, Amsterdam 1998, pp. 26-41.

Tilborgh, Louis van & Marije Vellekoop, coll, cat. *Vincent van Gogh. Schilderijen 1. Nederlandse periode 1881-1885*, Amsterdam (Van Gogh Museum) 1999.

Tilborgh, Louis van & Marije Vellekoop, Vincent van Gogh. Paintings 1. Dutch Period 1881-1885, cat. coll. Amsterdam (Van Gogh Museum), Zwolle 1999.

Tilborgh, Louis van, IJsbrand Hummelen, Cornelia Peres et al., *The potato eaters by Vincent van Gogh/De aardappeleters van Vincent van Gogh* (Cahier Vincent 5), Amsterdam/Zwolle 1993.

Tilborgh, Louis van et al., exhib. cat. *Van Gogh & Millet*, Paris (Musee d'Orsay) 1998.

Tilborgh, Louis van, Sjraar van Heugten, Philip Conisbee, Van Gogh & Millet, exh. cat. Amsterdam (Van Gogh Museum), Zwolle/Amsterdam 1988.

Tralbaut, Mark Edo, Vincent van Gogh in zijn Antwerpsche periode, Amsterdam 1948.

Tralbaut, Mark Edo, 'In Van Gogh's voetspoor te Nuenen en omgeving', De Toerist 11 (1955) 1 [June], p. 382.

Tralbaut, Mark Edo, Van Gogh. Debut & evolution, Amsterdam 1957.

Tralbaut, Mark Edo, Vincent van Gogh in Drenthe, Assen 1959.

Tralbaut, Mark Edo, 'Andre Bonger, l'ami des freres Van Gogh', Van Goghiana I (1963), pp. 5-54.

Tralbaut, Mark Edo, Vincent van Gogh, London 1969.

Tralbaut, Mark Edo, Van Gogh. Le mal aimé, Lausanne 1969.

Tralbaut, Mark Edo, 'Vincent van Gogh et Monticelli', Van Goghiana 7 (1970), pp. 29-48.

Trappeniers, Maureen, 'Catalogus', in: Van Uitert 1987 1988, pp. 130-241.

Tuch-Nijland, Nelly, 'Das Jugendwerk Van Goghs und sein erster Sammler: Hidde Nijiand', Baster Zeitung, 7 August 1945.

Uitert, Evert van, 'Uitgebloeide zonnebloemen', Openbaar kunstbezit 11 (1967) 8, not paginated.

Uitert, Evert van, Vincent van Gogh in creative competition. Four essays from Simiolus [1977-1982], Zutphen 1983 (diss. University of Amsterdam).

Uitert, Evert van, Carol M. Zemel, Tsukasa Kodera, Han van Crimpen, Martha Op de Coul, Cor van der Heijden, Maureen Trappeniers, Andrea Gasten, Van Gogh in Brabant, exh. cat. 's-Hertogenbosch (Noordbrabants Museum), Zwolie 1987.

Uitert, Evert van (ed.), exhib. cat. Van Gogh in Brabant. Schilderijen en tekeningen uit Etten en Nuenen, 's Hertogenbosch (Noordbrabants Museum) 1987-1988 (a).

Uitert, Evert van, 'Vincent van Gogh, boerenschilder', in: Van Uitert 1987-1988, pp. 14-46 (b).

Uitert, Evert van & Michael Hoyle (ed.), coll. cat. The Rijksmuseum Vincent van gogh, Amsterdam 1987.

Uitert, Evert van, Louis van Tilborgh & Sjraarvan Heugten, exhib. cat. Vincent van Gogh. Paintings, Amsterdam (Rijksmuseum Vincent van Gogh) 1990.

Vanbeselaere Waither, De Hollandse periode (1880-1885) in het werk van Vincent van Gogh, Amsterdam [1937].

Vellekoop, Marije & Sjraar van Heugten, coll. cat. Vincent van Gogh. Tekeningen 3. Antwerp en Paris, Amsterdam (Van Gogh Museum) 2001.

Venema, Adriaan, Kunsthandel in Nederland. 1940-1945, Amsterdam 1986.

Vergeest, Aukje, The French collection. Nineteenth-century French paintings in Dutch public collections, Amsterdam 2000.

Verzamelde brieven van Vincent van Gogh, supplemented and expanded by Ir. V.W. van Gogh, 1953, 4 vols., 5th ed., Amsterdam/Antwerp 1973.

Veth, Cornelis, Schoon Schip! Expertise naar echtheid en onechtheid inzake Vincent van Gogh, Amsterdam/Mechelen 1932.

Veth, Jan, 'Tentoonstelling van werken door Vincent van Gogh in de Amsterdamsche Panoramazaal', De Nieuwe Gids 8 (1892-1893) 1, pp. 427-431.

Visser-Nijland, M.A., 'Herinneringen aan mijn vader: Hidde Nijland', in De Muze van Hindeloopen. 40 jaar Hidde Nijland Stichting, Hindeloopen 1959, n.p.

Visser, W.J.A., 'Vincent van Gogh en 's Gravenhage', Geschiedkundige Vereniging 'Die Haghe' Jaarboek 1973, pp. 1-125.

Vital, Christophe, exhib. cat. Auguste Lepère 1849 1918, Fontenay le Comte (Musée de Fontenay-le-Comte)/Saint Jean de Monts (Palais des Congres) 1988.

Vollard, Ambroise, Recollections of a picture dealer, Boston 1936 (trans. V.M. MacDonald).

Vries, Dr. B.W. de, De Nederlandse papiernjverheid in de negentiende eeuw, The Hague 1957.

Welsh-Ovcharov, Bogomila, The early work of Charles Angrand and his contact with Vincent van Gogh, Utrecht/The Hague 1971.

Welsh-Ovcharov, Bogomila, Vincent van Gogh. His Paris period 1886-1888, Utrecht/The Hague 1976 [diss., published].

Welsh-Ovcharov, Bogomila, exhib. cat. Vincent van Gogh and the birth of Cloisonism, Toronto (Art Gallery of Ontario)/Amsterdam (Rijksmuseum Vincent van Gogh), 1981.

Welsh-Ovcharov, Bogomila, exhib. cat. Van Gogh à Paris, Paris (Musee d'Orsay) 1988.

Welsh-Ovcharov, Bogomila, 'The ownership of Vincent van Gogh's "Sunflowers", The Burlington Magazine 140 (1998) 3, pp. 184-192.

Wentinck, Charles, 'Stierf Vincent aan zijn familie?', Elsevier Geïllustreerd Maandblad 21 juli 1973, pp. 47-51.

Wintgens Hotte, Doris, Ankie de Jongh-Vermeulen (ed.), Dageraad van de Moderne Kunst. Leiden en omgeving 1890-1940, exh. cat. Leiden (Stedelijk Museum De Lakenhal), Zwolle 1999.

Wolk, Johannes van der, De schetsboeken van Vincent van Gogh, Amsterdam 1986.

Wolk, Johannes van der, 'Honderd jaar Kröller-Müller', in: Oxenaar et al. 1988, pp. 12-138.

Wolk, Johannes van der, 'Mrs Kroller and Vincentvan Gogh', in: Kōdera & Rosenberg 1993, pp. 377-396.

Wolk, Johannes van der, Ronald Pickvance & E.B.F. Pey, exhib. cat. Vincent van Gogh. Drawings, Otterlo (Rijksmuseum Kröller-Müller) 1990.

Wouters, Kees, 'Gek van Van Gogh. De verspreiding van het Nederlandse werk van Vincent van Gogh vanuit Breda', in Dirven & Wouters 2003, pp. 11-70.

Zemel, Carol, 'Het "Spook" in de machine. Van Gogh's schilderijen van wevers in Brabant', in: Van Uitert 1987-1988, pp. 47-58.

Zemel, Carol, Van Gogh's progress. Utopia, modernity and late nineteenth century art, Berkeley 1997.

Zola, Emile, L'Oeuvre, Paris 1983 (1886 1st ed.)

Exhibitions

1890
- Paris (Pavillon de la Ville de Paris), *Exposition de la Société des Artistes Independants. 4e exposition*
  22 March - 3 May

1891
- Paris (a) (Pavillon de la Ville de Paris), *Exposition de la Société des Artistes Independants: [Vincent van Gogh] Exposition posthume*
  20 March - 27 April
- Paris (b) (Le Barc de Boutteville), Ire Exposition des Peintres Impressionnistes et Symbolistes
  December

1892
- Rotterdam (Kunstzalen Oldenzeel), *Vincent van Gogh schilderijen en teekeningen*
  March
- The Hague (Haagsche Kunstkring), *Werken van Vincent van Gogh*
  16 May - 6 June
- Rotterdam (Kunstzalen Oldenzeel) Title unknown
  October - November

1892 - 1893
- Amsterdam (Kunstzaal Panoramagebouw), *Tentoonstelling der nagelaten werken van Vincent van Gogh*
  17 December - 5 February

1893
- Leiden (De Lakenhal) *Teekeningen van Vincent van Gogh*
  25 April - c. 9 May
- Copenhagen (Den Frie Udstilling), *Fortegnelse over Kunstvcerkerne paa den Frie Udstilling*
  25 March - end of May

1895
- The Hague (Haagsche Kunstkring) *Tentoonstelling van teekeningen van Vincent van Gogh*
  17 February - 3 March
- Paris (Galerie A. Vollard), *Exposition Van Gogh*
  4 - 30 June

1896
- Rotterdam (Kunstzalen Oldenzeel), *Tentoonstelling der werken wijlen Vincent van Gogh*
  March
- Paris (Galerie Vollard) Title unknown
  November

1897
- Dordrecht (Pictura) *Vincent van Gogh. Collectie Hidde Nijland*
  18 - 25 February

1898
- The Hague (Arts and Crafts Art Gallery) *Vincent van Gogh*
  dates unknown

1900 - 1901
- Rotterdam (Rotterdamsche Kunstkring) *Tentoonstelling van teekeningen van Vincent van Gogh*
  23 December - 10 February

1901
- Paris (Galerie Bernheim Jeune), *Exposition d'Oeuvres de Vincent van Gogh*
  15 - 31 March
- Berlin (Paul Cassirer), 3. *Kunstausstellung der Berliner Secession*
  8 May closing date unknown
- The Hague (Boschoord, Bezuidenhout), *Eerste Internationale Tentoonstelling*
  9 May - 12 June

1903
- Rotterdam (a) (Kunstzalen Oldenzeel) *Vincent van Gogh*
  4 January - 5 February
- Munich (Kgl. Kunstausstellungs - gebaude), *Secession*
  February - March
- Wiesbaden (Festsaale des Rathauses), *Ausstellung der Hollandische Secession*
  4 - 30 October
- Rotterdam (c) (Kunstzalen Oldenzeel), *Vincent van Gogh* (no catalogue known)
  November
- Rotterdam (b) (Kunstzalen Oldenzeel) *Vincent van Gogh*
  1 November - 13 December

1904
- Brussels (La Libre Esthetique), *Peintres Impressionistes*
  25 February - 29 March
- Groningen (Kunsthandel Scholtens & Zoon), *Vincent van Gogh* (no catalogue known)
  3 (?) - 19 March
- Dordrecht (Dordrechts Museum) *Verzameling Hidde Nijland. Tentoongesteld ter gelegenheid van de opening van het Dordrechts Museum*
  6 July - ?
- Rotterdam (Kunstzalen Oldenzeel), *Tentoonstelling van werken door Vincent van Gogh*
  10 November - 15 December
- Berlin (Paul Cassirer), [no title] (no catalogue known)
  December

1905
- Paris (Grandes Serres de l'Alma) *Exposition de la Societe des Artistes Independants, 21e exposition: Exposition retrospective Vincent van Gogh*
  24 March - 30 April
- Amsterdam (Stedelijk Museum) *Vincent van Gogh*
  15 July - 1 September
- Utrecht (Vereeniging ' Voor de Kunst'), *Vincent van Gogh*
  10 September - 1 October

1906
- Rotterdam (Kunstzalen Oldenzeel), *Vincent van Gogh*
  26 January - 28 February 1907
- Berlin (Ausstellungshaus am Kurfurstendamm), *13. Ausstellung der Berliner Secession*
  spring
- Mannheim (Städtische Kunsthalle), *Internationale Kunst und grosse Gartenbau Ausstellung*
  1 May - 20 October

1908
- Paris (a) (Galerie Eugène Druet), *Quelques Oeuvres de Vincent van Gogh*
  6 - 18 January
- Paris (b) (Galerie Bernheim Jeune), *Gent Tableaux de Vincent van Gogh*
  6 January - 1 February
- Munich (a) (Galerie W. Zimmermann), *Van Gogh / Gauguin*
  opening date unknown - 15 April
- Munich (b) (Moderne Kunsthandlung), *Vincent van Gogh*
  March - April
- Dresden (Emil Richter), *Vincent van Gogh / Paul Cézanne*
  April - May
- Frankfurt (Kunstverein), *Vincent van Gogh Ausstellung*
  14 - 28 June
- Zurich (Kunstlerhaus), *Vincent van Gogh, Cuno Amiet, Hans Emmenegger, Giovanni Giacometti*
  10 - 26 July
- Amsterdam (Kunstzalen C.M. vanGogh), *Vincent van Gogh*
  September
- Berlin (Paul Cassirer), *II. Ausstellung*
  15 October - 8 November

1909
- Bremen (Kunsthalle), *Leihausstellung von Gemalden, Zeichnungen und Bildwerken aus Brehmischem Privatbesitz*
  11 April - 8 May
- Rotterdam (RotterdamscheKunstkring), *Tentoonstelling van het Hollandsche stilleven in den loop der tijden*
  11 September - 10 October
- Paris (Galerie Eugène Druet), *Cinquante tableaux de Vincent van Gogh*
  8 - 20 November

1909 - 1910
- Munich (Moderne Kunsthandlung F.J. Brakl) / Frankfurt (Kunstverein) / Dresden (Galerie Ernst Arnold) / Chemnitz (Kunstsalon Gerstenberger), *Vincent van Gogh Munich*
  October - December; Frankfurt January; Dresden February - March; Chemnitz April

1910
- Brussels (La Libre Esthetique), *L'Evolution du Paysage*
  12 March - 17 April
- Rotterdam (Rotterdamsche Kunstkring), *Tentoonstelling van een aantal werken van Vincent van Gogh uitsluitend uit zijn Franschen tijd*
  11 June - 10 July
- Berlin (Paul Cassirer), *III Ausstellung. Vincent van Gogh 1853-1890*
  25 October - 20 November

1910 - 1911
- Rotterdam (Rotterdamsche Kunstkring), *Het dier in de beel dende kunst. Tentoonstelling van schilderijen, teekeningen en beeld houwwerk van Hollandsche meesters* (na 1840)
  17 December - 15 January

1911
- Amsterdam (Larensche Kunsthandel), *Vincent van Gogh*
  16 June - July
- Paris (Galerie Bernheim Jeune), *Le montagne*
  20 July - 5 August

1911 - 1912
- Hamburg (Galerie Commeter), [title unknown]
  10 November - March

1912
- Dresden (Galerie Ernst Arnold) / Breslau
  Ausstellung Vincent van Gogh 1853-1890 February
- Cologne (Stadtische Ausstellungs halle am AachenerTor), *Internationale Kunstausstellung des Sonderbundes westdeutscher Kunstfreunde und Kunstler zu Coln*
  25 May - 30 September
- Dusseldorf (Stadtische Kunsthalle), *Collection Marczell de Nemes*
  10 July - December

1913
- Brussels (La Libre Esthetique), *Interpretations du Midi*
  8 March - 13 April
- The Hague (Lange Voorhout 1), *Vincent van Gogh*
  July - 1 September

1914
- Antwerp (Zaal Comite voor Artistieke Werking), *Kunst van Heden*
  7 March - 5 April

1918
- The Hague (Haagsche Kunstkring) *Vincent van Gogh. Aquarellen, teekeningen en schetsen uit de Verzameting Hidde Nijland*
  6 - 29 April

1919
- Haarlem (Kunsthandel J.H. de Bois) *Moderne schilderijen en teekeningen*
  April

1924
- Amsterdam (Gebouw voor Beeldende Kunst) *Vincent van Gogh*
  March - April

1925
- Potsdam (Orangerie), *50 Fahre Hollandischer Malerei 1875-1925*
  summer

1927
- Paris (Galerie Bernheim-Jeune), *Vincent van Gogh. L'epoque Francaise*
  20 June - 2 July
- Basle (Kunsthalle) / Bern (Kunsthalle), *Vincent van Gogh 1853-1890. 143 Werke aus der Sammlung Kröller im Haag Basle*
  18 June - 4 September
  Bern 7 September - 17 October
- Brussels (Museum voor ModerneKunst), *Vincent van Gogh. 140 Werken der Verzameling Kroller, 's Gravenhage* [143 nos.]
  5 November - 4 December

1927 - 1928
- Berlin (Kunsthandlung OttoWacker), *Vincent van Gogh. Erste grosse Austellung seiner Zeichnungen und Aquarelle*
  6 December - 1 February
- Rotterdam (Museum Boymans), *Kersttentoonstelling in het Museum Boymans*
  23 December - 16 January

1928
- The Hague (Koninklijke Kunstzaal Kleykamp) *Vincent van Gogh. Aquarellen, teekeningen en schetsen uit de Verzamelinig Hidde Nijland*
  July
- Dusseldorf (Stadtische Kunsthalle), *Ausgewahlte Kunstwerke aus der Sammlung der Frau H. Kröller-Müller, Den Haag*
  1 August - 23 September
- Karlsruhe (Badische Kunsthalle), *Vincent van Gogh. 150 Werke aus der Sammlung Kröller im Haag* [143 cat.nos.]
  30 September - 9 December

1928 - 1929
- Berlin (National Galerie) *Vincent van Gogh. 143 Werke ans dem Besitz von Frau Kröller-Müller im Haag*
  28 December - 3 March

1929
- Hamburg (Kunstverein), *Vincent van Gogh. Sammlung Kröller im Haag*
  14 March - 21 May
- The Hague (Lange Voorhout 1), *Vincent van Gogh*
  1 July - 30 September

1930
- Amsterdam (Stedelijk Museum), *Vincent van Gogh en zijn tijdgenoten*
  6 September - 2 November
- The Hague (Gemeente Museum), *Vincent van Gogh*
  11 July - 2 October

1932
- The Hague (Gemeente Museum), *Vincent van Gogh uit de verzameling Kröller*
  25 June - 2 October

1935
- Haarlem (Kunsthandel J.H. de Bois) *Moderne prentkuntst en Hollandsche aquarellen*
  July - August
- Brussels (Palais des Beaux Arts), *L'Impressionnisme*
  15 June - 29 September

1935 - 1936
- New York (Museum of Modern Art) / Philadelphia (Philadelphia Museum of Art) / Boston (Museum of Fine Arts) / Cleveland (Cleveland Museum of Art) / San Francisco (The California Palace of the Legion of Honor) / Kansas City (William Rockhil Nelson Gallery of Ar and Atkins Museum)! Minneapolis (Minneapolis Institute of Art) / Chicago (The Art Institute of Chicago) / Detroit (The Detroit Institute of Art), *Vincent van Gogh*
  New York December - January;
  Philadelphia January - February;
  Boston 19 February - 15 March;
  Cleveland 25 March - 19 April;
  San Francisco April - May;
  Kansas City June - July;
  Minneapolis July - August;
  Chicago August - September;
  Detroit 6 - 28 October
- Rotterdam (Museum Boymans), *Fransche schilderijen uit de negentiende eeuw, benevens Jongkind, Vincent van Gogh*
  December - January

1937
- Paris (Les Nouveaux Musees, Quai de Tokyo) *La vie et l'oeuvre de Van Gogh*
  June - October

1938
- Venice, *XXI Biennale Esposizione Internationale d'Arte della Citta di Venezia*
  June - October
- Amsterdam (Kunsthandel Huinck & Scherjon), *Nederlandsche en Fransche kunst*
  15 October - 15 November

1940
- New York (Holland House), *Exhibition of paintings by Van Gogh*
  6 June - 19 July

1941
- Haarlem (Kunsthandel J.H. de Bois) *Moderne Schilderijen uit de 19de en 20ste eeuw*
  spring

1942
- Baltimore (The Baltimore Museum of Art) / Worchester, USA (Worchester Art Museum), *Paintings by Van Gogh*
  Baltimore 18 September - 18 October;
  Worchester 28 October - 28 November

1943 - 1944
- Indianapolis (John Herron Art Institute) / Cincinnati (Cincinnati Art Museum) / Ottawa (National Gallery of Canada), *An Exhibition of Modern Dutch Art, 14 paintings by Vincent van Gogh and work by contemporary Dutch Artists*
  Indianapolis 8 November - 12 December;
  Cincinnati 5 - 30 January;
  Ottawa 11 - 27 February

1945
- The Hague (Pulchri Studio), *Den Haag eert de Nederlandse Schilders van de 19e Eeuw*
  25 August - 30 September

1946
- Amsterdam (Stedelijk Museum), *5 generaties, tentoonstelling van schilderijen van 1800 tot heden* (cat. without nos.)
  12 July - 24 October

1946 - 1947
- Liège (Musée des Beaux-Arts) / Brussels (Musée des Beaux-Arts) / Mons (Musée des Beaux-Arts) *Vincent van Gogh*
  Liège 12 October - 3 November;
  Brussels 9 November - 19 December;
  Mons 27 December - January

1947
- Paris (Musée de l'orangerie) *Vincent van Gogh*
  24 January - 15 March
- Geneva (Musée Rath) *172 Oeuvres de Vincent van Gogh (1853-1890)*
  22 March - 20 April
- Basel (Kunsthalle) *Vincent van Gogh 1853-1890*
  11 October - 23 November

1947 - 1948
- London (Tate Gallery) / Birmingham (City Art Gallery) / Glasgow (Art Gallery) *Vincent van Gogh 1853-1890*
  London 10 December - 14 January;
  Birmingham 24 January - 14 February;
  Glasgow 21 February - 14 March

1948
- Bergen (Kunstforening) / Oslo (Kunstnernes Hus), *Vincent van Gogh. Malerier Tegninger*
  Bergen 23 March - 18 April;
  Oslo 24 April - 15 May
- Amsterdam (Stedelijk Museum), *Vincent van Gogh en zijn Nederlandse tijdgenoten* (cat. without nos.)
  25 June - 20 September
- The Hague (Gemeentemuseum) *Zeven Eeuwen*
  Den Haag 30 July - 26 September
- Meppel (location unknown) *Drents Landschap*
  dates unknown
- Venice, *Gli impressionisti alla XXIV Biennale di Venezia*
  6 June - 20 October

1949
- Gouda (Het Catharina Gasthuis) *Vincent van Gogh*
  13 April - 29 May

1949 - 1950
- New York (The Metropolitan Museum of Art) / Chicago (The Art Institute of Chicago) *Van Gogh Paintings and Drawings. A Special Loan Exhibition*
  New York 21 October - 15 January;
  Chicago 1 February - 16 April.

1950
- 's-Hertogenbosch (Centraal Noord Brabants Museum) / *Breda (Stedelijk Museum) Vincent van Gogh's*
  Hertogenbosch 11-26 March;
  Breda 29 March - April

1950 - 1951
- Leiden (Stedelijk Museum De Lakenhal) / Enschede (Rijksmuseum Twenthe) / Groningen (Museum voor Oudheden) / Leeuwarden (Friesch Museum) *Van Fantin - Latour tot Picasso*
  Leiden 14 October - 26 November;
  Enschede 6 January - 11 February;
  Groningen 16 February - 11 March;
  Leeuwarden 17 March - 8 April
- Paris (Musée National d'Art Mo derne), *Art Sacre, oeuvres francaises des XIX et XX siecles*
  29 November - 21 January

1952
- Milan (Palazzo Reale) *Vincent van Gogh. Dipinti e disegni*
  February - April
- Antwerp (Koninklijk Museum voor Schone Kunsten) *De arbeid in de kunst. Van Meunier tot Permeke*
  26 April - 30 June
- Paris (Bibliothèque Nationale) *Emile Zola*
  dates unknown

1953
- The Hague (Gemeentemuseum) *Vincent van Gogh 1853-1953*
  30 March - 17 May
- Otterlo (Rijksmuseum Kröller-Müller) / Amsterdam (Stedelijk Museum) *Eeuwfeest Vincent van Gogh 1853-1953*
  Otterlo 24 May - 19 July;
  Amsterdam 23 July - 20 September
- Berlin (Bezirksamt Tiergarten, Amt für Kunst) *Vincent van Gogh. Gemälde und Zeichnungen*
  dates unknown

1953 - 1954
- Saint Louis (City Art Museum) / Philadelphia (Museum of Art) / Toledo (Toledo Museum of Art) *Vincent van Gogh 1853-1890*
  Saint Louis 17 October-13 December;
  Philadelphia 2 January - 28 February;
  Toledo 7 March - 30 April

1954
- Recklinghausen (Stadtische Kunsthalle), *Zeugnisse europaischer Gemeinsamkeit. Meisterwerke der Malerei und Plastik aus europaischer Museen und Privatsammlungen*
  18 June - 30 July
- Arles (Musee Reattu), *La Provence et les peintres*
  1 July - 31 August
- Rotterdam (Museum Boymans), *Vier eeuwen stilleven in Frankrijk*
  10 July - 20 September
- Paris (Orangerie des Tuileries), *Van Gogh et les peintres d'Auverssur Oise*
  26 November - 28 February

1955
- Antwerp (a) (Koninklijk Museumvoor Schone Kunsten), *Kunst van heden*
  14 May - 12 June
- Antwerp (Comité voor Artistieke Werking) *Vincent van Gogh en zijn Hollandse tijdgenoten*
  15 May - 9 June
- Paris (Musée des Travaux-Publics) *Exposition internationale d'Industrie minérale*
  dates unknown
- Wormerveer (Ons Huis) *Arbeid in de Kunst*
  dates unknown
- Groningen (Pictura) *Tekeningen en Aquarellen van 19de eeuwse Nederlandse Schilders*
  dates unknown

1955 - 1956
- Liverpool (The Walker Art Gallery) / Manchester (City Art Gallery) / Newcastle (Laing Art Gallery), Vincent van Gogh. Paintings and drawings, *mainly from the collection of Ir. V. W. van Gogh*
  Liverpool 29 October - 10 December;
  Manchester 17 December - 4 February;
  Newcastle 11 February - 24 March

1956
- Eindhoven (Stedelijk Van Abbemuseum) *Van Gogh uit de Verzameling van het Rijksmuseum Kröller-Müller, Otterlo*
  28 January - 12 March
- Nuremberg (Fränkische Galerie) *Zeichnungen und Aquarelle von Vincent van Gogh aus dem Besitz des Rijksmuseums Kröller-Müller, Otterlo, Holland and von anderen Leihgebern*
  12 February - 11 March
- Amsterdam (Kunsthandel E.J. van Wisselingh & Co) *Vincent van Gogh 1853-1890. Quelques oeuvres de l'époque 1881-1886 provenant de collections particulières néerlandaises*
  20 February - 17 March
- Munich (Haus der Kunst) *Vincent van Gogh 1853-1890*
  October - December

1957
- Liège (Musee des Beaux Arts) / Eindhoven (Stedelijk Van Abbemuseum), *Natures mortes hollandaises 1550-1950 / Het Hollandse stilleven 1550-1950*
  Liege 16 March - 14 April;
  Eindhoven 20 April - 2 June
- Geneva (Musée d'art et d'histoire) *Art et Travail*
  14 June - 22 September
- Essen (Villa Hugel) *Vincent van Gogh (1853-1890). Leben und Schaffen*
  16 October - 15 December
- Vienna (Osterreichische Galerie im Oberen Belvedere) *Vincent van Gogh 1853-1890*
  February - March
- Vancouver (The Fine Arts Gallery, University of British Columbia) *The Changing Landscape of Holland*
  23 July - 29 August
- Tokyo (The Tokyo National Museum) / Kyoto (The Art Municipal Museum) *Vincent van Gogh. Collection Kröller-Müller Museum Otterlo*
  Tokyo 15 October - 25 November;
  Kyoto 3 - 27 December
- Essen (Villa Hugel), *Vincent van Gogh (1853 1890). Leben und Schaffen*
  16 October - 15 December

1958
- Paris (Musée National d'Art Moderne), *L'Art hollandais depuis Van Gogh*
  5 March - 20 April

1958 - 1959
- San Francisco (The M.H. de Young Memorial Museum) / Los Angeles (The Los Angeles County Museum) / Portland (The Portland Art Museum) / Seattle (The Seattle Art Museum) *Vincent van Gogh. Paintings and drawings*
  San Francisco 6 October - 30 November;
  Los Angeles 10 December - 18 January;
  Portland 28 January - 1 March;
  Seattle 7 March - 19 April
- Amsterdam (Rijksmuseum) *Dutch Drawings, Masterpieces offive centuries*
  October - June

- Schiedam (Stedelijk Museum), *Op een Blad Papier. Tekeningen en Aqiarellen uit het Rijksmuseum Kröller-Müller*
  December - January

1959
- Bordeaux (Mairie de Bordeaux), *La Decouverte de la Lumiere des Primitifs aux Impressionnistes*
  20 May - 31 July
- Recklinghausen (Stadtische Kunst halle), *Die Handschrift des Kunstiers*
  23 May - 5 July
- São Paulo (Museum de Arte Moderna) *5e Bienal do S. Paulo*
  September-December
- Aix-en-Provence (Pavillon de Vend me) *Van Gogh en Provence*
  3 October - 30 November

1960
- Paris (a) (Musée Jacquem art Andre), *Vincent van Gogh 1853-1890*
  February - March
- Brussels (Palais des Beaux Arts), *Le drame social dans l'art. De Goya a Picasso*
  21 May - 30 June
- London (Marlborough Fine ArtsLtd.), *Van Gogh Selfportraits*
  October
- Cuesmes (Ecoles Communales) *Vincent van Gogh*
  October
- Paris (b) (Institut Neerlandais), *Les Amis de Van Gogh*
  9 November - 17 December

1960 - 1961
- Montreal (The Montreal Museum of Fine Arts) / Ottawa (The National Gallery of Canada) / Winnipeg (The National Gallery Association) / Toronto (The Art Gallery of Toronto) *Vincent van Gogh. Paintings-Drawings*
  Montreal 6 October - 6 November;
  Ottawa 17 November - 18 December;
  Winnipeg 29 December - 31 January;
  Toronto 10 February - 12 March

1961
- Wolfsburg (Stadthalle), *Franzosische Malerei von Delacroix bis Picasso*
  8 April - 31 May
- Munich (Städtische Galerie Munchen) *Vincent van Gogh, Zeichtnungen und Aquarelle*
  May-June
- Recklinghausen (Stadtische Kunsthalle), *Polaritat. Das Apollinische und das Dionysische*
  2 June - 16 July
- Amsterdam (Stedelijk Museum), *Polariteit. Het Apollinische en Dionysische in de kunst*
  22 July - 18 September

1961 - 1962
- Melbourne (National Gallery of Victoria) / Launceston (Queen Victoria Museum and Art Gallery) / Sydney (Art Gallery of New South Wales) / Adelaide (National Gallery of South Australia), *Trends in Dutch Painting*

Melbourne 16 October - November;
Launceston 21 November - 4 December;
Sydney 14 December - 4 January;
Adelaide unknown
- Brussels (Palais des Beaux-Arts) *250e anniversaire de l'Academie des Beaux - Arts de Bruxelles*
  dates unknown

1962
- Brussels (Musee des Beaux Arts) / Otterlo (Rijksmuseum Kröller-Müller), *Le Groupe des XX et son temps / De Twintig en hun tijdgenoten*
  Brussels 17 February - 8 April;
  Otterlo 15 April - 17 June
- London (Marlborough Fine Arts Ltd.) *Van Gogh's life in his drawings. Van Gogh's relationship with Siqnac*
  May - June
- Warsaw (Muzeum Narodowe w Warszawie), *Vincent van Gogh, obrazy i rysunki. Wystawa dzil ze zbiorou muzeon holenderskich*
  8 - 18 October

1962 - 1963
- Tel Aviv (Tel Aviv Museum, Helena Rubinstein Pavilion) / Haifa (Museum of Modern Art), *Vincent van Gogh*
  Tel Aviv 30 December - 14 February;
  Haifa 20 February - 20 March

1963
- Hamburg (Kunstverein), *Wegbereiter der modernen Malerei Cézanne-Gauguin Van Gogh Seurat*
  4 May - 14 July
- Amsterdam (Stedelijk Museum) *150 jaar Nederlandse Kunst. Schilderjen, beelden, tekeningen, grafiek 1813-1963*
  6 July - 29 September

1964
- Recklinghausen (Stadtische Kunst halle), *Torso- das Unvollendete als kunstlerische Form*
  14 May - 19 July
- Kassel (Alte Galerie) *internationale Aussreliung Documenta III*
  27 June - 5 October

1964 - 1965
- Delft (Stedelijk Museum Het Prinsenhof) / Antwerp (Koninklijk Museum voor Schone Kunsten), *De schilder in zijn wereld*
  Delft 19 December - 24 January;
  Antwerp 6 February - 14 March

1966
- Belgrade (Narodni Muzejna), *Vincent van Gogh. Collection Kröller-Müller Otterlo*
  30 October - 20 December
- Arnhem (Gemeentemuseum) *Zestig schilderijen en tekeningen van Vincent van Gogh uit het Rijksmuseum Kröller- Müller te Otterlo*
  22 January - 27 February
- Paris (Institut Neerlandais) / Albi (Musee Toulouse - Lautrec) *Vincent van Gogh. Dessinateur*
  28 January - 20 March

1967
- Montreal (Expo '67. International Fine Arts Exhibition), *Man and his world*
  28 April - 27 October

1970
- Frankfurt (Frankfurter Kunstverein) *Vincent van Gogh. Zeichnungen und Aquarelle*
  30 April - 21 June

1971
- Moscow (Pushkin Museum) / Leningrad (Hermitage), *Vincent van Gogh*
  Moscow 15 April 30 May;
  Leningrad 13 June - 31 July

1971 - 1972
- Charleroi (Palais des Beaux-Arts) / Antwerp (ICC) / Paris (Institut Neerlandais) / Lyon (Musee des Beaux Arts) *Cent dessins du Musée Kröller-Müller*
  Charleroi September;
  Antwerp October - November;
  Paris December - January;
  Lyon February - March

1972 - 1973
- Munich (Haus der Kunst) *Das Aquarell von 1400 bis 1950*
  14 October - 7 January

1973 - 1974
- New York (The Museum of Modern Art) / Chicago (The Art Institute) / Ottawa (The National Gallery of Canada) / San Antonio (Marion Koogler McNay Art Institute) / Mexico City (The Museum of Modern Art) *Drawings from the Kröller-Müller National Museum Otterlo*
  New York May - August;
  Chicago September - October;
  Ottawa November - January;
  San Antonio January - March;
  Mexico City March - June

1974
- London (Courtauld Institute Galleries) / Newcastle-upon-Tyne (Hatton Gallery, University Newcastle-upon-Tyne) *Drawins from the Kröller- Müller National Museum, Otterlo*
  November - December

1979
- Seoul (Sejong Cultural Centre), *Dutch landscape painting of the nineteenth century*
  8 - 22 October

1980
- Mons (Musée des Beaux Arts), *Van Gogh et la Belgique*
  3 October - 30 November

1980 - 1981
- Amsterdam (Van Gogh Museum), *Vincent van Gogh in zijn Hollandse jaren. Kijk op stad en land door Van Gogh en zijn tijdgenoten 1870-1890*
  13 December - 22 March

1981
- Toronto (The Art Gallery of Ontario) / Amsterdam (Van Gogh Museum), *Vincent van Gogh and the Birth of Cloisonism* Toronto 24 January - 22 March; Amsterdam 9 April - 14 June

1983
- Paris (Grand Palais) / London (Royal Academy of Arts) / The Hague (Gemeentemuseum), *De Haagse School. Hollandse meesters van de 19de eeuw* Paris 15 January - 28 March; London 16 April - 10 July; The Hague 5 August - 31 October

1984
- New York (The Metropolitan Museum of Art), *Van Gogh in Arles* 18 October - 30 December

1984 - 1985
- Copenhagen (Ordrupgaard Samlingen), *Gauguin og Van Gogh 'Kobenhaven' 1893* 12 December - 10 February

1985 - 1986
- Tokyo (The National Museum of Western Art) / Nagoya (City Art Museum), *Vincent van Gogh* Tokyo 12 October - 8 December; Nagoya 21 December - 2 February

1986
- Osaka (The National Museum of Art), *Vincent van Gogh from Dutch Collections. Religion Humanity Nature* 21 February - 31 March

1986 - 1987
- Hull (Ferens Art Gallery) / Nottingham (Nottingham University Art Gallery) / York (York Art Gallery) / Exeter (Royal Albert Memorial Museum), *Don't trust the label* Hull 9 August - 14 September; Nottingham 22 September - 25 October; York 1 November - 7 December; Exeter 20 December - 24 January
- New York (The Metropolitan-Museum of Art), *Van Gogh in Saint Rémy and Auvers* 12 November - 22 March

1987 - 1988
- 's Hertogenbosch (Noordbrabants Museum), *Van Gogh in Brabant. Schilderijen en tekeningen uit Etten en Nuenen* 2 November - 10 January

1988
- Amsterdam (Van Gogh Museum), *'Een soort van Bijbel.' De collectie houtgravures van Vincent van Gogh* (no catalogue) 24 January - 13 March
- Rome (Galeria Nazionale d'Arte Moderna e Contemporanea), *Vincent van Gogh* 28 January - 4 April
- Paris (Musee d'Orsay), *Van Gogh a Paris* 2 February - 15 May

1988 - 1989
- Amsterdam (Van Gogh Museum), *Van Gogh & Millet* 9 December - 16 February

1989
- Arles (Ancien Hopital Van Gogh), *Van Gogh et Aries (Exposition du Centenaire)* 4 February - 15 May

1990
- Amsterdam (Van Gogh Museum), *Vincent van Gogh. Schilderijen* 30 March - 29 July
- Otterio (Kröller-Müller Museum) *Vincent van Gogh. Tekeningen* 30 March - 29 July
- The Hague (Haags Historisch Museum) *Vincent van Gogh en Den Haagv* 8 September - 18 November

1990 - 1991
- Essen (Museum Folkwang) / Amsterdam (Van Gogh Museum), *Vincent van Gogh en de moderne kunst 1890-1914* Essen 11 August - 4 November; Amsterdam 16 November - 18 February

1991
- Aarhus (Aarhus Kunstmuseum), *Northern Romantic Painting 1790-1990* September - November
- Amsterdam (Rijksmuseum) / Tokyo (The National Museum of Western Art), *Imitatie / Inspiratie. De invloed van Japan op de Nederlandse kunst / Imitation and inspiration. Japanese influence on Dutch art from 1650 to the present* Amsterdam 25 April - 26 June; Tokyo October - November

1992
- London (Barbican Art Gallery), *Van Gogh in England. Portrait of the Artist as a Young Man* 27 February - 4 May

1993
- Amsterdam (Rijksmuseum) *Kunst, hennis en cornmcrcie. De kunsthandelaar J.H. de Bois (1878-1946)* 23 January - 2 May
- Amsterdam (Van Gogh Museum), *The potato eaters by Vincent van Gogh / De aardappeleters van Vincent van Gogh* 11 June - 29 August

1993 - 1994
- Melbourne (National Gallery of Victoria) / Brisbane (Queensland Art Gallery), *Van Gogh. His sources, genius and influence* Melbourne 19 November - 16 January; Brisbane 22 January - 13 March

1995
- Hamburg (Hamburger Kunsthalle), *Van Gogh. Die Pariser Selbstbildnisse* 17 March - 28 May
- Amsterdam (Van Gogh Museum) *Vincent van Gogh. Het grafisch werk* 19 May - 27 April

1995 - 1996
- Yokohama (Yokohama Museum of Art) / Nagoya (City Art Museum), *Vincent van Gogh Collection from the Kröller Müller Museum, Otterlo, The Netherlands* Yokohama 9 December - 11 February; Nagoya 17 February - 22 March

1996
- Vienna (Bank Austria Kunst - forum), *Van Gogh und die Haager Schule* 28 February - 27 May

1996 - 1997
- Brussels (Galerie van het Gemeentekrediet) / Cologne (Wallraf Richartz Museum), *Kunst voor fijnproevers* Brussels 19 November - 23 February; Cologne March - September

1997
- Venice (Palazzo Grassi), *Flemish and Dutch Painting. From Van Gogh, Ensor, Magritte, Mondrian to contemporary artists* 16 March - 13 July
- Amsterdam (Van Gogh Museum) *Vincent van Gogh, tekeningen. Nuenen 1883-1885* 20 June - 12 October

1998
- Sagamihara (Citizen's Gallery) / Kobe (Daimaru Museum) / Ashikaga (Museum of Art) / Hamada (Children's Museum of Art), *Flower Painting from Van Gogh to Mondrian* Sagamihara 10 January - 8 March; Kobe 2 - 14 April; Ashikaga 18 April - 28 June; Hamada 4 July - 30 August

1999
- Leiden (Stedelijk Museum De Lakenhal) *Dageraad van de moderne kunst. Leiden en omgeving 1890-1940* 2 April - 29 August

1999 - 2000
- Tokyo (Bunkamura Museum of Art) / Fukuoka (Fukuoka Art Museum), *Vincent van Gogh from the Kröller-Müller Museum* (cat. without nos.) Tokyo 19 November - 23 January; Fukuoka 1 February - 23 March

2000
- Detroit (The Detroit Institute of Art), *Van Gogh: Face to Face* (cat. without nos.) 12 March - 4 June
- Brussels (Paleis voor Schone Kunsten) *Brussels, kruispunt van culturen* 8 September - 5 November

2000 - 2001
- Boston (Museum of Fine Arts) / Philadelphia (Philadelphia Museum of Art), *Van Gogh: Face to Face* (cat. without nos.) Boston 2 July - 24 September;

Philadelphia 22 October - 14 January
- Detroit (The Detroit Institute of Art) / Boston (Museum of Fine Arts) / Philadelphia (Philadelphia Museum of Art) *Van Gogh: Face to Face*
Detroit 12 March - 4 June;
Boston 2 July - 24 September;
Philadelphia 22 October - 14 January 2001
- Saint Louis (City Art Museum) / Frankfurt (Stadelsches Kunstinstitut) *Vincent van Gogh and the Painters of the Petit Boulevard / Vincent van Gogh und die Maler des Petit Boulevard*
Saint Louis 17 February - 13 May;
Frankfurt 8 June - 2 September

2001
- New York (Museum of Modern Art), *Van Gogh's Postman: The Many Faces of Joseph Roulin* (no catalogue)
1 February - 15 May
- Saint Louis (City Art Museum) / Frankfurt (Städelsches Kunstinstitut), *Vincent van Gogh and the painters of the Petit Boulevard* (cat. without nos.)
Saint Louis 17 February - 13 May;
Frankfurt 8 June - 2 September

2001 - 2002
- Chicago (The Art Institute of Chicago) / Amsterdam (Van Gogh Museum), *Van Gogh and Gauguin. The Studio of the South / Van Gogh en Gauguin. Het atelier van het zuiden*
Chicago 22 September 13 January;
Amsterdam 9 February - 2 June
- Washington (The Phillips Collection) / Boston (Museum of Fine Arts), *Impressionist and PostImpressionist Still Life Painting*
Washington 22 September - 13 January;
Boston 17 February - 9 June

2002
- Apeldoorn (Paleis Het Loo), *Vorstelijk Vee op Het Loo. Nederlandse huisdierrassen aan de wand en in de wei*
9 May - 28 July
- Sapporo (Hokkaido Museum of Modern Art) / Kobe (Hyogo Prefectural Museum of Modern Art) *Vincent & Theo van Gogh*
Sapporo 5 July - 25 August;
Kobe 7 September - 4 November

2002 - 2003
- Bremen (Kunsthalle) / Toledo (Toledo Museum of Art) *Van Gogh: Felder, Das Monfeld und der Künstlerstreit / Van Gogh: Fields (the exhibition travelled on to Toledo without the works from the Kröller-Müller museum)*
19 October - 26 January

2003 - 2004
- Otterlo (Kröller-Müller Museum) *Vincent en Helene - ter gelegenheid van de 150e verjaardag van Van Gogh*
14 February - 4 January
- Rotterdam (Kunsthal) *Roken in de kunst. Van Jan Steen tot Pablo Picasso*
13 December - 14 March

2004
- Amsterdam (Van Gogh Museum) *Edouard Manet, Impressions of the Sea*
18 June - 10 October

2004 - 2005
- Seattle (Seattle Art Museum) / Atlanta (High Museum of Art) *Van Gogh to Mondrian: Modern Art from the Kröller-Müller Museum*
Seattle 29 May - 12 September;
Atlanta 19 October - 16 January
- Amsterdam (Van Gogh Museum) *Art Nouveau Bing*
26 November - 27 February

2004 - 2006
- Otterlo (Kröller-Müller Museum) *De favorieten van Helene*
10 August - 1 April

2005
- The Hague (Gemeentemuseum) *De Haagse School en de jonge Van Gogh*
5 February - 16 May
- Tokyo (The National Museum of Modern Art) / Osaka (The National Museum Osaka) / Nagoya (The Aichi Prefectural Museum of Art) *Van Gogh in Context*
Tokyo 23 March - 22 May;
Osaka 31 May - 18 July;
Nagoya 26 July - 25 September
- Dordrecht (Dordrechts Museum) *Dromen van Dordrecht. Buitenlandse kunstenaars schilderen Dordrech*
3 April - 21 August
- Bonn (Kunst-und Ausstellungshalle der Bundesrepublik Deutschland) *Crossart. From Van Gogh to Beuys. Masterpieces of Modern Art from ten German and Dutch Museums*
12 August - 6 November
- Amsterdam (Van Gogh Museum) / New York (The Metropolitan Museum of Art) *Van Gosh tekenaar. De meesterwerken / Vincent van Gogh: the drawings*
Amsterdam 2 July - 18 September;
New York 11 October-31 December
- Amsterdam (Van Gogh Museum) *Presentatie aankoop Van Goqh tekening*
1 - 18 September

2005 - 2006
- Brescia (Museo di Santa Giulia) *Gauguin-Van Gogh, L'aventura del colore nuovo*
22 October - 26 March

2006
- Amsterdam (Van Gogh Museum) *10 jaar verzamelen, 1997-2006*
1 March - 16 April

2006 - 2007
- Otterlo (Kröller-Müller Museum) *De kunstpaus, H.P. Bremmer*
14 October - 25 February
- Dallas (Dallas Museum of Art) *Van Gogh's Sheaves of Wheat*
22 October - 7 January

- Brescia (Museo di Santa Giulia) *Turner e gli impressionisti*
28 October - 25 March
- Amsterdam (Van Gogh Museum) *Vincent van Gogh en het Expressionisme*
24 November - 4 March
- Budapest (Budapest Museum of Fine Arts) *Van Gogh in Budapest*
1 December - 1 April

2007 - 2008
- Otterlo (Kröller-Müller Museum) *Het raadsel van 'dubbel-Ingres' - Van Goghs tekeningen in het Kröller-Müller Museum opnieuw bekeken*
11 October - 27 January
- Seoul (Museum of Art) *Van Gogh: Voyage into the myth*
24 November - 16 March

2008 - 2009
- New York (The Museum of Modern Art) / Amsterdam (Van Gogh Museum) *Van Gogh and the Colors of the Night*
New York 21 September - 5 January;
Amsterdam 13 February - 7 June
- Brescia (Museo di Santa Giulia) *Van Gogh. Disegni e dipinti. Capolavori dal Kröller-Müller Museum*
18 October - 25 January

2009
- Basel (Kunstmuseum Basel) *Vincent van Gogh - Between Earth and Heaven: The Landscapes*
26 April - 27 September

2009 - 2010
- Taipei (National Museum of History) *Van Gogh: the Flaming Soul*
11 December - 28 March

國家圖書館出版品預行編目資料

燃燒的靈魂：梵谷 ＝ The flaming soul: Van
Gogh's drawings and paintings ／ 泰歐・梅登多
普（Teio Meedendorp），歐克耶・斐黑斯特
（Aukje Vergeest），庫勒穆勒美術館作；國立
歷史博物館編輯委員會編輯. ~ 初版. ~ 臺北
市：史博館, 民98.12
　　面：　公分
參考書目：面
ISBN 978-986-02-0970-9（平裝）

1. 梵谷（Van Gogh, Vincent, 1853-1890）　　2.
繪畫　3. 藝術評論
947.5　　　　　　　　　　　　　　　98021841

The Flaming Soul
Van Gogh's
Drawings and Paintings 燃燒的靈魂 梵谷

總發行人	黃永川	Publisher	HUANG Yung-Chuan
出版者	國立歷史博物館	Commissioner	National Museum of History
	10066臺北市南海路49號		49, Nan Hai Rd., Taipei, Taiwan, R.O.C. 10066
	電話：02-23610270		Tel : +886-2-23610270
	傳真：02-23610171		Fax : +886-2-23610171
	網站：www.nmh.gov.tw		http://www.nmh.gov.tw
作者	泰歐・梅登多普	Authors	Teio MEEDENDORP
	歐克耶・斐黑斯特		Aukje VERGEEST
	庫勒穆勒美術館		The Kröller-Müller Museum
總策畫	高玉珍	Curator	Pauline KAO
編輯	國立歷史博物館編輯委員會	Editorial Committee	Editorial Committee of National Museum of History
執行編輯	賴貞儀	Editor	LAI Jen-Yi
展覽行政	張慈安	Exhibition Coordinator	CHANG Tzu-An
翻譯	林瑞堂、吳長釗、張慈安、賴貞儀	Translators	LIN Juei Tang, WU Chang-Chao, CHANG Tzu-An, LAI Jen-Yi
美術設計	陳伶倩、關月菱	Art Designers	CHEN Linh-Chien, KUAN Yueh-Ling
總務	許志榮	Chief General Affairs	HSU Chih-Jung
會計	劉營珠	Chief Accountant	LIU Ying-Chu
印製	四海電子彩色製版股份有限公司	Printing	Suhai Design and Production
出版日期	中華民國 98 年 12 月	Publication Date	December 2009
版次	初版	Edition	First Edition
定價	新台幣1,000元	Price	NT$ 1,000
展售處	國立歷史博物館文化服務處	Museum Shop	Cultural Service Department of National Museum of History
	10066臺北市南海路49號		49, Nan Hai Rd., Taipei, Taiwan, R.O.C. 10066
	電話：02-2361-0270		Tel: +886-2-2361-0270
	五南文化廣場台中總店		Wunanbooks
	40042台中市中山路6號		6, Chung Shan Rd., Taichung, Taiwan, R.O.C. 40042
	電話：04-22260330		Tel: +886-4-22260330
	國家書店松江門市		Songjiang Department of Government Bookstore
	10485台北市松江路209號1樓		209, Songjiang Rd., Taipei, Taiwan, R.O.C. 10485
	電話：02-25180207		Tel: +886-2-25180207
	國家網路書店		Government Online Bookstore
	http://www.govbooks.com.tw		http://www.govbooks.com.tw
統一編號	1009803545	GPN	1009803545
國際書號	978-986-02-0970-9（平裝）	ISBN	978-986-02-0970-9 (pbk)